A HISTORY OF BRITISH WOOD ENGRAVING

Frontispiece – William T. Rawlinson:
Graveyard of the Giants, 1968.
27.7 x 37.75cm

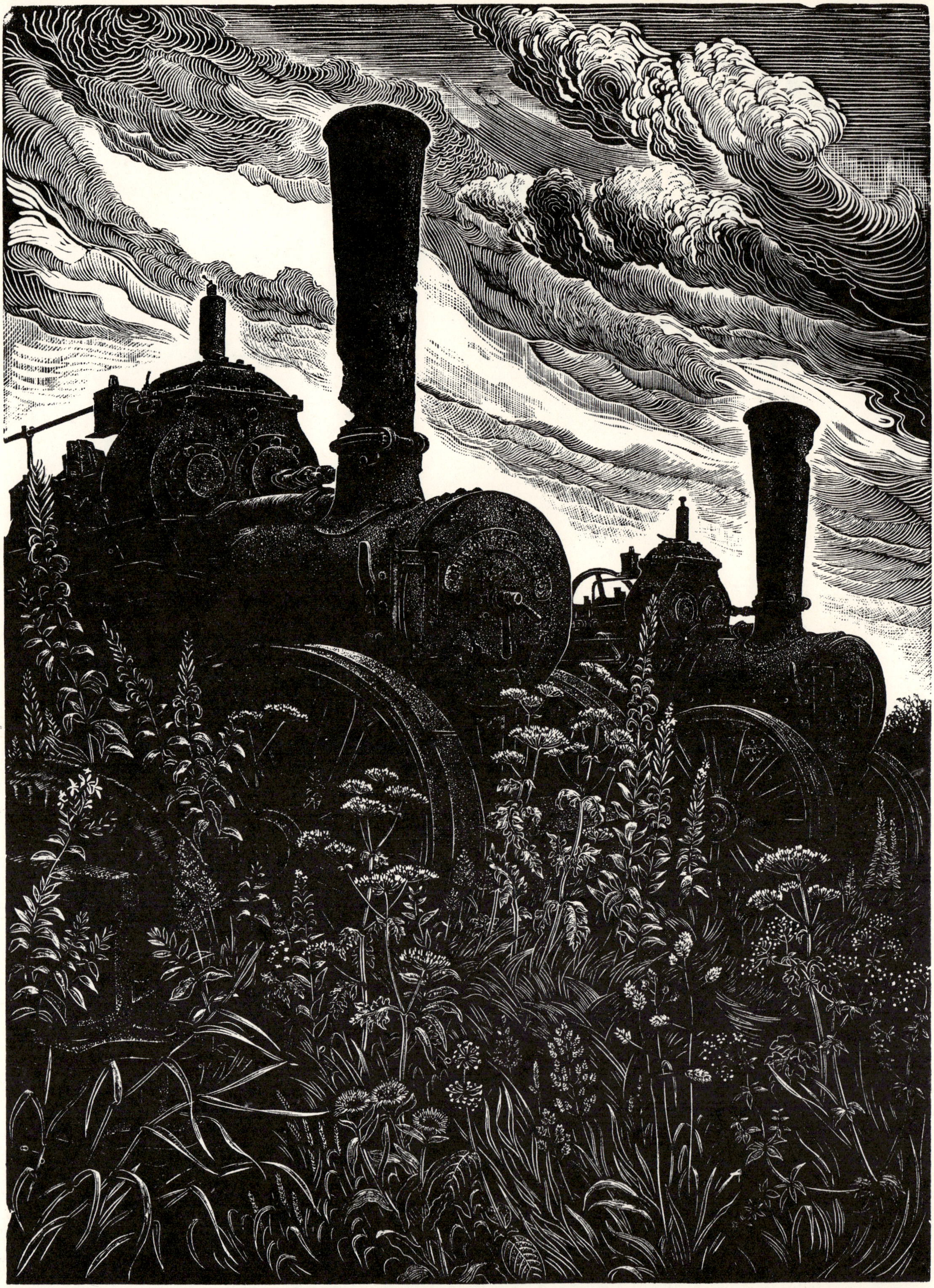

A HISTORY OF BRITISH

WOOD ENGRAVING

BY ALBERT GARRETT

MIDAS BOOKS

Also by Albert Garrett,
The Wood Engravings and Drawings
of Iain Macnab of Barachastlain

First published in 1978
by Midas Books
12 Dene Way, Speldhurst,
Tunbridge Wells, Kent TN3 0NX

ISBN 0 85936 077 6

Designed and produced by
Mechanick Exercises, London.

Set in Monotype Plantin by
South Bucks Typesetters Ltd.
Beaconsfield

Reproduction by
Pembury Litho Plates Ltd.
Pembury, Tunbridge Wells.

Printed and bound in Great Britain by
R. J. Acford, Industrial Estate, Chichester, Sussex.

CONTENTS

ILLUSTRATIONS

FOREWORD

It has been well said that 'the aim of the historian, like that of the artist, is to enlarge our picture of the world, to give us a new way of looking at things'. In his new book *A History of British Wood Engraving* Mr Albert Garrett brings together and fuses these two aims. This he is well fitted to do being not only a distinguished artist and President of the Society of Wood Engravers but also an author and biographer. That he should have brought his talents to bear on an historical survey of wood engraving constitutes an important event; that he should have made the subject the basis of such a magnificent and exhaustive work is doubly important. Many have written short studies of wood engraving but no one has previously written a comprehensive historical and analytical account such as this. The book therefore fills a long-felt want.

The development in Britain during the earlier part of the twentieth century of a school of wood engraving had far-reaching effects and ranks as a movement of major concern in the world of art. This school reintroduced and re-established the artist-engraver using the white line as the basis of his aestheticism. These artist-engravers were also bound by a common philosophy. Rejecting entirely the role of reproducers of illustrations played by the nineteenth-century engravers, they, with their new vision of the world, incorporated their feelings for places and things into their designs and realised that wood engraving was superbly fitted for this process. They sought for the spirit of a place or event and fused ideas and vision with scenes and happenings. Out of the magic and mystery of relationships they wove the fabric of their pictures. A hint of this is obtained even from the titles of the reproductions in this book. To choose but a few of them, there are Gertrude Hermes's *More people* and *Undercurrents*; George Mackley's *Broken willow*; Robert Gibbings's engravings from *The Glory of Life*; Paul Nash's *Breakwater* and John Nash's *Flowers and Faces.*

The common philosophy shared by these engravers, and based on their objective vision and insight into their world, was combined with their common aestheticism to make a school whose impact was immense. Their pictures were not limited by the narrow confines of galleries but were much used to illustrate fine books and thus communicated their message to the four corners of the globe. Indeed wood engraving is an art form particularly adapted to communication. Its shining whites and rich blacks have great impact and are well able to impress their message on the mind.

Since the days of Thomas Bewick, wood engraving has been used to convey and to highlight the thoughts and feelings which move the minds of artist-engravers. Bewick in the preface to his sixth edition of *British Birds* wrote 'When I first undertook my labours in natural history, my strongest motive was to lead the minds of youth to the study of the delightful pursuit. . . . Little was I then aware that children of a larger growth, and even minds illumined with talent and hearts warm with liberality, would have caught from my exertions the kindred feeling, and extended the popularity of my labours farther than the indulgence of my fondest hopes.' Bewick's experience has been repeated again and again; there can be few aspects of human thought and activity into which insight has not been given by successive generations of wood engravers, or which wood engravers have not highlighted or brought into focus. This, together with the fact that as Albert Garrett has stated 'a fine drawing gives a heightened sense of reality', makes the subject of particular attraction. It also makes it one of daunting size and complexity. This is particularly so when it is appreciated, again as Garrett has stated, concerning artists and their experience, that 'each work progresses until in maturity a single drawing can be charged with the meaning of a lifetime's experience. Time is layered and matrixed in a single drawing'. Albert Garrett's own engraved studies of time and life development, of the balance and poise of ideas, form an important contribution to this field.

The history of wood engraving epitomizes the history of our culture and in this history Albert Garrett synthesizes and presents in microcosm much of the essential part of that culture. It is a work superbly executed; it will be enjoyed and have relevance and importance to generations not only of artists but of all interested in the world about them.

PROFESSOR ALAN W. WOODRUFF

ACKNOWLEDGEMENTS

I am indebted to Professor Alan W. Woodruff, who in his perceptive foreword emphasises the human values of visual communication and the historical role played by engraving. A physician of his stature who is also a sensitive wood engraver understands the importance of these values.

My special thanks to Stanley T. E. Lawrence, the famous blockmaker, who provided the engravings for [82] and [393] and who is a living *Who's Who* of engraving in many countries. If you want to find your way around in engraving, do not ask a practitioner: ask Stanley Lawrence. However, if you want engravings then you must ask the practitioners and I want to thank them all sincerely for their magnificent contributions and for the information and data they have provided. It is gratifying to know that this information is accurate – they wrote it! This co-operation should save future historians much frustration.

Some of the engravers provided valuable historical information without which this book would have been less comprehensive. My grateful thanks to Helen Binyon (Eric Ravilious); Enid Marx (St Andrews engravers); Pauline Clark (William Abercrombie document); George Buday (Hungarian folk lore); Rachel Reckitt and Ernest Fedarb (Tom Chadwick); Monica Poole (John Farleigh); Winifred and Alison McKenzie (St Andrews engravers); Hilary Paynter (Portsmouth School); William T. Rawlinson (Hans Holbein and John Greenwood) and Richard Shirley Smith (David Jones).

A collection of very early wood engravings was required from art galleries, public and national libraries and institutions scattered throughout the world. Everywhere I found the staffs of these establishments most kind, helpful and very efficient; it was a pleasure to work with them. I wish to thank the staff of the British Museum, and in particular its Photographic Department and the Natural History Section; British Library; Victoria and Albert Museum; Tate Gallery; Ashmolean Museum; Institute of Archaeology; Bodleian Library; Royal Botanical Gardens; Royal Society of Arts; Arts Council of Great Britain; Royal College of Physicians; National Library of Scotland; Louvre Museum; Bibliothèque National de France, Cabinet d'Estampes; Ministère des Affaires Culturelles, Paris; Musées Nationaux, St Germain-en-Laye; Institute Royal des Sciences Naturelles de Belgique; Etruscan Museum; Nostra Nazional; Albertina Museum; William Rockhill Nelson Gallery of Art; the Metropolitan Museum of New York; Fogg Art Museum, Harvard University; The Art Museum, Princeton University – and a special thank you to Professor Kiyofusa Narita, Director of the Paper Museum, Tokyo and Malcolm Fry of the Royal Society of Painter-Etchers and Engravers.

Valuable information and photographs were provided by James Ingram of P. & D. Colnaghi; the Leicester Galleries, London; and Magdalene Street Gallery, Cambridge. I wish to thank them, the Paul Nash Trust and Thomas Yoseloff of the Golden Cockerel Press for permission to reproduce wood engravings.

Sifting through a stock of prints and documents left by master engravers was exciting for me, but not so enjoyable for Mrs Ella Webb, Mrs Helen Macnab, the late Mrs Mary Buckland-Wright, Mrs Elsie Farleigh, Mrs Guy Malet and Mrs Roberta Sekalski, all of whom worked without reserve to ensure that the late wood engravers' works reproduced, gave a true picture of their stature. Their contribution to the history is of vital importance.

Viewpoints other than those of the author are essential for a lively narrative, and my thanks are due to the following publishers for quotations. Christopher Sandford for "Cockalorum" Golden Cockerel Press, John Rewald for "Camille Pisarro. Letters to his son Lucien", The Guardian for Thomas Sturge Moore, the Sunday Times for Frank Rutter, The Architect for Eric Gill, the Studio International for John Farleigh, Clare Leighton for her "Modern Wood Engraving", Punch 1897 for the Charles Keene and Phil May engravings, the Sylvan Press for John Farleigh, Constable and Co for the "Black girl in her search for God", Kenneth Lindley for "The Woodblock Engravers", Lund Humphries for "Gabo", the Abbé Breuil executors for Palaeolithic drawings and James Ravilious for permission to reproduce his father's engravings.

I wish to thank Anthony Reid for his help and support of Ralph Chubb in whose stature we both believe and Peter Fung and Peter Swan for their guidance on Chinese stone pictures, and Douglas J. Walton, Eastcote Studios for special photography.

Mr Henry Larken of the London College of Printing gave great assistance in many different ways with this book, and his untiring help is most warmly acknowledged.

INTRODUCTION

The purpose of this book is to show that there is now a British school of wood engraving with a common philosophical vision and a dominant aesthetic language to which many artists have made personal contributions. To enable the reader to appreciate the full range of ideas and expression, the root sources in antiquity from which the school draws inspiration have been summarized.

This book provides the first opportunity to bring together the work of a large number of artists and to set down an account of their activities which have contributed to the establishment of the British school. Because there is no adequate record of the activities of wood engravers in Britain, it is academically important that this serious gap in art history is closed. The British school has arisen as a strong and clear-cut reaction against the commercialism of the eighteenth and nineteenth centuries, and in so doing has effected a revival of the art of wood engraving.

The presence of a British school is evident from the comprehensive collection of reproductions shown in this book, from which the reader can make a personal judgement on the scope and quality of the engravings. In the majority of cases the original prints have been photographed and where this has not been possible, reproductions of the best quality have been used. Although great care has been taken in photography and in printing, it is inevitable that there should be some loss of detail in these two processes when an original print has to be reduced in order to be accommodated in the page size. In these instances, the aim has been to give a good impression of the original engraving.

I am not an historian and this volume has been prepared from the point of view of a wood engraver interested in the past, the present, and having an eye to the future. An important factor involved in producing this work is the necessity to present an historical record whilst many of the artists are still living and producing engravings. From the point of view of writing art history, most historians establish a comfortable time gap between themselves and their subject. This was made clear to me when I was a student at Slade. The history professor, Rudolf Whittkower (who died in 1971) was asked to criticise our end-of-year exhibition. He gave us a delightful comment containing the grain of truth when he said 'I never feel happy unless there is at least one hundred years between the work and myself'.

To make more complete the summary of antiquity influencing the engravers of the British school, it has been necessary to introduce aspects of Palaeolithic art and of the engraving of armour; two areas not usually included by the art historian in one book.

As a teacher, I am concerned that students and collectors should be encouraged to investigate situations and individuals, and to form their own opinions. To this end, the book has been designed to enable the reader to find information quickly and sources of reference identified.

Because of the considerable variation in the use of the terms 'wood engraving', 'woodcut', 'black-line technique' and 'white-line technique', it is necessary to make my own interpretation clear, and this is particularly important when one considers the confusion that exists in applying the terms 'wood engraving' and 'woodcut'. This confusion is in no way eased by the existing literature on the subject.

Whilst people unhesitatingly refer to a 'woodcut', a copper engraving is never called a 'coppercut' and there appears to be no confusion in the terms used in water colour and in oil painting. Even in a widely-studied area such as the Danube school, books published in many countries are almost equally divided between the use of the terms 'wood engraving' and 'woodcut', though occasionally one encounters a book (usually of German origin) in which the more correct term 'formschneider' is used in reference to the Danube school. In Europe, the woodcut started as a debased wood engraving, produced by craftsmen who were not creative engravers and it is surprising that the early European woodcuts have enjoyed popularity and are reproduced frequently. Because of the lack of creative ability in the journeyman xylographers, there was no development in early woodcuts in Europe by reason of the fact that the craftsmen lacked an understanding of the way to develop the medium. In its creative form, the art of the woodcut started in China involving artists of sensitivity, and much later the art flourished in Japan. The woodcut, brought to considerable heights of expression in the nineteenth and twentieth centuries, is basically a two-dimensional medium and in consequence is limited.

Like copper engraving, wood engraving is a fundamental discipline whereas the preparation of a woodcut is not a fundamental discipline. There are only three fundamental disciplines in art: painting, sculpture, and engraving. In most countries, universities structure their arts faculties on these three disciplines. A fundamental discipline is a basic image-forming process through which a final statement can be made, either in two-, three-, or four-dimensional form.

A wood engraving must be cut with the sharp steel point of a burin. The wood must be very hard; end-grained boxwood is generally used though other end-grained timbers have been employed in recent times. In any period, the best engraving is always that executed on very hard materials (wood, copper, steel, glass, or stone).

The black-line technique in wood engraving shows the black line on a white background. A black line is left standing on the block and the white areas are cut away low enough so that they do not receive a film of printing ink. The earliest known black-line wood engravings can be seen in the reproductions of the *Diamond Sutra* and the *Tripitaka* from China, and the technique continued as a tradition into the nineteenth century. The black-line technique can be used creatively or employed in commercial art to imitate a drawing.

A white-line wood engraving shows the white line on a black background. A white line is incised with a burin into the surface of the material being engraved. When the surface of the block is inked, the white line, being below the surface of the block, receives no ink and in consequence, is not printed on the paper.

Unlike engraving on wood or metal, the woodcut is produced on soft materials. The wood engravers of the twentieth century developed the European form of the woodcut and through their experiments in the use of softer materials turned linoleum into a medium for printing in colour. The European techniques of the woodcut and the linocut evolved from the white-line technique of engraving. A woodcut is precisely what the name suggests: it is cut with a knife, chisel, and a range of gouges. The nature of these tools requires the scale of cutting to be very much larger than is the case with engraving.

Whilst colour can be (and sometimes is) used in engraving, it does not mean that the colour is qualified and, in fact, engraving is not a medium for colour because there is no development from the flat, unbroken film of ink. All the leading wood engravers of the twentieth century have experimented in the use of colour and agree that the use of colour in wood engraving is purely decorative and spatially arbitrary. The woodcut, like the linocut, is a good medium for the use of colour and although it is a two-dimensional image, the woodcut can give an illusion of three-dimensional quality by the superimposition of one plate of colour upon another in a trichromatic layering system. Because this book deals only with wood engraving, no reproductions of woodcuts or linocuts are shown in order that there might be no confusion in comparison of techniques.

This book contains some personal reminiscences because, as a practising wood engraver, I have had the privilege of meeting important artists and studying and working with many of them. These reminiscences and the statements of individuals are employed to aid a full appreciation of the artists' work, and in so doing, I hope to have expressed some of the thoughts and concepts of the engravers of my time.

It is unfortunate that a great deal of the work of the British school is contained in the books published by private presses and not all of this material is available in public collections. Thus, much of the work can be seen only in the copies of books in the possession of private collectors, many of whom do not live in Britain. Even if all of these books could be exhibited together, they could only be opened at one page at a time and to view the contents in a serious study would demand an enormous amount of time and present an insurmountable problem of security. However, it is hoped that the reproductions shown in this volume will ease the situation and improve the understanding.

The illustrations are, of course, a personal choice. My selection has been made from the wood engravers who, in my view, are contributing something to the art of engraving; the contributors include artists, illustrators and designers. Because of the element of personal choice, I am aware that I can be accused of bias but it is hoped that such will not be too evident; any artist must be prepared to stand by what he considers to be good or bad art. It is unfortunate that in one instance I could not obtain a reproduction because of restrictions of copyright of a book.

In the book there are a few references to establishments that were started many years ago and are still in existence but whose title has been amended in the passage of time. For the purpose of rapid identification, the modern title is used throughout.

History is never complete and by the time this book is read events will have taken place which will be worthy of a mention in the annals of wood engraving. This is not a matter for regret but rather an indication that wood engraving is a living thing, and that the British school of wood engraving is evolving continuously, changing its range and scope as its membership expands. One of the striking features of the school is its special national quality – and in art, this quality is seen only in the work of the best practitioners. This is something of which to be proud because it will be with us for far longer than the present vogue of what is called the 'international style' in art.

For economic reasons, the demands of commerce have a limited call upon wood engraving, but while there are artists of the quality and vision of many of those who are mentioned in this book, and the presence of a number of young people preparing for a career in which the technique will be used, the art of wood engraving will continue to be employed as a unique form of expression.

Eastcote 1977 ALBERT GARRETT

1 IN THE BEGINNING THERE WAS ENGRAVING

Primitive man had an urgent need to create a visual image for communication but had no models on which such a language could be based. He chose to make his first ventures in visual communication by means of engraving on cave walls and from this he progressed to sculpture and painting. The sites selected by Palaeolithic man were underground caves in which there was little or no light, which suggests that his engravings were done at a period when the primitive oil lamp had been developed. The confrontation with an irregular stone surface in a cold and dark cave must have caused Palaeolithic man to engage in some fundamental thinking, especially as some caves had permanent lakes or small streams, or walls that were continually moist.

The first Palaeolithic work to be discovered was engravings of mammoths on rock, ivory and pebbles. They were found by Edouard Lartet in 1864 in the deposits of La Madeleine cave in the Dordogne area of France.[1] These engravings were Upper Palaeolithic and Franco-Cantabrian in style and were probably done as early as 30,000 BC.

The urge to communicate visually carried with it a desire for permanency of record and soon it was discovered that an incised line in a hard material was more permanent than a mark with coloured clay, and that an engraving could convey more information than a flat area of natural pigment. Palaeolithic man appears to have had a strong faith in a future; had this not been so he would not have gone to the trouble of making tools to engrave lines that would last. Moreover, it requires a high degree of skill to fashion a burin from flint and it has very little use other than for engraving. The urge for permanency is also emphasized by the fact that Palaeolithic man never destroyed or obliterated old work but often incorporated it into new pictures, thus giving rise to the layered engravings [4]. Despite the difficulty of fashioning tools from flint, primitive man produced sturdy burins in this material and gave them graver-like points. It was his success in making burins that enabled him to embark upon engraving schemes of a very grand scale.

During the Middle and Upper Palaeolithic periods, hammer stones were used to shape flints and this development in tool-making has enabled the caves of Altamira and Font-de-Gaume to be classified as Magdalenian IV.

Palaeolithic man found that he could apply and hold colour in an engraved line by rubbing pigments into the grooves, though he did not do this solely for decorative purposes. Pigments were to hand in the natural earth and dyes could be extracted from plants which had a much higher permanency rating than some modern synthetic colourings. Primitive man discovered that when an incised image is illuminated, one side of the incision becomes a light-reflecting plane. This phenomenon enables the image to be seen in illumination of low energy. The lighting conditions obtaining in caves are always minimal, and at very low energy levels the human eye could detect the detail of an engraving but not that of an image of flat pigment.

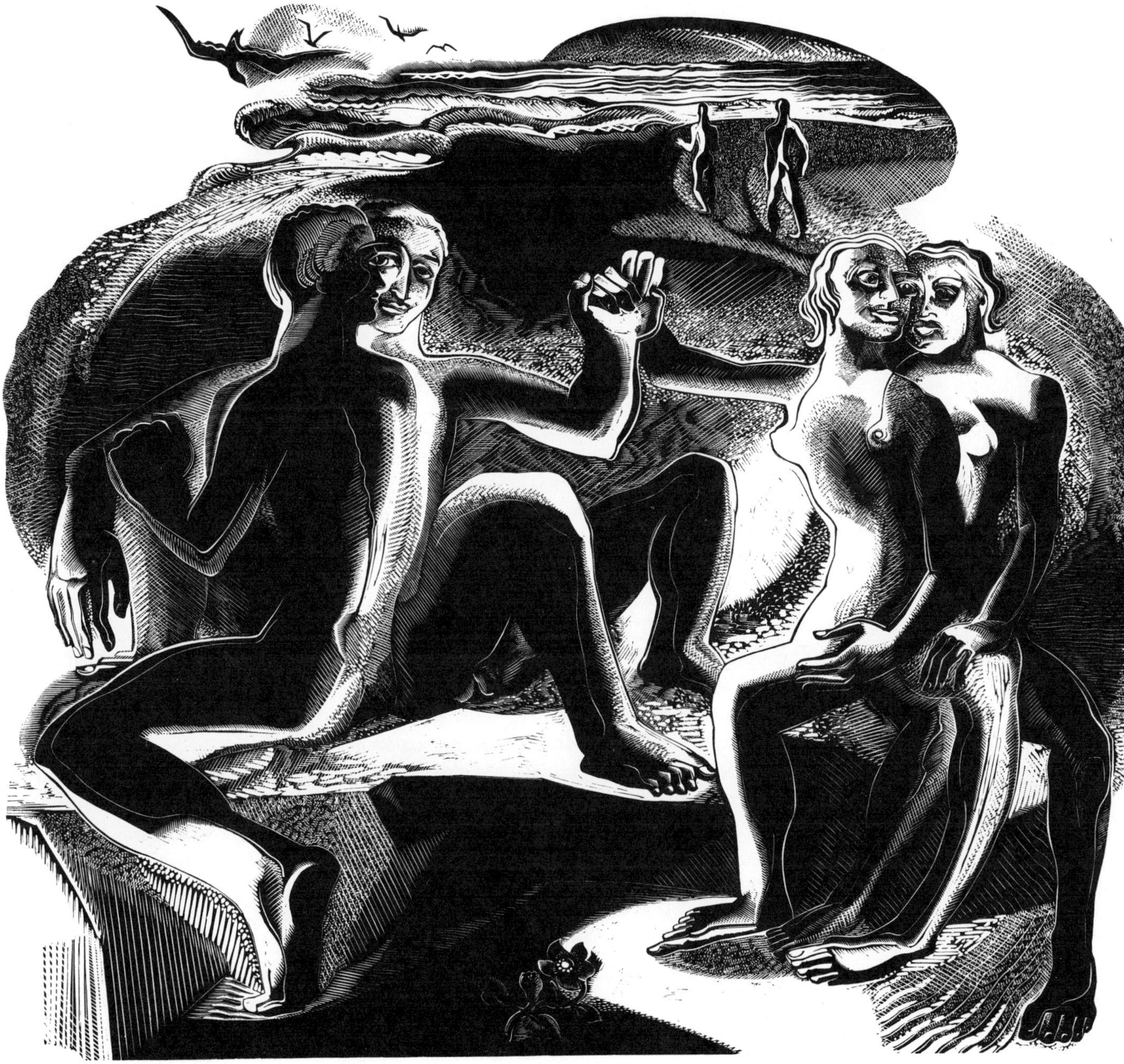

[1] Gertrude Hermes: *More People*, 1935. 48.8 x 44.5cm

Though he would have been unable to identify them, Palaeolithic man used the basic laws of light reflection in the employment of large areas of light-coloured surfaces to provide additional sources of reflection. This understanding of the behaviour of light influenced his power of overall composition though it is an appreciation for which he is usually given little credit.

The caverns used by Palaeolithic man were created by erosion and in some cases the action of water and sand has endowed the caves with fantastic formations and smooth polished surfaces. The majority of the caves were formed in limestone of varying types; only a few in other kinds of rock have been discovered. Despite the perfection of his flint tools, primitive man does not appear to have employed the technique of flattening surfaces but has developed the exploitation of the natural environment in the cave in a very clever manner. His engravings of animals that

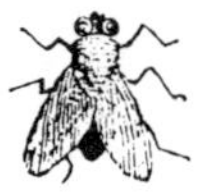

[2] Thomas Bewick: *House Fly.*

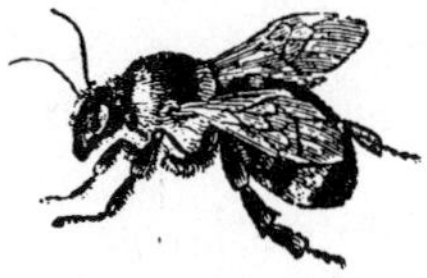

[3] Thomas Bewick: *Bumble Bee.*

run in harmony with the natural form of the rock surface and his success in expressing the joy of living and the spirit of the hunt do not relate to the traditional image of the brutal caveman.

In the Franco-Cantabrian area there are a number of caves containing primitive art. The six large ones are Altamira, Font-de-Gaume, Les Combarelles, Lascaux, Niaux, and Trois Frères. In all these caves, Palaeolithic man shows an instinctive understanding of his material, its right use, and the exploitation of its possibilities, thus giving to his art its most striking quality – that of intense vitality.

The much-travelled wood engraver, Robert Gibbings, showed the reaction of a modern engraver to the art of Lascaux in his book *Coming down the Seine* published in 1953. The engraving is remarkably accurate and in the book Gibbings sets down some of his reactions to the Cave of Lascaux. His vivid descriptions show how profoundly moved he was by this primitive art. He wrote, 'Wherever one stands in the caves the effect on the mind is the same – overwhelming. But they have left an awesome sanctuary, the most impressive picture gallery that I have ever entered.'[2]

Upper Palaeolithic man inhabited caves over a wide area of Europe and in addition to southern France and Spain, paintings and engravings occur in Belgium and in the Scandinavian-Krelian area, the engravings being found as far north as the White Sea. The cave art of Spain shows a greater sophistication of design and perspective while in the rock paintings of South Africa, perspective is represented by the superimposition of figures and a sequential reduction in the size of the images.

The study of primitive art as depicted in the cave paintings and engravings is fascinating. Apart from the consideration of technique of execution and of the purpose of the engravings, there is the interesting speculation as to the nature of the gatherings that might be assumed to have taken place in the halls and galleries of the caves, some of which were in perpetual darkness.

Palaeolithic man's ability to draw animals expressively in all their complexity of form and movement was brilliant. Each engraving is an individual portrait of the animal; yet portraits of primitive man himself are avoided and man is represented by rudimentary and symbolic drawings. Probably the nearest to a portrait image of

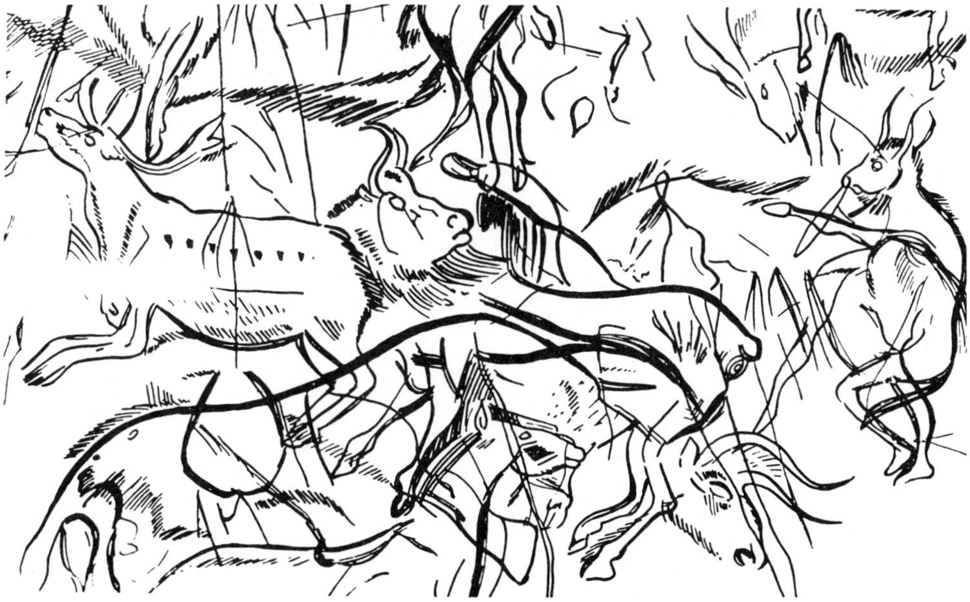

[4] Layered engravings after Breuil. The half human ithyphallic man (extreme right) measures 20cm and may be playing upon a musical bow.

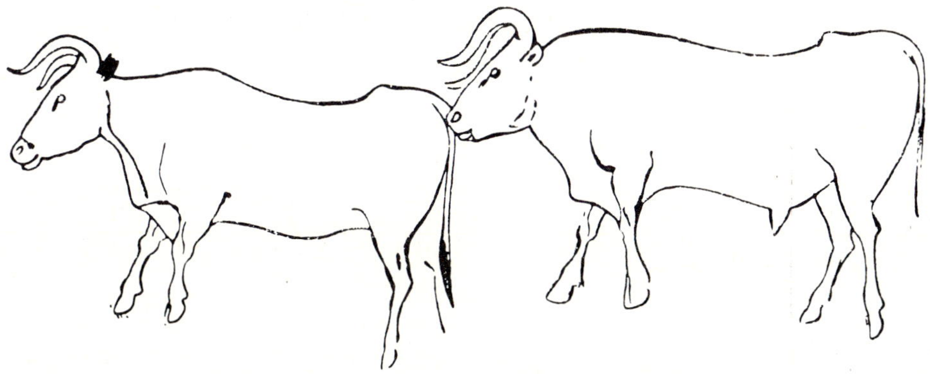

[5] *Bos primigenius*, reminiscent of modern cattle. Upper Palaeolithic engraving.

a man is in the Cave of Lascaux, although the engraving is a two-dimensional symbol. It is evident that Palaeolithic man had the skill to depict the human figure if he so desired but it could well be that there was a religious or social taboo to showing a human being in a cave picture.

It is evident that the composition at Lascaux evolved from the conscious selection of units in relation to the continuously undulating environment of the cave walls, roof and floor. By using the bulges of the rock surface for anatomical features of animals, Palaeolithic man showed a surprising ability to achieve a relationship between his need to express an idea and the environment in which that expression was to be achieved.

Altamira, the next cave in importance to Lascaux, was discovered in 1869 and is the first cave in which Upper Palaeolithic engravings were found. Despite being dismissed as forgeries by the Congress of Anthropology and Prehistoric Archaeology at Lisbon in 1880, the paintings and engravings in Altamira are now highly regarded and special permission has to be obtained for filming or photography.

In 1895 E. Rivière discovered paintings and engravings in the La Mouthe cave in the Dordogne.[3] A year later, F. Daleau was able to decipher several engravings in the Pair-non-Pair cave in the Gironde area, and the fact that the images were partially covered by thick deposits won them immediate recognition from the experts. In 1901, Henri Breuil and his collaborators L. Capitan and D. Peyrony discovered the Les Combarelles cave near Les Eyzies and found the cavern richly adorned with engravings. In the same year the three explorers reported the discovery of the Font-de-Gaume cave also in the Vezère Valley near Les Eyzies.

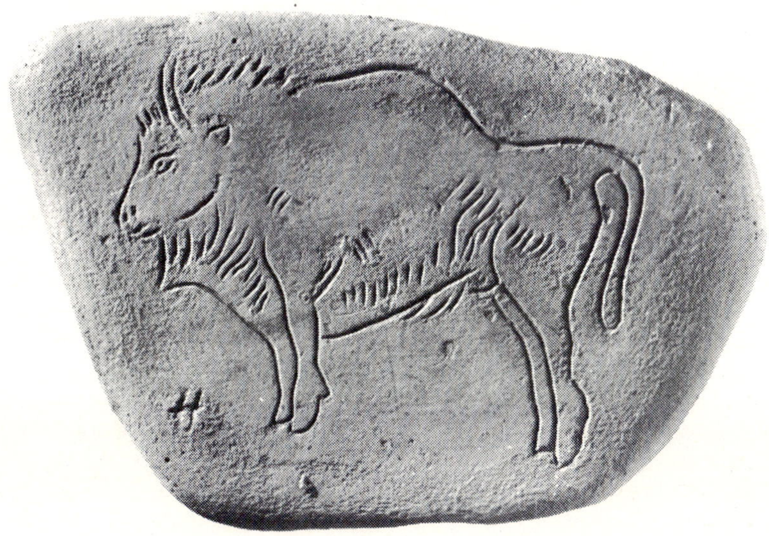

[6] Engraving of a bison on a pebble from Laugerie Basse. Possibly a preparatory sketch for a larger work. Length 10cm

[7] Reindeer engraved on reindeer antler from Kesslerloch near Thayngen. Late Magdalenian. Length 8.25cm

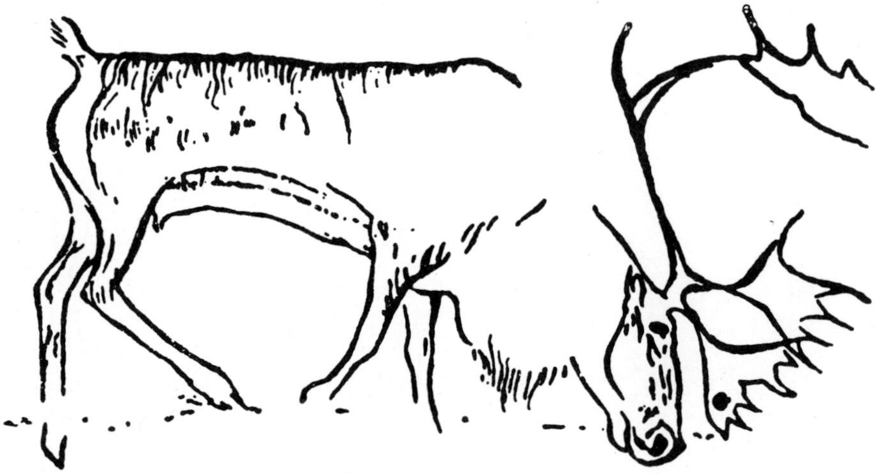

Font-de-Gaume is Magdalenian in period and style and the cave comprises a long narrow corridor with galleries branching off. Unfortunately, the cavern is exposed to continual variations of air and temperature and much of the painting has deteriorated. The work is now difficult to recognise and it is necessary to refer to the reconstructions by Breuil[4] for identification. Breuil has also listed the animals found in Les Combarelles where there are some 300 engravings of which 291 have been deciphered.

One of the largest caves to be found is the Caverne des Trois Frères at Montesquien-Avantes in the Ariège. This cave was discovered in 1914 by Count Henri Begouen and his three sons – hence the name 'the three brothers'.[5] The walls of the cave carry a large number of overlapping engravings [4] and three periods are represented, Aurignacian, Perigordian and Magdalenian. The time-layered engraving shown in [4] presents a symphony of animals wild in energy and also a half-human figure. The illustration is based on Breuil's study of the engraving and according to him the bison-headed, ithyphallic man seen springing and dancing might be playing a musical bow.

The cave of La Madeleine, discovered in 1952 by M. Bessac, is near the town of Montauban on the River Tarn.[6] Its engravings are of the Magdalenian period and include two nude female figures rendered in naturalistic style and facing each other. Reindeer antler engravings were found on the floor of the cave and one of these is the Rain Myth believed to be a literal illustration of the legend of that name and a theme seen in other cave engravings.

[8] Wild ass from the cave Caladei Genovesi. Height 25.0cm

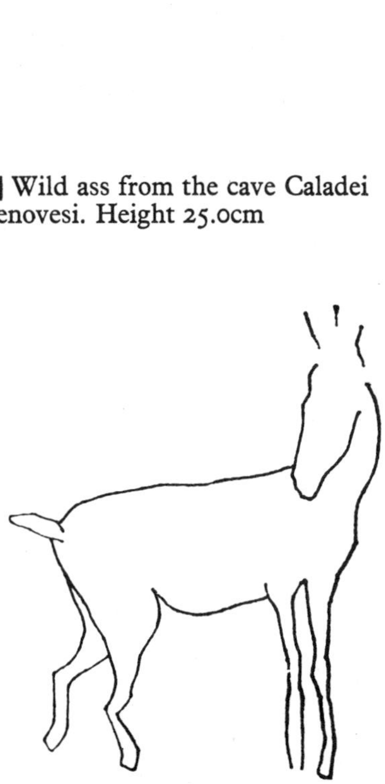

In the middle of the village of Teyjat in the northern Dordogne region is the cave of La Mairie, discovered by Peyrony in 1903 and containing some fine engravings of animals.[7] Peyrony also discovered more engravings nearby at Bernifal and the work is in a fluent Magdalenian style. The engraving Bos Primigenius [5], also from Teyjat, shows how little cows have changed in forty thousand years.

Niaux is a spectacular and gigantic cave overlooking a valley in the Pyrenees near Tarascon-sur-Ariège. The cave was discovered in 1866 by Dr Garrigou but no special significance was given to its art until the paintings were authenticated in 1906 as Ice Age art.[8] The black animal paintings in this cave are Magdalenian in style and in one of the chambers there are engravings cut into the clay floor.

In considering primitive engraving, the question must arise as to how Palaeolithic man got his training. It is suggested that the most competent men were assigned to engraving the animals while the less skilled were given the task of depicting the symbols. How did primitive man ascertain the degree of skill in the engravers of his time? Perhaps animal skins could have been used to test draughtsmanship (in the absence of paper or vellum) but it is evident that space on cave walls was reserved for the gifted engraver and not employed for practice.

In the book *The Art of the Stone Age*,[9] a solution to the problem of training is offered: 'It may be assumed that the Ice Age artists, who were trained in a kind of art school, were simultaneously the tribal magicians and the only men privileged to have access to the subterranean stations.' This idea of magicians did not impress Robert Gibbings on his visit to Lascaux, and it is difficult to find any historical record to support this notion.

It is possible that some of the engraved pebbles, reindeer horn and bone pieces found in the caves can provide some evidence of training activity. The engraved bison shown in [6] might well be the work of a student; if the engraving is analysed, a number of inaccuracies can be identified as the kind of errors a student might make. While evidence of organised training is scanty, the extraordinary unity of quality that prevails in the art of the caves, covering a very large area and a considerable span of time, can only assume the presence of 'schools' and the provision of some kind of training.

In his cave art, primitive man shows no interest in the fauna or any trace of a landscape surrounding the animals. Had he done so, it would have given him

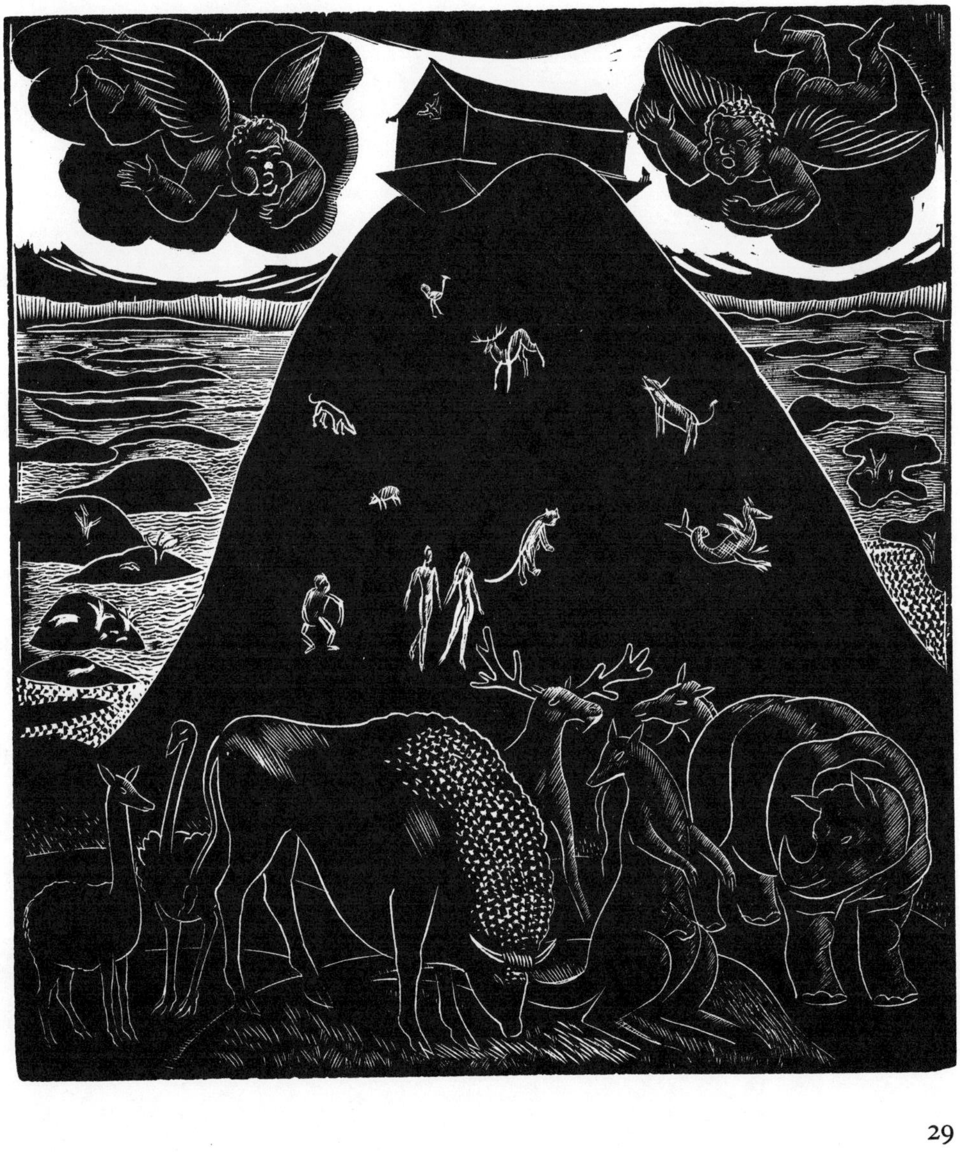

[9] Leon Underwood: *The Ark*, endpiece to *Animalia* 1926. 16.0 x 18.0cm

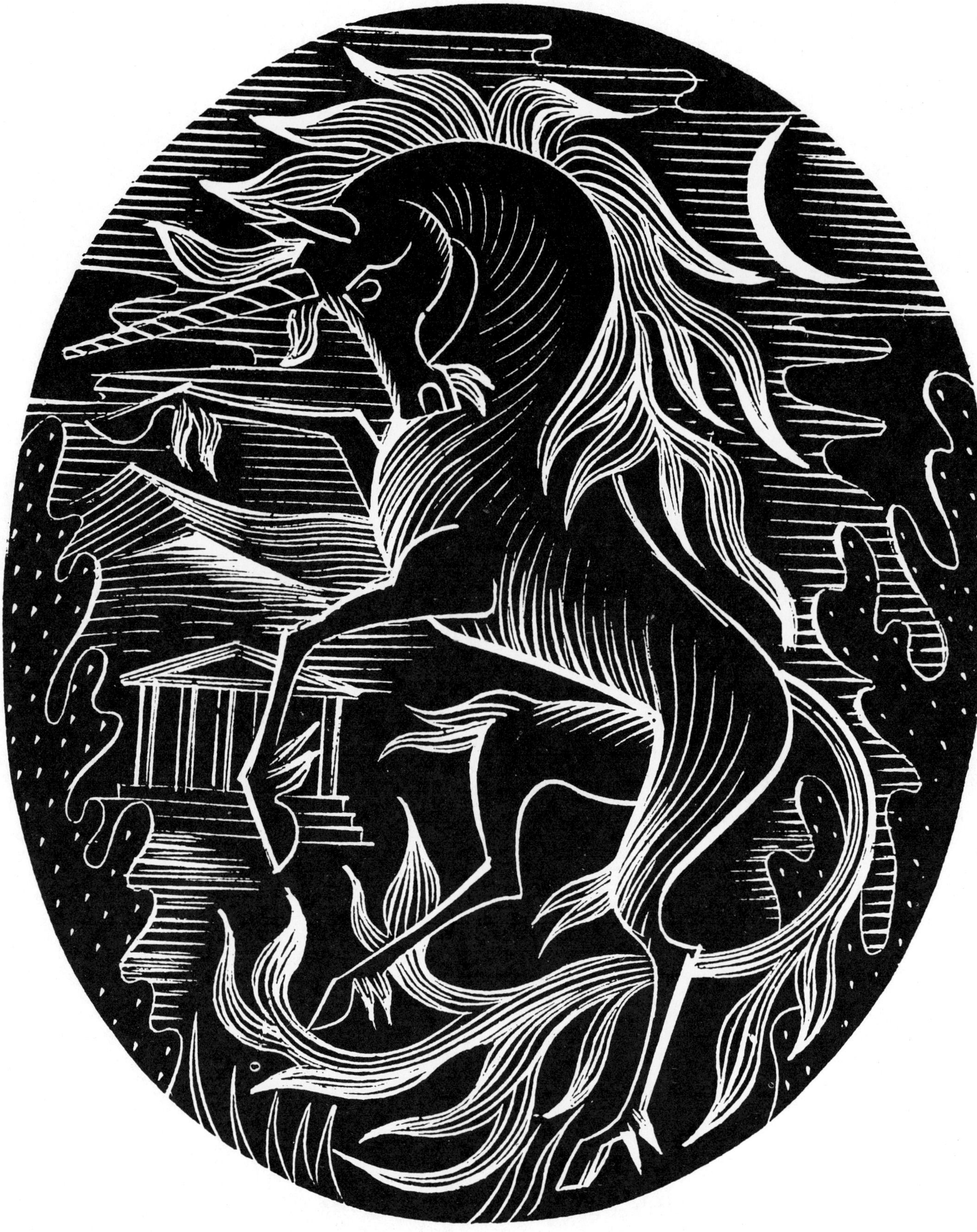

[10] John Farleigh: *The Unicorn*, Brewer's Society, 1946. 6.7 x 8.2cm

problems of perspective and thereby involved him with geometry and a much different space perspective – a development that was to come very much later. The only trace of fauna appearing in Palaeolithic art is found in a cave on the small island of Levanzo off the west coast of Sicily. The engravings in this small cave are Franco-Cantabrian in style and were not discovered until 1950 [8]. They are covered with a dark patina and are very well preserved.

Primitive art has exercised an influence on twentieth-century engravers. Writing of the Lascaux cave, David Jones stated: 'Works which have since proved a reassurance to us all that man, already twenty to forty thousand years ago, whatever his limitations or capabilities was capable of superb artistry. In some respects we have not equalled that artistry, let alone surpassed it.'[10] It was Picasso who said, 'To me there is no past or future in art. If a work of art cannot live always in the present it must not be considered at all. The art of the Greeks or of the Egyptians, of the great painters who lived in other times, is not art of the past; perhaps it is more alive today than it ever was.'

The art of the caves certainly came alive again in the engraving developments of the twentieth century and is probably best summed up in the Chinese Taoist statement, 'No point of time is long ago nor by lapse of ages has it grown old'.[11] In 1925, Leon Underwood visited the cave at Altamira and was the first of the young engravers of the twentieth century to do so. He viewed Altamira lying on his back (though since that time the floor has been lowered) and using acetylene lamps which have different colour-rendering properties from the Palaeolithic oil lamps. Regardless of the poor viewing conditions, these paintings had a profound effect on Underwood. He was impressed by the quality of the drawing and said of the Magdalenian artist, 'To draw like this suggested that he must have been at a pitch of intellectual and artistic development entirely at odds with the accepted ideas of material progress and our assumption of a direct relationship between technological and mental civilisation.' Underwood did not accept the anthropological theory that the paintings were part of supernatural rites.

In the first half of the twentieth century, the influence of prehistoric art was beginning to take root in the young experimental artists. In Britain, the period December 1948 to January 1949 became memorable because the seminal exhibition *40,000 Years of Modern Art* was held in the Academy Hall, Oxford Street, London. This exhibition was a traumatic experience for the public. With the exception of sculptors such as Epstein, Moore, Underwood, Brzeska, McWilliam, Hepworth, Arp, Brancusi, Giacometti, Lipchitz and Modigliani, the world of prehistoric and primitive art was not seen as an influence on the development of art but as something far below the cultural eye – a curio that was never a work of art.

The influences of primitive art manifested themselves in two main channels of expression: geometric and non-geometric. The geometric negroid forms of Africa were taken to heart by Picasso, Braque, Matisse, Vlaminck, Derain, Epstein and Brzeska, whereas the non-geometric world of Palaeolithic art affected the development of Klee, Miró, Ernst, Moore, Brancusi, Hepworth, Underwood, Arp and others. Picasso, Braque and Matisse adopted Cézanne's dictum that nature and form was comprised of the cube, prism and sphere. These artists had an understanding of geometry and used this knowledge to make their Cubism more geometric, giving it the flavour of Hellenic art. Being Europeans, they also adapted negroid art forms to serve their own purposes even though Cubism and negroid art are separate art forms. Eventually the Cubists found that their limited conceptions of space brought the development of Cubism to an end.

Leon Underwood's wood engraving *The Ark* [9] is a seminal work in the development of the twentieth-century revival of wood engraving. This work was published in 1926, a year after his visit to Altamira, and it was used as an end-piece in his book *Animalia*. However, there is one very important difference between this wood engraving and its Palaeolithic source: Ice Age draughtsmen were realists in vision whereas Underwood's vision in this work is romantic, no doubt due to his interest in William Blake.

REFERENCES

1 Giedion, S. *The Eternal Present*, Oxford University Press, London, 1962
2 Gibbings, R. *Coming down the Seine*, Dent, London, 1953
3 Powell, T. G. E. *Prehistoric Art*, Thames & Hudson, London, 1966
4 Bandi and others *The Art of the Stone Age*, Methuen, London 1960
5 Bandi, *The Art of the Stone Age*
6 Bandi, *The Art of the Stone Age*
7 Bandi, *The Art of the Stone Age*
8 *Encyclopedia of World Art, Vol XI*, McGraw Hill, London, 1966
9 Bandi, *The Art of the Stone Age*
10 Attwater, D. *A Cell of Good Living*, Chapman, London, 1969
11 Sickman & Soper *The Art and Architecture of China* (Pelican History of Art), Penguin Books, London, 1956

2 FROM STONE TO METAL BURINS

In the Mesolithic and Neolithic periods, cave art deteriorated progressively until it became a means of expression achieved by the use of rudimentary symbols. The cave art which continued beyond the Bronze Age is primitive in the sense that it was done by a race of people of inferior development to that of Palaeolithic man.

Between the achievement of the Upper Palaeolithic period and the next great development in art near the end of the Bronze Age, there is a vast space in time of which there is scant knowledge and very little evidence. Probably about 2500 BC, the Megalithic stone monuments of Stonehenge (in England), Carnac (in Brittany) and New Grange (in Ireland) were being erected, though little is known of the civilisations that were responsible. Similarly, there is little information on the nature and development of art between Palaeolithic man and the attainments of Greek art. However, it seems evident that engraving was rediscovered before the beginning of the period known as the Iron Age.

By the time that Greek art had reached a maturity of development, there had been a change in the dominant image and with it a change from a non-geometric world to one that was fully geometric and mathematical and inhabited by an individual who, from about 300 BC onwards, can be called 'Euclidean man'. Whilst Palaeolithic man had no architecture in the permanent sense, geometric man developed the permanent building and did so to such a degree of success that between 447 and 432 BC he erected the Parthenon, a structure that continues to exert an influence on architectural thought.

The human portrait as a clear art form began to emerge in the Middle Stone Age (about 6000 BC) and developed progressively over a very long period. With this development came European man's geometric thinking and realist objective vision which was to drive him to become dominated by perspective. Whilst eventually this dominance was to become complete in Europe, perspective was never totally accepted in China where it was used only when required and Chinese art continues to be interpretative in terms of the dominant philosophy of the period.

Metal working in iron began in the Neolithic age, about 3500 BC and metal working in copper, bronze and gold began in approximately 2500 BC. Metal burins were to lead to precision in art and to the superb attainments of Greek art. Engraving with metal into metal was later to lead to an achievement of even greater precision during the Italian Renaissance.

The introduction of metal working into the Mediterranean countries and into China was to effect a drastic change of scale from the massive Palaeolithic friezes extending for several metres on cave walls to the smaller Greek and Etruscan circular metal *cistae* a few centimetres in diameter.

There is considerable literature dealing with Greek architecture, sculpture, painting and pottery. Engraving played a smaller but very real part in the full spectrum of Greek art. The Greeks were able to cast in bronze and thereby make burins and there is always the possibility that burins may also have been cast in iron. The precision and very sharp cutting of Greek engraving indicates that the metal of their burins was hard and tough and could hold good cutting edges.

The Greek engraved bronzes were found on widely scattered sites, but the products come mostly from a comparatively limited region and many were found at the site of Praeneste. These engraved works consisted of toilet-cases and mirrors which were ornamented with incised metal-engraved outline designs. The Italians gave the name *graffiti* to metal engravings which may be regarded as the forerunners of the modern art of metal engraving. The quality of Greek engraving is comparable to the standard of painting of the period.

The Greek toilet-cases are known as *cistae* but are sometimes called mystic

[11] Bronze coffer with engravings from Praeneste. The two statuettes of ephebes on the lid serve as a handle. Hellenistic art.

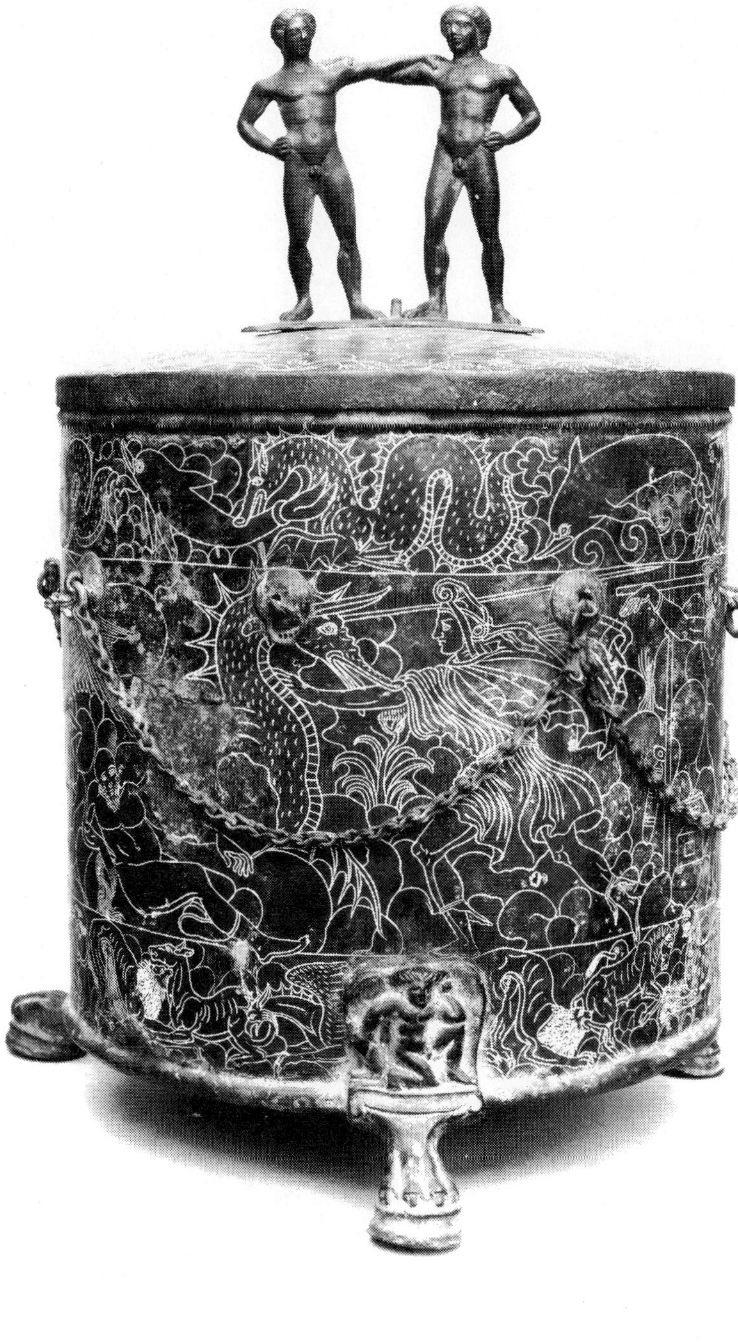

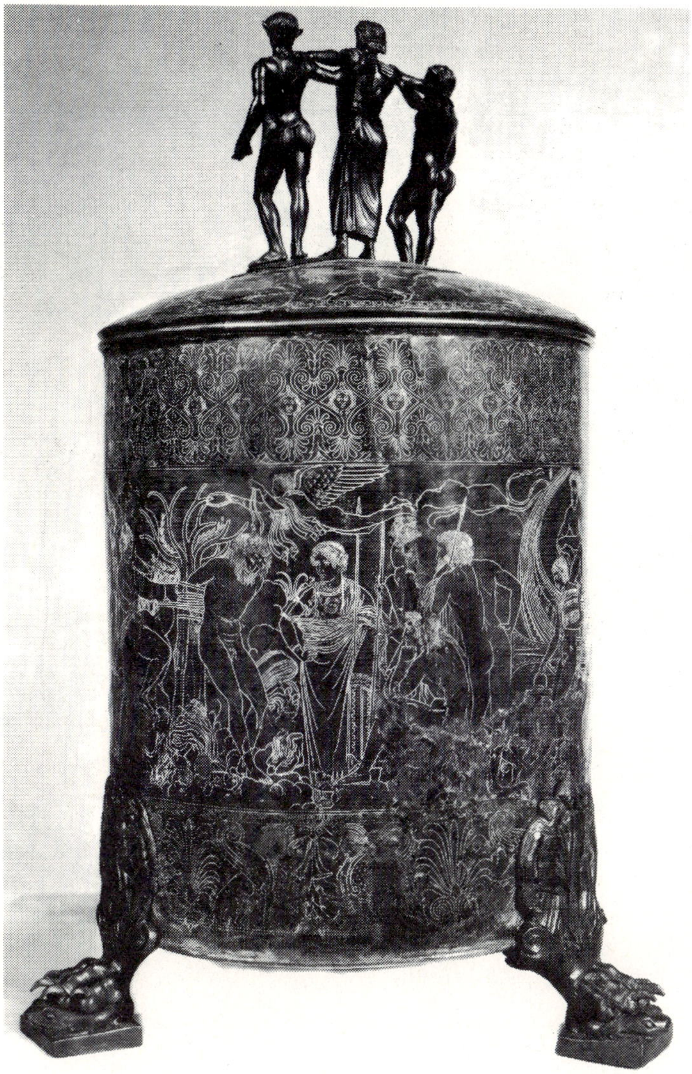

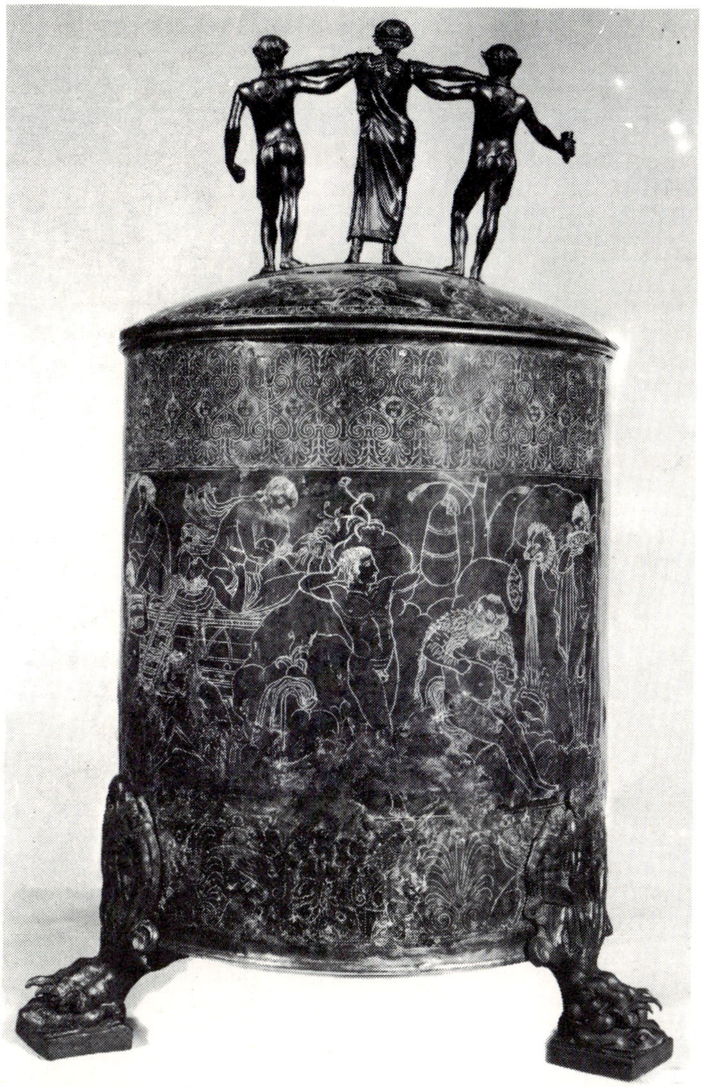

[12] The Ficoroni coffer or *cista* engraved on bronze.

[13] The Ficoroni coffer. Engraved decorations on the lid and sides represent episodes of the myth of the Argonauts.

cistae because they were erroneously supposed to have been intended for use in the mysteries. By a similar error mirrors were taken to be sacrificial plates. In fact, the *cistae* were ordinary dressing- or jewel- cases and mirrors. These metal decorations are, of course, one-off pieces of engraving.

Most of these objects in bronze have been found in central Italy, partly in Etruria and some in Latium. A very small number of bronze discs have been discovered in the Greek island of Aegina. These discs are engraved in the severe archaic style with figures of men engaged in athletic exercises. A disc now in the British Museum is engraved on both sides with this type of subject. These discs provide evidence that, as in other arts, the Greeks led in the skills of engraving.

In terms of modern engraving, John Farleigh understood the purity of Greek engraving and largely formed his style upon the few known examples. Like the Greek engraver, he also understood the human form and could express it. In his most successful work, George Bernard Shaw's *The Adventures of the Black Girl in her Search for God*, Farleigh is seen at his best. The absolute economy of the rendering of the young black girl's body set against the light translucent structure and image of God is remarkable.

The Etruscans hold an interesting position among the peoples of antiquity. Their history in the Italian Peninsula began in the early part of the seventh century

[14] John Buckland-Wright:
Composition No. 5 1935. 13.0 x 18.0cm

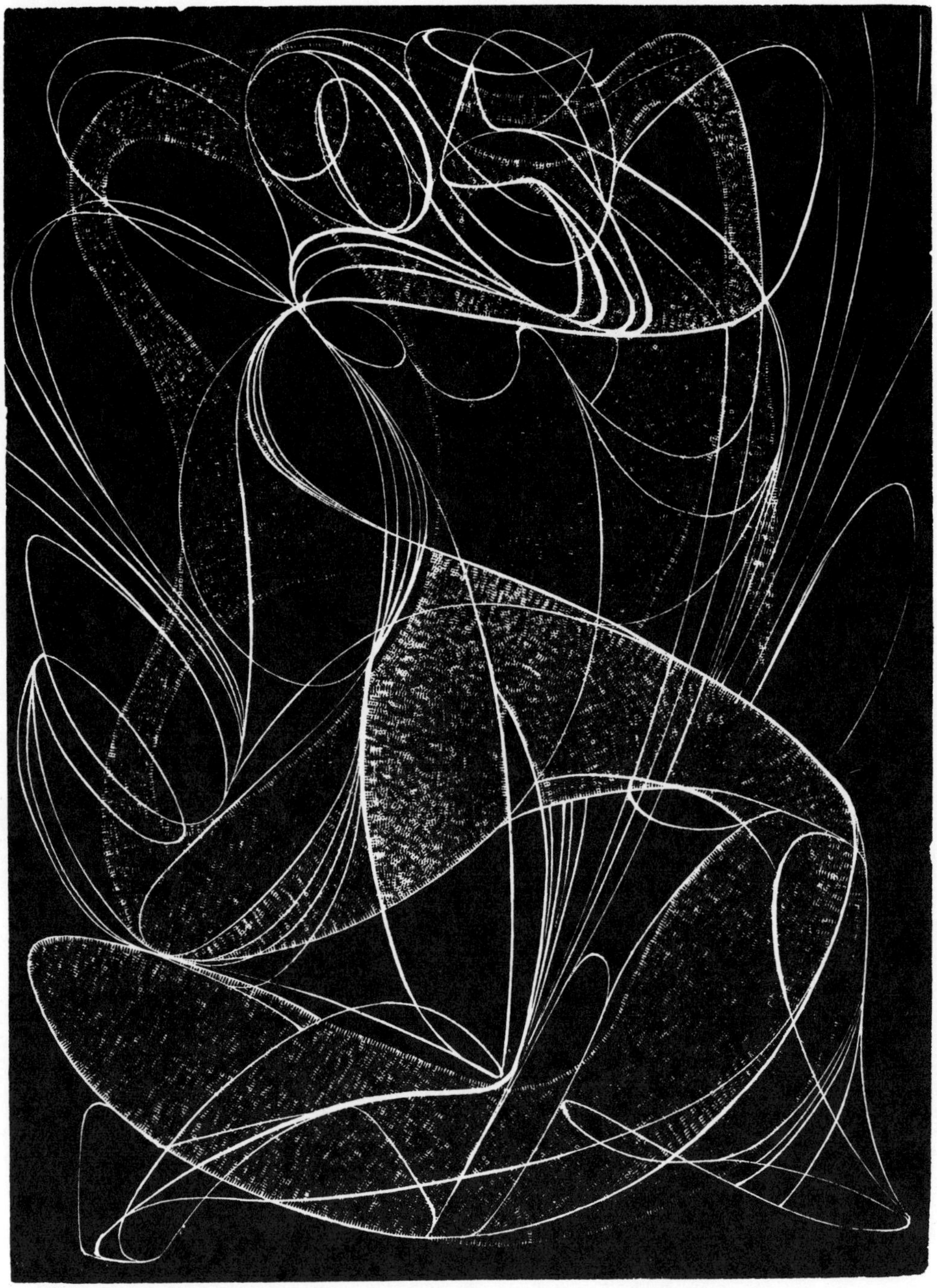

BC and ended shortly before the beginning of the Christian era, yet the origin of the Etruscans, like their language, is obscure. They absorbed elements of the pre-Hellenic Greek and oriental cultures and their art was influenced by certain aspects of the early Greek archaic styles.

Early Etruria was the land lying between the River Tiber, the River Arne and the sea, with the important towns along the coast. From about 1400 BC Italy was in the Apennine Bronze Age contemporary with the latter part of the Middle Bronze Age of central Europe. Because of the scarcity of tin as one of the principle ingredients of bronze, the tin mines of Etruria were of considerable interest to the Mycenaeans as the nearest source of the metal to Greece.

Although engraving plays only a small role in Greek and Etruscan art, the quality is very high. The Etruscans excelled in engraving on metal with the burin and thousands of mirrors and coffers have been discovered.

Etruscan mirrors are in the shape of a disc of metal, one surface of which is carefully polished to reflect the light. The other face is engraved or in relief, but the engraved mirror is the more common in Etruria. Toilet mirrors and other objects for the toilet or for use as ornament were kept in sensitively designed, elegant bronze coffers, which were usually cylindrical and sometimes square or oval in shape. Small sensitive pieces of sculpture were used as lid handles and for the feet. Coffers were usually decorated with a series of engraved scenes in the form of a frieze. The majority of coffers that have been discovered are of the Hellenic period of the fourth century BC and a large number of these were made in the Etrusco-Latin town of Praeneste which had become the main centre of production.

In 535 BC the Etruscans repulsed the Massaliotes of Corsica from the Italian coast in a naval battle at Alalia and then in 474 BC they attacked Cumae, but were routed by Hieron of Syracuse. The Etruscan navy was annihilated.

Etruscan artists of all periods produced engravings in gold, silver and bronze and even the early examples of art are compositions requiring the application of skill and imagination to the existing knowledge of formal pictorial structure. There is a wide range of subject matter and as new objects are discovered the range of Etruscan art increases. Each piece, because it is engraved, is a one-off work. Most of the pictorial content seems inspired by Greek myths and the artists probably became familiar with the prevailing style through sketches, models and vases, though they did not always interpret the precise meaning of the myths that were depicted in the Greek models.

[15] The Diamond Sutra, printed A.D. 868. The wood engraving shows the Buddha addressing Subhuti, an aged disciple.

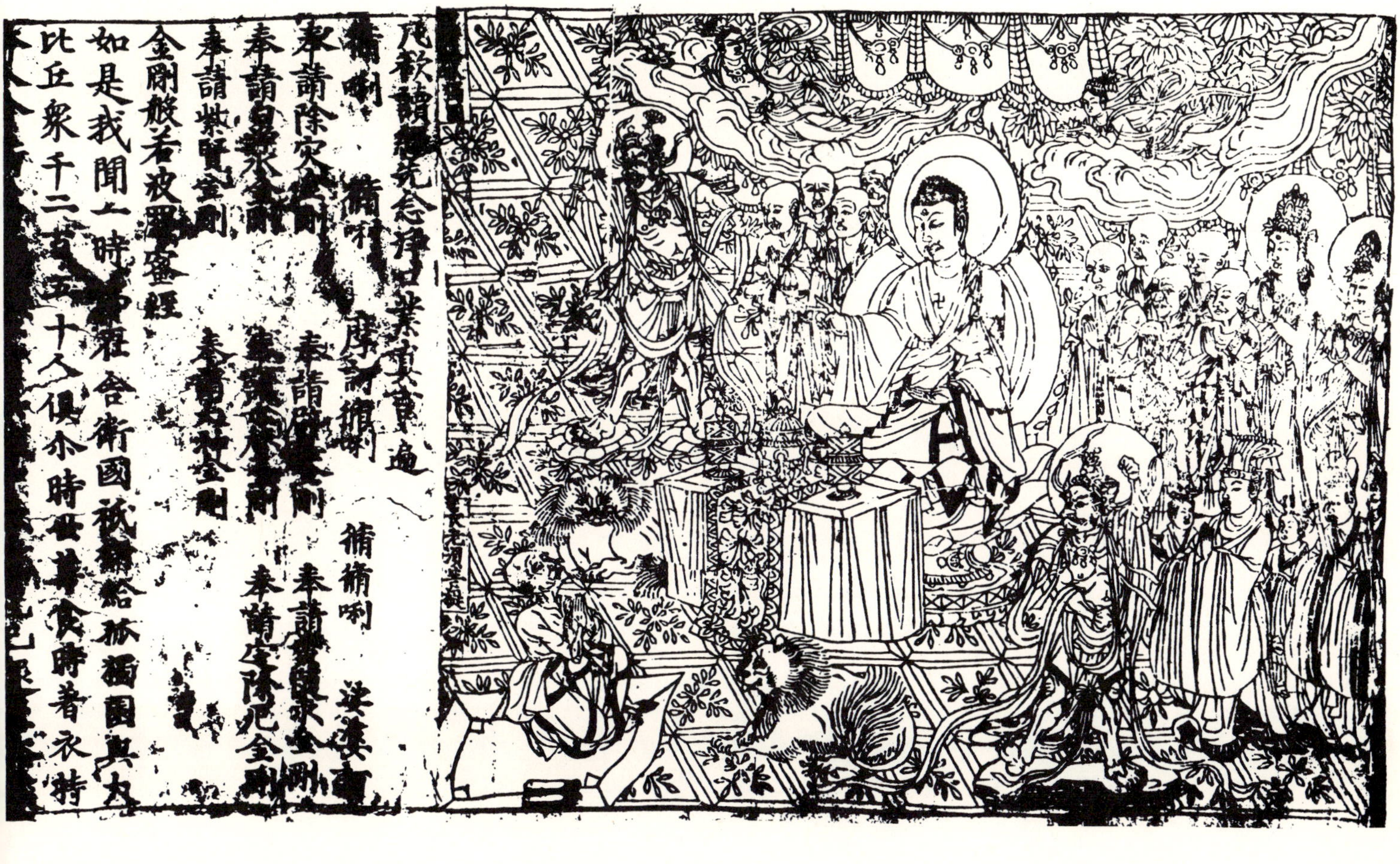

經頌云非因亦非果真際淨名經云畢竟空寂舍

因果亦歸空

泯融性相泯絕果因淨若太空童今

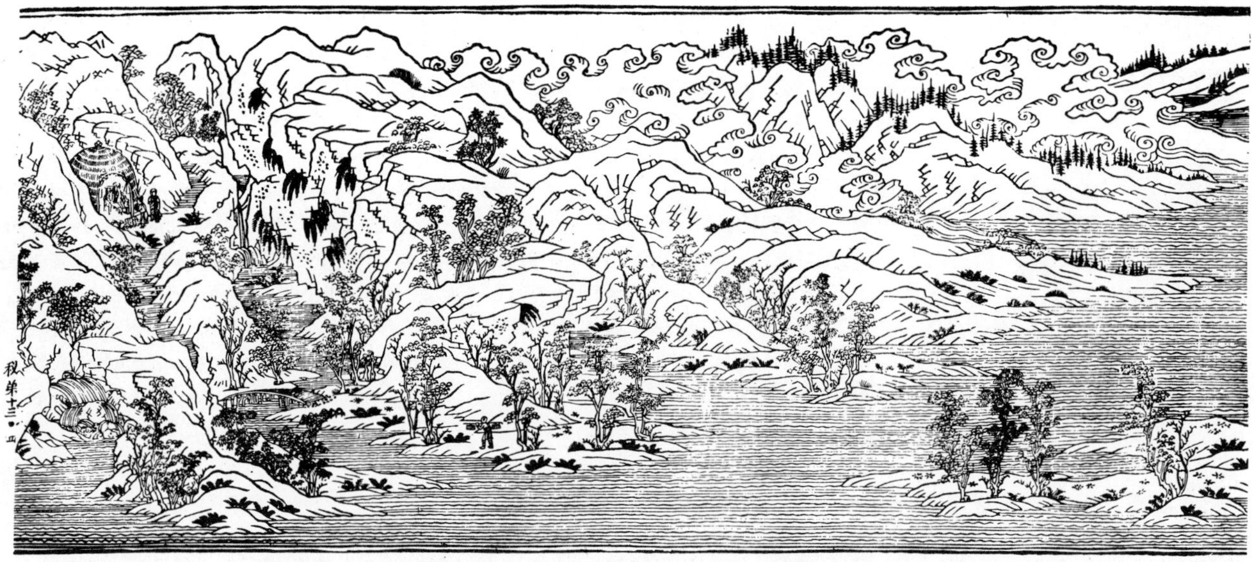

義切方求法

言前了義方日切求句下尋名誠非得法諒唯神會豈是心知法華經云是法非思量分別之所能解

韜光迷自通

冈象玄珠

知見香之所熏修方至廣作佛事之因益濟利樂克家智身之土淨名經云欲淨其土當淨其心隨其心淨即佛土淨

福種因無失

淨心福種誠為無漏

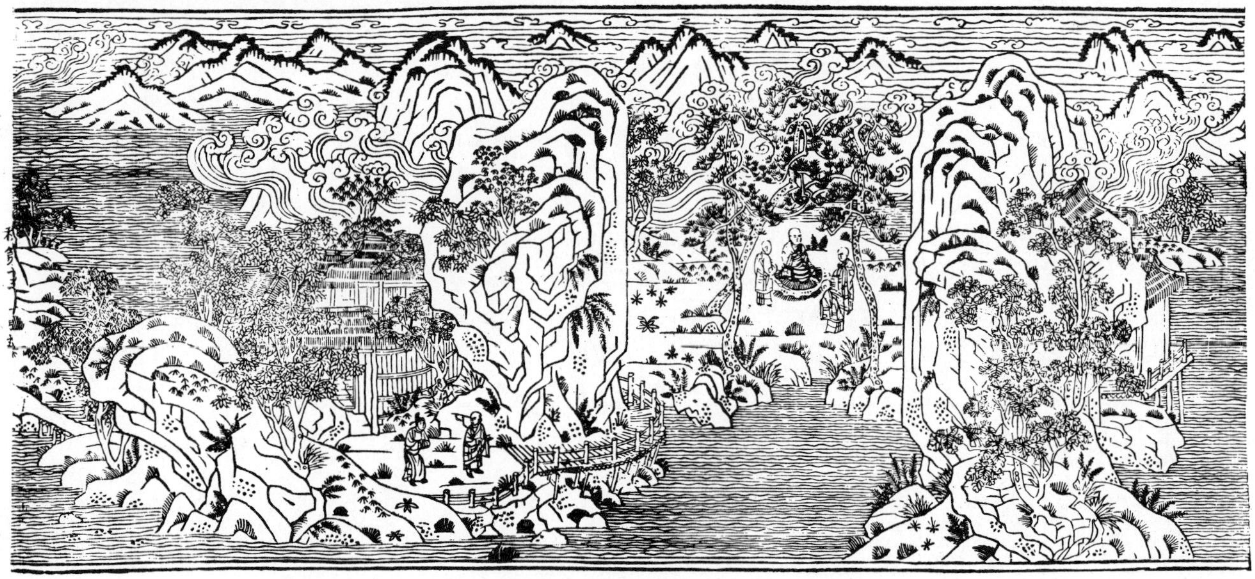

智願過諸已

謂佛智願超諸十地出過二乘已證解脫瑜伽論云如實安立清淨妙智為一切有情起此願故

其如見不同

唯識論云其如見道

於性中業累所昏如水發聞無量義疏云亦名妙法蓮華

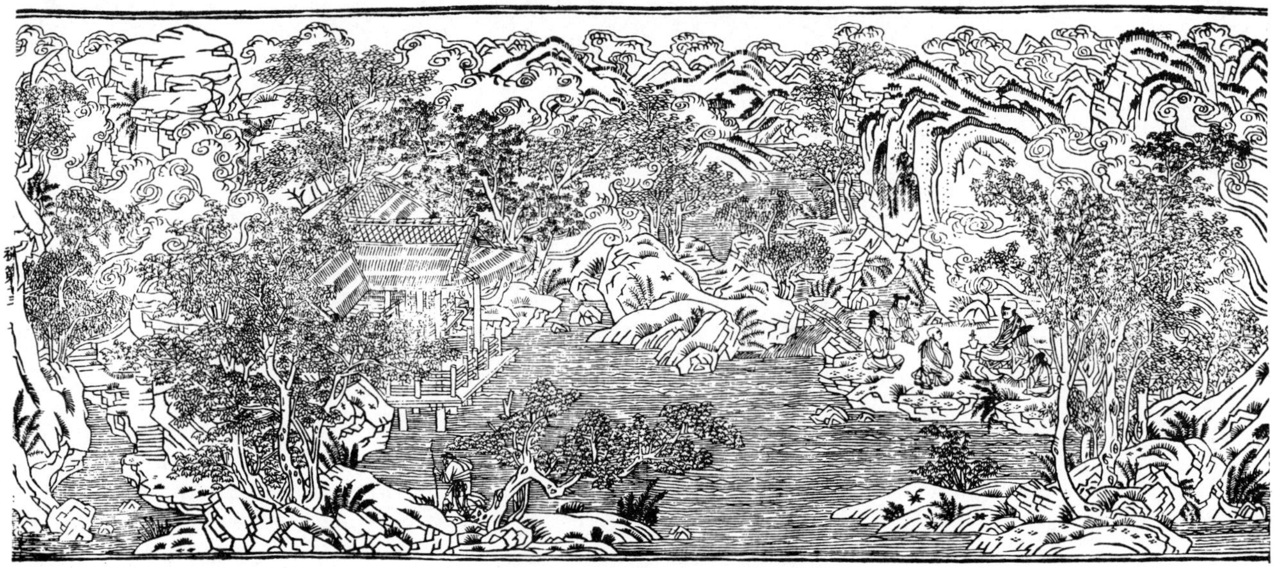

解即祛煩惱

解即妙解祛即遣除煩惱如明來暗謝智起惑忘唯識論

[16, 17, 18] Landscapes from the *Sung Imperial Commentary on Chinese Tripitaka.* 53.0 x 22.7cm

Probably the finest, best-known and most appreciated masterpiece from Palestrina, the ancient Praeneste, is the *cista* or toilet case known as the *Ficoroni cista*, which was discovered by chance some twenty-five miles from Rome in 1786 by the antiquarian Francesco Ficoroni. It is now housed in the Soprintendenza Alle Antichita Dell' Etruria Meridionale in the Villa Guilia, Rome [12 and 13]. This large cylindrical bronze coffer with finely engraved decorations on its lid and sides dates from probably 330 BC. The artist shows a superb mastery of art, composition and fluency in handling the engraving, which is continuous around the cylinder. Drawing, foreshortening, anatomy and structure are remarkably confident. The artist's signature inscribed on the coffer is that of Novios Plautios. Many writers and historians assess this casket engraving as one of the finest known monuments of pictorial art.

Engravings on coffers and mirrors were often interpretations of painted compositions and the marvellously engraved scenes on the Ficoroni coffer depicting the legend of the Argonauts might well have been an interpretation of the painting of the Argonauts executed by Cydias of Cnidus and mentioned by Pliny the Elder.[1] The wood engraving of the centre section was done in 1880 and correctly reflects the quality of the original work, showing the detail more clearly than would be possible in a photograph.

The engraving of the *Ficoroni cista* is not only a superb example of classical art but is also a work in which copper engraving is seen in technical perfection. Among the twentieth-century artists inspired by the Ficoroni coffer was John Buckland-Wright who used it to demonstrate to his students the perfection that can be obtained in copper engraving. Buckland-Wright's own attainment was of the same high order as that of the engraver of the coffer, as is evident from his engraving *Composition No 5* [14] which shows how well defined his technical skill was at its peak of perfection. His expression of the subject matter shows wonderful depth of feeling and the engraving is an example of space concepts very close to those of the sculptor Gabo.

The Bronze Age technology developed in China in the Shang dynasty, 1523 to 1027 BC, and it is evident today that casting in bronze was practised there centuries before casting was even thought of in Europe. For many years scholars were unable to understand how advanced bronze-casting techniques could appear suddenly and in a mature form and this led to the theory that bronze casting had been introduced into China fully developed. However, in recent excavations prototypes have been unearthed which have proved the theory wrong. These prototypes are thin and the decoration rudimentary, thus it is almost certain that bronze casting was developed by the Chinese themselves.

Archaeological excavations in China have revealed a very large number of tombs of the Shang dynasty and of the Chou dynasty which succeeded it. Many of these tombs contained sacrifical remains of slaves – sometimes as many as thirty bodies – though by the end of the Bronze Age the sacrifice of human beings had given way to a sacrifice symbolized by the placing of a wooden or pottery model in the tomb.

In 1971 a new tomb was discovered at Linchengchiao of the late Autumn and Spring period 770 to 475 BC. Timber was found in this tomb held together by bronze nails. These nails were strong and sufficiently tough to pierce cypress timber planks of eight centimetres in thickness. The nails formed a complicated jigsaw pattern. Having produced bronze nails, obviously it was a straightforward matter to produce metal burins, which could be either pushed by hand or used with a mallet.

Throughout its history, Chinese writing has remained calligraphic and the

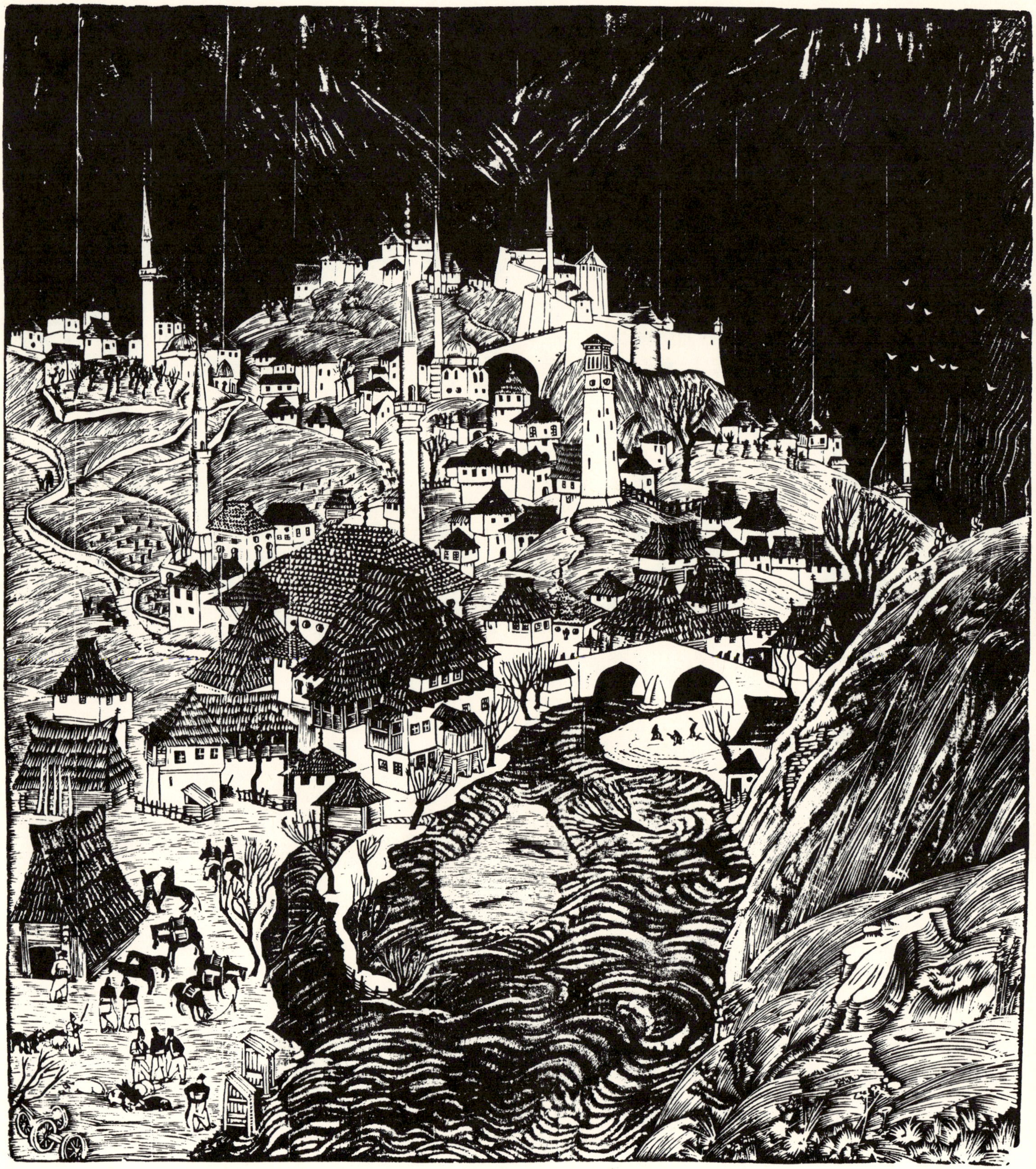

[19] Bernard Rice: *Town of Travnik in Bosnia*, 1925. 36.3 x 40.75cm

[20] *Le Bois Protat*, 1370 (fragment)
23.0 x 60.0cm

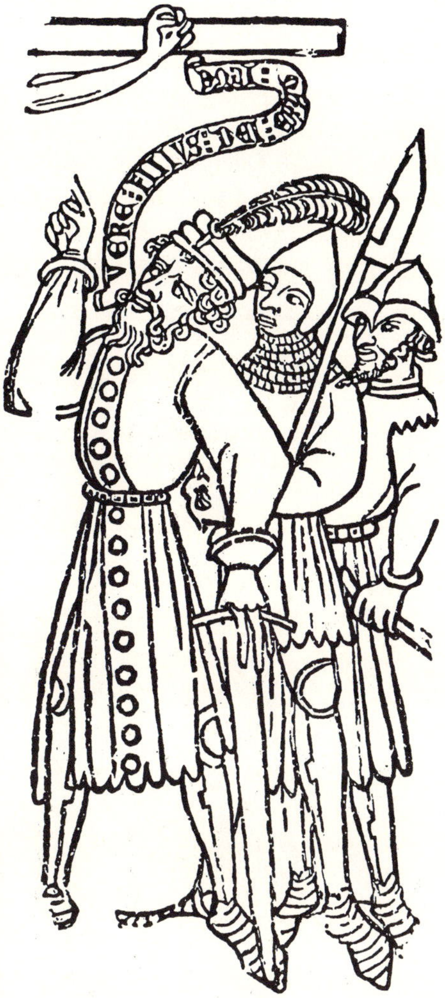

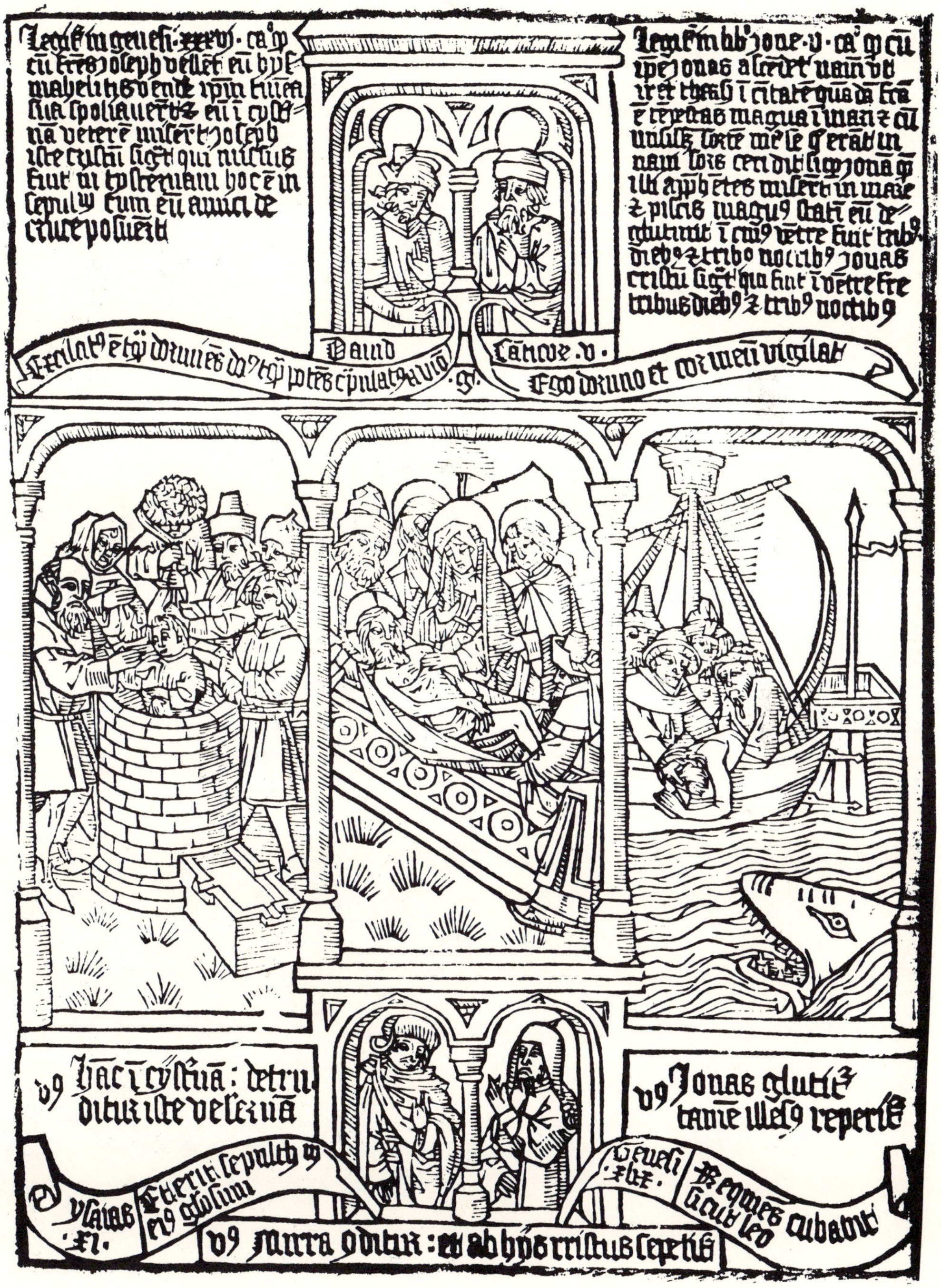

[21] An illustration from *Biblia Pauperum*, 1470.
Page size 20.0 x 27.0cm

earliest examples are those of the Shang dynasty incised, engraved or written on scapula bones. Many thousands of these inscribed bones have been recovered from tombs. They were used for the practice of scapulamancy, a type of divination in which an oracle is asked for answers to questions inscribed on the bone. Fire was then applied and according to the nature of the cracks which appeared the answers were divined. These bones have provided large quantities of important historical and philological information from the characters incised or engraved on them.

In the Chou dynasty jade began to be used in Chinese art. Decoration on early jades was produced by raised or incised lines engraved or cut. During the Shang dynasty the Chinese mastered the technique of shaping and drilling this extremely hard stone.

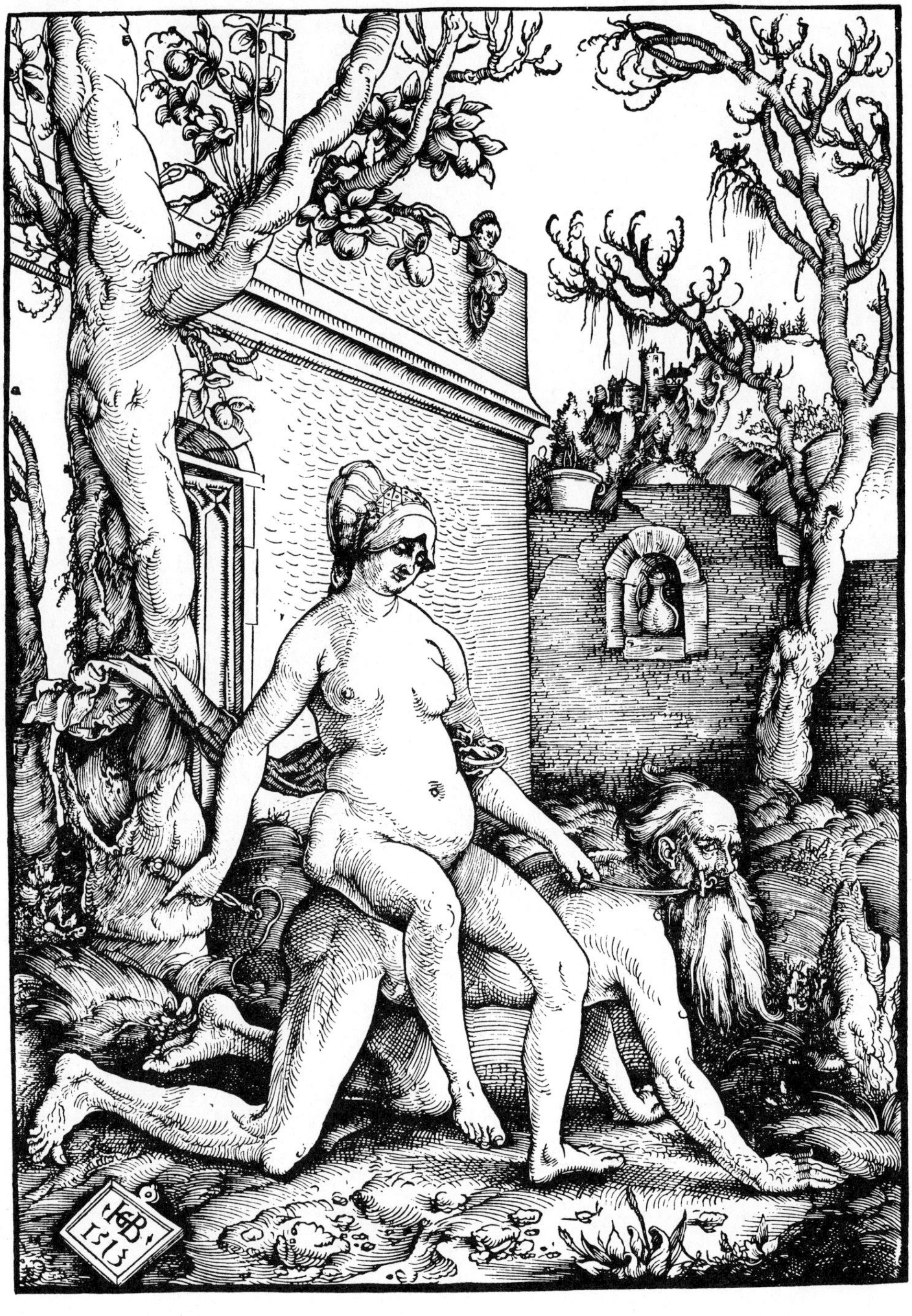

[22] Hans Baldung Grien: *Aristotle and Phyllis*, 1513.

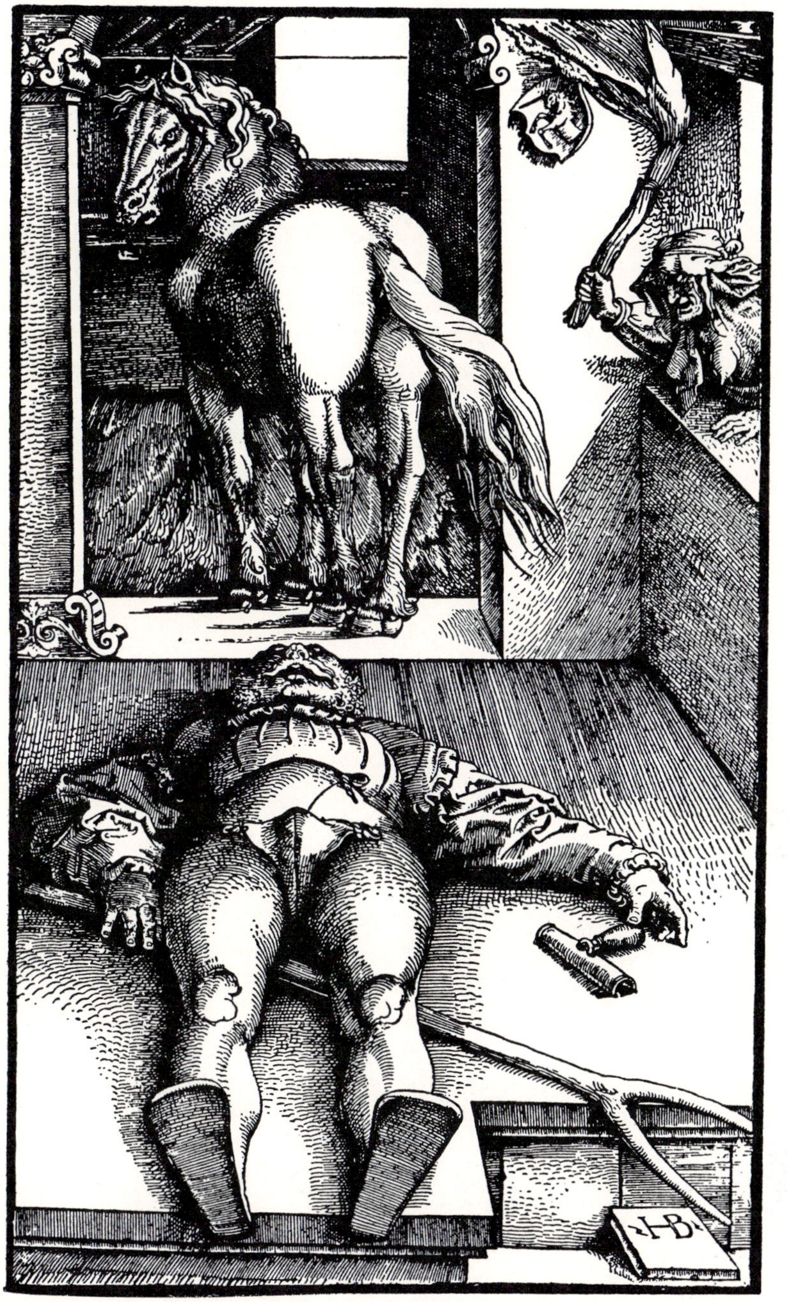

[23] Hans Baldung Grien: *The Groom Bewitched*, 1544. 19.7 x 33.7cm

During the first century BC the Chinese carved and engraved inscriptions on stone tablets or directly on to rocks. Stone tablets appear in the tombs and some were later set up in gardens and monasteries. Famous people, poets and thinkers had their writings engraved on tablets of this kind.

The early development of stone pictures gave rise to the practice of 'rubbing' known in China as *ta-pen*, and this technique of reproduction is a predecessor of the art of printing. *Ta-pen* originated as a means of copying and disseminating the inscriptions and stories engraved on the stone. The rubbing was made on thin, highly absorbent paper using an ink of simple structure. The stone inscriptions are valued as a source material for historical research and for their calligraphy.

The world's oldest 'book' was printed in China and the date in the colophon is translated to read that the work was printed on 11 May AD 868 to the order of Wang Chieh for his parents, though the location of the printing is unknown. The work was purchased for the British Museum by Sir Aurel Stein when he visited Tun-huang in 1908 and 1909.

The 'book' is known as the *Diamond Sutra* [15] and is really a scroll of paper printed from large blocks. Originally the paper was stained yellow but exposure to light has given parts of it a greyish tone. The scroll commences with a black-line engraving showing the Buddha preaching to his aged disciple Subhuti, and the work shows a maturity of skill indicating that the artist already had considerable experience.

Commenting on the *Sutra*, Arthur M. Hind says, 'But to judge from the accomplishment of its art there is little doubt that it must have its predecessors.'[2] The quality of the engraving of the *Diamond Sutra* does not compare so well with the outstanding quality of the three wood engravings from the *Tripitaka* [16, 17 and 18]. In both works the wood engraving is executed so as to simulate the drawn line, to which it is faithful up to the point where the character of engraving is still evident.

In addition to the *Diamond Sutra*, Sir Aurel Stein was also responsible for the discovery of some of the earliest-known Chinese wood engravings (in the *formschneider* black-line technique) in the cave of the 'Thousand Buddhas' near Tun-huang in Eastern Turkestan on the western frontier of China.[3] Together with the *Diamond Sutra* this material has helped to form the currently-held opinion that printing techniques originated in China with the use of wood blocks, rather than in India as was thought at one period.

Confucius lived from 551 to 479 BC and the Chinese version of his name is K'ung fu-tzu. Shortly after his death his disciples recorded his philosophy and sayings in

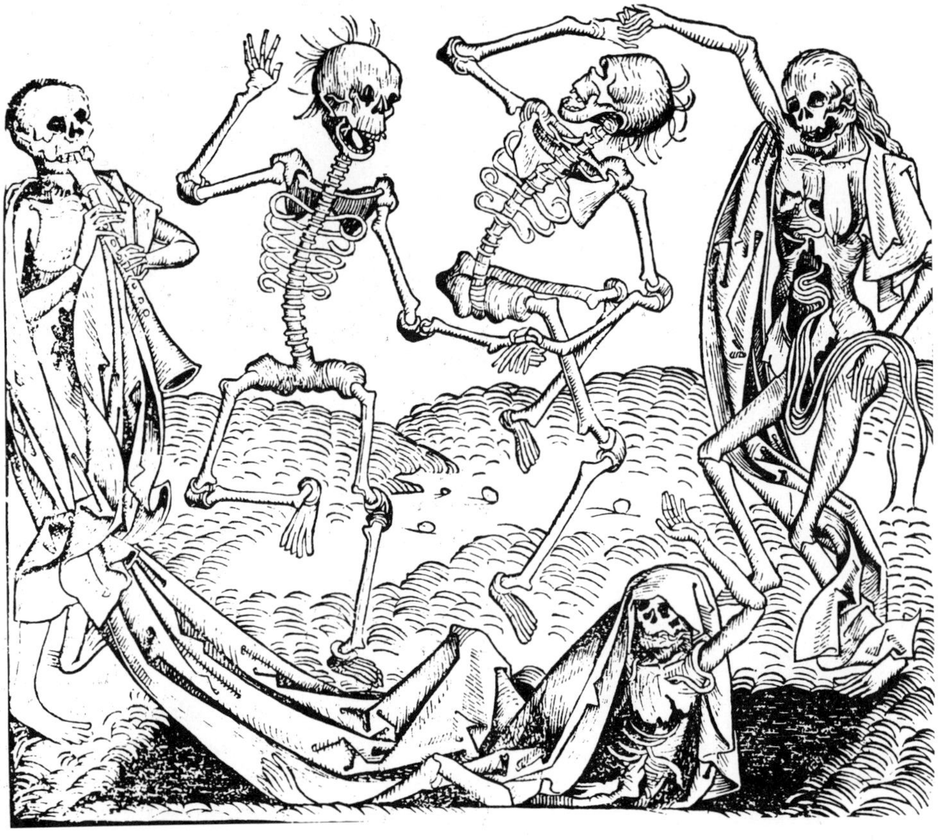

[24] Michael Wolgemut: *Dance of the Dead*, from the *Nuremberg Chronicle*, 1493.

the famous *Analects*. These stone tablets became known as the 'stone classics'. The rubbings of the Confucian texts taken from the stone pictures on to paper are likely to be among the first examples of duplicated pictorial images, which centuries later were to develop into compositions like the *Diamond Sutra*.

Landscape art began in the Han dynasty and reached a climax in the Sung dynasty (AD 960 to 1280) but prior to this primitive 'books' had developed using the techniques of hand copying, though the product was not recognisable as a 'book' in the European sense.

As early as AD 600 there is evidence of early printing in connection with the Taoist developments in China, in which there was emphasis on the physical aspects of nature. The Taoist priests made seals in wood (vin) which were carved and engraved in such subjects as the constellations, the sun and the moon. There are records that printed paper money was issued in the Pao-li era (AD 825 to 826) and dictionaries were first printed in the time of Wen-tsung (AD 827 to 840). One of the oldest items of printing so far recorded from China is a charm printed from wood on a single sheet and showing a six-armed *Bodhisattra* figure in the centre of Sanskrit words written in *Lantsa* letters. The print is dated AD 757 and was discovered in 1944 during the excavation of a T'ang dynasty tomb in the town of Ch'eng-tu, Szechwan.

Stone pictures made their appearance in China in the Han dynasty, a period during which China developed from a feudal system towards a unified state. Many of the early Chinese stone pictures were discovered in tombs and some of the work was extensive, as in the Hasiao-tang Shan tomb in the Shantung province where an entire wall is devoted to the depiction of a procession of a god of thunder. This was done before AD 129. A second tomb of Wu Liang-tz'u is famous for its stone pictures and was erected between AD 145 and 168. Within the last two decades, Han reliefs and stone pictures have been discovered on numerous sites.

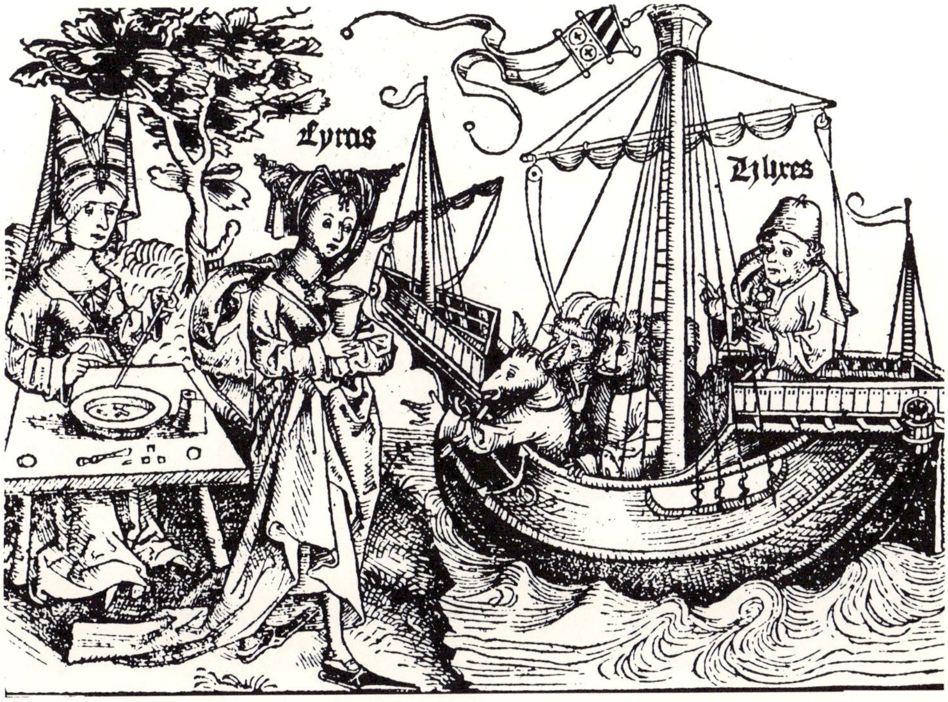

[25] Michael Wolgemut (shop): *Circe and Odysseus*, 1493.

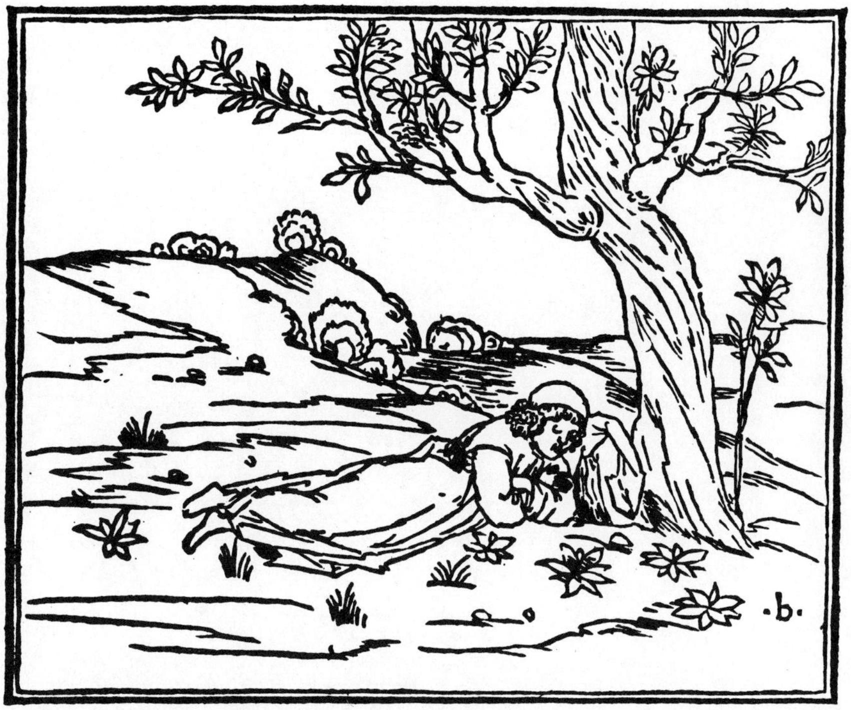

POLIPHILO QVIVI NARRA, CHE GLI PARVE ANCORA DI DORMIRE, ET ALTRONDE IN SOMNO RITROVARSE IN VNA CONVALLE, LAQVALE NEL FINE ERA SERATA DE VNA MIRABILE CLAVSVRA CVM VNA PORTENTOSA PYRAMIDE, DE ADMIRATIONE DIGNA, ET VNO EXCELSO OBELISCO DE SOPRA. LAQVALE CVM DILIGENTIA ET PIACERE SVBTILMENTE LA CONSIDEROE.

LA SPAVENTEVOLE SILVA, ET CONSTIPATO Nemore euaſo, & gli primi altri lochi per el dolce ſomno che ſe hauea per le feſſe & proſternate mébre diſfuſo relicti, me ritrouai di nouo in uno piu delectabile ſito aſſai piu che el præcedente. Elquale non era de monti horridi, & crepidinoſe rupe intorniato, ne falcato di ſtrumoſi iugi. Ma compoſitamente de grate montagniole di non tropo altecia. Siluoſe di giouani quercioli, di roburi, fraxini & Carpini, & di frondoſi Eſculi, & Ilice, & di teneri Coryli, & di Alni, & di Tilie, & di Opio, & de infructuoſi Oleaſtri, diſpoſiti ſecondo laſpecto de gli arboriferi Colli. Et giu al piano erano grate ſiluule di altri ſiluatici

[26] A page from the *Hypnerotomachia Poliphili*. Venice. Produced by Aldus Manutius, December 1499. Engraving 13.25 x 11.75cm Page 19.15 x 27.8cm

Chinese stone pictures are not reliefs in the sense of being sculptural reliefs or bas-reliefs as in the western conception of sculpture, based upon the Greek ideas. The majority of stone pictures are engraved and rarely come into focus in the western historical studies of Chinese art, most western writers and historians referring to them as sculpture.

In 1968 evidence of casting in iron in China was found upon the discovery of the tomb of Liu Sheng, Prince Ching of Chungshan of the Western Han dynasty (206 BC to AD 24) and the tomb of his wife Tou Wan; both tombs were found in the Lingshan Mountain of Mancheng. The tombs were of gigantic size, cut deep into the rock and were sealed with an iron wall which had been cast on the site, which was a truly amazing feat for that time.

When the tomb of Liu Sheng was finally opened by dynamite, it was found to contain over 2800 objects including the now famous jade funerary suit of Prince Liu Sheng made from 2690 pieces of jade sewn together with gold thread. With these iron-casting techniques, craftsmen were able to make very hard iron burins and chisels for engraving on stone.

The introduction of Buddhism into China began the development of large-scale sculpture with a concentration on the human form. The human figure had been depicted earlier in the Han dynasty but examples are scarce compared with the proliferation of images under the influence of Buddhism.

In China historians attach a major importance to the period around the second and third centuries AD, which marks the end of the Han and Wei dynasties, as a significant turning point in their history. Stone reliefs, which continue into modern times, lost their earlier central importance as a means of expressing pictorial art and calligraphy. Painting on paper and silk developed as distinctive arts in which brush work reached its pre-eminence in Chinese painting. Chinese Buddhist art began and bronzes were in decline.

The Han reliefs and stone pictures are remarkable for their supreme craftsmanship. The craftsmen developed skills which enabled them to cut stone virtually with the freedom and flexibility of brush strokes on paper and silk. This craftsmanship linked and related the stone picture not to sculpture but to painting.[4]

Some magnificent wood engravings have recently come to light and their excellence is of a very high order.[5] These landscape prints of the Northern Sung dynasty from the Sung Imperial Commentary on the Chinese *Tripitaka* dated AD 1108 were engraved some time between AD 984 and 991 [16, 17 and 18]. No explanation is available as to why they were not printed until nearly a century later. In 1962 the prints were acquired by the Fogg Art Museum, Harvard University. These landscape prints are older than any other landscape prints known and are of an unfamiliar character. The engravings were used to illustrate an important Buddhist book called *Yu-chih Pi-tsang-ch'uan*. The engraving is in pure black line, anticipating the German *formschneider* technique of engraving. Representation of natural images is highly abstracted, as would be expected from China, where by this time philosophies were being influenced by Buddhism.

Each cut in the engravings bears only the mark of the engraving tool and the purity of execution is such that a series of radial burin incisions moving to a common centre provide the convention for a bunch of leaves on a tree. A fern leaf arises from the same action but with the central radiation opened out along a curve. Each short line is curved and is the body curve of the engraver controlling the cutting pressure of the block as it is turned into the resisting burin. The engraving of the

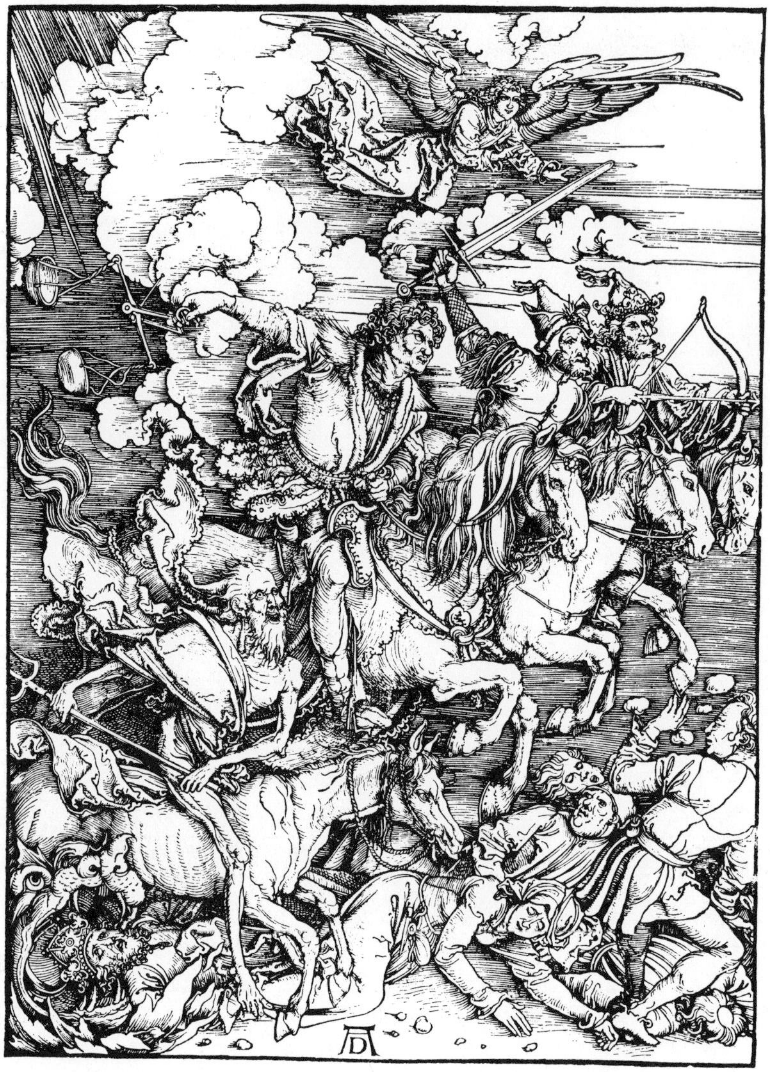

[27] Albrecht Dürer: *Death, Famine, War and Plague*, from *The Apocalypse*, 1497/8. 28.2 x 38.8cm

water is based upon a curved line, interspersed by alternating single unbroken straight lines with double unbroken straight lines. Variations in the water's surface are achieved by increasing or decreasing the thickness of the black-line curve or changing the rhythms of one single and two black-line combinations.

The degree of abstraction between the clouds, water, trees, buildings, rocks, mountains and people is equal. This achievement is largely due to the size of the burin; the smallest detail and the convention units combine to form an image. The degree of observation is equal in all parts. The compressed expression of the engraver's total experience, and the intense and relative consistency throughout all these works result in a remarkable achievement. Engraving of this purity is very rare. The cleanness, monumentality and unity from rocks to mountains arise from the engraving of the small unit multiplied into the greater mass of the mountain, the rhythms being similar, changing only in their sequence and the emphasis of the length of the body curvature.

The textures in these landscapes are suggested by the manner in which the lines are engraved but no attempt is made to imitate natural textures and the end result is strictly the engraving solution. Individuals portrayed in compositions occupy a minor position in the overall concept and the detail allocated to them is of a limited scope.

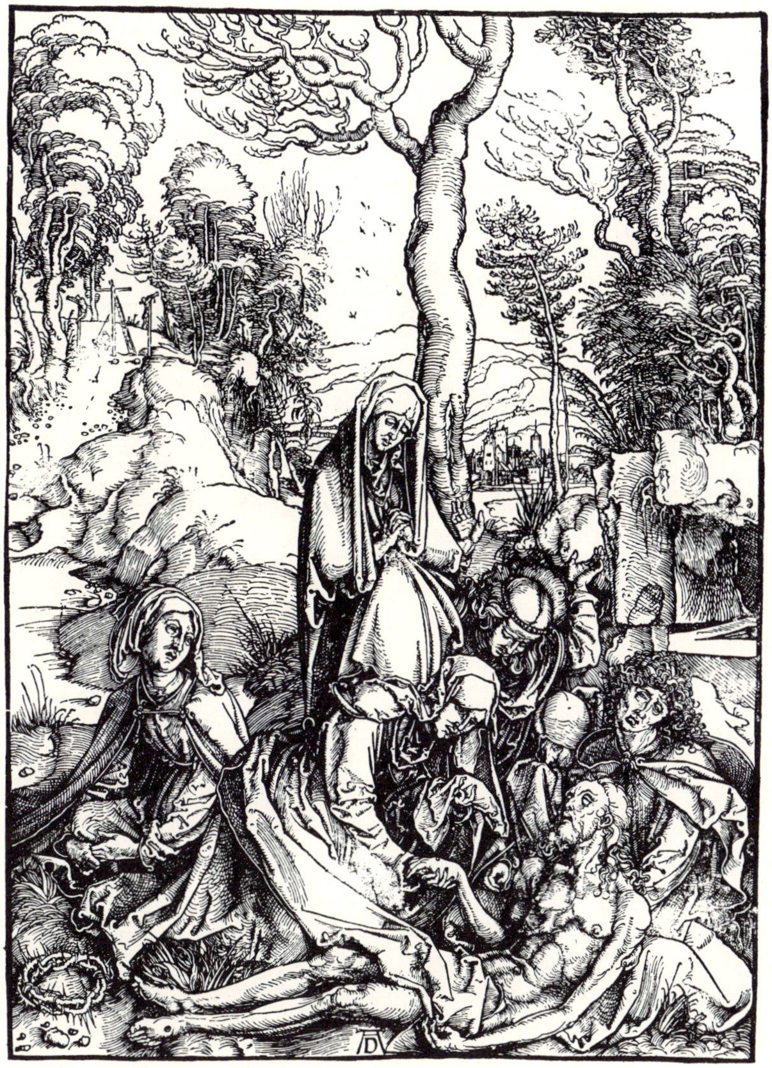

[28] Albrecht Dürer: *The Lamentation of Christ*, 1498/9. 27.5 x 38.7cm

Such stylistic unity suggests the artists were very mature in experience and possessed great sensitivity. Work of this quality and profundity points to the fact that there must have been other, similar engraving done in the period. The quality, sensitivity and stylistic unity supports the view that these three prints were engraved and produced directly by the artist rather than a *formschneider* type of engraver. They have a similarity in technique to the fourteenth- and fifteenth-century Danube school and, together with the *Diamond Sutra*, are the earliest examples of prints showing the creative engraving of the black-line technique, continually changing in shape throughout its length.

The *Tripitaka* prints are masterly examples of the skill with which the artists impart just sufficient information to enable the scene to be interpreted correctly by the sensitive viewer. Inhibited by his preoccupation with perspective, the western artist cannot accommodate this concept of communication because his sense of perspective is so structured that he must omit no detail. The Chinese are interested in space but to a lesser degree than are Europeans. They render space as a psychological experience and the *Tripitaka* engravings are superb examples of this philosophy.

The pictures of the *Tripitaka* engravings illustrate the Chinese philosophy embodying the concept of the observer having an ability to move, even from one

[29] Albrecht Dürer: *The Holy Family with Three Hares.* 28.1 x 38.7cm

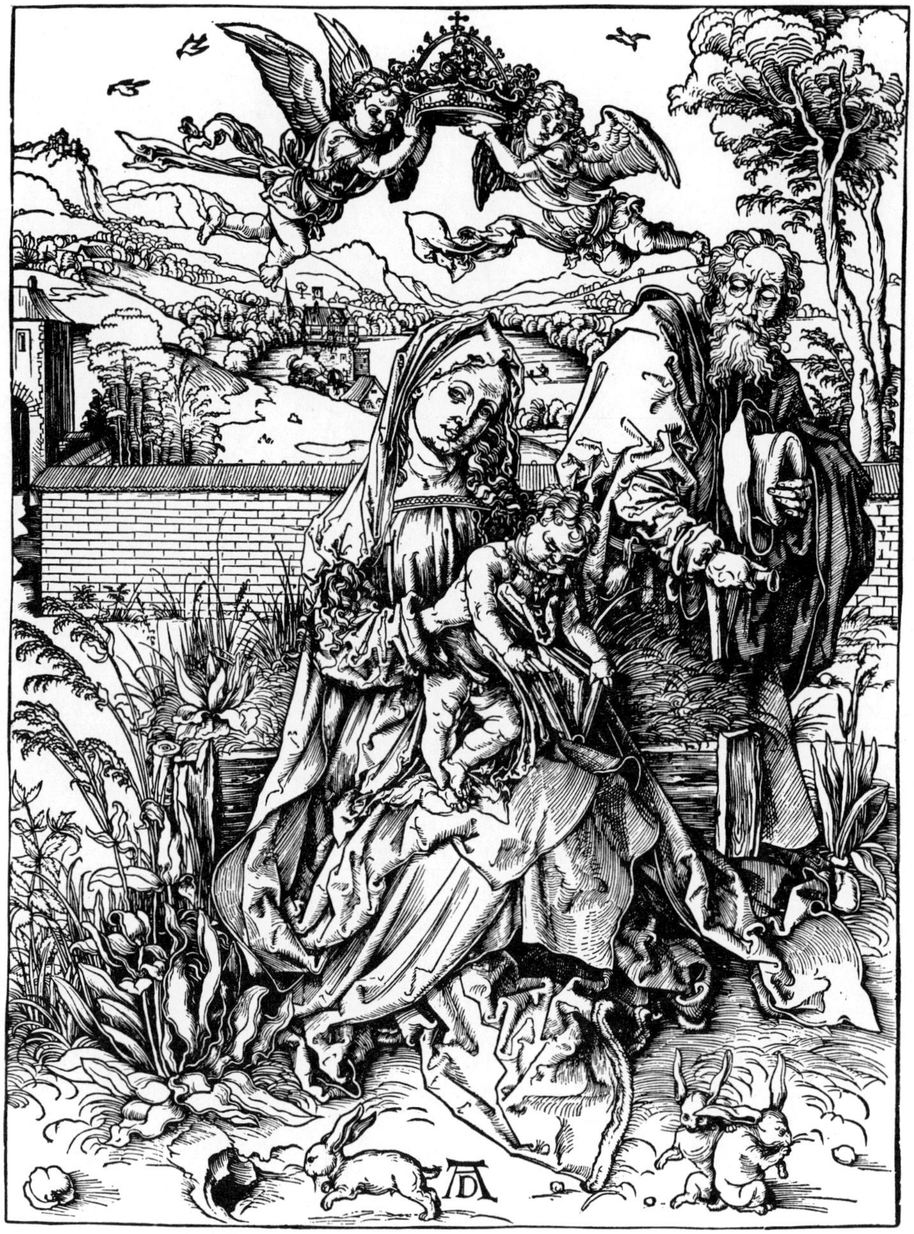

side of an object to another, thus achieving a panoramic view which, in theory, can be of any length. This is born out beautifully if the *Tripitaka* landscapes are laid end to end; the panorama is virtually continuous, as if the artist had walked for many miles. The viewpoint is a high one and the horizon line is to all intents and purposes the top edge in all four landscapes. This gives them a unity and common denominator. The depth and recession can be read as the progression of clearly defined and continuous space planes.

The influence of very early Chinese engraving can be seen in the work of two modern engravers, Gertrude Hermes and Bernard Rice. The image-forming

[30] Albrecht Dürer: The engraved long-grained wood block for *The Holy Family with Three Hares.*

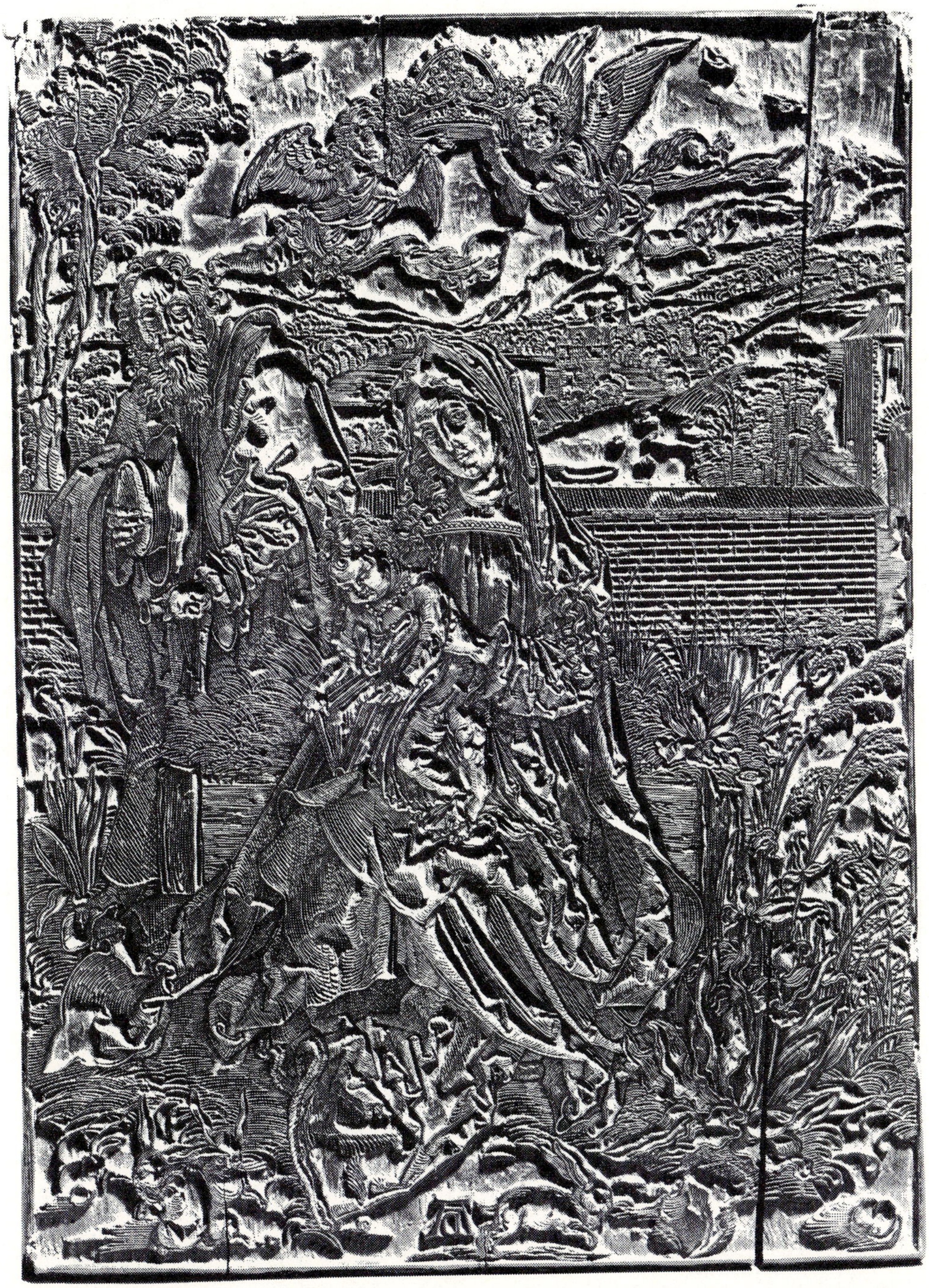

process analysed in the *Tripitaka* prints bears a very close relationship to the Hermes image-forming process, though these works were unknown in Britain when Hermes was at the language-forming stage of her development. However, she was well versed in the other early Chinese engravings. In the aspects of engraving language, Hermes, perhaps more than any other modern artist, has given new life to the very oldest language and extended it into modern times.

Likewise, Bernard Rice had no opportunity to study the *Tripitaka* landscapes when he was engraving in wood. In some respects, his print *Town of Travnick in Bosnia* 1925 [19] is almost anticipating them in style but not technique. However, Rice is very conversant with Chinese art; he has absorbed some of its character and sensitivity and the influence appears as a natural component of his style. In engrav-

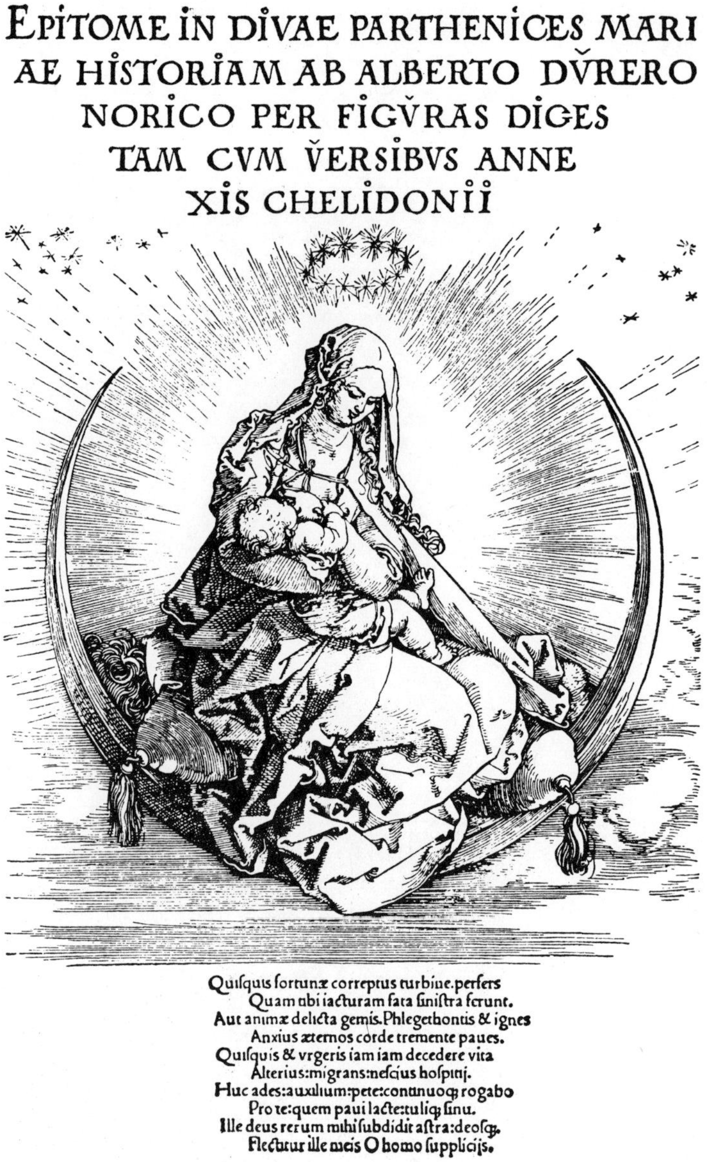

[31] Albrecht Dürer: Title-page of *The Life of the Virgin*, 1511. 19.1 x 20.1cm

ing he is a rebel and non-conformist. He engraved *Town of Travnick* when only two years out of the Royal Academy Schools.

The techniques used by Rice are dependent upon a great knowledge of the behaviour of timber and the possession of the skill necessary to produce a successful engraving – a task that is not as easy as it may appear. Rice is approaching wood engraving as a painter which accounts for his interest in light and shadow. The light and space concept in the *Tripitaka* prints is purely philosophical but Rice is approaching the physical nature of light in black and white as did the French Impressionists. His atmospheric technique established an independence of viewpoint at a time when the younger generation of this century were hammering out the white-line creed, which set him apart from the purists of the white-line engraving. However, he is a brilliant artist though he has never received the recognition that he richly deserves.

The early example of the *Diamond Sutra*, AD 868, and the later example of the Tripitaka, AD 1108, though separated by over two centuries, show the high standard of development achieved and maintained in Chinese wood engraving.

[32] Albrecht Dürer: *St Christopher*, 1511. 21.2 x 21.3cm

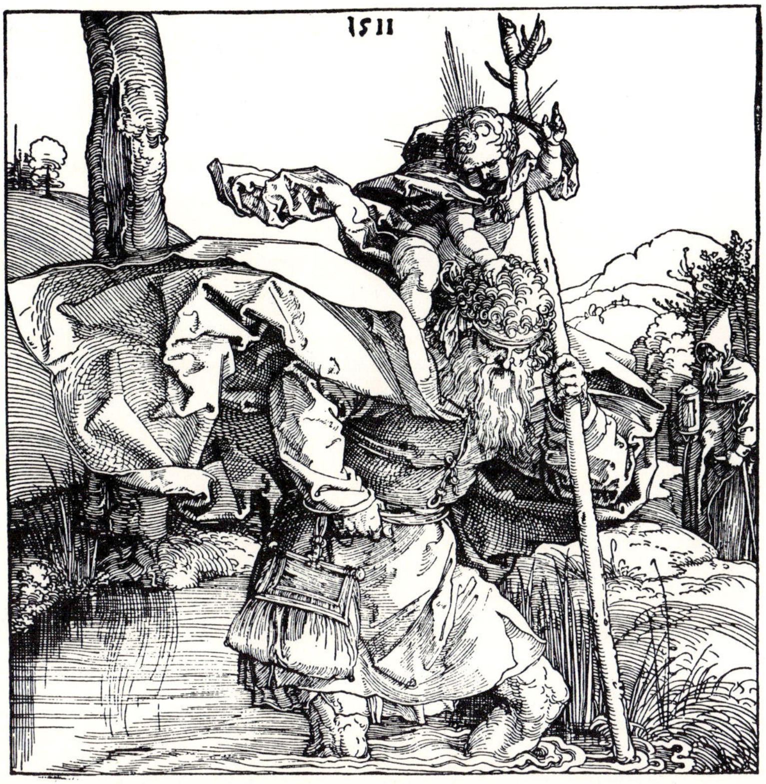

[33] Albrecht Dürer: *The Last Supper*, 1523. 30.2 x 21.4cm

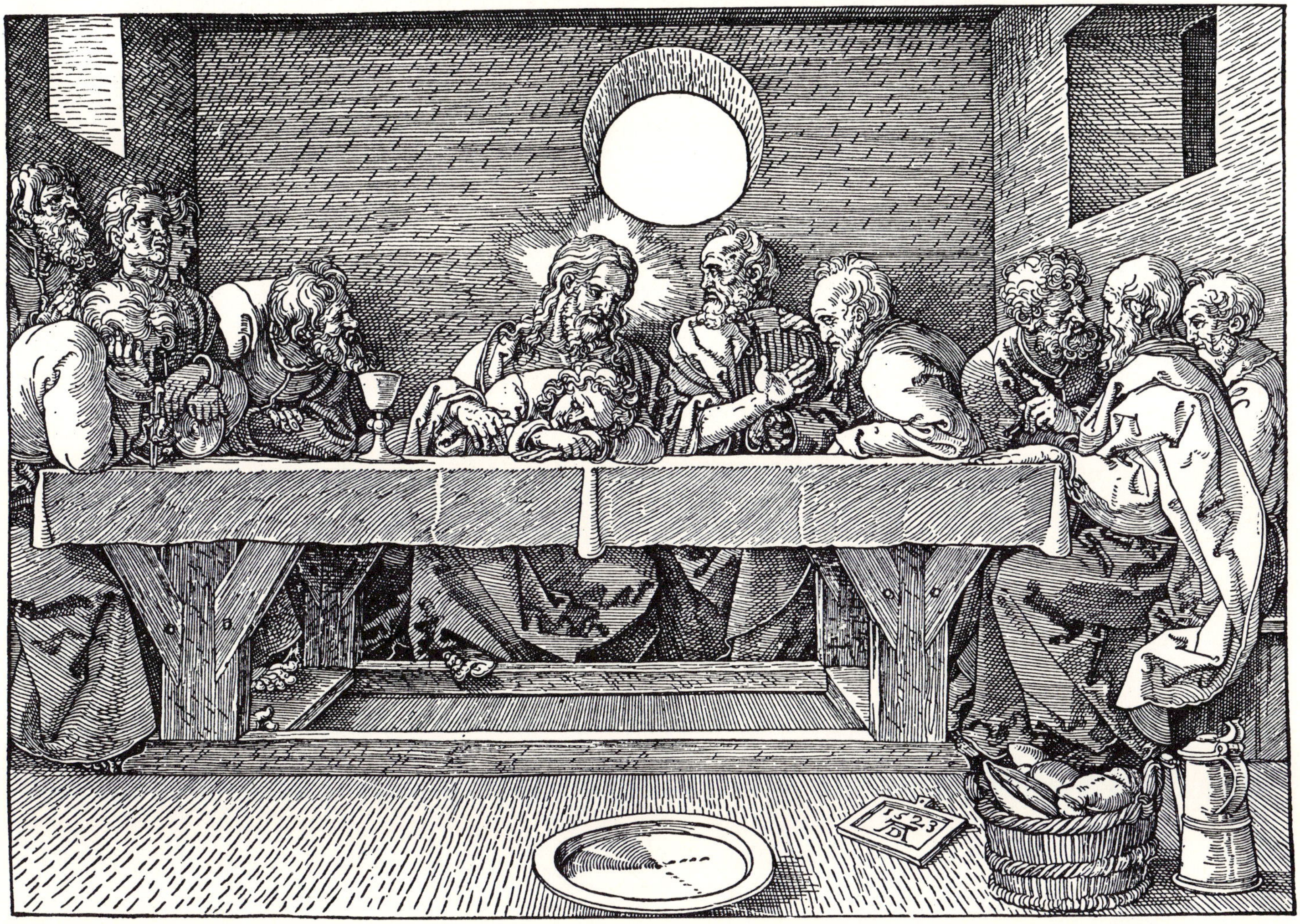

However, about the time that printing was being developed in Europe the woodcut made its appearance in China. It is thought that this technique evolved from the work of two eminent literati painters, T'ang Yin (1470 to 1523) and Ch'in Ying (1510 to 1551). Incidents from the work of these two men were repeated in early woodcuts and the more erotic subjects were specially favoured.

Towards the end of the Ming dynasty, 1368 to 1643, two compendiums appeared which were very significant: *The Mustard Seed Garden Manual*,[6] 1689, and *The Ten Bamboo Studio*[7] 1630. The latter work was begun in 1619 by Hu Chêng-Yen (1582 to 1672) whose skill in seal cutting had brought him to the decoration of writing paper and then to this more ambitious book. The complete work comprises sixteen volumes containing one hundred and eighty-six woodcuts. The work contains poems and fine calligraphy and many of the illustrations are in colour.

Contemporary sources make it evident that some ten engravers worked permanently in the studio of Hu Cheng-Yen who treated them as creative artists and gave constant advice on the production of the work. The woodcuts were translations of Cheng-Yen's delicate watercolours and the engravers achieved graduated tones in the printing surfaces, heightening effects by sensitive inking and accurate register. *The Ten Bamboo Studio* marks a golden age in early Chinese colour printing.

The British school of wood engraving has found considerable inspiration from the work of the Palaeolithic artists and the early Chinese engravers. However, this inspiration was given to a redevelopment of an art and did not come as part of the continual evolution of technique. The cave art of primitive man remained buried for many centuries and exercised no influence on early wood engraving or upon its commercial development. The early Chinese engraving remained in obscurity and made almost no contribution to development until recent times.

Thus, although the British school of wood engraving has academic roots in Europe and Asia, the development of wood engraving as a commercial item was not a continual process and appears to have been a separate evolution of part of European art.

REFERENCES

1 Woltman & Woerverman *History of Painting: Medieval, Vol I*, Kegan Paul, London, 1880
2 Francis, F. (ed) *Treasures of the British Museum*, Thames & Hudson, London, 1971
3 Sickman & Soper *The Art and Architecture of China* (Pelican History of Art), Penguin Books, London, 1956
4 Swann, P. *The Art of China, Korea and Japan*, Thames & Hudson, London, 1963
5 Loehr, M. *Chinese Landscape*, Belknap, Harvard, Mass., 1968
6 Speiser, W. *China*, Methuen, London, 1960
7 Sickman & Soper *The Art and Architecture of China*

3 THE FORMSCHNEIDER ENGRAVERS

Until the fourteenth century, the repository of pictorial and literary expression in France and Germany was the one-off illuminated manuscript. The situation was ripe for change to the introduction of the processes of mass reproduction of illustration and text. However, this development could not begin until paper had become available, wood engraving techniques perfected and a satisfactory method of printing invented.

Papermaking was first established in China. It is thought that the technique was known in AD 65 but the process was not officially reported until AD 105. It took a very long time for papermaking to travel from China to Europe where the first paper was probably made in Spain about AD 1150. In Italy, the Fabriano mills were active in 1276 while France was making paper near Troyes in 1438.

There is scant evidence that the wood-engraving techniques of China and Japan found their way to Europe though there were a small number of prints in circulation there. It seems that the need to illustrate books and other printed material created a demand for artists to produce a picture on a surface that could be printed. The presence of engraving as an established technique in armour and similar material gave the artists the inspiration to experiment in a softer substance. The use of wood must have been reasonably obvious, thus giving rise to the art of woodcut and the establishment of the European image print which led to the block book.

The use of wood in the printing of textiles had long been customary. The specimens of textiles extant from the period of Coptic art in the early years of Christianity were probably printed from wood, although it is unlikely that any of the actual blocks have survived. It appears that a long-grained plank of wood was employed to provide the printing image for textiles in Europe. In 1898 at the Abbey La Ferté-sur-Grosne near Dijon, in what was the Duchy of Burgundy, Protat discovered a fragment of a wood block engraved on both sides [20].

Known as the *Bois Protat* after its discoverer, the block is thought to have been engraved between 1370 and 1380. The images are linear drawings of the utmost simplicity and the fragment shows signs of considerable use. The block is 25mm in thickness but it has been estimated that the complete image would have been larger than the maximum size of paper available in the fourteenth century, thus suggesting that it was used for textile printing.

Prints for card playing were the next wood engravings to arrive on the European scene in 1377. The designs were cut on wood and the prints coloured with the aid of stencils, or hand coloured with transparent washes. Prints were also produced for pilgrimages and usually depicted incidents from the life of Christ or representations of favourite saints. These prints were crude images probably produced by monks and distributed through churches, monasteries and county fairs. It was not long before their manufacture became a new trade and by the end of the fourteenth century the process had so developed that it was possible to make wood engravings of considerable size and complexity.

About 1430 the block book began to appear in Europe. This was a logical development from the issue of a single image print in which a collection of prints were issued as one book. From this came the page containing both a picture and a few lines of explanatory text. The block book was intended as a cheap substitute for the illuminated manuscript and it had a very short life, being superseded by the process of printing from movable type, an invention already in its initial stages of development when the block book began to be published.

Examples of block books from France and Burgundy are *Ars Moriendi*, an *Apocalypse*, the *Biblia Pauperum* and the *Speculum Humanae Salvationis*. The *Biblia Pauperum* and the *Speculum Humanae Salvationis* are adaptations of manuscript versions. The illustrations concentrate on the temptations of unbelief, despair and avarice, all of which attack the dying, and text and pictures were all engraved on the same block. The *Biblia Pauperum* first appeared in manuscript at

[34] Hans Burgkmair: *Herald* from *The Triumph of Maximilian I*, 1526.

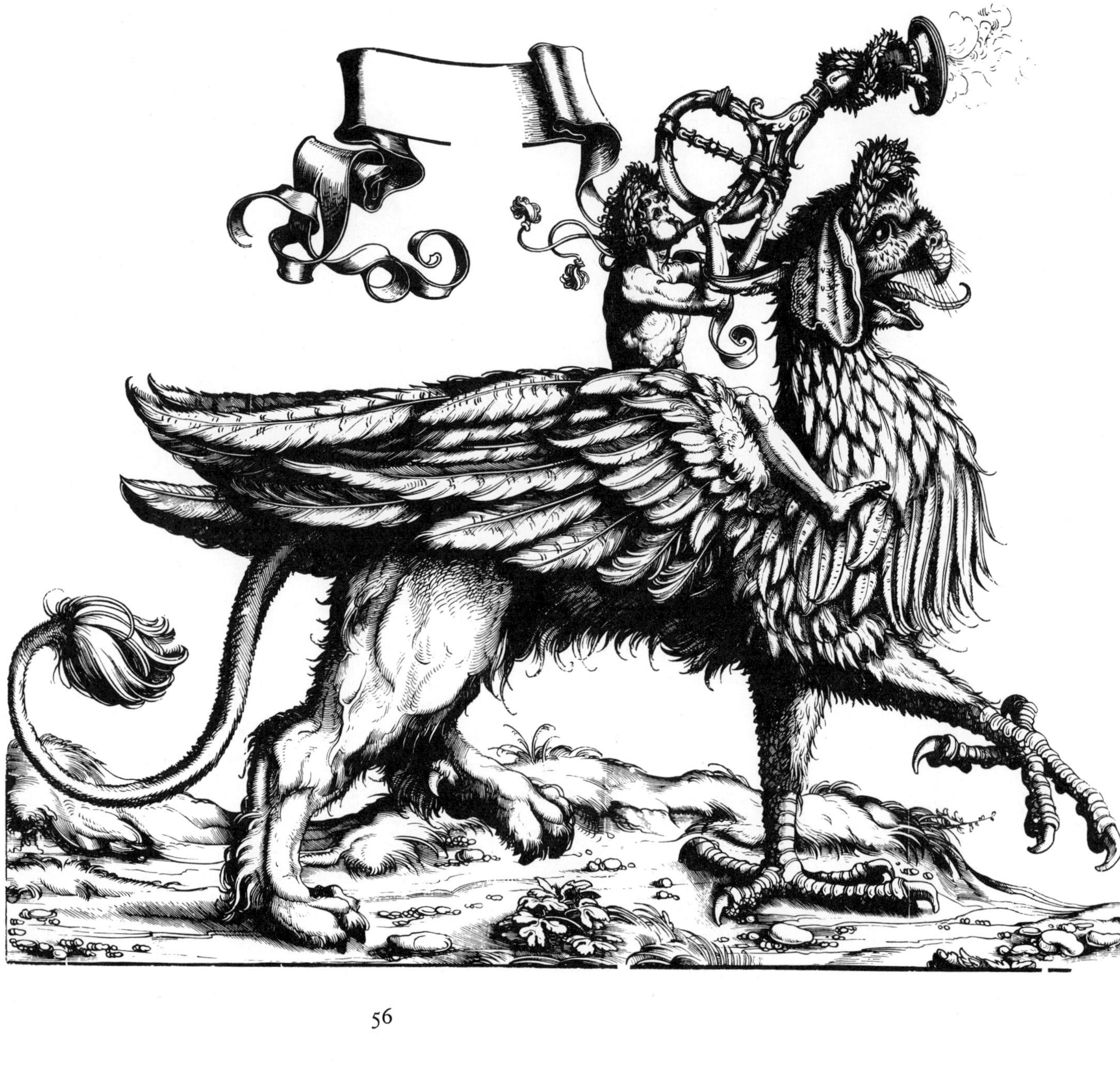

the end of the thirteenth century and was intended for the layman who had limited literacy [21]. The *Speculum Humanae Salvationis*, first found in manuscript in 1324, was a book of the same kind but with more text. It told stories of the Virgin and of Christ. The first printed edition of 1450 had forty plates and another ten were added in subsequent editions between 1470 and 1480.

The *Biblia Pauperum* served to direct the reader to a devotional existence and to prepare him for the life hereafter, and the illustrations propagated the Christian theme. The *Biblia Pauperum* was popular in France and Germany but is seen only in limited issues elsewhere in Europe.

[35] Hans Burgkmair: *Five men on horseback, with shields that jump up into the air in pieces* from *The Triumph of Maximilian I*, 1526.

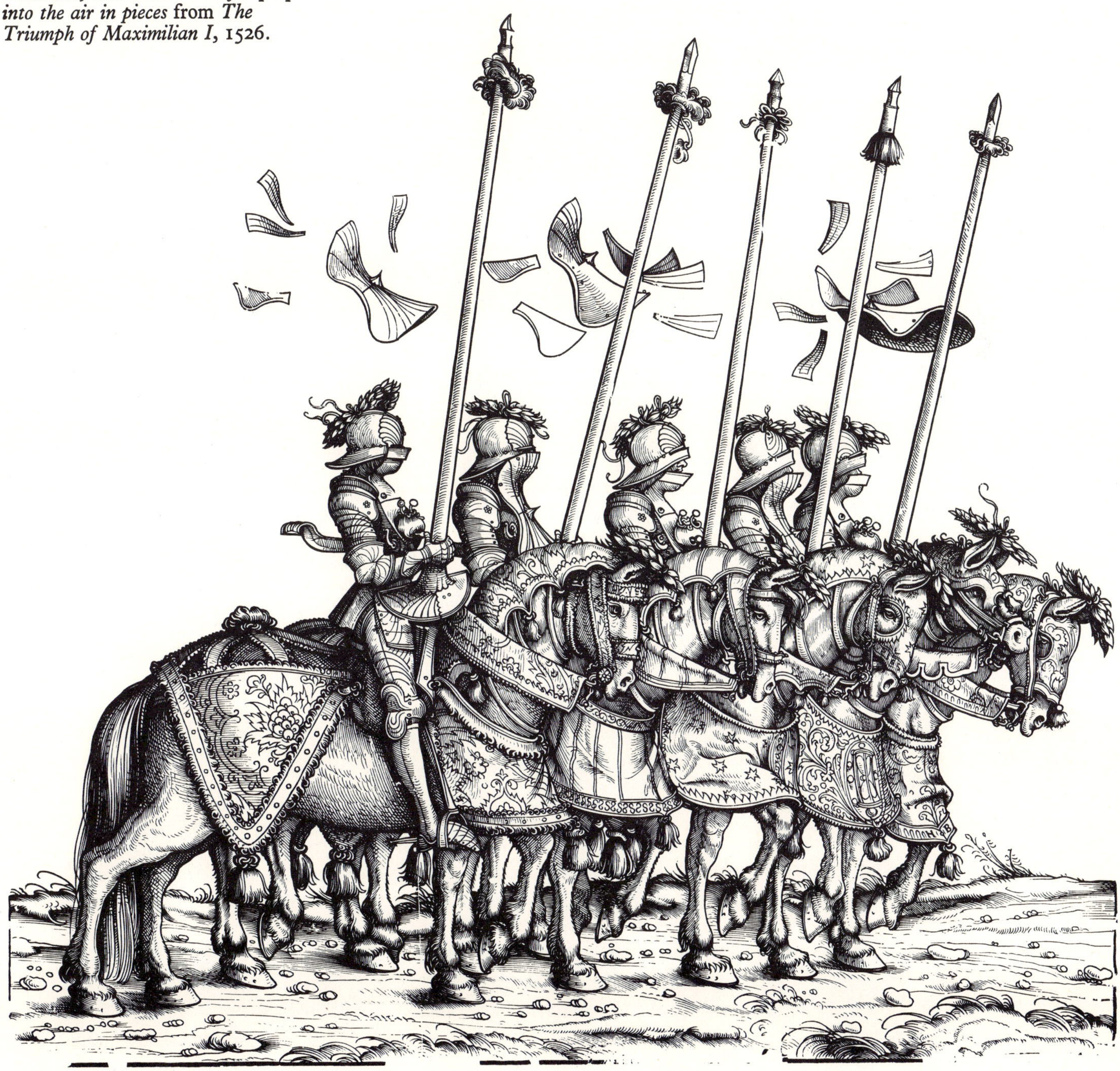

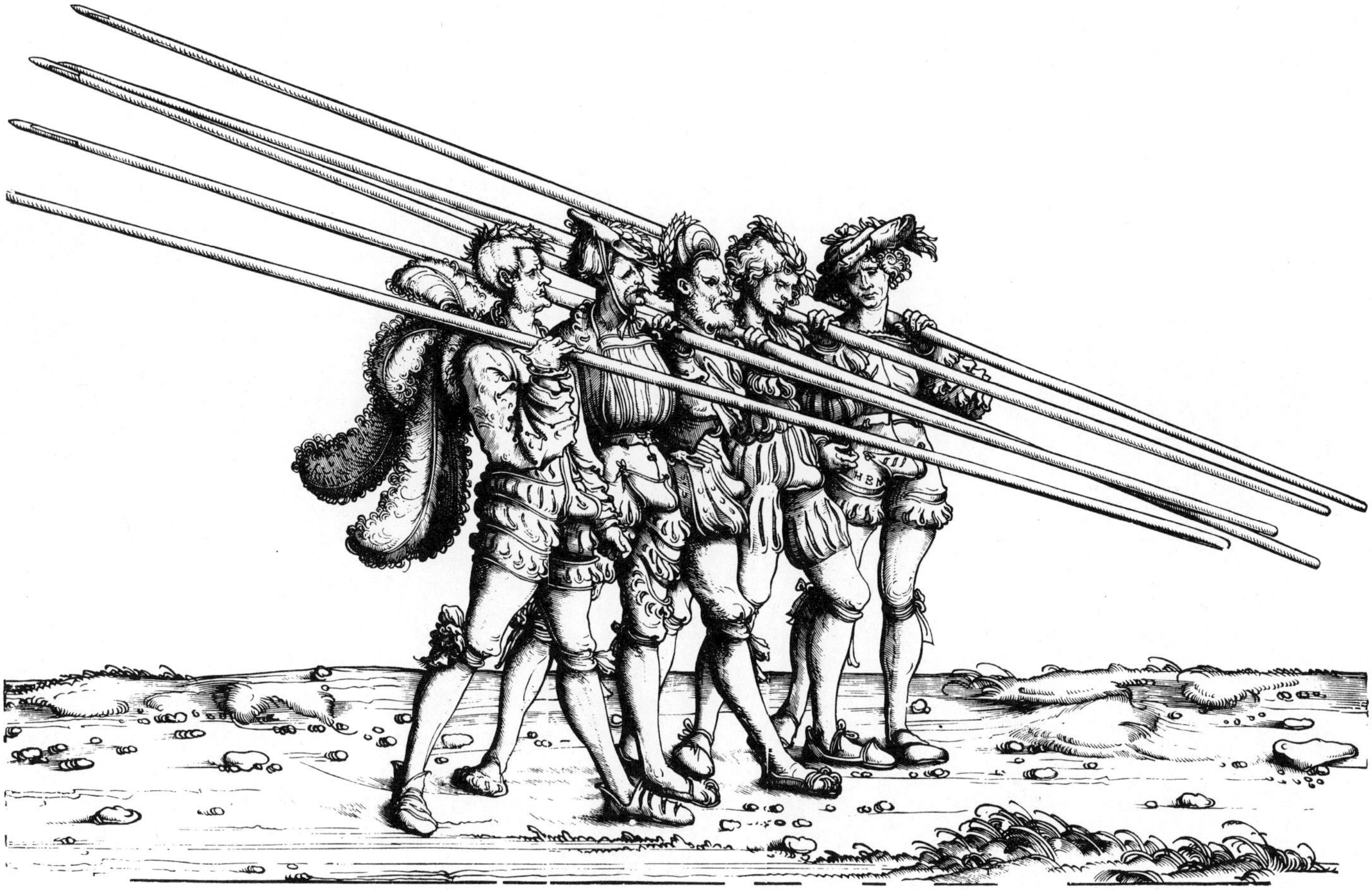

[36] Hans Burgkmair: *Five men with lances* from *The Triumph of Maximilian I*, 1526.

In the fifteenth century there was an increase in the number of people who could read and, together with a need for learning, this created a demand for an easier method of reproducing a manuscript than by the laborious cutting of text matter on wood. The demand was met when Johann Gutenberg invented a mould from which separate metal letters could be cast in quantity.

Gutenberg was born in Mainz between 1394 and 1399 and was a member of the Gensfleisch family, one of the patrician class. Mainz was well known for the skill of its workers in precious metals and as a young man Gutenberg became familiar with casting techniques, a skill that was later to help him with his invention.

One of the problems in the mass production of metal type was the casting of small letters in quantity. Gutenberg's invention of a successful mould and the development of a suitable alloy was a major breakthrough. The precise date of the invention is difficult to identify because of the need to keep the process a secret. However, in order to secure capital, Gutenburg entered into partnership in 1438 with three men, one of whom was Andreas Dritzehn. Soon after the partnership was established Dritzehn died and his two brothers, Georg and Claus, took legal action to acquire his part of the agreement. From the legal proceedings recorded when the case was heard at Strasbourg there is evidence of printing equipment though no printed material has survived.

Between 1444 and 1448 Gutenburg left Strasbourg and returned to Mainz where, in 1450, he borrowed money from Johann Fust, a lawyer and goldsmith, ostensibly for the purpose of printing a folio Bible. Never a very good manager, Gutenberg soon exhausted the loan and sought another from Fust who then became a partner in the business. Because no payment of interest or capital was

[37] Albrecht Altdorfer: *Luxemburg*, from *The Triumph of Maximilian I*, 1526.

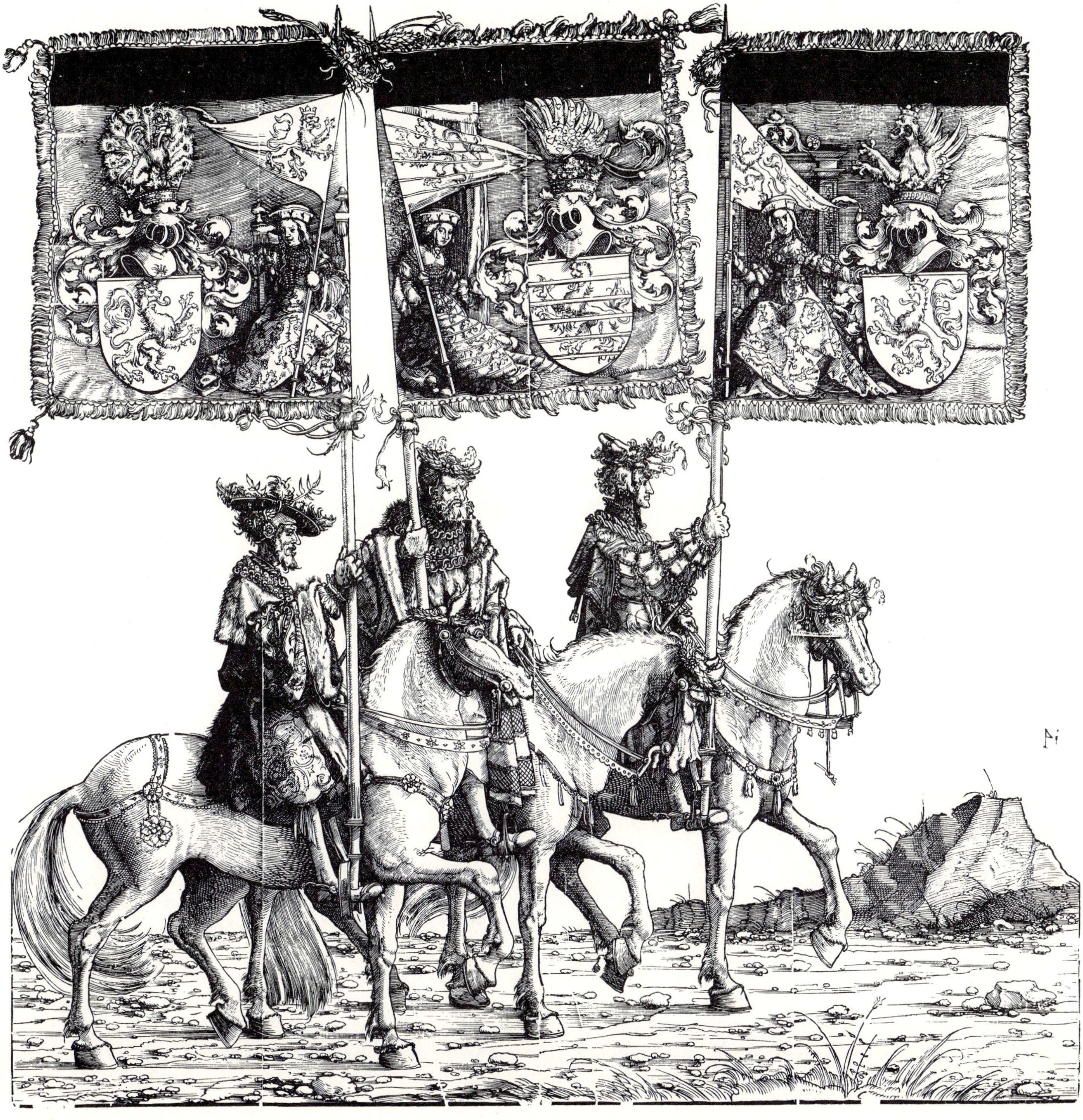

forthcoming, Fust sued Gutenberg to recover his money – by then a substantial amount – and the case was heard in 1455. Judgement was given against Gutenberg and in default of payment, equipment and stock equal to the value of the money due was passed to Fust who then ran the press with the technical assistance of Peter Schoeffer.[1] While no details of the press are known, the size of the folio Bible, it comprised 643 leaves, suggests that its production occupied six presses simultaneously.

Little is known of Gutenberg's occupation after he left the press though some authorities think he may have printed another Bible, the 36-line, in 1457, of which nine copies have survived. Despite the many problems that beset Gutenberg for most of his life, he eventually became a pensioner of the Archbishop of Mainz in 1465. He died in 1468.

The early printers did not find it necessary to record the details of their development, seeming to be too busy with the production of other people's work. Thus the name of Gutenburg does not appear in any of the work that is attributed to him. Nevertheless, his achievements were considerable: the typographic mould, the effective alloy for casting, a printing press – which he probably had built on the principle of a wine press – and the development of an ink that would cover metal letters adequately.

The spread of printing by the use of movable type brought with it a demand for pictures but many of the early book illustrations were, unhappily, not the best examples of the art of the engraver. Most of the wood blocks used in early printing were cut anonymously and it was not until the end of the fifteenth century that individual artists can be identified and then only occasionally. In 1486, Breydenbach published an account of his travels in Palestine and the book, *Peregrinationes in Terram Sanctam*, was illustrated by Erhard Reuwich who accompanied him.[2] Not only did he do the drawings but he also cut the blocks. This may well be one of the first references to a book illustrator, as well as being an early example of collaboration between author and artist.

During the fifteenth and sixteenth centuries a unique print school developed in the German towns of Nuremberg, Wittenberg, Augsburg, Regensburg and Strasbourg. Among the Nuremberg artists was the painter and engraver Michael Wolgemut (1434 to 1519) and his great disciple Albrecht Dürer (1471 to 1528) and the sculptors Adam Kraft, Peter Vischer (1455 to 1529) and Veit Stoss (1447 to 1533). The studio of Michael Wolgemut was organised to produce all that was required of the professional artists of the time and it was to assume a very important historical significance. This significance was almost parallel in scope and achievement to that of the twentieth-century Bauhaus at Weimar and Dessau. In many ways Walter Gropius (1883 to 1969), the architect and founder of Bauhaus, incorporated the concepts embodied in the Wolgemut studios and other similar enterprises along the Rhine.

During the fifteenth and sixteenth centuries, science and art were part of wealth and civic welfare. Through engraving and the multiple production of prints and books, education was more adequately supported and thus was able to meet the needs of a wider spectrum of the population. This placed upon the artists the responsibility of giving the reading public correct visual information and, later, with the rise of the news book, pictorial news relevant to the time.

[38] Albrecht Altdorfer: *Austria*, from *The Triumph of Maximilian I*, 1526.

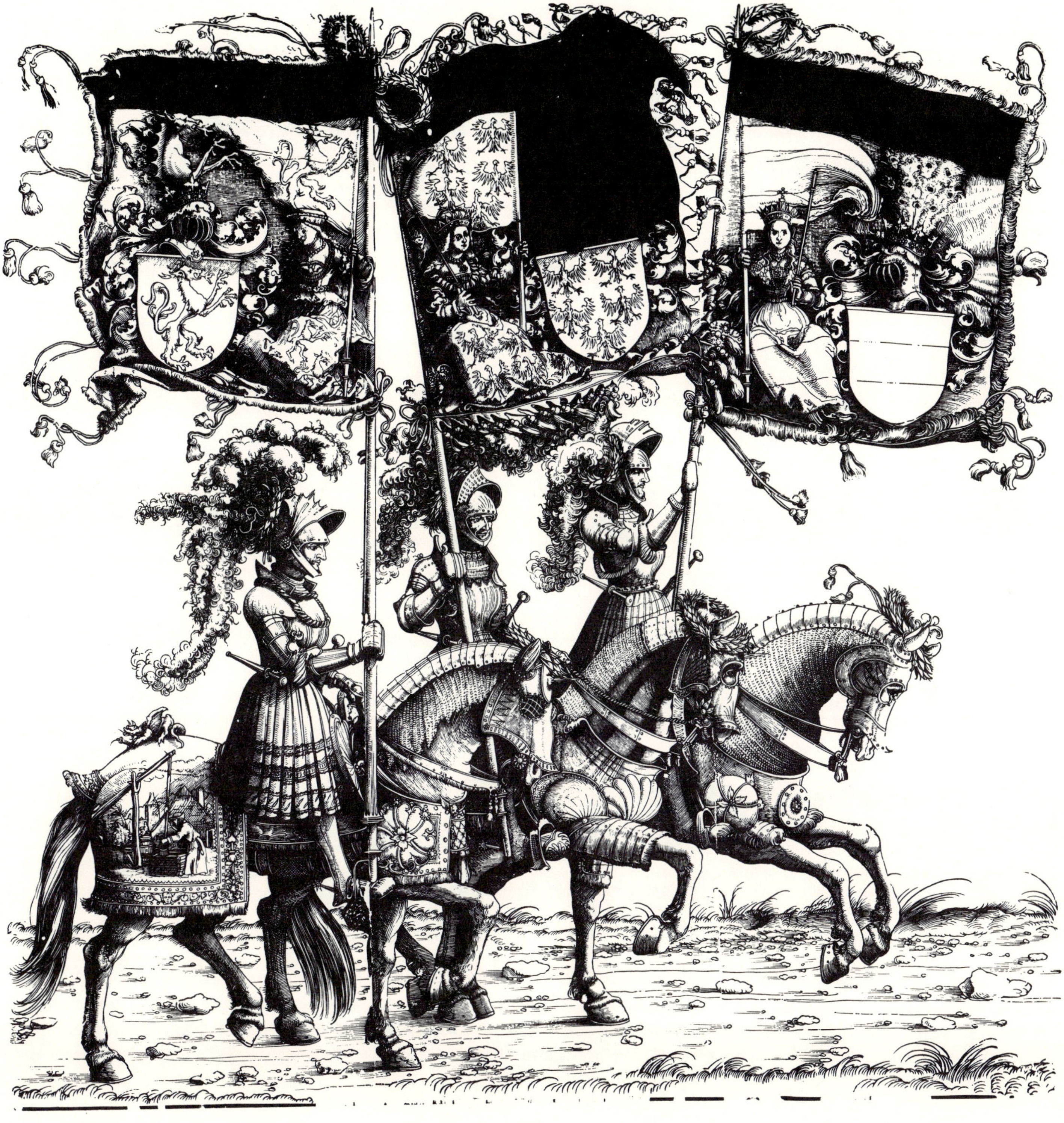

[39] Hans Springinklee: *Battle before The Rouanne*, from *The Triumph of Maximilian I*, 1526.

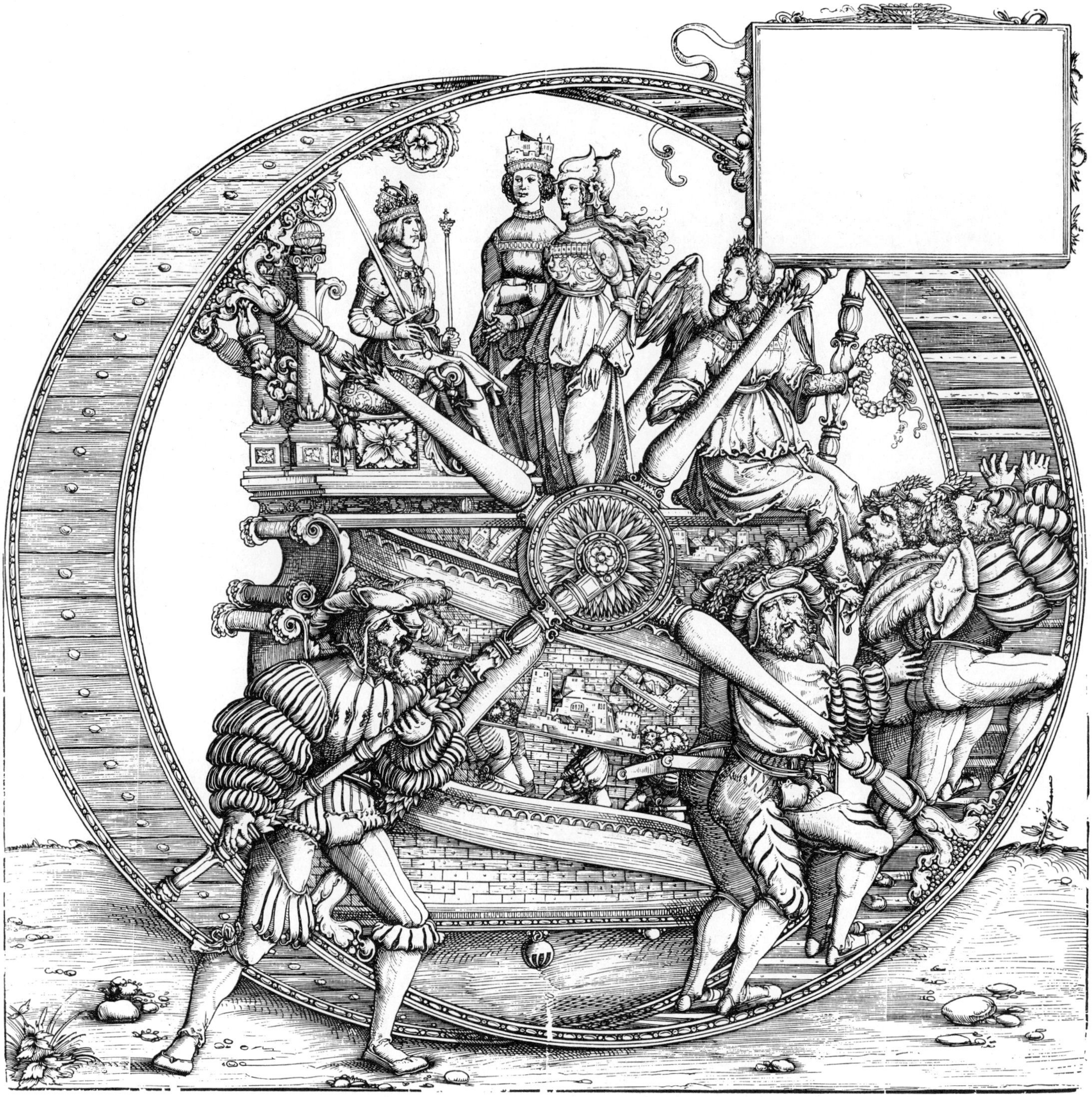

The demand for the reproduction of visual information led to the establishment of the *formschneider* engraving technique. During the fifteenth century there were five main centres where the *formschneiders* were at work, and each centre was associated with a master artist who was trained as a painter-engraver. Dürer and his pupils were at work in Nuremberg; in Wittenberg, Lucas Cranach the Elder (1472 to 1553) was working; Albrecht Altdorfer (1480 to 1538) was active in

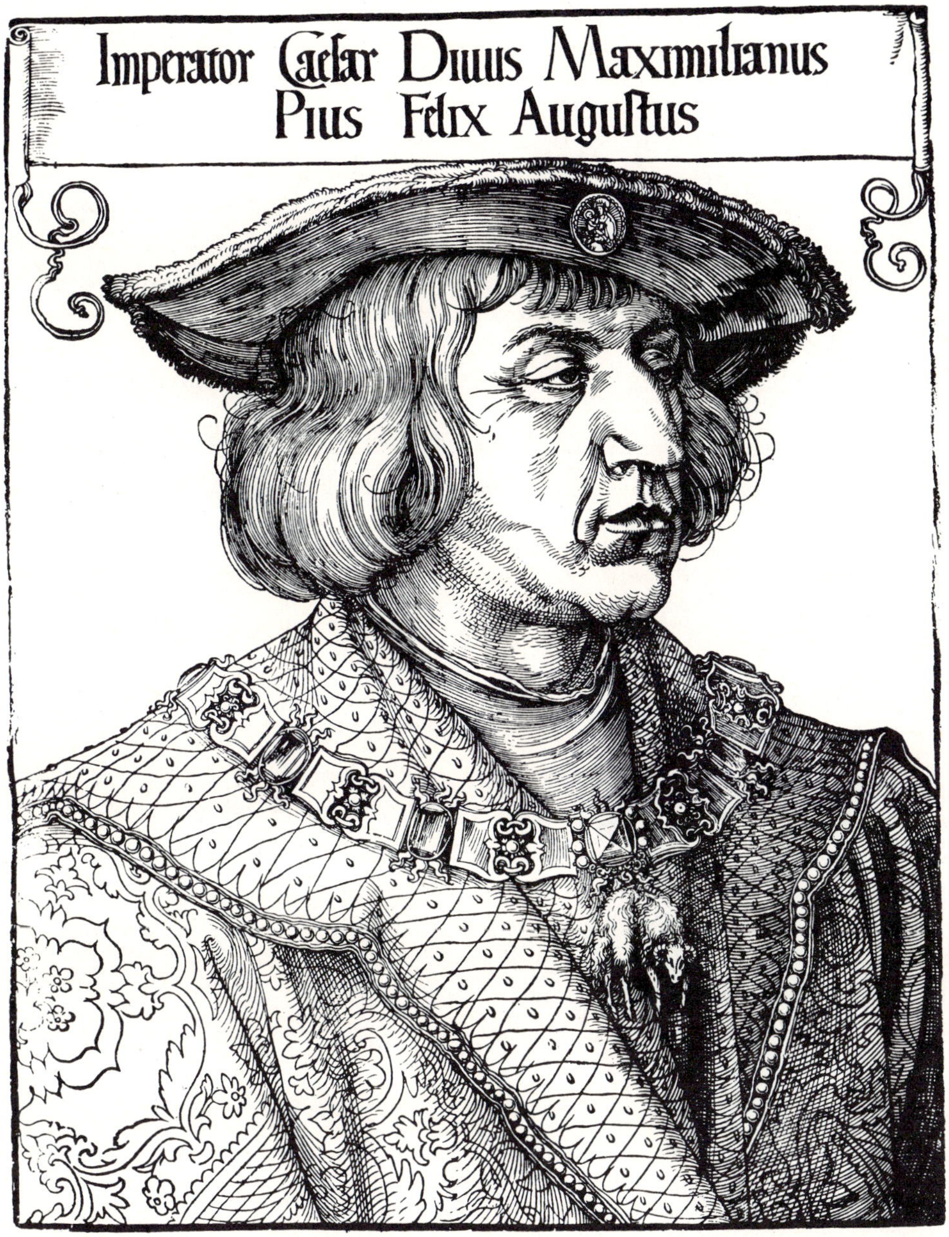

[40] Albrecht Dürer: A *formschneider* engraving of Maximilian I, probably completed after the Emperor's death. 31.9 x 41.4cm

Regensburg; at Augsburg Hans Burgkmair the Elder (1475 to 1531) was working, having been trained by the brilliant copper engraver Martin Schongauer (1445 to 1495). Burgkmair was the father-in-law of the Elder Holbein; his production in engraving amounted to seven hundred works. Hans Baldung Grien (1484 to 1545), Grünewald (1455 to 1528), whose real name was Mathis Neithardt, Johann Ulrich Wecklin (first work appeared 1508, died 1520) and Hans Weiditz (c. 1500 to 1536) were all working in Strasbourg.

Hans Baldung Grien was a gifted student of Dürer's workshop until 1509. He settled in Strasbourg and then moved to Freiburg across the Rhine where he lived from 1511 to 1516. Baldung's activity extended from the reign of Maximilian I into the time of Charles V. His personal style was significant, mannered and self contained and his engraving was heightened by the use of the *chiaroscuro* technique of cross-hatching. He was a fine draughtsman and engraver but displayed a penchant for the macabre [22].

[41 – 48] Hans Holbein the Younger: *The Temptation*; *Adam tills the Soil*; *The Preacher*; *The Miser*; *The Knight*; *The Duchess*; *The Ploughman*; *The Last Judgement*; all from *The Dance of Death*, 1538. 5.0 x 6.5cm

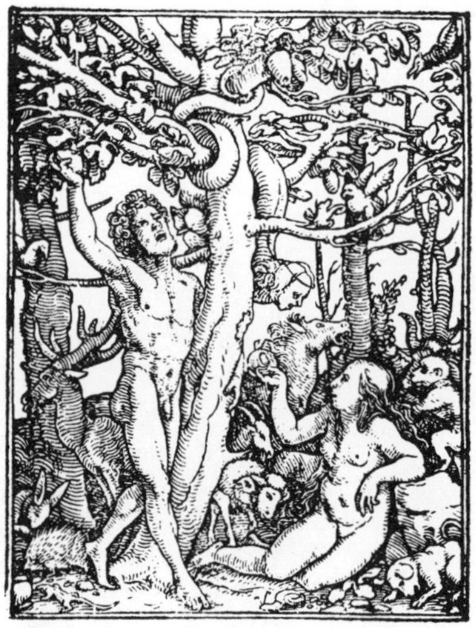

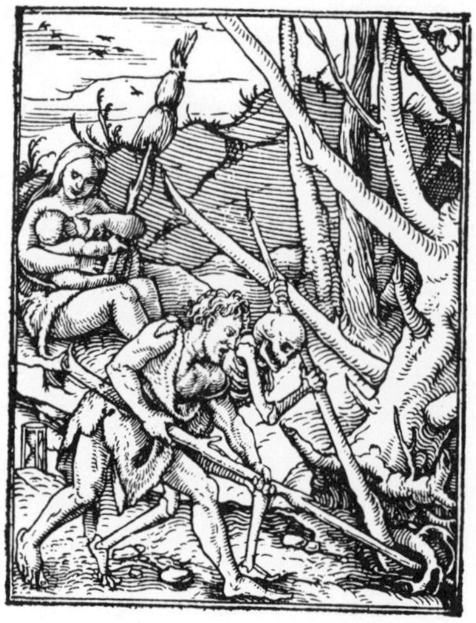

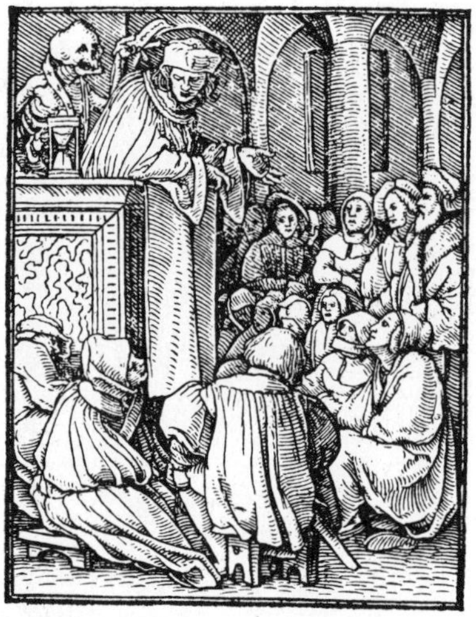

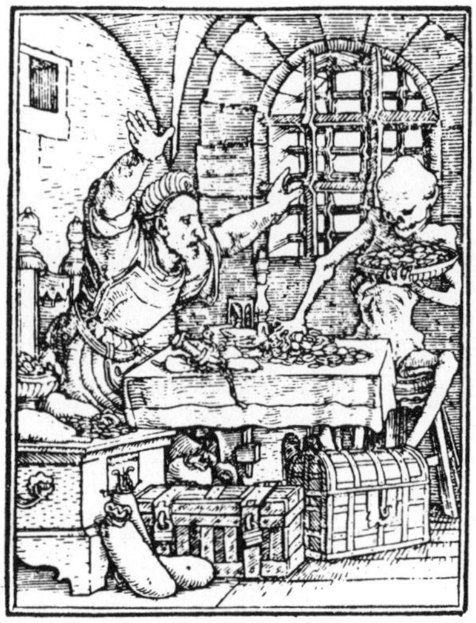

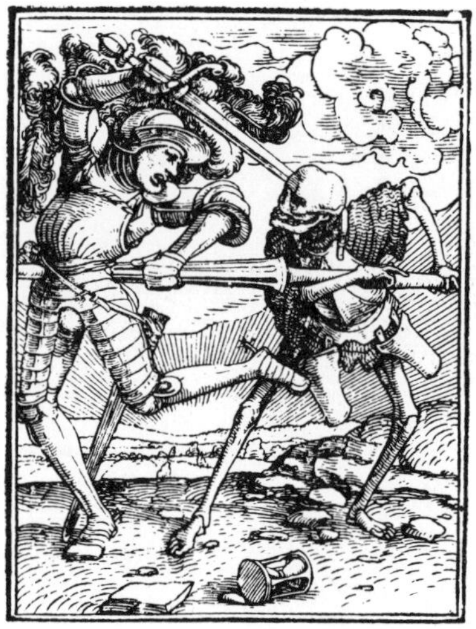

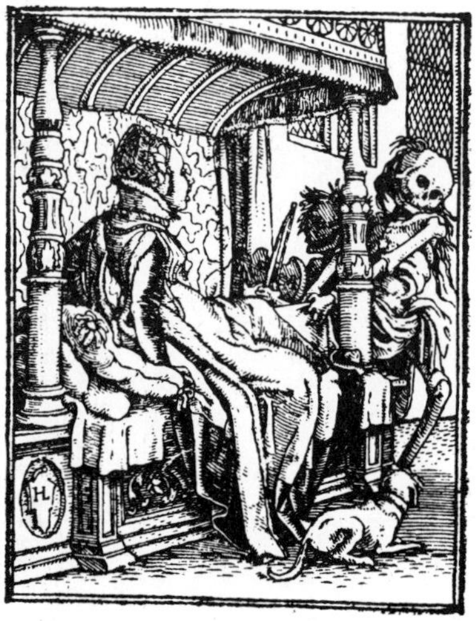

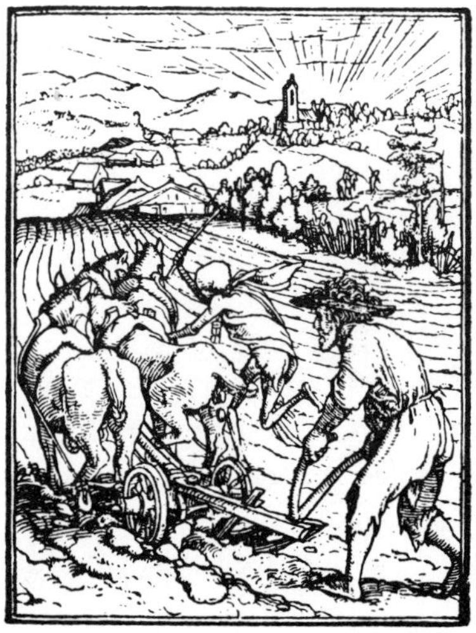

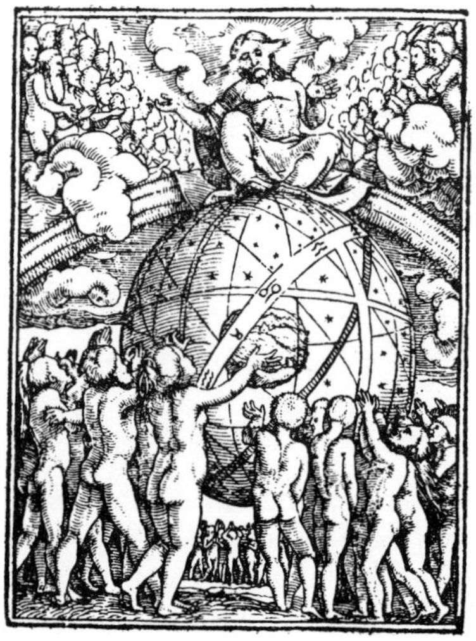

Grünewald the painter-engraver was trained by Schongauer and became a teacher of the young Dürer from 1492 until 1494 when Dürer was working in the Upper Rhinish towns. Grünewald rejoined him again in Nuremberg from 1499 until 1502 after Dürer had completed his *Apocalypse* series and helped him to cope with the publishing demands for his work. In 1500 Grünewald had produced his engravings for Koberger's publication *The Revelations of Saint Bridget of Sweden.* At this time both artists were affected by the influence of the Italian Renaissance and were breaking away from the medieval tradition. Grünewald introduced into the Danube school the technique of dry-point etching of which he remained the finest exponent, only to be overshadowed later by Rembrandt. The *Isenheim Altarpiece* (1513 to 1515) was Grünewald's greatest masterpiece.

Lucas Cranach the Elder, a German painter-engraver and book illustrator, was an important German artist and was court painter to the Electors of Saxony from 1508, a position he held under three successive Electors. Cranach was enobled, served as a burgomaster and ran a large workshop which combined a studio, an apothecary shop and a printing and bookselling establishment. He was deeply committed to the Reformation and to Martin Luther's *Das Newe Testament Deutzsch* printed by Melchior Lother. Cranach was a personal friend of Luther and many of his wood engravings were designed to promote the Protestant cause. Twenty-one full-page *formschneider* engravings are generally attributed to Cranach in Luther's *New Testament* published in Wittenberg in September 1522. Luther's Bible, his greatest achievement, had the effect of unifying the two German languages of the time, the 'high' and the 'low' German, the 'high' winning over the 'low' form. The first edition of the Bible is sometimes known as the *Septemberbibel.* Cranach's engravings are of a polemical character. After the first edition of the New Testament in 1522, over eighty editions had appeared by 1534 when the complete Bible was published.

In the sixteenth century craftsmen engravers, or 'commercial' engravers, worked in very close contact with the leading artists of the various studios and developed a form of print making that made possible a substantial step forward in the production of images and illustrated books. The object was to multiply the drawings of the artists of the period because not only did the prints stand in their own right as works of art but they also made a very important contribution to the development of illustration.

Engravers were also coming into *formschneider* engraving from the flourishing production of firearms for sport and armour, which developed in the several centres. Without the patronage of the aristocracy the engravers could not have existed in sufficient numbers. The designers of firearms and armour were taking intaglio prints or impressions on paper to record their decorative designs engraved on the metal. These prints formed a file to safeguard the engravers from repeating a previous client's design. The earlier methods of decorating firearms and armour by various etching processes gave way to engraving as the design developed in precision and sophistication, because engraving gave the highly desirable jewel-like accuracy of cut to match the increasing precision of design. It was much more in keeping with the development of the mechanical exactitude of the armour and weapons. In order to make a print from a design, the engraved lines were filled with stiff ink. Paper was then placed on the engraving and pressure applied by burnishing. This had the effect of pulling the ink out of the lines.

The wood-block engravers were known as *formschneiders.* They worked their blocks on the long grain of the timber in the plank with the point of the burin but did not use the end grain as is the practice in modern wood engraving. The devel-

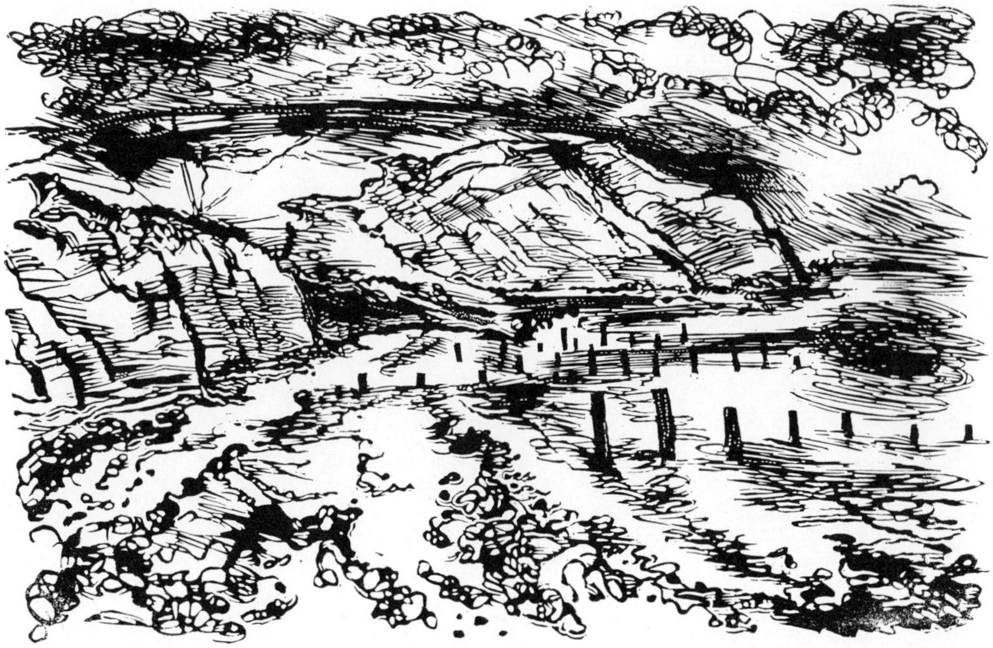

[49] Kenneth Lindley: *Dorset Coast*, 1969. 19.5 x 12.5cm

opment of *formschneider* engraving was to give rise to a significant co-operative art form made possible by division of labour. There were three stages involved in the production of the block: a master artist produced a drawing, a draughtsman transferred the drawing to the block which was then engraved by the *formschneider*. (Sometimes the master artist would draw direct on to the block.) The printer then took an impression from the finished and inked block to complete the process. A similar division of labour was to be developed again by the nineteenth-century commercial engravers in their efforts to supply newspapers and periodicals with much-demanded illustrations.

The blocks cut by the Danube school [30] were from the long-grained plank and the timber used was usually pearwood or cherry, each with an even and close-grained texture. Sometimes, however, the harder oak was used. This timber also had good inking properties. A mixture of woodcutting and engraving techniques were used to produce a *formschneider* print but its engraver did not develop either wood engraving or woodcutting in its own right. The *formschneider* was a reproductive engraver only and a similar function was performed by the commercial engraver of the eighteenth and nineteenth centuries, but on a larger scale. However, the *formschneider* engraver worked as an individual who was concerned with the complete drawing and the interpretation of it in an engraving. The commercial engraver was involved in the mass production processes as part of a team which demanded complete subjugation of individuality.

Thomas Bewick (1753 to 1828) engraved two of the smallest blocks to be produced in his time *House fly* and *Bumble bee* [2 and 3] and both were engraved on end-grained boxwood. In comparison it should be noted that a *formschneider* engraving was usually of a reasonably large size because the long-grained timber could not have been used for very small work with success.

Holbein's *Dance of Death* series of prints [41 to 48] were some of the smallest and certainly the finest of engravings, but they were composed within the *formschneider* terms, as were his two lovable donkeys *Two Art Critics* [400]. With the exception of the genius of Holbein in producing small work, it was the large dimensions of the prints that enabled the *formschneider* to be successful and to serve the educational and social function which was so important at the time. Although today we have photographic facilities for reduction, very small engravings are still important for the simple reason that photographic reduction sometimes produces a printing image in which the fine detail of the original is lost.

Albrecht Dürer (1471 to 1528) was born in Nuremberg and was to become the most important and gifted draughtsman in that city. He was also to exercise very considerable influence on the development of *formschneider* engraving. Despite the fact that he wanted to be a painter his father apprenticed him as an illustrator in the Michael Wolgemut studio where he worked from 1486 to 1490.

In the Wolgemut studio, altarpieces and religious pictures were produced as well as engraving and *formschneider* prints for book illustration. Wolgemut was primarily responsible for the development of *formschneider* techniques and his own output in this field was considerable. The best known of the books illustrated by the Wolgemut studio are the *Schatzbehalter* 1491 and the *Nuremberg Chronicle*,

[50] Eric Ravilious: *Sussex Landscape*, 1933. 16.2 x 13.0cm

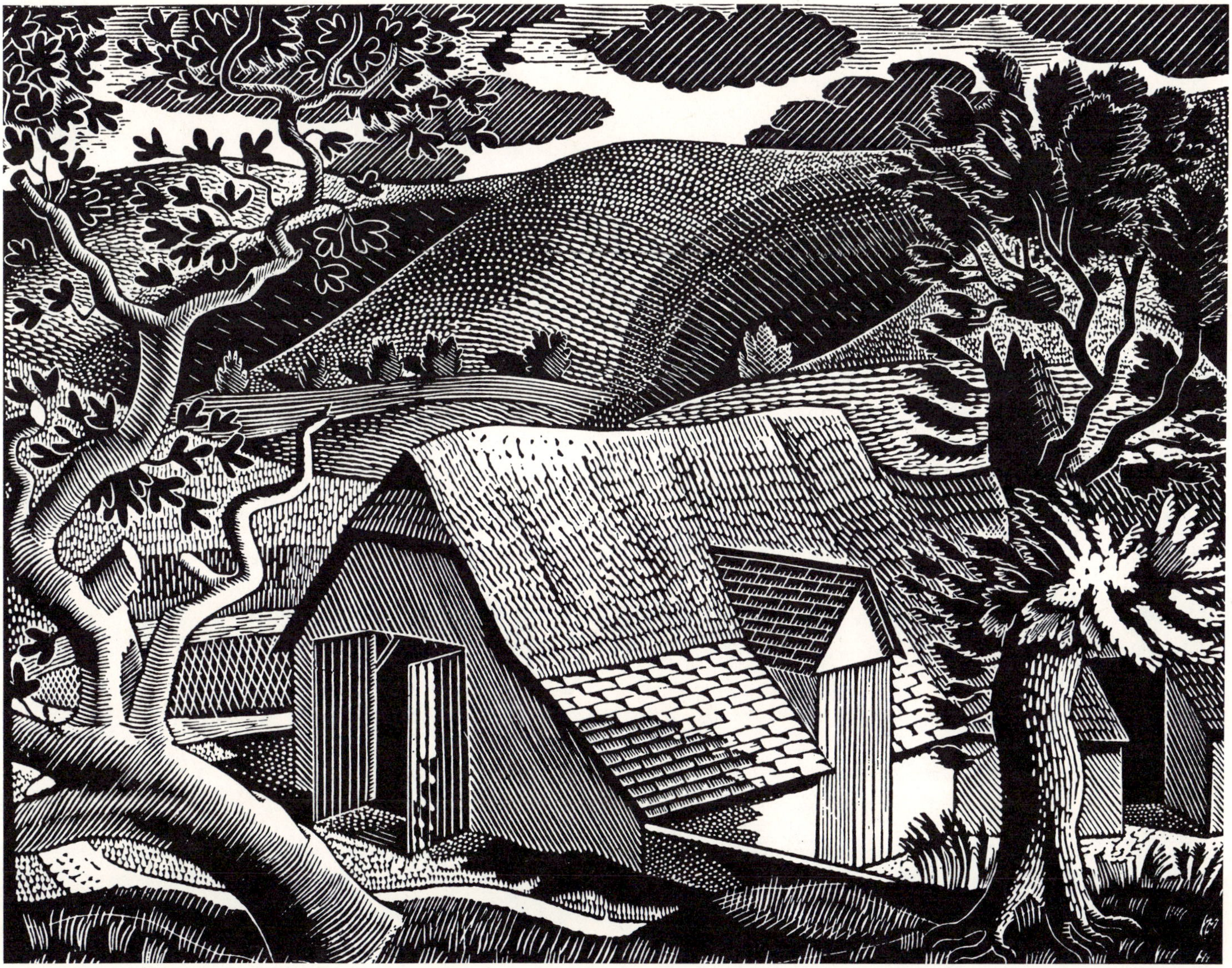

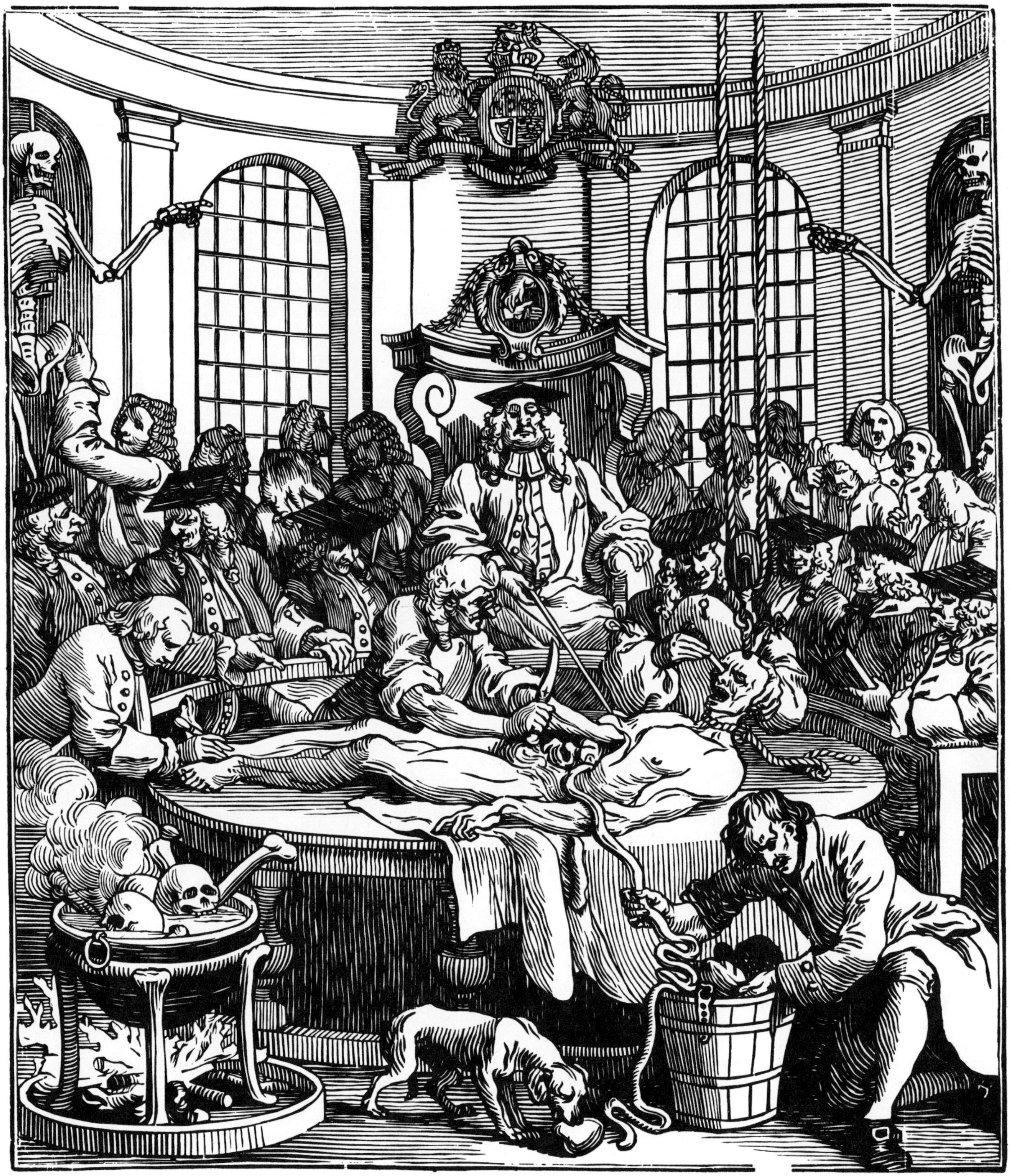

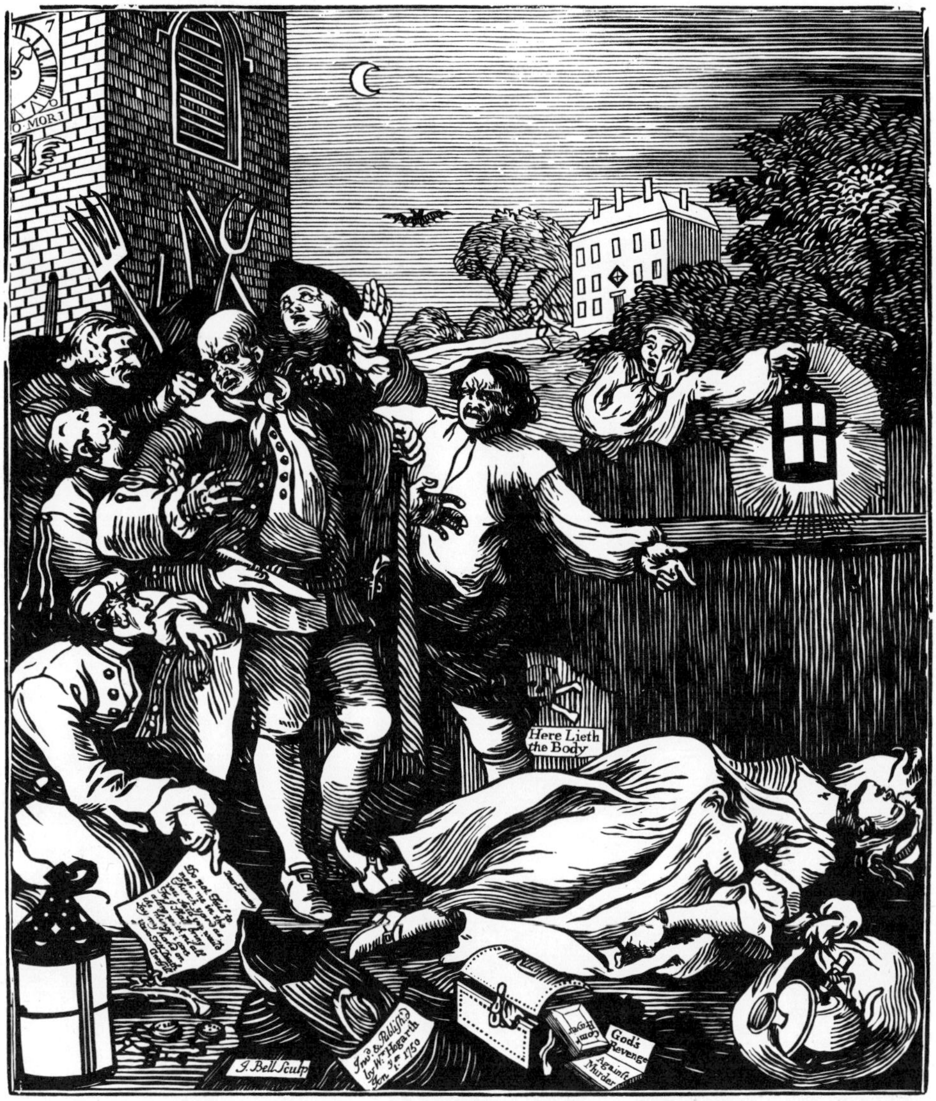

[51, 52] William Hogarth: *The Reward of Cruelty*. 38.2 x 44.8cm; *Cruelty in Perfection*. 37.8 x 44.8cm; both engraved by John Bell, 1750.

first edition 1493, [24 and 25]. Both of these works were published by Koberger (Dürer's godfather) who founded a large and well-organised business which at one period was said to house twenty-five presses and a very substantial work force.

In the colophon of the *Nuremberg Chronicle* it states that the artists responsible were Wolgemut and Wilhelm Pleydenwurff. Some of the prints in the *Chronicle* are approximately 18.5 x 28.5cm and it contains about 652 different blocks which are repeated at intervals giving a total of 1809 pictures. The copy of the book in the Royal College of Physicians Library in London was printed in 1497 and is a third edition, though Panofsky in his *The Life and Art of Albrecht Dürer* describes only one edition. The subject matter concerns saints, martyrs and religious teaching. The book is 7.5cm in thickness and the page size is 25.5cm by 38.25cm. Pages are set in double column and the column width is 7cm. The letter form is the Medieval Gothic. The ink is a black of remarkably good density. Though profusely illustrated, the book contains only one full-page illustration. Throughout the *Nuremberg Chronicle* there are no solid black areas larger than a centimetre square while the white areas are numerous. The texture of the paper gives the book a certain rough character and in some of the illustrations there is evidence of inadequate inking and unequal pressure. The engravings in the book are of two kinds: one variety

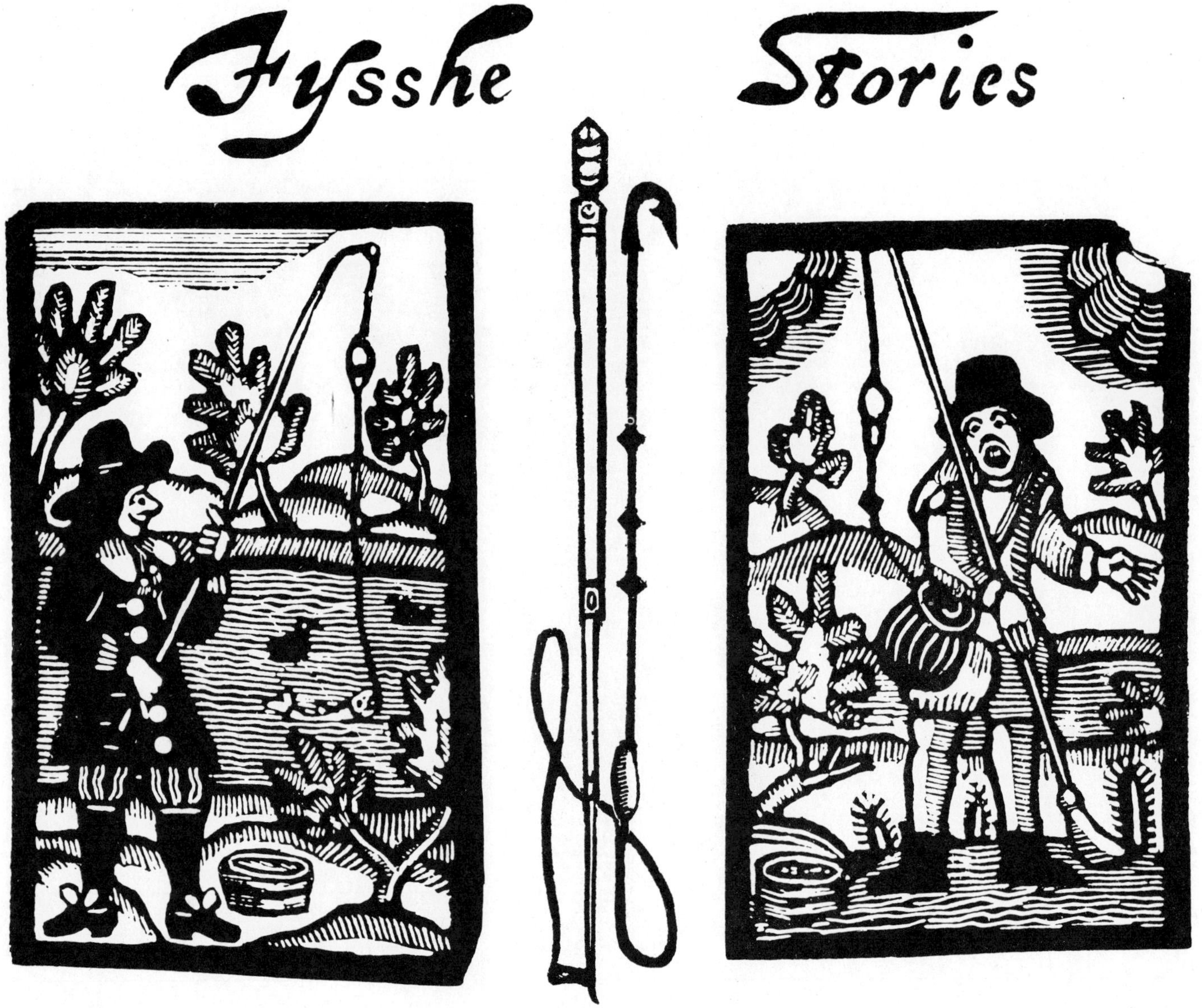

[53] Joseph Crawhall: Blocks from *The Compleatest Angling Booke that ever was Writ*, 1859. 18.0 x 12.0cm

is about the size of a normal postage stamp and the other extends across the double column of text matter.

There is considerable repetition of illustrations and in some cases the same block appears wherever there is a specific reference to the subject it depicts. It has been suggested that this technique was employed to help those of limited reading ability to follow the text matter.

Formschneider engraving was also practised in the north of Italy but in no way did it develop to the heights of skill and perfection seen in Germany. However, one Italian book printed in Venice is of major importance and among the most famous of all printed books: the *Hypnerotomachia Poliphili* or *Strife of Love in a Dream* [26] by Francesco Colonna. It was produced by Aldus Manutius in December 1499 and his punch cutter Francesco Griffo of Bologna cut the Roman type used in the work. The book displays an exceptionally fine harmony between the balance of line and type. There are 172 engraved illustrations by an unknown artist. The Italian paper used is whiter and finer in texture than German paper. This book was to serve as a model for engraving and design for the English nineteenth-century black-line engravers such as Ricketts and Shannon.

[54] Sir Frederick Leighton: An illustration from George Eliot's *Romola*, engraved by W. J. Linton. 10.25 x 15.8cm

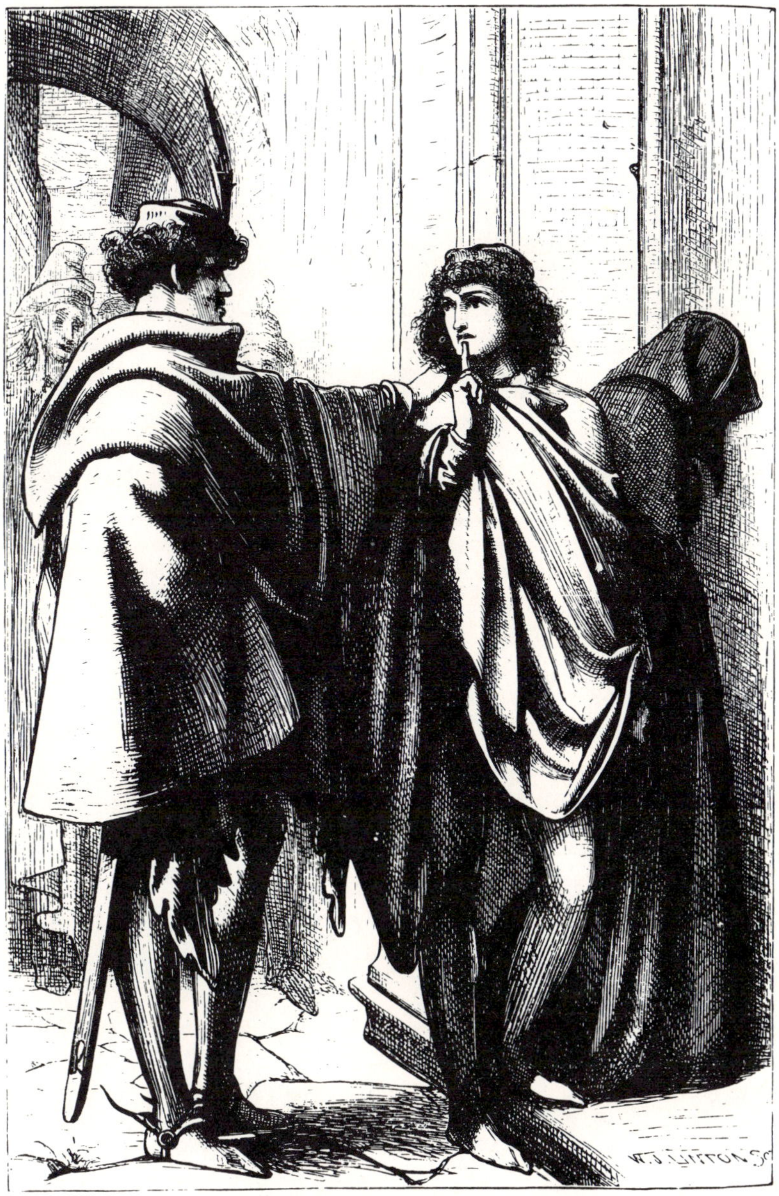

The length of time needed to produce illustrations could only be reduced by the introduction of many artists and craftsmen, which was the working principle of the Wolgemut studio. A black-line *formschneider* print, designed by Wolgemut, appears in the *Schatzbehalter* but it is very difficult to distinguish one artist's work from another in this book and the illustrations are generally clumsy and mediocre in design.

The Wolgemut studio used Dürer as a craftsman and a designer of prints and this gained him admission into the circle of the Nuremberg book illustrators. His output was very large during his early formative years when he is believed to have done most of the block engraving himself. Some of the prints are signed and were issued by Dürer personally. Other prints are unsigned and were produced for other publishers.

The attribution of an unsigned print to a specific artist presents problems because of the fact that the print concerned might be the work of an incompetent block draughtsman copying an original engraving. The conditions under which *formschneiders* worked and the strain upon eyesight tended to shorten their productive lives, while the economic necessity to continue working for as long as possible, despite physical shortcomings, could well result in inferior copies of work that in its original form was excellent. Dürer suffered this indignity and on occasions some of his drawings were engraved in a wretched manner. Some of the best Dürer prints were cut by the *formschneiders* Wolfgang Resch and Hieronymus Andreas. It is thought that Andreas was known by the familiar name of 'Formschneider' and that this was the origin of the title in its application to all reproductive engravers. The name is still used in Germany. It was Andreas who was responsible for cutting Maximilian's massive project of the 192 prints comprising the *Triumphal Arch* which was started in 1512 and had the overall measurements of approximately 350cm by 25cm.

Dürer lived for fifty-seven years and at times his life was unhappy and difficult, yet in his art he is continually in a state of transition. By the time his style had formed he was confronted with a complex situation arising from the developing Renaissance movement in Italy. The Renaissance movement meant a sharp return to the concepts of classical art that were manifested in Greek art. Yet it meant more than that because its political and religious changes were to culminate in the Reformation.

Dürer was in sympathy with many of these changes and his work reflects the onslaught of the Renaissance in a gradual change of style. He became a convert to

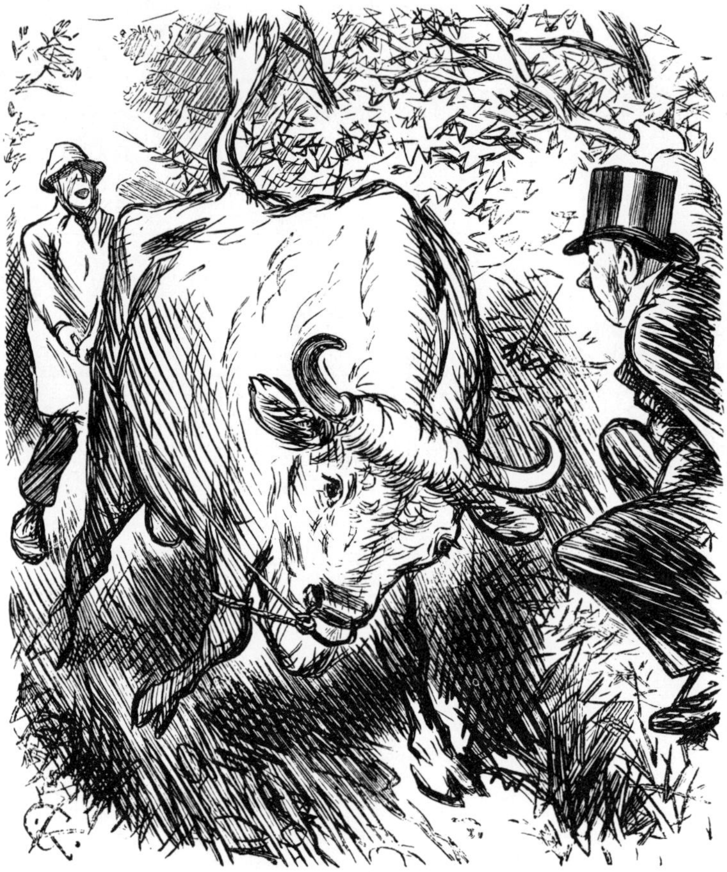

[55] Charles Samuel Keene: A pen drawing engraved and reproduced in *Punch*, 2 June 1879. 9.5 x 11.5cm

REASSURING!

Old Gent (suddenly turning corner in narrow lane). "Oh!—I say!—Is he?—Will he?"—*(Backing into Hedge.)*—"Can he?"——

Peasant. "Don't take no Notice of 'im, Sir! I've got a wee bit Check on 'im if he runs!!"

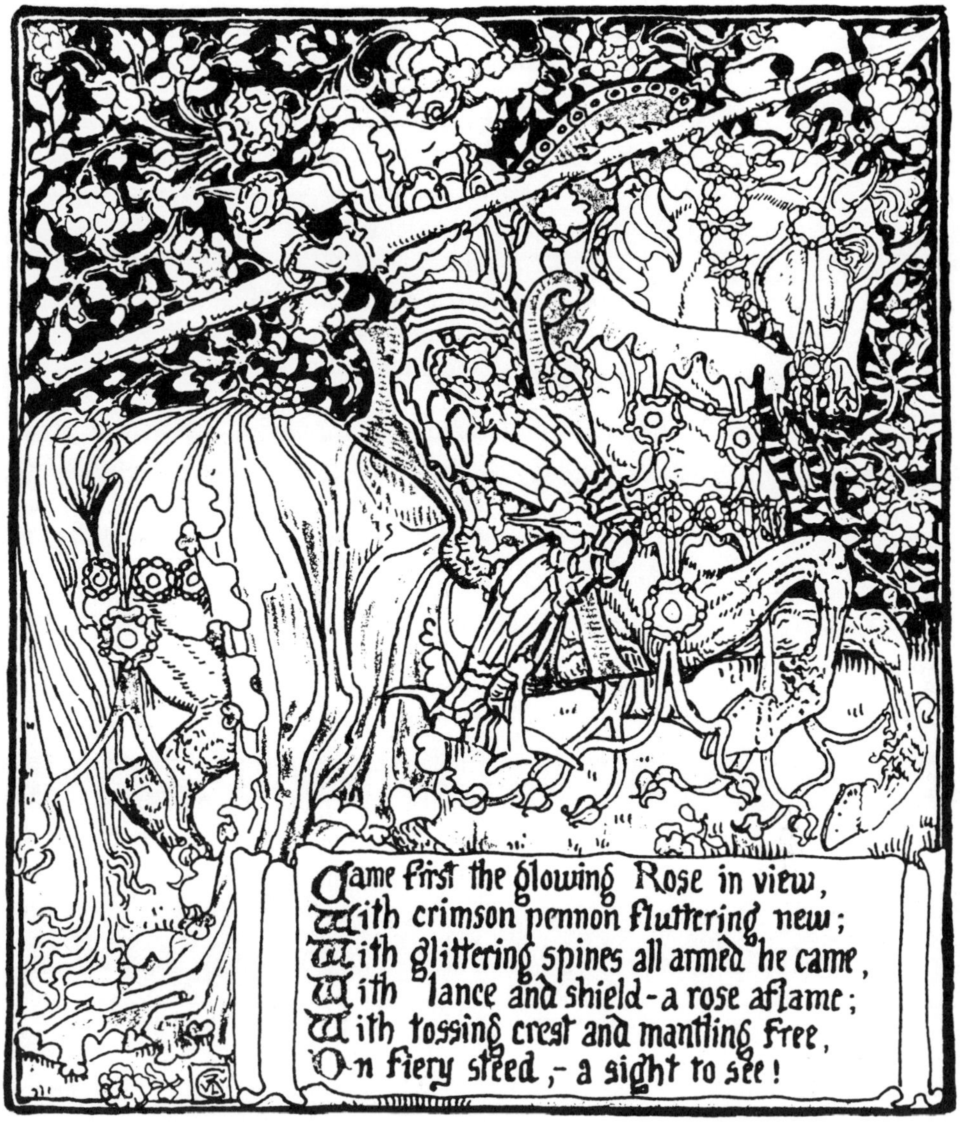

[56] Walter Crane: Illustration to the *Queen Summer* adapted by Crane and Morris for a wallpaper design, 1891. 15.0 x 17.25cm

Lutheranism and his conversion led him into a severe spiritual crisis. To some extent religion influenced his choice of subject and mode of expression. As an artist he was highly intellectual with a wide spectrum of interests. His power for work and his concentration were phenomenal, which accounts for his large output. He engraved in copper, made drypoints and etched on iron. However, in the prints made during the last few years of his life there is a sharp decline in both number and quality.

Dürer's technique and attention to detail was fabulous, but as an originator of the grand composition, which he attempted on so many occasions, he was at times weak and often disjointed. His insistence on detail led him into the irritating habit of including flourishes everywhere and at every opportunity. It was his intellectual interest in detail which induced him to compose with bits and pieces. When his prints were completed, the all-embracing, rhythmical and flowing structure which is a feature of Renaissance art very often eluded him. The early prints show him completely at ease in the Medieval tradition; these prints are very Gothic in style but awkward in composition. However, he did begin to absorb the concepts of the Renaissance and some of the middle and late period prints are masterpieces of composition. This success was after his first visit to Italy and his introduction to the master engravings of Andrea Mantegna (1431 to 1506).

The earliest Italian copper engravings which can be considered as creative are not dated before about 1460. Among the early engravers was Marcantonio Raimondis whose creative prints appeared in the first decade of the sixteenth century. Raimondis was born in Bologna between 1480 and 1530 and he was largely responsible for popularizing the works of Raphael through his engravings. The first Italian engravers never achieved the same perfection of technique as their German predecessors. During Dürer's first visit to Italy in 1494 he did drawings of the early Italian engravings. Nine of these drawings are in the British Museum. He also copied two of Mantegna's engravings and these drawings are in the Victoria and Albert Museum. The sophistication of the geometric, mathematical and volumetric expression embracing Renaissance compositional concepts, where detail was strictly sublimated to structure, eluded Dürer, despite the fact that he was talented in mathematics. It would appear that Dürer the mathematician was of little use to Dürer as a composer. He was concerned with the infinite complexity

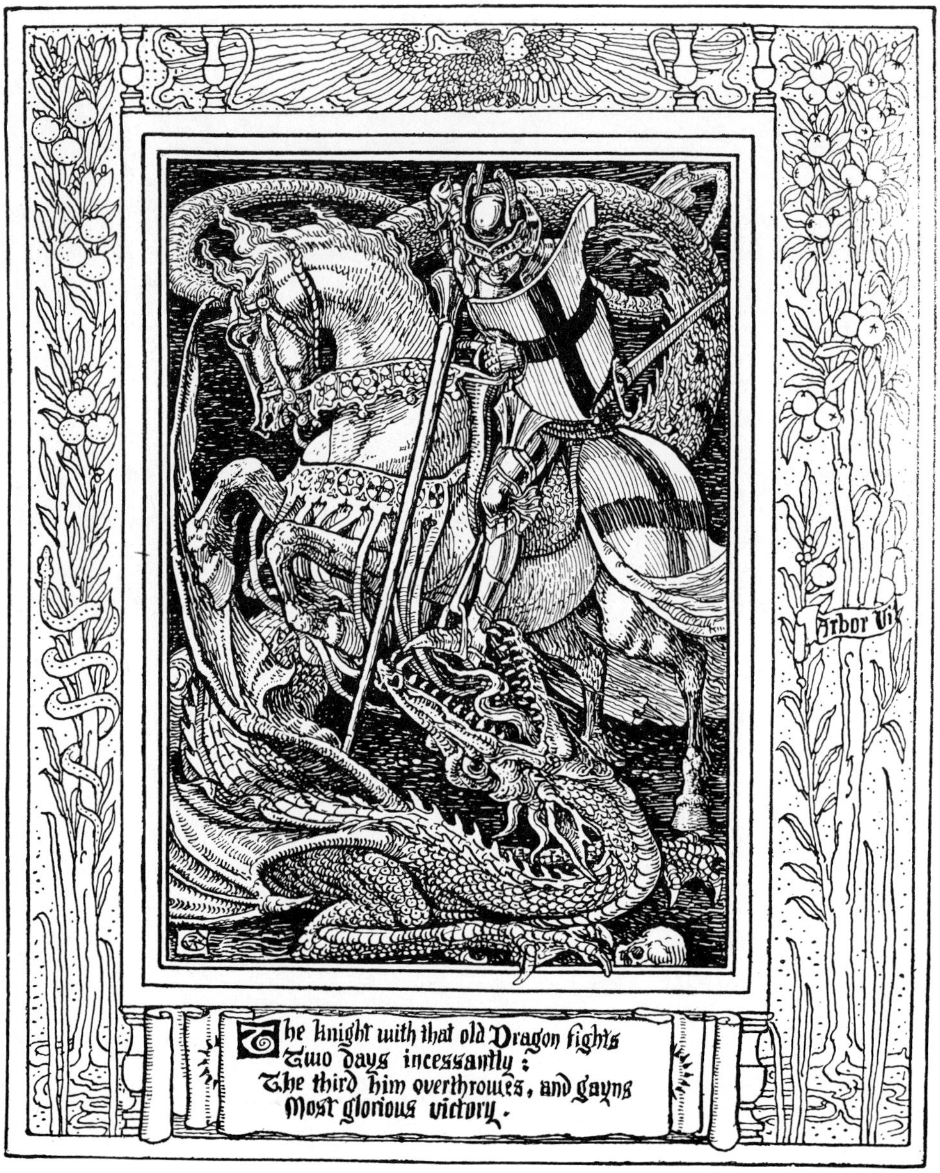

[57] Walter Crane: Illustration to Spencer's *Faerie Queen*, 1894.

of creation but failed to achieve that fusion of conflicting elements which is good design.

Another engraving influence in the life of Dürer was the work of Antonio Pollaiuolo (1432 to 1498). He was the first great artist of the Renaissance to work creatively by engraving copper. The only other great artist to engrave on copper was Mantegna whose work in this medium appeared towards the end of his life. There is only one work signed by Pollaiuolo, *The Ten Nudes*. The precise date of this work has not yet been determined but it was produced in the artist's mature years. There are several prints of the engraving extant in various collections but the copies vary in the quality of the printing. While the copy in the Uffizi Gallery in Milan is probably the most widely known, the print in the collection of Prince Lichtenstein at Feldsberg is the best example.

Vasari describes the earliest works executed by Pollaiuolo as *Paci*, small engraved

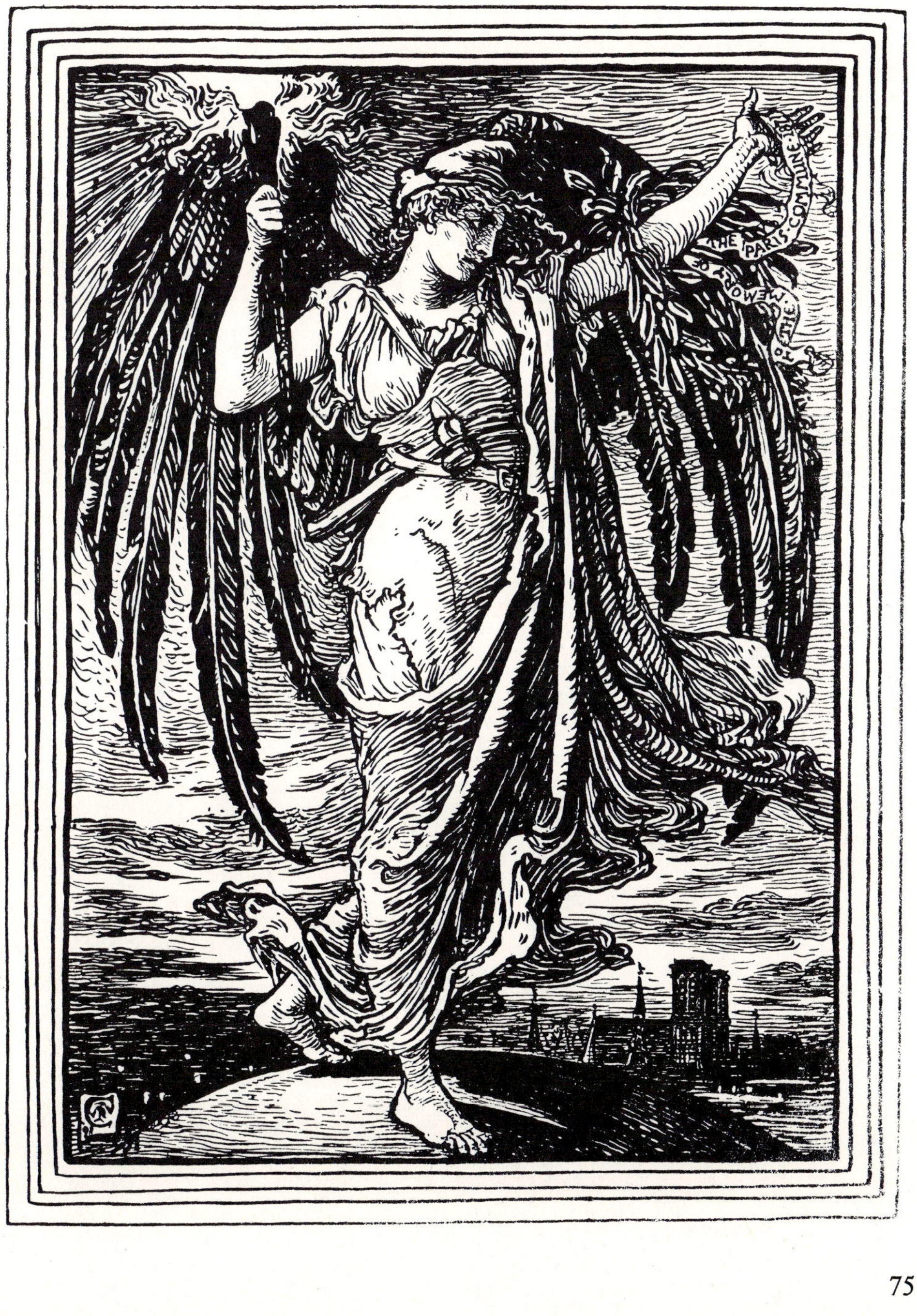

[58] Walter Crane: Cartoon for the *Socialist Cause*, 1886 – 1896.

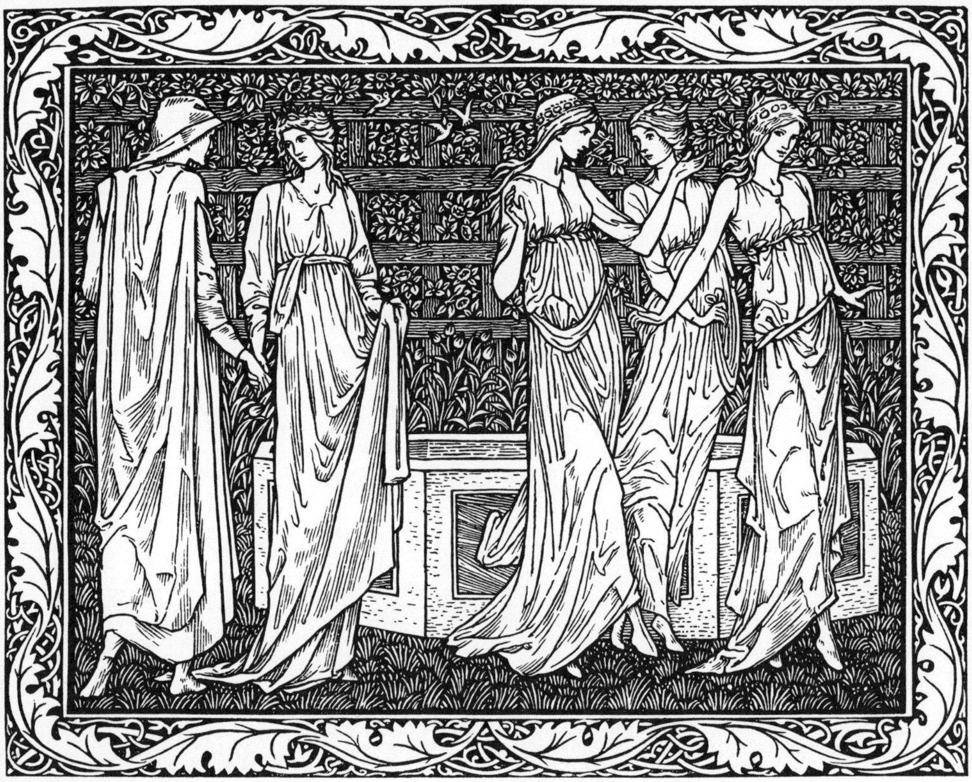

Have litel thought but on hir play.
Hir lemman was bisyde alway,
In swich a gyse, that he hir kiste
At alle tymes that him liste,
That al the daunce mighte it see;
They make no force of privetee;
For who spak of hem yvel or wel,
They were ashamed never a del,
But men mighte seen hem kisse there,
As it two yonge douves were.
For yong was thilke bachelere,
Of beaute wot I noon his pere;
And he was right of swich an age
As Youthe his leef, and swich corage.
THE lusty folk thus daunced there,
And also other that with hem were,
That weren alle of hir meynee;
Ful hende folk, and wys, and free,
And folk of fair port, trewely,
Ther weren alle comunly.
WHAN I hadde seen the countenaunces
Of hem that ladden thus these daunces,
Than hadde I wil to goon & see
The gardin that so lyked me,
And loken on these faire loreres,
On pyn-trees, cedres, and oliveres.
The daunces than y-ended were;
For many of hem that daunced there
Were with hir loves went awey
Under the trees to have hir pley.
A, lord! they lived lustily!
A gret fool were he, sikerly,
That nolde, his thankes, swich lyf lede!
For this dar I seyn, out of drede,
That whoso mighte so wel fare,
For better lyf thurte him not care;
For ther nis so good paradys
As have a love at his devys.
OUT of that place wente I tho,
And in that gardin gan I go,
Pleying along ful merily.
The God of Love ful hastely
Unto him Swete-Loking clepte,
No lenger wolde he that he kepte
His bowe of golde, that shoon so bright.
He bad him bende it anon-right;
And he ful sone it sette on ende,
And at a braid he gan it bende,
And took him of his arowes fyve,
Ful sharpe and redy for to dryve.
Now God that sit in magestee
Fro deedly woundes kepe me,
If so be that he wol me shete;

[59] Page from the *Kelmscott Chaucer*, *The Romaunt of the Rose.* Illustration by Burne-Jones, engraved by W. H. Hooper, 1896.

[60] A pen drawing by Phil May, engraved and reproduced in *Punch*, 1897. 11.75 x 18.8cm

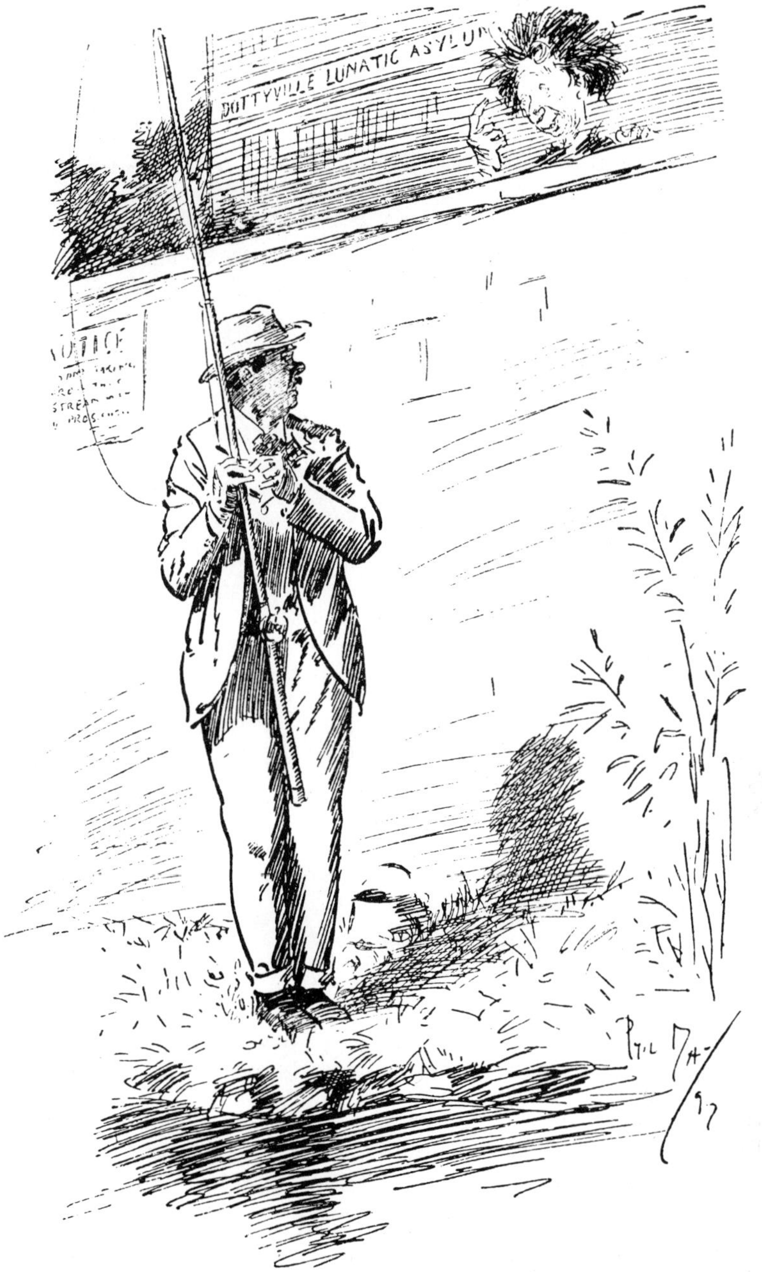

Lunatic (suddenly popping his head over wall). "WHAT ARE YOU DOING THERE?"
Brown. "FISHING." *Lunatic.* "CAUGHT ANYTHING?" *Brown.* "NO."
Lunatic. "HOW LONG HAVE YOU BEEN THERE?" *Brown.* "SIX HOURS."
Lunatic. "*COME INSIDE!*"

plaques of precious metal enclosed in jewelled frames for liturgical purposes. Fifteenth-century *Paci* were generally made in the *niello* technique, a word derived from *higellum*, the black enamel with which the engraved lines were filled. None of the *Paci* of Pollaiuolo is in existence, having been melted down in time of war or otherwise destroyed.

Pollaiuolo's engraving shows the influence of the *niello* technique in the different shading of the background by which the figures are set into relief and it has a fine decorative value. It is a work displaying two different techniques of expression.

The *niello* influence in Pollaiuolo's engraving is shown in the very limited space

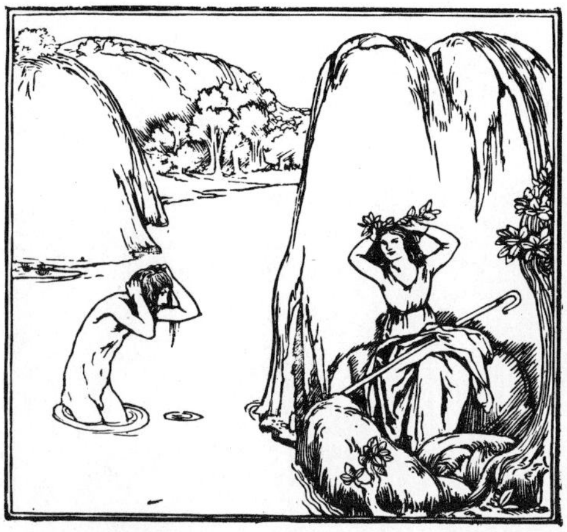

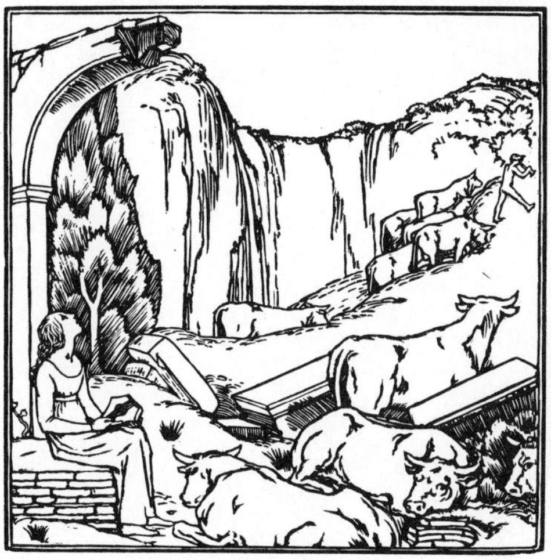

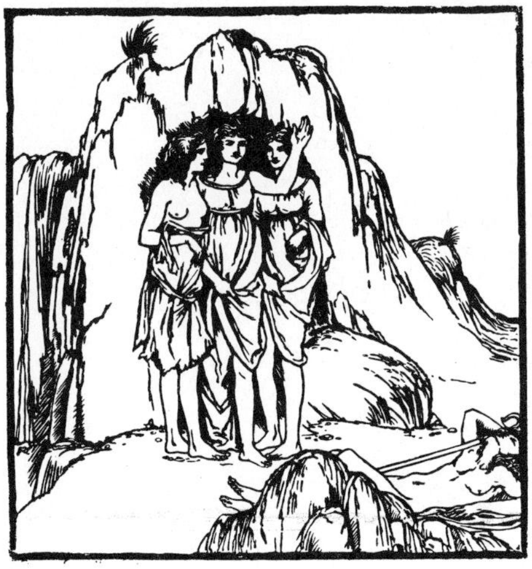

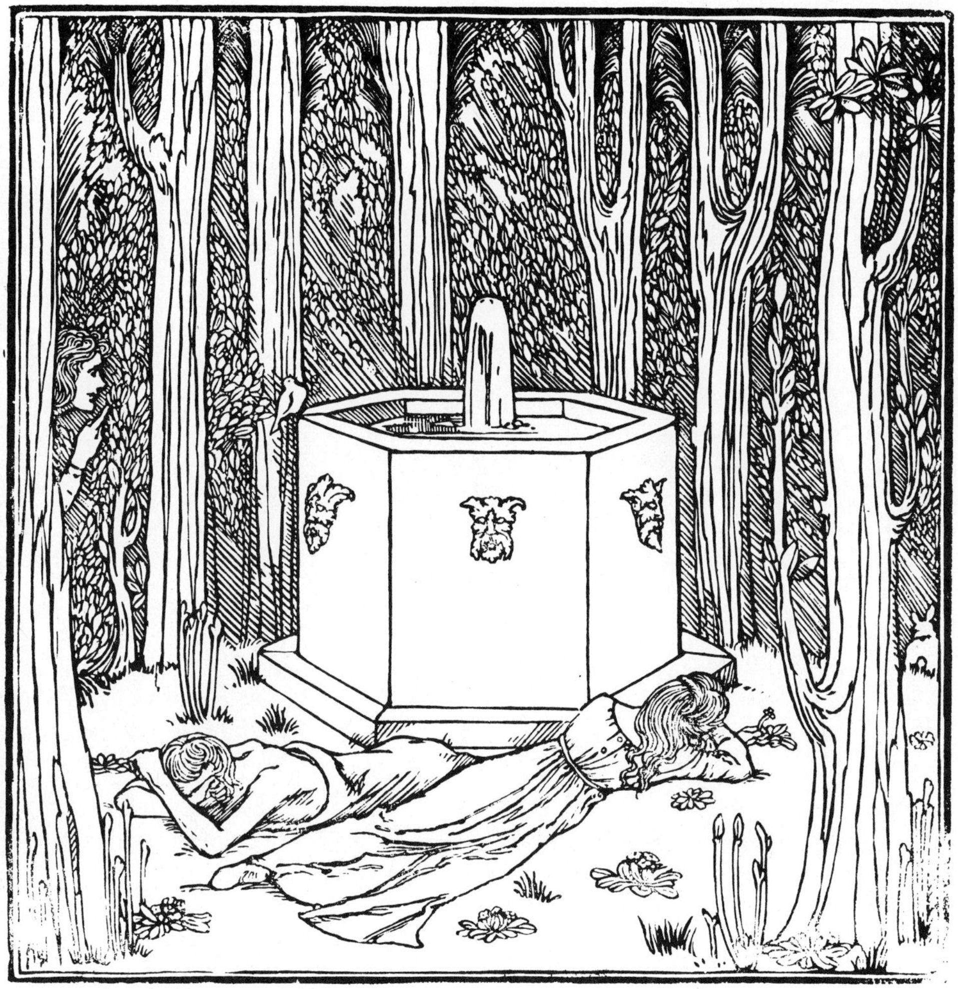

occupied and the rendering of the figures as bas-relief. This is also characteristic of Mantegna's engravings. In the work of both artists the weight of volume and the solidity of the figures flow through the composition as a continuous rhythmic structure; an essential attribute of good engraving. The peculiarities of Pollaiuolo's technique appear also in the engravings of Mantegna and it is probable that the latter adopted them from him. Dr Kristeller suggests that it was *The Ten Nudes* which gave Mantegna the inspiration to master the technique of engraving.[3] However, open-line engraving was practised by the Paduan followers of Mantegna as early as 1460 to 1470.

In Dürer's *Head of St John* can be seen the clear influence of Mantegna, both in the expression and in the classical treatment of the hair. The figure of *St Christopher* [32] is a repetition of the *Bacchus* in Mantegna's engraving. At the same time that Dürer's drawing and composition was influenced by Mantegna, his engraving came under the formative influence of Martin Schongauer who was a brilliant performer in copper engraving. In his work all the elements of style arising from the rendering of the image, volume and space were fused. Before Schongauer's influence, Dürer's engraving on wood or copper was awkward in style with a cleavage between the rendering of solids, space and light. Later he showed a better understanding and more confident fusion of these elements.

[61 – 64] Illustrations by Charles Shannon.

Dürer married in July 1494 and settled in Nuremberg and was ready for another big leap forward in his art. During the next ten years his output of engravings and

[65] Illustration by Charles Ricketts. 12.5 x 22.5cm

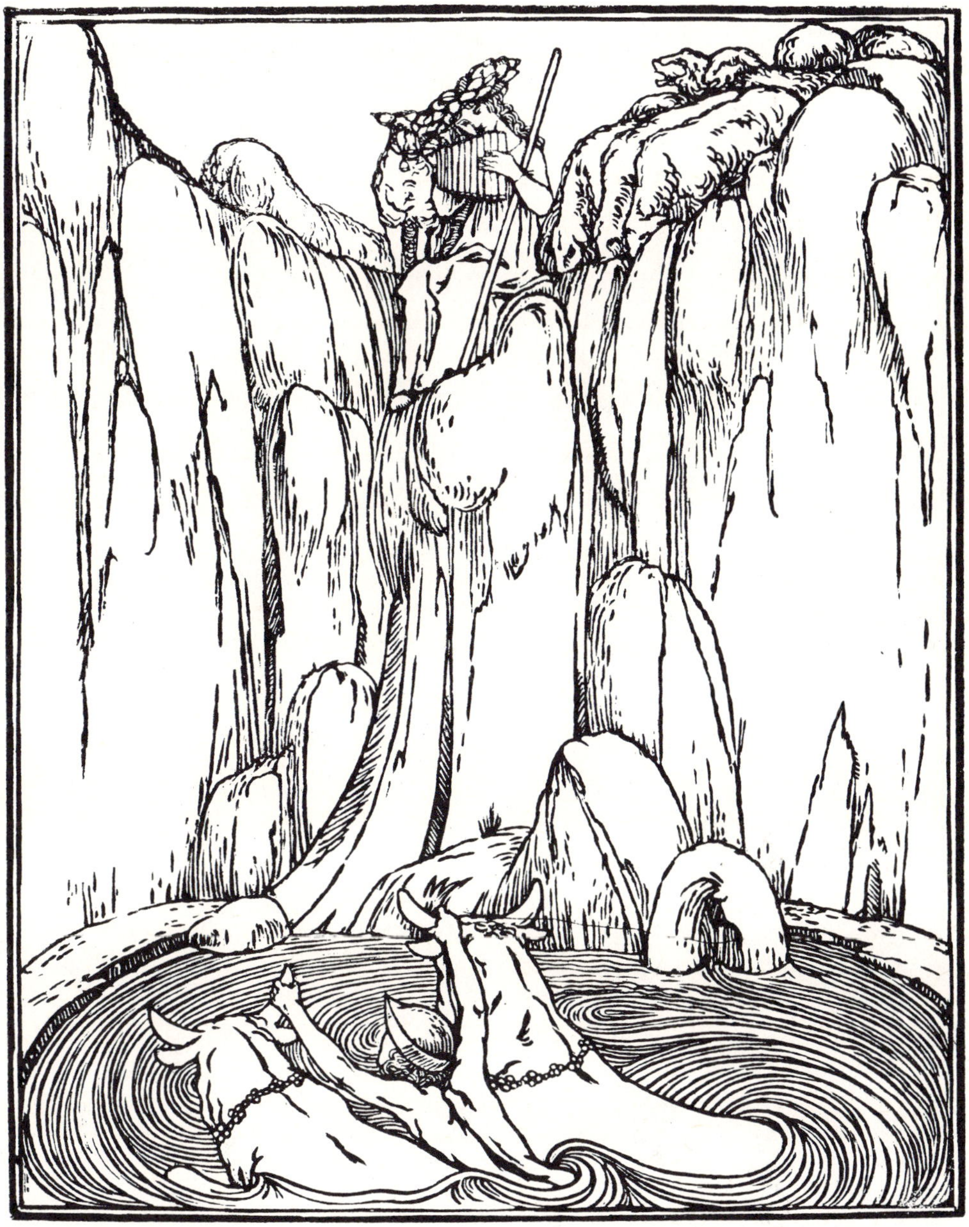

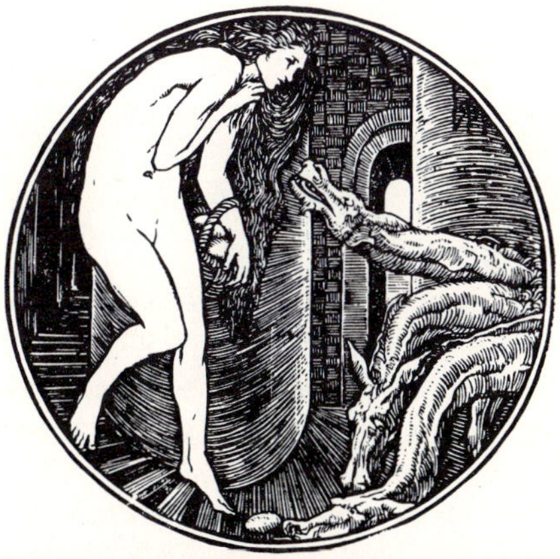

[66] Charles Ricketts: *The Descent into Hell* from *The Marriage of Cupid and Psyche*, 1897.

prints was substantial. In 1498 he produced *Apocalypse* which, at the time of its publication, was a new type of illustrated book [27]. The subject matter of *Apocalypse* is taken from the last book of the New Testament and Dürer's engravings, like Leonardo da Vinci's *The Last Supper*, belong to that category of works of art termed 'masterpieces'. They form part of a number of flawless works that sum up tradition and establish new standards.

The work shows the distinct stylistic influence of Mantegna and took about two years to produce. The illustrations comprise a series of fifteen *formschneider* engravings of an average size of 282 x 388mm, and seem to have been designed to be viewed separately from the text matter which is set in black letter. The book was published in two editions, one with German text and the other in Latin, and the engravings are beautifully balanced by the double-column text matter.

While superficially the book can be identified as having been designed and printed by the artist, Dürer was not a printer and it is likely that it was printed by Koberger,

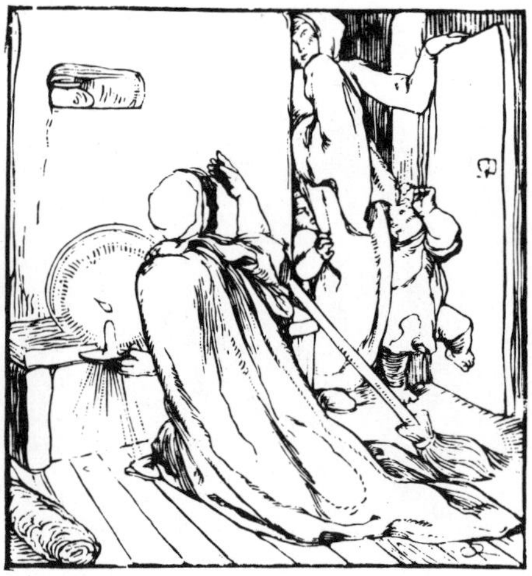

[67] Charles Ricket: *The Lost Piece of Silver* from *The Parables*, 1903. 7.7 x 8.5cm

whose type appears to have been used for the setting of the text. It seems likely that Dürer designed the complete work. If this is correct, he created a precedent for a wood engraver to design and illustrate a complete book. This practice was not seen again until the twentieth century when it reappeared for a short period in the revival of wood engraving as part of the private press movement.

Dürer's second book was the *Large Passion* which comprises eleven prints and was published in 1511 [28]. This book, which he began in 1499, did not reach the public in a complete form.

He began to work on his third great series, the *Life of the Virgin*, sometimes referred to as the *Little Passion*, between 1500 and 1505 [31]. The whole series, with a frontispiece, was issued in 1511. Several *formschneiders* were employed on the work and their competence varied throughout the series. However, despite the *formschneiders*, some of these prints show Dürer's style in its full maturity. The engravings – a little smaller than those of the other two books – are 29.8cm high and 21.1cm wide. In these engravings of the Virgin greys predominate over the previous emphasis on solid blacks and whites. These dominant greys show a marked change and sublimation in Dürer's technique.

Dürer's fourth book, the *Small Passion* was also published in 1511 though two of the prints are dated 1509 and two 1510. The work consists of thirty-six subjects and a title page and is smaller than his other books. In dealing with the quantity of detail that Dürer demanded in the small scale, there is little doubt that the *formschneider* engravers encountered the limitation of using a long-grained plank.

In these four books, a further refinement of design was made which adds a complication to the definition of the term 'block book'. It is usual to consider a block book as one in which both the text and the illustrations have been printed from wood blocks. Panofsky describes each of Dürer's books as block books but

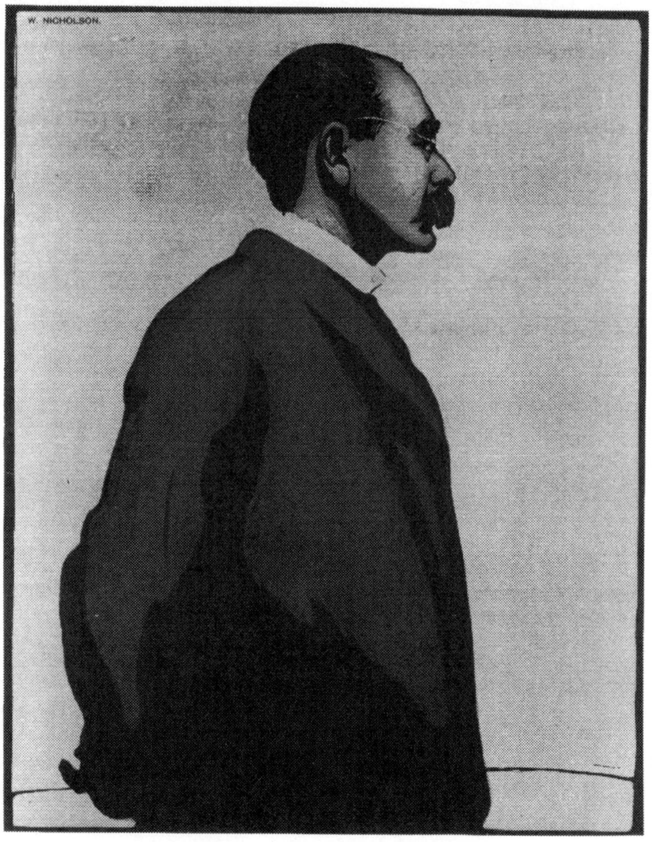

[68] William Nicholson: *Portrait of Rudyard Kipling*. Issued as a supplement to *The New Review* October 1897. Printed black and brown on cream paper.

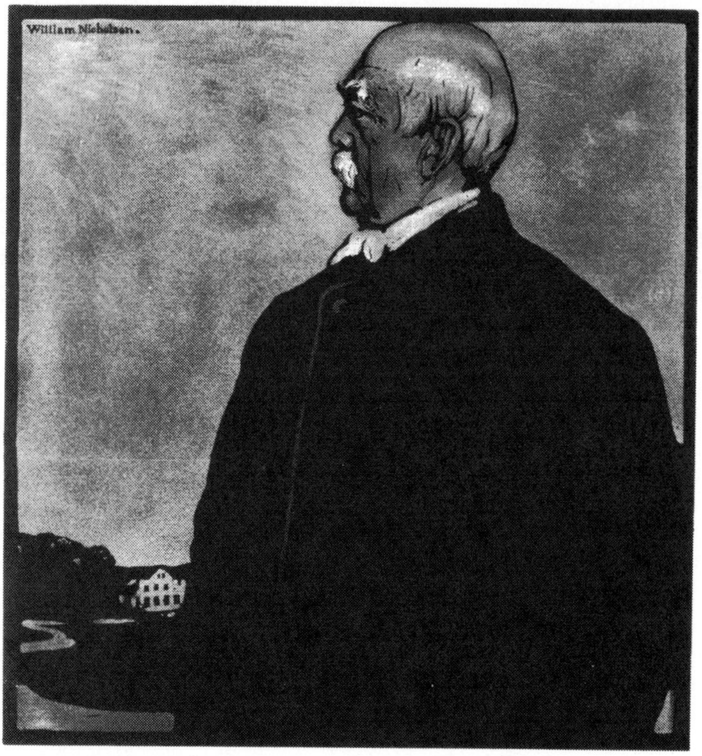

[69] William Nicholson: *Portrait of Prince Bismarck*. Issued as a supplement to *The New Review* December 1897. Printed black and brown on cream paper.

[70] Lucien Pissarro: *Roses d'Antan* from *l'Image*, 1896. 10.25 x 9.7cm

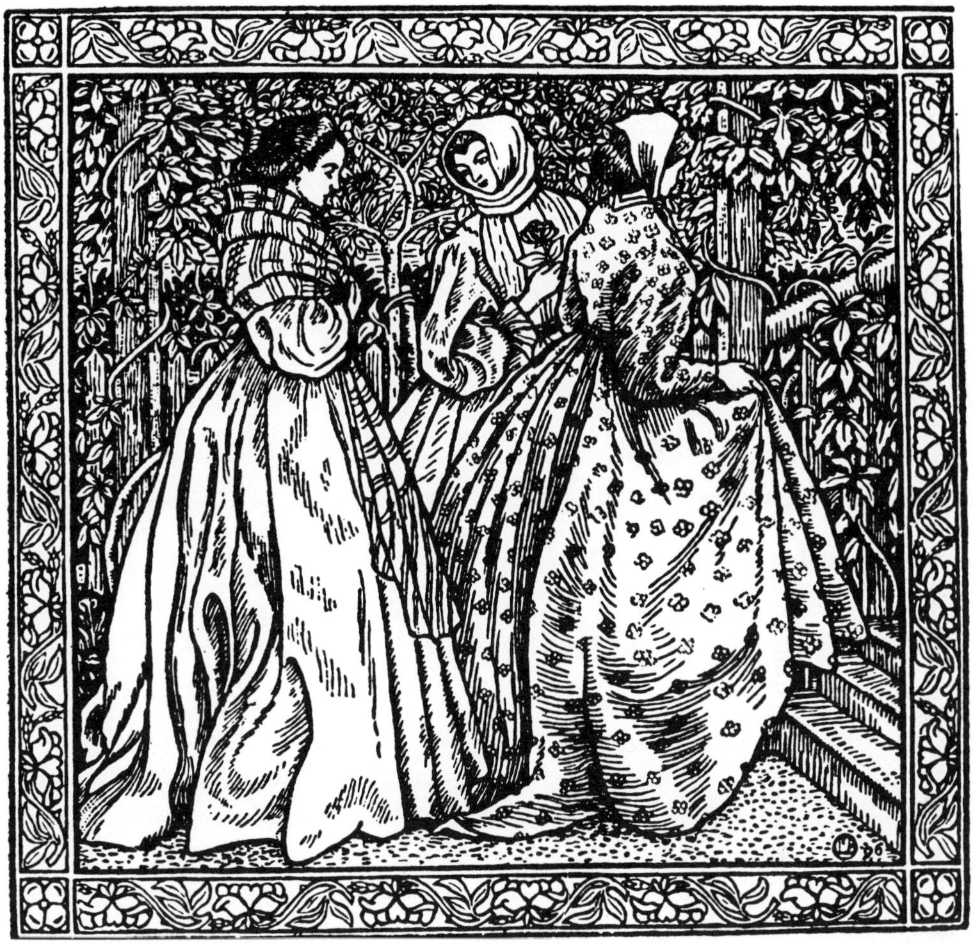

A. M. Hind in his book *An Introduction to a History of the Woodcut* suggests that the books cannot be given this classification and quotes the use of Koberger's type in the *Apocalypse*.[4]

The most remarkable small *formschneider* prints are Holbein's series *The Dance of Death* which are only 5cm by 6.5cm. Holbein, four years older than Dürer and a master of composition, adhered to the Renaissance teaching that the flow of detail through a unified structure could be controlled like the flow of water through a tap. He was very fortunate in having the services of Lutzelburger, one of the most skilful *formschneiders*. Lutzelburger could engrave on a small scale because Holbein as a master kept his detail under control.

Formschneider engraving was at its best between 1509 and 1512, a relatively short period. Through Dürer's efforts, engraving reached its complete development. When the publication of his three great books made such a marked impression he fell a victim to the will of a potentate who had no genuine feelings for his democratic art but intended to make its technical perfection serve his own ambitious purposes. The *formschneider* print had reached the attention of the court and the Emperor Maximilian I (1459 to 1519) wanted to use this art form to portray personal and dynastic matters which hitherto had been the exclusive domain of the more aristocratic engravings.

Maximilian was an exaggerated, extravagant and ambitious character who glorified in proficiency in tournaments, jousts, pageants and other forms of sport demanding

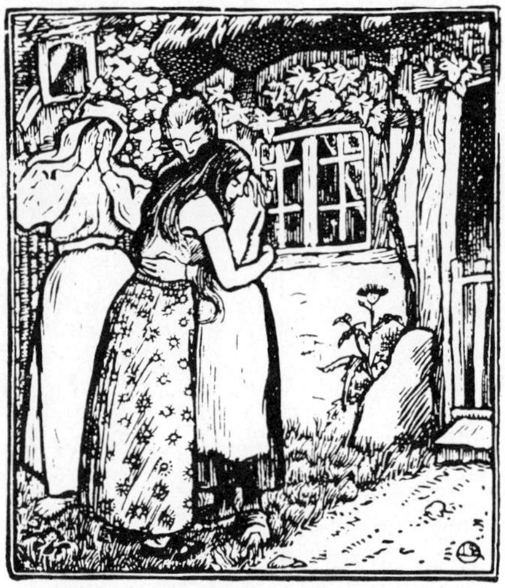

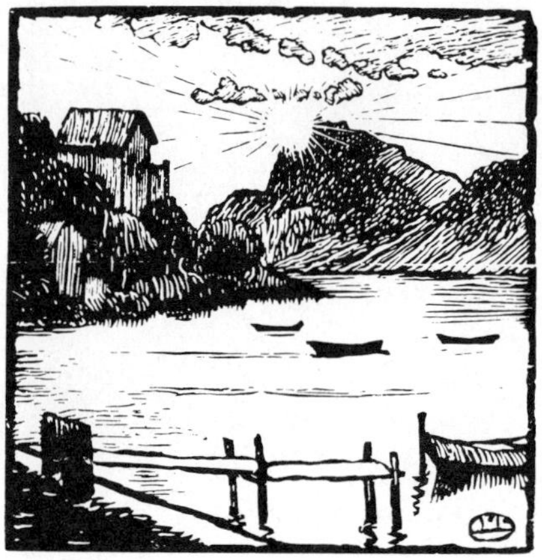

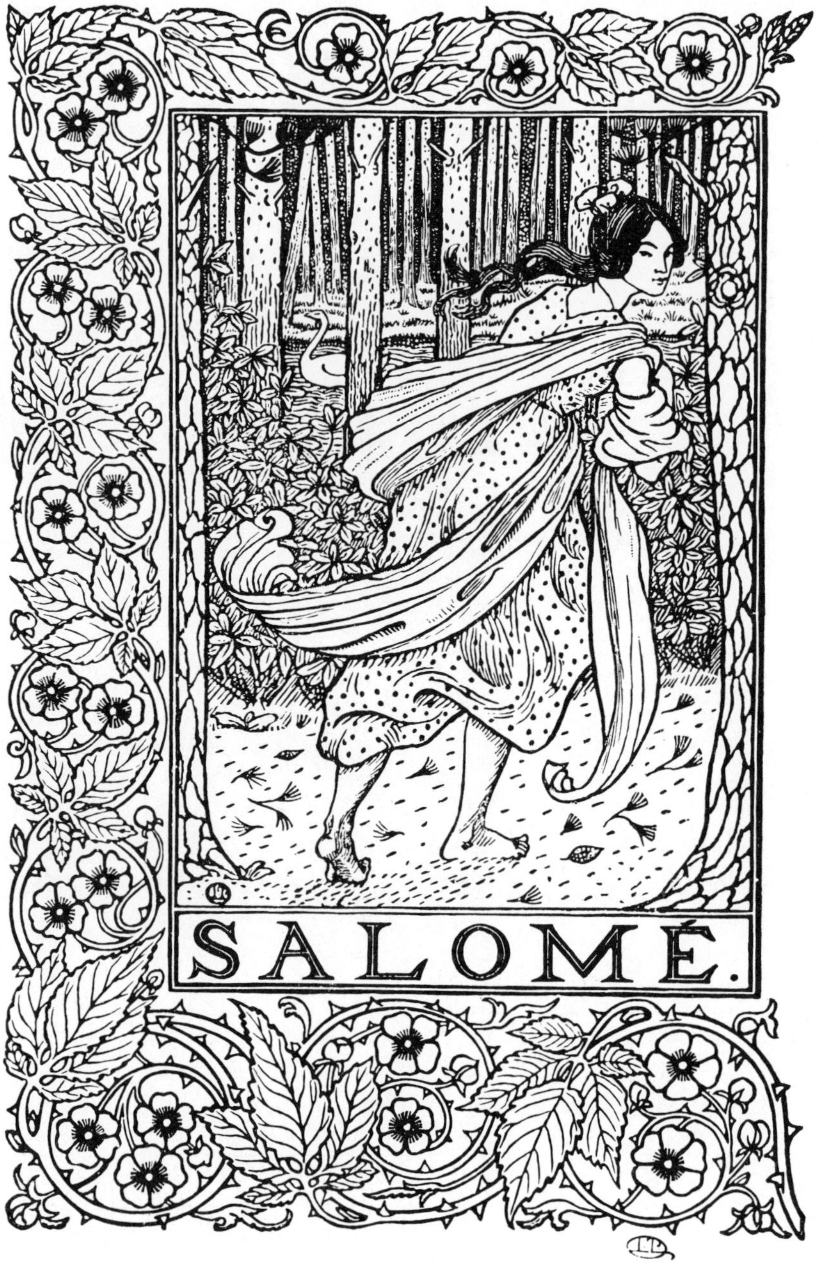

[71] Lucien Pissarro: From *The Book of Ruth and the Book of Esther*, 1896. 6.6 x 7.6cm

[72] Lucien Pissarro: *La Pointe de Cargoussa*, 1897. 7.5 x 7.7cm

[73] Lucien Pissarro: *Salome*, frontispiece for *Les Moralités Légendaires* Vol I, 1897. 12.0 x 18.5cm

chivalrous display. Everything he did was larger than life but he was lacking in any sense of aesthetic fitness, control or direction. Because he was Emperor of Germany, his armour and firearms had to be more ambitious in design and more highly decorated than those of any other prince. His exploits had to be perpetuated and glorified in a grand *Triumphal Arch* which was to take the form of the largest *formschneider* print project ever undertaken.

Maximilian commanded a school of artists who could satisfy his desire for masses of pictorial detail. Aesthetically there was certainly no point in producing such an extravaganza. Discussion for this flamboyant work probably took place during the Emperor's visit to Nuremberg from 4 to 12 February 1512. The *Triumphal Arch* was conceived as a single-sheet project printed from 192 individual blocks. Overall measurements were approximately 348cm high and 294.5cm wide. The design of the architectural structure was assigned to the architect Jörg Kölderer of the upper Inn Valley, Innsbruck in the Tyrol. Kölderer's arch followed the pattern of the *Arcus Triumphalus* in Rome. Kölderer, though mentioned as an

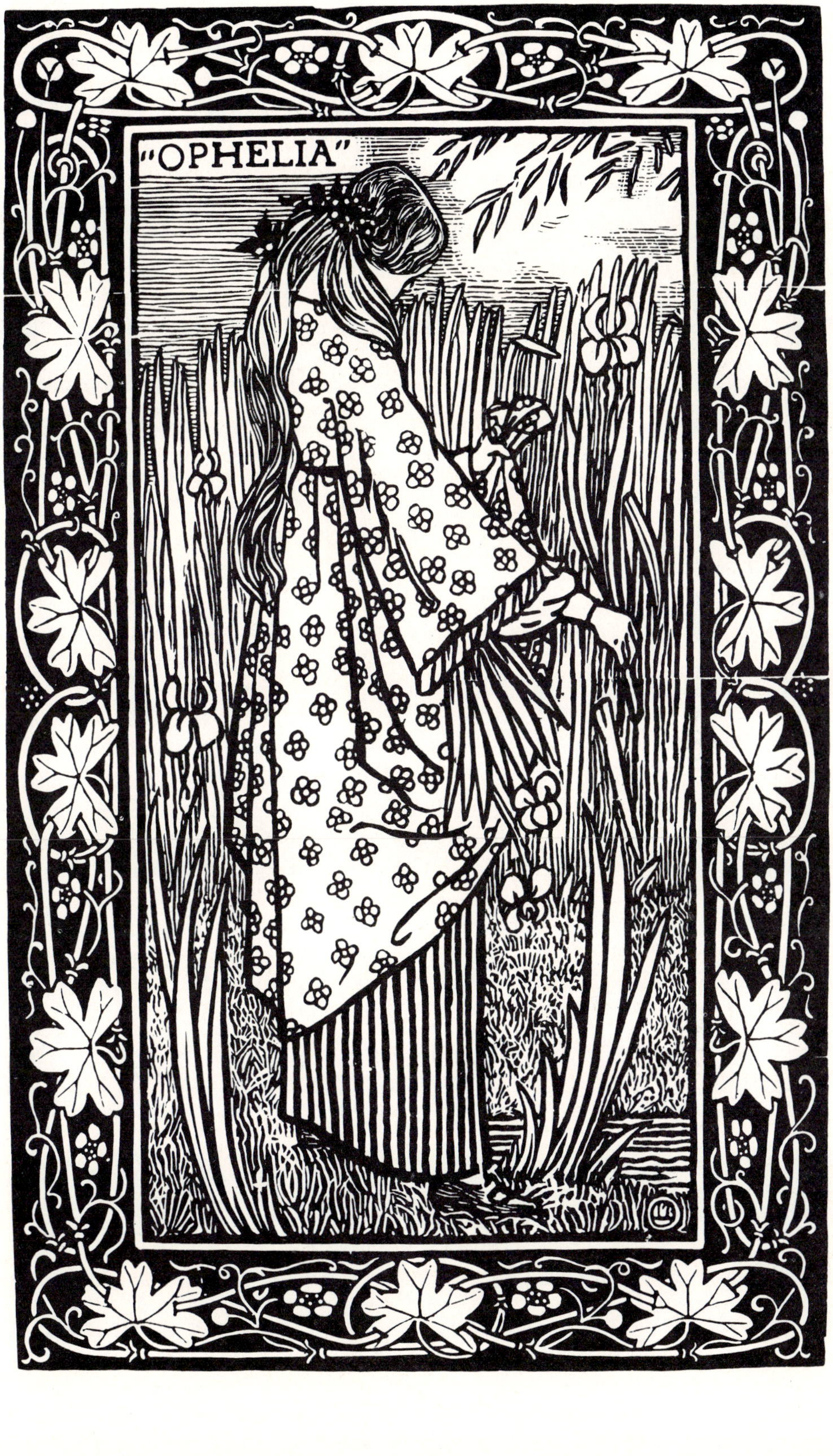

[74] Lucien Pissarro: *Ophelia*, frontispiece for *Les Moralités Légendaires* Vol II, 1898. 11.5 x 18.6cm

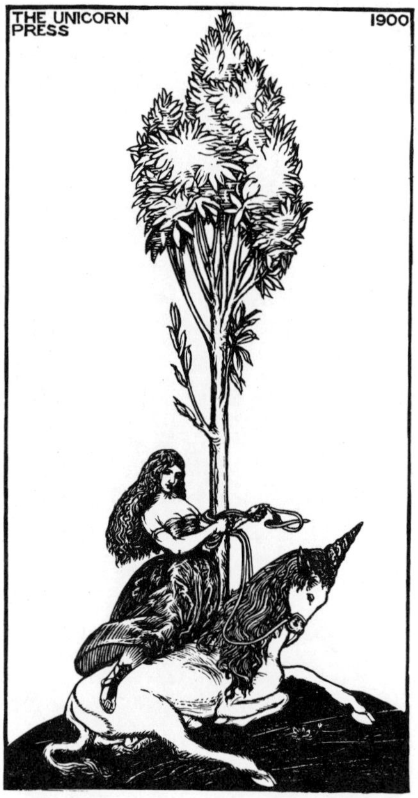

[75] Thomas Sturge Moore: *The Unicorn Impress*, 1900. 9.0 x 17.6cm

architect, was also a painter influenced by the Danube school. He was first commissioned by the court at Innsbruck in 1497 and in 1498 became Court Painter to Maximilian. In 1518 he became Court Architect and held both offices under Charles V and Ferdinand until his death in 1540.

Maximilian was surrounded by many very talented artists who, had they so desired, could have advised against this ill-considered project. However, in the fashion of the period it was unthinkable that such advice should be offered and, as professionals, the artists carried out the Emperor's demands in order to remain in employment. Thus, although Dürer was appointed as chief designer, he was powerless to direct artistic activity to more profitable projects and his own contribution was minute in proportion to that from artists of lesser ability.

Maximilian was not content with only one extravaganza and ordered another the *Triumphal Procession* to supplement the *Triumphal Arch.* He conceived this work and in 1512 gave the necessary instructions to his secretary Marx Treitz-Snurwein. Dürer yet again found himself in the unfortunate position of being forced to work in a minor role. Approximately half the blocks were designed by Burgkmair and the remainder shared by Beck, Altdorfer, Huber, Schäuffelein, Springinklee and Dürer. Burgkmair of Augsburg had been in the Emperor's service for many years and Dürer had to prove his worth in drawings and prints in competition with this Augsburg artist. Like Dürer, Burgkmair responded to the influence of the Italian Renaissance but his art lacked the enquiring depth of Dürer who at that time had become quite scientific. Burgkmair, in contrast, expressed gaiety and freedom and had an inexhaustible imagination in narration [34, 35 and 36]. He took a delight in decorative splendour expressed with a mature dignity. From 1510 his work was engraved by the excellent *formschneider* Jost de Negker (1485 to 1544) who came from Antwerp. Burgkmair started producing prints in 1508 and was quickly in the forefront of engraving in Augsburg.

The blocks for the *Triumphal Procession* were not produced until 1516 to 1518. Maximilian died in 1519 and publication of the work was interrupted. An incomplete series of prints from the blocks was published in 1526, by order and at the expense of the Archduke Ferdinand, brother and successor of Charles V, but the complete series of 137 blocks was not issued until 1883 and 1884.

A number of portrait drawings by Burgkmair have been preserved. The earliest known drawing by the Augsburg painter and engraver is a self-portrait dated 1497 or 1498 which shows the young artist dressed as for a wedding. About twenty studies of heads and portraits by him are known, most of them drawn in chalk or charcoal.

Dürer is reputed to have made more than 250 drawings for the *Triumphal Procession* but to have taken only five prints, and in the final version his contribution to this princely extravagance was *Wedding of Maximilian* and *Mary of Burgundy.* Burgkmair provided most of the engravings for the *Procession.* In this work he is comparable with Dürer but like Schongauer he was more at ease with the Renaissance flow of Mantegna and Pollaiuolo.

However, Maximilian aroused some enthusiasm for Dürer's forty-five marginal works in the last big book-publishing project, the famous *Prayer-book of Maximilian I.* This prayer-book was compiled, arranged and in certain sections even worded, from Maximilian's wishes. It was probably intended for the members of the Order of St George which the Emperor had revived in connection with his dream of a great new crusade. Johann Schönsperger the Elder of Augsburg was the printer and a statement in the colophon says that the printing was finished on 30 December 1513.

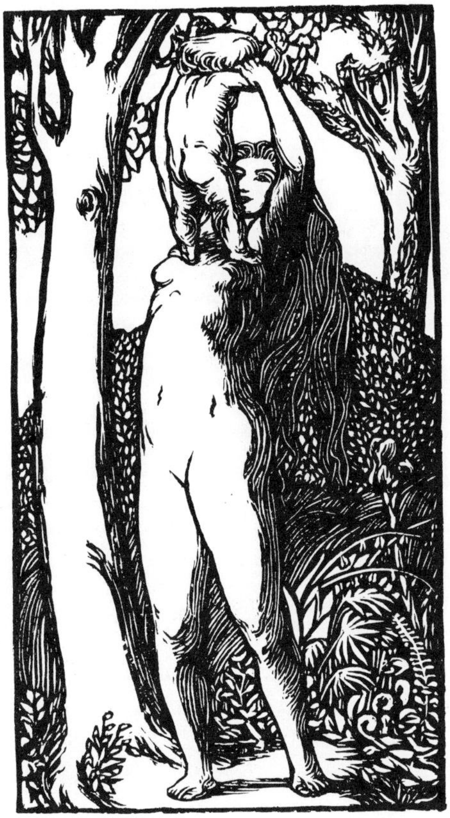

[76] Thomas Sturge Moore: *Little Mother*. 6.0 x 10.75cm

[77] Edward Gordon Craig: *View over Florence*, 1908. 12.5 x 3.4cm

Five specimens of this prayer-book are known. However, they do not in themselves constitute a real or final edition. They are all different and none is really complete. The 1513 examples are most likely to be proofing copies and as such were subject to changes and additions before the final publication. In the prayer-book, illustrations no longer try to compete with text. Alongside the powerful black letter the linear designs would have appeared weak. The thin black lines are heavily outweighted by the dense black masses. In 1515 Dürer interrupted his work on the prayer-book and several other artists were instructed to continue in the pattern set by Dürer. These artists included Lucas Cranach, Hans Burgkmair, Hans Baldung Grien, Jörg Breu the Elder (1480 to 1536) of Augsburg and, according to some, Albrecht Altdorfer (1480 to 1538) who made twenty-eight marginal drawings.

Altdorfer was a landscape painter, working in Regensburg from 1505 onwards and most probably born there. He had knowledge of the art of Dürer and Mantegna. Through his improvised borrowings from Italy, he created a serene style expressing an ideal view of the world, which was in contrast to the much harsher Danube school. He was quite unmoved by new problems of form, by perspective and proportion. From 1526 until his death he was employed as the town architect of Regensburg. It is unusual that as an architect he never mastered perspective. Altdorfer worked on the corner towers of Maximilian's *Triumphal Arch* and the illustrations in [37] and [38] show his engravings for the *Triumphal Procession*. His style is rich, delicate and sensitive, as indeed are his painted landscapes. Altdorfer is dominantly a picturesque artist which is a common attribute of architects.

The type used in the prayer-book was designed for the work by Vincenz Roeker who was one of Maximilian's secretaries. The design is based on the bold *lettre brisée* script which was used in liturgical manuscripts produced in the first half of the fifteenth century. The type face was designed to simulate the free play of the pen. Because the text of the prayer-book is continuous the illustrations are confined to the margins. The small drawings produced by Dürer are a lovable experience compared with the more ponderous allegorical prints. In these drawings he succeeds triumphantly in dispersing the thin line between imagination and visual reality.

Dürer also thought in terms of colour for the prayer-book in its final edition. Two things are known concerning this aspect of colour. Firstly, the royal copy, one of the five, which is part in the Staatsbibliothek in Munich and part in the Museum at Besançon, has painted initials and is accurately ruled with pink lines, drawn by pen after printing in order to simulate a hand-decorated manuscript. The second thing is that Dürer's drawings were rendered in coloured inks. His choice of hues was red, violet and olive green but each drawing is in one colour only.

Probably the first printing in colour was the *Mainz Psalter* of 1457. Colour printing was seen in Augsburg with Erhard Ratdolt's liturgical book *Missale*

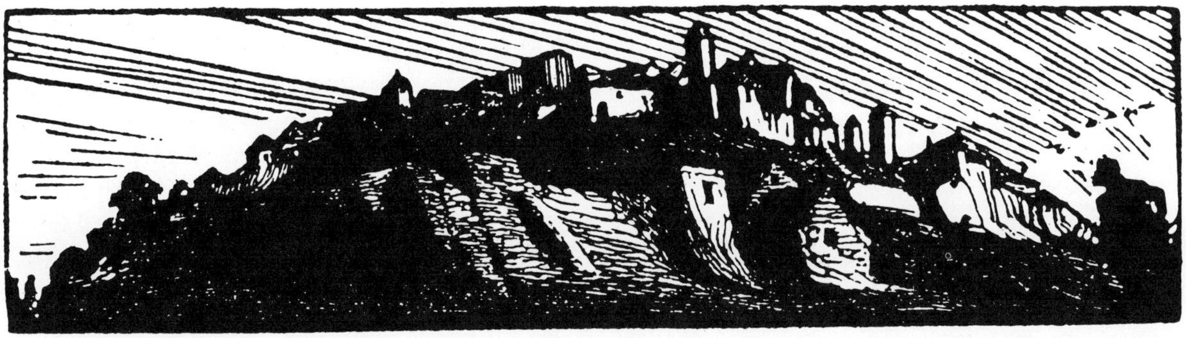

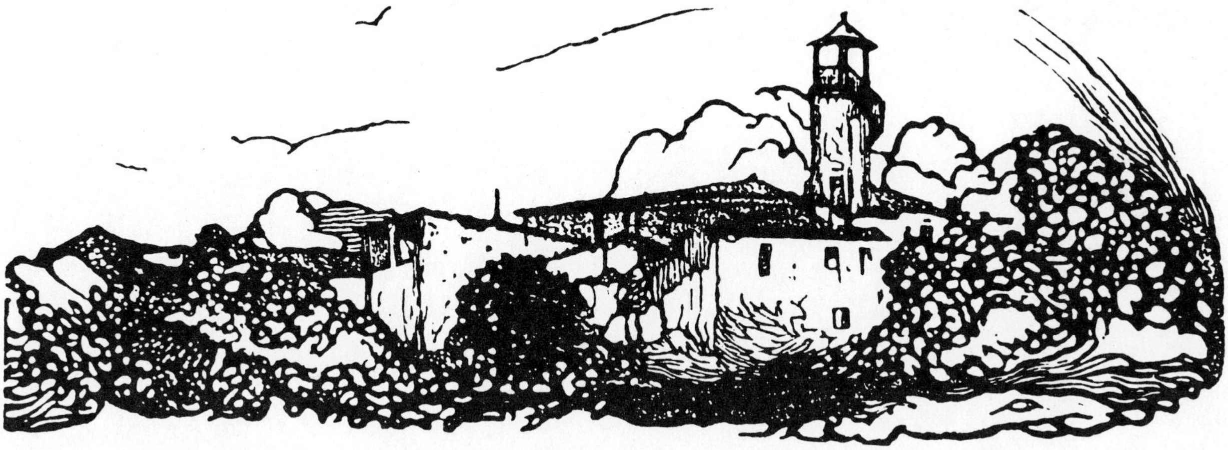

[78] Edward Gordon Craig: *Torre dei Diavoli*, 1908. 13.0 x 4.7cm

Aquileiense of 1494. Ratdolt (1447 to 1528) worked in Venice up to 1486 and thereafter at Augsburg until 1528. He was one of the most accomplished of the early printers. One of his early works of colour printing was the *Euclid Elementa*, Venice 25 May 1482, and the colour was used mainly as a solid tint.

In 1508 Hans Burgkmair had produced a colour print entitled *The Emperor Maximilian I on Horseback*. Lucas Cranach the Elder produced a colour print *St Christopher* dated 1506 although the blocks were finally finished in 1509. Hans Baldung Grien produced his colour print *The Witches* in 1510. The technique of colour printing spread quickly, as did every new development in the Rhine area.

The technique of tinted engraving gave rise to the term *clair-obscur*. Whilst Ratdolt of Augsburg had been working in this technique, including the printing of gold, since 1494, the major impetus and further development came from the Flemish *formschneider* Jost de Negker of Antwerp. He settled in Augsburg a little before 1508 and remained there until 1544. Some authorities attribute the invention of the coloured engraving to him.

At the beginning of the sixteenth century and largely through the influence of Dürer, the art of perspective was developing and leading to a clarification of three-dimensional form and space rendering and the end of the Medieval traditions. Colour was used to define space planes, within the perspective structure, such as foreground, middle distance and the horizon. This technique was to continue through to the nineteenth and early twentieth century print making.

During the Augsburg Diet of the summer of 1518, Dürer is known to have made several large-scale portrait drawings. Among them are the portraits of Maximilian I drawn on 28 June 1518 and of Jacob Fugger the Rich, Cardinal Albrecht of Brandenburg and a portrait said to be of Cardinal Lang von Wellenburg of Salzburg. These drawings were transcribed into other works during the next two years. The Fugger drawing was used for a painting in Munich in 1520. Albrecht of Brandenburg's portrait was used for the engraving *The Small Cardinal*. The drawing of Maximilian I was used not only for two paintings in Vienna and Nuremberg but also for a large *formschneider* engraving [40] which, as in the case of the two paintings, was most likely not completed until after the Emperor's death in 1519. It is this print which has been responsible for the image of Maximilian I becoming so well known. A second portrait was engraved and published the following year by Hans Weiditz, using the Dürer portrait as a model, and in 1520 Lucas van Leyden repeated Dürer's portrait in one of his best-known prints. Dürer captures the noble aloofness and the natural benevolence of Maximilian I but at

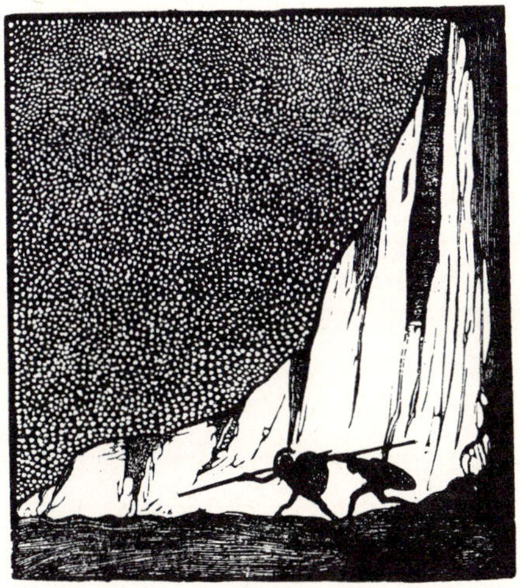

[79] Edward Gordon Craig: *The Vikings*, 1908. 8.0 x 9.0cm

the same time he draws the fatigue and disillusionment overtaking the sitter. This print is remarkable for its clarity, economy and brilliance of line, each quality in its turn defining the form. The lines in themselves bear little relation to the incidental light but build up to a masterly overall impression. By their freedom the simple black lines characterizing this engraving belittle the fabulous skill required to produce them on the wood block.

As a patron, Maximilian exercised a major influence on the development of armour and firearms. As the mechanical accuracy of weapons increased so did the intricacy of ornament upon them. The principal techniques used in decoration were first etching and then engraving, which took over from etching because it was a more precise technique. Because it had been worked out by the skill of the armourers, etching was able to be adopted by artists as a developed technique.

While Dürer was in Augsburg he became acquainted with the technique of etching. The earliest datable work, etched on iron, is a genre piece by Urs Graf dated 1513. Dürer most probably became acquainted with the new technique through his collaboration with such armourers as Koloman Colman of Augsburg whom he supplied with designs for Maximilian's silvered armour.

Dürer's first etching is undated and known as *The Desperate Man*. It is based upon a portrait drawing of 1514. Amongst others there are two etchings dated 1515 entitled *A Man of Sorrows Seated* and *Agony in the Garden*. Within a very few years the artists of the Rhine were using the etching process liberally.

Many of Maximilian's projects failed through lack of money and Dürer did not always receive full payment for his work. Eventually the Emperor awarded Dürer a pension of a hundred florins a year though the payment of the pension proved to be irregular. With the death of Maximilian in 1519, Dürer lost a patron who, even if not always solvent, was of generous intent. His death marked the end of an era and came at a time when Dürer was preoccupied with the teachings of Martin Luther and with the cause of Protestantism, in which he never faltered.

Through the sixteenth century a constant supply of ornamental designs was issued to armourers and firearm makers by the engravers of Nuremberg and Augsburg from such exponents as Peter Flotner, Virgil Solis, one of the best book illustrators of the time, and later Jost Amman and Paul Flindt. In both the sixteenth and seventeenth centuries the European princes and noblemen maintained one or more gunmaker amongst the artists and craftsmen attached to their courts. The most spectacular of these court artists were the two brothers Emanuel and Daniel Sadeler who came from Antwerp to work at the court of Maximilian I in Munich and later at the court of Emperor Rudolf II in Prague. In 1610 Daniel returned to Munich where he continued to decorate arms until his death in 1632.

The gunmaking centres each had their own clearly defined styles and these local styles persisted for long periods. Normally the gun stock would be decorated with carving or bone inlay and the lock and mounts with engraving. When a richly-ornamented gun was required the services of a professional engraver were obtained. It was the practice in the gunmaker's workshop for the engraver to take a proof of the designs he had executed on the metal parts and these were retained as a record of the design, which in most cases was exclusive to the individual weapon.

Nuremberg and Augsburg were also the largest manufacturing centres of sporting weapons. The majority of engraved decoration of sixteenth- and seventeenth-century guns and armour in German culture can be traced back to the work of one or other of a small group of south German engravers. Towards the end of

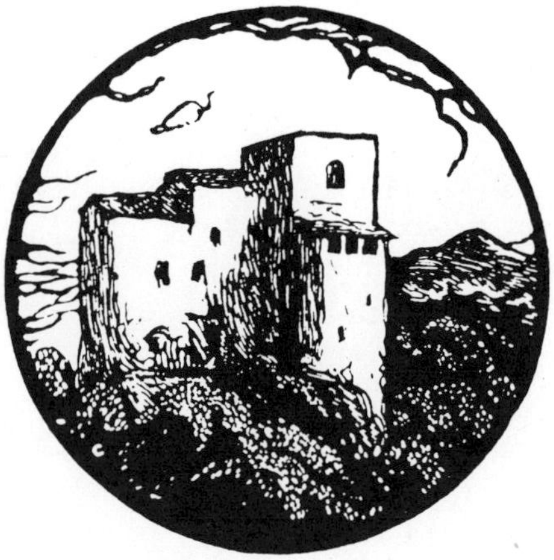

[80] Edward Gordon Craig: *A City*, 1907. Diameter 6.6cm

the sixteenth century, designs by the French artist Etienne Delaune (1518 to 1583) were common and used in particular by the Munich school. This master engraver spent some years in Germany and many of his designs were published there.

With the rising demand for decorated engraved firearms, the engravers found it worth while to issue books of ornaments designed to be used and copied directly by the gunmakers without the need for adaptation. One of the earliest of these 'book' series of engravings is of wheel-locks of the French type which are attributed to a follower of the French engraver Androciet Ducerceau. They date from the end of the sixteenth century. These were followed by a whole series of designs for firearm engravings produced by Parisian artists who dominated the market for designs for gun engraving.

For most European princes it was a point of honour to excel at the hunt. Maximilian endeavoured to perpetuate his own exploits by having published illustrated accounts of them in such books as *Theuerdank* and *Der Weisskunig*. The latter is an allegorical autobiography of the Emperor written by his secretaries, in which he appears as the 'White King'. Hans Burgkmair produced 117 of the 251 engravings for this work. The 1517 first edition of the *Theuerdank* was produced by Maximilian's Court Painter Johann Schönsperger the Elder (1481 to 1523) in Nuremberg and in it a black line *formschneider* print illustrates Maximilian I killing a boar with his new type of boar sword. Maximilian's *Theuerdank* or *The Knight of Adventurous Thoughts* is a thin disguise for the Emperor himself. It is a long poem of Maximilian's youth and his courtship of Mary of Burgundy who died five years after their marriage. Most of the 118 engravings were by Hans Leonhard Schäuffelein (1480 to 1540) but fourteen were by Burgkmair. The *formschneider* engravings were produced by Jost von Negker.

We are inclined to overlook the fact that engravers had to be aware of new techniques and equipment used in the scenes they illustrated. Dürer makes it evident that he was up to date in new developments because he shows the new boar swords in his engravings of *The Promenade* and *The Ensign Bearer* of 1500 and in his print of *The Martyrdom of St Catherine*. In this engraving he shows a boar

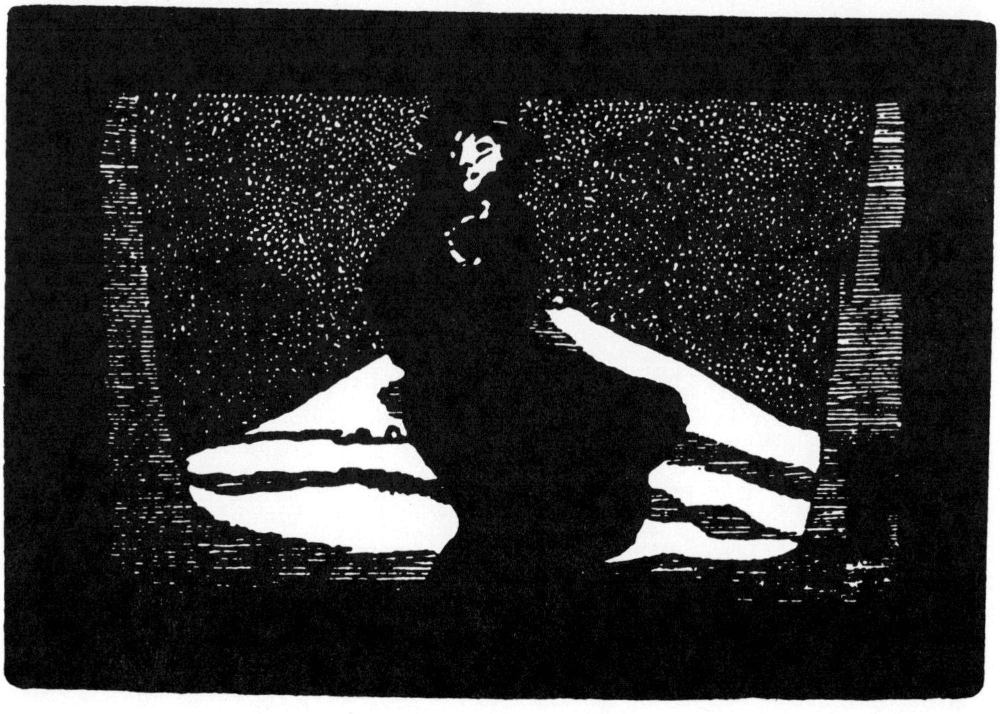

[81] Edward Gordon Craig: *January*, 1905, 10.5 x 7.0cm

sword of much plainer construction with two staghorn plates riveted on either side of the tang as a grip. This most recent form of grip, with the rivet heads and washers made prominent by decoration, was to become a characteristic feature of hunting swords and knives of the period. In Dürer's engraving *St Eustace and the Mystical Stag* the saint is carrying a very up-to-date 'hand and a half' sword. Its long blade was to be used for cutting or thrusting against a large animal from horseback. The average length of the sword was one and a half metres. Dürer also illustrates the new form of the composite bow in the prints of *The Martyrdom of St Sebastian*, *Death, Famine, War and Plague* [27] and *St Michael Fighting the Dragon.*

In Maximilian's *Triumphal Procession* Hans Burgkmair illustrated one group which consisted of five boar hunters on horseback each carrying what were described as their new boar swords and hunting spears. He illustrates the chamois and ibex hunters in this work as having an extra sheath to hold the blades of their spears.

Designs for gun and sword were also produced by Heinrich Aldegraver, Urs Graf and Hans Sebald Behan. Urs Graf (1485 to 1527) draws typical knife-daggers in detail in his print *The Dancing Peasant Couple* of 1525. Typical knife-daggers of the late fifteenth and early sixteenth century can be seen in the engravings by Dürer of *The Cook and his Wife* and *The Three Peasants.* Of a similar character are the knives carried by hunters in the tapestry known as *Les Chasses de Maximilian* which was woven in 1525 and now hangs in the Louvre.

Starting from the second half of the fifteenth century the armourers and firearm designers in Italy developed an engraving technique called *niello*, similar to Pollaiuolo's *niello* engraving for *Paci. Niello* engraving turns up a little later in the sixteenth century in Persian armour. This technique in Persian armour and firearms is sometimes described as *tula* or *toula. Niello* plates were plates with engraved designs filled in with a black composition of metallic alloys, silver, copper and a small proportion of lead. The plate or metal part was then heated in the fire and rubbed over with borax; it was replaced in the fire for a short time then left to cool and afterwards burnished. This engraving technique was not taken up by the European artists in general but it gave rise to the art form known in Russia as 'black art' which appeared early in the seventeenth century.

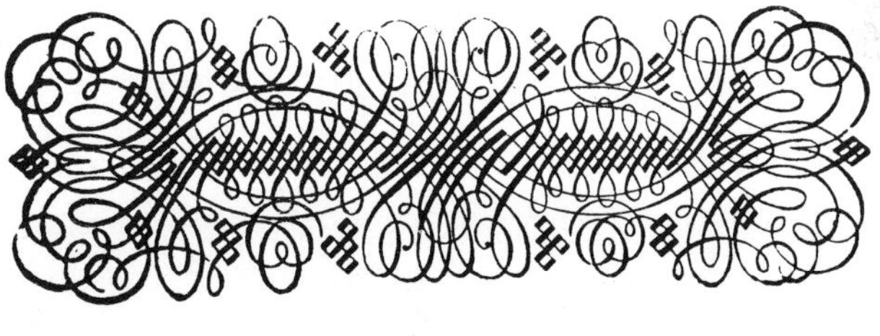

[82] Kate Greenaway: *Endpiece.* 8.0 x 2.6cm

During the sixteenth century the Danube school ceased to be the focus of engraving in all its richness and greatness. Yet there was still a young German artist who was to gain a leading position in engraving and become Court Painter to Henry VIII later in the century. This was Holbein the Younger, the great humanist, draughtsman and painter.

Hans Holbein the Elder had three sons, Ambrosius, Hans the Younger and Bruno; all became painters. Hans the Younger was born in or near Augsburg in 1467 or 1468 and his initial training took place in his native Germany. About 1514

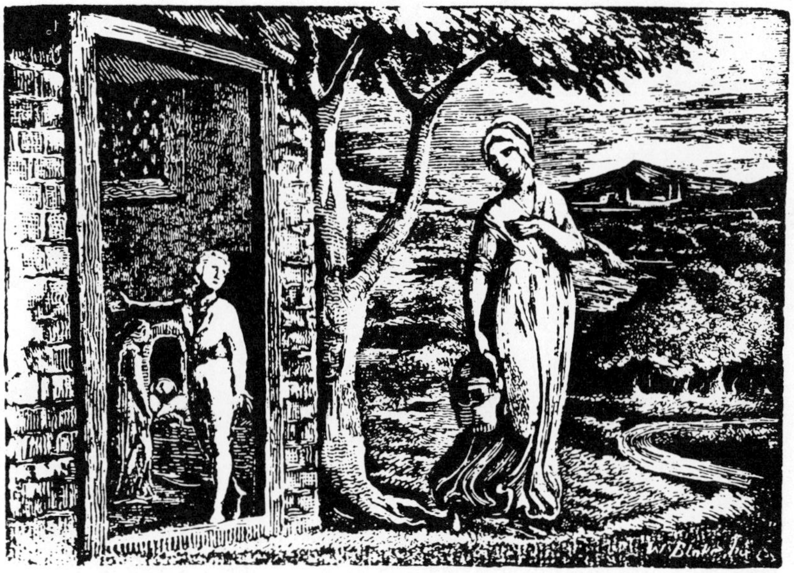

[83] William Blake: Illustration from *Little Tom the Sailor*, 1821. 10.4 x 7.4cm

he moved to Basle with his elder brother Ambrosius and there joined the establishment of the scholar-printer Johnn Froben, for whom he designed a border for the 1518 edition of More's *Utopia*.

Between 1527 and 1530 he began drawings for the *Dance of Death* [41 to 48] and his work was copied by armoury engravers upon sheaths of some Swiss and South German daggers. He did several pen and ink drawings of the hilts and sheaths of rapiers, daggers and a hunting sword.

Holbein's drawings for the *Dance of Death* developed into a series which was completed in 1538 and it is believed that the *formschneider* Hans Lützelburger did the engraving. Despite the fact that the *Dance of Death* is a very well-known series of illustrations, very little is known of Lützelburger who so sensitively followed Holbein's drawings.

In 1522 a large *formschneider* print representing the fight of peasants and a naked man in a wood, after the device of an unknown master, and with the monogram NH, bears the inscription 'Hans LevczelbVrger Fvrmschnider 1.5.22.' This is yet further evidence that these engravers were known as *formschneiders*. In Holbein's *Dance of Death* there is one print *The Duchess* [46] showing Lützelburger's monogram HL which is believed to have been engraved between 1527 and 1530.

Holbein's drawing is completely free from the medieval German tradition and the prints are very light for a German production, there being no large black or white areas: the images are light grey. Holbein's last work in the series *The Last Judgement* [48] is a masterly composition, possibly one of the largest in scale of conception yet contained within the smallest dimensions.

Numerous artists were to follow with other *Dance of Death* series, but none is comparable in quality to Holbein's grim inspiration. The series consists of forty-one engravings each 5cm wide and 6.5cm in height but a compositional flow and structure make the engravings appear larger than the actual dimensions. Their drawing is extremely sensitive, clear and strong despite the very small space, indicating that Holbein must have possessed an unusual understanding and sympathy for the work of the *formschneider*. In his overall production he drew nearly 1200 designs for wood and metal prints. His *Dance of Death* was conceived at the outset to avoid the need for words. Here is a case of a master craftsman in drawing avoiding the use of explanatory text and it is ironic that more than three

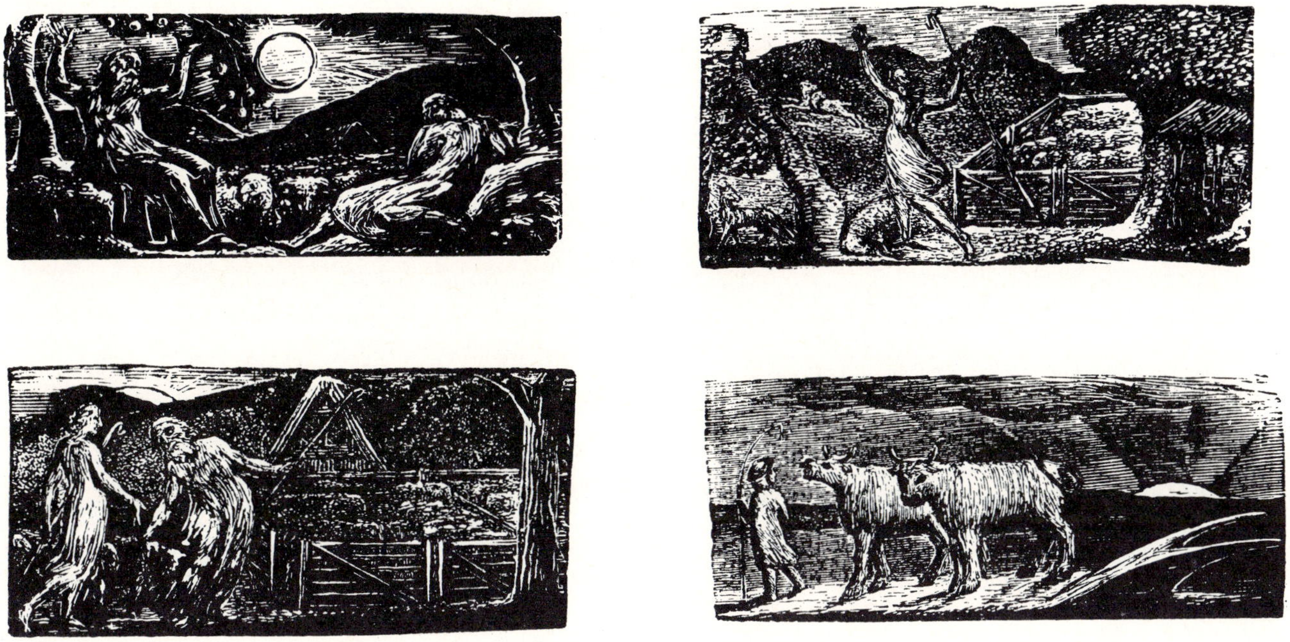

[84 – 87] William Blake: Illustrations from *Virgil's Eclogues*, 1821. 7.5 x 3.4cm

hundred years later a master craftsman in writing, Charles Dickens, offered his publisher one hundred pounds not to supply illustration to his books.

The *Dance of Death* was first published as a small book in 1538 in the Lyons edition by the Brothers Trechfel. In this edition there are forty-one leaves with passages from the Bible in Latin and with French verses by Giles Corrozet.

Holbein developed a style of portrait painting which combined the classical mode of the Renaissance with his own brilliant linear technique. By 1523 he had executed a series of portraits of Erasmus (1466 to 1536) and in 1526 received an urgent communication from Erasmus who had gone from Basle to England and wished to effect a meeting between Sir Thomas More and the artist. At that time, Holbein was worried about the religious troubles on the Continent and was glad to accept the invitation to meet More, with whom he stayed until early in 1528.

Thomas More introduced Holbein to Henry VIII. Henry appointed Holbein Court Painter with apartments in the royal palace, an ample salary and additional payment for his pictures, thus giving him a secure position in English art. After a short visit to Germany in 1528, Holbein settled in London in 1532.

Most historians write only of Holbein as a great portrait painter, rarely mentioning his superb humanist engravings. He is a much more rounded personality than the history books usually present. Perhaps his secure post as Court Painter prevented him from achieving his full stature in the other forms of expression for which he had more than ample talent. The engraving *Two Art Critics* [400] is never seen in the art history of Holbein, yet it is a lovable crack at life and evidence of the fact that Holbein was not completely concerned with official portraits, but was also very human. He spent most of his time in the circle around Thomas More and died in the London Plague of 1543 to 1544.

Henry VIII was responsible for starting the custom of engraving armour in England and his patronage of this art was continued by Elizabeth I. A number of engraved suits of armour can be seen in the collection at the Tower of London. The armourers' workshops at Greenwich, where much of the work was carried out, were closed in 1637.

[88] Samuel Palmer: *Harvest under a Crescent Moon*, 1826. 7.75 x 2.6cm

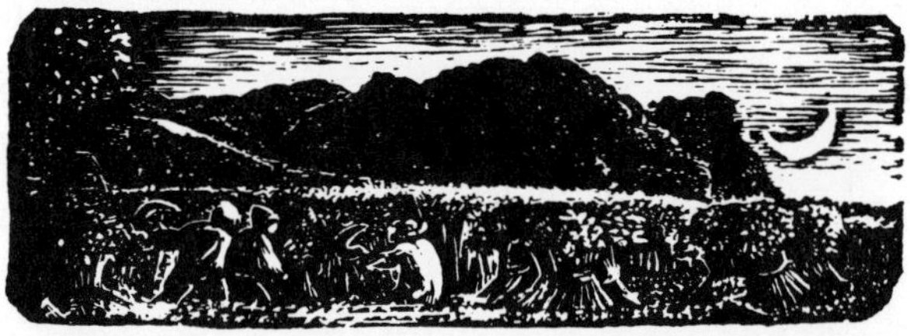

The seventeenth and eighteenth centuries concentrated on the production of large quantities of books to serve the growing educational and governmental needs and because of this demand, engraving became very commercially orientated. Wood engraving of the quality of the Danube school disappeared from the better quality book. This excellence of illustration was not to be seen again until it was revived in the late nineteenth and the twentieth centuries.

The first book to be illustrated with metal engravings was produced in 1477 by the German printer Nicolaus Laurentii in Florence, but the process did not gain momentum before the middle of the sixteenth century when the intaglio processes of copper engraving and copper etching began to take the place of wood engraving. At that time, intaglio printing was a much slower process than relief printing, but because labour was cheap and time was not pressing, this difference was of little account.

However, wood engraving continued to be used for cheap books. The art deteriorated to the level of very crude work and probably started what is now termed 'commercial art', which followed a policy that anything was good enough for a reading public unable to afford a high purchase price.

REFERENCES

1 Scholderer, V. *Fifty Essays*, Hertzberger, Amsterdam, 1966
2 Steinberg, S. H. *Five Hundred Years of Printing*, Penguin Books, London, 1966
3 Hind, A. M. *An Introduction to a History of the Woodcut, Vol I*, Dover, New York, 1963
4 Hind *An Introduction to a History of the Woodcut*

4 THE BLACK-LINE TRANSITIONAL ENGRAVERS

The use of end-grained timber for wood engraving was certainly an important and significant development but unfortunately it is not possible to state with any precision the name of the first engraver to use end-grained boxwood. This is not an uncommon situation because artists, like printers, were often so busy expressing other people's creative ideas that they omitted to record their own. The development of the use of end-grained wood is usually attributed to Jean-Michel Papillon although some historians record the discovery as being by Foy of Lyons. Papillon (1698 to 1775) was a French wood engraver, an engraving historian and a collector of ancient engravings. He is known to have had some five thousand wood engravings and wood-cuts. His work consists of head and tail pieces for books, a large number of pictorial alphabets, book plates, frontispieces and vignettes. The French consider him as a modest practitioner of engraving. He was skilful but not strongly creative. His smallest block was less than a square centimetre and he engraved four landscapes with figures on blocks less than the size of a normal postage stamp.

In the seventeenth century the skill of engraving on wood had deteriorated and because of this publishers favoured copper engraving as a means of providing illustrations for the better quality product.

The earliest record in France of Papillon's writing is 1760, when he attempted to popularize the new method but was unsuccessful. There seems to be agreement that in the middle of the eighteenth century Papillon, then in Paris, engraved for the first time with the burin on the end-grained hard wood block. From the collection of his engravings executed from 1745 to 1767 which are in the British Museum, it appears that most of his work was engraved on the end-grained block and the texture is exceptionally sharp and clean. Among the items in the British Museum collection there is certainly no evidence of his having designed for long-grained timber. In fact, Papillon was obviously so pleased with what could be done with end-grained boxwood that he became preoccupied with a particular spiral cloud which just could not have been obtained on the long-grained timber. His smallest engraving could no more have been done on long-grained wood than could Bewick's *House Fly* [2]. Papillon used both the black and white lines in his wood engravings.

It was unfortunate that Papillon lived before his time and it was many years before wood engraving was revived, although Hogarth made an attempt to use it in 1750. Hogarth (1697 to 1764) was interested in wood engraving solely as a reproductive medium and he employed wood instead of copper for the last two plates of his series *Progress of Cruelty*. The attempt was meritorious but was not successful financially.

The standard of wood engraving in the eighteenth century was so low that Walpole, writing about 1770 of Papillon's recently published book *Traité Historique et Pratique de la Gravure au Bois* expressed doubt whether the author would ever,

[89] Edward Calvert: *The Ploughman*, 1827. 12.9 x 8.4cm

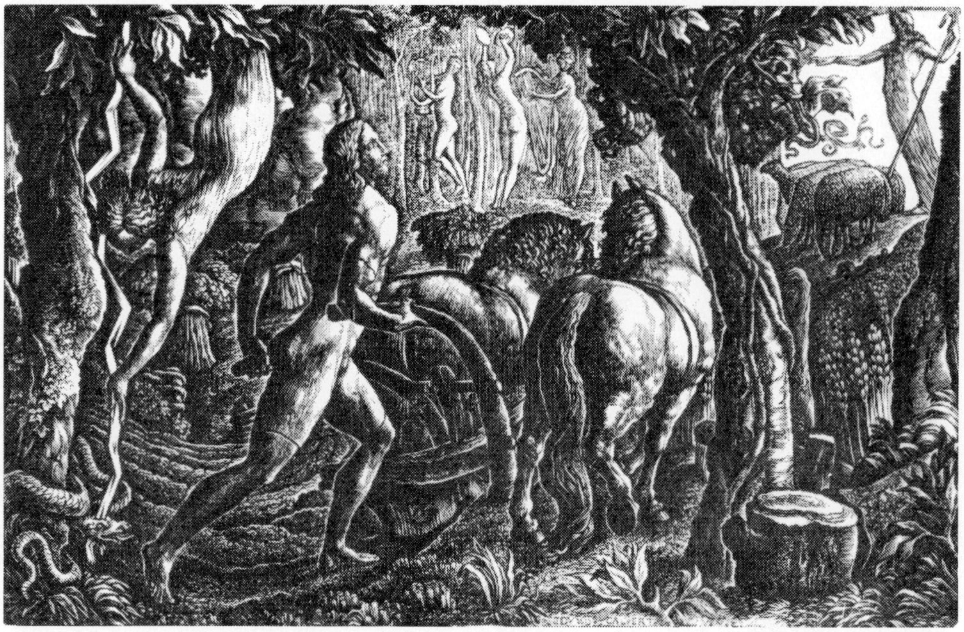

as he wished 'persuade the world to return to wooden cuts'. As end-grained timber as used by Papillon is of little use for the woodcut, perhaps Walpole was responsible for starting the confusion of terms in the use of 'woodcut' when 'wood engraving' is being described.

In the nineteenth century there were sufficient wood engravers working in Britain to make it possible to refer to the developing British school of wood engraving as belonging to this period. The development sprang from a double 'tap root' with each branch having an approximately equal and parallel time span. These two roots are termed 'black-line' and 'white-line' and each merits separate consideration.

In dealing with the black-line transitional engravers, Whistler is taken as the starting point although he was not an engraver. The white-line development described in Chapter 5 drew its inspiration from William Blake and its technical development from Thomas Bewick. The exponents of both techniques worked concurrently but in neither technique did the engravers venture into the other form.

The black-line root, stemming from Whistlerian concepts, proved to be weaker aesthetically than the white-line root, and eventually its epitaph was read by Thomas Sturge Moore when he was invited by the Society of Wood Engravers to address its members and the public at its exhibition held in Manchester in 1927. From 1920 onwards the white-line technique dominated and eventually the black-line ceased to be common practice. Previous to 1920 the two roots had been vaguely defined but never clearly separated.

During the late 1800s it became apparent that there were signs of an impending change in art and this change eventually expanded into a revolution. Despite the fact that people tend to assume that a revolution cannot last, or adopt a neutral attitude towards its causes, the change in art continues and is in progress today.

In 1859 an American artist, James Abbott McNeil Whistler (1834 to 1903) moved into London's art world. He was unusually voluble, sardonically witty and astringently provocative. His student days had been spent in Paris and he had experienced considerable development before coming to London. Whistler's first residence in London was in rooms in Wapping and he first exhibited at the Royal Academy in 1859 when he showed two etchings. However, his time was divided between France and England and it was not until about 1860 that he settled in London permanently.

[90] Edward Calvert: *The Cyder Feast*, 1828. 12.9 x 7.7cm

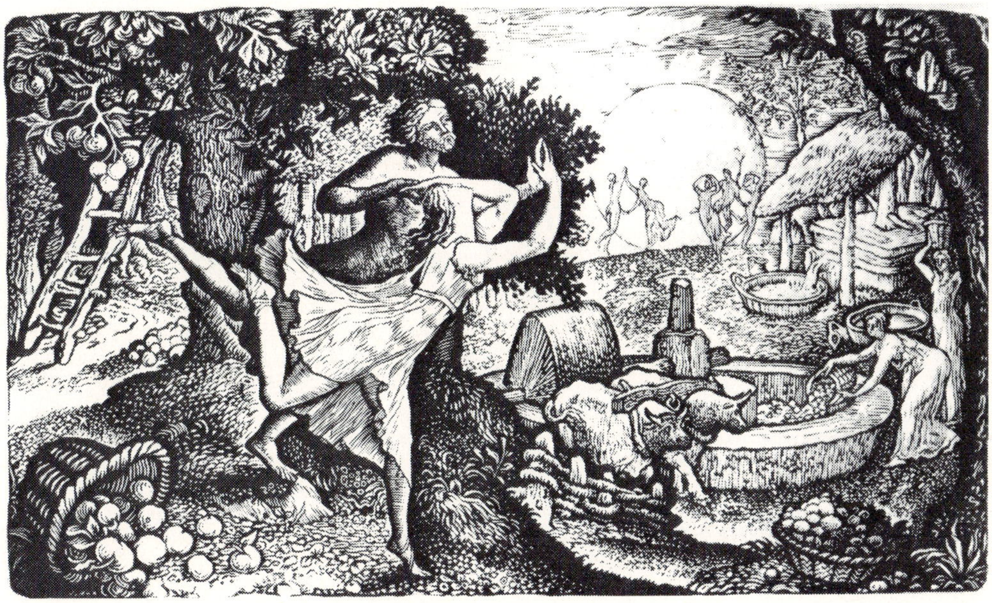

By the middle of the nineteenth century Whistler was strongly affected by the Japanese prints of the Ukeyoye school, which are the classic examples of the art of the Japanese woodcut. These woodcuts were being produced while Hogarth, Reynolds, Gainsborough, Chardin, Fragonard and Goya were still painting.

Whistler produced new aesthetic experiences both in painting and in the sphere of etching, and these were to give him authority in attacking established traditions in art. Today his work is still highly valued and respected on both sides of the English Channel. The aesthetic doctrine, formed during his period in Paris, is known as 'Art for art's sake'. In France the aesthetic movement of the nineteenth century was set in motion by Baudelaire and Gautier. The latter crystallized Whistler's philosophy with his term *l'art pour l'art*, defining it as referring to 'a man for whom the visible world exists'. The concept dealt with a world of form and a language of aesthetics.

At this period art in England was dominated by literary and moral values; the word 'aesthetic' was hated and the subject was looked upon as a German branch of philosophical enquiry, to be regarded with contempt and suspicion. Today, of course, aesthetics are recognised as part of philosophy.

Whistler expounded his aesthetic creed at his Ten O'Clock Lecture which he delivered first in Prince's Hall, London in 1885 and repeated at the Universities of Oxford and Cambridge and also at the Grosvenor Gallery in Dieppe. He stated that art has no didactic purpose or popular purpose and that only an *élite* can appreciate art.[1] He said: 'The artist is born to pick and choose and group with science, the elements, that the result may be beautiful – as a musician gathers his notes and forms his chords until he brings forth from chaos glorious harmony.' This was contrary to the scientific ideas of the developing French Impressionism of his time. In his statements Whistler was reiterating Baudelaire's comments of about forty years earlier. His attitude is typical of the confusion about the nature and purpose of art that existed during the nineteenth century. Despite his aesthetic theory of 'art for art's sake' he was influenced by three masters of Realism, Courbet, Rembrandt and Velasquez, although his own aesthetic concept of art was far removed from any form of realistic thinking. His aesthetic concepts were finally shattered by Cézanne.

His introduction to the art of the Japanese print had a strong influence on his

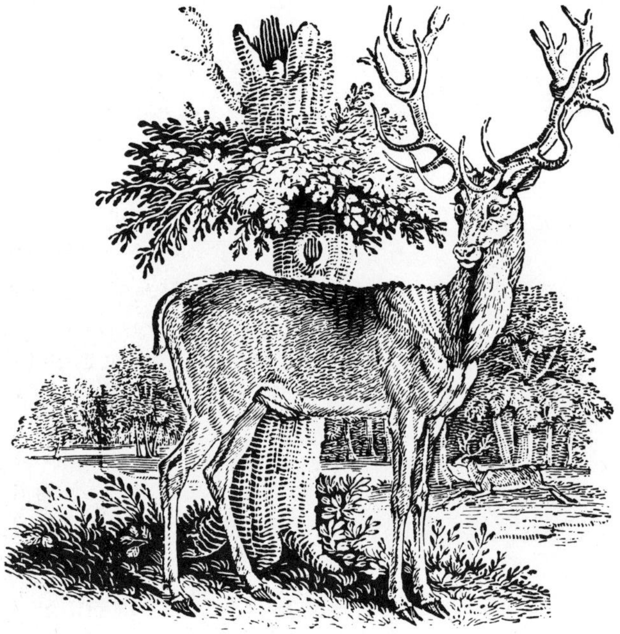

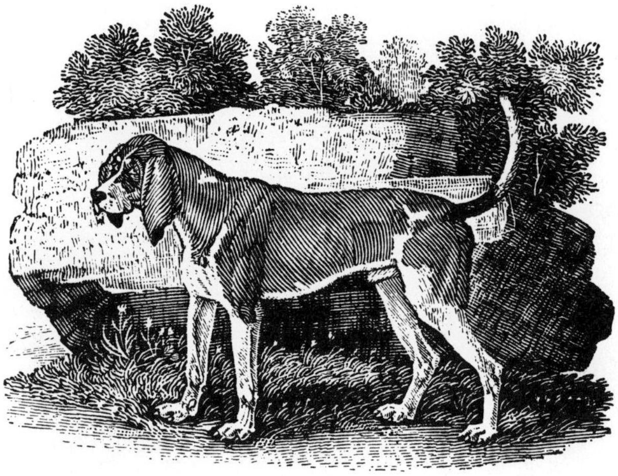

[91] Thomas Bewick: *The Stag* from *Quadrupeds*, 1790. 8.0 x 8.25cm

[92] Thomas Bewick: *The Old English Hound* from *Quadrupeds*, 1790. 8.0 x 6.0cm

subject matter and shape, but the two-dimensional world of shape added to the dimensional confusion of space measurement. It is somewhat paradoxical that Whistler accepted the Japanese print, which was wholly orientated as a popular art form, yet declared in his doctrine that there was no such thing as popular art or art for the people.

In 1877 Whistler exhibited eight pictures at the Grosvenor Gallery and included his *The Golden Girl*, *Harmony in Yellow and Gold*, *The Falling Rocket* and *Nocturne in Black and Gold*. Ruskin (1819 to 1900) took a strong dislike to these works and said so in no uncertain terms. Ruskin caused Whistler to sue him for libel. The lawsuit was heard in 1878 and the farthing damages awarded to Whistler were face saving. Had he been less touchy he might well have shrugged his shoulders and dismissed the old man's outburst.

Whistler's influence on art and artists was particularly marked in etching. At that time reputations were made on the techniques of wiping and biting the plate, rather than on art and content. Craftsmen masqueraded as artists, believing that a flamboyant title was more important than the art content.

It can be claimed that Whistler was the first English artist to base his works on the development of purely formal values, which sharply contrasted the literary values so dominant in Victorian art and the Pre-Raphaelite Brotherhood. He strongly desired to secure the divorce of art from the world in general and its separation from everything except aesthetic emotion, but his policy proved to be an ivory tower. After the nineteenth century art became very closely bound up with life and directly engaged in solving the problems of the twentieth-century form.

In 1898 the International Society of Sculptors, Painters and Engravers, with Whistler as president, was founded to promote the Impressionist theories of art which, at that time and for a long time afterwards, were an absolute anathema to the Royal Academy which has never welcomed any rebellion against its accepted standards. The International Society held its exhibitions at the Royal Institute Galleries in Piccadilly. These galleries were built by the Institute in 1880 and were completely lost to art when they were closed in 1967. During the first three years of its life, the Society showed works by Degas, Manet, Monet and Camille Pissarro.

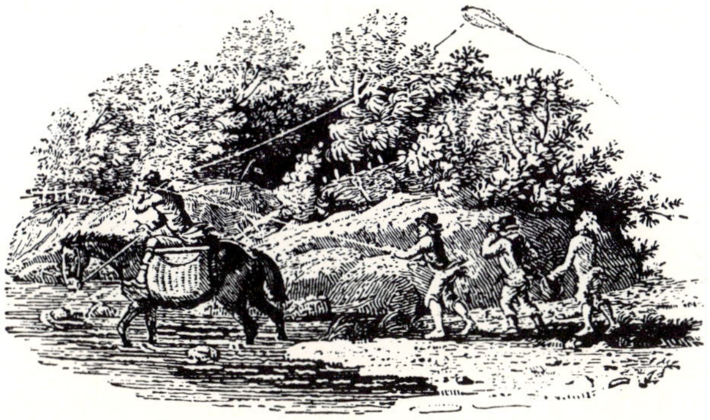

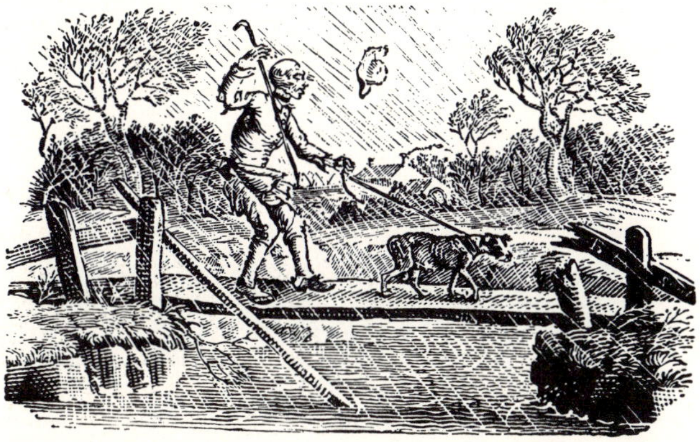

[93] Thomas Bewick: *Kite Flying* from *Quadrupeds*, 1790. 8.0 x 4.5cm

[94] Thomas Bewick: *The Blind Man Crossing the Bridge* from *Quadrupeds*, 1790. 8.3 x 5.0cm

In a letter to his son Lucien in 1883, Pissarro wrote, 'I wouldn't want to be an aesthete, at least like those across the Channel. "Aestheticism" is a kind of romanticism more or less combined with trickery, it means breaking for oneself a crooked road. They would have liked to make something like that out of Impressionism, which really should be nothing more than a theory of observation, without entailing the loss of fantasy, freedom, grandeur, all that makes for great art. But not eccentricity to make sensitive people swoon.'

Realism has never been the strongest and most prevailing force in the history of art; classicism has held this major role but realism has always been the sharp corrective force against stalemate, formula, form disintegration and boredom. These objective, realistic and science-based concepts were quite contrary to Whistler's 'art for art's sake'. The leading Impressionist artists of France held him in high regard and Camille Pissarro said in 1887 'Whistler is very artistic, he is a showman but nevertheless an artist.'[2] Had this respect not been in evidence in Paris, Whistler would not have been able to do the vitally important work of introducing the French Impressionists to London for younger generations, because the Impressionists were very fussy as to how their works were handled and where they were exhibited. Whistler usually receives very little credit for this achievement, which also, incidentally, indicated the liberal side of his character in supporting a style of art so different from his own.

[95] Thomas Bewick: *The Farmyard* from *History of British Birds* Vol I, 1797. 8.25 x 7.5cm

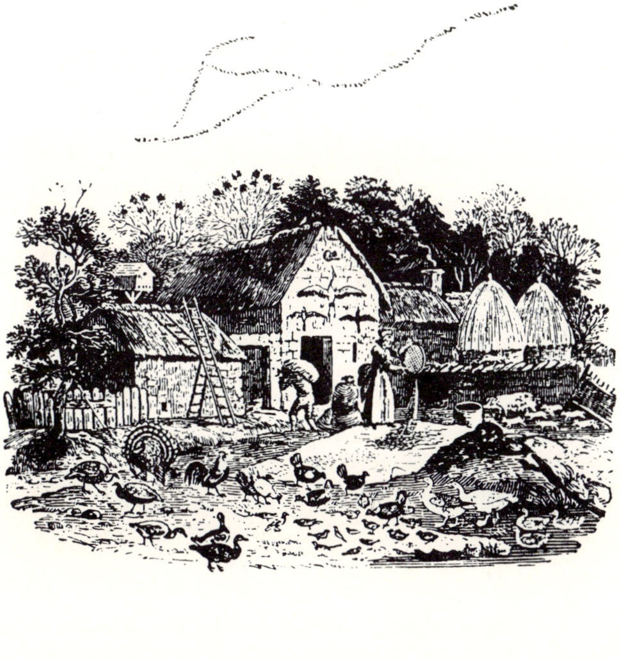

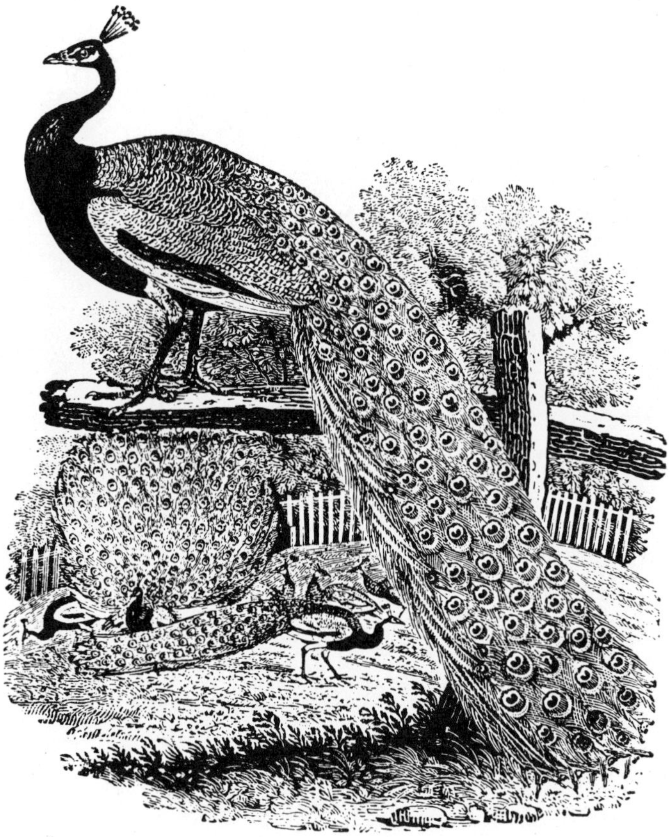

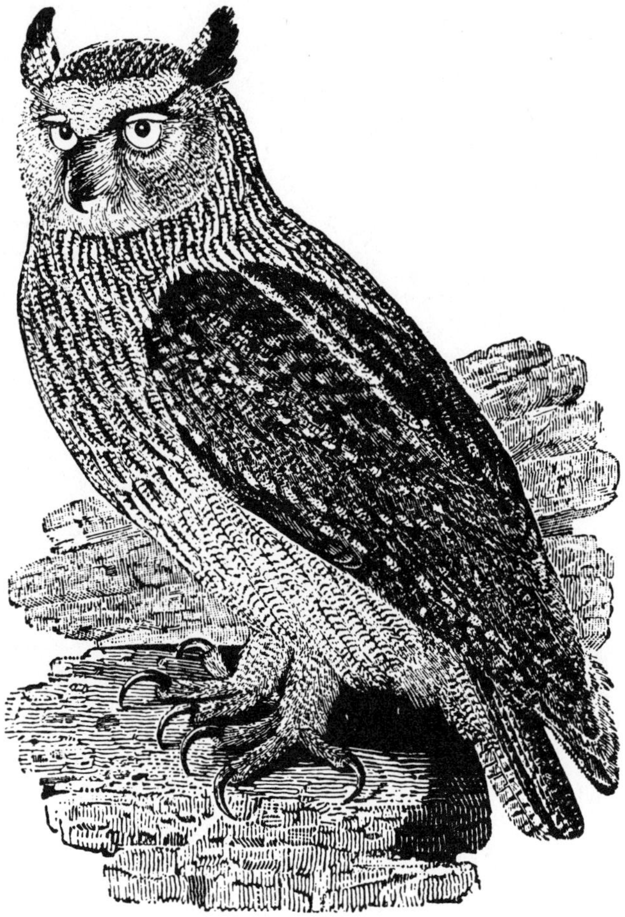

[96] Thomas Bewick: *The Peacock* from *History of British Birds* Vol I, 1797. 8.75 x 10.5cm

[97] Thomas Bewick: *The Eagle Owl* from *History of British Birds* Vol I, 1797. 8.0 x 12.0cm

[98] Thomas Bewick: *Feather* from *History of British Birds* Vol I, 1797.

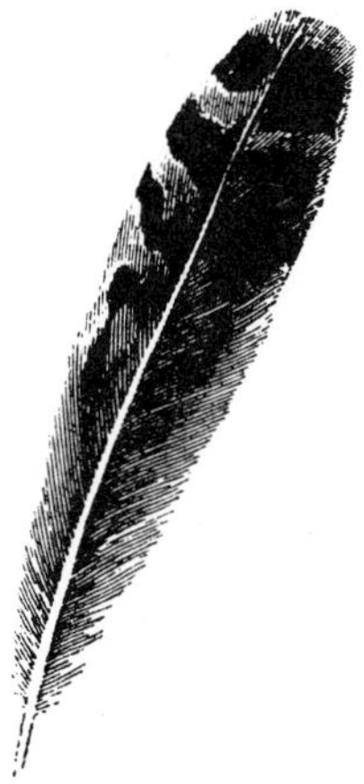

He became the lens between the forward-thinking artists in London and those in Paris. In Paris his friends were Fantin-Latour, Courbet, Manet, Legros, Braquemond and Baudelaire, the poet and critic. It was a situation for which he was peculiarly well fitted because he practised most of the branches of art excepting sculpture and engraving. In 1886 he was elected President of the Royal Society of British Artists whose galleries were in Suffolk Street, London. At the exhibitions of the Society pictures were hung up to the ceiling and opera glasses provided for the public. Hanging of this nature gave rise to the term 'skied' and artists today still use this word as part of their terminology. A similar state of affairs existed at the Royal Academy, where exhibition space was at a premium.

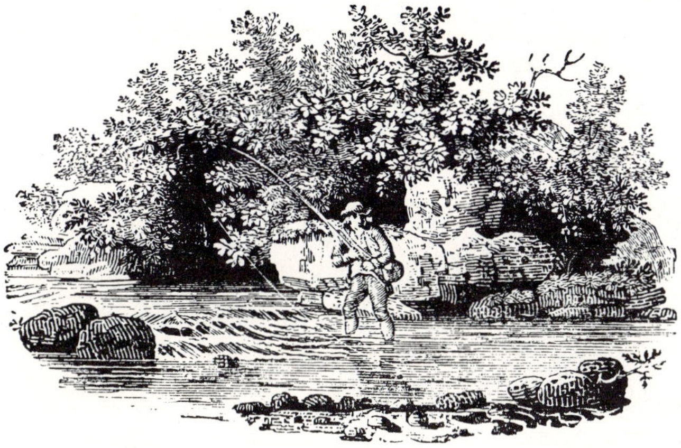

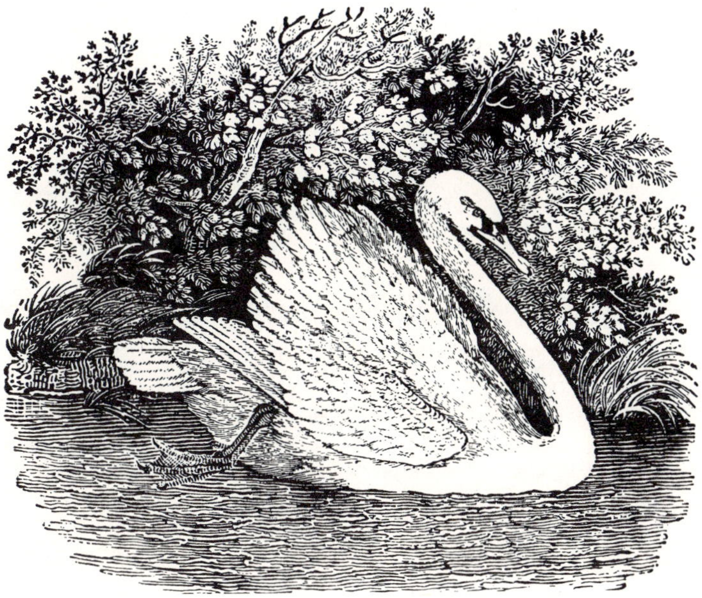

[99] Thomas Bewick: *The Angler* from *History of British Birds* Vol II, 1804. 8.5 x 5.5cm

[100] Thomas Bewick: *The Mute Swan* from *History of British Birds* Vol II, 1804. 9.3 x 8.1cm

The Suffolk Street galleries were designed for the Royal Society of British Artists by John Nash in 1823, at the time when he was redesigning London from St James's Park to Regent's Park, which was probably the first and last successful exercise in town planning for London.

Whistler was largely responsible for obtaining the Royal Charter for the Society, which was granted in 1887. He held the office of President for two years then resigned in a fit of temper because he could not get his own way over decorations and repairs. The innovations which he brought to the Society, including the paintings by Claude Monet and other advanced artists, proved too much for it. He changed the existing customs of hanging pictures separated by an inch of space and extending to the ceiling, to the present-day system of three lines, one at eye level, one above and one below. Today this arrangement is in the process of being broken down, except at the Royal Academy, and individual spacing is gaining in favour. Whistler draped the large gallery walls and put in a false ceiling but the cost brought the Society into financial difficulties. The whole situation became so tense that he felt obliged to resign.

With the onset of the Franco-Prussian War in 1870, Camille Pissarro fled from Louveciennes in France to England where he joined Claude Monet at Lower Norwood. While in London both these artists started their study of Turner's works. The Pissarro family exemplified the French artists' traditional pride in being *peintres-graveurs*. They were expected to be equally proficient in painting and engraving. Four of Camille's children became painters, in fact Lucien began to draw at a very early age: a remarkable family! At that time there was a very wide gulf between the art of London and that of Paris. Camille was only interested in the work of Turner and Whistler.

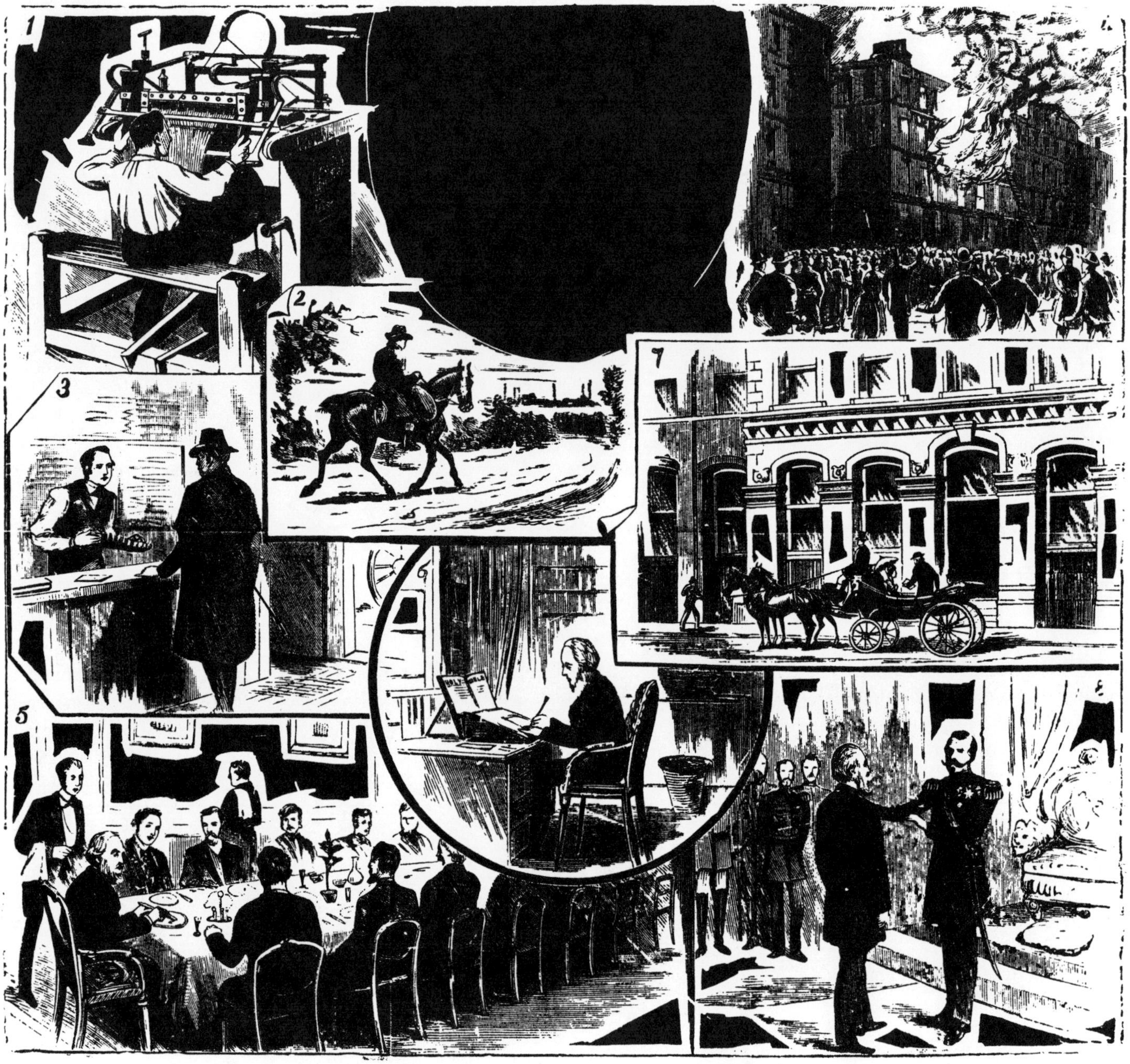
1
2
3
5
6
7

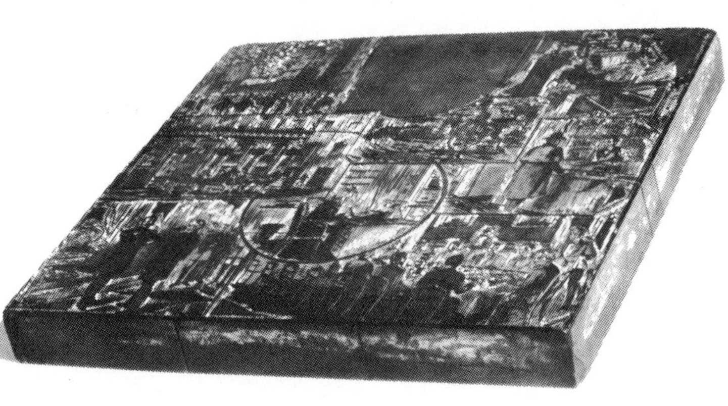

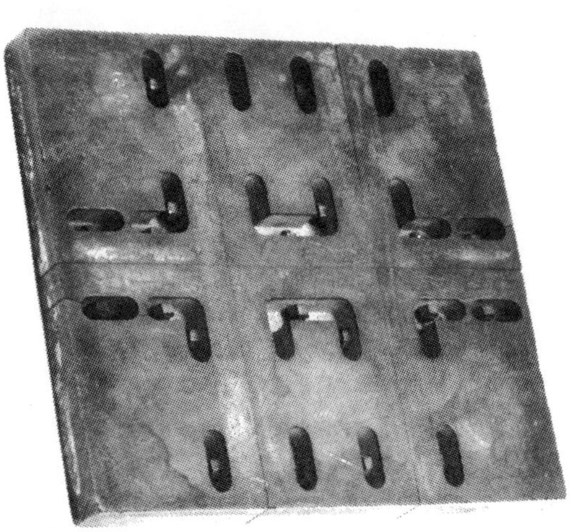

When they returned to France in 1871 the family lived at Pontoise where Camille joined Cézanne. Like most of the Impressionists, Camille was very politically orientated as an anarchist but he never took an active or violent part in public life and at the height of the Commune in Paris he was in exile in London. In 1894 when strong measures were taken against the anarchist riots, the family fled to Belgium. During the early nineties Camille was involved in the political movements of the extreme left.

The tradition of print making practised by Camille was carried on by Lucien and later by Lucien's daughter Orovida Pissarro (1893 to 1968). Camille became a British subject in 1916.

In 1883 Lucien Pissarro, then twenty years of age, came to London on the initiative of his father to learn English. He stayed with relations in Holloway and worked for a period with Weber and Company, the music publishers of New Bond Street. He settled in England permanently in 1893. Lucien Pissarro (1863 to 1944) became interested in wood engravings from contact with the French wood engraver Auguste Lepère in Paris and while in Paris contributed wood engravings to the publication *L'Image littéraire et artistique* which was published by Floury, Paris 1896/7 [70].

The master engravers in Paris at that time were Lepère, Steinlen, Vierge and Gustave Dore. Lepère assured Lucien that he would be successful in France, that 'the English movement is waking up the sleepy heads and there will certainly be a serious revival'. He wrote that Lucien ought to assist this movement with his talent and experience: 'It is a question, I say this in confidence, of not allowing the vulgarizers to take the lead.'[3]

In the eighteenth and early nineteenth centuries, both wood engraving and copper engraving and etching were valued only as a means of reproducing drawings, designs and even paintings. In May 1883, Whistler's brother-in-law, the well-known surgeon Sir Francis Seymour Haden (1810 to 1910) read a paper before the Society of Arts, now the Royal Society of Arts, in which he made the first effective appeal to be heard in favour of recognising these techniques as a means for producing original work. The arguments he used were authoritative and have meaning for the present time. In dealing with the claims of etching and engraving to rank as fine arts he wanted: '. . . to compare, without regard to the process employed or the person employing it, the practice of the painter-etcher, who is an original artist, with that of the modern engraver, who is not an original artist, and by the discussion which I hope will follow such comparison, to arrive at an intelligible conclusion as to the comparative claims of the two to be considered fine art.' He continued by describing and contrasting the deadness of the reproductive engraving with creative etching. Of the reproductive engraving he said: 'Now I would respectfully submit that this strange departure from all forms of natural representation on the part of the engraver, and his adoption of a set of symbols which he learnt in his apprenticeship and which he will transmit to his successors, and which in no respect differ from the symbols employed by the heraldic engraver, can only be explained by the fact that his task is a mechanical one and that the brain impulse necessary to the exercise of the creative faculty, and therefore of the art faculty, is in abeyance.'

Haden then defined the *peinture-gravure* tradition: 'All forms of engraving, in short, whatever the process employed in their production, divide themselves necessarily and naturally into two kinds, those which are original and those which are not; those which, under the name of painting-engraving, or etching, were

[101] Illustration from *The Christian Herald*, 1885. 22.0 x 20.0cm

[102] Front view of the block used for the illustration from *The Christian Herald*.

[103] Back view of the block shown in [102] showing the bolting system.

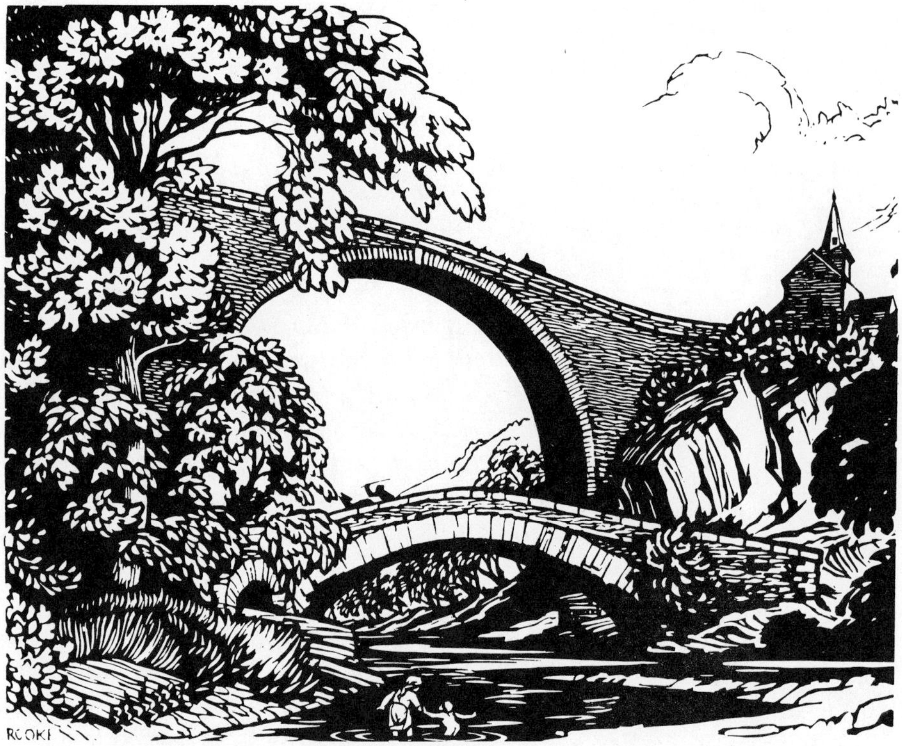

[104] Noel Rooke: *The Two Bridges*, 1914. 18.25 x 15.25cm

practised by the great masters of painting who were their own engravers, and by means of which we are able to obtain, even in this remote day, work as original as their painting and at a comparatively moderate cost; and those by which, under the common term of engraving, the design of the painter is reproduced upon the plate by other minds and other hands.'

In his paper Haden took to task the Royal Academy for its treatment of the painter-engravers and etchers. He said: 'Turning now to the class of modern original engravers, the etchers – the pariahs of the Academy – they consist of a number of persons, some of them painters and some of them artists seeking to make a profession out of original engraving who, in the belief that a return to that art in its pure forms is still possible, have formed themselves into a society for its promotion. This association, under the name of the Society of Painter-Etchers, succeeded the old Etching Club and consists, at present, of about a hundred original engravers who meet once a year to exhibit their works, observe progress and comment on the ostracism to which they are being subjected by the Royal Academy. Their idea is that a return to the original form of engraving, as it was practised by the great masters of painting, would be an advantage to art. Their wonder is that such an idea should meet with no encouragement in an academy of arts.'

The Society to which Sir Francis Haden made reference became the Royal Society of Painter-Etchers in 1889. Paris was quick to see the advantages of an organisation on similar lines and in 1890 a group of painter-engravers formed the Société des Peintres-Graveurs Français which is still functioning. It is interesting to note that while the Royal Academy has continued to exhibit some engravings and etchings, it has never been able to stage an exhibition that is in any way comparable to those of the Royal Society of Painter-Etchers and Engravers.

Haden's etching needle was employed as skilfully as his surgeon's scalpel and his etchings became as well known in Paris as they were in London.

Six years later Charles Ricketts (1866 to 1931) and Charles Hazelwood Shannon (1863 to 1937) were inspired by the principles of Haden and also the principles, though not the practice, of William Morris. Morris made a similar protest in favour of original wood engraving and woodcutting. He was born in Walthamstow in 1834 and died in 1896. He was educated at Marlborough and Exeter College, Oxford. Closely associated with the Pre-Raphaelite Brotherhood, he was a particular friend of Sir Edward Colley Burne-Jones. After Oxford he was articled as an architect to George Edmund Street but turned from architecture to painting on the advice of Rossetti. Morris practised professionally as an artist from 1857 to 1862. In 1874, nine years before Haden's lecture, he set up his own company. When it had become established he began to devote a lot of time to lectures and Socialist theories. He was one who disapproved of wayward eclecticism. His primary concern was for an art of high quality and craftsmanship that could be made available to and within reach of 'Everyone' or 'Everyman', the term Morris used to indicate people in general. His political philosophy was sound in building Everyman into his concept but in practice it can never be achieved.

William Morris was an exceptionally good designer and a good businessman. He insisted on designing the work in all the numerous fields of art and craft in which he was interested. He is the outstanding figure in the Arts and Crafts Movement and led the redevelopment of the private press with the book as its principal product, while Ricketts dominated the world of commercially produced books. Morris's earliest excursion in book design dates from 1889. In 1890 he started the Kelmscott Press at Hammersmith, for which he designed type founts, ornamental letters and borders. He issued fifty-three books from the Kelmscott Press, comprising his own works, reprints of English classics and various smaller books, originals and translations.

The Kelmscott *Chaucer* is Morris's finest contribution to the world of fine books and an astounding production, despite its *Art Nouveau* flavour and profuse decoration. It has 556 pages printed in black and red. There are eighty-seven *formschneider* prints after drawings by Burne-Jones, innumerable ornamented borders and twenty-six large initial words. The ornaments and large initial letters were all drawn and engraved by Morris, who also designed the binding. The paper

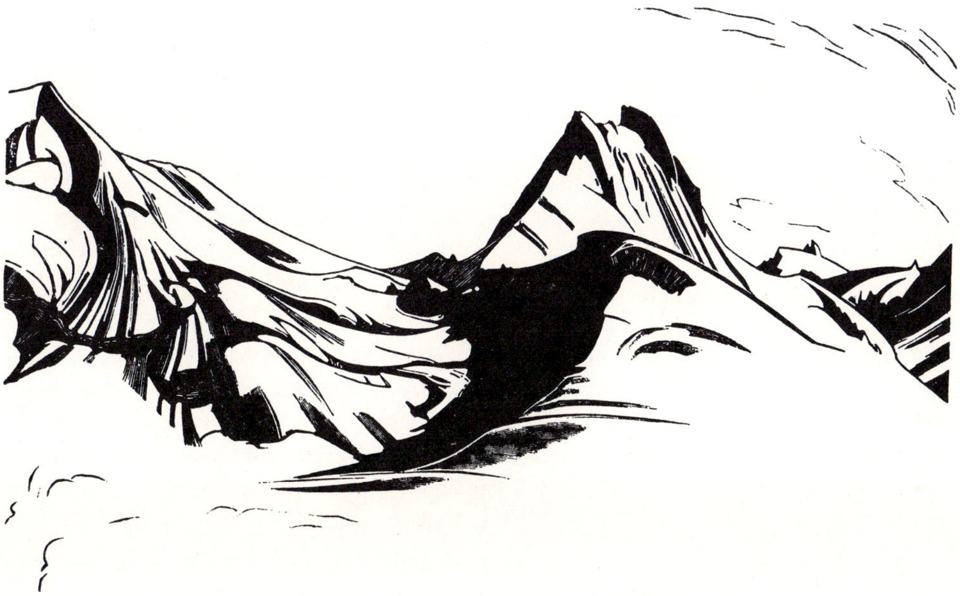

[105] Noel Rooke: *Zinal Rothhorn.* 15.25 x 9.75cm

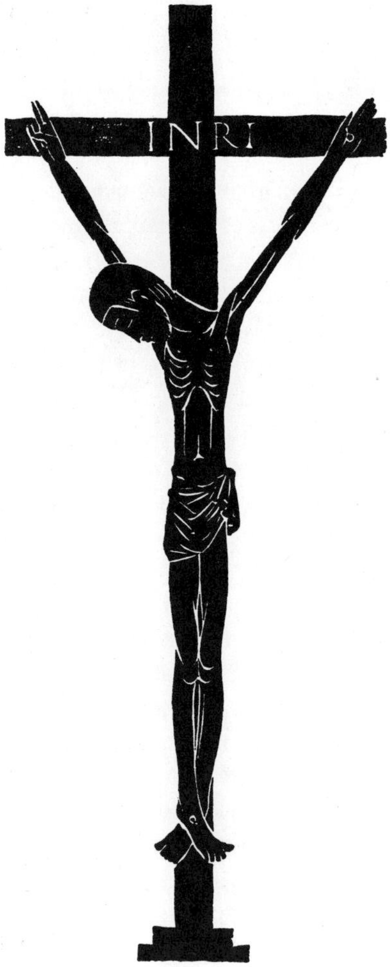

[106] Eric Gill: *Crucifix*, 1913. 7.2 x 18.1cm

was specially made, entirely from linen, and the book was issued as a limited edition of 438 copies. Work was started on 1 August 1892 and completed on 8 May 1896. Morris died four months after the great work was finished.

The Kelmscott *Chaucer* is a massive production, devised by a designer rather than by an artist. It misses the whole point of Dürer's concept of the artist-designed and produced book as an integrated whole. The *Chaucer* illustrations were engraved by the *formschneider* engraver W. H. Hooper. They are usually described as admirable but they are stiff, wooden and formulistic [59]. Bearing very little relation to the quality of the Danube school, they fit exactly into Haden's description of reproductive engraving.

It is well known that Burne-Jones, Morris's friend, had little or no knowledge of drawing for engraving, although he provided many drawings for Morris's books. The drawings executed by Burne-Jones had to go through a very protracted translation process: R. Catterson-Smith had to redraw them in ink, then they were revised by Burne-Jones and then transferred to the photosensitized block to be engraved by W. H. Hooper, who spent about one week on each block.

In quality and expressive sensitivity the *Chaucer* engravings bear no relation to the lively, springy engraving of the drawings of Charles Keene or Phil May reproduced in Punch in 1897 [55, 60]. Throughout *Chaucer* Morris achieved a uniform greyness and skilfully attained an effect which was midway between absolute black and absolute white. The book proved to be a very important step forward in achieving unity in all aspects of book production but it in no way helped the artist to produce and design the kind of books which were to be such an important feature of twentieth-century creative engraving.

Walter Crane (1845 to 1915), a disciple of Morris who was a wood engraver and designer of books, made a considerable contribution to the design and production of children's books. His father was a lithographer and portrait artist. In 1857 Crane moved to London from the family home in Chester to begin an apprenticeship to W. J. Linton, who recognised his designing skills and encouraged him with his drawing. Crane gained a wide experience of all kinds of engraving before leaving Linton in 1862 to become an independent book illustrator. The oil painting of Walter Crane, executed by G. F. Watts in 1891, which hangs in the National Portrait Gallery, shows a man with a profile that suggests a strong character. The portrait gives the impression of a person who is sensitive and intellectual.

Oscar Wilde appreciated Crane's talent and they became friends. When Wilde was the editor of *Women's World*, a fashion magazine, he published a Crane drawing and reviewed Crane's book *Flora's Feast*. Later Wilde commissioned Crane to illustrate his book *The Happy Prince*.

In addition to illustrating books, Crane designed tapestry and stained glass for Morris and Company. He adapted his book illustration *The Goose Girl* for tapestry and in 1886 followed it with stained glass designs for a private house called *Clare Lawn* at East Sheen near London. During the 1860s Crane was attracted to the work of Rossetti, Hunt and Millais. Stylistically he followed the tradition of black-line engraving in which he was trained by Linton. While in Linton's employ Crane did work as a court reporter-artist. Linton's firm was noted for the engraving of Christina Rossetti's poem *Golden Market* and Sir Frederick Leighton's paintings and drawings [54].

It was not until 1865 that Crane started working on children's books (then known as toy books) which were to establish his renown during the seventies and eighties.

[107] Eric Gill: Christmas card design, 1916. 5.24 x 5.2cm

[108] Eric Gill: *Madonna and Child with Chalice*, 1916. 4.4 x 5.1cm

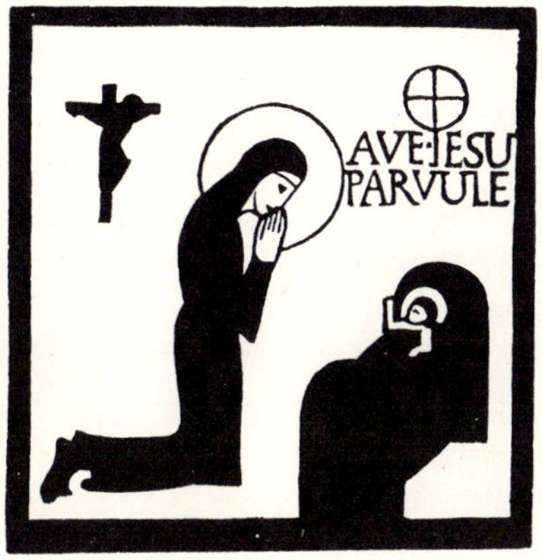

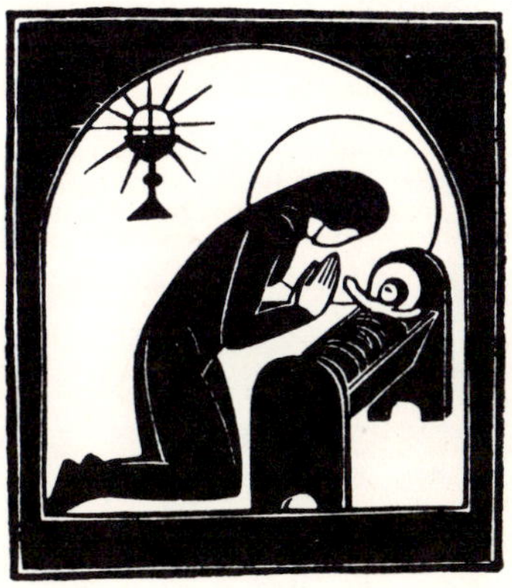

His early toy books such as *Cock Robin*, *Dame Trot and her Comical Cat* and *The House that Jack Built* were published by Warne and Co in 1865-66 and sold for sixpence each. His *The Baby's Opera* was published by Edmund Evans in 1877 and was followed in 1878 by *The Baby's Bouquet*. These two books combined music, illustrations, colour and rhymes fused into good, sensitive design. Most of his wood engraving illustrations are very sensitive but Victorian in detail, colour and texture.

Crane's use of colour in his engravings is remarkably sensitive and individualistic, as is evident in his employment of closely related colours of low chroma. He had a keen understanding of the principles and usage of discord which is the reversal of the natural order of the hues in the light spectrum. The principle of discord was first defined by the physicist Rood.[4]

The principle of colour discord appears to have faded from use at the end of the Victorian period and was absent from modern work until some ten years ago when interest was revived. In terms of Crane's colour vocabulary, present-day work appears thin, cold and mean. Today his books are being reproduced by photolithography but at a standard which does not represent the original work adequately.

Crane was not altogether happy about the style of *Art Nouveau*, and he wrote of it thus: 'That strange decorative disease; must it be to the grave I must come before I can understand?'[5] Despite the *Art Nouveau* style of Ricketts and Shannon, Crane produced many illustrations for their Vale Press books. Ricketts and Shannon managed the Vale Press from 1896 to 1904 in partnership with Llewellyn Macon, a well-to-do lawyer. During that time approximately forty-five books were produced.

Crane was also an important influence in teaching. From 1893 to 1896 he was Director of Design at the Manchester Municipal School of Art, having previously taught at the South Kensington School of Art. He was Principal of the Royal College of Art from 1896 to 1899. Despite his many achievements, Walter Crane occupied a minor position in the British school of wood engraving because his style was not capable of extensive development.

The Kelmscott style of book design became popular in America and encouraged the establishment of many private presses. It also had the effect of making a number of commercial publishers improve their book design. In American productions engraving was superseded by the new process of photo-engraving which came into being soon after the Kelmscott *Chaucer*, though it is doubtful whether Morris would have used the process. Morris's decorative borders and fine taste persisted, but there was also a large body of work which was tasteless, merely imitation of Morris's style and overwhelmingly decorated.

[109] Edward Wadsworth: *Newcastle*, 1913. 10.0 x 14.0cm

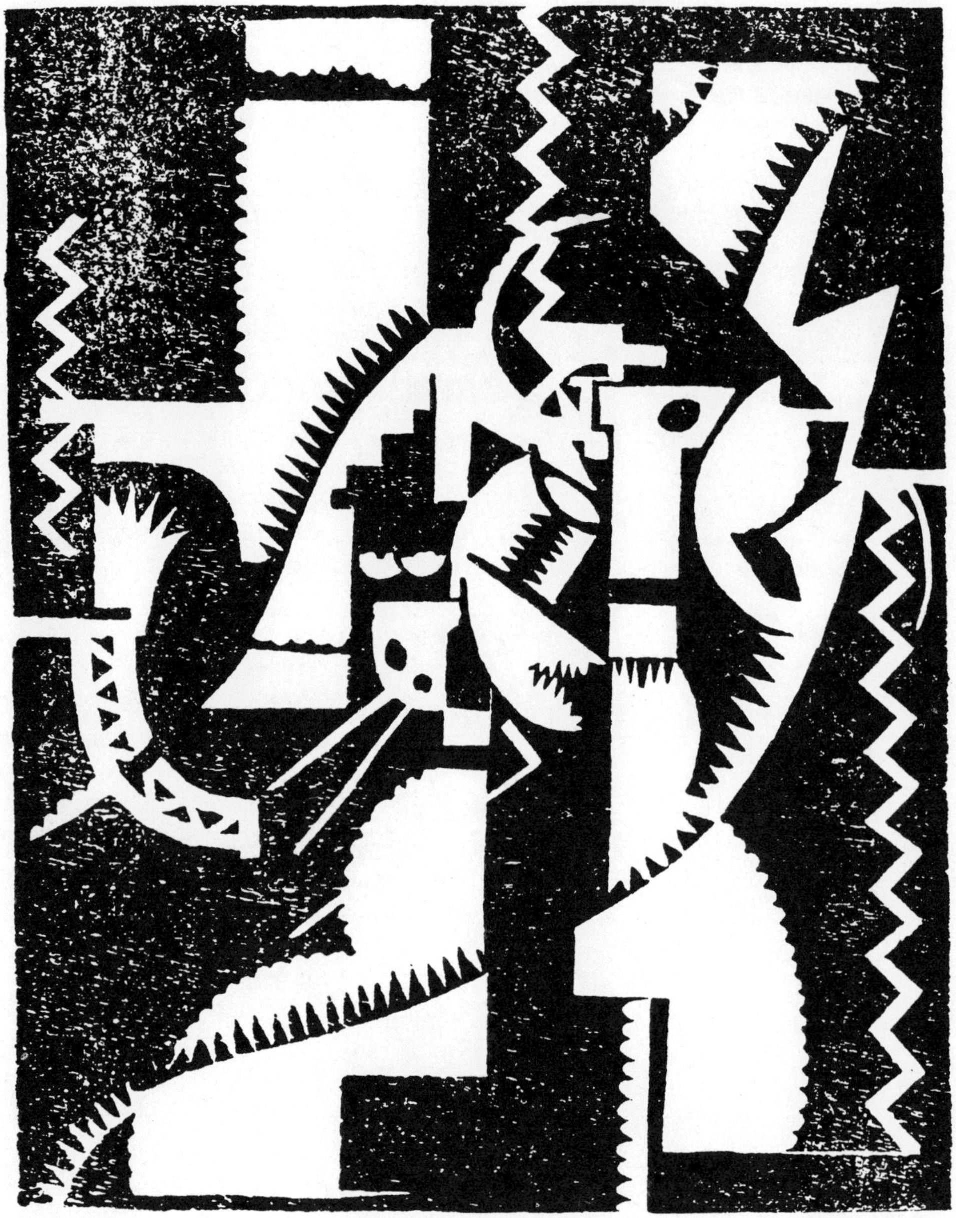

Morris and the Arts and Crafts movement stimulated a lot of interest in the well-designed book, both for the commercial press and the private press. As a wood engraver he had a large output but he did not expand his technique in the creative sense.

Charles Ricketts and Charles Shannon met as students in 1884 when they were members of the long-forgotten Lambeth Art School. They were apprenticed to a wood engraver together and continued to work with each other all their lives as creative painter-engravers in partnership. Their shared interests led them to set up a joint household for the practice of art. Oscar Wilde said of their home in the Vale, Chelsea: 'A house where you will never be bored'. Both Ricketts and Shannon were unashamedly literary in outlook. They shared a common aestheticism and were strongly opposed to the new scientific vision and aesthetic realism of the French Impressionists and Post-Impressionists.

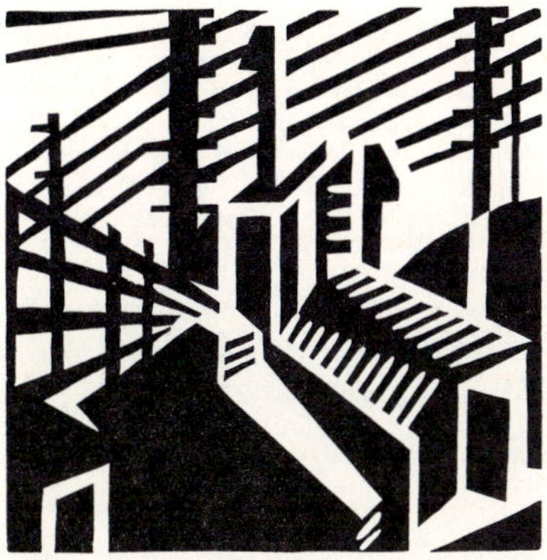

[110] Edward Wadsworth: *Platelayers' sheds*, 1914. 7.6 x 7.6cm

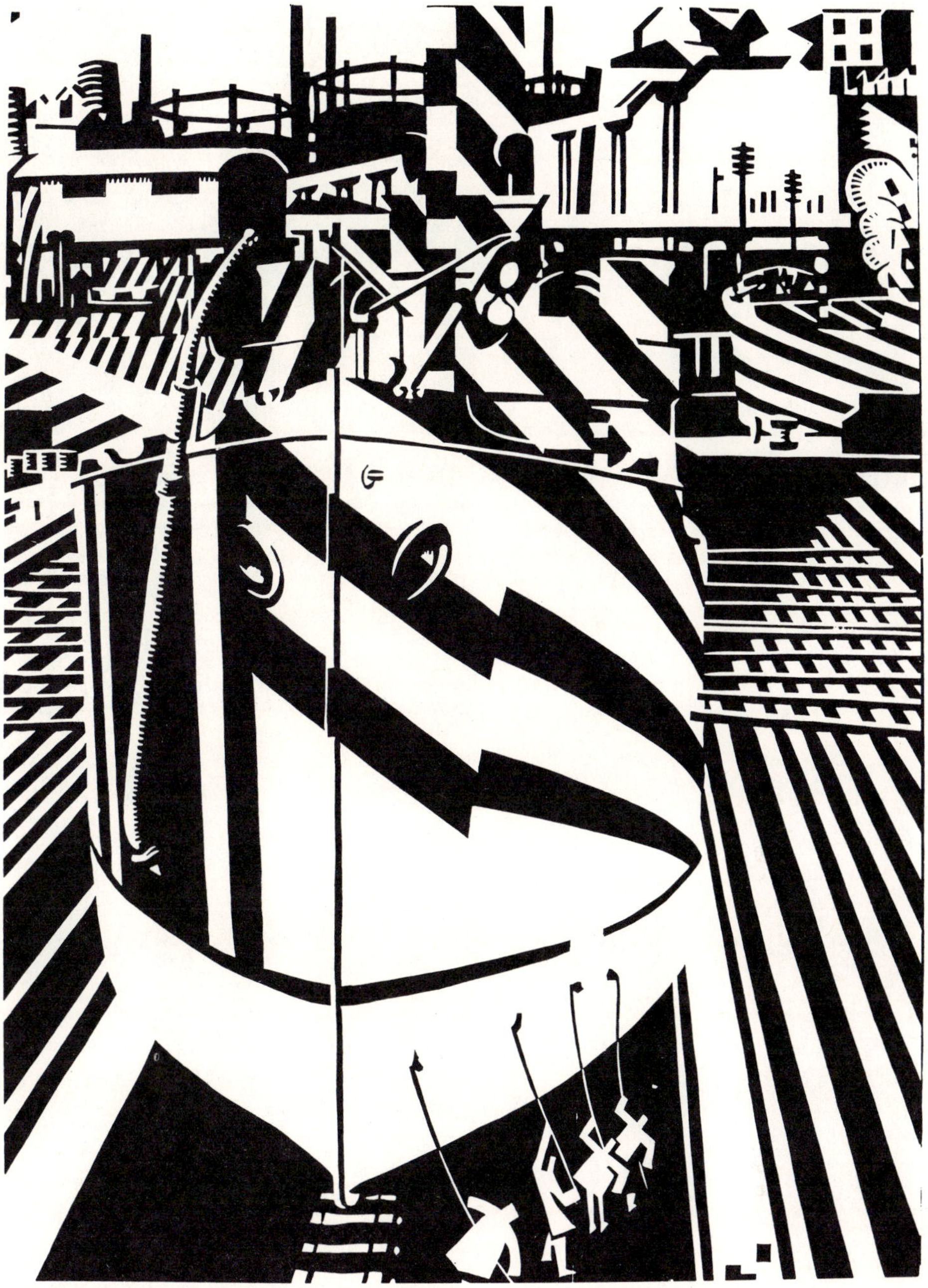

[111] Edward Wadsworth: *In Drydock*, 1918. 18.5 x 24.75cm

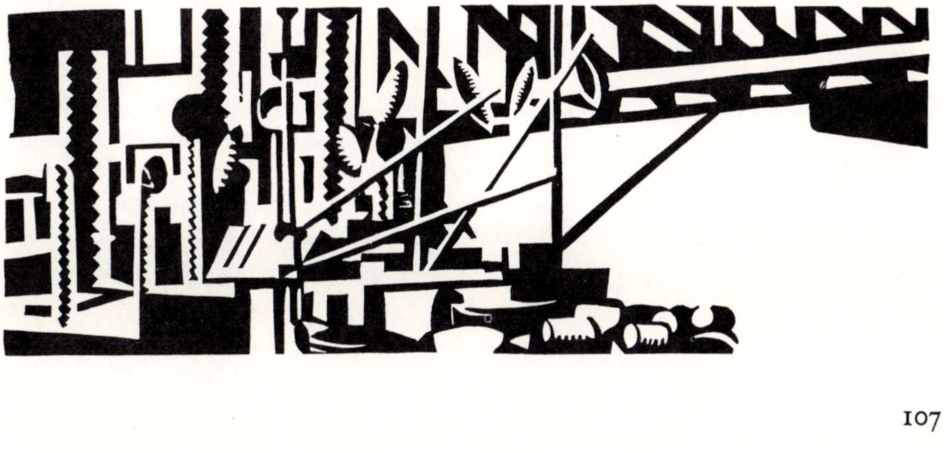

[112] Edward Wadsworth: *Camouflage*, 1918. 18.4 x 6.75cm

[113] Edward Wadsworth: *Black Country*, 1919. 14.5 x 11.0cm

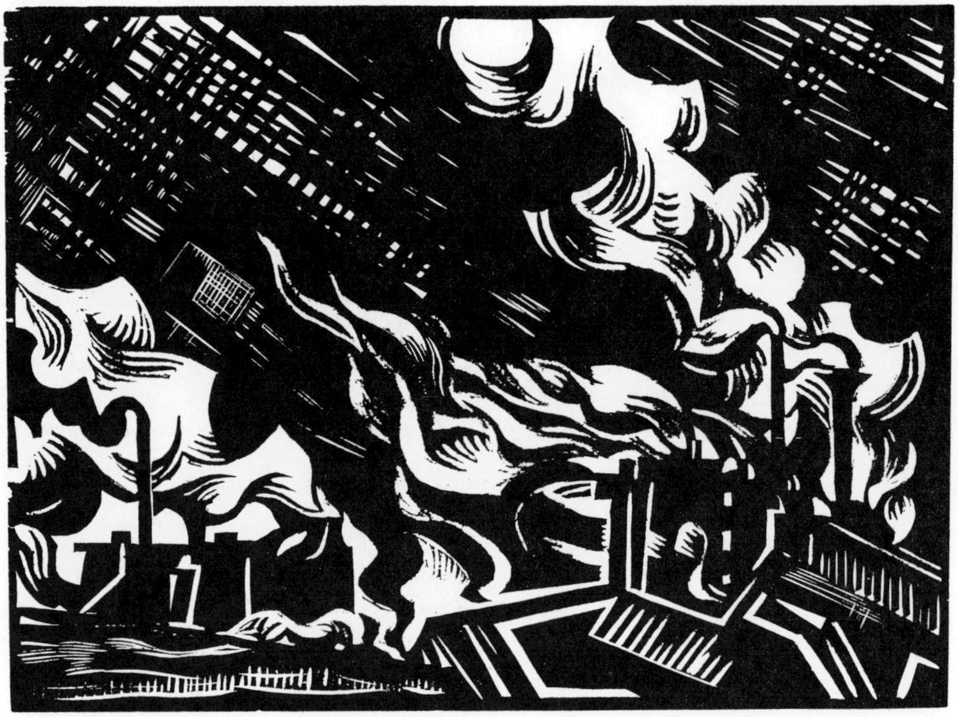

These two artists had a love for eighteenth-century France and the art of Japan, but they also clung to the most conservative classicism of the nineteenth century. This latter art form had run to seed and become a sickly form of Grecian narcissistic naturalism which had to die. Ricketts and Shannon cultivated the most delicate and refined appreciation, distilling it until it became a quintessence in an existence to which music, literature and painting contributed.

The rumblings of bigger things to come were already in the air. Roger Fry, then a young man, was a frequent visitor to the home of the two artists in the Vale and he learned from Ricketts the values to which he aspired. Both the artists were deeply affected by the work of Dürer and also of Puvis de Chavannes (1824 to 1898). The influence of Dürer can be seen as a technical one in their engravings, from the use of the black line and an occasional use of the white line. It appears that the realism of Dürer had little effect on either man. Similarly, the urgency to expand education through a democratic art and technical development could not have meant much to them. Their art had refinement but not urgency, it had academic learning in ample measure yet was divorced from reality. Neither of these artists was very concerned about the aesthetics of engraving – a subject that did not raise its head until the twentieth century.

These two artists' literary interests laid the foundations of the great scholarship which was to distinguish them both, especially in the field of illustration and book design. Very early in their careers they met Thomas Sturge Moore (1870 to 1944), the poet and wood engraver, and found that he was a kindred spirit who shared their passionate and exclusive devotion to the arts. The meeting took place in 1885 when Ricketts and Shannon were sharing a drab room in Kennington Road in South London.

Although not dependent on art for a livelihood, the artists' lifelong friend Sturge Moore was a sensitive and gifted wood engraver who consistently influenced them. Sturge Moore was persuaded to attend the same art school as Ricketts and Shannon where he won a prize of thirty shillings which was to be spent on a book.

[114] Edward Wadsworth: *Blast Furnaces*, 1919. 17.9 x 13.5cm

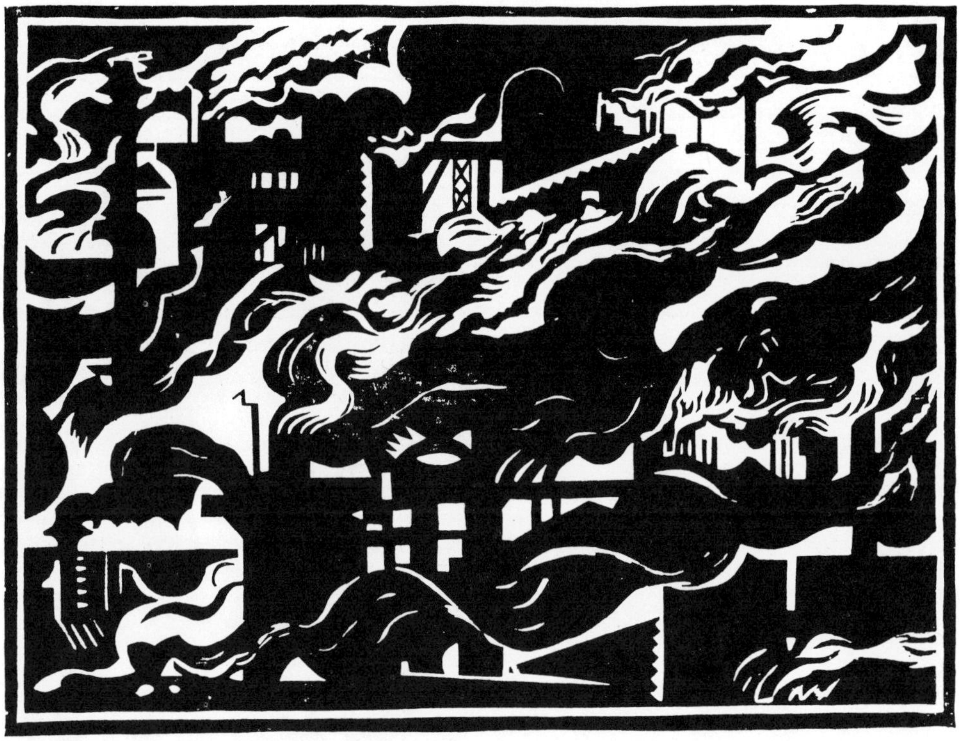

However, he insisted on being allowed to buy two prints by Katsuchika Hokusai (1761 to 1849).

It was several years after this prize distribution that Hokusai was acknowledged as one of the world's great master artists and draughtsmen. His output was enormous and he worked as an artist for seventy years, thus being able to be regarded as the 'grandfather' of the twentieth-century serial development in painting and engraving, and the time study of form which is a unique feature of present-day art.

One of the Hokusai woodcuts in Ricketts' and Shannon's collection was *Fuji Above the Lightning No 9* which was published between 1823 and 1829 by Yeijudo. Hokusai did a series of thirty-six views of Fuji and eventually extended it to forty-six. Each was a separate study of Fuji in all its different moods. He produced a considerable number of series of which the eight *Famous Waterfalls* is perhaps the best known. The most extensive was the *Fifty-three Stages of the Tokaido Road.* The Fuji series comprised a set of studies of the one subject, whereas the other series are either variations on a theme or the projection of a story in pictorial terms.

[115] Philip Hagreen: *The Profiteer*, 1916. 3.8 x 4.3cm

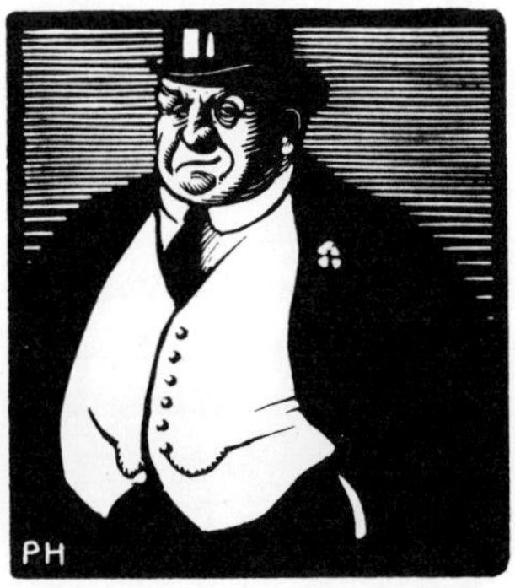

Perhaps it was the *Fuji* series which inspired Monet to make fifteen studies of the same haystack, the series of twenty studies of Rouen Cathedral, the twenty *Poplars* and the *Nympheas* series. Monet's studies of single subjects were the precursors of the recent development of the American serial painters group.

In the later part of the nineteenth century inspiration was again to come from France, where the genius of Carpeaux had rescued sculpture from the malaise of decline and the disturbances of 1870. Carpeaux sent his pupil sculptor Dalou to teach at the Lambeth Art School. He also sent to England the painter Tissot while Camille and Lucien Pissarro and Monet were at Norwood.

Lucien Pissarro met Ricketts, Shannon and Sturge Moore and found them sympathetic company. These four engravers formed themselves into the Dial Group and most of their production was in fine books. Lucien was also introduced to Whistler, and his early work was influenced by the English engravers. He was also influenced by Morris's Kelmscott *Chaucer*, which worried Camille Pissarro.

[116] Robert Gibbings: *Mellaha, Malta*, 1919. Diameter 19.2cm

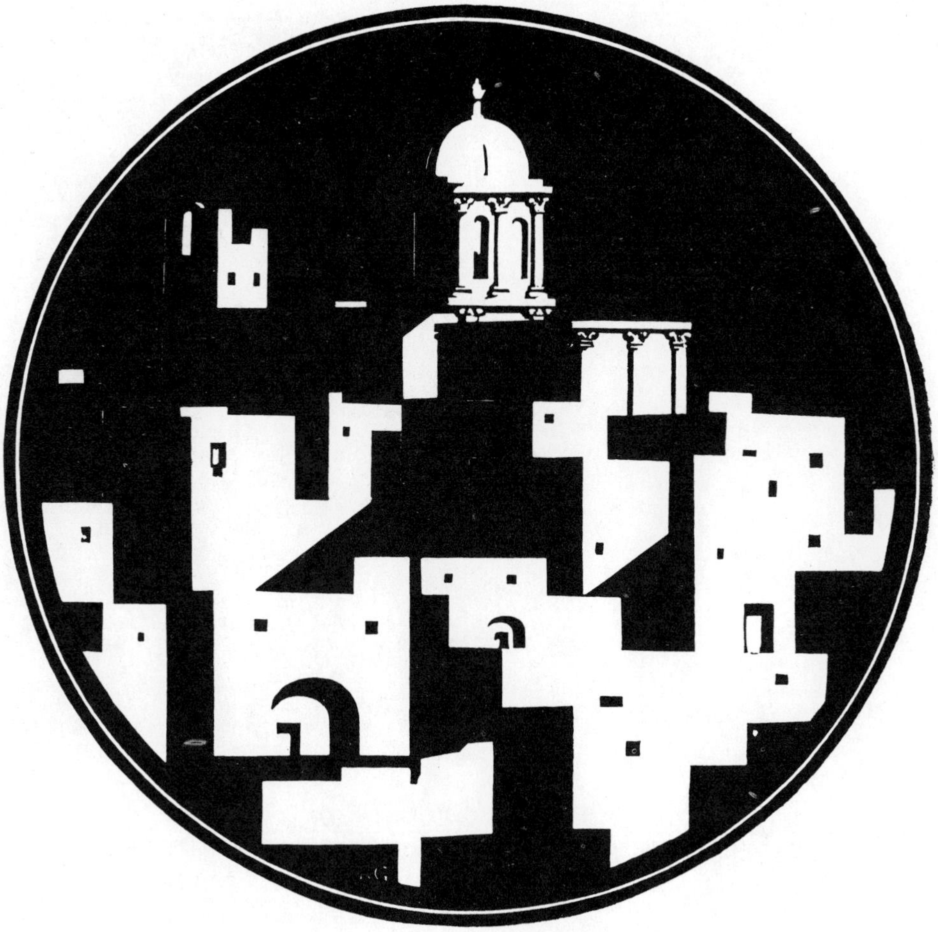

In a letter to Lucien he wrote: 'I do not doubt that Morris's books are as beautiful as Gothic art, but it must not be forgotten that the Gothic artists were inventors and that we have to perform not better, which is impossible, but differently and following our own bent. With this in view you would have to disregard friend Ricketts, who is of course a charming man but who, from the point of view of art, seems to stray from the true direction which is the return to nature. We have today a general concept inherited from our great modern painters, hence we have a tradition of modern art and I am for following this tradition while we inflect it in terms of our individual points of view. Well then, is this the path of Ricketts? No. It has been my view for a long time that it is not a question of pretty "Italian elegance" but of using our eyes a bit and disregarding what is style.'

During his early years as a wood engraver Lucien was continually under instruction and guidance from Camille, though he had made up his mind to stay in England and he liked the English engravers. Gradually he formed his own individual style after working through these influences and became a pure engraver making a considerable contribution to the British school.

In 1894 Lucien had founded his own Eragny Press named by Camille after the Pissarro home in Normandy. This was one of the first private presses to be set up by an artist for the production of his own works. He designed a fount of type for his personal use and called it Brook after his studio at Stamford Brook, Hammersmith, where he lived and worked. He had set an example which was to lead to the development of several other private presses that were founded in the first half of the twentieth century.

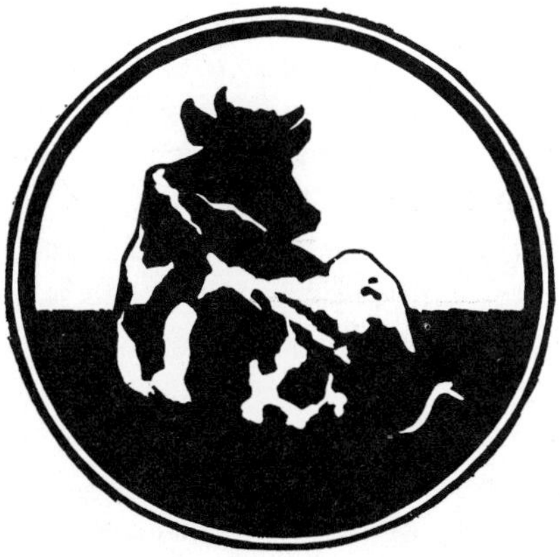

[117] Robert Gibbings: *Cow*, 1920. Diameter 6.2cm

[118] Paul Nash: *Promenade No 1*, 1920. 14.6 x 11.5cm

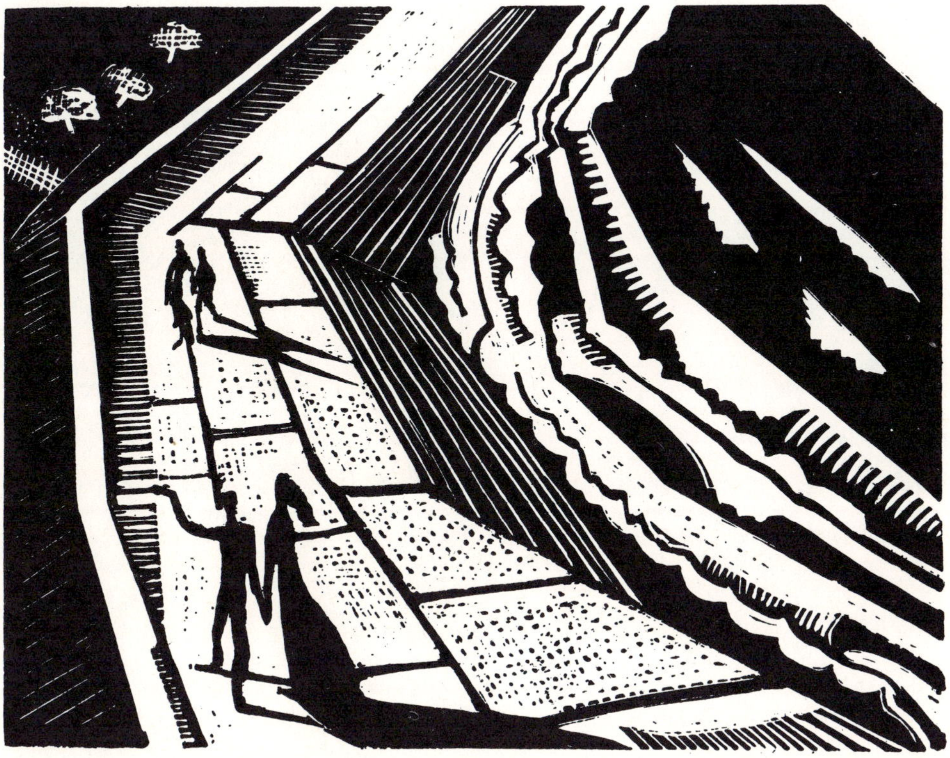

In 1893 Ricketts and Shannon worked for nearly a year designing and engraving thirty-seven wood engravings for the Greek pastoral romance *Daphnis and Chloe* from an Elizabethan English translation which they had discovered. The inspiration for this book was the *Hypnerotomachia* of 1499 [26]. *Daphnis and Chloe* is widely considered the first work of modern times to have illustrations produced by the artist and the page arranged by him. Ricketts became not only an important artist and literary figure but also a foremost connoisseur of drawings. He was a benefactor to the British Museum Prints and Drawings Department, one of his significant gifts to the Museum being a masterly drawing fragment *Roof of a Building* by G. B. Tiepolo (1696 to 1770).

[119] John Nash: *Sheep and Lambs*, 1920. 5.8 x 7.75cm

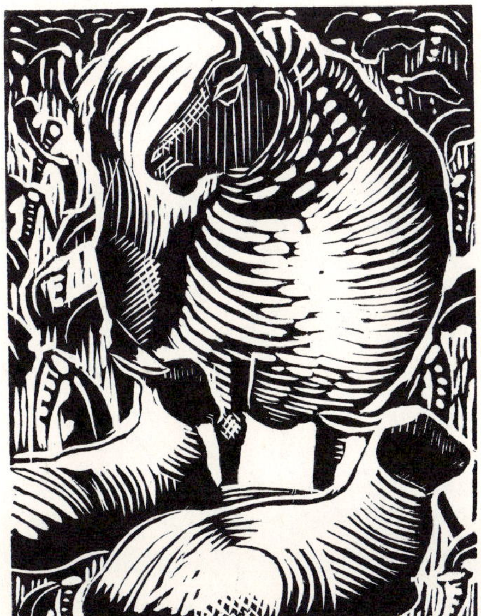

Ricketts and Shannon are chiefly remembered for their designs and engravings for Oscar Wilde's books. Wilde and Ricketts were friends; this friendship lasted through all the bitterness from which Wilde was to suffer after his trial in 1895 and subsequent imprisonment. Wilde had very enlightened views on book illustration. When discussing a future book of his poetry with Ricketts and Shannon, he said that the illustrations were not to be taken from anything in the book, only suggested by it, for in his opinion literature, being more graphic than painting, should never be illustrated in itself but solely by what it evoked. He asked Ricketts and Shannon to design wood engravings and illustrate his book *A House of Pomegranates* 1891. He loved good books that were beautifully printed and handsomely bound. Ricketts wrote of Wilde that he secured work for him as a designer of books and bindings from successive publishers and that it seemed that when Wilde was not giving people ideas he was getting them jobs. Ricketts thought him 'The kindliest and most generous of men I ever met and the most richly endowed in intellect. In intellect and humility he is the largest type I have come across.' He expressed these views in his book *Recollections of Oscar Wilde* 1932.[6]

The last book to be published by the Vale Press was Ricketts' *Biography of the*

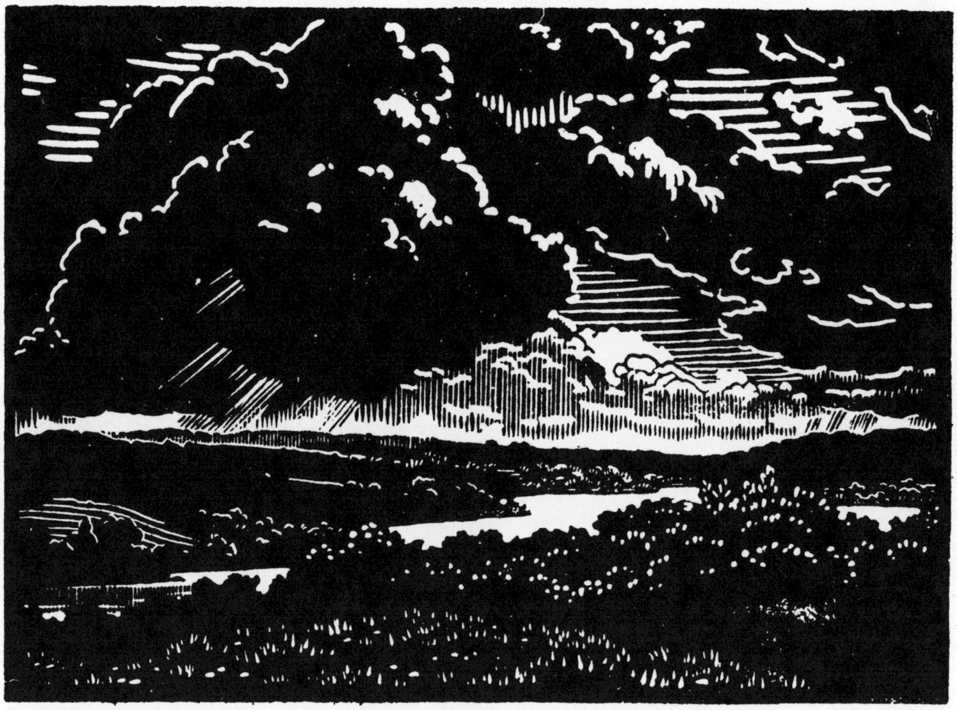

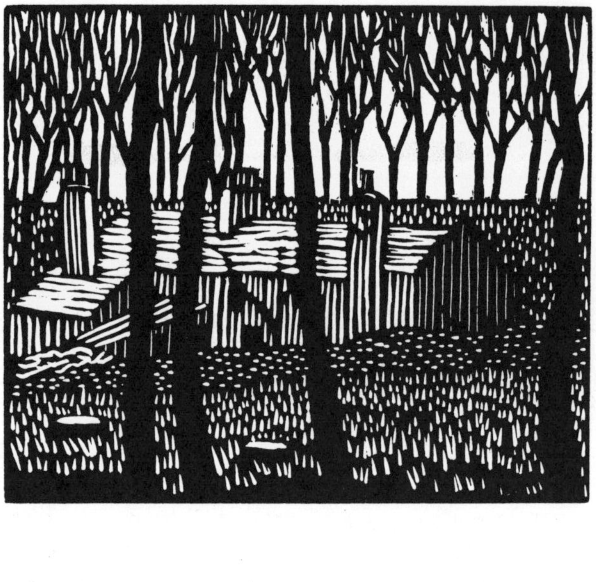

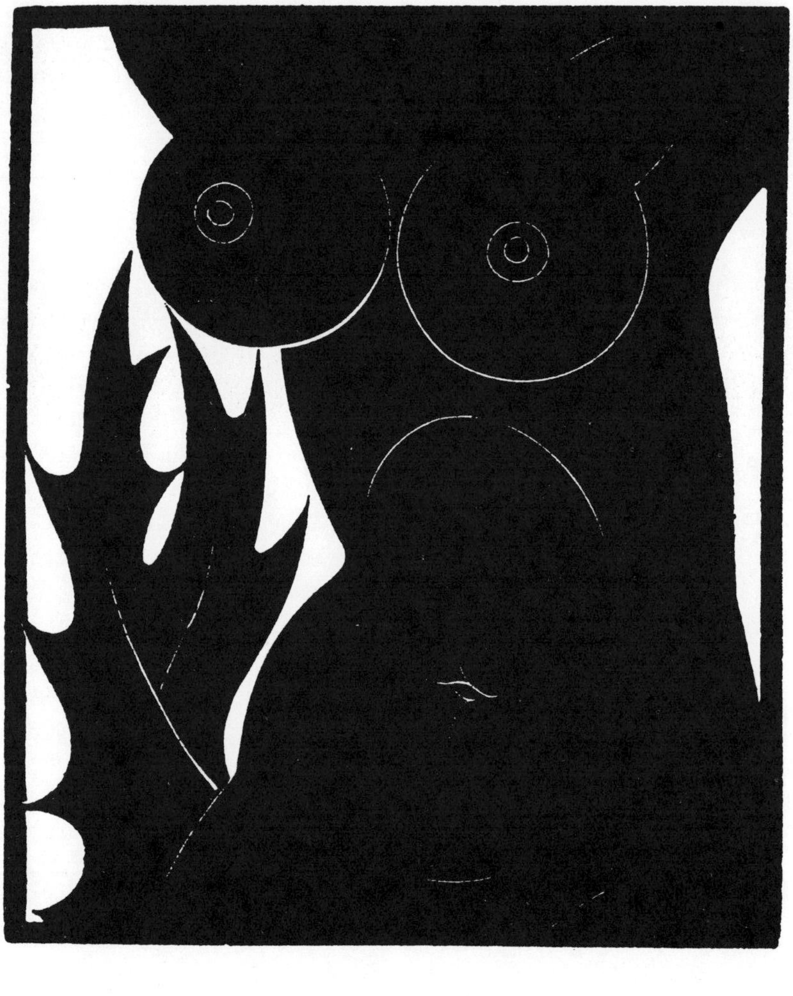

[120] Philip Hagreen: *From the Walls of Thelema*, 1920.

[121] Edward Montgomery Dickey: *The House in the Wood*, 1920. 7.6 x 6.2cm

[122] Eric Gill: *The thorn in the Flesh*, 1921. 10.5 x 12.5cm

Vale Press 1904. This book displays a very close affinity in style to Morris's Kelmscott *Chaucer*. In common with Aubrey Beardsley, the drawing and engraving style of Ricketts has a manifestation of elegance and a very personal hedonism. He was the supreme exponent of the *Art Nouveau* style. When he closed his Vale Press in 1904 he cast the matrices and punches of his type into the Thames.

Ricketts' other long-standing friend, Sturge Moore, was an exponent of both the black and white line in a single work, but the black line always dominated in his engraving. He had a small but sensitive production. He is better known as a poet than as an engraver and as an artist he is underestimated and somewhat neglected. There was no purist approach to visual form where he was concerned, neither for that matter was he concerned very much with the formal relationships between space and solids or light as a physical manifestation. Like his friends he was firmly based in literary concepts. Stylistically he is close to the Pre-Raphaelites and in particular to Sir Edward Burne-Jones.

The majority of Sturge Moore's engravings are small illustrations for books rather than autonomous prints in their own right. As an artist he viewed the world in Wordsworthian terms with Burne-Jones's sentimentality applied to the human form and to nature and natural forms. His wood engravings are imaginative and generous in spirit. His line is lyrical, but the mixture of black and white line gives his engravings something of the character of drawings. This quality of engraving was to become something of an anathema in the twentieth century.

The concept of engraving as a fundamental discipline did not interest Moore very much. His interests and his world of art were to be eclipsed by the inevitable form changes that were to affect not only him but others of his generation. He had no interest in the aesthetics of Whistler yet failed to establish his own aesthetics because his scope of production was too small.

In the younger generation of artists Moore met an earthy earnestness which he failed to understand and was therefore unsympathetic to their cause. He gave his views on art in his book *Art and Life* in which he wrote: 'I see it, in maturing, refining as much as possible from Egyptian pylons to Gothic needles, from Hindoo poems twenty thousand lines long to the tirades of Byron. Form in becoming skilful, attenuates. That is why there are neither beautiful nor ugly subjects and why, from the point of view of sheer art, an axiom might almost be laid down that there is no subject, style being in itself an absolute manner of seeing things.'[7] Moore failed to understand that the refining and maturing process at a tangent to visual reality is the language of decadence. The onslaught of the more objective Impressionists and the development of the modern world was hitting him hard. For him, subject matter was of greater importance than the form in which that subject matter would be expressed. The process he describes can be seen historically as always appearing in the decline of a culture or at the end of a cultural period. Maturing and refining is all that there is left when the creative fires of a cultural period have burned out.

In 1939, Sturge Moore collected and compiled letters and journals of Charles Ricketts in a book called *Self-Portrait* edited by Cecil Lewis.

Within the Dial Group there was the uneasy situation of Lucien Pissarro steering a delicate course between the severe French aesthetic principles on the one hand and the sentimental English aesthetic concepts on the other hand. Ricketts was anxious to start a new movement and he urged Lucien to join, but the idea proved abortive.

Without Lucien, Ricketts' ideas of a new movement did not stand much chance of success. Camille's counsel prevailed; he told Lucien: 'The new movement

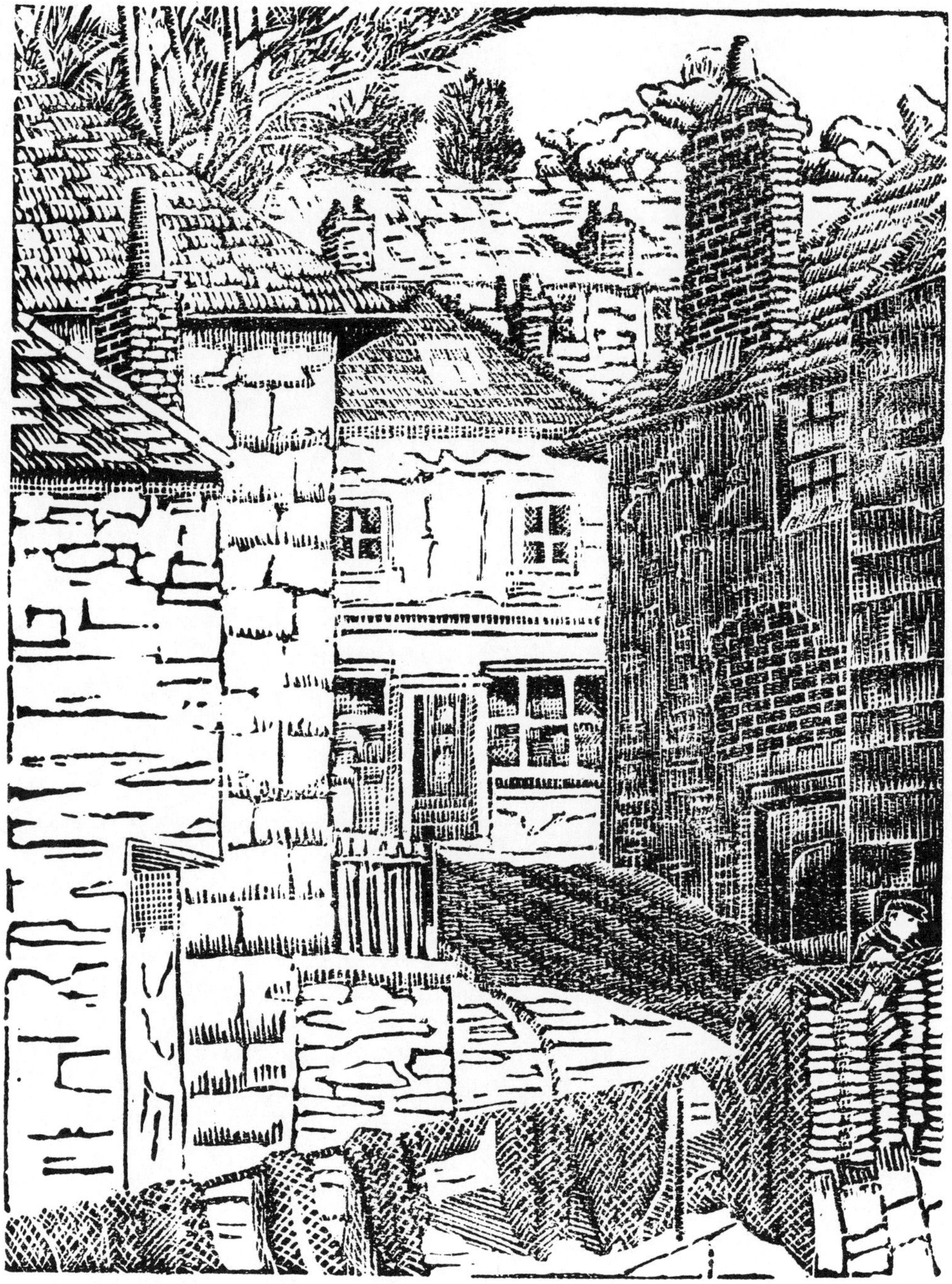

[123] Charles Ginner: *A Cornish Village*, 1921. 16.5 x 22.4cm

Ricketts ironically urges you to support seems to be absurd, at least for you, since this neo-catholic movement dovetails with the reactionary turn of the upper bourgeoisie, which is fearful of the rising anarchist philosophy. Damn' it, neo-catholicism may be in style for a bit, but since real belief is necessary for it to succeed, the chances are that it won't get very far, everybody cannot be as sick as Huysmans is.' This statement indicates that Camille held strong views on the new movement and he can be said to have influenced British wood engraving by being instrumental in delaying or even diverting a movement that was of good intent but led by the wrong people.

Despite the great difference between the political backgrounds of Charles Ricketts and Lucien Pissarro, the friendship between the two men lasted a long time.

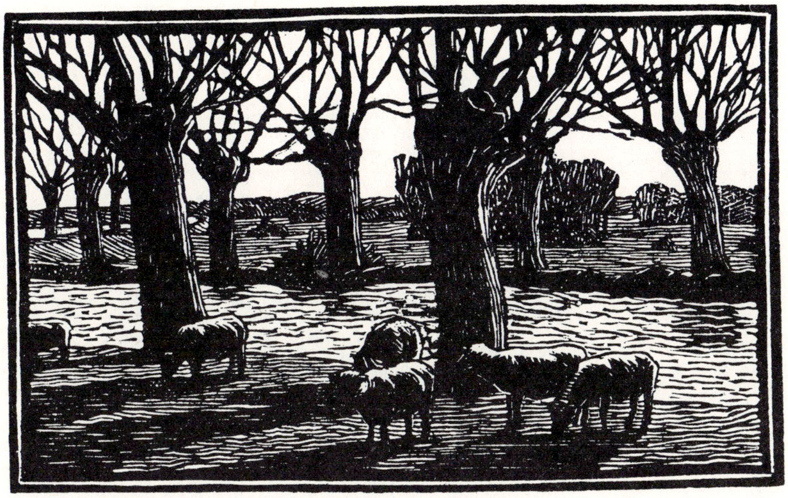

[124] Gwendolen Raverat: *Sheep by the River*, 1921.

At the beginning of the twentieth century, the concept behind the art of engraving changed. The style of the nineteenth century demanded that an engraving should appear as the reproduction of a drawing or painting but at the start of the new century the art of wood engraving began to take on a creative aspect that was to make it stand in its own right as art. This development started when the ranks of the reproductive engravers were strengthened by sympathetic links with the creative genius of men like Edward Gordon Craig (1872 to 1966).

Like Whistler in his painting and etching, Craig was to introduce into wood engraving an aesthetic form, centred upon formal values and the expression of aesthetic emotion. Craig's art was to be spread far and wide through wood engraving, the woodcut, the book and the theatre. Of all these transitional engravers it was Craig who saw the early meanings of the impending revolution in art and who was to carry the aesthetics of his time and the new changing order into wood engraving and the theatre.

Craig's early engravings show the prevailing influence of *Art Nouveau*. Eventually he helped to found the Society of Wood Engravers and as a result he gradually adopted some of the aesthetics of white-line engraving although he never fully adopted the creed but used it as and when he wished. Thus, Craig's engraving is both black-line and white-line. The sensitivity of his woodcuts is outstanding though most of his work is small in its dimensions. He used his wood engraving and woodcuts to exploit his work for the theatre.

Edward Henry Gordon Craig was surrounded by talented people in the arts from birth. His mother, the famous actress Ellen Terry, became Sir Henry Irving's leading lady. At the age of sixteen years she married the painter George Frederick Watts (1817 to 1904) who was then forty-seven years old. It was his second marriage, his first having failed, and it lasted only sixteen months. He and Ellen Terry separated in 1865 but Watts did not agree to a divorce until twenty years later.

In 1865 Ellen Terry fell in love with the celebrated architect Edward William Godwin (1833 to 1886) and they set up home together at Stevenage. The first child born to Ellen Terry was Edith (1869 to 1947) and the second was Edward Henry Gordon who took the name of Craig in later life. He was born at Stevenage on 16 January 1872. Even when very young these two children were given an exceptional training in literature, art and the theatre. Children's books illustrated by Walter Crane were the only ones considered suitable by their mother for her

[125] Thomas Sturge Moore: *The Young Man who left his Sheet and fled away naked*, 1921. 12.25 x 7.4cm

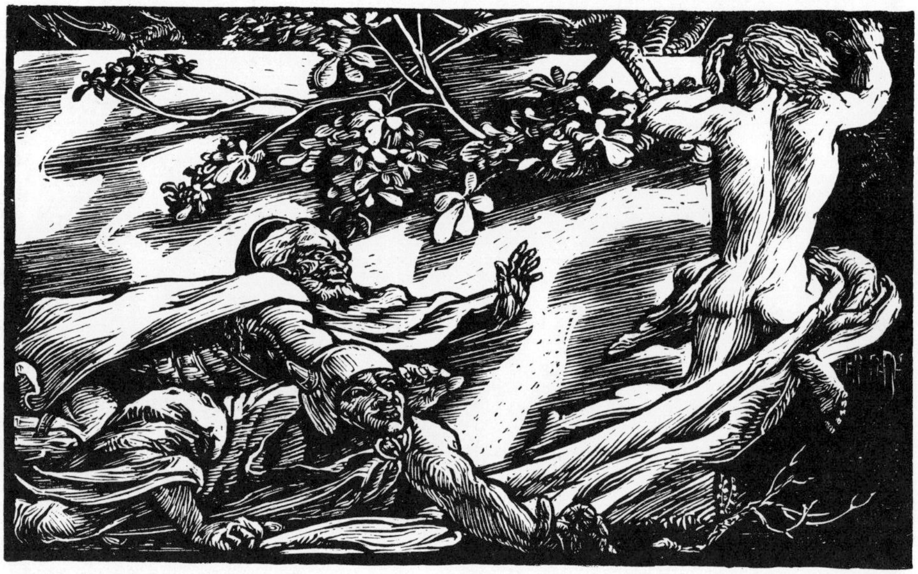

children in the early stages of their development and she is reputed to have forbidden access to any other books. She expected her son to become a good actor, then an artist of originality and finally to aspire to new developments in the art of the theatre. Edward achieved all these things and acted in his first play *Olivia* at the age of six years, on 28 March 1878 at the Royal Court Theatre. Gordon Craig's father, Edward Godwin, was a significant and talented architect who designed and worked sympathetically with Whistler's Aesthetic movement, the Pre-Raphaelites and William Morris's Arts and Crafts movement. In the mid-sixties he was on close terms with Whistler. Like Whistler and Sturge Moore, he was an admirer of Greek as well as Japanese art and he designed interiors and furniture which show a marked Japanese influence.

In 1876 Edward Godwin worked on the Bedford Park project and built a number of houses and studios, including his own home. His most controversial house was White House in Tite Street, Chelsea, which he designed for Whistler between 1877 and 1878. Whistler required a house with a comfortable but sparsely furnished interior in the Japanese style and containing a small theatre and spacious studio suitable for opening as an atelier for his increasing circle of young admirers.

While employed in London as an actor, Edward Gordon Craig spent a lot of time studying in libraries and galleries. He moved to Uxbridge in 1893. From 1899 he began to devote his time to drawing and engraving and he began the production of *Dido and Aeneas* in that year. He produced his first wood engravings in 1895 to help his stage designs.

From Uxbridge Craig discovered the then small village at Denham where his near neighbours were William Nicholson and James Pryde, Nicholson's brother-in-law. Visiting these two men brought Craig into contact with the idea and the expression of wood engraving in the hands of a creative artist as distinct from a professional commercial engraver and Nicholson showed Craig the way to hold the block and the burin. In considering Craig's work some writers have remarked that Nicholson did not give much away in describing technique but the two men were of such a calibre that a satisfactory relationship would have been established very quickly.

In two of the books produced by Nicholson the engravings were printed in black and the areas of colour added lithographically. In using this mixture of printing techniques, Nicholson not only offended some of the purists of his day but was ahead of his time. He anticipated the current commonly used method of employing more than one printing process, although it is only the very competent artist who is able to achieve success in this method of reproduction.

Further, by designing his own books and engraving illustrations for them in the painter-engraver tradition, Nicholson started a trend that was to have considerable influence in wood engraving, although it is doubtful that his work would have had its full development had it not been for the activities of the elder Joseph Crawhall (1821 to 1896), the Victorian chap-book artist and writer. Joseph Crawhall worked for Ye Leadenhall Press of Newcastle and produced a series of light-hearted, naive and unintentionally humorous chap-books. His main productions were *Newcastle Fishers, Garlands* 1864, *Chaplets from Coquet-side* 1873, *Border Notes and Mixty-Maxty* 1880, *Chap-book Chaplets* 1883, *Olde ffrendes wyth New Faces* 1883 and *Wallet-booke* 1885. These cheap productions were sold by hawking them around Newcastle. They were intended for a semi-literate public – hence the naive style

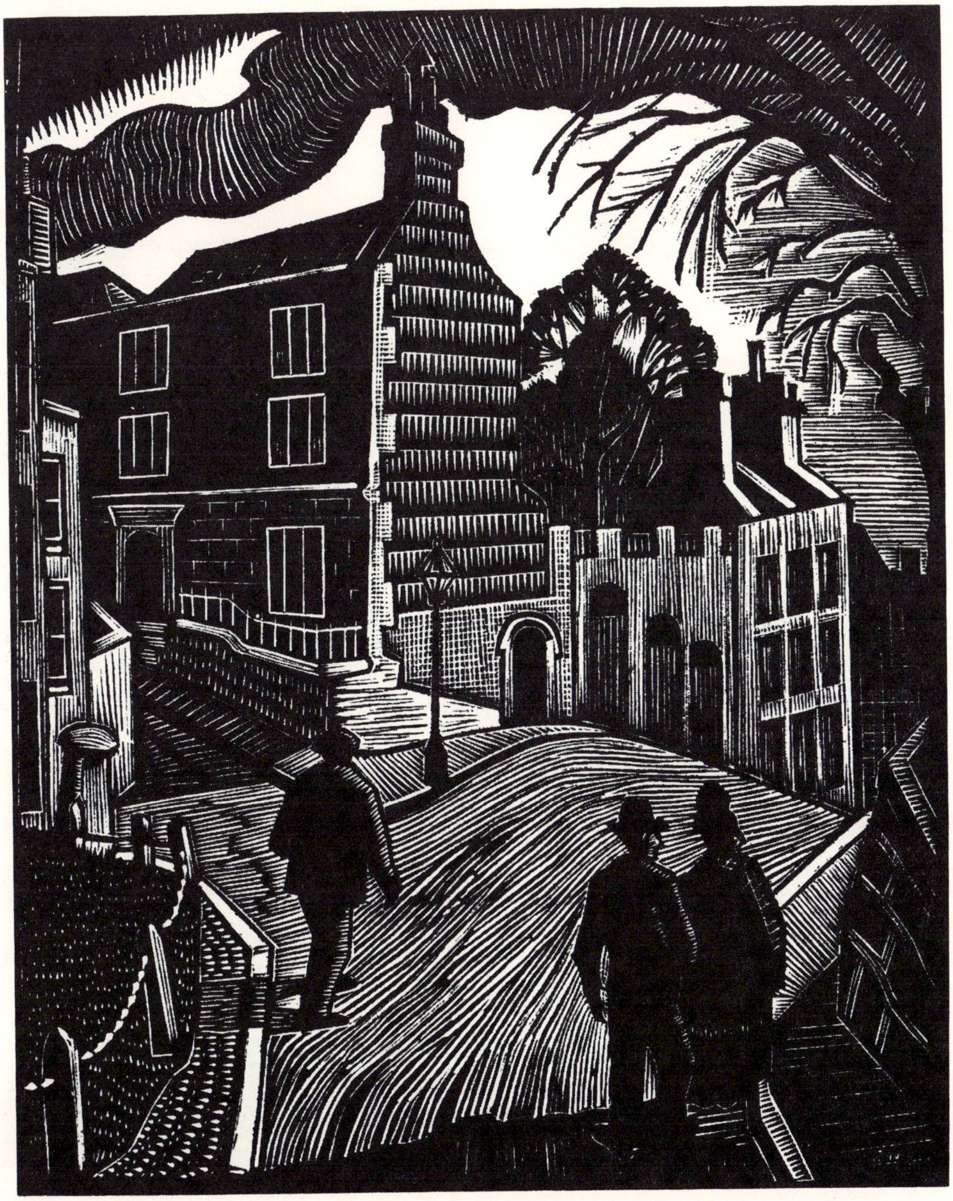

[126] Ethelbert White: *Holy Bush Hill, Hampstead*, 1921.
13.25 x 16.5cm

of design and the crude engraving. Crawhall was a creative engraver but appears deliberately not to have developed his talent. In [53] the hand of the sophisticated designer can be seen in the triangular relationship of the three fishing rods linking the two blocks with the lettering above.

Crawhall had a good sense of design and could assemble a book as a craftsman but his more ambitious books in colour were not successful technically. In 1889 he assembled a large collection of his blocks and published them without a text in a book called *Impresses Quaint*. He is the Newcastle version of Mexico's Posada (1851 to 1913) though there was much less fun in Posada's violent political world. Crawhall's son, Joseph Crawhall the younger, (1860 to 1913) became an eminent animal and bird painter.

Nicholson's best-known image prints are the portrait of the ageing Queen Victoria and the engraved advertisement for Rowntree's Select Cocoa. Both were issued by the Beggarstaff Brothers. He shows most of the characteristics of Whistler's aesthetic form in his early paintings, with his love of elegance and the distinguished and vertical pose. He was also associated with the stage and his engravings, which are frequently mistaken for woodcuts, have a theatrical quality about them.

Edward Gordon Craig had a common interest with Nicholson in the theatre, engraving and the woodcut. From 1889 until 1897 Craig was a member of Henry Irving's company at the Lyceum Theatre in London but he became increasingly dissatisfied with acting. He gave up the stage in 1897, despite the fact that he was

[127] Paul Nash: *Places*, 1922.

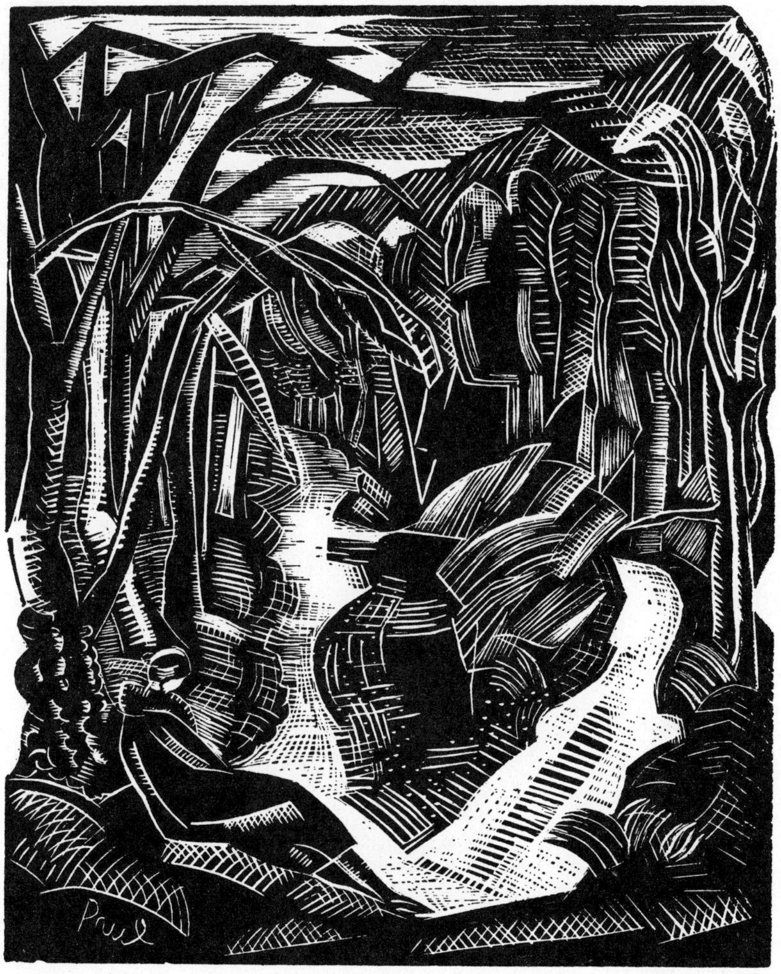

[128] Paul Nash: *Black Poplar Pond*, 1922. 11.5 x 15.3cm

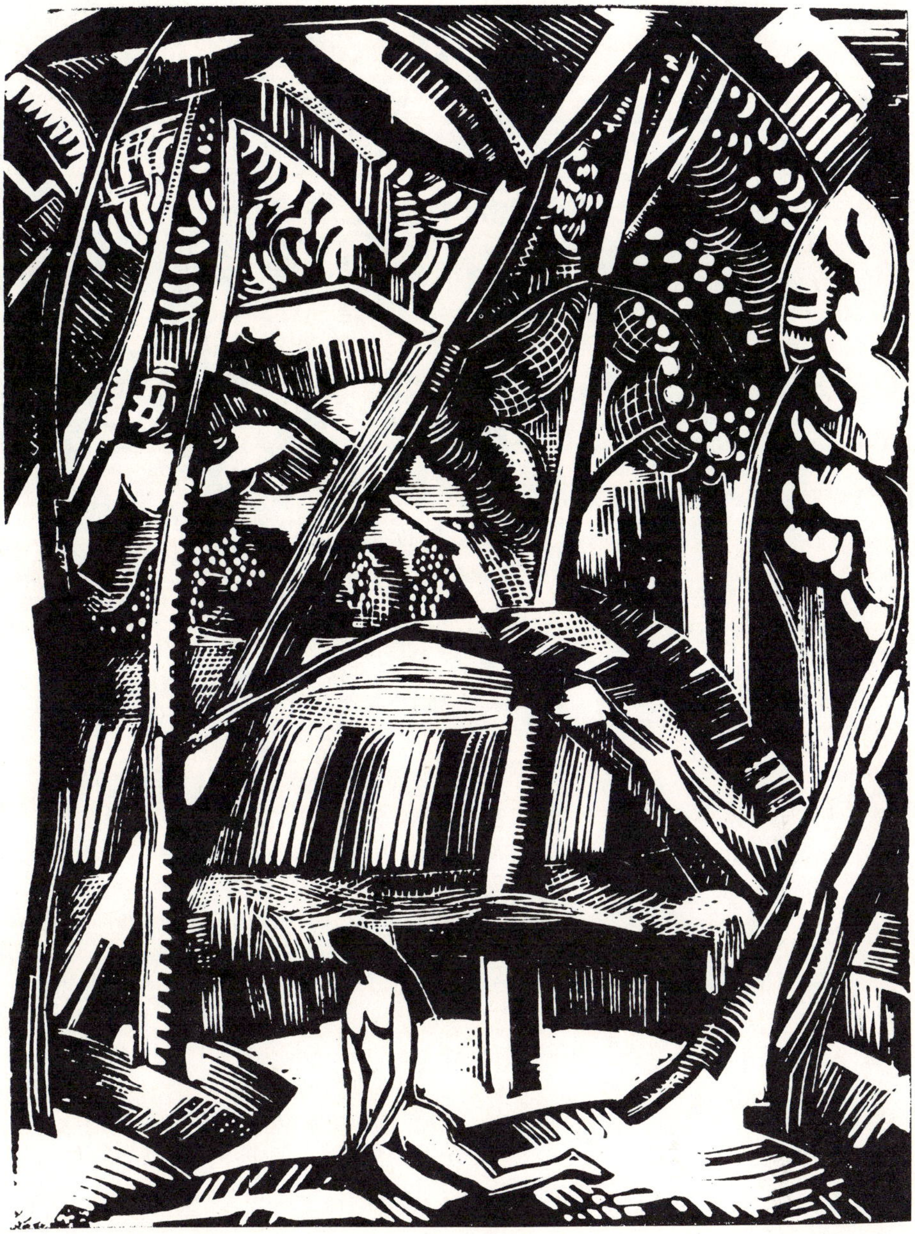

richly endowed with voice, presence, intelligence and the technique natural to one born into the theatre.

However, Craig did not leave the world of the theatre entirely when he became a graphic artist, designer and wood engraver – in this latter field of expression his sensitivity was to prove exceptional. As a theatrical designer and producer his ideas were revolutionary. His first stage production was an adaptation of de Musset's *On ne badine pas avec l'amour* which was seen in Uxbridge in 1893 and in which he played the part of Perdican.

When he was in Germany with Isadora Duncan in 1905 he evolved his great idea for a new kind of kinetic theatre – a synthesis of form, light, scene, figures, movement and sound. He was thinking in abstract terms on the fundamental elements of the theatre, although this kind of abstract thinking never entered his engraving and pictorial world of form which remained representational throughout and romantic in source and inspiration.

[129] Gwendolen Raverat:
Bowl Players in France, 1922.
15.25 x 10.4cm

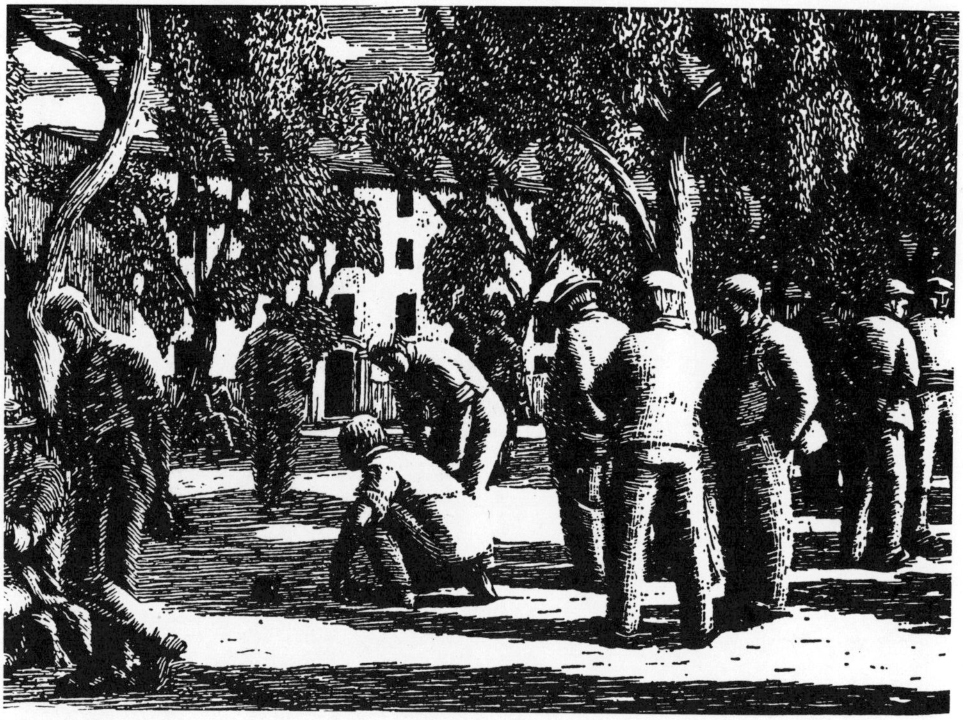

Craig found that the theatre was controlled by hard-headed businessmen who were not particularly interested in reforming the theatre as an art. It seemed to him that a revolution in theatrical design and production was very necessary and the vested interests in the theatre presented a situation so commercially orientated that eventually it led to his leaving England to settle abroad. On leaving England he made his first home in Northern Italy at the Villa Raggio in Rapallo and from 1925 until his death in 1966 he lived in Genoa.

Craig found himself in the forefront of the struggle against theatrical realism, which in visual art would be termed naturalism, i.e. the imitation of nature. In some respects he was also against the nineteenth-century practice of the dominating perspective creating the illusion of naturalism. Nineteenth-century theatres in Europe had become addicted to the use of mechanical devices in the production of spectacle, requiring an army of men to operate stage machinery.

Those who saw the Craig productions found them striking in their simplicity, and the distribution of colour over large areas afforded a stimulating theatrical experience. His insistence on simplicity of treatment was fanatical. A new sense of space and form had arrived on stage which was the very antithesis of the elaborate, ornate, naturalistic concepts of production then surrounding the theatre and Irving.

Craig was not alone in his concepts for the reform of theatrical design. On the Continent, the Swiss born Adolphe François Appia (1852 to 1928) had similar ideas and ambitions and was working for the operatic stage. He introduced multi-level floors and independent movable light sources. In 1892 he stripped the stage of all its decorative clutter and used only the basic forms of decoration for his production of *Das Rheingold* and *Die Walküre.*

Appia received some early encouragement from Richard Wagner's new opera house at Bayreuth, which gave an impetus to his theories on the application of light, form and movement. In 1923 he designed the revolutionary production of *Tristam und Isolde* for La Scala in Milan.

For Appia it was the realism of traditional style in production which spoilt the whole art form. In the 1890s he wrote his first papers on production and made his first sketches for the stage designs for Wagner's musical dramas. From 1900 onwards he devoted his whole career to stage production and became recognised as a great exponent of modern movement in theatre production. Appia's development was independent of that of Gordon Craig who was his younger contemporary and friend. Craig considered Appia's most beautiful design to be his huge multi-level stage production of Gluck's opera *Orpheus and Eurydice* at Dresden. Appia had demonstrated the new art of the theatre at Bayreuth by 1892 and in England Craig had made his demonstration of movement, light and form by 1903. Both men were to meet similar problems of opposition and frustration and both had their greatest works ahead of them.

Modern theatrical art began with these two far-seeing artists. The connections between the theatre and engraving are important, the 'light in motion' concept of the theatre, as opposed to the previous 'fixed light' concept was to move into wood engraving through Craig and also through Noel Rooke. To understand and appreciate fully the art of Craig, his engravings and woodcuts must be seen as the work of a great artist of the theatre.

Craig's source of inspiration came from his study of the simplicity of early Italian art and architecture. He studied in detail the works of Duccio, Sebastiano Serlio and the early Renaissance painters. He also studied the early Renaissance buildings. Their interiors demonstrated simplicity by mass, sensitively modified by texture, which became obscured when overtaken by the full complexity of the Renaissance development of overflowing energy, massive scale and an abundance of detail. It is typical of Craig that he had a sensitivity of design which enabled him

[130] Gwendolen Raverat: *Jeu de Boules, Vence*, 1922. 16.5 x 11.0cm

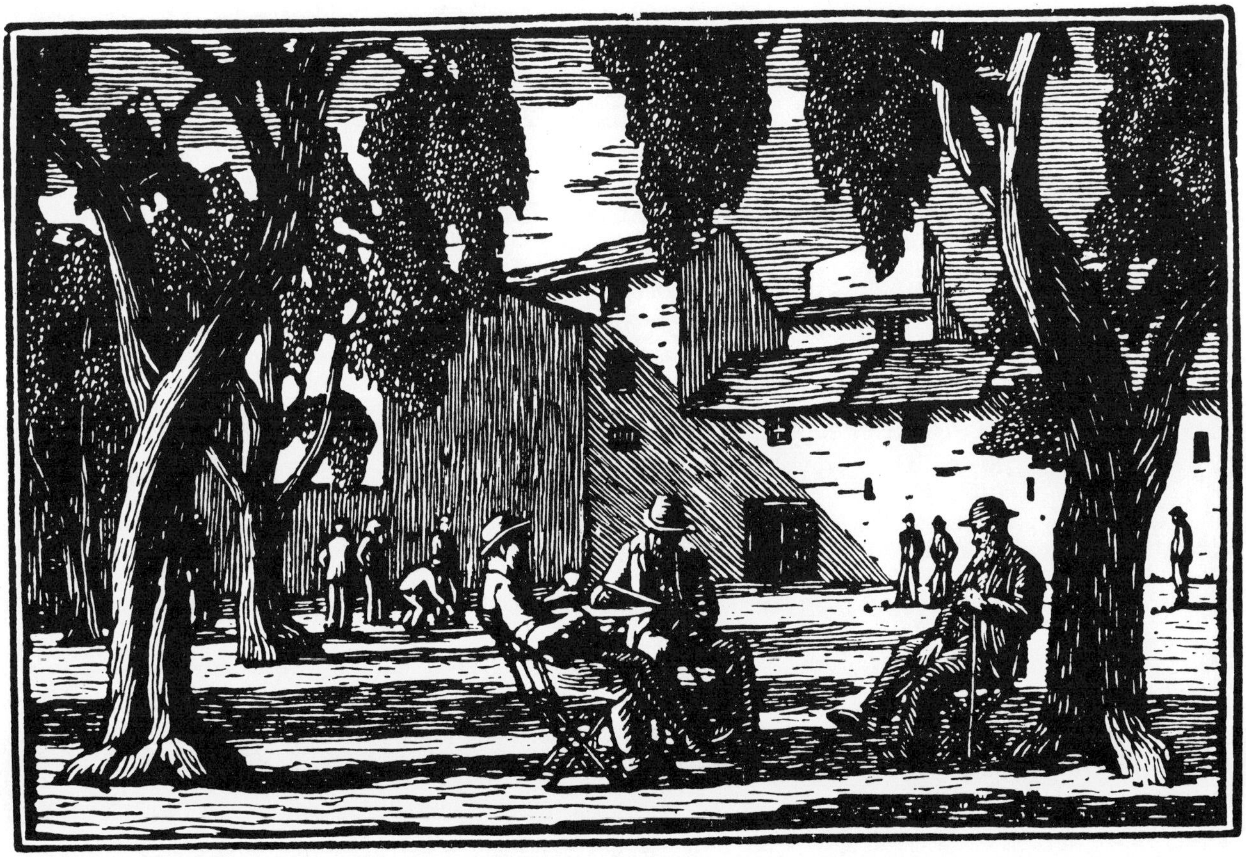

to select the early and pre-Renaissance art as a basis for new concepts. In terms of architecture, the religious building is not far removed from the theatre because it has an impressive concept of space, interesting texture and colour in its decoration and ritual.

As an artist, Craig was now on the way to a glorious maturity of style. The early influence of *Art Nouveau* was disappearing and his engravings were becoming more expressive and sensitive. His views had influence in America and Europe and are expressed in his book *Towards a New Theatre.*[8] He believed that the director should control all aspects of theatrical production, including the design of the stage sets. His dream was a school for the study of the art of the theatre, in its complete form and not merely for stage design. He was thinking in terms of concepts of reform for the whole of the art of the theatre because his own talent covered the whole range of that art. His school, for which he fought so hard and long, was never established in Britain but eventually he found a generous backer in Lord Howard de Walden and in 1913 opened his School for the Art of the Theatre in Florence. It was known as the Arena Goldoni and was an open-air theatre with workrooms, storerooms and offices. It served Craig ideally as a headquarters for publishing *The Mask* between 1908 and 1929. It was publication of *The Mask* which did most to advance his cause and his reputation.

In the matter of skill, Craig placed a high value on drawing and gave the then young Bernard Meninsky (1891 to 1950) his first teaching post at the Arena Goldoni. Meninsky was later to become famous as a draughtsman though underrated as a painter. At the Arena Goldoni, Craig had thirty students and had held three exhibitions of their work prior to the declaration of war in 1914. When the war began, the students departed, funds from England ceased and the school had to be closed.

REFERENCES

1 Whistler, J. A. M. *The Gentle Art of Making Enemies*, Heinemann, London, 1890
2 Rewald, J. *Camille Pissarro: Letters to his Son Lucien*, Kegan Paul, London, 1945
3 Rewald, *Camille Pissarro: Letters to his Son Lucien*
4 Rood, O. N. *Modern Chromatics*, Kegan Paul, London, 1879
5 Crane, W. *An Artist's Reminiscences*, Methuen, London, 1907
6 Ricketts, C. *Recollections of Oscar Wilde*, Nonesuch Press, London, 1932
7 Moore, T. S. *The Vinedresser* (Art and Life series), Methuen, London, 1899
8 Craig, E. G. *Towards a New Theatre*, Dent, London, 1912

5 THE PRECURSORS OF THE WHITE-LINE TECHNIQUE

The artists exercising the most direct influence on the twentieth-century engravers up to the Second World War were Albrecht Dürer (1471 to 1528), Thomas Bewick (1753 to 1828) and William Blake (1757 to 1827). Blake's lifelong admiration was for Dürer whose metal engraving *Melancholia* was always to hand, as was Milton's *Il Penseroso*.

Between the two wars, the aesthetic philosophy of twentieth-century engraving was to be infused with new inspiration by the underground galleries of Lascaux and Altamira. There was very little of technical value to the engravers in concepts resulting in 'isms', which were devised and developed chiefly in the interests of painting and sculptural expression and which flowed continuously through the early part of the twentieth century. From the point of view of engraving the most important of the 'isms' were Impressionism, Cubism, Expressionism and also abstraction as seen in the Bauhaus and the School of Paris. All of these were, in fact, fundamental concepts. The reason why the engravers got so little from these various languages was that very few of the aesthetic concepts were workable in engraving because it is a discipline that is essentially linear and the engravers had to revert to the early high peaks of achievement in engraving to enable them to achieve a revival of man's first fundamental discipline.

No engraver can achieve success if his drawing is weak and inarticulate. This stricture influences the ebb and flow of engraving through time. Blake was a fine draughtsman and his work shows his love of linear emphasis and formal design. The linear dominance in his work lessens his influence in painting but not in engraving. It is the draughtsman in Blake that gives the sharp, accurate intensity to his images and poetry. His sensitivity was so highly developed that even the 'hack' work brought to him by well-meaning friends to help him financially was executed with a skill that made his superb draughtsmanship very evident.

As a boy, Blake wanted to be a painter but his father wished to ensure that his son could earn a reasonable living. Consequently, at the age of fourteen, in 1772, Blake was apprenticed for a period of seven years to the engraver Basire of the Society of Antiquaries. The nature of the training he received enabled Blake to create his unique illuminated and engraved books which are the most important part of his production in visual art. His unsurpassed intaglio engraving is seen in his *Book of Job* which appeared in 1825. At the end of his apprenticeship in 1778, Blake became a student in the newly-formed Royal Academy for a short time.

Like his contemporary Thomas Bewick, Blake realised the nature of the situation in commercial engraving and saw that the superb craft skill required in reproductive engraving had no spark of creative life. Therefore, as soon as independence and opportunity arrived, with the end of apprenticeship, both Blake and Bewick turned wood engraving back into the realm of art, using the white-line technique instead of the black-line which lingered on from the *formschneider* tradition. To

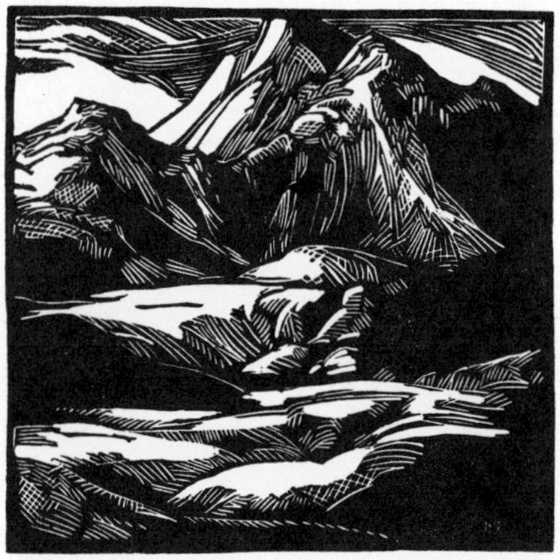

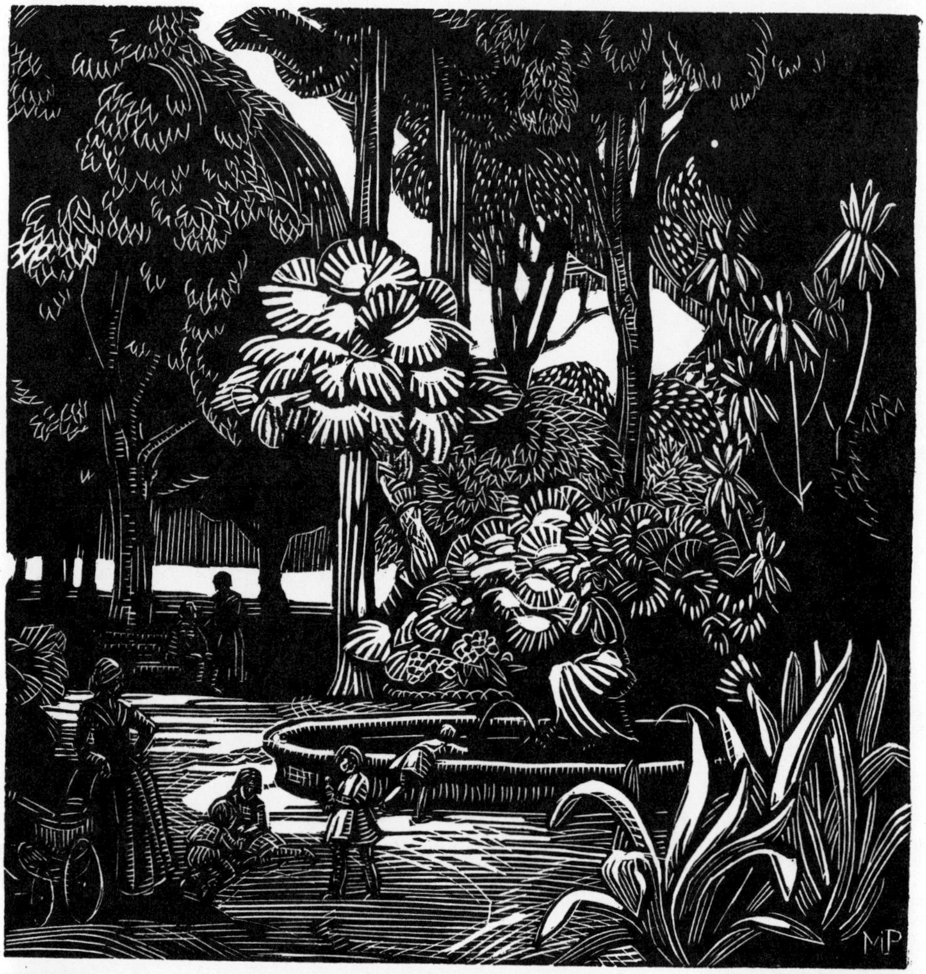

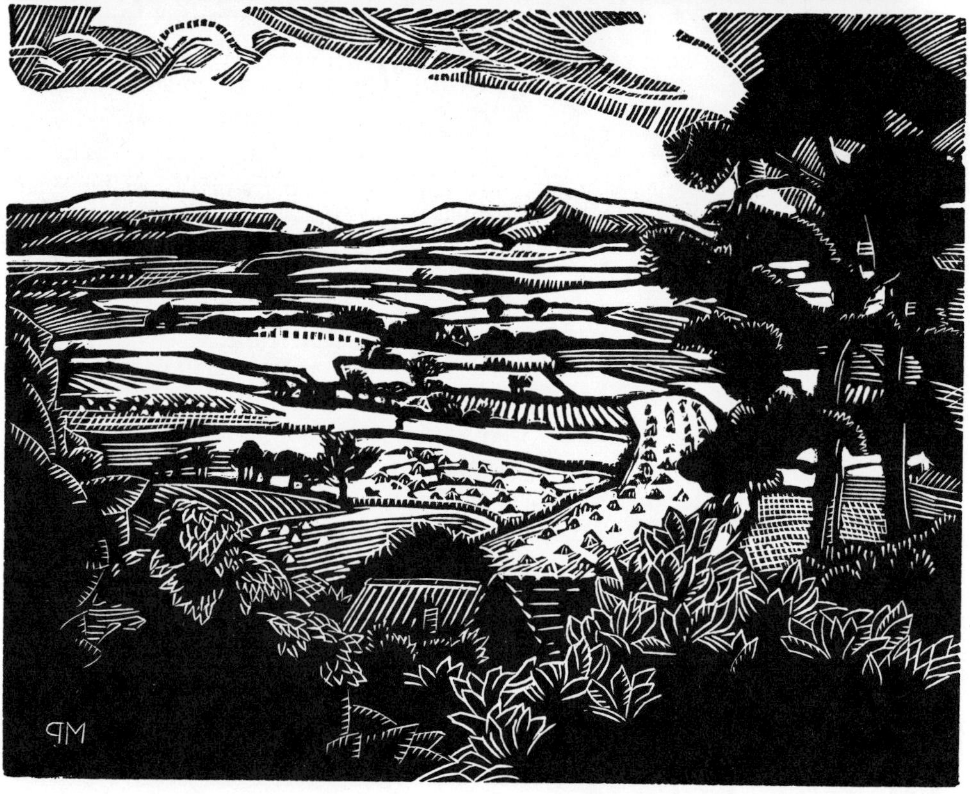

[131] Margaret Pilkington: *August*, 1924. 9.25 x 9.25cm

[132] Margaret Pilkington: *The Fountain, Burghese Gardens*, 1924. 12.0 x 12.75cm

[133] Margaret Pilkington: *The Cheshire Plain*, 1925. 12.75 x 10.25cm

[134] Margaret Pilkington: *Perugia*, 1925. 12.5 x 18.0cm

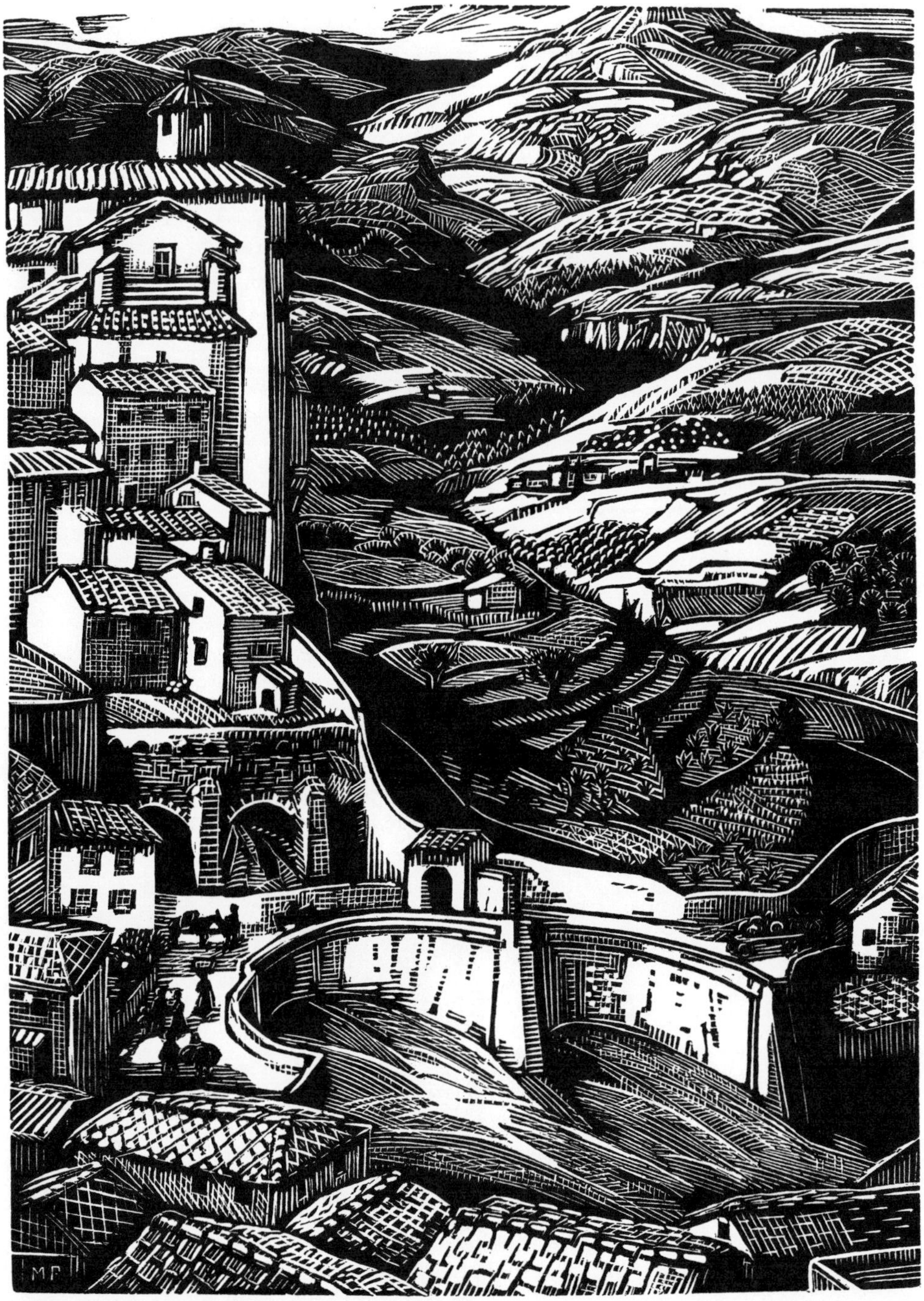

suggest, as some writers do, that engraving inhibited Blake as a painter is a misunderstanding of the nature of engraving as a fundamental discipline. It was the linear element of the persistent draughtsman which got in the way of Blake the painter, because as soon as he engraved he became a great artist, but he never attained this distinction as a painter.

Engraving released a very important part of Blake's creative genius and from existing literature it is evident how he stood in regard to the engraving of his time. The fashionable engravers of the period were Bartolozzi, Schiavonetti, Strange and Woollett, who were soft in style but polished; yet Blake scorned them all. The fact that he followed the black-line tradition and was concerned mainly with effects resembling drawing rather than engraving did not divert Blake from his purpose.

[135] Ethelbert White: Illustration from *The Story of my Heart*, 1923. 11.25 x 8.6cm

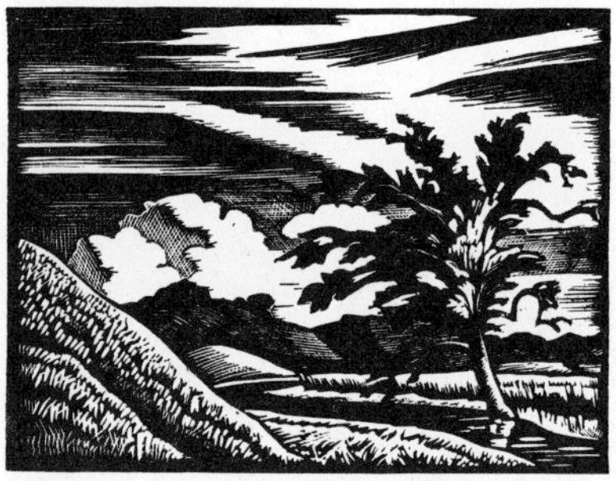

An outstanding example of pure poetry forged out of the conditions of 'hack' work is seen in Blake's achievement as a wood engraver in Thornton's edition of *Eclogues of Virgil* [84 to 87]. It is a simple and splendid instance of sheer genius transforming rudimentary craft into art.

Blake's seven-year apprenticeship to the engraver Basire was not an unbearable chore; the real burden of commercial art followed directly afterwards when he had to face the reality of earning a living. Basire sent Blake out for two years to draw antiquity for the Society and make drawings of monuments, buildings and the older churches. At this period Blake was able to study Gothic art which was to form his style in visual art. It was an influence which stayed with him throughout his life, though it was a language quite foreign to eighteenth-century art and made Blake at odds with the time in which he lived.

For Blake, the Gothic style was seen as the ultimate expression of the Christian religion. He said: 'Grecian is mathematical form; the Gothic is living form. Mathematical form is eternal in the reasoning memory; living form is eternal existence.'[1] The mathematical and geometric proportions were not clearly understood in Blake's time, and the monumentality of Renaissance art, so dear to

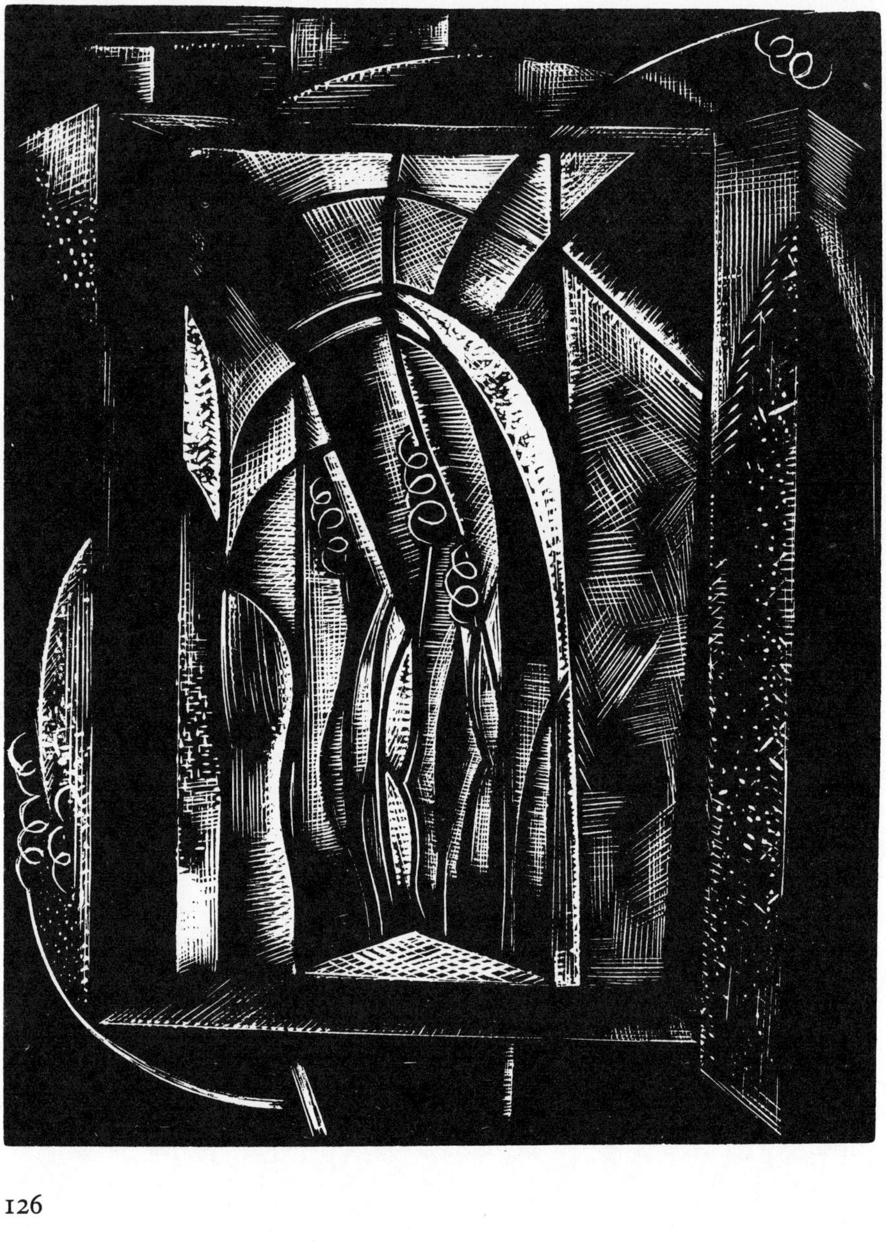

[136] Paul Nash: *Coronilla*, 1925. 9.1 x 11.7cm

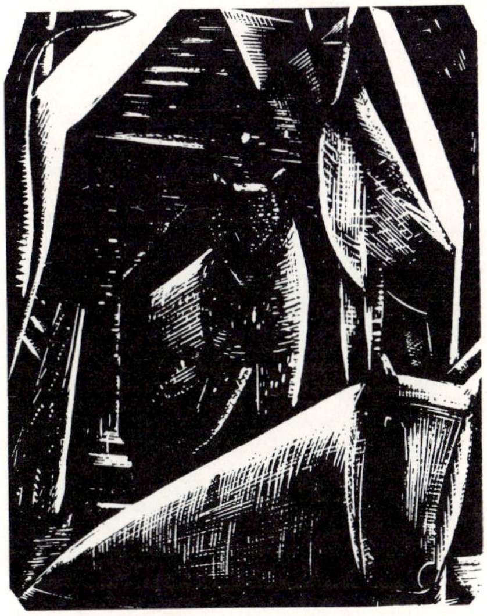

[137] Paul Nash: *Cattle and creeping thing* from *Genesis*, 1924. 8.9 x 11.5cm

Reynolds, was an anathema to Blake. He could not tolerate it. Had Basire been able to send him to Lascaux and Altamira to pursue antiquity a little further and see the art of man before geometry and mathematics were thought of, the impact of a non-secular religious art might well have changed the course which Blake followed. He was obsessed by colour. He used it romantically but failed to render colour as light and space. Had he been able to see the use of colour in Palaeolithic art in the Dordogne caves, he might well have been able to infuse his concept of light with more technical understanding. This had to be done eventually by Constable (1776 to 1837) and Turner (1775 to 1851) who were followed in their turn by the French Impressionists and ultimately by Cézanne (1839 to 1906).

Blake never related his linear emphasis of form with light. He started off with the black-line commercial *formschneider* tradition, completely anglicized because in the drawing schools of his time a black line meant little more than a division between two forms. However, in the few wood engravings for Thornton's *Virgil* he reversed his training in the black-line tradition and, perhaps in desperation, moved into the white-line – as did Bewick at Newcastle.

Both Blake and Bewick failed to develop the full potential of linear light beyond their immediate needs. However, Bewick carried the technical development further than Blake, though as small works of art Blake's wood engravings are inspired in their breadth of conception and simplicity of rendering. These small works are none the less responsible for an influence out of all proportion to their size. They were an inspiration to artist friends of Blake's later life and above all to Samuel Palmer (1805 to 1881) whose own individual art owes so much to these wood engravings.

In 1818, at the age of sixty-one, Blake was introduced to John Linnell (1792 to 1882). Linnell, then in his twenties, was a pupil of John Varley and a promising portrait and landscape painter with a distinctive style. He was a man of fierce and eccentric religious beliefs and an almost Biblical atmosphere surrounded his home life and family. Blake held his admiration and affection and it was largely through his friendship with Linnell that a group of young artists was to form around him in the latter part of his life. Of this group it was Samuel Palmer and Edward Calvert who were to take up wood engraving and produce significant works in the white-line technique.

In 1824 when he was half-way through his illustrations to *Job*, Blake was introduced to Samuel Palmer who was then nineteen years old. When Palmer went to visit Blake at Fountain Court, Strand, London, he used to kiss the threshold when he arrived.

The friendship between Blake and Palmer lasted for some two years when it was overshadowed by a breakdown in Palmer's health. By 1826 he was living at Shoreham near Sevenoaks in Kent. He remained there for about seven years, living in a cottage named Waterhouse, where he played the violin and sang. Eventually, music gave way to visual art and with Edward Calvert and George Richmond, Palmer formed the Shoreham Group. On only one occasion did William Blake join the Group at his friend's home in Shoreham.

One wood engraving by Palmer is called *Harvest under a Crescent Moon* [88]. Several drawings and paintings of this subject were made which show Palmer's studies of this hilly landscape taken from different perspective viewpoints and eye levels. This engraving by Palmer was not printed until 1920 when five prints were taken from the block. There are no known earlier impressions.

Blake's wood engravings had a lasting influence on his friend Edward Calvert (1799 to 1883), a native of Appledore in Devonshire. Calvert studied under James

[138] Paul Nash: *The sun and the moon* from *Genesis*, 1924. 8.9 x 11.5cm

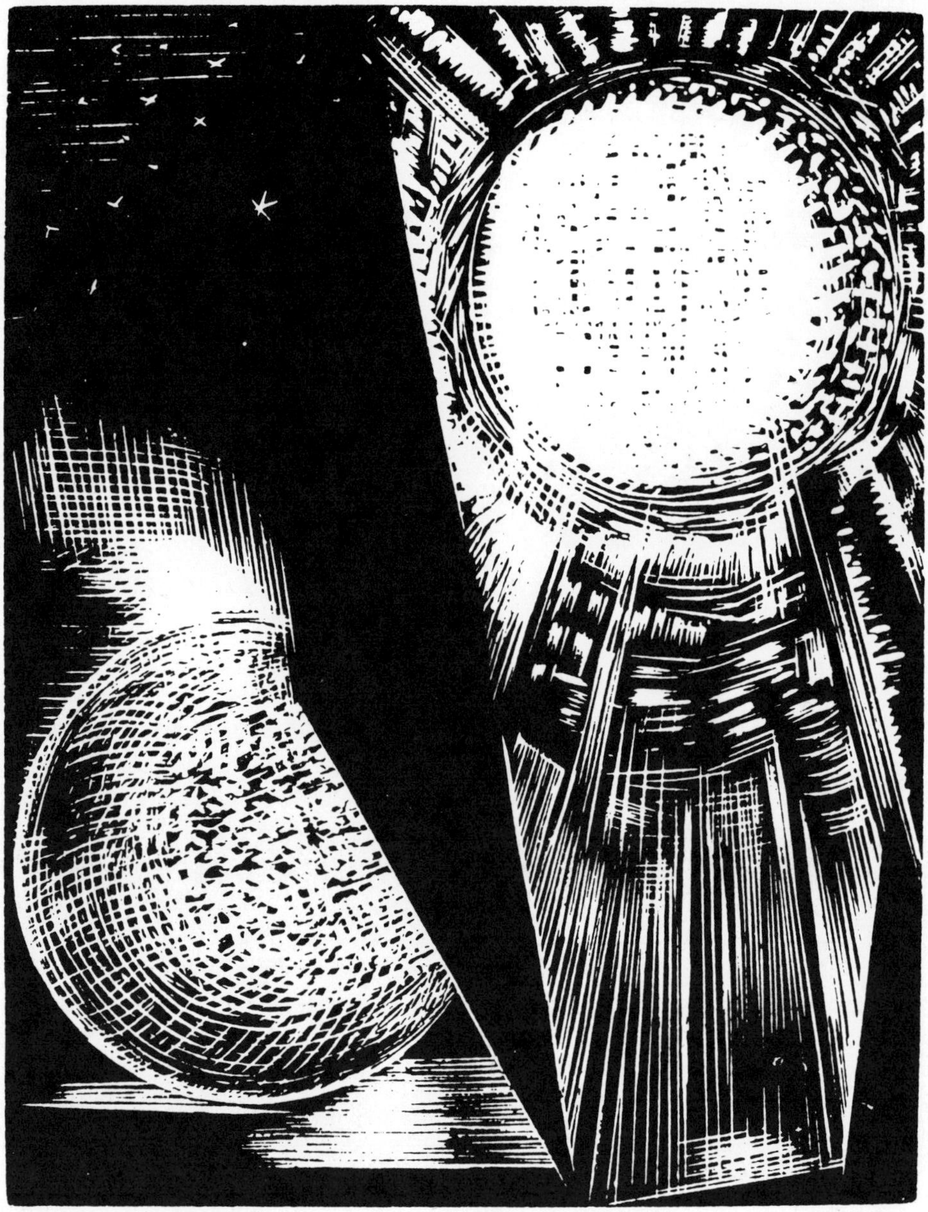

Ball and A. B. Johns of Plymouth and later he moved to London to become a student at the Royal Academy Schools. He was also a friend of George Richmond who was the youngest member of the Shoreham Group. Later the Group was joined by the painters Henry Walter (1790 to 1849) and Francis Oliver Finch (1802 to 1862). Calvert's first painting was exhibited at the Royal Academy in 1825.

The work of Blake gave rise to a pastoral school of romantic landscape art characterized by a sensuous tenderness of form, religious revivalism and rustic simplicity, making a unique contribution to British art. The spirit of the Shoreham Group flourished for a short period, but creative energy left the members as they grew older. For a time the Group was in a state of communal ecstasy of primitive Christian vision.

Calvert's block for the *Ploughmen* [89] was originally lettered 'Seen in the kingdom of heaven by vision through Jesus Christ our Saviour' but it was also known under the title of 'Christian ploughing the last furrow of life'. His block for the *Cyder Feast*, engraved in 1828, was also originally lettered in religious terms: 'Edwd. Calvert inven.et. sculp. by the Gift of God in Christ'.

[139] Paul Nash: *The division of light from the darkness* from *Genesis*, 1924. 8.9 x 11.5cm

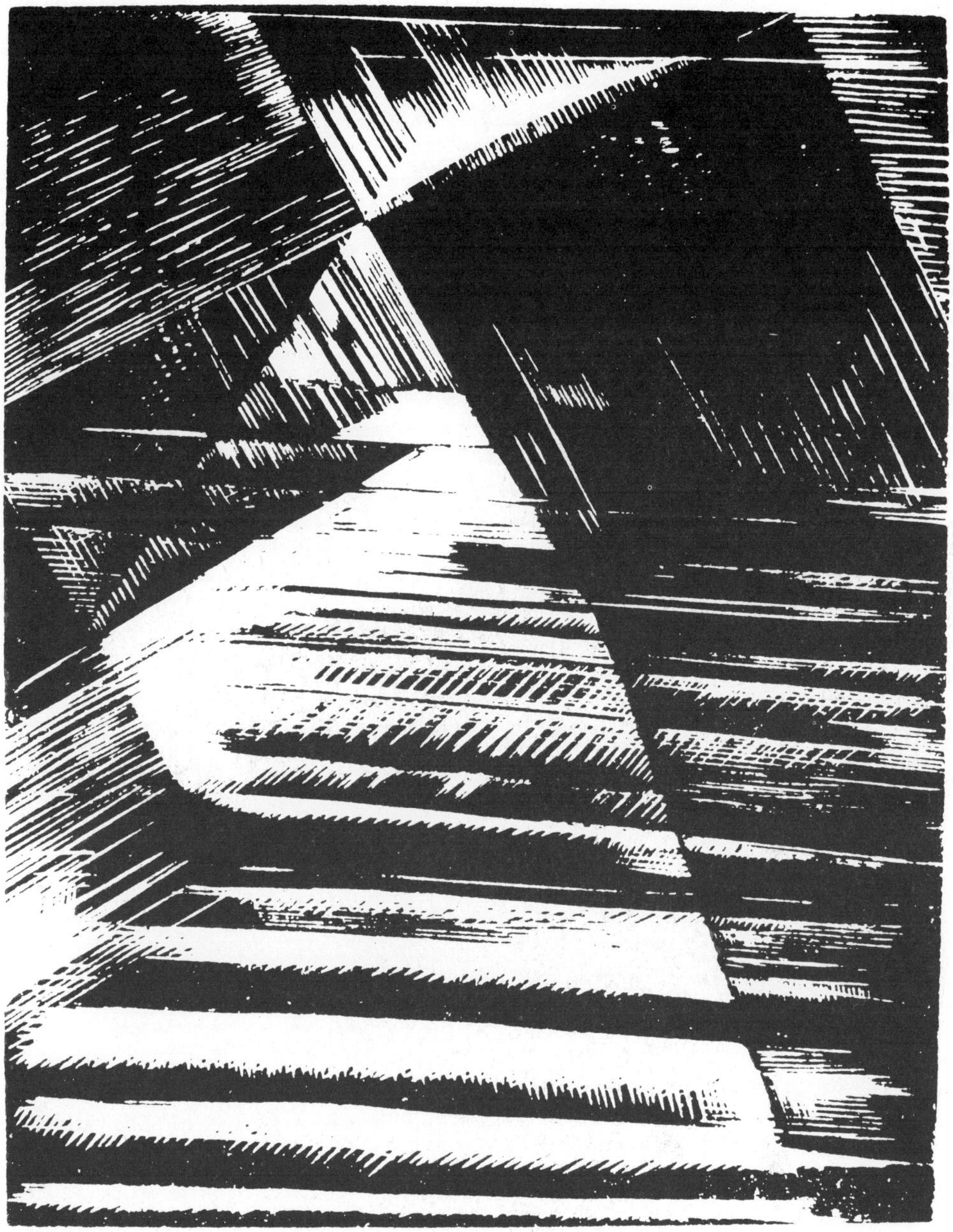

In producing romantic art based upon religious concepts, the Shoreham Group represented an artists' circle the like of which was not to be seen again until Eric Gill formed his group at Ditchling in the 1920s.

Palmer began etching in about 1850 and ten out of thirteen etchings produced by him were done in Kensington. These etchings were to prove a fruitful influence upon the youthful Graham Sutherland. Palmer's work finally ceased with the break-up of his family and his failing health. Because of adverse circumstances and the difficulty of earning a living, his total output was small but it was of very high quality. His contribution to British romantic art is secure in history.

Thomas Bewick outlived Blake by one year. These two influential engravers are not known to have met each other; Blake lived in London and liked it whereas Bewick hated it and loved his native Newcastle. Wordsworth wrote in a lyrical ballad, 'Oh that the genius of Bewick were mine'. Charlotte Brontë at sixteen years

[140] Edward Gordon Craig:
Robinson Crusoe, 1925. 9.25 x 11.25cm

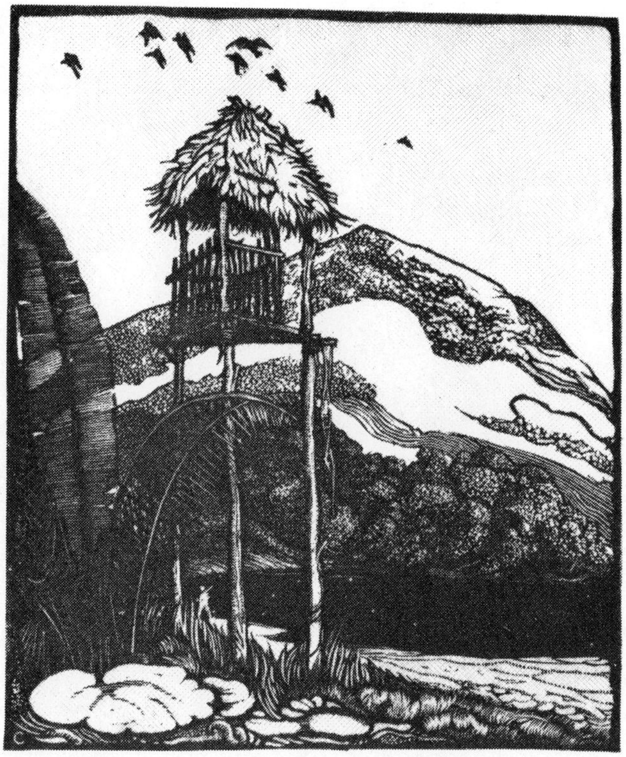

of age also wrote a poem about Bewick, and the book which Jane Eyre found so exciting at the beginning of her story was Bewick's *History of British Birds*.[2]

Thomas Bewick (1753 to 1828) was four years senior in age to Blake. Though now a famous national figure, Blake failed to achieve recognition as a poet and artist during his lifetime. Bewick, however, not only achieved a remarkable reputation in his lifetime but has become even more famous in the twentieth century. As an artist Bewick had two clear-cut qualities: a remarkable consistency of form and a lucid and concise language based upon the white line of wood engraving. In his long working life he was industrious and his singleness of vision was devoted to the perfection of skill rather than to extending his art; in his case art appears as a by-product of application and faith.

Bewick attracted the attention of Thomas Carlyle (1797 to 1881) and John Ruskin (1819 to 1900). Carlyle read Bewick's *Memoir* published in 1862 and described the artist in a letter he wrote to his friend Ruskin. Ruskin saw the value of the draughtsman and engraver and recommended the *Memoir* for his drawing students. In writing to Carlyle, John Ruskin commented that the only qualification of his admiration was that Bewick, untrained, unhelped, but also unharmed, could draw the poor, but not the rich; he could draw the pig but not a Venus – because he was not a gentleman. Ruskin regretted a little Bewick's love of ugliness which 'is in the English soul, to be found in Hogarth and Cruikshank'.[3]

In some of Bewick's works, the animals are crude and awkward and unrelated to their environment. This shows a lack of self-criticism and an unsureness of critical aesthetic values. It is a very easy thing for an accomplished artist to fall in love with a subject and become so completely submerged by it that he does not attain his full potential. However, this is a happier situation than that of the artist whose ambitions are in excess of his talent.

Writers have blurred the edges between Bewick's important technical achievement and his value and influence as an artist. Today his stylistic influence is

[141] Edward Gordon Craig: *The Ghost of Hamlet's Father*, 1925.

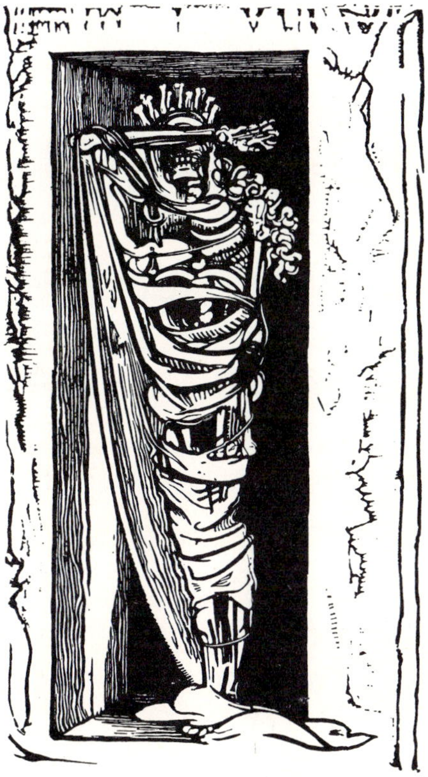

considerable among book illustrators and less so among other artists. He is remarkable in that he reversed the whole process of wood engraving from the predominantly black-line *formschneider* commercial reproductive tradition to the white-line.

Bewick made the very first move to restore the art of wood engraving to the status of creative art. However, he was not the first artist to use end-grained boxwood; the first book known to have been illustrated with end-grained blocks using the black-line *formschneider* technique is Howell's *Medulla Historiae Anglicanae* of 1712.

Bewick was an exceptionally accurate artist and had an intense interest in materials, texture and light. It is likely that it was his interest in the illumination of a surface to disclose details of its structure and texture that led him to develop his white-line technique. In using white line, Bewick had to be aware of the behaviour of light to a far greater extent than those engravers using black line. If an engraving of Ricketts or of Shannon is examined it will be noted that the engraver could only suggest white light in an artificial manner – a difficulty encountered by all who used the black-line technique.

In Bewick's three little landscapes *Kite flying* [93], *The Farmyard* [95] and *The Angler* [99] he illuminates all the forms with light. This important aspect of Bewick escaped comment from both Carlyle and Ruskin but it was to be appreciated fifty years later by the French Impressionists and 120 years later by the white-line school of the twentieth century – even so, this quality in Bewick's work is still not fully understood. He thought in terms of reproducing the effect of light and of how much to cut away and how much to leave. In so doing he was controlling the total distribution of the light available.

In using white line, Bewick has the double advantage of texture creation, by its being naturally drawn in the white line, with the addition of a natural field of texture arising from the black area left between closely-spaced white line. His creative use of these advantages has fascinated engravers ever since. Most of his engraving occupies an area of only a few square centimetres. Obviously he had no notion that in the twentieth century his work would become fashionable and would be enlarged photographically to dimensions of several square metres to be used as murals in coffee bars and as backdrops for window displays in the large stores. The accuracy of detail in these small engravings is such that even in a photographic enlargement of considerable size, the essential spirit and detail of the engraving remains accurate.

[142] Eric Gill: Illustration from *The Song of Songs*, 1925. 9.5 x 6.5cm

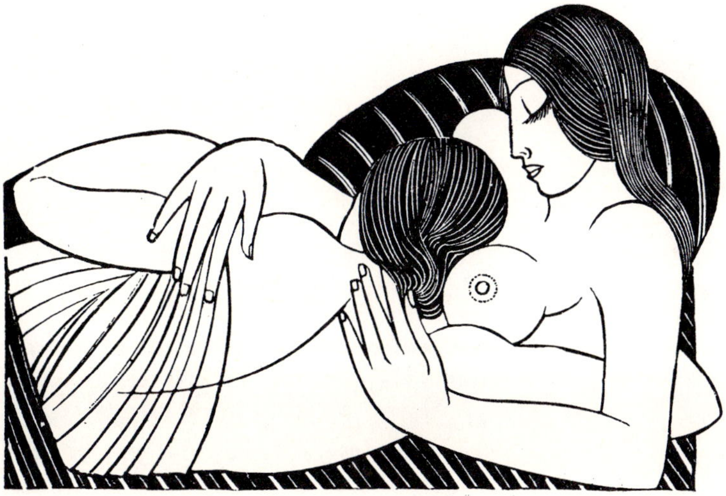

He was one of eight children of a farmer and was born at Cherryburn House at Ovingham in Northumberland; a part of the old building stands today. His old shop in St Nicholas Churchyard still exists with his name scratched in a window. A tablet records the shop's history.

In the eighteenth century Newcastle was a centre for engraving and this skill was highly regarded. On 1 October 1767, Bewick was apprenticed to a Newcastle engraver named Ralph Beilby whose work covered a very wide range of items: ornaments, tail-pieces, diagrams and rough designs for magazines and book illustration. In Beilby's business they also engraved all sorts of objects. The Beilby family had been glass artists for several generations and they were instrumental in developing enamelled glass in the eighteenth and early nineteenth centuries. Bewick records quite a lot of information on the Beilby glass artists in his *Memoir*. He produced a number of books, the most famous of which are *General History of Quadrupeds* and *History of British Birds*. His largest engraving is *The Wild Bull at Chillingham* [395]. It was a commissioned work and Bewick considered it his finest engraving. A smaller version of the Chillingham bull appears in *General History of Quadrupeds*. Bewick's largest engraving has another claim to fame because of the accident that befell the block. He left the block near a

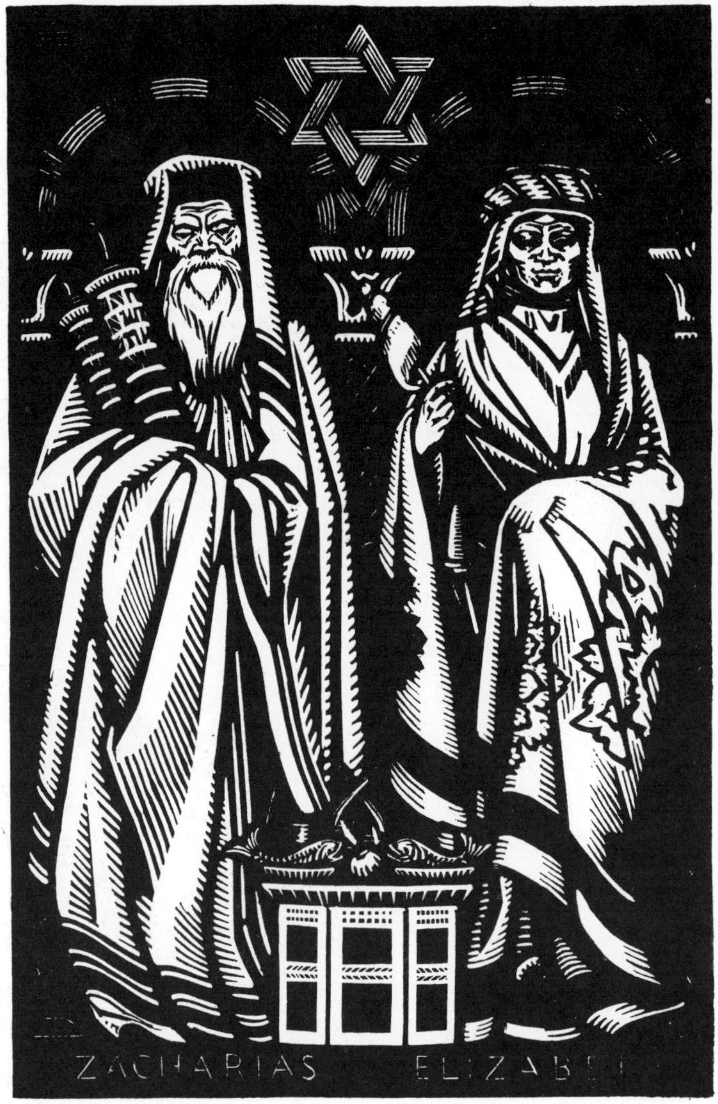

[143] Noel Rooke: *The Visitation*, 1925. 9.5 x 13.0cm

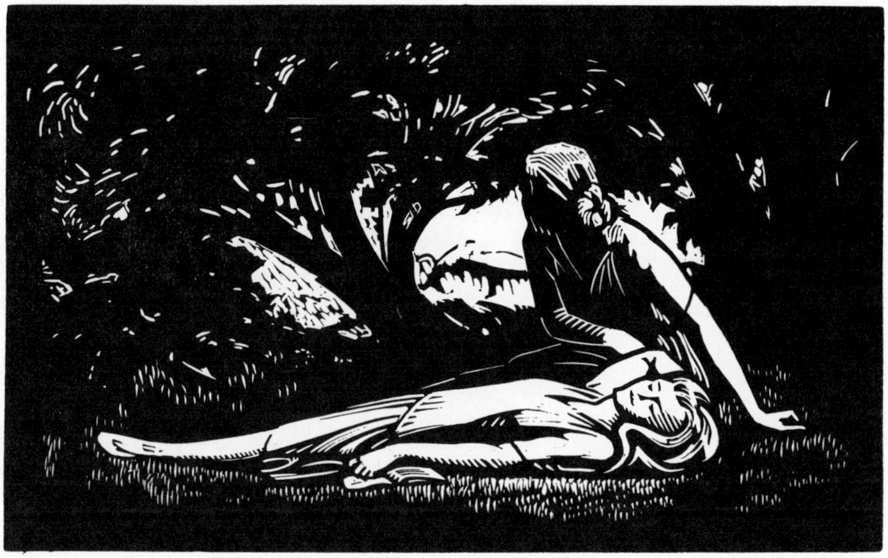

[144] Noel Rooke: *Woodland*, 1925. 14.0 x 8.5cm

window in his workshop over the weekend and by Monday morning the sun's rays had split the wood due to the sharp rise in temperature during the day and a rapid fall at night. Fortunately, the block was able to be clamped together, fixed in a gun-metal frame and further impressions taken. The few prints taken before the disaster have become rare collectors' items.

In 1799 Bewick was commissioned by a menagerie proprietor to do an engraving 19cm by 13.5cm of a lion, an elephant, a tiger and a zebra. These engravings are large by Bewick's standards and are by no means his best; indeed they are rather clumsy and fall far below the quality of illustration in the Chillingham bull engraving. The animals are not fused with the environment and background and, in the case of the elephant in particular, the relationship between the two elements is naïve. It is difficult to understand how Bewick could have approved the engraving and it it likely that the background was cut by another engraver. In the case of the lion, the whole is unmistakably the work of Bewick, although the relationship between the lion and its environment still leaves a lot to be desired. It is in his larger works that Bewick's limitations are apparent.

Appreciation of an unusual kind was given to Bewick's work in 1843 when William Yarrell, writing in a *History of British Birds* recorded: 'Among a considerable number, which had been forwarded to the London markets for sale, I was fortunate enough to select five examples of the new species . . . I described them in a paper read before the Linnean Society and proposed to call it Bewick's Swan, thus devoting it to the memory of one whose beautiful and animated delineation of subjects in natural history entitle him to this tribute.'[4]

Two of Bewick's students, Jackson and Chatto, wrote an authoritative historical treatise on wood engraving published in 1839.[5] In this book the authors wrote that Bewick is 'said to have invented a graver with a fine groove at the point which enabled him to cut the outlines by a single operation.' There is little doubt that he used this tool in the engraving of *The Old English Hound* [92].

The nineteenth century saw the rise of an increasing demand upon the publishers of books, periodicals and newspapers for the rapid production of illustrations, the need for pictorial news being particularly pressing. Publishers had a choice of two techniques: that of engraving on metal or that of engraving on wood, as was being

[145] Leon Underwood: *Co-Eternal*, 1925. 9.3 x 14.5cm

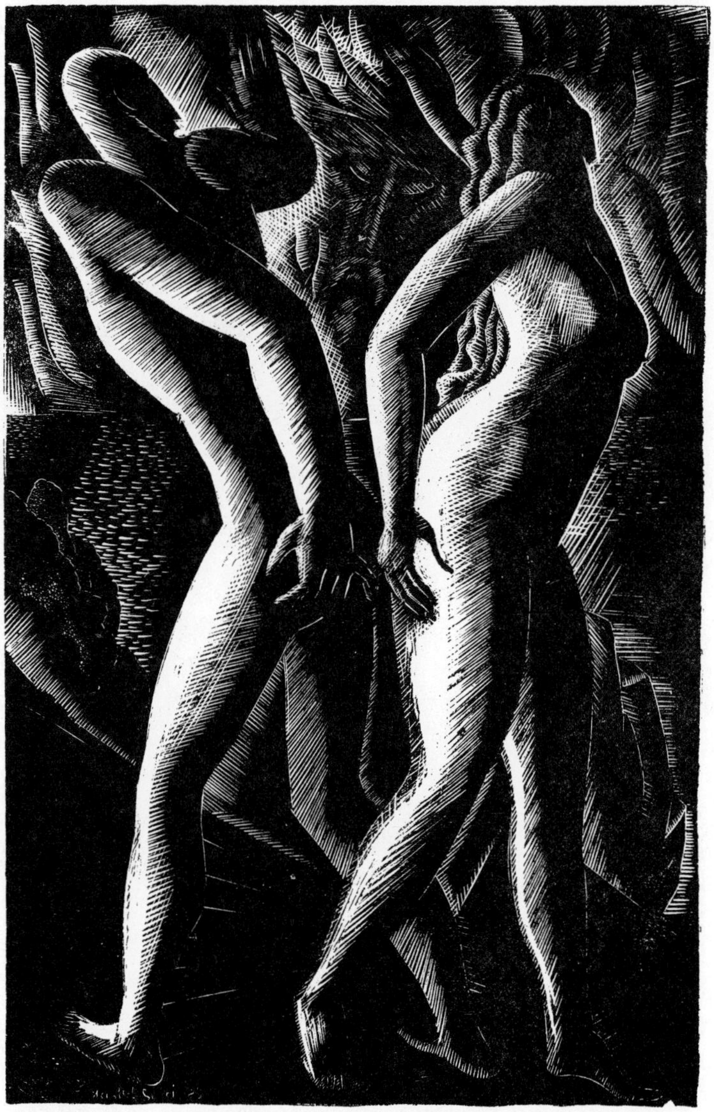

so brilliantly demonstrated by Bewick. Wood had the advantage over metal because it was easy to repair or replace – an adjustment not so easily made in metal. Bewick's skill in producing graphic detail in engraving on end-grained boxwood indicated to the publishers the potential of this technique, though it was cost and time taken to produce an illustration that finally decided the matter.

The process for the mass production of books, periodicals, and newspapers in the nineteenth century was a relief technique. Despite the invention of Karl Klic in photogravure and of Alios Senefelder in lithography, methods of printing from intaglio and planographic surfaces had not been developed to include books, periodicals or newspapers, though the separate printing of copper-plate engravings by the intaglio process was seen in book production. Commercial demands in mass printing of illustrations had two essential requirements: clarity of image and speed of production. Wood engraving met the first of these requirements thus the method of engraving used by Bewick became the principal technique employed for the production of illustrations and the era of commercial reproductive engraving began.

It was ironical that Bewick should train many of the commercial craftsmen in his workshop in Newcastle. Among his students and apprentices were his son Robert Elliot Bewick, his younger brother John Bewick, Charlton Nesbit, Luke

Clennell, George Gray, John Thurston, Robert Johnson, William Temple, William Harvey, Henry Hole, Henry White and a man named Anderson. Despite the fact that the training given by Bewick imparted a high degree of craftsmanship, it could not develop creative ability where it did not exist and none of Bewick's pupils emerged as an artist.

The second requirement of mass production – that of speed – could not be met without a substantial division of labour in order to get the engraving done rapidly. This latter point was of urgent consideration because of pictorial news; the time between the event and the publication in print was very important.

Thus, the division of labour in producing an engraving was inevitable but it demanded that the engravers had to subject themselves to anonymity. In the provision of a labour force to meet the demand, Bewick's pupils were invaluable

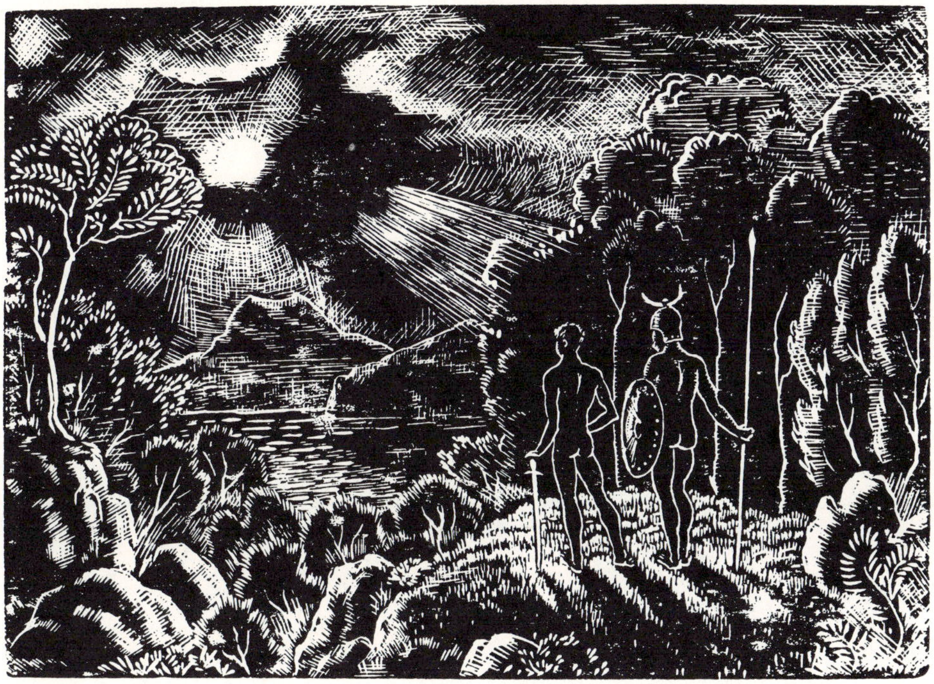

[146] Ralph Chubb: Illustration from *A Fable of Love and War*, 1925. 12.75 x 9.0cm

because they could also instruct others in the requisite craft skill and help to maintain the number of personnel needed. Eventually, all of Bewick's students moved to London where they quickly lost sight of his white line and employed the black line of the *formschneider* engraver.

The speed by which illustrations could be produced was increased substantially when, in 1860, Charles Wells devised a method of bolting together small blocks of wood in order to provide a large printing image. This method permitted an engraving to be made up of two, four, six or even eight pieces, thus a single illustration could be divided between a number of engravers. On completion of the individual block, the separate engravings were bolted together and then finished by a senior engraver in such a manner that the joins did not show in the final printed impression. This technique was developed to a very high degree of craftsmanship [102 and 103].

The skill of commercial wood engraving reached its zenith about the time of the Great Exhibition of 1851. Thereafter it slowly declined until it was finally eclipsed between 1885 and 1890 when the zincograph, based on an invention of Firmin Gillot in 1850 and developed by his son Charles in 1872, came into increasing use.

Following the work of Niepce (1765 to 1833) and Daguerre (1787 to 1857), a successful process of photography was evolved by William Henry Fox Talbot (1800 to 1877) whose Calotype process can be said to have been the foundation of press photography. The increasing use of the camera following Talbot's invention eventually removed the last vestige of wood engraving from the commercial scene.

The pressure of production increased during the later days of the nineteenth century and this pressure has been maintained, especially in the field of periodicals and newspapers. An example is seen in the production of *The Engineer*, a weekly publication which continues to serve the engineering profession. About 1870 this magazine required ten days in which to achieve publication; today, a photograph can be accepted one day before its appearance in the magazine. There is no place for the artist wood engraver within this industrial framework.

[147] Eric Ravilious: *Sussex Church*, 1926.

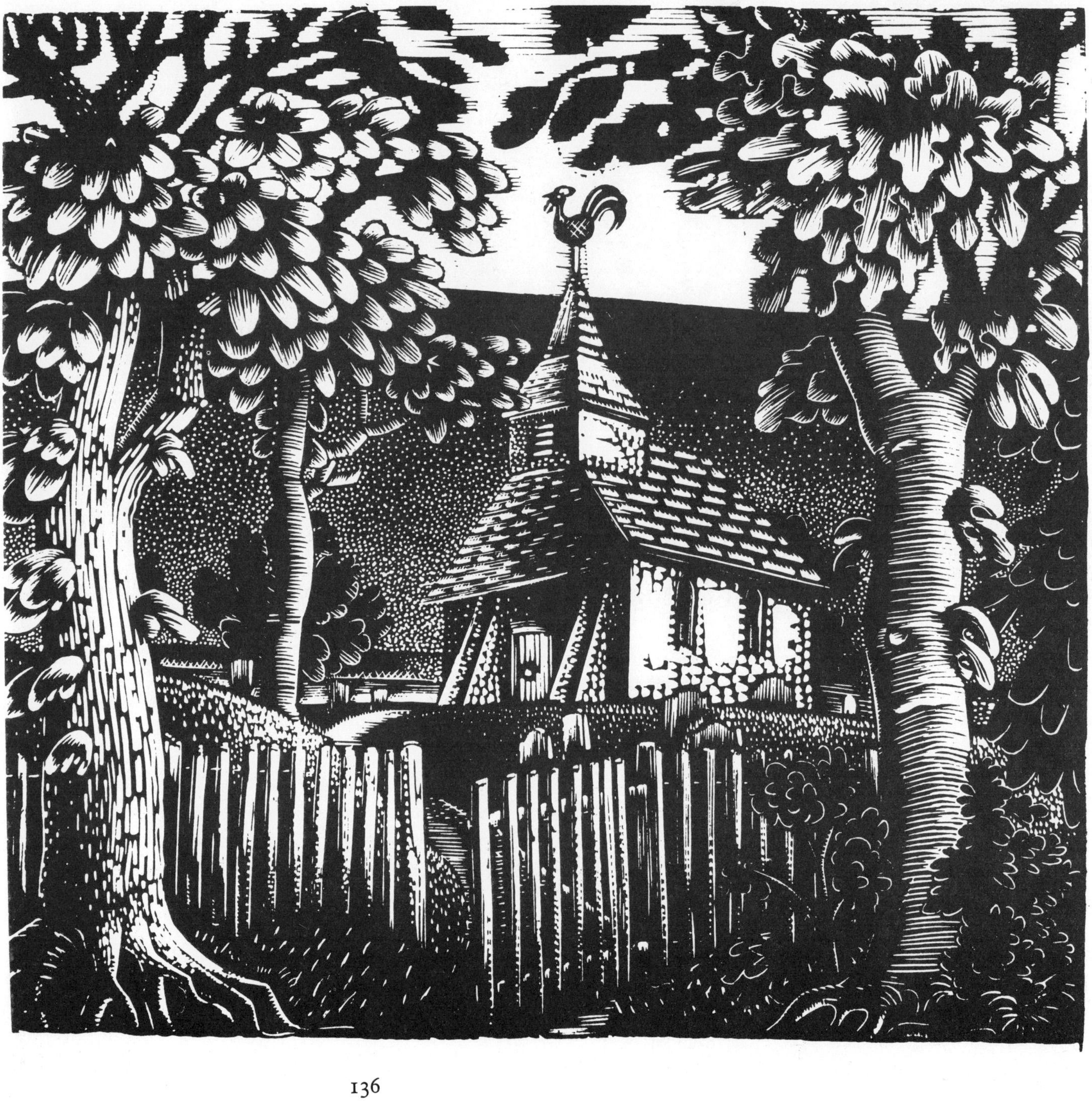

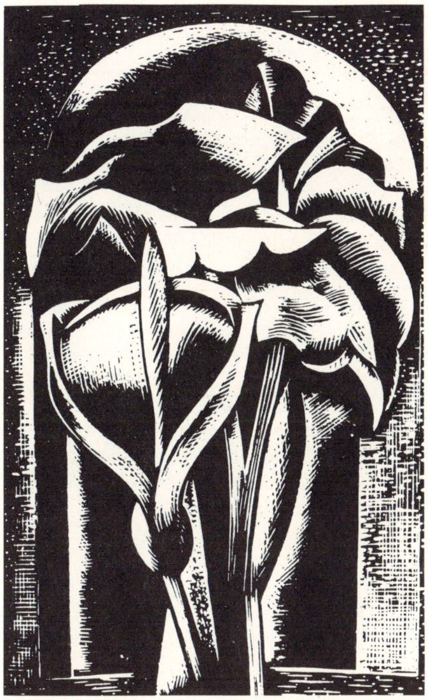

[148] Paul Nash: *Design of Flowers*, 1926. 9.5 x 15.25cm

Joseph Cundall writing in his book of 1895 *A Brief History of Wood Engraving from its Invention*, states: 'Owing to the invention of various mechanical processes, and the perfection to which photography has risen, the art of wood engraving would seem to be in danger of becoming extinct. This is by no means the real case, for the brilliant band of wood engravers which has formed in America still continues to give us excellent examples of their skill, and especially we may mention the inimitable copies of paintings by the old masters by Timothy Coles, whose rendering of Paul Potter's *Young Bull* excites our warmest admiration.'[6]

Discussing the English scene he writes: 'In England, under the influence of Mr William Morris and his followers, a revival of this interesting craft as practised in the fifteenth century has been set on foot in some of the Schools of Art – notably at Birmingham where in 1893 the students issued a *Book of Carols* illustrated with original designs, some of which were cut by the students themselves. This revival of the earlier and purer methods of engraving coupled with a careful study of the possibilities of the art, may be taken as a sign that by no means the last chapter on the history of engraving on wood has yet been written.'

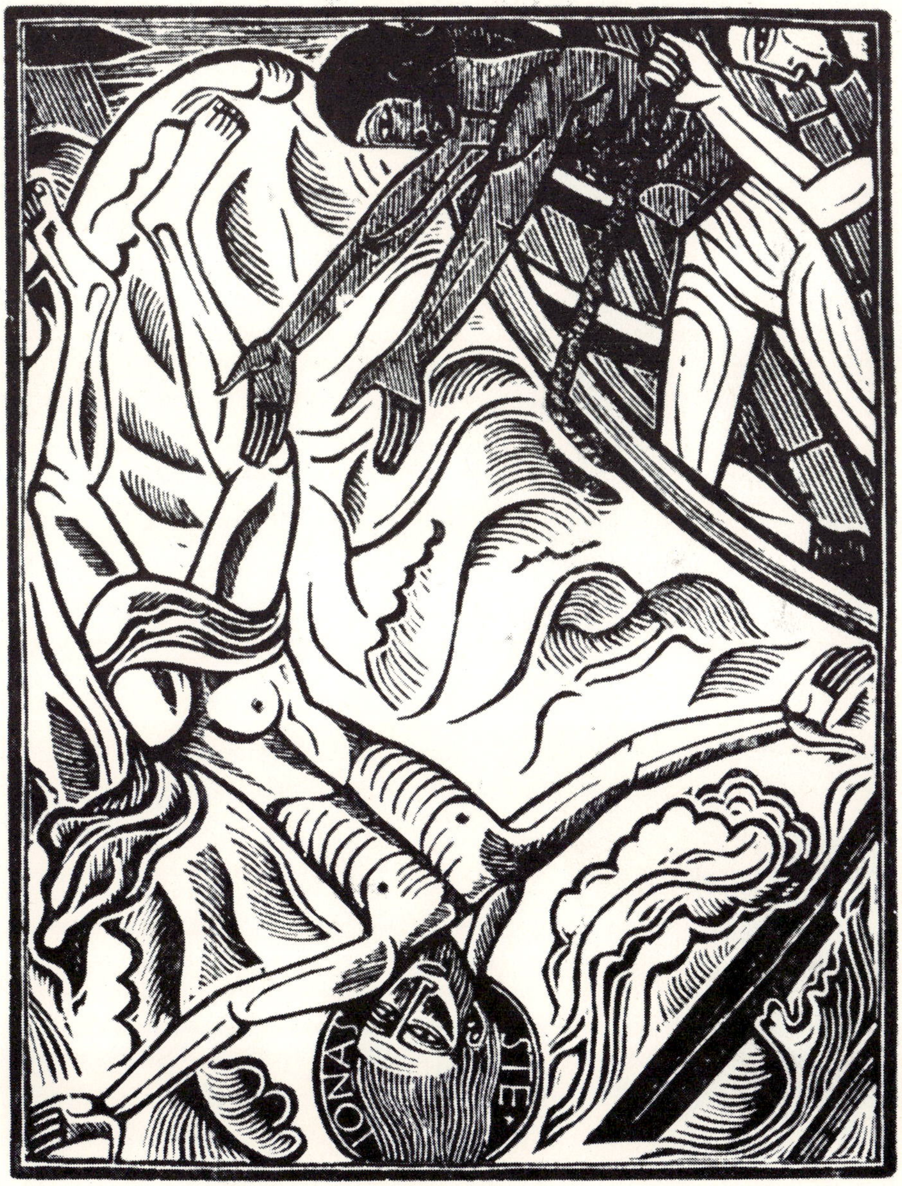

[149] David Jones: *Jonah* from *The Book of Jonah*, 1926.

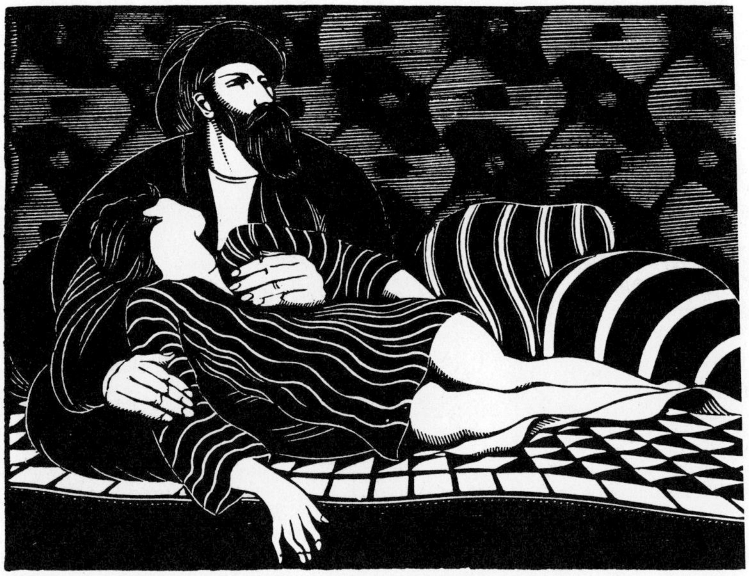

[150] Robert Gibbings: *Red Wine*, 1926. 10.2 x 7.5cm

In American wood engraving and magazine production a bitter controversy had broken out between the old and very senior artist wood engraver W. J. Linton and the young engravers Timothy Coles and Henry Marsh. An attack was published by Linton in 1879 in the *Atlantic Monthly.*

The editor of *Scribners Magazine* wrote in defence of the two young engravers: 'But from the moment Scribners began to avail itself of the art of photographic pictures upon the wood, a great development took place because that presented at once to the public the work of the best artists. The men who hitherto had been shut away from us could draw and paint their pictures which could then be photographed upon the block; and the pictures themselves could all be preserved, so that as the engraver cut away his picture on the block, he had always the original before him, not only as a guide, but as an inspirer.'

For a young man, Coles's work for Scribners was brilliant and he was unwittingly caught up in the pressures of his time. Whilst pursuing goodness, he lacked the wisdom and experience to see more than one move ahead and was in fact the very means through which creative engraving was to die completely. Coles and Linton were at variance in their opinions of the dominating illustration requirements and the situation between the two men could not be resolved.

Linton was defending the art of engraving as a fundamental discipline whereas Coles and the younger American engravers were caught up in the world of the facsimile. They were also at cross purposes with the aesthetics of form. Had the subject been understood as its presence in the world of art demanded, the sad argument would not have arisen.

In an issue of *Scribners Magazine* the editor wrote of Linton: ' . . . his *Atlantic* paper contains no word of praise for the exquisite work that has been done by Mr Henry Marsh; indeed, not even the slightest mention of what can fairly be called the greatest single engraving enterprise in the world – Mr Marsh's woodcuts in Harris's *Insects Injurious to Vegetation.*' In the *Atlantic Monthly* Linton replied: 'There is not a line left'.

The demands on the resources of the craft engravers caused individual commercial engravers to develop skills other than those which rightly belonged to their medium. For one thing the creative artists whose eyes and hand recorded the event or scene, were naturally not willing to have their individualities and techniques blunted and sometimes slaughtered by the engravers. Therefore, the engravers

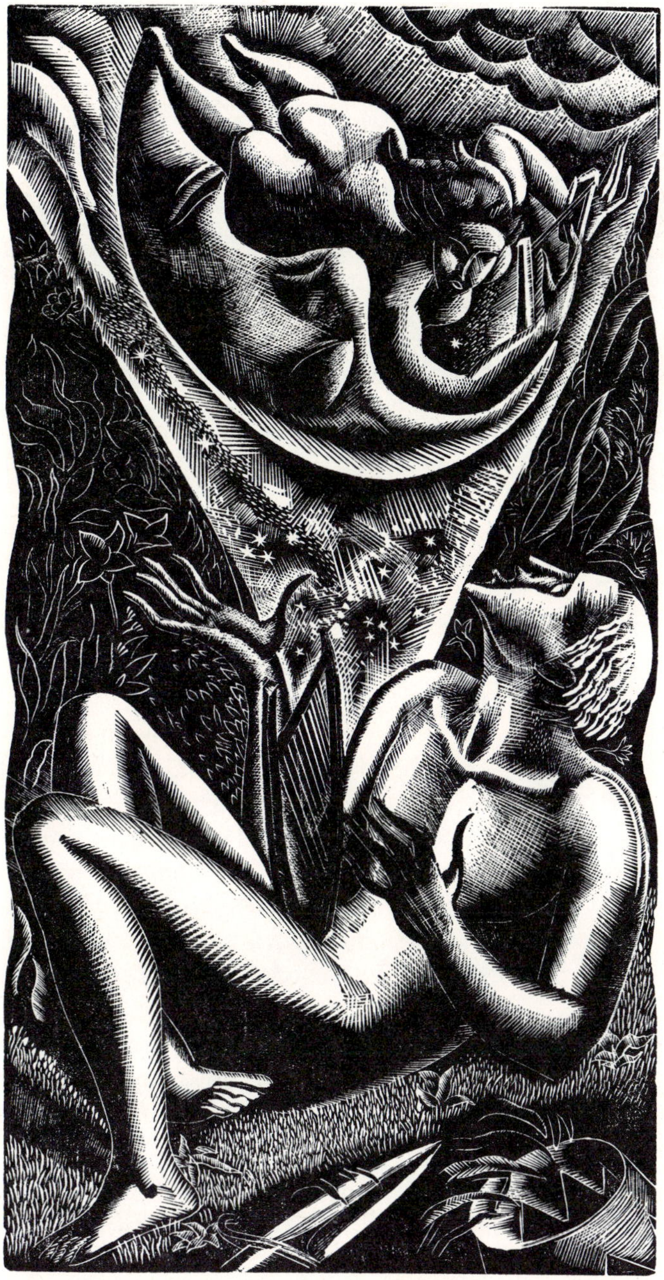

[151] Leon Underwood: Frontispiece from *The Music Behind the Moon*, 1926. 8.75 x 17.0cm

turned their skills to facsimile interpretations of the artists' drawings, which for press work were rendered in pen line and the degree of their success and skill must be admitted [55 and 60].

The commercial engravers were interpreters, working in a period when the standards of draughtsmanship were very high. If the artist decided to live by commissions from publishers he had to acquire confidence of expression through the exacting, uncompromising and revealing pen. This forming factor is so often overlooked in their critical evaluation. However, few of the artists of the time had much conception of the sense and limitations of wood engraving, and drew as the spirit willed them. Nevertheless, all the artists expected the commercial engravers to produce a facsimile copy of every penstroke and took it for granted that an acceptable rendering of their wash drawings would appear. Though artists and engravers seemed to have entrenched themselves firmly in the basic forms of large-

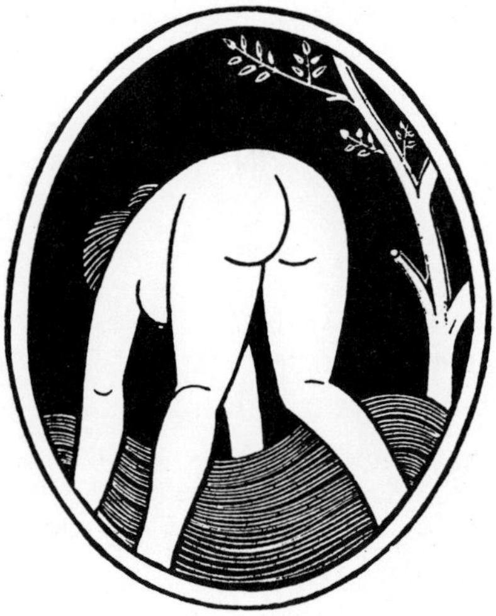

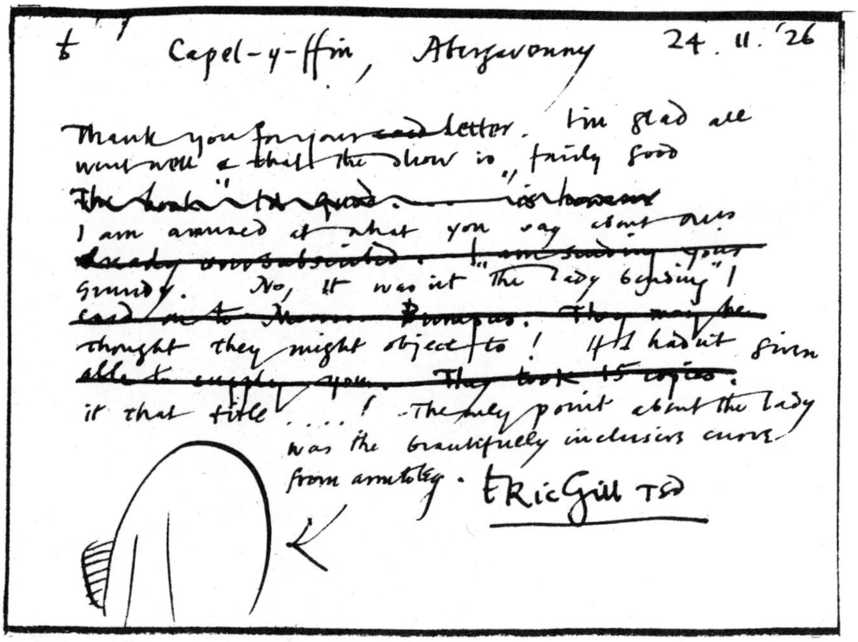

[152] Eric Gill: *Woman bending*, 1926. 4.8 x 6.0cm

[153] Eric Gill: Postcard to Margaret Pilkington, 1926

scale illustration, it was only a question of time before their manual skills were threatened by the application of the new technology of photography.

The commercial engravers' immediate reply to the new development was a stiffening of their ranks and attempts to attain even greater skill. Multiple tools were brought out which would cut several fine white lines at one time; these tools were made of an exceptionally tough steel by Rubin of Paris. Only a small number were made and most of them have now found their way into the kits of the creative engravers of the twentieth century or to museums. Modern versions of these tools bear no comparison in fineness and cutting qualities with those made by Rubin. With the improved tools the commercial engravers aimed at fascimile reproductions of the newly-introduced photographs; to show their skill in handling tone or variations of grey they even 'interpreted' paintings.

Thus, in the nineteenth century, the art of wood engraving lost all its identity in the anonymity of reproductive engraving and even today it is too frequently regarded as a disreputable ghost. It should be remembered that wood engraving was part of commerce and also that it contributed substantially to education in that the school books of the nineteenth century relied upon the skills of the reproductive engraver for their illustrations. Although the nineteenth century ended with a disappearance of creative wood engraving, the twentieth century started with an attempt to revive the skill as a creative art.

The architect William Richard Lethaby (1857 to 1931) designed and built the Central School of Arts and Crafts in Southampton Row, London. The school was completed in 1908 and still functions today under the title of the Central School of Art and Design. In its original form, the Central School played a major role in the revival of wood engraving and print making as a creative art form.

In many respects Lethaby anticipated Walter Gropius's concepts of the twentieth-century Bauhaus where art, craft and the machine were to be eventually resolved into a single concept. Lethaby did not believe that genius was the answer to better design but thought, 'Art should be everywhere. It cannot exist in isolation or one man thick: it must be a thousand men thick. . . . It is only by bettering the whole body of building that we shall be able to raise the summit.'[7]

As both Principal of the Central School of Arts and Crafts from 1896 to 1911 and Professor of Design at the Royal College of Art from 1900 to 1918, he was to bring together a group of thinkers and artists who were to become famous. Lethaby was the first Professor of Design to be appointed at the Royal College and he was also Surveyor to Westminster Abbey. As a pioneer of new developments he, more than anyone, interpreted the concepts and philosophy of Ruskin and Morris to the students of his time.

As far back as 1888 when the Arts and Crafts Society held its first exhibition, artists and craftsmen were fighting for change and quality in art. The Society, from its foundation in 1886, existed solely as an exhibition society to bring together the work of artists every three years. The first president was the wood engraver and book designer Walter Crane (1845 to 1915) and other outstanding members were Emery Walker, Cobden Sanderson, William de Morgan, Philip Webb and William Lethaby. These men drew their encouragement from William Morris, who assisted in the founding of the Society.

Walter Crane was strongly influenced by the Pre-Raphaelites and in common with William Morris had strong socialist ideals. His involvement in politics led him (with George Bernard Shaw) to join the Socialist League in 1883. His cartoons [58] became a weekly feature in socialist magazines and he also gave lectures at the meetings of Shaw's Fabian Society.

In 1884, Crane became the first President of the Art Workers' Guild which had

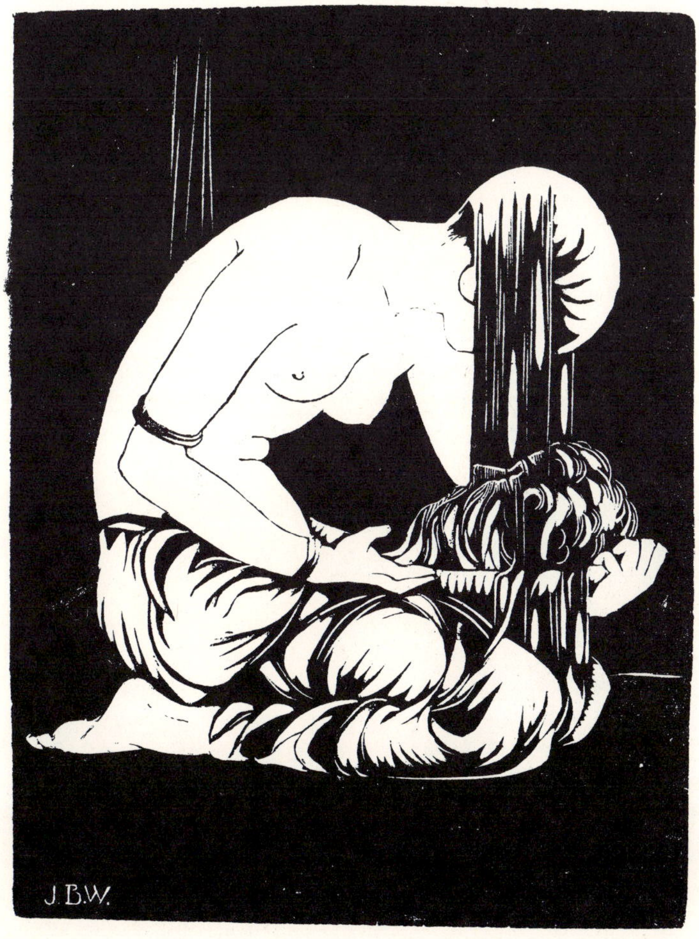

[154] John Buckland-Wright: *Salome*, 1926. 9.0 x 12.0cm

been formed by Lethaby and his friend Philip Webb in order to combine artists, designers and architects. Lethaby was elected Master of the Guild in 1911.

In the early part of the 1900s architects liked to be considered artists, though this is not now the general professional view. The Art Workers' Guild was started because the architects and artists felt that one of the main reasons for the decline of the arts was the gap that existed between architecture, painting and sculpture. It was believed that real art arose from unity of all the visual arts and architecture.

The influence of the Art Workers' Guild was considerable although it never sought publicity and worked through other bodies. Finding that the Royal Academy blankly refused to show the crafts, the Guild took steps to set up two new bodies: the Arts and Crafts Exhibition Society and the Design and Industries Association.

The primary purpose of the Arts and Crafts Movement was the revival and improvement of craftsmanship in all the constructive and decorative arts. It had a creed which was to encourage a proper pride in honest work. In this Lethaby was an enthusiastic supporter, although he was not opposed to the machine to the same degree as Ruskin and Morris.

Lethaby was very active in attracting highly competent staff to the Central School of Arts and Crafts and one such man was the calligrapher Edward Johnston (1872 to 1944). Lethaby saw some of Johnston's manuscripts and suggested that his skill was such that he should teach calligraphy. There was no class in this subject at the Central School at the time because it appeared that nobody knew enough about it to be able to teach it. Johnston thought he was coming to the Central School as a student and on arrival was surprised to find that he was required to teach.

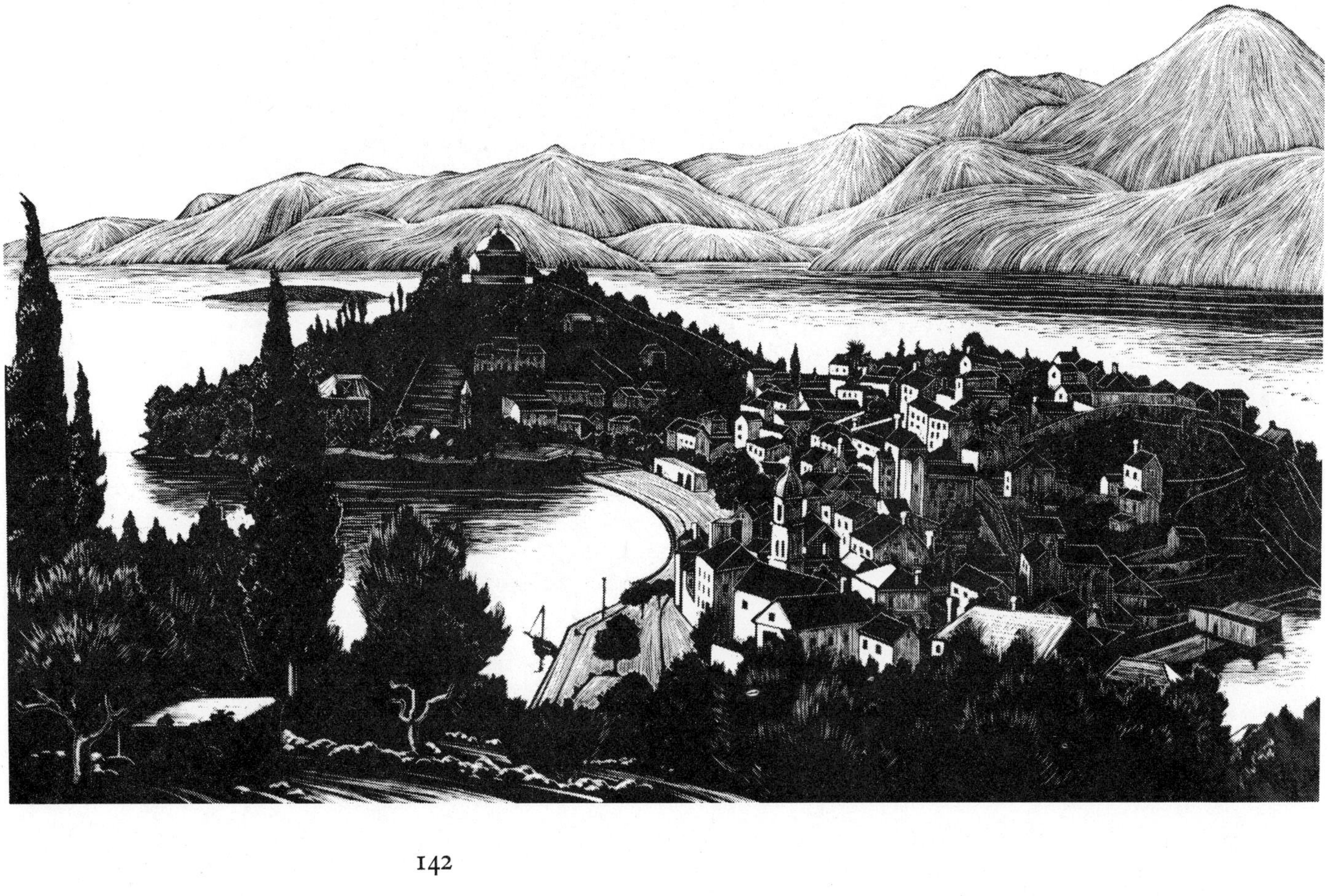

[155] Clare Leighton: *Saftat*, 1926. 30.5 x 20.0cm

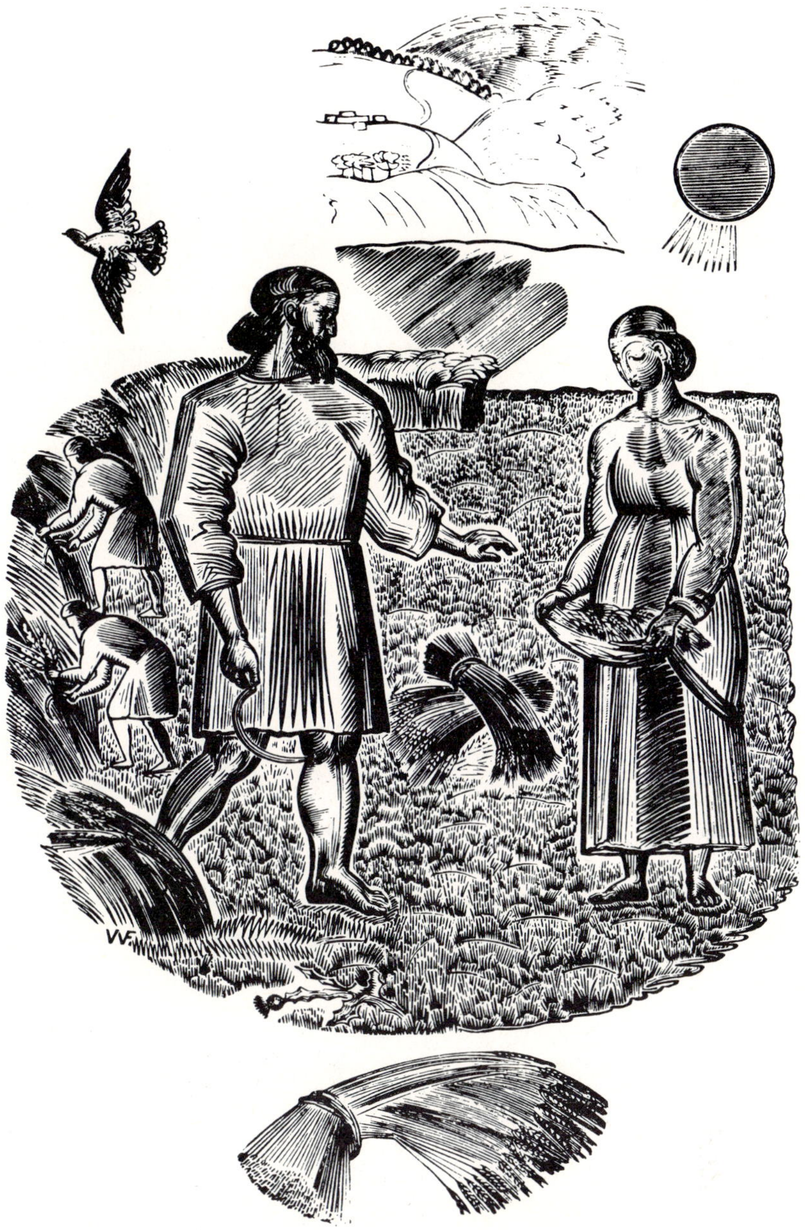

[156] Wladimir Favorsky: Illustration from *The Book of Ruth*, 1925. 9.5 x 14.5cm

Johnston started his career as a teacher in 1899 and his first class consisted of seven students. He had a very active mind and considerable clarity of thought but he was deliberate both in speech and movement. This characteristic was so marked that at times he could give the impression of lassitude. His first class of seven included two remarkable students: Noel Rooke and Eric Gill, both of whom were to have a lasting impact not only on the art of lettering but on wood engraving as well. Gill refers to Johnston as the teacher and leader he had been looking for: the man who profoundly altered the whole course of his life and all his ways of thinking. Johnston had made the apparently simple discovery that the nature and form of a letter was determined by the form of the tool used to make it. This discovery was to lead to the foundation of modern calligraphy.

In 1906 Edward Johnston published his book *Writing, Illuminating and Lettering*, a work now regarded as a classic. In October 1912 he took a house in Ditchling in Sussex where his neighbour was his former pupil Eric Gill. Here Johnston designed

[157] John F. Greenwood: *The Ethelbert Gate, Norwich*, 1926. 13.5 x 19.0cm

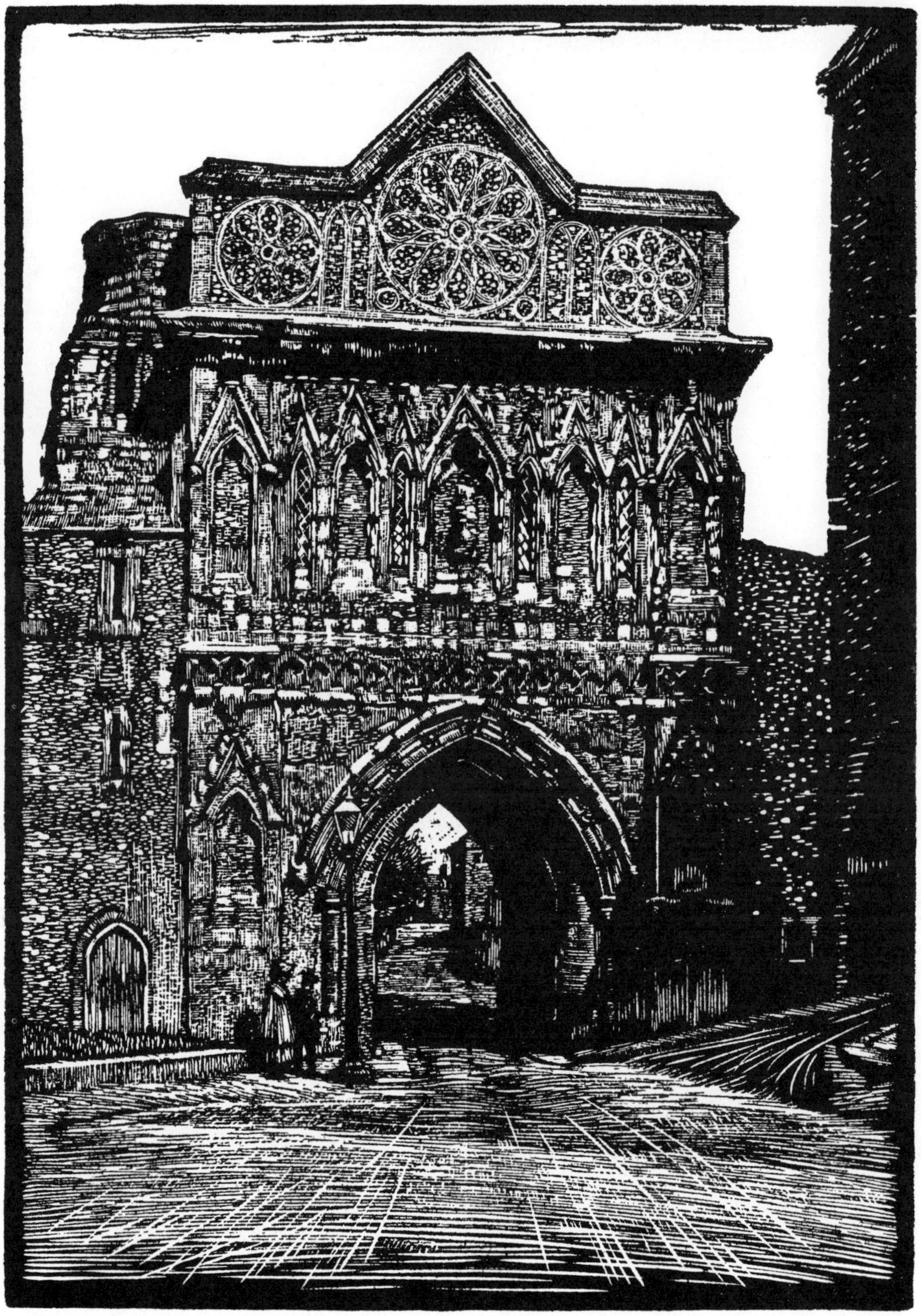

a block letter alphabet for the London Underground which influenced Gill in designing an alphabet which was eventually issued as a typeface called 'Gill Sans'.

Johnston's statement 'The form of a letter is determined by the form of the tool used to make it' must have had a lot of meaning for his student Noel Rooke. Johnston was approaching the future conception of wood engraving and in teaching his students he was planting seeds in a very rich soil. In 1904 Rooke turned to wood engraving after a lot of discussion with Johnston about his dissatisfaction with the reproductions of his drawings by the photographic process and commercial engravers. He discovered that the end-grained wood block was a distorting method of reproducing pencil and pen drawings. This in turn led to his discovery that a

[158] Ethelbert White: *The Rick Yard*, 1926. 7.6 x 6.2cm

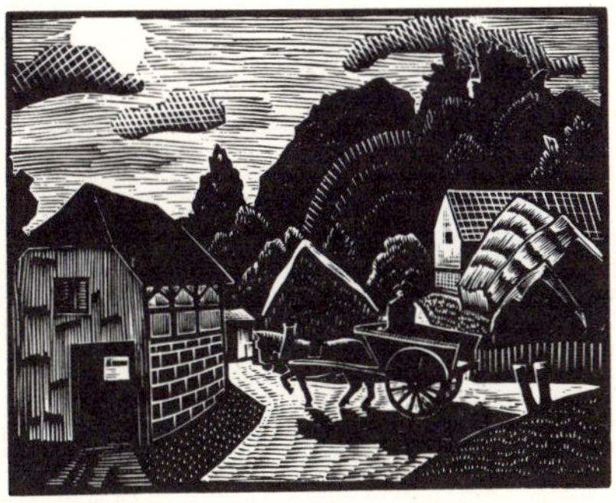

wood engraving could only be an original work of art if it was designed by the artist, graver or burin in hand, using incisions determined by the tool and medium itself and not by forcing it to represent something other than itself. Thus Rooke was applying Johnston's teaching to another means of expression.

Rooke began to experiment with a designed engraving using the shapes made naturally by the engraving tools. He sought the advice of Lucien Pissarro who, whilst wishing to be helpful, could not sympathize with Rooke's enthusiasm for a burin-designed technique. The idea cut clean across Pissarro's concepts of the black line. By that time Pissarro's world was formed; his art concept was stronger than his wish for experiment in form and he wished to continue to be free to apply both his black-line and white-line techniques as constituent parts of his art concept only.

Pissarro made no attempt whatsoever to join the new white-line school, though he consorted and exhibited with members of the Society of Wood Engravers. He was in the position of the *peintre-graveur* where any change of concept must be embodied in the total, which in his case was painting.

His former fellow student, Eric Gill, welcomed Rooke's idea however, and the two men set to work to evolve the new language and concepts which were to give rise to a national school of wood engraving.

In 1905 Noel Rooke became a teacher of book illustration at the Central School. Although he had made a number of wood engravings he was not allowed to teach this subject until 1912 when, against some opposition, permission was given. Among his early pupils in wood engraving were Vivien Gribble, Rachael Marshall (later Mrs David Garnett) and Robert Gibbings. In 1914 Rooke became Head of the School of Book Illustration at the Central School and in the same year experimented in the use of colour in wood engraving. He continued to be active as a teacher of wood engraving for some thirty years.

Robert Gibbings's background was quite different from that of Gill, with whom he had many qualities in common. Gibbings and Gill were both outsize personalities and both were born of clerical families. Gibbings's father was the Reverend Edward Gibbings who was a canon of Cork Cathedral.

Gibbings began his art education in 1912 at the Slade School of Fine Art before studying at the Central School under Rooke. When he started there he had not thought seriously about wood engraving but Rooke declared that it would help him to express form. In 1913 Gibbings did his first wood engraving called *The Two Pigs*, drawing in pure silhouette. In the same year Gibbings obtained the Slade Certificate in Drawing in the first class. On leaving the Central School he was awarded its Art Diploma of Honour.

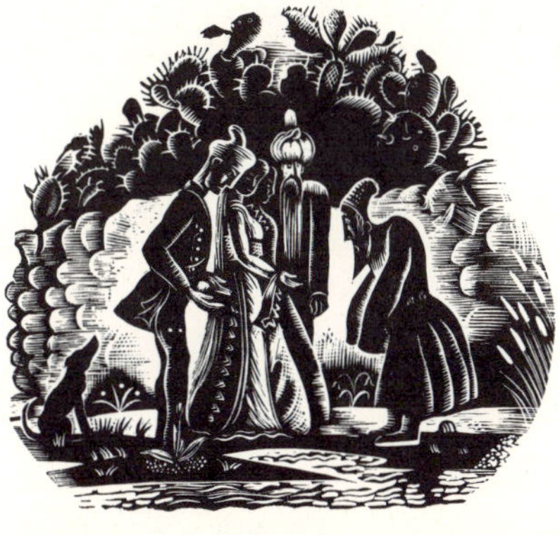

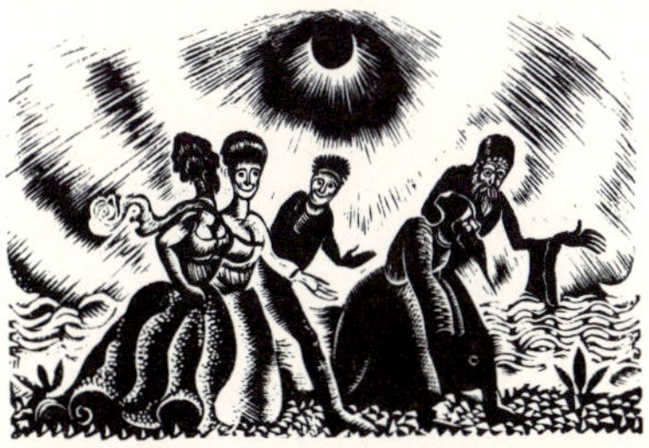

[159] Douglas Percy Bliss: Two illustrations from *Rasselas*, 1926.

During the years just prior to the First World War there was an engraver working separately and apart from the Central School group. This was Gwendolen Mary Raverat (1885 to 1957) who was a member of a remarkable family. She was the daughter of Sir George Howard Darwin, a professor of astronomy, and her grandfather was Charles Darwin. Her early childhood was spent in Cambridge and she started drawing at the age of ten. Before the war she was a member of a group of intellectual young people of whom Rupert Brooke was the most prominent. Gwendolen Raverat joined the Slade in 1908 and studied under Frederick Brown and Henry Tonks. When she left the Slade she went to Paris to the Sorbonne where she met and married Jacques Pierre Raverat, a fellow student.

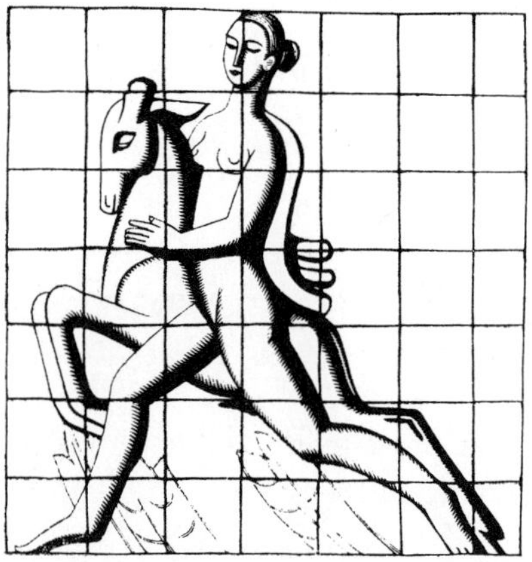

[160] John Ralph Beedham: *Diana*, from a sketch drawn by Vernon Hill, 1926. 8.75 x 9.25cm

Gwendolen drew her inspiration from the wood engraving of Bewick but unfortunately during her studentship at the Slade there was no interest in wood engraving. Thomas Balston writes in his book *English Wood Engraving 1900-1950*, 'She had the luck to obtain some instruction from her cousin Eleanor Monsell – Mrs Bernard Darwin – who had begun to cut and engrave wood blocks as early as 1898, but soon desisted owing to the pressure of other work. By 1914 Gwendolen Raverat had nearly sixty blocks to her credit.'[8]

Her subjects were figures and landscape. In style her art was fluid, relaxed and painter-like in conception and at no time did she come under the design influence of Rooke, Gill or Gibbings. She was very friendly with Gill who often visited the Raverat home. She was an impressionist in style and technique. Her engraving is calm and tonal change flows gently across her work expressing a grey world so different from the unrelenting black and white counterpoint of the group at the Central. The aesthetics of her engraving steered clear of decoration and her handling of light is masterly. Although she had a high regard for Bewick, she never shared his intense interest in the texture of materials and her long friendship with Gill did not influence her style of engraving. It was closely akin to the style of the French wood engraver Auguste Lepère whose work had not at that time been seen in this country.

Despite the impressionistic style of Raverat, it is generally accepted that the British school of wood engraving, to which she has made a memorable contribution, is design orientated rather than impressionistic. Gwendolen Raverat developed independently as a white-line engraver. Her work appeared in *Spring Morning* a book by Francis Cornford published by the Poetry Bookshop in 1915. This was the first book to be illustrated with white-line wood engravings.

The background and career of Eric Gill was substantially different from that of his fellow student Noel Rooke. Gill came from a family of eleven children; his father was the Reverend Arthur Tidman Gill. Though he was born into a Nonconformist religious family, Eric Gill was to adopt the Roman Catholic faith in

[161] Eric Ravilious: *Boy Birdsnesting*, 1927. 13.2 x 8.75cm

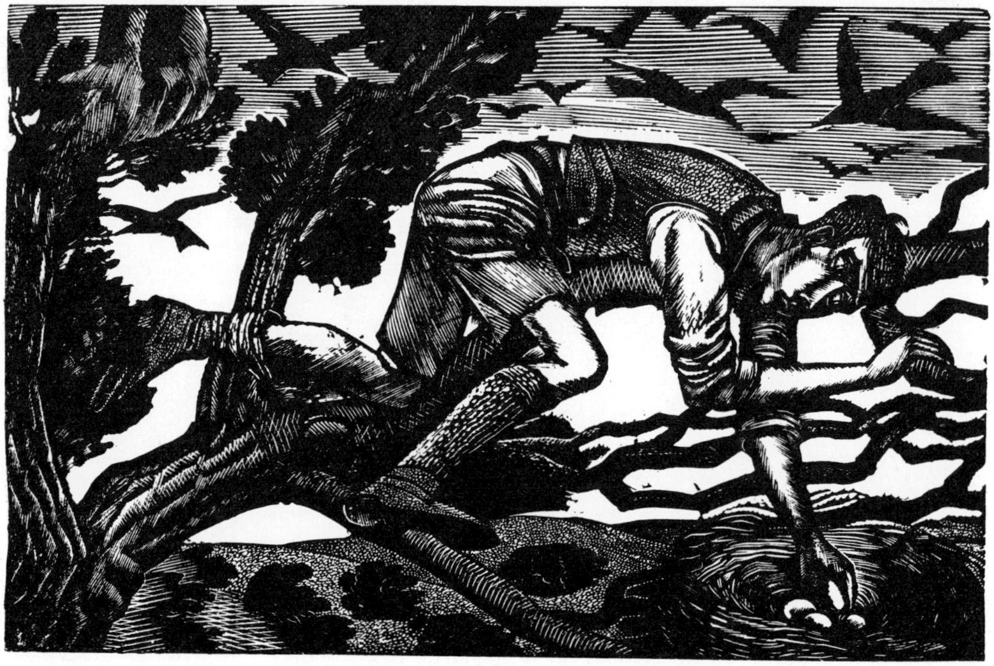

later life. Politics were an important influence and he subscribed to a down-to-earth form of socialism rather than the more rarified Fabian version.

Gill's father had wanted to be an artist and he taught his son perspective. He sent him to Chichester Technical and Art School as a day student and there Eric Gill developed a talent for lettering which later was to make him famous as a typographer. In 1900 he secured a job in the office of W. H. Caroe, the architect of the Ecclesiastical Commissioners in London. This kindled an interest in architecture which Gill retained throughout his life and which strongly influenced his principles of design and construction.

When he was a student at the Central School, he was encouraged by Lethaby not to limit himself to lettering but to take up carving in stone and so widen his scope of expression. Eventually Gill became one of Britain's finest stone-carving sculptors.

For some time Gill was associated with Edward Johnston in engraving letters and small devices. He shared a home with Johnston at Hammersmith and the two

[162] John Nash: *Daphne Laureola*, from *Poisonous Plants*, 1927. 10.75 x 15.3cm

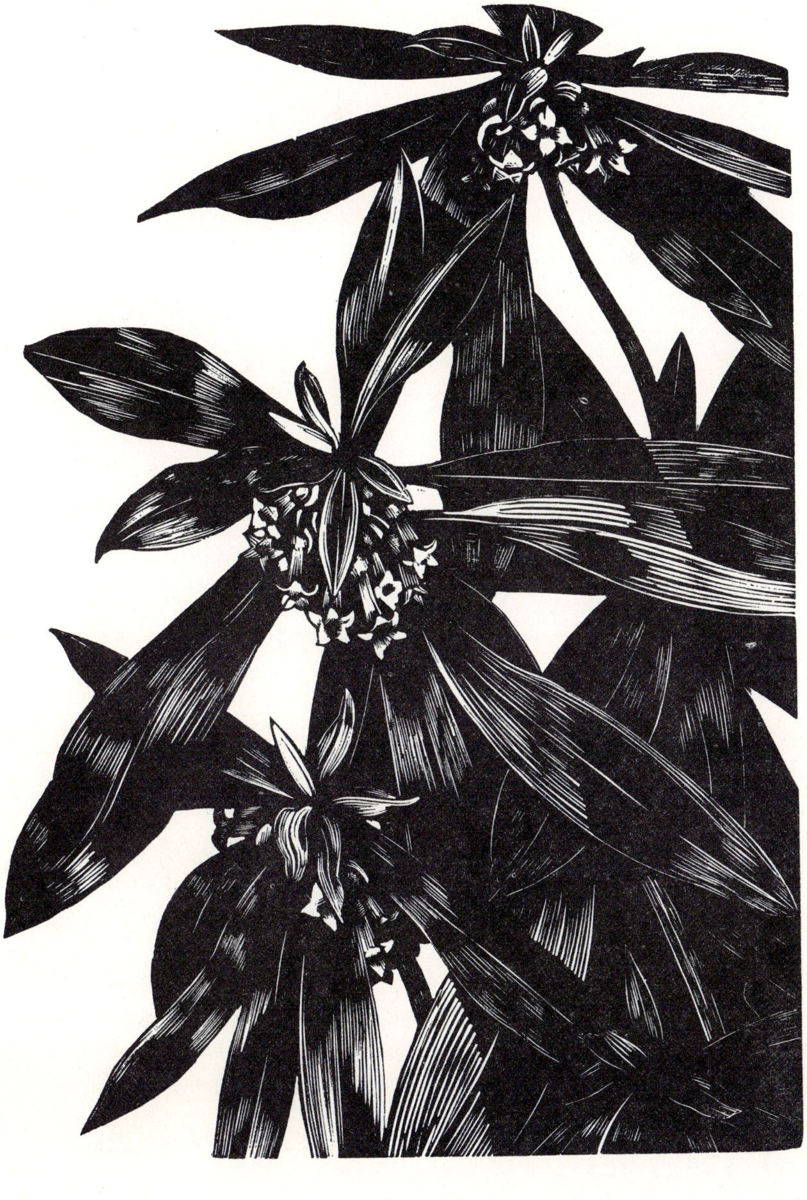

[163] David Jones: *Noah*, from *The Chester Play of the Deluge*, 1927. 14.3 x 16.5cm

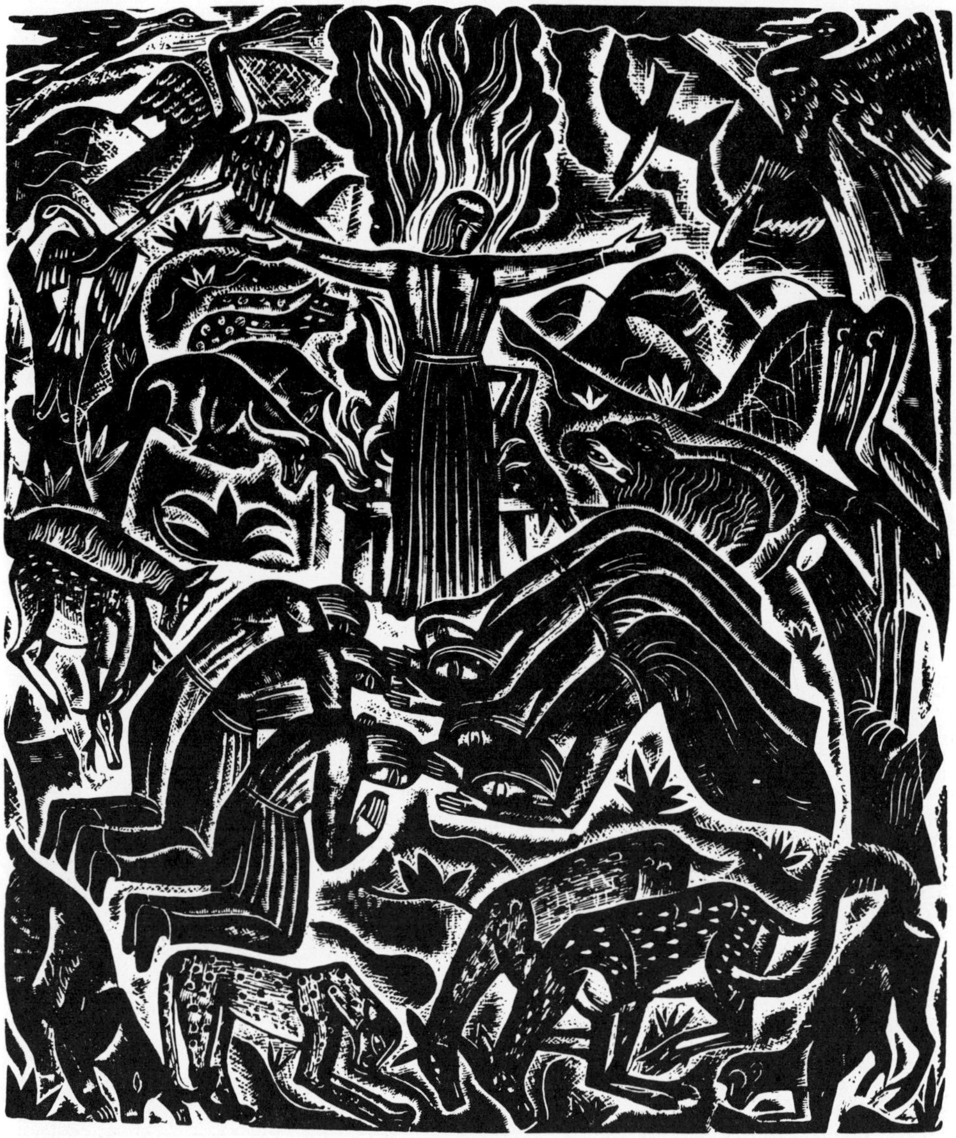

men proved to be sympathetic companions. Johnston's views on art and craft at that time are pertinent today and were similar to those held by Gill, 'I object to destroyers of creeds who have no equivalent ready to offer for the shelter they have pulled down. I object to the appeal to "science" combined with unscientific statement. I object to rhetoric displacing logic.'

In the early part of the twentieth century, Gill produced only a few small blocks. In 1904 he was busy earning his living by teaching gilding at the Central School and in 1905 taught lettering at the Paddington Institute. At this time, he was receiving commissions for architectural lettering which kept him solvent.

By 1907 Gill had realised that he needed more space for his growing family and for his increasing work in lettering, sculpture and wood engraving. He bought a pleasant Georgian house named 'Sopers' in the main street of Ditchling; the building still carries the same name. Here he was joined by Joseph Cribb who was his assistant in sculpture and lettering for many years. In the new location, Gill soon found himself the centre of a community of artists and craftsmen, though this did not occur intentionally; he just had the personality that attracted artists.

In art Gill was precise; as a thinker he was tenacious but sometimes inspiringly right and at times badly wrong. As a craftsman he expressed his precision and tenacity as a quality to support his statement 'Without philosophy man cannot know what he makes; without religion he cannot know why.'[9] As an artist his philosophy can be said to be his national monument.

There is a certain coldness in the perfection of Gill's craftsmanship and there is a flawlessness in his skill which gives his work a certain God-like character which some people cannot recognise. For those who can study Gill, there is the excitement of the discovery of a great thinker, the philosopher through form who was equally conversant with the meaning and conduct of human life. He said: 'Art must be allowed to express the life of the senses as well as the life of the spirit, and to do so without evasion.'[10]

In his art and writing Gill expressed a way of life in which art and religion were inseparable. He saw modern art as primarily a religious movement, away from frivolity, hypocrisy and flattery and from worship of mammon. Although in many ways he had Victorian streaks in his make-up, he accepted the art of his time, he contributed to it and extended his experience of it. To have meaning for subsequent generations an artist must firstly be of his own time; Gill was one of the last great artist craftsmen to carry the torch lit by Ruskin and Morris.

[164] Bernard Rice: *Decent from the Cross*, 1927. 29.8 x 23.0cm

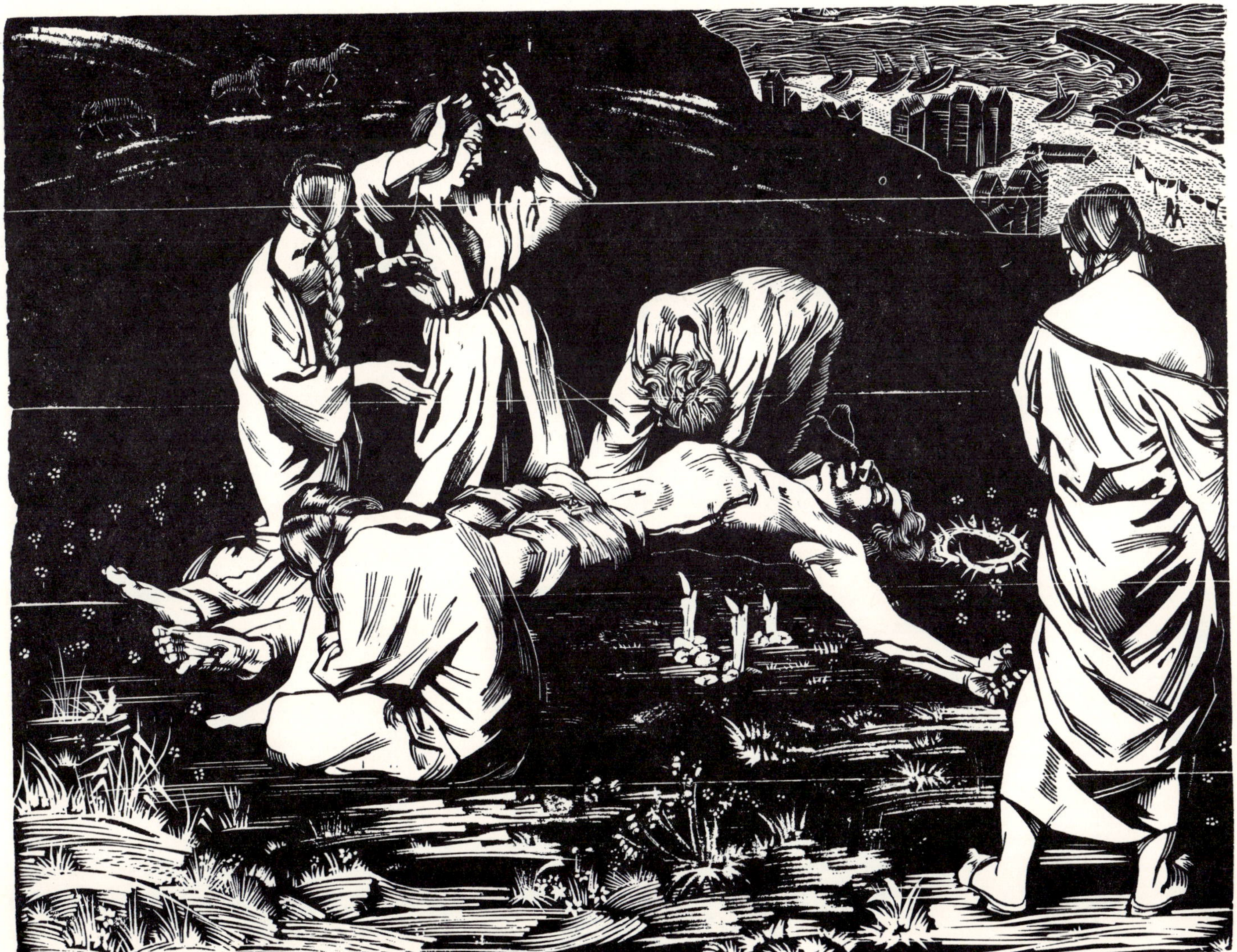

[165] John Farleigh: *Hemlock*, 1928.

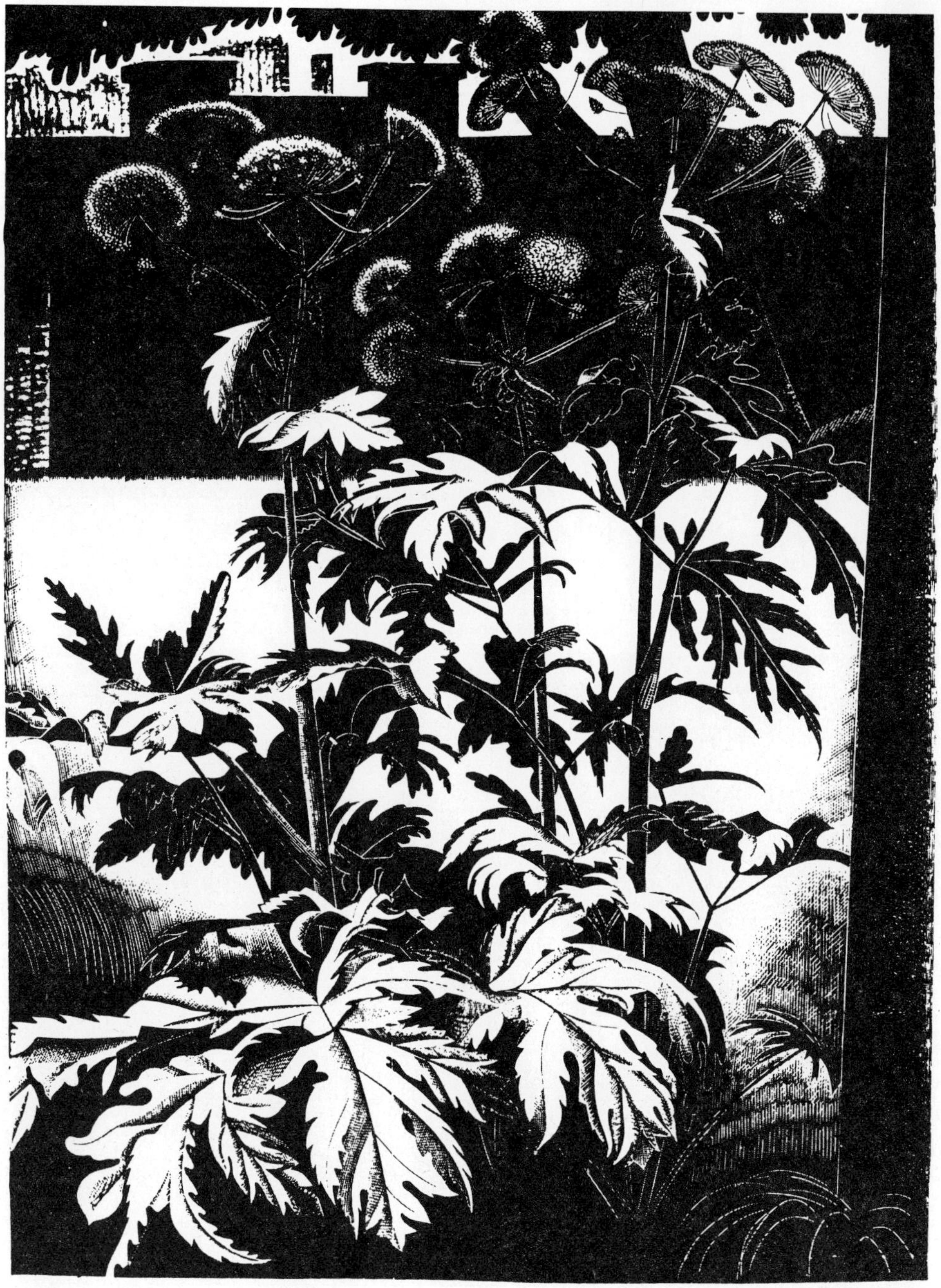

Eric Gill was very friendly with Roger Fry. 1910 was an eventful year for the modern movement of art: Fry came to the conclusion that no significant art was being produced in Britain; at best there was the New English Art Club though he resigned from its jury in 1908. Fry went to Paris to choose pictures for an exhibition that would introduce the 'new art' to Britain. He was helped by the dramatic critic Desmond MacCarthy.

In 1910 two exhibitions were organised by Roger Fry, the first in Brighton and then the important one at the Grafton Galleries in London. The effect of the latter was extraordinary and it was to split the art world asunder. It contained a number of paintings by Manet, including the *Bar of the Folies-Bergère*, twenty-one by Cézanne, forty-one by Gauguin, twenty-one by Van Gogh and two landscapes by Georges Seurat. There was also a certain proportion of works by living artists, mainly of the group called *Les Fauves*, or wild men. The group's leader was Henri Matisse. In this exhibition, Gill showed his garden statue which held its own with Matisse's *Pose de Nu*, Vlaminck's *Rouen*, Flandrin's *Paysage* and Picasso's *Nature Morte*.

In a letter to Rothenstein discussing the exhibition Gill wrote: 'All the critics are tearing one another's eyes over it and the sheep and the goats are inextricably mixed up. . . . As a matter of fact those who like it show their pluck, and those who don't show either great intelligence or else great stupidity. The show quite obviously represents a reaction and a transition and so if, like Fry, you are a factor in that reaction and transition then you like the show. If, like MacColl and Robert Ross,

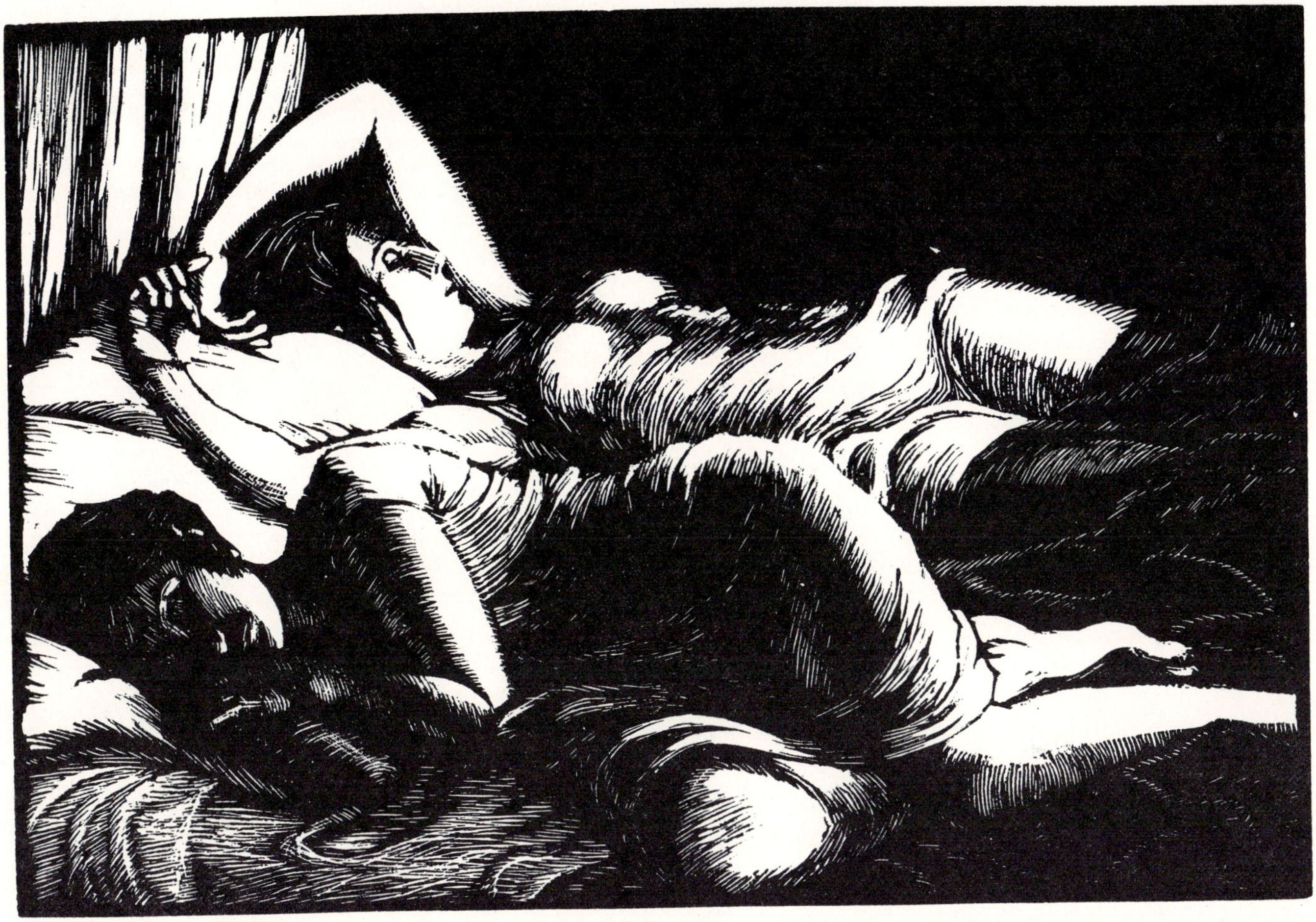

[166] Gwendolen Raverat: *The Sleepers*, 1928. 17.75 x 12.0cm

you are too inseparably connected with the things reacted against and the generation from which it is a transition, then you don't like it! If, on the other hand, you are like me and John and McEvoy and Epstein then, feeling yourself beyond the reaction and beyond the transition, you have a right to feel superior to Mr Henri Matisse.'[11]

In this letter Gill discloses exactly how he stood in face of the challenge; it is a letter from a very clear mind and written as of one of them. However, the public took a very poor view of the exhibition and threatened to burn it down. Police had to be stationed at the Gallery to keep law and order. One of the critics, Robert Ross, expressed a most dispeptic view when he wrote in the *Morning Post* 7 November 1910: 'A date more favourable than the fifth of November for revealing the existence of a widespread plot to destroy the whole fabric of European painting

[167] Eric Ravilious: *The Holy Children* from *Apocrypha*, 1929. 12.75 x 18.0cm

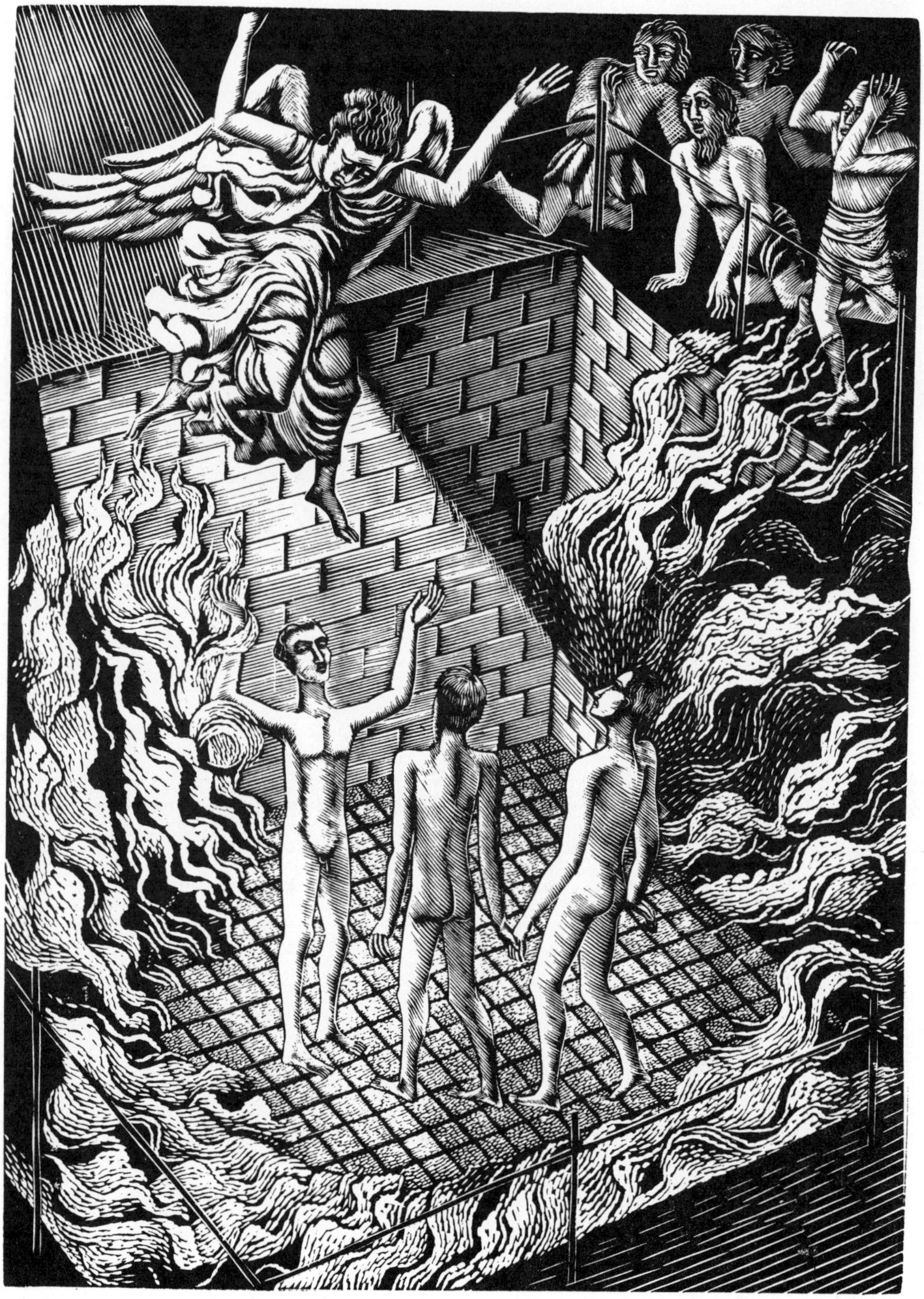

could hardly have been chosen. . . . If the movement is spreading . . . it should be treated like the rat plague in Suffolk. The source of the infection (i.e. the pictures) ought to be destroyed.'

However, Roger Fry kept up his spirits and held another exhibition in 1912. For all those concerned with the production of art these exhibitions placed before the art world a new standard as typified by the work of Cézanne. Fry was to continue his work of interpreting Cézanne and at that time there was no critic better qualified; whatever faults Fry may have had, no one wrote better criticisms.

From 1912 onwards art was to experience drastic change in conceptions of form and space as these two aspects were subjected to considerable research, which is still in progress. One of the first casualties in this examination of aesthetics was William Rothenstein's academic Fabian socialism. The Fabians and associates of Rothenstein saw Fry as content to go no higher than Cézanne but what they failed to see was that in their Englishness, as typified by the New English Art Club, the politics of Fabian socialism and of religion was not art and would not in itself produce significant artists.

However, it is possible for an artist to be religious yet have an art expression that is purely aesthetic and nothing to do with the subject matter of religion. Such an artist is usually of a very high calibre and has an expression that is manifest in the quality of line, form, colour and space, in the use of his tool, whether it be brush, burin or chisel. Both Cézanne and Gill had this calibre; Gill's art was religious in its expression and the denominational variant did not amount to much where his art was concerned. Van Gogh is a supreme example of a religious artist in paint with no secular denominational subject matter, although Gill failed to recognise this outstanding quality in Van Gogh. Artists can be blind and insensitive in the recognition of new and significant talent, as can critics, and this was one of

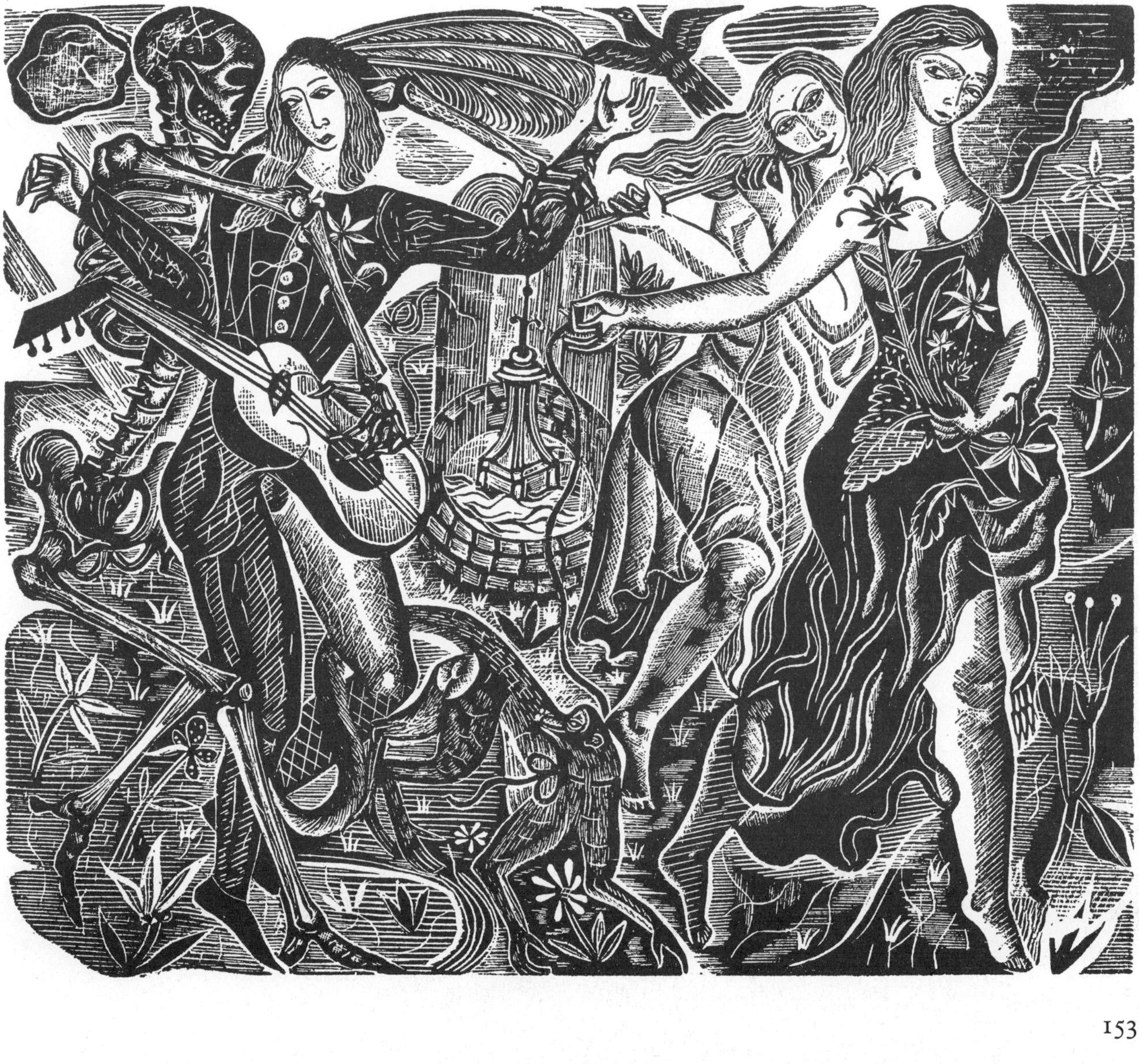

[168] David Jones: *Everyman*, 1929. 16.8 x 14.3cm

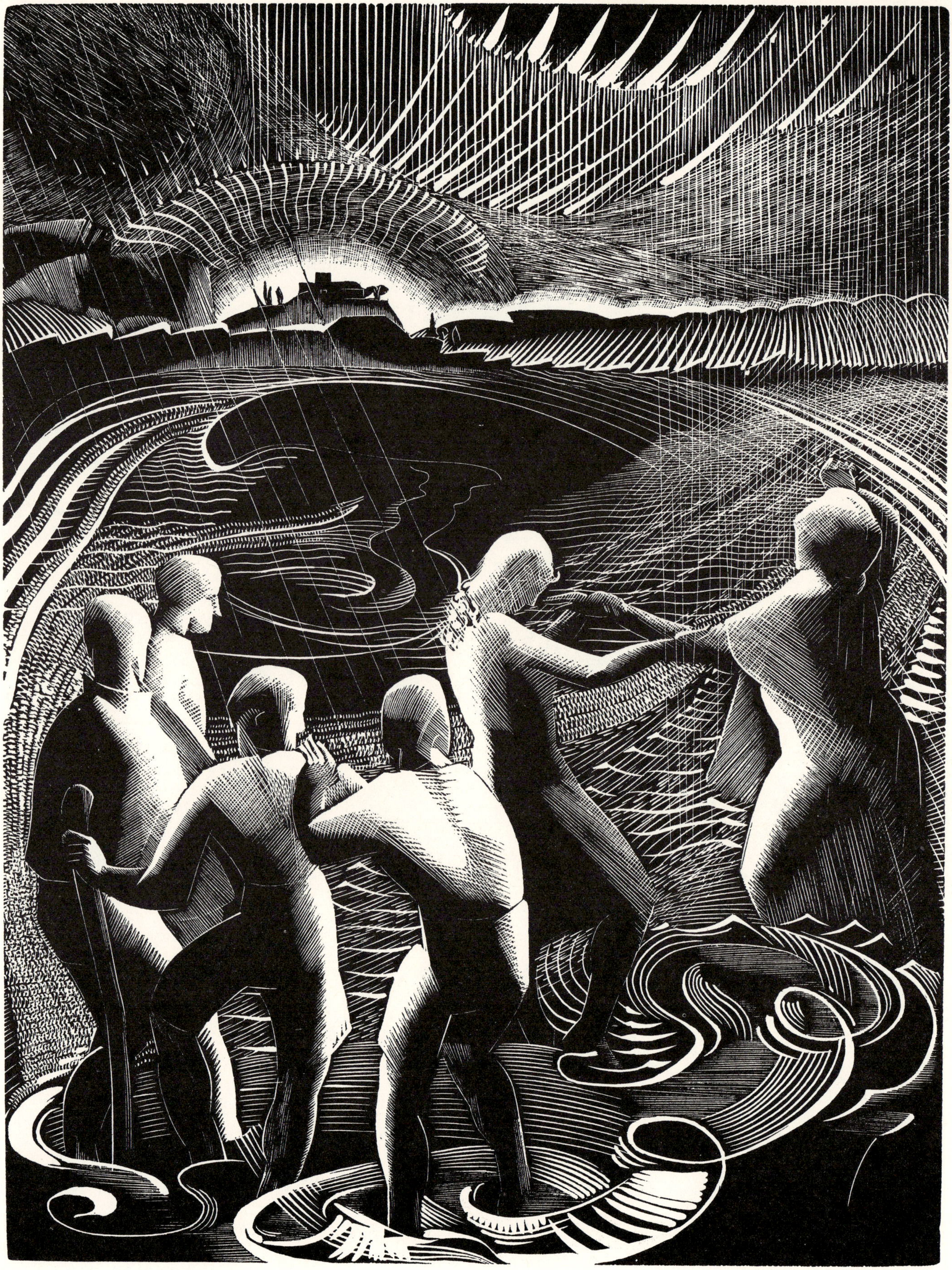

[169] Gertrude Hermes: *The Slough of Despond*, 1928. 17.75 x 23.75cm

the reasons why Gill often appeared awkward and blundering. He was a very practical person and it seems that he saw in Roman Catholicism the kind of religion best suited to his deep-rooted feelings. Yet the intensity of his religious motivation made him never completely at ease with other artists. Being completely absorbed in one religious doctrine he was not interested in creating anything pertaining to a new religion.

Eric Gill was one of the most outstanding religious artists Britain has produced in this century. William Blake was another outstanding religious artist, though his artistic expression was not as God-like as that of Gill. In outlook Gill was both radical and conservative; he had a powerful mind but was blessed with a boyish wide-eyed optimism. The boyishness of his character was with him until the end and he appeared never to grow old. He said he would dignify his own status, even if he could not dignify other people's and in this respect his wood engravings have a remarkably personal quality.[12]

Like John Farleigh, Gill was something of an extension of the ideals of William Morris. The socialism of Morris was based on a concept of a better quality in life for everyone; but because his productions were exclusive and expensive, his conception of art being for the people could not become a reality. Gill's socialist beliefs, though strongly held and hotly defended, were different from those of Morris in that they were simpler and more manageable in concept. Because Gill had an orderly mind in his own art, he was able to live a better and fuller life as an artist.

Having moved to Sussex in 1907, Gill became the focal point for a collection of friends, and they formed what was known as the Ditchling Community. This group developed naturally because it comprised a small band of like-minded people trying to link together in a communal existence; it succeeded because it was small. Had the group been large it would have failed because of the complications which arise when the application of the ideas of a large group is attempted. The Ditchling Community had a private chapel where visiting priests said Mass and where Compline was recited daily. It is evident that the Community regarded the daily Missal as of greater consequence than the daily newspaper.

Gill's assistant sculptor, Joseph Cribb, was the first of his friends to take up residence at Ditchling. Edward Johnston went to live there in 1912 and Ralph John Beedham also joined the Ditchling Community. The role he played is remarkable for its human interest, his fabulous skill and, in particular, for his contribution in the early days of the British school of wood engraving [160]. He was a commercial reproductive engraver who was unable to draw and never engraved any work which he had created.

Beedham was probably the last *formschneider* to be trained in Britain. When he was apprenticed in 1893 the development of photography had been in progress for some fifty years and in its application to printing was arriving at the point where it was to take the place of wood engraving. By the time that Beedham had completed six years of his apprenticeship, both the line and the half-tone plates were in commercial use. Although he witnessed the decline of wood engraving in periodical and newspaper production, Beedham understood the need for the technical revolution and was in sympathy with the concept of engraving becoming creative.

Beedham engraved his last block at the age of eighty-three years. There can be very few who have been able to engrave to this age; most engravers have been forc-

[170] Iain Macnab: *Le Quai de Isle, Annecy*, 1929. 26.5 x 29.0cm

ed to give it up much earlier due to failing eyesight. Ralph John Beedham died in 1975 having remained active both physically and mentally until his final illness.

Beedham was an instructor of wood engraving at the School of Photo-engraving at Bolt Court, London. Among his best students were Mabel Alleyne and Joan Hassall who speaks very highly of him as a teacher. Hassall's engraving technique is traditional and she uses both the black line and the white line having been trained outside the didactic white-line school. The names of Beedham and Hassall will always be linked together and Joan Hassall's craft standards are such that Beedham approved the link.

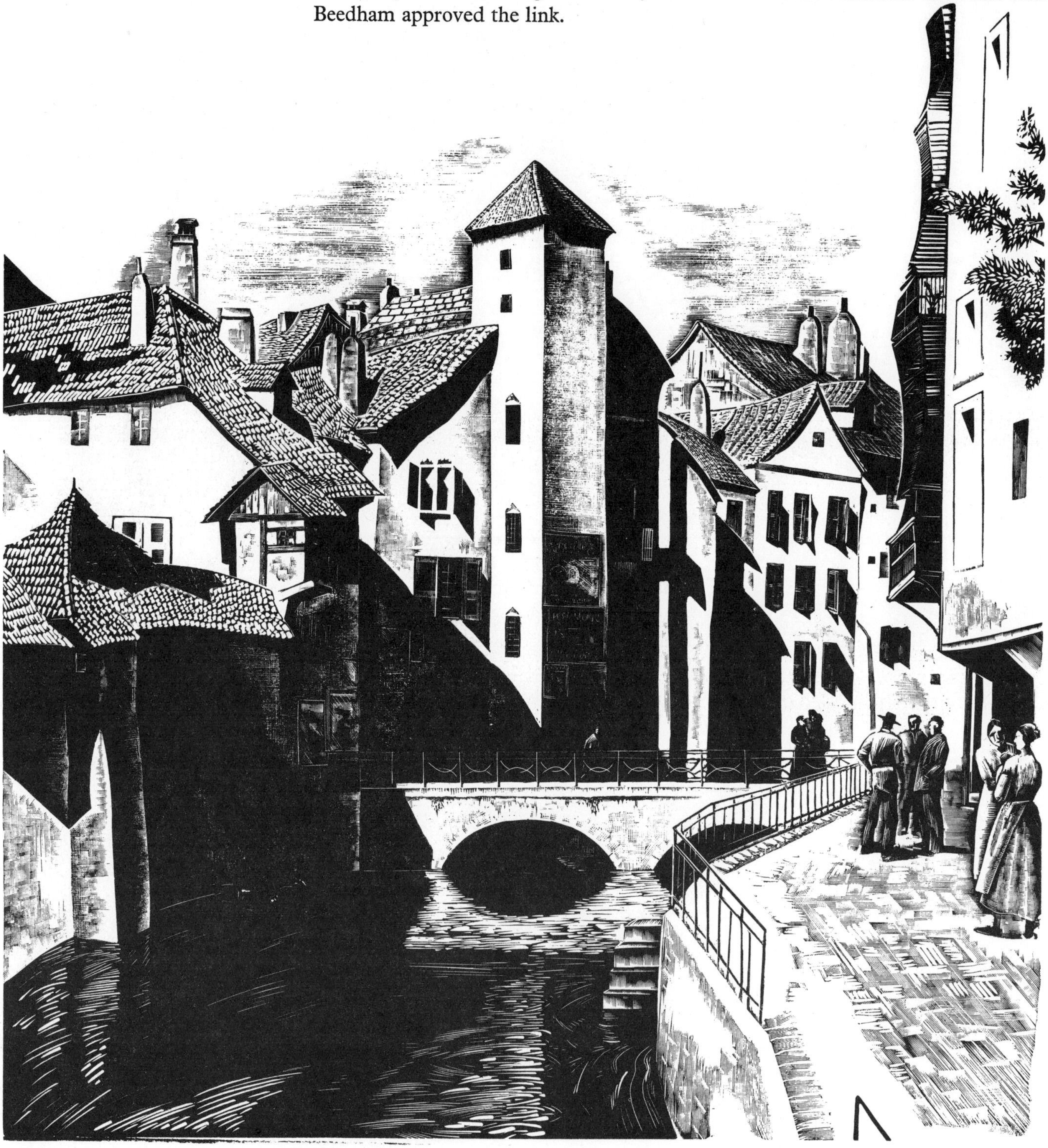

When Beedham joined Gill at Ditchling in the early 1920s, Gill instructed him in lettering and Beedham became his assistant in this and remained so until Gill died. One of his tasks was to clear the numerous white areas from the engravings of both Gill and Gibbings. Most of these blocks were used in book illustration and neither Gill nor Gibbings could have achieved their volume of book illustrations without Beedham's work. Beedham established a long friendship with both men

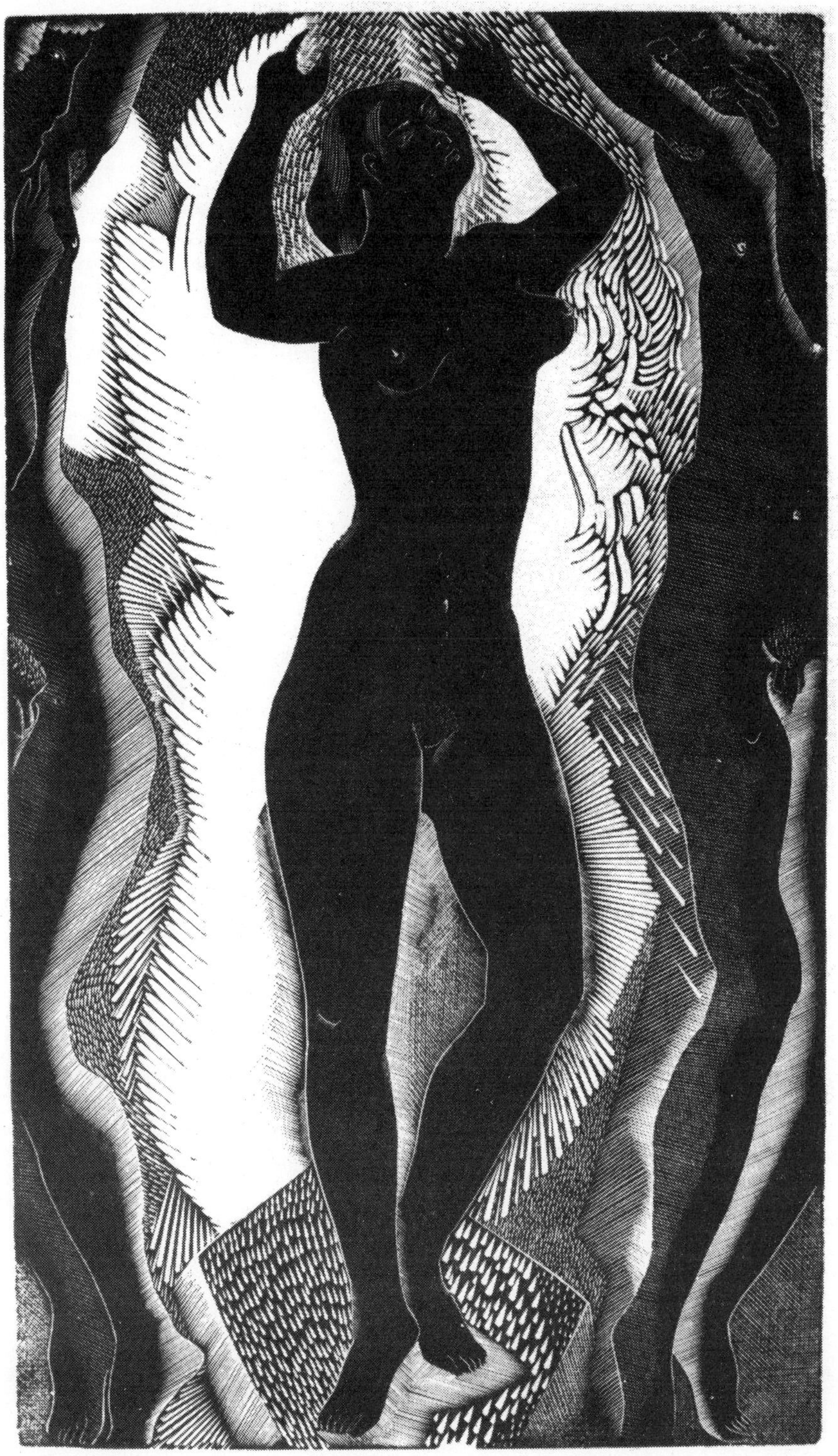

[171] Blair Hughes-Stanton: *Emancipation of Woman*, 1929. 10.1 x 18.1cm

[172] Clare Leighton: *Boston Cod*, 1929. 20.5 x 23.75cm

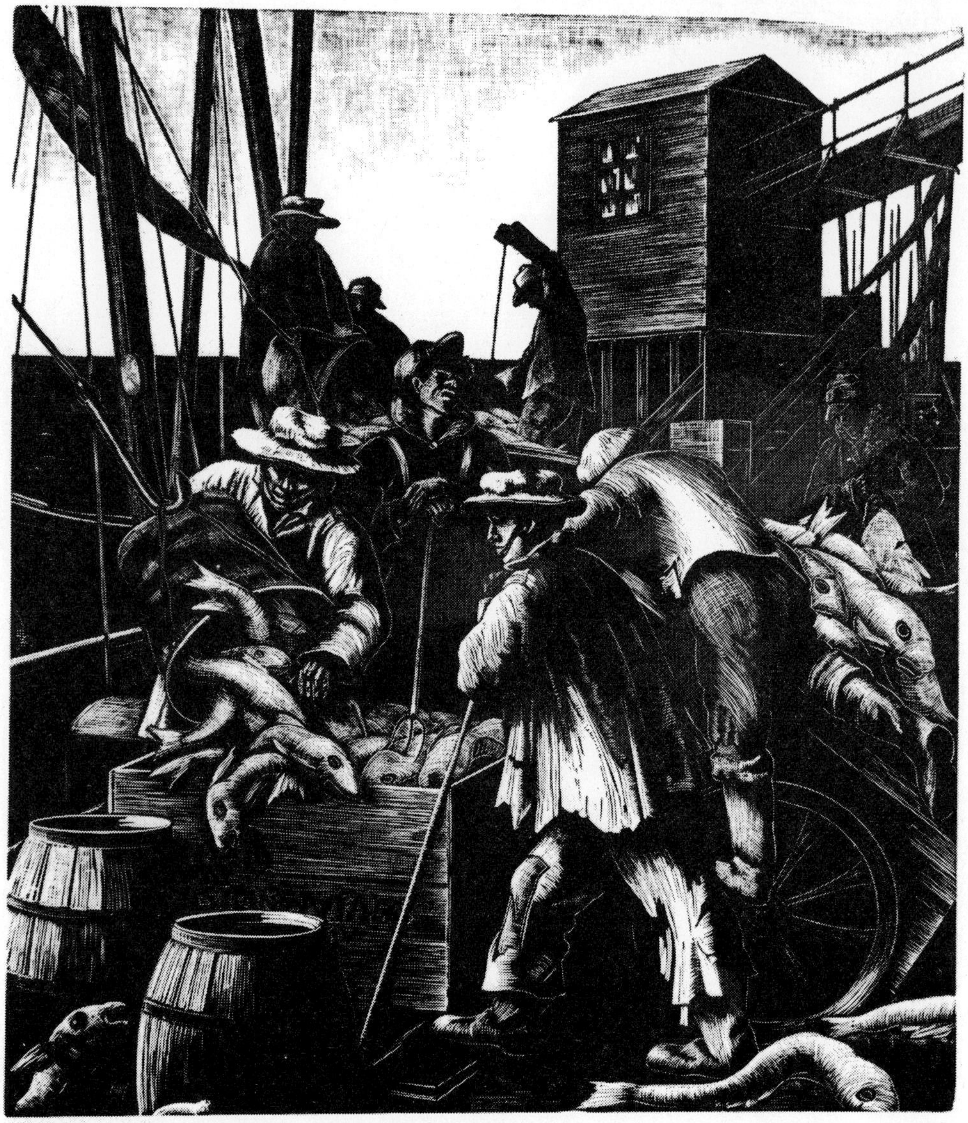

but some of the other creative engravers were anything but kindly disposed to the *formschneider* in their midst.

Beedham also did some work for John Farleigh and the Curwin Press. In his *Graven Image* Farleigh wrote, 'I admit that a firm table is useful, especially when clearing out a lot of wood. It is an arduous job, but the muscles of the wrist and arm become sufficient in time. I have since handed on all clearing to the skilful craftsman John Beedham, now that I have enough work to justify the small extra expense. John Beedham is the only man I know who can be trusted to clear a block. An exquisite engraver of the reproduction school, he has recently reissued an excellent little textbook on engraving that every engraver should read.'[13]

The Ditchling experiment was soon to be interrupted by the outbreak of war in 1914 and Gill enrolled in the Home Defence Brigade. He knew nothing of the causes and politics of war because he was ignorant of foreign affairs, his mind working only in art and religion. Eventually he was conscripted for service in the Army in which he spent a few uneventful months.

In 1915 the Gill family moved to a larger house and Hilary Pepler, a member of

[173] Nora S. Unwin: *Teazle and Grasses*, 1929. 12.75 x 17.5cm

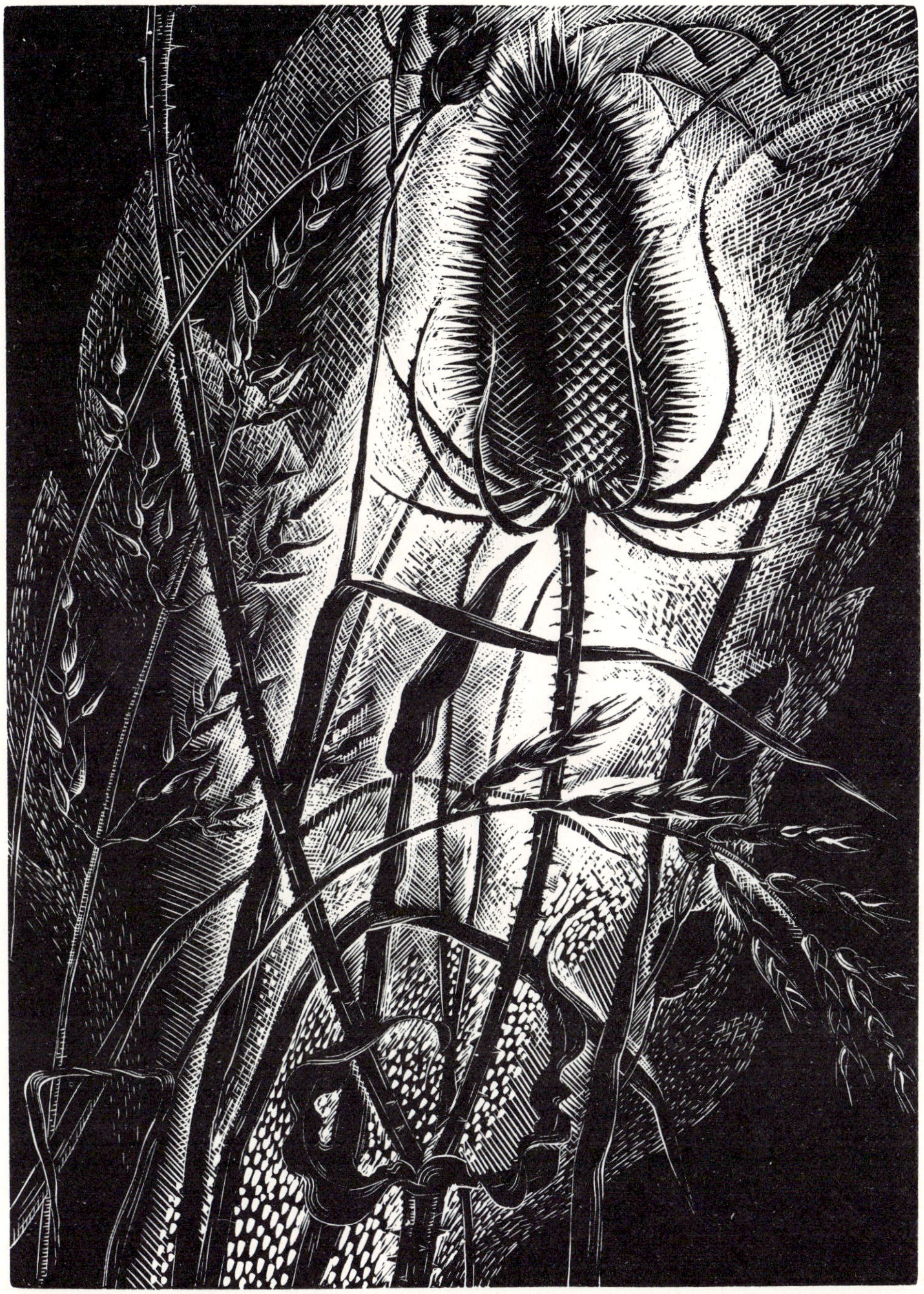

a Quaker family and friend of Johnston and Gill, settled at 'Sopers'. Pepler set up his Ditchling Press at 'Sopers' in 1916. His modest equipment consisted of an early Stanhope press, a folio Albion press and two fonts of Caslon Old Face type.

Pepler's first book *Devil's Devices* was illustrated by Gill. He also published a well-known and appreciated series of Christmas cards from carefully selected wood engravers.

In January 1921 David Jones was brought down to Ditchling by a friend after serving in the Welch Fusiliers. Of all Gill's pupils David Jones was the only one gifted with creative genius. Indeed he had this quality to a far greater degree than Gill.

The Ditchling Community was now dividing into two camps. Financial prob-

[174] Douglas Percy Bliss: *The Figure Heads*, 1929. 18.25 x 18.5cm

lems arose and it became evident that whilst there was little that was wrong with the principles of the Community as a whole, the realisation of them was not always possible. In 1924 Gill resigned his membership of the Guild of St Joseph and St Dominic and he moved to Capel-y-ffin in the Ewyas Valley in the Black Mountains north of Abergavenny.

He became established in the new workshop very quickly and between 1925 and 1926 had prepared designs for an alphabet which was taken up by the Monotype Corporation and issued as the typeface Perpetua, making its first appearance as

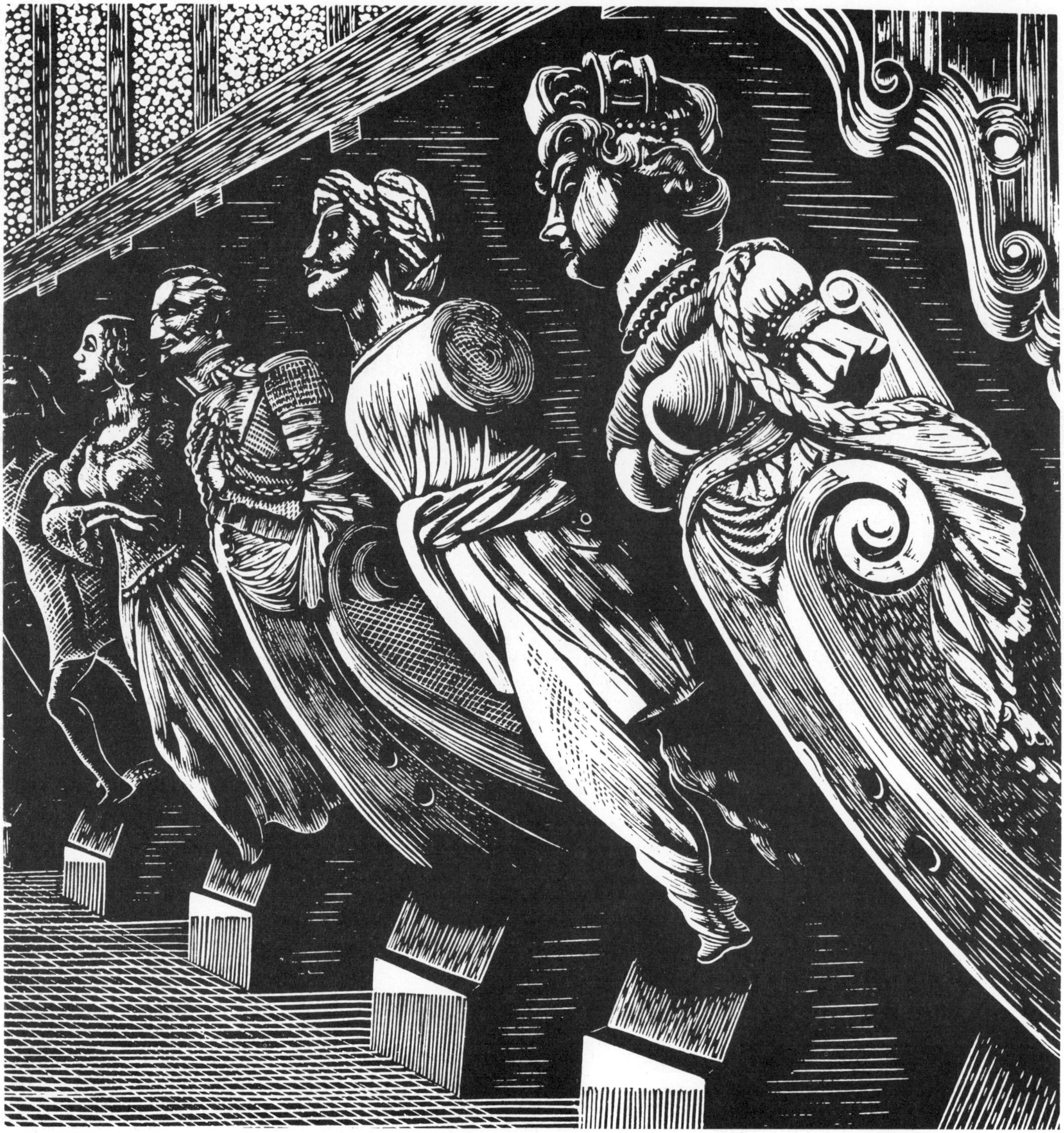

such in Gill's book *Art Nonsense and Other Essays* published in 1929. The contact with the Monotype Corporation was through Stanley Morison, who was aware of a link that Gill had had with Johnston when the latter designed his sans type, and Morison persuaded Gill to work on his ideas for a sans alphabet in 1927. This was eventually issued by the corporation as Gill Sans and is Gill's most famous exercise in type design. Among the other type faces he designed are Aries, executed for the exclusive use of the Stourton Press in 1932 but not used until about 1934, and the Golden Cockerel type cast in 1929 by the Caslon Foundry and first used in the Press's production of *The Hundredth Story* in 1930.

When he left Ditchling Gill became separated from Robert Gibbings whose war experience was quite different to that of Gill. At the outbreak of war Gibbings

[175] John Nash: *Judith and Holofernes* from *Apocrypha: the Book of Judith*, 1929. 12.5 x 18.0cm

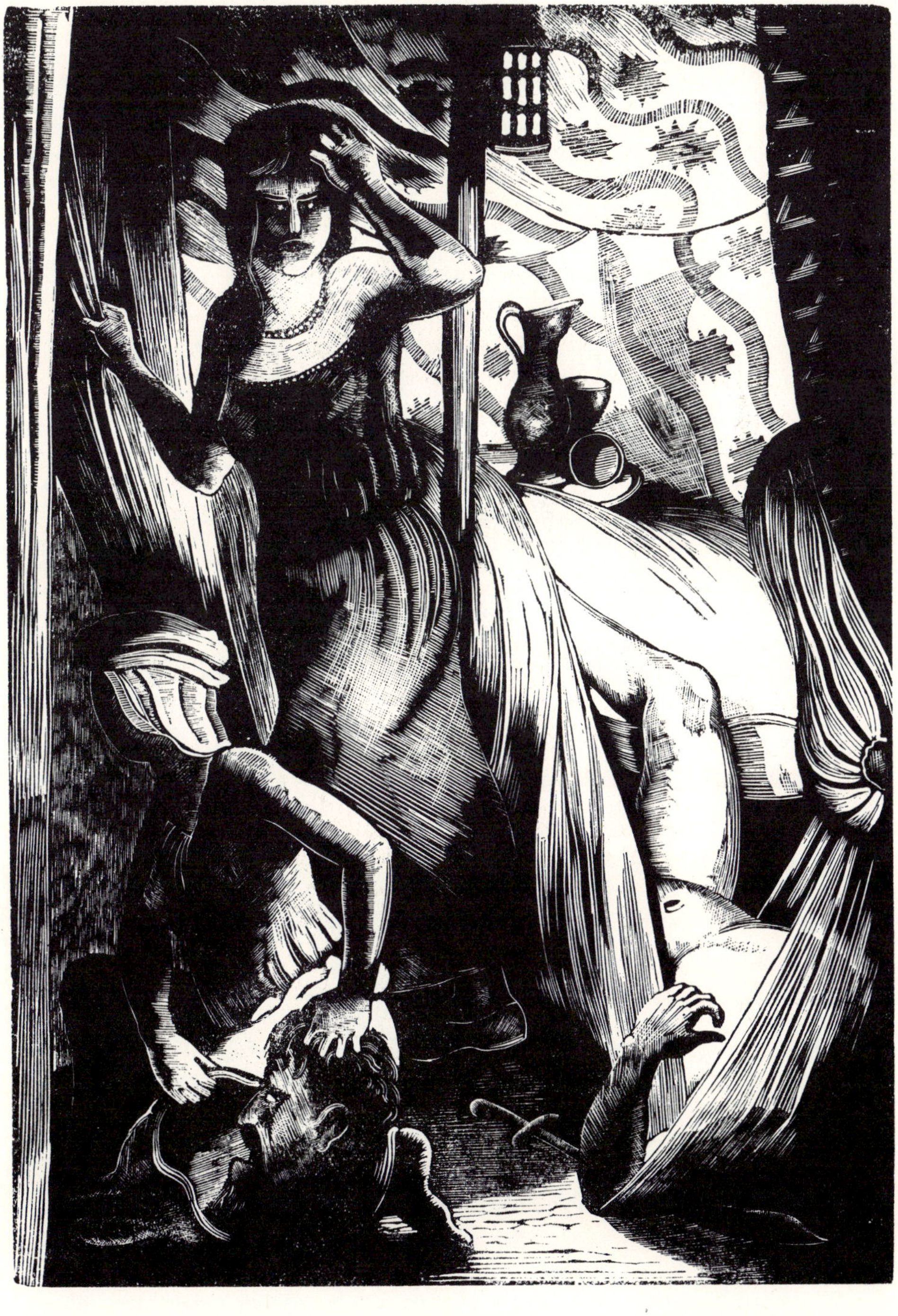

[176] Gertrude Hermes: *Tree of Life*, 1930. 18.5 x 26.5cm

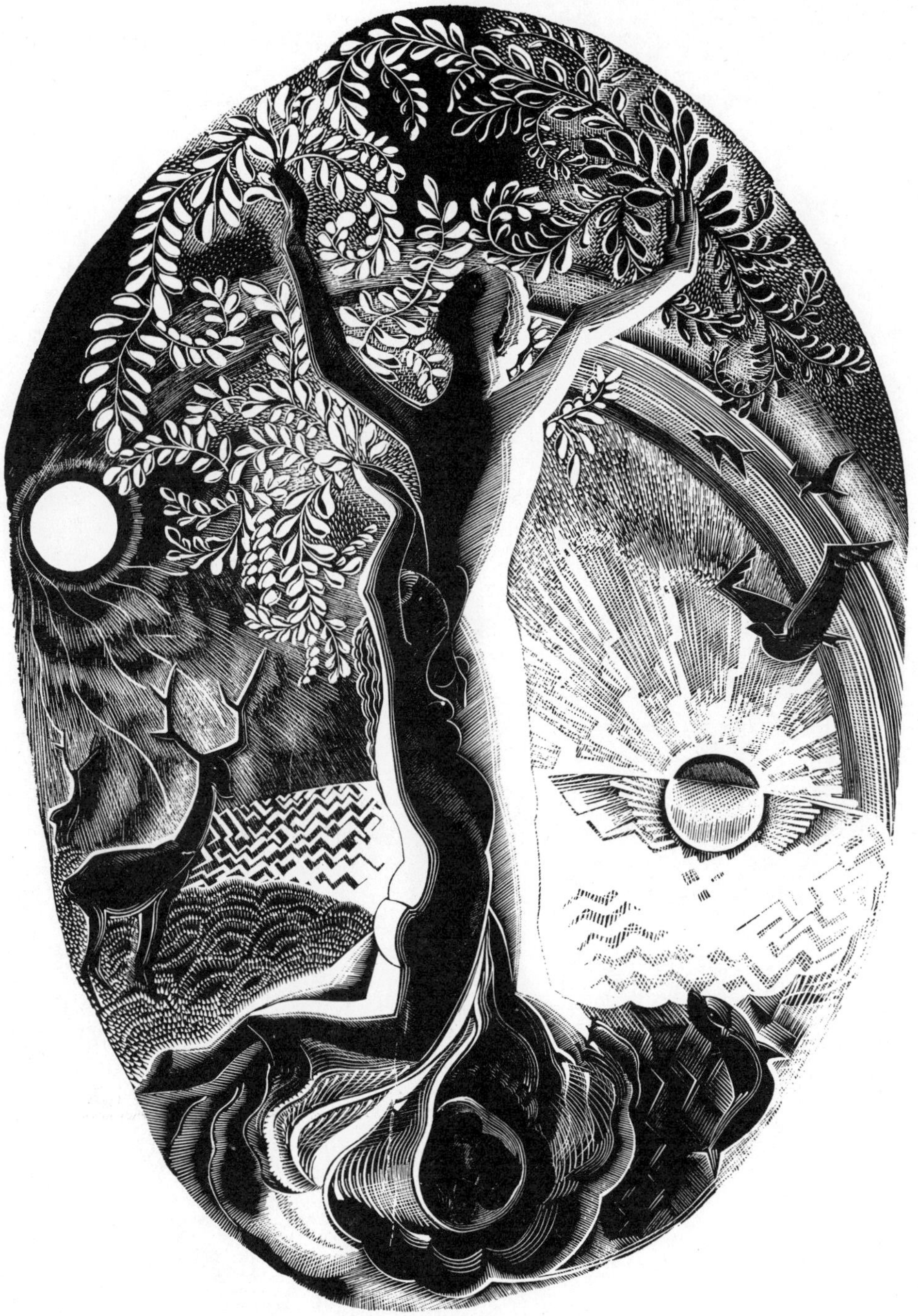

was gazetted as a second lieutenant in the 4th Battalion, Royal Munster Fusiliers. He found himself in the Gallipoli and Dardanelles campaigns but a piece of shrapnel through his neck ended his active soldiering. It meant a long period in hospital and an opportunity to get to know Malta. The island is the subject of several of his wood engravings. It was not until 1918 that it became possible for Gibbings to regard art as a full-time occupation. After the armistice he settled in London and married.

The reforming process of creative wood engraving was intensified quite independently from the influence of the Central School. Wyndham Lewis was developing his aesthetic concepts, which were to become known as 'Vorticism'. This was one

[177] Gertrude Hermes: *Waterlilies*, 1930. 13.5 x 23.25cm

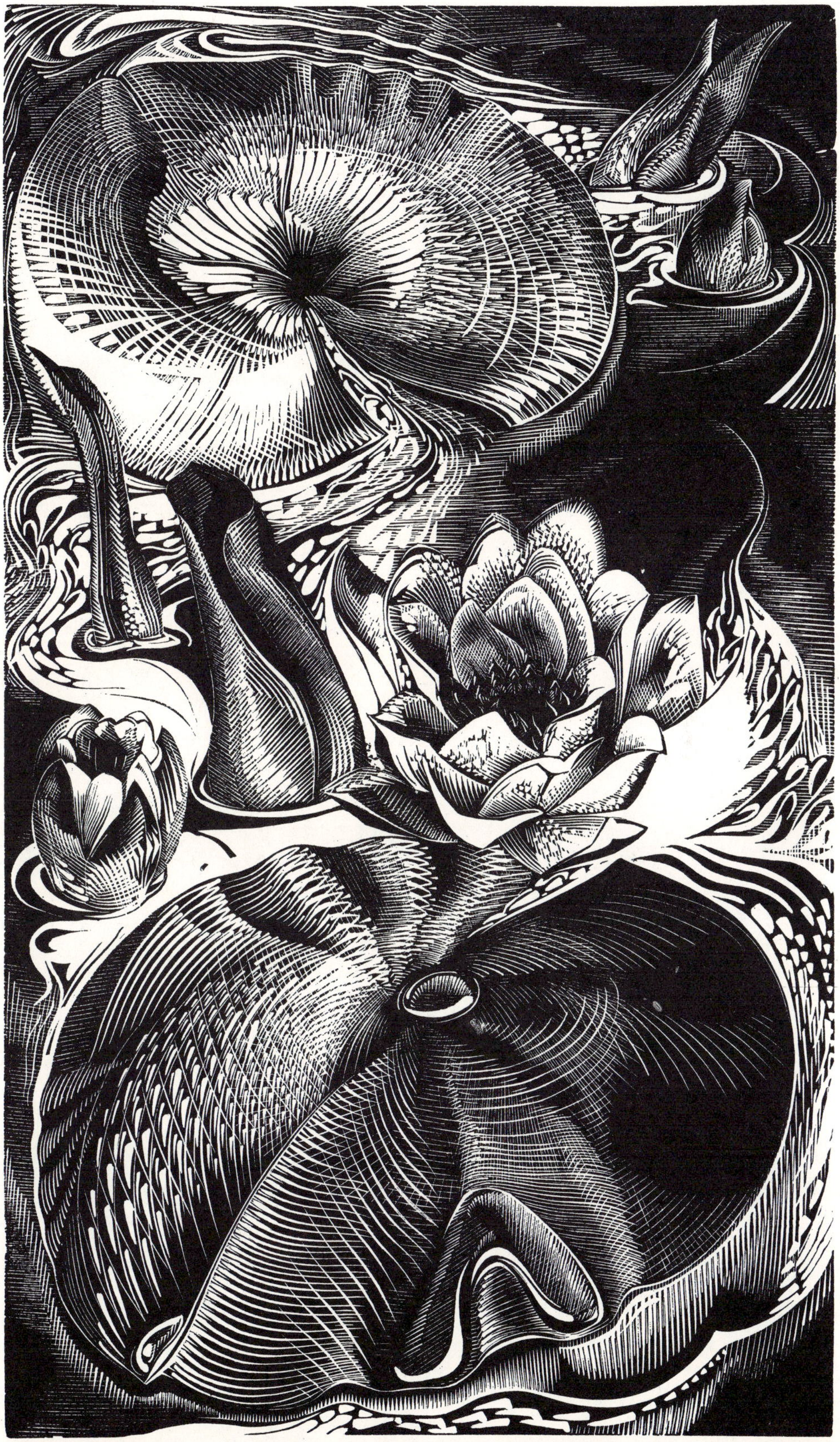

of the first direct manifestations of the revolt sparked off by Roger Fry's Post-Impressionist exhibitions. It was also the only entirely English 'ism'. It was Lewis's friend Ezra Pound who christened the movement as 'Vorticism'. The Vorticists were Edward Wadsworth, Henri Gaudier-Brzeska, William Roberts, Frederick Etchells, Jessie Dismorr and Helen Saunders. Later Michael Ayrton and Merlin Evans were influenced by Vorticism. Lewis's work was included in Roger Fry's second Post-Impressionist exhibition in October 1912.

Lewis wrote of his aims: 'As regards visual Vorticism, it was dogmatically anti-real. It was my ultimate aim to exclude from painting the everyday visual real altogether. The aim was to build up a visual language as abstract as music. The colour green would not be confined, or related, to what was green in nature – such as grass, leaves, etc; in the matter of form a shape represented by fish remained a form independent of the animal, and could be made use of in a universe in which there are no fish.'[14]

He also wrote: 'Another thing to remember is that I consider the world of machinery as real to us, or more so, as nature's forms, such as trees and so forth; and that machine forms have an equal right to exist in our canvases. I found colleagues who came from the industrial north, like Wadsworth, more ready to accept my views in this respect.'

From 1913 to 1920, Edward Wadsworth produced a series of wood engravings of the ships and dry docks at Liverpool. His interest in engineering and work on camouflaged ships is very apparent. This series of camouflaged ships was among the first works of the new school to attract wide public notice. They had a marked influence on the work of many contemporary engravers. Wadsworth was a completely independent artist and was looking for a medium that would give him scope for his bold and abstracted renderings of natural objects. He appears to have had little contact with the Central School group.

Wadsworth's prints have been persistently described as woodcuts but they are wood engravings; the precision of his angles could not have been achieved with a knife or gouge. As wood engravings the prints are virtually modern versions of a black-line *formschneider* print and as such they are also engraved drawings. Wadsworth was not really interested in the art of engraving, only in using it to serve his purposes for the occasion. Nevertheless his work represents an early experiment in the reform of wood engraving as a creative process.

REFERENCES

1 Selincourt *William Blake*, Duckworth, London, 1909
2 Brontë, Charlotte *Jane Eyre*, Collins, 1973
3 Rayner, John *Wood Engraving of Thomas Bewick*, Penguin Books, London, 1947
4 Yarrell, W. *History of British Birds*, London, 1843
5 Chatto and Jackson *A Treatise on Wood Engraving*, Knight, London, 1839
6 Cundall, J. *A Brief History of Wood Engraving from its Invention*, Sampson Low, London, 1895
7 MacColl, D. S. *Confessions of a Keeper and Other Papers*, Maclehose, London, 1931
8 Balston, T. *English Wood Engraving* 1900-1950, Art and Technics, London, 1951
9 Speaight, R. *The Life of Eric Gill*, Methuen, London, 1966
10 Speaight *The Life of Eric Gill*
11 Speaight *The Life of Eric Gill*
12 Speaight *The Life of Eric Gill*
13 Farleigh, J. *Graven Image*, Macmillan, London, 1940
14 *Engravings by the English Society of Wood Engravers* (exhibition catalogue), Carnegie Institute, Pittsburg, 1940

6 THEY KISSED THE CHAINS THAT BOUND THEM

The vigorous growth in wood engraving in the years immediately after the First World War was due in part to the excitement felt by the post-war generation in the rediscovery of a medium that had lain dormant for so long under the avalanche of commercialism, and also to the fact that the concepts were being clarified. The white-line aesthetics were firmly established and they continue to be seen in current developments.

Robert Gibbings had obtained his second commission for a wood engraving which was for a book plate for which he received a fee of three guineas. Gibbings's early wood engravings were all small, simple and tentative [117]. In 1922 he received his first commission for book illustration for Jonathan Cape's publication of an edition of Samuel Butler's *Erewhon.* His second book illustration commission came from Harold M. Taylor who was the owner and founder of the Golden Cockerel Press. The commission was for ten wood engravings for a limited *de luxe* edition of Brantôme's *La Vie des Dames Galantes.*

In view of the income from these commissions, Gibbings felt that one room in Chelsea was justified. No sooner had he obtained the room than a letter arrived from Harold Taylor's wife to inform him that her husband, already ill, had suffered a relapse. This news meant that his first big project was in jeopardy. A friend of Gibbings said, 'Why don't you buy the Press. It's just what you want.' Gibbings answered that he did not have the money. His friend replied 'I'll lend it to you. Go down on Monday and, if you like it, buy it.' Gibbings, who never hesitated in making decisions, went down on the Monday and bought it. The Golden Cockerel Press was to be the beginning of an exciting adventure and magnificent achievement. Gibbings was to come out of the venture rich in attainment and with great satisfaction of the soul, but financially disappointed; he just kept himself going with very little to spare and in the end went bankrupt. Today, of course, his books fetch considerable sums when they are sold.

The Golden Cockerel Press was the instrument which enabled Gibbings to develop as a designer of books. This was a natural corollary to his training from Rooke. Gibbings's energy, so apparent in his wood engravings, expresses the quickness and fullness of life and its urgency. No one has done this quite as well as he. In studying form, he was not concerned as artists usually are with the development and exploitation of it for its own sake, but as a means to an end. Gibbings wished to illustrate and his approach to form had to serve the call of illustration. He also wished to share his feelings of joy with others and this helped to make him an extrovert personality. He had rare vision and his strength, toughness and wit enabled him to express sensitivity within a powerful structure. Brutal strength dominates his early work and sensitivity is released during the middle and late periods. His technical skill is a constant feature through his life and is an outstanding element of the work of the British school of wood engraving.

From the beginning to the end of his career, Gibbings was a superb and clear-sighted illustrator and designer. As an artist he was the illustrator's dynamo and as an engraver he purified his language of form. He was a creator of memorable images and possibly our best-loved book illustrator.

He wrote to a number of artists inviting their co-operation. Oddly enough, Eric Gill was the only one to refuse, his grounds being that Gibbings was not a Catholic! However, Gibbings made another approach and this time he succeeded. Gill's acquaintance with Robert and Moira Gibbings ripened very quickly. He paid several visits to their house adjoining the Press at Waltham St Lawrence, where Gibbings had built a hut studio surrounded by trees at the bottom of the garden. Gill was soon engraving Gibbings's portrait. It was in collaboration with Gibbings at the Golden Cockerel Press that Gill did his best work in the field of book design and wood engraving.

On 27 March 1920 Robert Gibbings met Lucien Pissarro, E. Dickey, Noel Rooke, Sidney Lee and Philip Hagreen in the latter's studio, with a view to bringing wood engravers together to form their own society. It was agreed that they should meet in each other's studios and this practice was maintained into the seventies. At

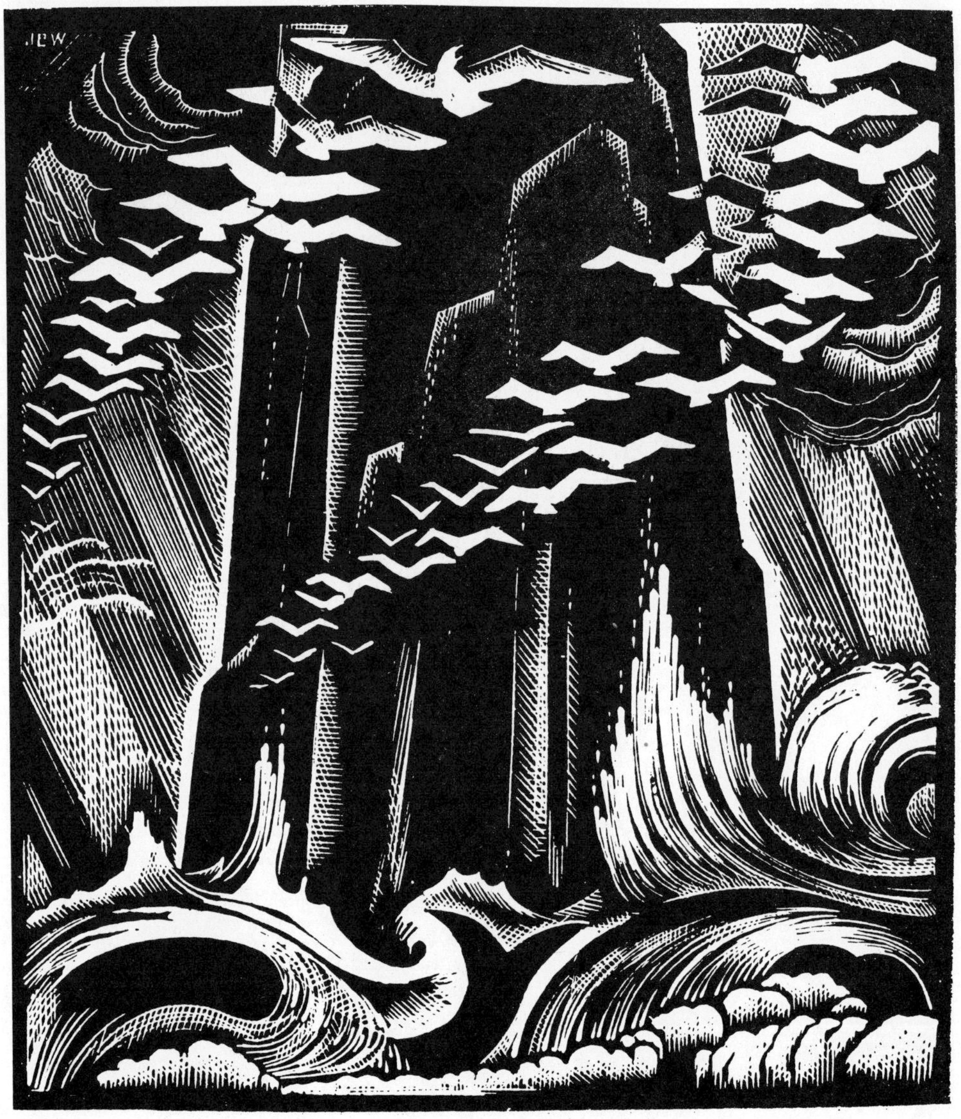

[178] John Buckland-Wright: Illustration from *The Collected Sonnets of John Keats*, 1930. 10.2 x 11.5cm

[179] Robert Gibbings: *Blogg's Pond*, approx 1930. 12.1 x 17.0cm

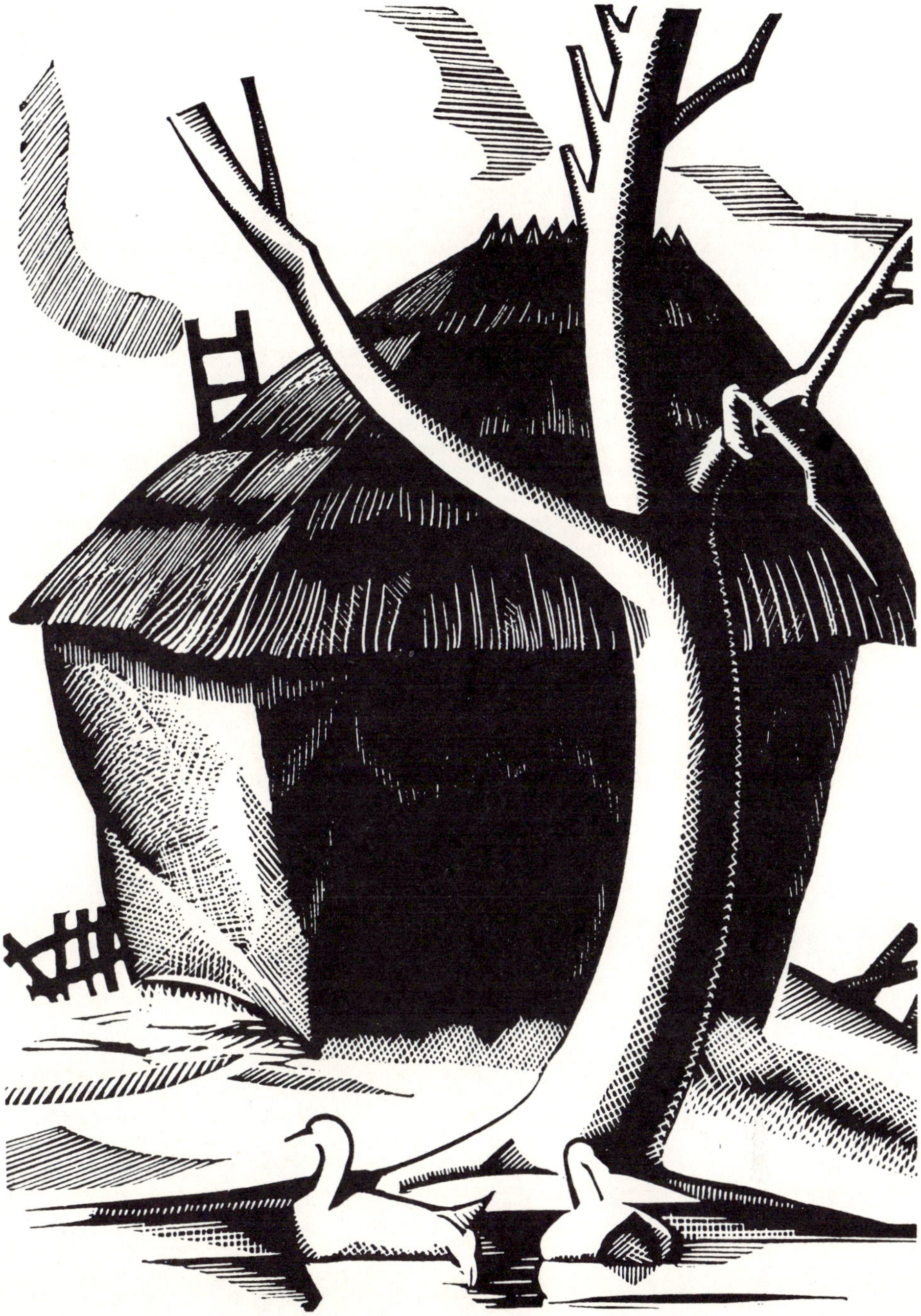

the first meeting the first resolution was 'That this Society be called the Bewick Club'.

Eric Gill, John Nash, Gwendolen Raverat, Sturge Moore and Gordon Craig were invited to foundership and they accepted. Wadsworth, Ricketts, Shannon, Ginner and Lucien Pissarro's brother Rodo were also invited but did not accept.

The Society's policy was laid down in the resolution 'The purpose of the Society is to hold exhibitions devoted solely to woodcutting and engraving by the European method.' At the fourth meeting held in 1920 it was agreed that the Society be called the Society of Wood Engravers. The Chenil Gallery in Kings Road Chelsea agreed the terms for the first exhibition, held in November 1920.

Gill made the wood engraving concept quite clear in the statement he wrote for the December issue of *The Architect* on the first exhibition of the Society of Wood Engravers. 'Membership of the Society is confined to those who use the European method of wood engraving. This method, distinguished from the Japanese or Eastern method by the fact that prints are obtained by means of the printing press, is more suitable to the tradition and temperament of European artists, and is of greater utility in connection with book production and decoration. . . .

'The modern world has been led to attach an absurd value to mere representation, and to judge all works from a mere imitation of natural form. There is, however, at the present time, by the mercy of God, a tendency to realise again the intrinsic value of a work of art as opposed to its extrinsic or sentimental value, and, in this matter, wood engraving is especially valuable, for the exact imitation of nature, which in paint or etching is comparatively easy and natural, is in wood engraving both difficult and unnatural. The wood engraver is forced by his material to have some respect for the thing in itself and to place an absolute value upon the art of drawing.'[1]

The first exhibition was a resounding success and attracted a very large response from the press. Some 133 inches of column cuttings came in from the national newspapers and magazines of all kinds. This was the more remarkable in view of the fact that, as exhibitions go, it was a small one with very small works all in black and white except for one work in colour by John Nash and another by Robert Gibbings. There was a total of ninety-one prints by seventeen wood engravers and the press reports made it evident that new developments in prints were afoot.

Two of the transitional black-line wood engravers joined the Society: Lucien Pissarro and Edward Gordon Craig who also worked in the woodcut technique. Both were to make an important contribution to the school and at the same time to develop wood engraving as they wished.

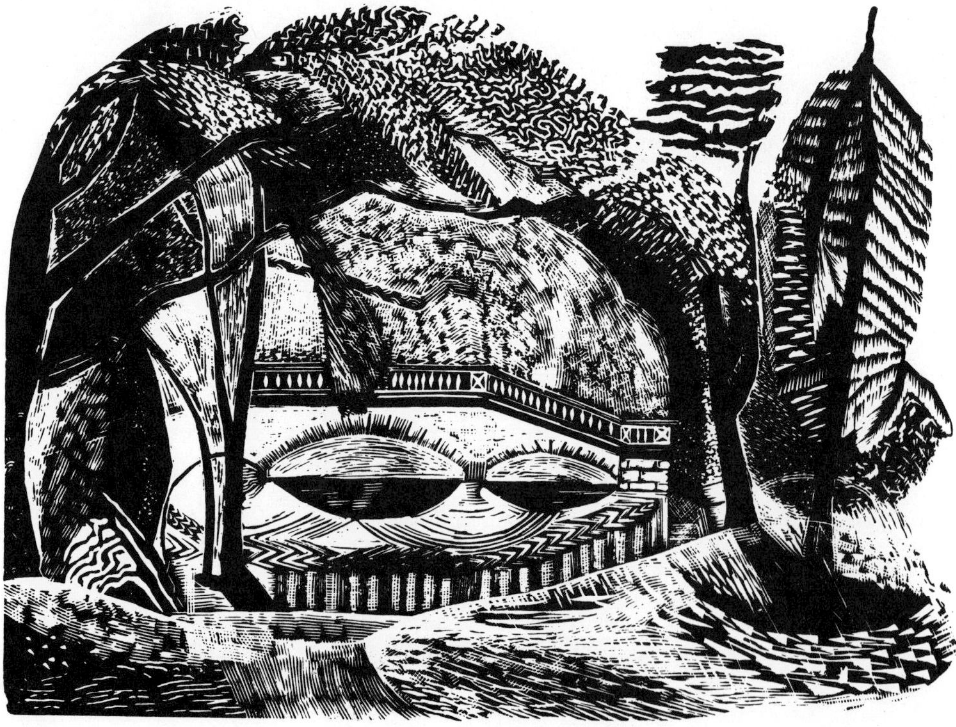

[180] Enid Marx: *Kenwood Folly*, 1930. 14.0 x 10.8cm

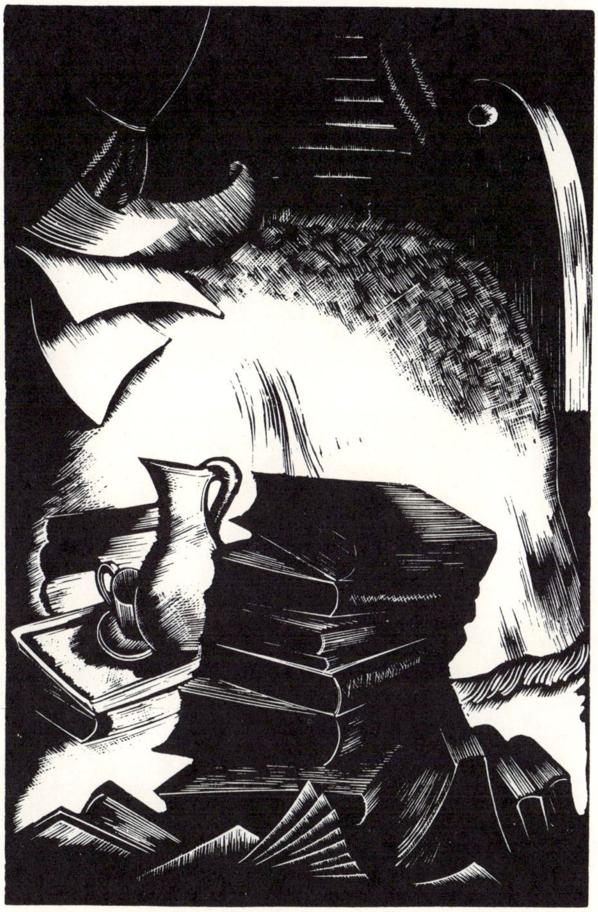

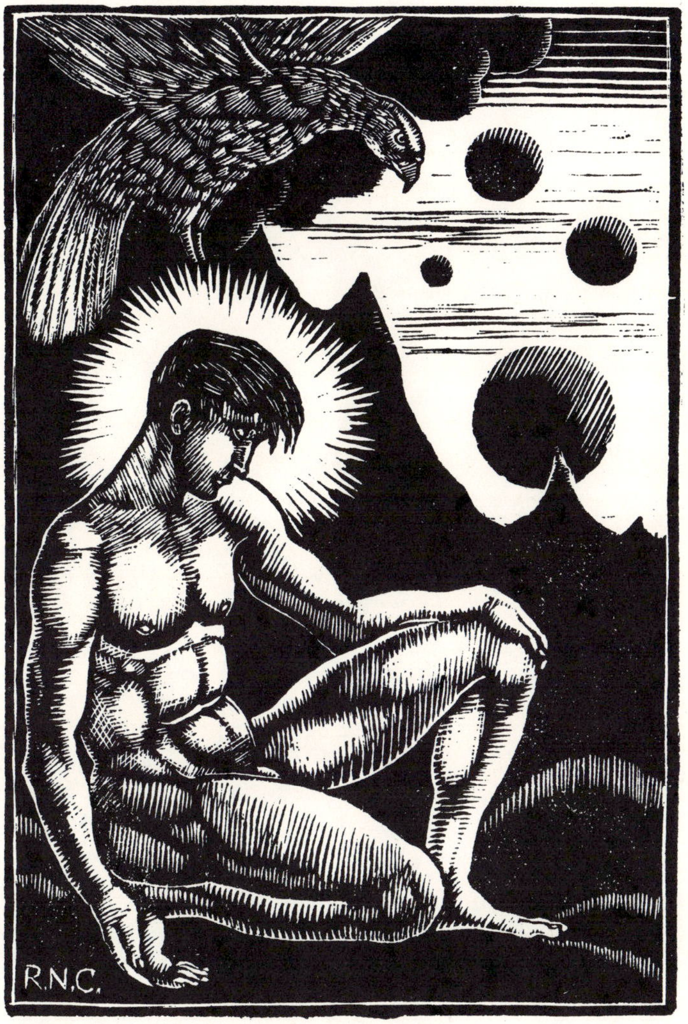

[181] John Nash: Illustration from *Celeste*, 1930. 7.9 x 12.0cm

[182] Ralph Chubb: *Mankind*, 1930. 9.0 x 13.5cm

By coincidence the Colnaghi Gallery had opened an exhibition of the work of the French wood engraver, the late Auguste Lepère (1849 to 1918) at the same time as the Society of Wood Engravers' exhibition. Lepère was a very mature master of the art whereas the members of the Society were very young. In style Lepère was painter-like and impressionistic and a true *peintre-graveur*.

Lepère and Pierre Gusman, another veteran engraver and historian, together founded the *Société des Graveurs sur Bois* in Paris in 1897. This society published *L'Image* under the artistic editorship of Tony Beltrand and Auguste Lepère, but it ran for one year only. In 1900 Lepère and Beltrand designed colour wood engravings for J. Richepin's book *Paysages et Coins de Rues* in Paris (*La Collection des Dix*). Gusman was also experimenting with colour using the *chiaroscuro* technique, or *clair obscur* of the Danube school. Colour was also being used for books by the engravers Pissarro, Gibbings and Rooke.

In Germany it was Carl Theodor Thiemann, born in 1881, who pioneered the revival of creative wood engraving. His work dates from about 1908. Thiemann spent most of his life near Dachau. He studied in Prague and his work was exhibited frequently in Munich and Vienna. Contemporary with Thiemann, a school of Russian wood engraving, stemming from the inspiration of the renowned Wladimir Favorsky (1886 to 1964) developed a creative revival and trained many brilliant students.

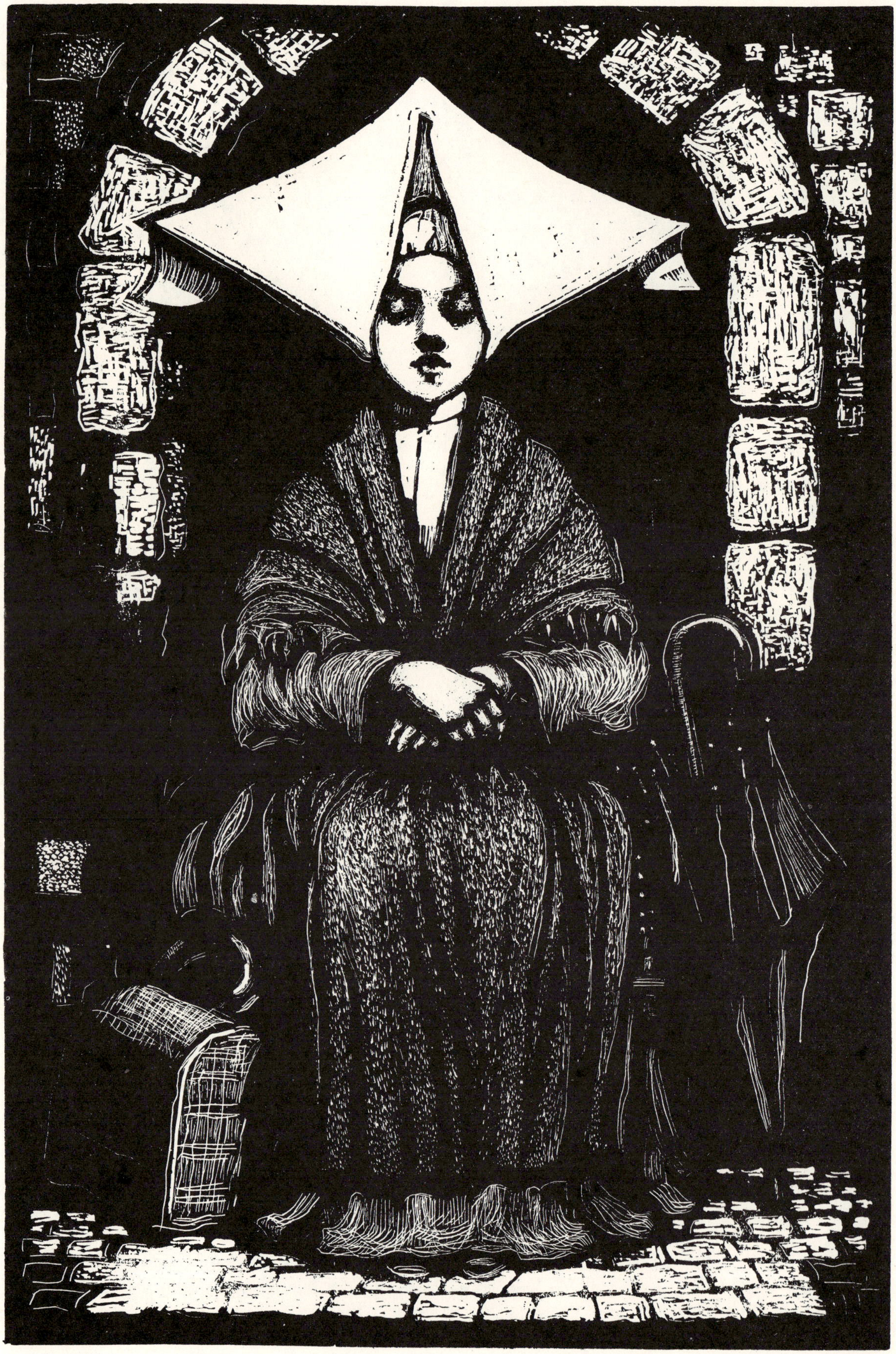

[183] Annabel Kidston: *A Traveller*, 1930. 15.5 x 23.0cm

The *Jewish Guardian* fired the first critical shot at the young English wood engravers. Their critic wrote: 'I am pleased to see that the wood engravers have formed themselves into a Society and that they are holding a very interesting little show at the Chenil Gallery by the Town Hall in Kings Road, Chelsea. Doubtless this hanging of such engravings side by side in collected form will bear in on their producers that they are working in a very narrow and limited groove, not justified by the legitimate limitations of their craft. . . .

'Let them examine the earlier, and best, work of Auguste Lepère now on exhibition elsewhere and they will see what free and expressive work was done by him, and many others, on lines which they have been taught to depise.'[2]

This was good writing and was indeed sharp comment but with the exception of Gwendolen Raverat, who was influenced by Lepère, the young engravers had no interest in the Lepère 'impression'. It was these young engravers who were to win a world-wide reputation and they were aware of the problems of establishing a new concept.

Charles Marriott, affectionately known as the 'incorruptible Marriott' did not quite appreciate the intentions of the engravers and in *Outlook* he wrote: 'The very merits of the first annual exhibition of the Society of Wood Engravers, at the Chenil Gallery, provoke a melancholy reflection, followed, however, by a hope of something beyond art as it is commonly understood. The melancholy reflection is that we have come to a state in which artists are driven to seize as an opportunity what their forefathers regarded as a limitation. They have learnt to "kiss their chains". No praise of the woodcut can conceal the fact that it is a more difficult way of doing something that could be done easily.'[3]

Marriott did not realise that these artists, in their research, were seeking a language of designed engraving. This was one of the reasons for the works being so small, although rarely have such small works been so highly charged with meaning. Marriott was unaware of the difference between drawing and the fundamental discipline of engraving. It was engraving that the exhibitors exploited and not the effects of drawing.

The critic of the *Athenaeum* was sensitive to the engravers' aims, he wrote: 'Certainly a great many artists, both in England and France, are now turning to this medium, no doubt because its limitations necessitate a certain formality of treatment which is congenial to the trend of modern art, while affording at the same time an incitement to technical invention. . . . Now, after a long interval, the wood is again being used as a medium for direct artistic expression. . . .'

There was also a lot of discussion in the press on the arrival of cheap works of art. Engraving once again, as with the Danube school, was to play a role which was both public and educational. In the foreword to the Society of Wood Engravers' second exhibition in November 1921, Campbell Dodgson expressed the scope of wood engraving when he wrote: 'The exhibition will prove again, as the first did, that woodcuts are not only suitable for illustrations, book plates, or the ornamentation of leaflets, ballads and other petty progeny of the printing press, but also, what is still insufficiently recognised, that they make, when framed, an excellent effect in the decoration of small rooms such as most of the collecting world inhabits in days when the burden of taxes is heavy and large engravings after Landseer have lost their charm, and Axel Haig's cathedrals bore us, and oil paintings are hateful if bad and much too expensive if good.'[4]

The second exhibition of the Society of Wood Engravers in 1921 brought two new artists into its membership, the landscape painter Ethelbert White and Paul Nash, and the third exhibition in November 1922 saw the introduction of Charles

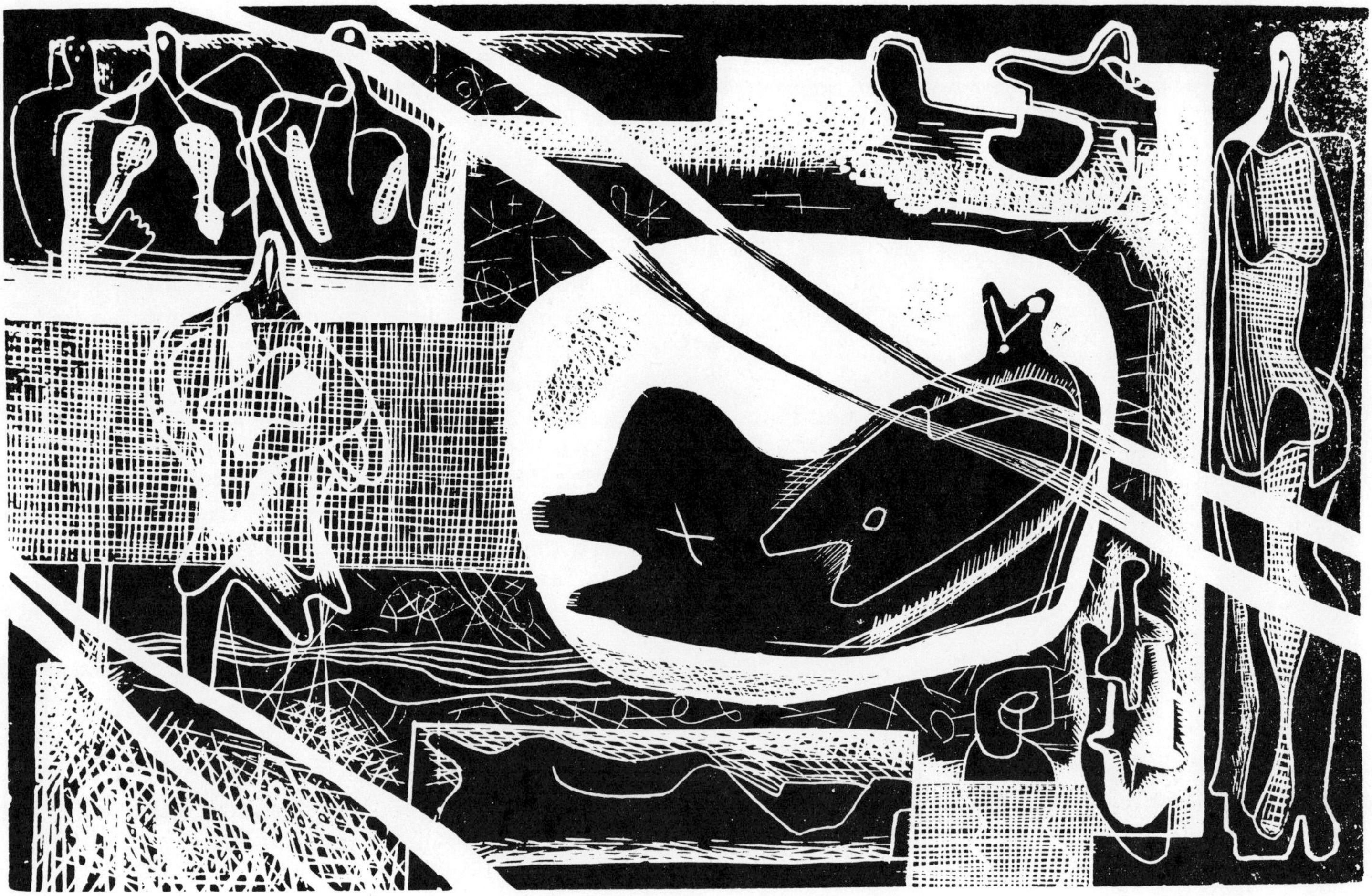

[184] Henry Moore: *Figures. Sculptures.* 1931. 19.6 x 12.75cm

Ginner and David Jones. At the 1922 exhibition, the *Manchester Guardian* commented: 'The method of illustration will not please everybody – there are those people to whom mere black and white are more or less anathema – nor will the treatment of the subject in many instances be wholly acceptable. But for all that, the exhibition is strong in its particular characteristics. Here and there, particularly in the studies by Paul Nash, there are tendencies which we do not like, so freed do they seem from the commonly accepted rules of pictures.'[5]

The catalogue of the 1922 exhibition carried Eric Gill's symbol for the first time [388]. He designed it for the Society and it has appeared on all letterheadings since. It has also been used freely on posters and catalogues and similar material. The first block [387] with the letters W E had to be modified so as not to restrict the Society to wood engraving.

Paul Nash and John Nash his brother, four years his junior, were sons of William Henry Nash, the Recorder of Abingdon. Though there was no art tradition in the family both men were destined to become important artists, each in his own right, and they were to make a considerable contribution to the British school of wood engraving. It was Paul who encouraged John to paint and John who persuaded Paul to take up wood engraving. He was an artist with wide overall vision and a deep sense of elemental nature. His interpretation of English landscape is romantic in the Blake and Sutherland tradition. He introduced the language of Cubism and Surrealism into English art. John is also a landscape painter but with a more objective eye than Paul. His vision is intellectually informed and he analyses visual

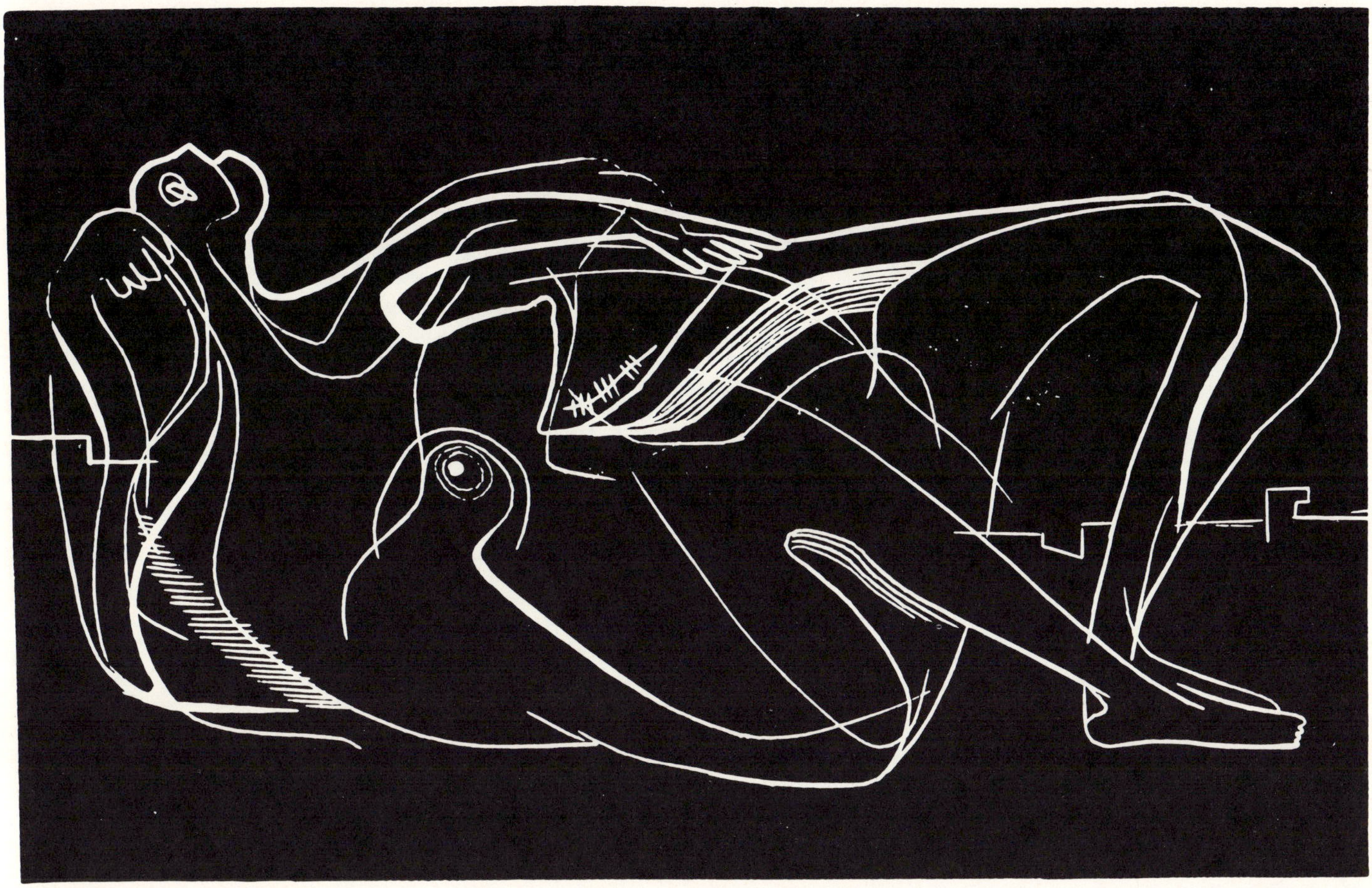

[185] Henry Moore: *Reclining Nude*, 1931. 16.1 x 10.1cm

experiences objectively. In engraving his visual form discoveries are sharpened by the precision of his burin, and his engraving has some of the lovable qualities of Robert Gibbings's quickness of life.

On leaving school in 1906 Paul Nash began attending art classes during the evening at the School of Photo-engraving and Lithography at Bolt Court, London and he continued studying at evening classes until 1909. In 1907 he began a short period of study at the Chelsea Polytechnic and extended his studies from 1910 to 1911 at the Slade School of Fine Art. In his early formative years he came under the influence of Rossetti and Blake, whose small wood engravings for Thornton's *Virgil* had an idyllic mysticism that fascinated Nash and provided an inspiration that he never lost.

Paul Nash held his first one man exhibition in 1912 at the Carfax Gallery. This event took place soon after the cataclysmic days of the Post-Impressionist exhibitions at the Grafton Galleries in November 1910 and January 1912. He caught the interest of Sir William Rothenstein who purchased his drawing *The Falling Stars* which was very close to Blake's romanticism in spirit. The one man show gave Nash courage and self-confidence and led to an invitation to exhibit with the New English Art Club.

When war broke out in 1914 he enlisted in the Artists Rifles and was assigned to home service. Later he was gazetted as second lieutenant in the 3rd Hampshire Regiment and served on the Ypres Salient. Eventually he was wounded and sent back to England with broken ribs and was invalided out of the Army.

When Nash had recovered, John Buchan recommended him as an artist to the

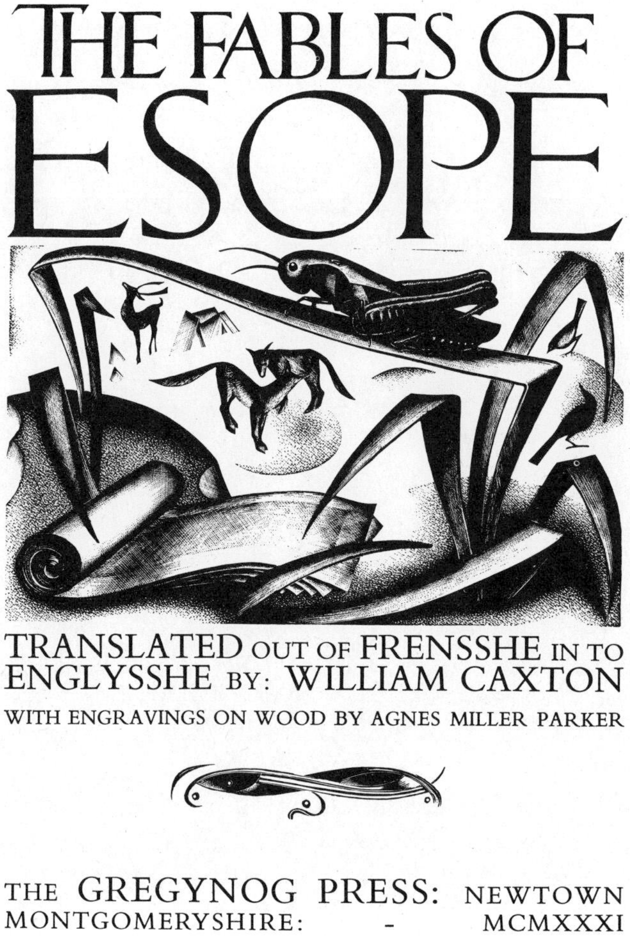

THE FABLES OF ESOPE

TRANSLATED OUT OF FRENSSHE IN TO ENGLYSSHE BY: WILLIAM CAXTON

WITH ENGRAVINGS ON WOOD BY AGNES MILLER PARKER

THE GREGYNOG PRESS: NEWTOWN MONTGOMERYSHIRE: - MCMXXXI

[186] Agnes Miller Parker:
Title page from *Fables of Aesop*, 1931.
Page size 21.5 x 30.5cm

War Office. He returned to France as an official artist in 1917 and again found himself at Vimy. He found the job of war artist threw him into more danger than when he had been there fighting. His experiences made a profound impression on him and gave a deeper meaning to his art form. In 1918 he held a small exhibition of drawings and watercolours done in the trenches at the Leicester Galleries and it was at this point that he gained the interest of Herbert Read who had had similar experiences and was impressed with the truth of Nash's rendering of the horror of war. The unpleasant experiences of the war had a maturing effect on Nash and after the 1918 exhibition he emerged as one of the foremost English artists.

From the Cubist influence, Paul Nash was acquiring a means of structural control which he always sublimated to his native romantic imagination. These qualities made themselves felt at his next exhibition at the Leicester Galleries in 1924. By this time he had exhibited seventeen wood engravings with the Society of Wood Engravers.

About 1919 he formed a friendship with Eric Fitch Daglish and both were invited to become members of the Society in 1922. Daglish was a pupil of Nash's for wood engraving. Three of his works were exhibited at the opening exhibition of the Society of Wood Engravers in 1920. He was a very fine draughtsman and a sensitive engraver, chiefly of animals and birds, and he illustrated his own books with his wood engravings. Daglish was a professional naturalist and writer and published many books through J. M. Dent between 1926 and 1948. His fame as an engraver rests upon his superb craftsmanship and expert knowledge of his subject though he never moved out of the role of the naturalist. During the 1920s he lived at Dymchurch, very near to Paul Nash.

John Nash had no formal training at an art school and his outlook and style as an artist are very different from those of his brother. It was Paul who dissuaded John from having an art school training, but he exercised a formative influence over his brother's development by sharing the knowledge gained in his own formal training. In some ways this accounts for John's pictorial innocence and objective vision; he was the realist and Paul the poet. They both developed an interest in the Norwich school of painting and in particular Cotman, Cozens and Girtin.

1913 was an important year for John Nash because he had his first one man show at the Dorien Leigh Gallery. This exhibition brought him into the orbit of the realist artists of Fitzroy Street. At this time they were expanding the Camden Town Group into the London Group which held its first exhibition in London in 1914.

[187] Iain Macnab: *Corsican Landscape*, 1931. 25.4 x 20.3cm

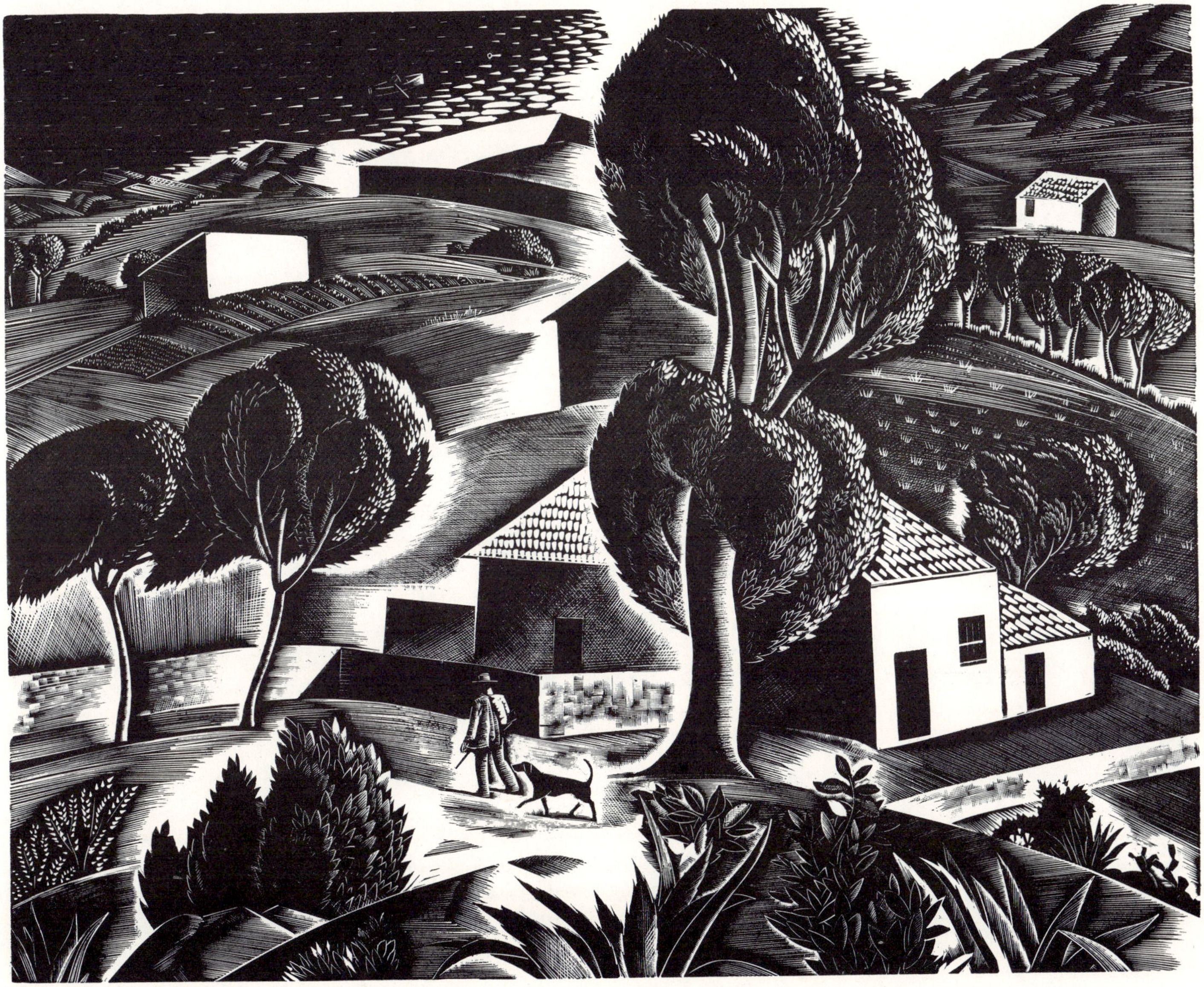

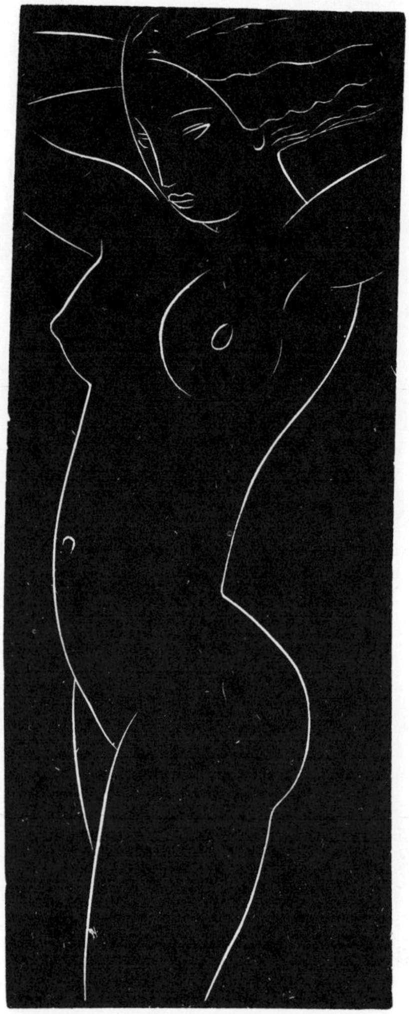

[188] John Buckland-Wright: *Nude*, E, 1931. 5.1 x 13.25cm

In the Fitzroy Group, John Nash met Bevan, Ginner, Gilman, Gore and Lucien Pissarro. What is particularly interesting in the case of the latter is that when the Nash brothers started engraving neither of them adopted Pissarro's black-line technique and both worked in the new white-line.

A close examination of John Nash's engravings gives the feeling that life has much to offer, even if it be only an engraving of a flower or a pig [119]. His innocence and freshness of outlook has led him to emphasise the sharp-cut quality of engraving and this expresses the essence of living and the appreciation of forms. John Nash's engravings of the human form, of flowers and of plants have a realism that is quite scientific in its observation and crispness of expression. Despite the fact that they are small works, the engravings are important in the British school because they stand out as unique studies of natural structures, progression and rhythm, surface texture, accurate three-dimensional rendering and shape expression.

In all, John Nash has illustrated twenty-five books of which seven are in wood engraving. Three of these books were produced by the Golden Cockerel Press and one by the Cresset Press. The contribution of John Nash to the art of book illustration is marked by his directness of observation and drawing, his literary awareness and search for visual truth. Nash's early wood engraving *Sheep and Lambs* shows his severe and simple honesty, form observation and the pure volumetric form arising from it. This engraving is one of the first to indicate the future development of wood engraving. *Daphne laureola* from *Poisonous Plants* issued by John Nash in 1927 [162] is a famous image and a remarkable engraving using considerable economy of means. The few white lines carefully defining the undulations of the leaf surfaces are solely responsible for the black leaves appearing highly polished in the matt black ink, a phenomenon which is psycho-physical. This effect is heightened through each line being the right length and shape, which is a subtlety often missed; such experiences and sensitivity are rare in art. He also uses the light lines on the leaves to describe two large arcs which hold the composition together. These two arcs are only drawn in part and the complete line is interpreted by the viewer – the Chinese philosophical economy of understatement. Nash's geometry is not superficially superimposed on the subject, but has been found and extracted from it and in this work he is demonstrating the French principle of abstraction in his own way. This engraving is the essential John Nash.

Nash is the complete artist and can move logically and freely through the world of plants, animals, landscape and human beings with confidence. As the visual realist he can be seen at his most complex in *Judith and Holofernes* [175]. The inherent drama in this subject is sublimated to the point where it has to re-evolve gradually. There is not a single flourish or imperfect line anywhere, neither is there one too many in this mass of articulated human limbs intertwined and related by folds and fabric everywhere. The even distribution of blacks, white and greys, which in lesser hands could be so boring, are in Nash's work all elements used to emphasise the glorious rhythms and their counterpoint. This white-line engraving will stand favourable comparison with any black-line engraving of the Danube school though its outstanding qualities are not immediately apparent. Only two tools have been used for the engraving and there is no concession to decoration or pattern-making for their own sakes. The engraving is an autonomous work of art in its own right and it sets standards for illustration.

In the 1920s the Society of Wood Engravers was pouring a great deal of energy into promoting wood engraving and the 1921 exhibition went to Oxford; the 1922 and 1924 exhibitions went to the Whitworth Gallery in Manchester. Not content

[189] Leon Underwood: Illustration from *The Island*, 1931. 10.0 x 20.5cm

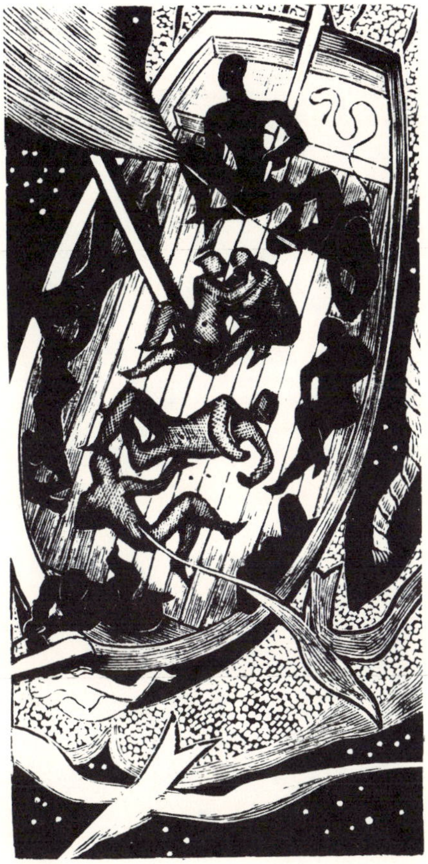

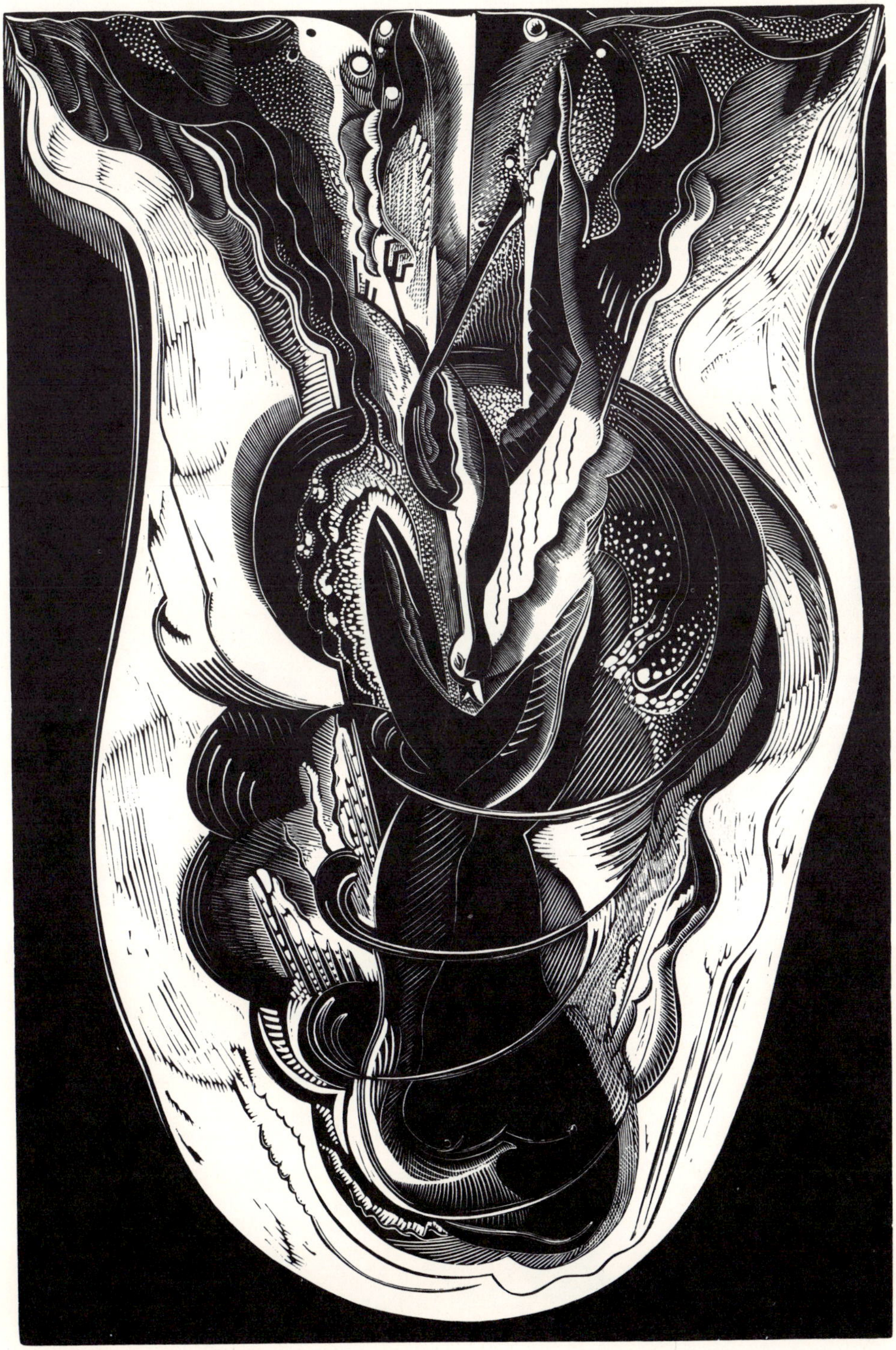

[190] Gertrude Hermes: *Fathomless Sounding*, 1932. 25.15 x 38.1cm

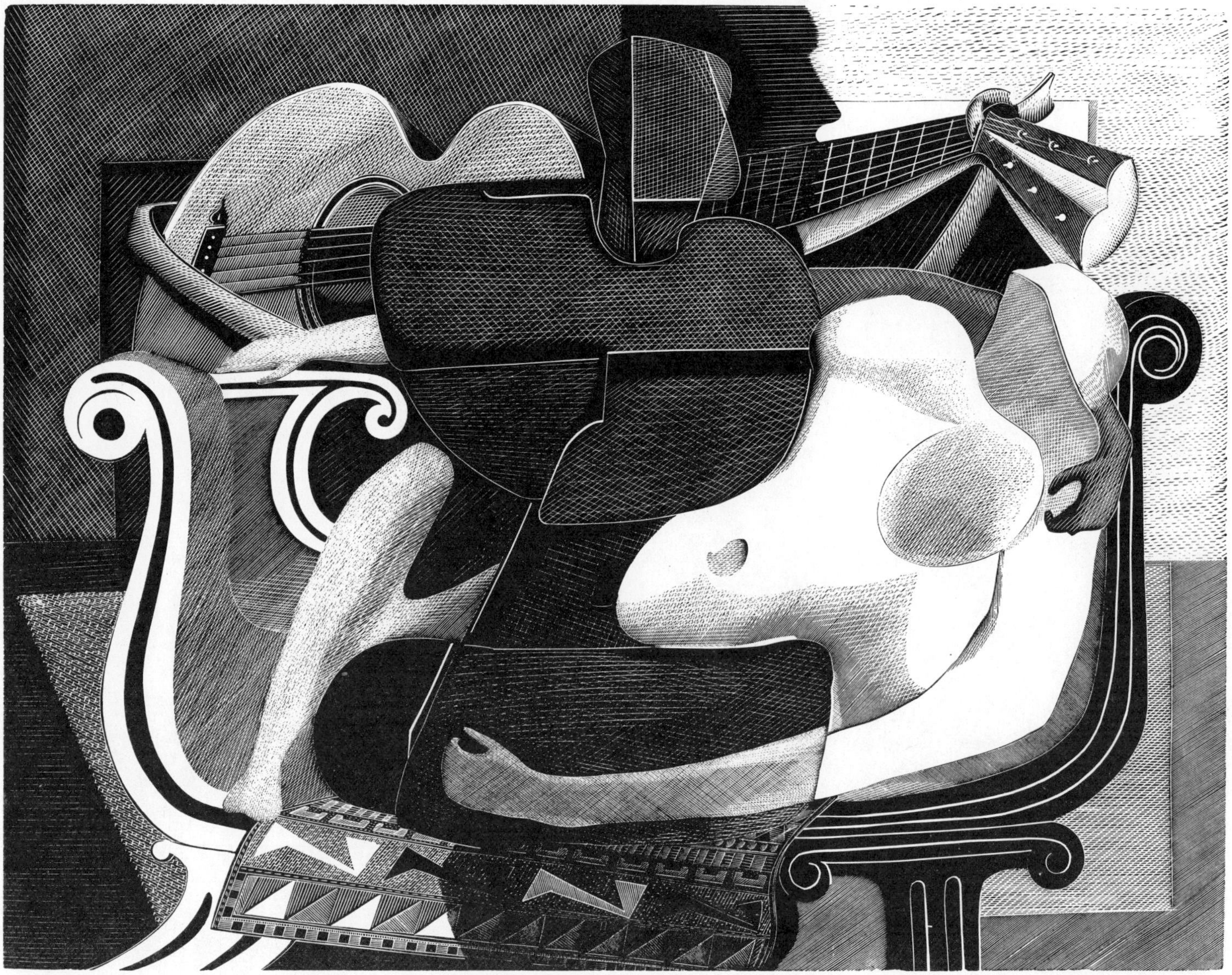

[191] Blair Hughes-Stanton: *Figures I*, 1937. 29.3 x 23.0cm

to confine its activities to Britain, the Society organised its first overseas exhibition in 1923 at the Department of Fine Arts, Carnegie Institute, Pittsburg, where the work of twenty-one engravers was exhibited.

The 1925 annual exhibition of the Society was marked by the inclusion of the first exhibited works of the then young unknowns, David Jones, Gertrude Hermes and John Farleigh. All three were to increase the range of expression; to make white-line engraving a vehicle for unique creative vision – and to become eventually major engravers of the new British school.

In 1923 and 1924 the Society's annual exhibitions were held at Arthur E. Howell's St George's Gallery. In 1925 it moved to the Redfern Gallery, then in Old Bond Street, run by Rex Nankivel and continued showing there until the gallery moved to Cork Street in 1936. The Society of Wood Engravers was probably the first society to place its exhibition programme in the hands of art dealers. The new generation of engravers was very professionally orientated, and for artists they were unusually businesslike.

In commenting on the 1924 exhibition of the Society, the press noted the exhibits of Eric Fitch Daglish and John F. Greenwood but not those of David

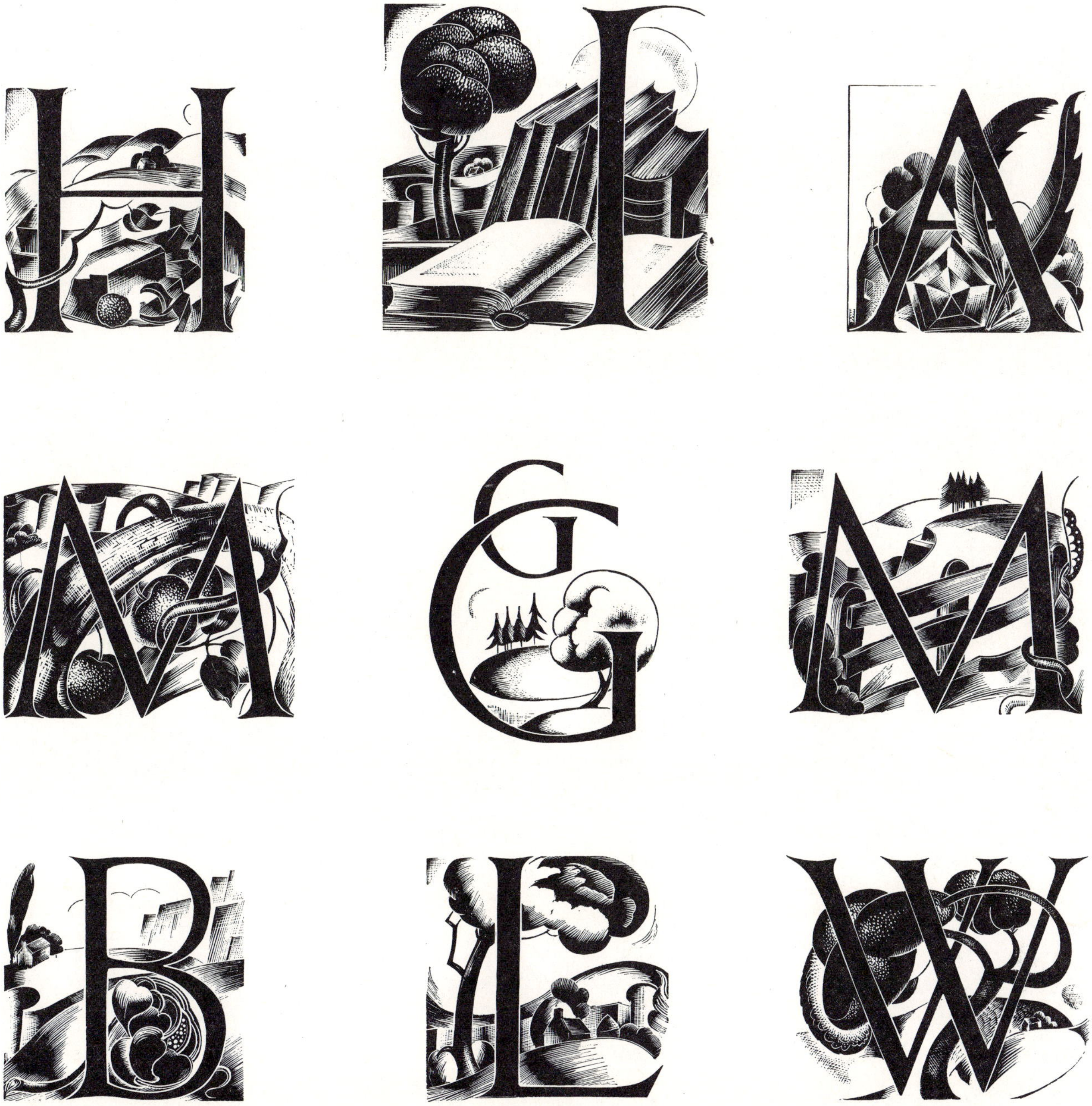

[192] William MacCance: *Initials*
from *Fables of Aesop*, 1932.
20.25 x 20.25cm

[193] John R. Biggs: *Ox House, Shaftesbury*, 1932. 7.5 x 12.75cm

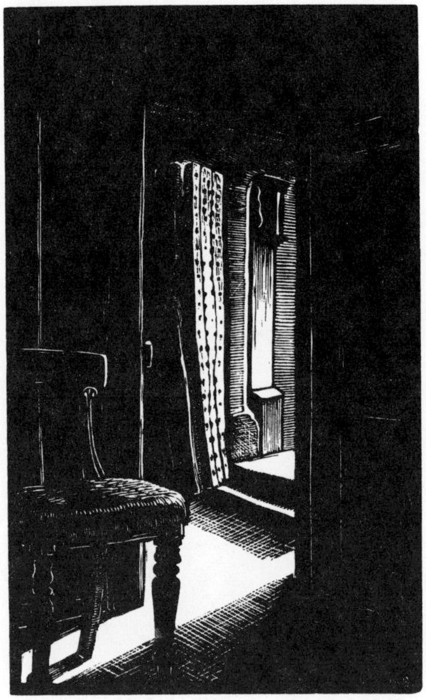

Jones. This was surprising because David Jones's art is highly concentrated and full of surprises for the sensitive viewer. There is no label or dominant stylistic influence which fits. In content his art stems largely from the poetry of William Blake and the painter El Greco, but Jones has understood the art of Palaeolithic man better than most. Like the Nash brothers, Jones's most favoured medium after wood engraving is the watercolour. Both Paul Nash and David Jones worked in engraving to forge the overall language of their various media. In their approach to the subject of war expressed in art, Jones was transcendental and classical whereas Paul Nash was partly objective and partly romantic. Nash never completely clarified these two opposing elements in his make up.

Both David Jones and Paul Nash were to develop into major artists, Jones being a natural engraver whose burin opens the flow to life and to his images. He is in the grand tradition of painter-graver and a Jones engraving, whether in wood or copper, could not exist in another medium. With great economy he achieves complex images and maximum movement. His wood engraving is of the pure white-line concept and he uses a pencil beam of delicate white light illuminating and delineating his subjects and their structure and environment just sufficiently to identify them. He has never approached wood engraving from the point of view of exploiting it as a medium; he uses it as a means to an end. He is an artist using the medium as he finds it. His copper engraving technique is virtually his white-line engraving reversed to give a black-line image.

Jones is an original artist who stands alone, independent of the aesthetic form movements which have crossed his time and space. It is only in his composition and structure that traces of Cubism and abstract thinking are evident. In English art such quality exponents are rare. He was not afraid to drive his aesthetics home or to be unfashionable for his time. Jones must, in this position, be given time for the full appreciation to run parallel with this achievement. The formal language of Paul Nash had a continental airing while he lived and thereby appreciation came much earlier in his lifetime. Jones's formal language is as personal as is his closeness to the Arthurian legend and his Franciscan devotion to animals and all things living.

[194] Tom Chadwick: *Lorton, Cumberland*, 1932. 19.25 x 8.5cm

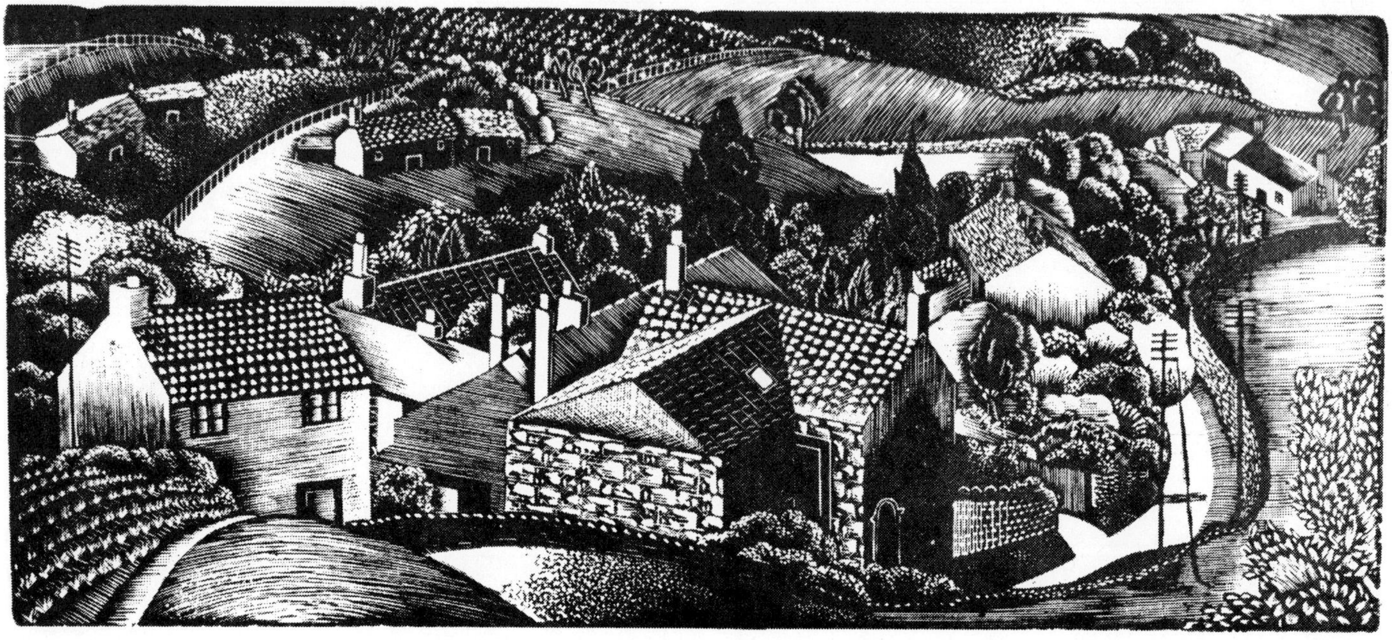

[195] Lettice Sandford: Illustration from *Thalamos*, 1932. 10.8 x 18.5cm

[196] Lettice Sandford: Illustration from *Sappho*, 1932. 8.5 x 14.75cm

David Jones is a superb draughtsman and together with another of similar quality, Gaudier-Brzeska, has produced some of the finest animal drawings of the century. Iain Macnab has said that where drawing is concerned we still need to retain the word 'magic'. Bernard Meninsky also used the word when writing of the art of drawing and 'magic' is a very adequate way to describe such a drawing as Jones's *Lynx*. It has the magic of the Palaeolithic artist in the cave, a quality rarely seen in the work of modern or geometric man. With a few fine lines, a few light tones and a few dark strokes of emphasis so accurately placed, the artist is able to sum up virtually everything the animal is, does and fears. Yet the artist, through the drawing, expresses a Franciscan love and sheer joy. The sublimation of anatomy and structure is such that the observer puts it all together. Understatement of this quality is usually only associated with Chinese philosophy rather than the direct European style of expression.

He started his formal training in art at the Camberwell School of Art in 1909. Here he firstly became aware of the French Post-Impressionists through his tutors A. S. Hartrick, Reginald Savage and Herbert Cole. Jones speaks well of the teaching of Hartrick who had known Gauguin and Van Gogh in Paris; thus Jones

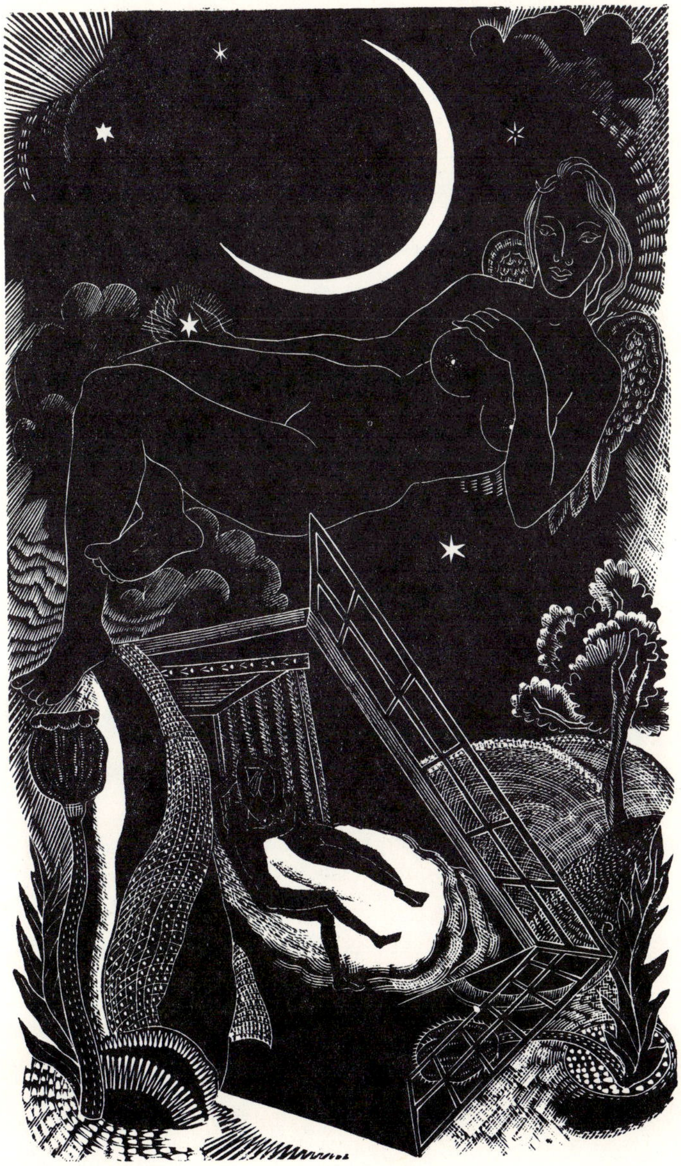

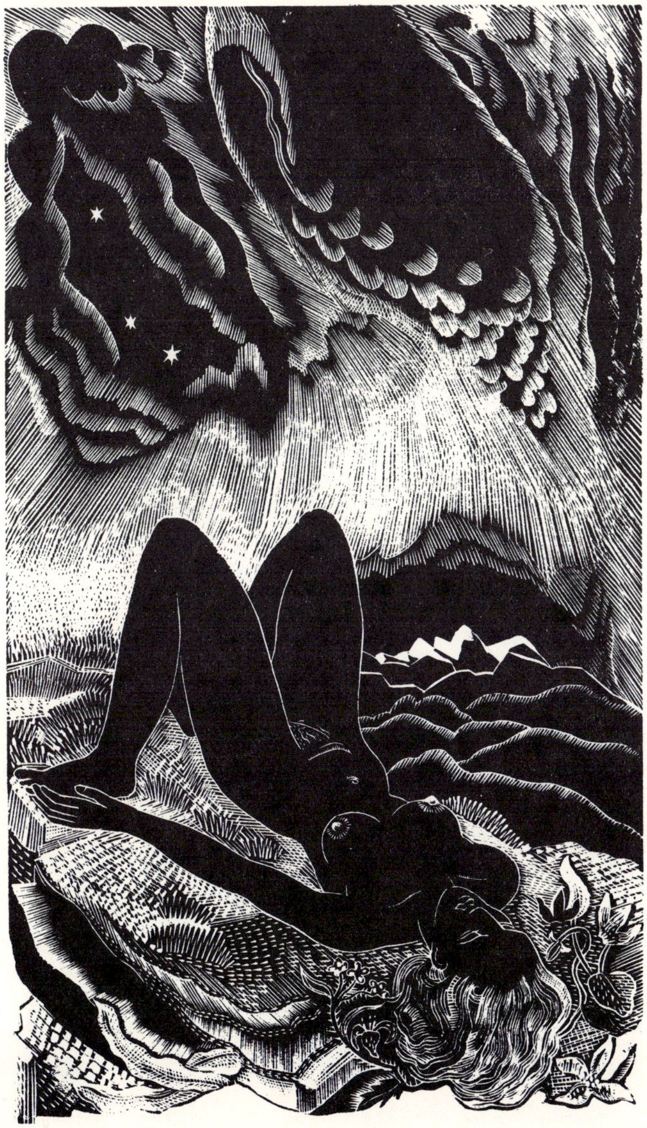

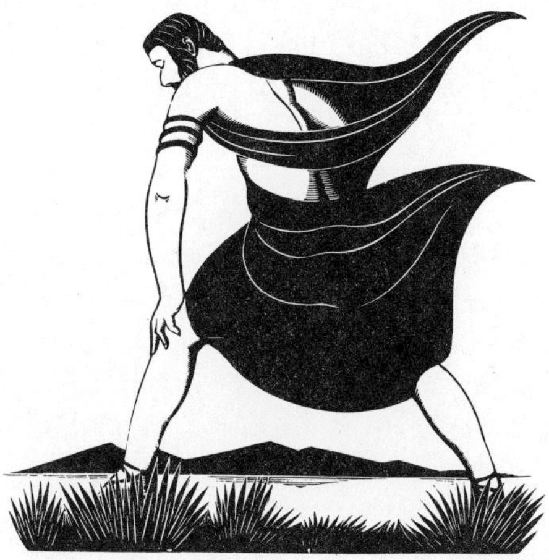

[197] Robert Gibbings: Illustration from *Hyperion* by John Keats, 1932. 12.5 x 12.75cm

heard of the modern French movement first hand. His career was later interrupted by the outbreak of war and in 1915 he joined the Royal Welch Fusiliers with whom he served in the trenches on the Western Front in France until 1918.

With the aid of a government grant he resumed his art studies in 1919 at the Westminster School of Art under Walter Bayes and Bernard Meninsky and it was there that he resolved his previously muddled thinking on art. Walter Bayes emphasised the need for mastering the aesthetics and craft of art in order to become articulate and gave the necessary guidance for his students to achieve this. No student having a real potential could fail to benefit from Meninsky's life class. Thirty years later Jones was to confirm this teaching in his book *Anathemata*, 1952, when he wrote: 'It is axiomatic that the function of the artist is to make things *sub specie aeternitatis*'.[6] The evidence of the philosophy of Bayes is seen in Jones's statement, 'There must be no mugging-up, no "ought to know" or "try to feel", for only what is actually loved and known can be seen *sub specie aeternitatis.*'

In 1921 David Jones was received into the Roman Catholic Church and with increasing pace began to show evidence of a religious symbolism in his work. Coupled with the Welsh-inspired imagery, this gave rise to composition in which both factors are lovingly coaxed into an environment where everything is resolved and fused. In his symbolism, the art of David Jones can never be separated from his religious beliefs.

In the same year that he became a Catholic, Jones was introduced into Ditchling by Eric Gill. He never became a member of the Guild of St Joseph but stayed at Ditchling for four years, living with one of the families in the settlement and learning wood engraving from Desmond Chute. For David Jones wood engraving became a major medium and one that was particularly suited to the fine sense of craftsmanship which he had gained from his father.

In 1925 Jones moved to Gill's new workshop at Capel-y-ffin where Gill had taken up residence in 1924. The influence of Eric Gill made a lasting impression on David Jones.

In moving to Wales Jones was seeking a quieter place to work and to clarify his aesthetic individuality which at this time was still unresolved. The Welsh landscape, mountain valleys and the rocks by the Pembrokeshire shore, enabled him to find himself as an artist. Two visits to Caldy Island and a period in the monastery there were important to him as an artist.

In 1925 he did his first work for the Golden Cockerel Press when he illustrated an edition of *Gulliver's Travels* published in two volumes with forty wood engravings. His second Golden Cockerel Press book *The Book of Jonah* appeared in 1926 and the third work was *The History of Pompey the Little, or the Adventures of a Lap Dog* by Francis Coventry. His final work for the Golden Cockerel Press was *The Chester Play of the Deluge* in 1927 which contained ten of his wood engravings and occupied the major part of his time in that year.

In 1927 he left Wales and went back to live with his parents. He was invited to join the Society of Wood Engravers in the same year, and he remained a member until his death.

In 1928 he engraved on copper a series of illustrations for an edition of Coleridge's *Rime of the Ancient Mariner* and for grace and eloquence these engravings stand out among intaglio prints.

During 1924 the members of the Society of Wood Engravers were hotly debating a possible change of gallery and dealer from St George's and Mr Howell to the

Redfern and Rex Nankivel. This was to prove a wrench to friendships and loyalties and in 1926 a splinter group was formed under the title of the English Wood Engraving Society. They held their first exhibition at St George's Gallery thus continuing a link with the dealer Howell. Meanwhile the original Society transferred to the Redfern Gallery. Throughout their separate existence, the two societies continued to hold their exhibitions at the same time with the same opening date. In the minutes of the original Society is the following entry: 'It was resolved that the Society of Wood Engravers shall observe a friendly attitude towards the new Society.'

The leader of the new English Wood Engraving Society was Edward Gordon Craig, despite the fact that he was then living permanently in Italy – an indication of his importance in English engraving.

The artists showing at the English Society's first exhibition were Gordon Craig, Ethelbert White, John F. Greenwood, Leon Underwood and his most talented students Blair Hughes-Stanton and Gertrude Hermes, and a young engraver named Douglas Percy Bliss. Amongst these 'revolutionaries' John F. Greenwood appeared as a continuation of the Bewick tradition, rather than a revival of it. He was not caught up in the reforming process of engraving, but he was a brilliant craftsman and had a natural sympathy for the wood. This style of engraving from Bewick through Gwendolen Raverat and John F. Greenwood continued through the century in the work of Reynolds Stone and William T. Rawlinson.

The energy of the original Society was at a high level and its members were not content to rest on their laurels. The Society took its 1927 exhibition to Liverpool and Manchester; these events were financed by cash from sales. The Society has never received any official financial support.

At Manchester in 1927 Thomas Sturge Moore addressed the new movement when he was invited to open the Society of Wood Engravers' exhibition at Mount

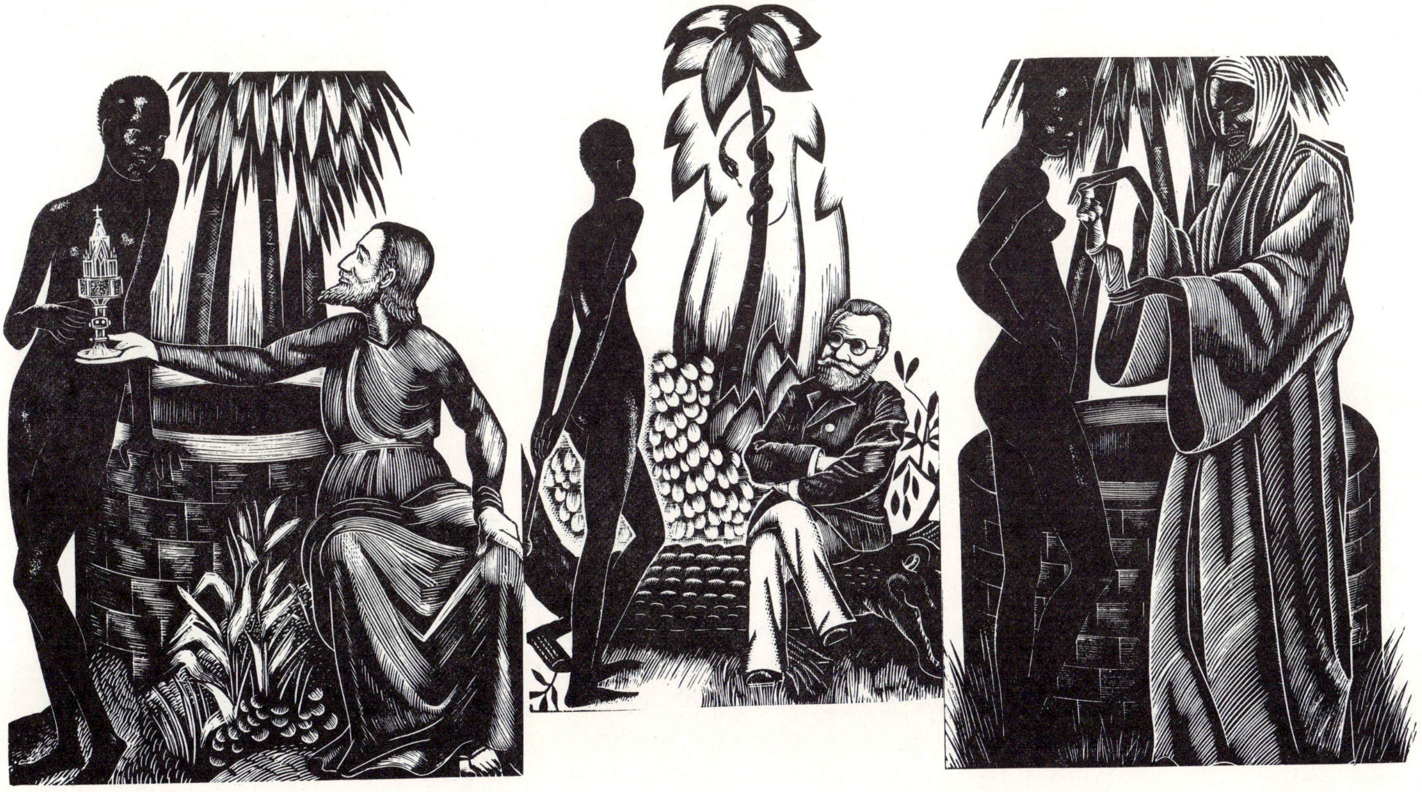

[198 – 200] John Farleigh: Illustrations from *The Adventures of the Black Girl in her Search for God*, 1932.

[201] Lettice Sandford: Illustration from *Hero and Leander*, 1933. 12.1 x 18.6cm

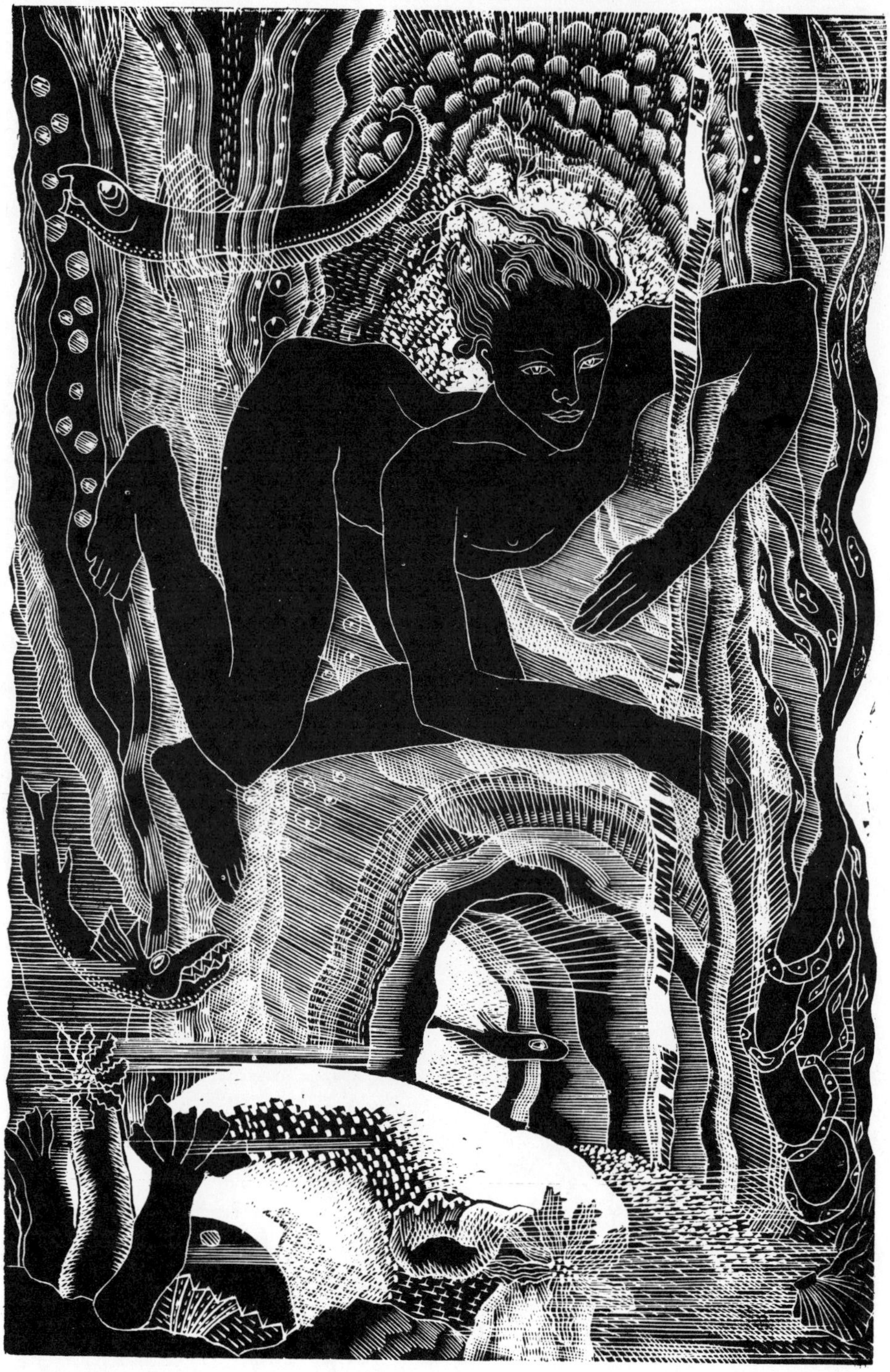

Street, the event being presided over by Lawrence Haward, the Curator of the Manchester City Art Gallery. Sturge Moore delivered a sharp censure tempered with little praise to the 'engravers of the white-line brigade'. His theme was based upon aesthetic values and was in itself a good subject for a poet to take, but nobody in the philosophy of aesthetics could have been farther removed from the philosophical outlook of these young engravers than Sturge Moore. He also used this opportunity to make his transitional position as an engraver quite clear in relation to the artists and to members of the Mancunian public, who were in no way prepared to accept the aesthetic onslaught which the London engravers were mount-

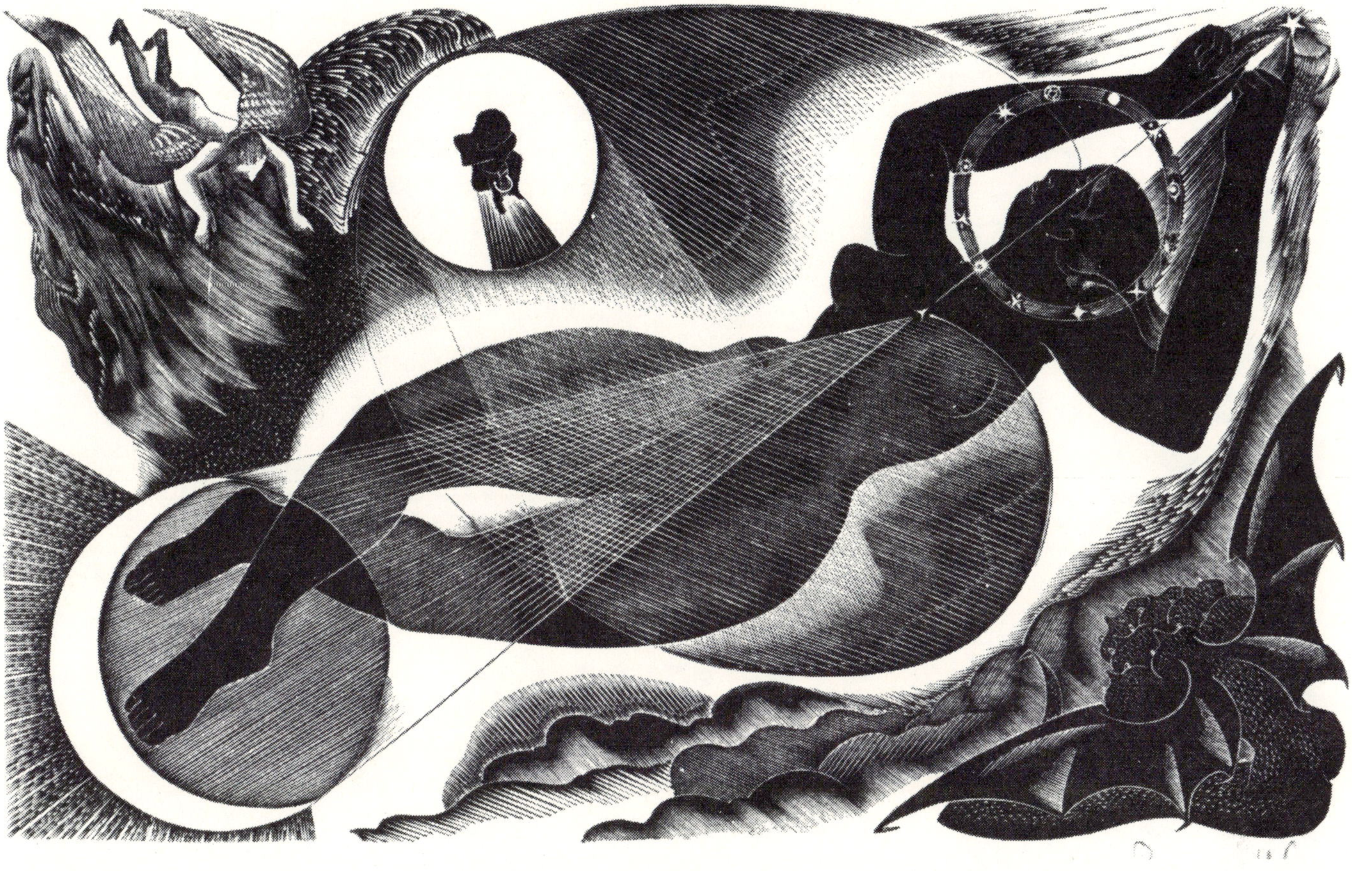

[202] Blair Hughes-Stanton: *The Woman in Heaven* from *Revelations of St John*, 1933. 12.5 x 7.6cm

ing. Sturge Moore also used the occasion to give advice on the technique of wood engraving.

Among the artists exhibiting at the Manchester event were Eric Gill, Robert Gibbings, Noel Rooke, Paul and John Nash, Lucien Pissarro, Gwendolen Raverat, Margaret Pilkington, Clare Leighton, Edward Gordon Craig and Eric Ravilious. A strong team!

Sturge Moore was among the first wood engravers of the black-line tradition to be invited to membership of the newly-formed Society of Wood Engravers in 1920 and he accepted. However, when asked to pay his subscriptions in 1923 he refused and resigned. He never exhibited any work with the Society. In 1924 Edward Craig had proposed him for re-election together with the election of Nicholson, Ricketts and Shannon, but the proposal was defeated.

In his address at Manchester, Sturge Moore said: 'Today we saw the commercial value of works of art – etchings were a case in point – in the process of being violently divorced from their aesthetic value by skilful dealing, just as drapers and costumiers scientifically divorce that of silks and patterned stuffs from the cost price of such materials by a manipulation of the fashions. The snob and herd instincts of some sections of the public might be flattered for the benefit of a trade until taste was entirely enervated.'[7]

He went on to say that without perceiving, alas, what was afoot, many artists and scholars played into the hands of these perverters of taste. But aesthetic value could never derive from movements, crazes or fashions; it depended wholly on individual private experience.

To his own eyes many modern woodcuts and engravings looked like translations

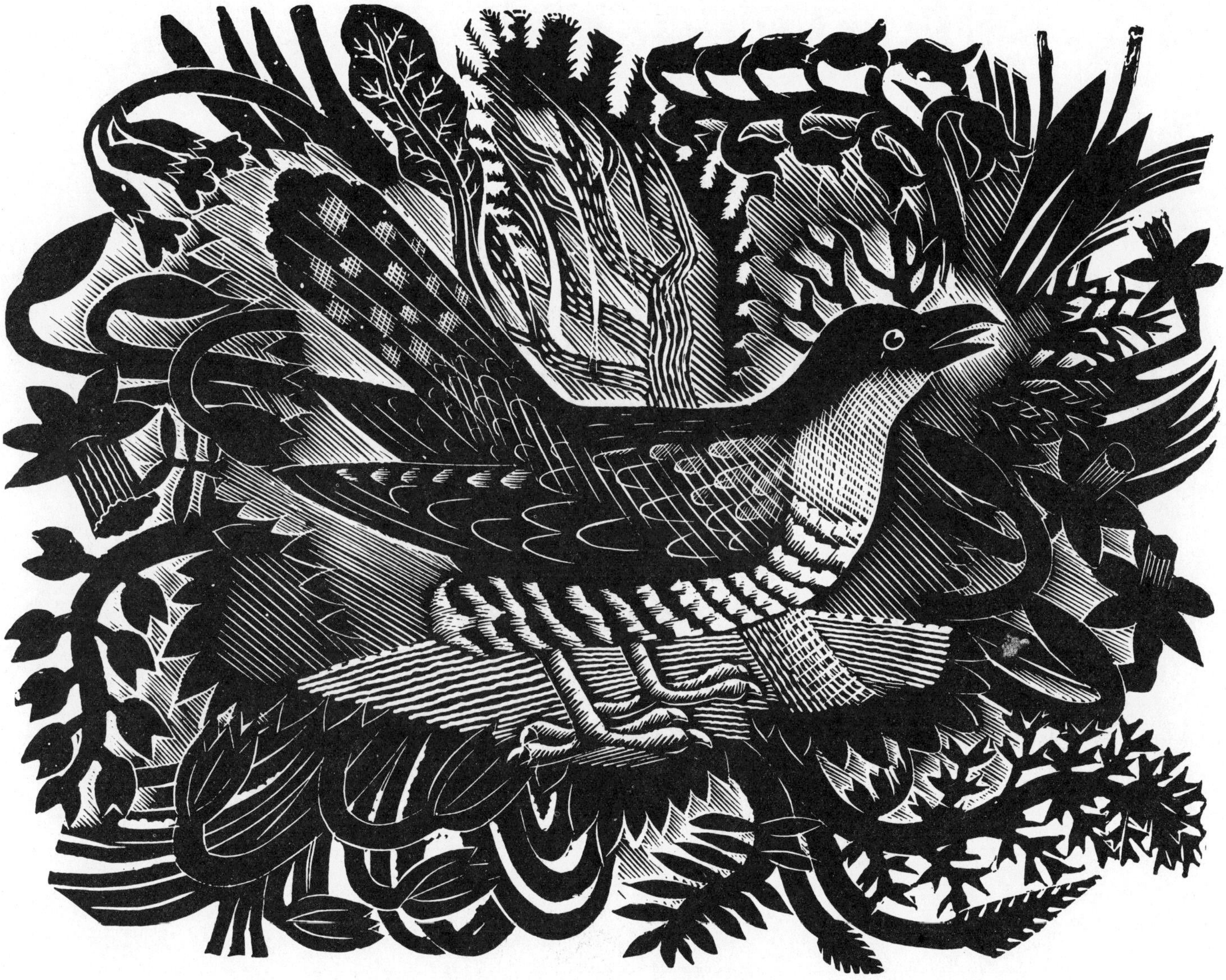

[203] Eric Ravilious: Illustration for *The Cornhill Magazine*, 1933.

[204] Agnes Miller Parker: Illustration from *Welsh Gypsy Folk Tales*, 1933. 10.5 x 7.0cm

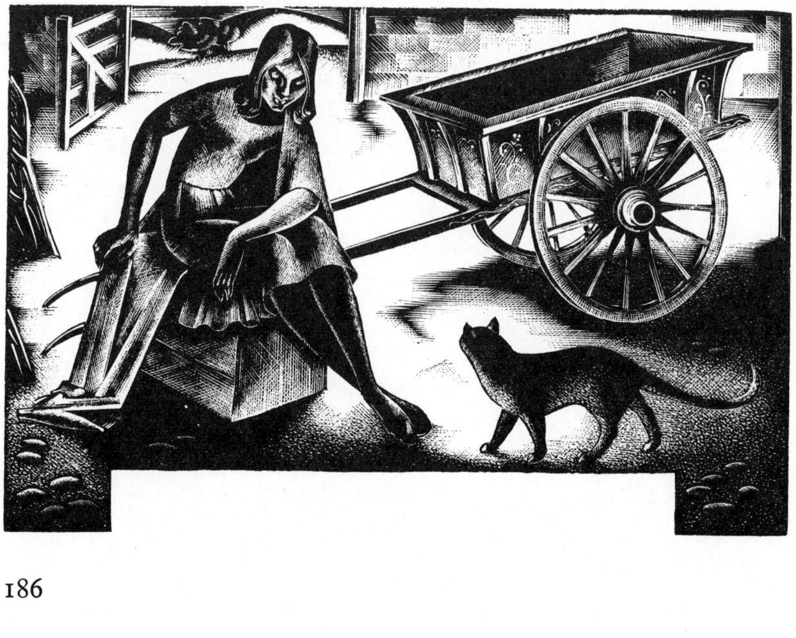

from photographs or commonplace sketches into a language of flat blacks and whites, more or less simplified. Such a translation might be proof of ingenious application, but had no necessary relation to creative art. Yet it formed the basis of the current idea of what a woodcut style consisted of. This infantile blunder influenced artists of real power and sensibility to their hurt. But, on the other hand, the public and critics were led away to believe that to recognise some general characteristic was to appreciate art, or that to detect this or that master's workmanship was to admire his art.

Sturge Moore advised his fellow 'wood-scorpers' to be careful not to drop into mere translation, and the public to make sure that they really admired and were not merely pleased to recognise what they praised or bought. He urged both artists

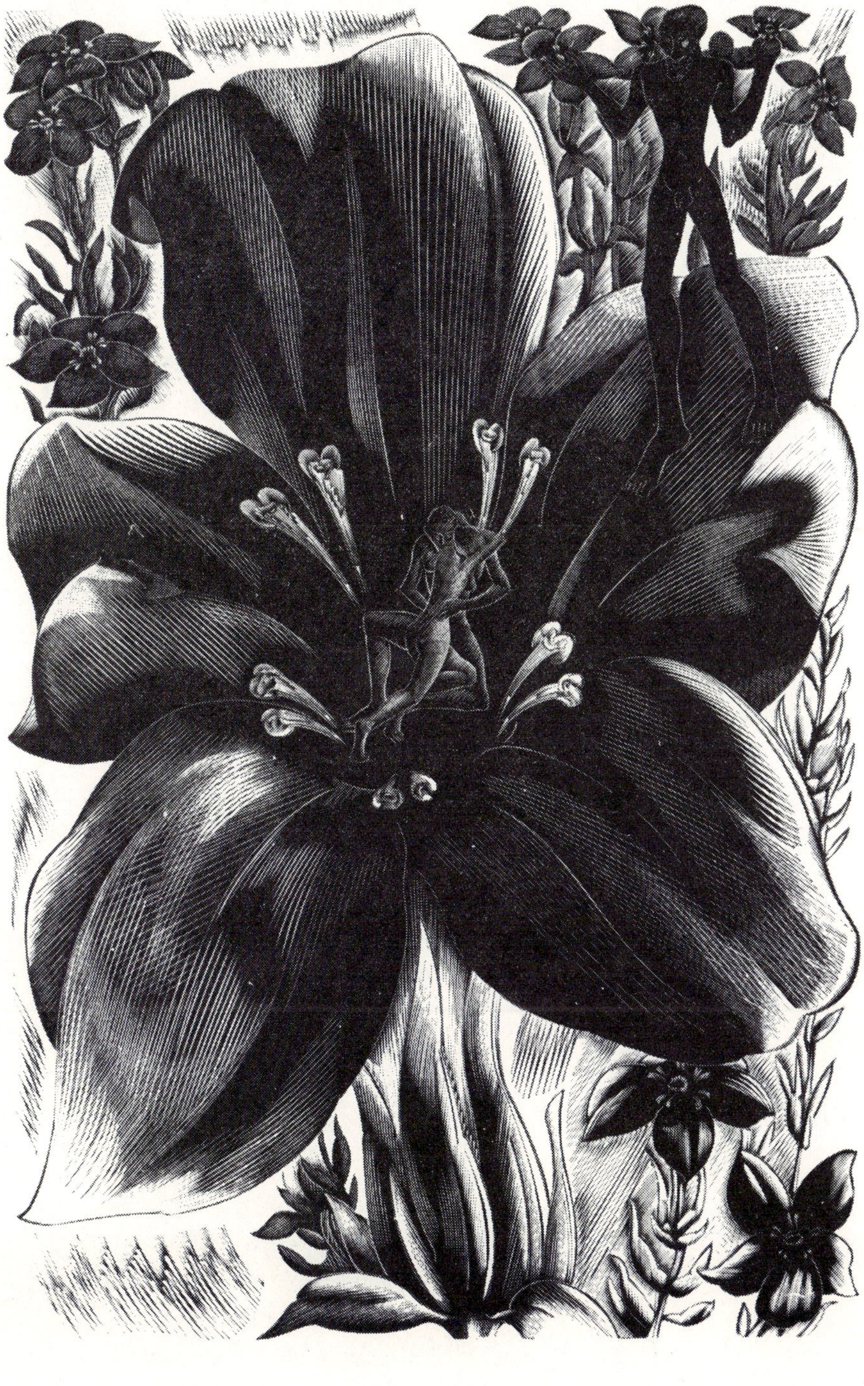

[205] Blair Hughes-Stanton: *Gentian* from *The Ship of Death*, 1934. 9.75 x 15.5cm

and public to beware of becoming the dupes of fashions, crazes and theories, for art consisted wholly of exceptions, individual successes; general traits that these shared with other less nicely organised works were always comparatively unimportant.

Wood engraving, he said in conclusion, was a peculiarly friendly art, and permitted the most gradual focusing of an artist's preferences, with endless opportunities for revision. These comments of Sturge Moore might be claimed to mark the end of the development of black-line transitional engraving and the final echo of Whistler's Aesthetic Movement.

[206] Robert Gibbings: Illustration from *Glory of Life*, 1934. 15.4 x 21.75cm

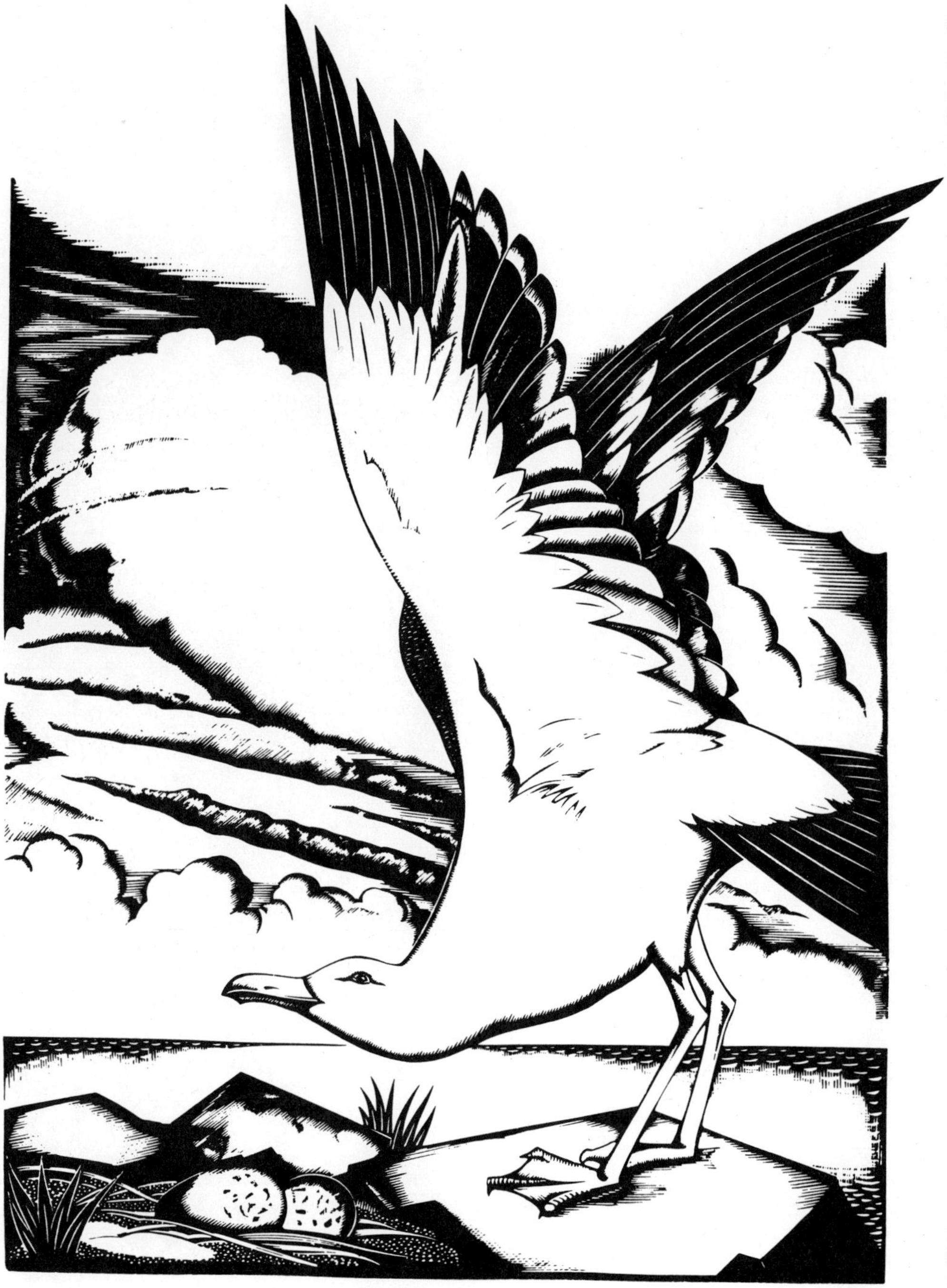

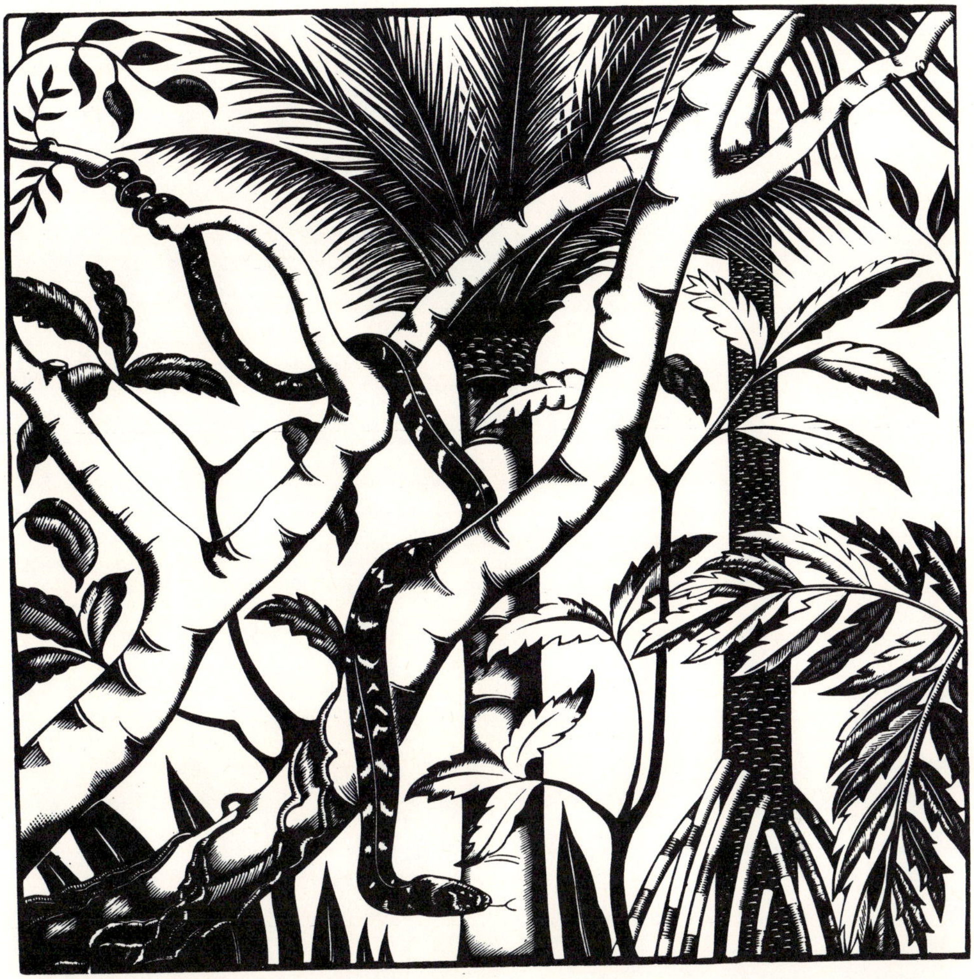

[207] Robert Gibbings: Illustration from *Glory of Life*, 1934. 15.25 x 15.25cm

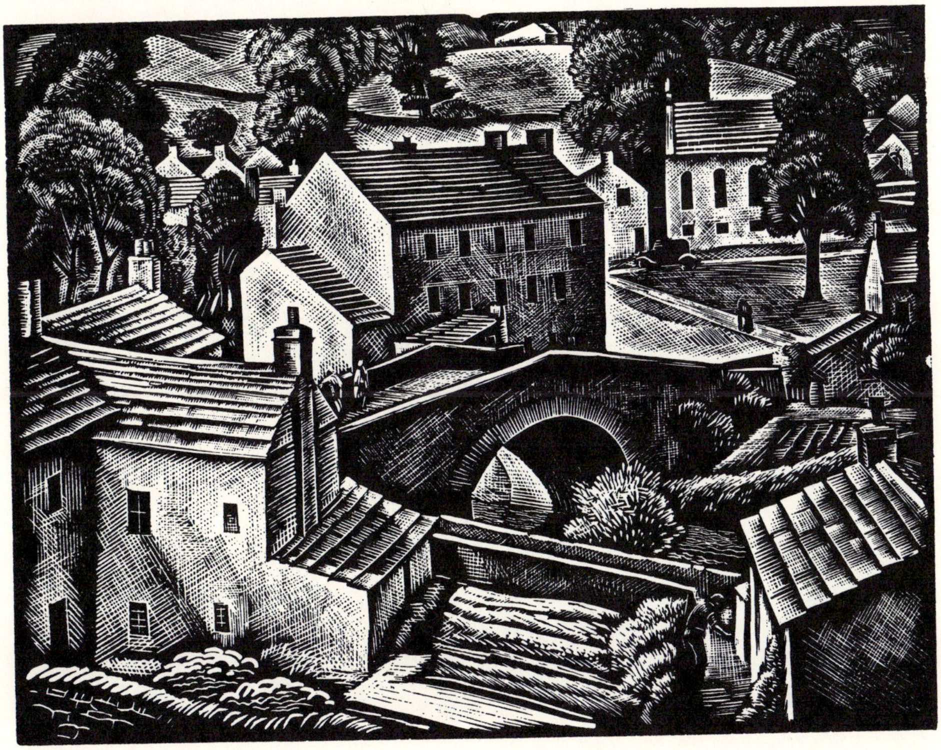

[208] John F. Greenwood: *Village*, 1934. 14.5 x 11.25cm

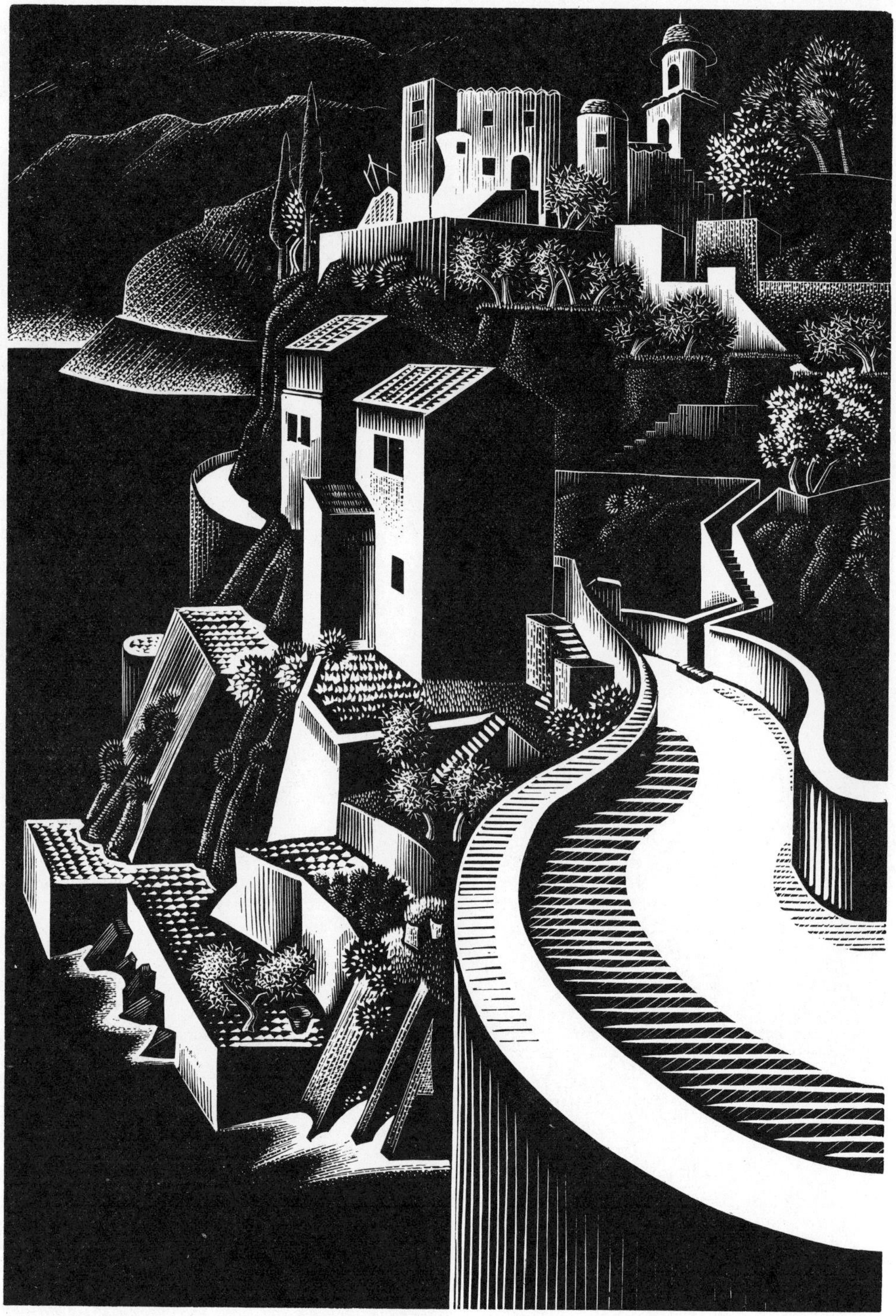

[209] Alison McKenzie: *Road to Sorrento*, 1934. 15.35 x 22.5cm

The Society's exhibitions of 1928, 1929 and 1930 mirrored the new talents of Clare Leighton and John Farleigh. Leighton has many talents; she is an illustrator of books, a designer of stained glass, a mosaic artist and an author. As an artist, her exactitude and nobility of form and truth are akin to the style of Eric Gill.

Clare Leighton's art is characterized by the large swinging curvatures which delineate her strong sense of volume. These long engraved lines were a new experience in wood engraving. Long lines do of course appear frequently in the work of Gill, but the nature of Leighton's lines is so different. A long line by Gill is as taut as a tuned violin string; a Leighton line is as relaxed as a broken one. Gwendolen Raverat has this relaxed quality but her lines are always short.

The unity of Leighton's rhythmic curvature is the body curve movement. Technically she is much less experimental than, for instance, Gertrude Hermes. Yet Leighton was the first wood engraver to show the way to the shimmering silvery greys which are unique to fine cutting in wood engraving. In her book *Wood Engraving and Woodcuts* published in 1932, she introduces three Russian engravers, Michael Pikov, Sakhnorskaya and Alexis Kravchenko. Of the Kravchenko illustration to *Quiet Don* she describes the special greys: 'There is the same strong silvery quality in this print that is so often in modern Russian wood engravings. The sparkle upon the water in this print is uncanny and though the regularity of the lines in the sky might seem almost mechanical, yet it has an exciting feeling to it. The whole engraving is sensitive and beautiful in colour.'[8]

Leighton then considers Sakhnorskaya's print *Woman in the 1905 Revolution* and says: 'There is a strength and an aliveness about this Soviet school of modern wood engraving that is unequalled – whereas the English allow themselves to be perhaps too much dominated by craftsmanship, and the Germans have little

[210] Blair Hughes-Stanton: *Family*, 1935. 27.75 x 16.8cm

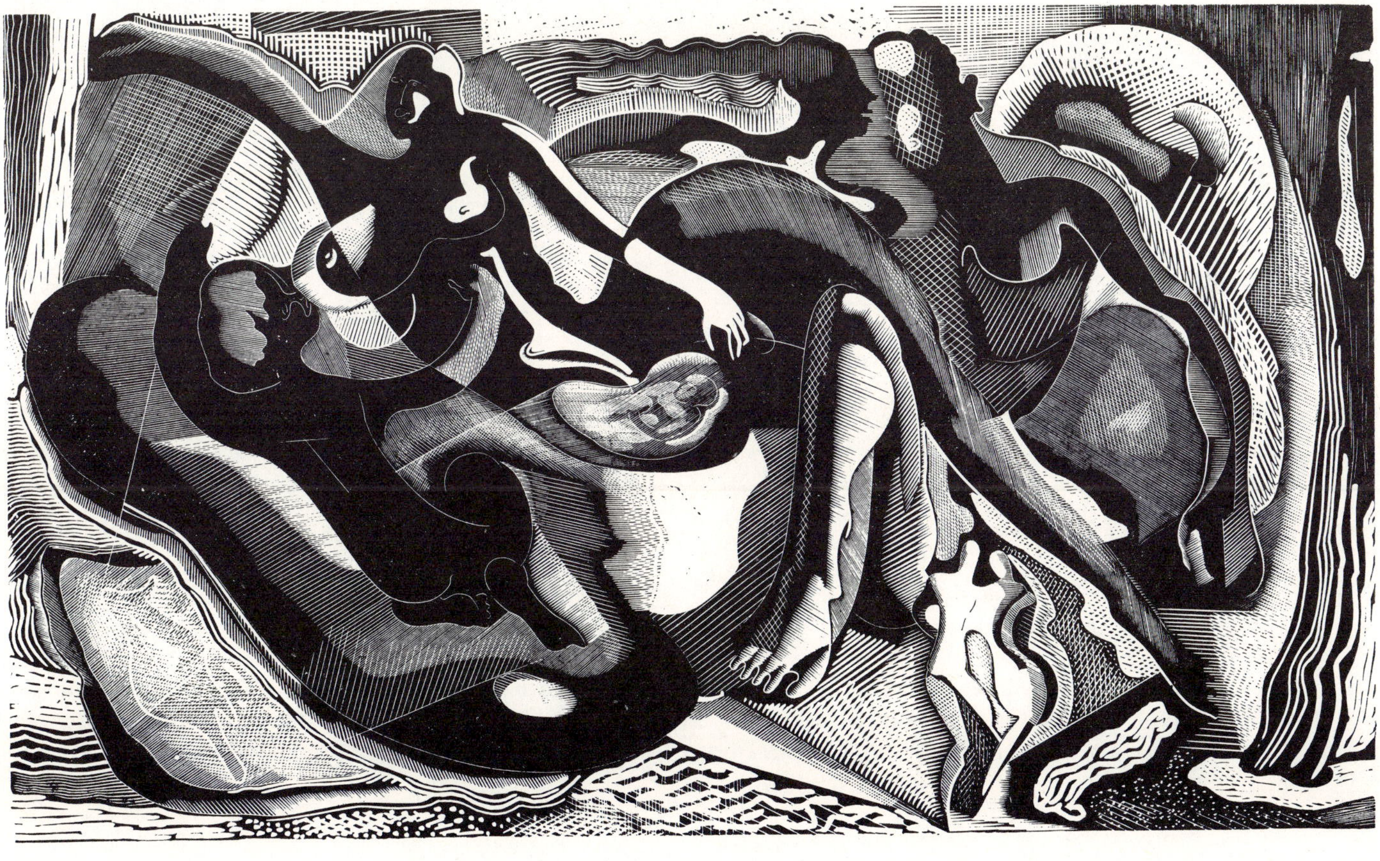

[211] John Nash: *Summer* from *Flowers and Faces*, 1935. 13.0 x 16.5cm

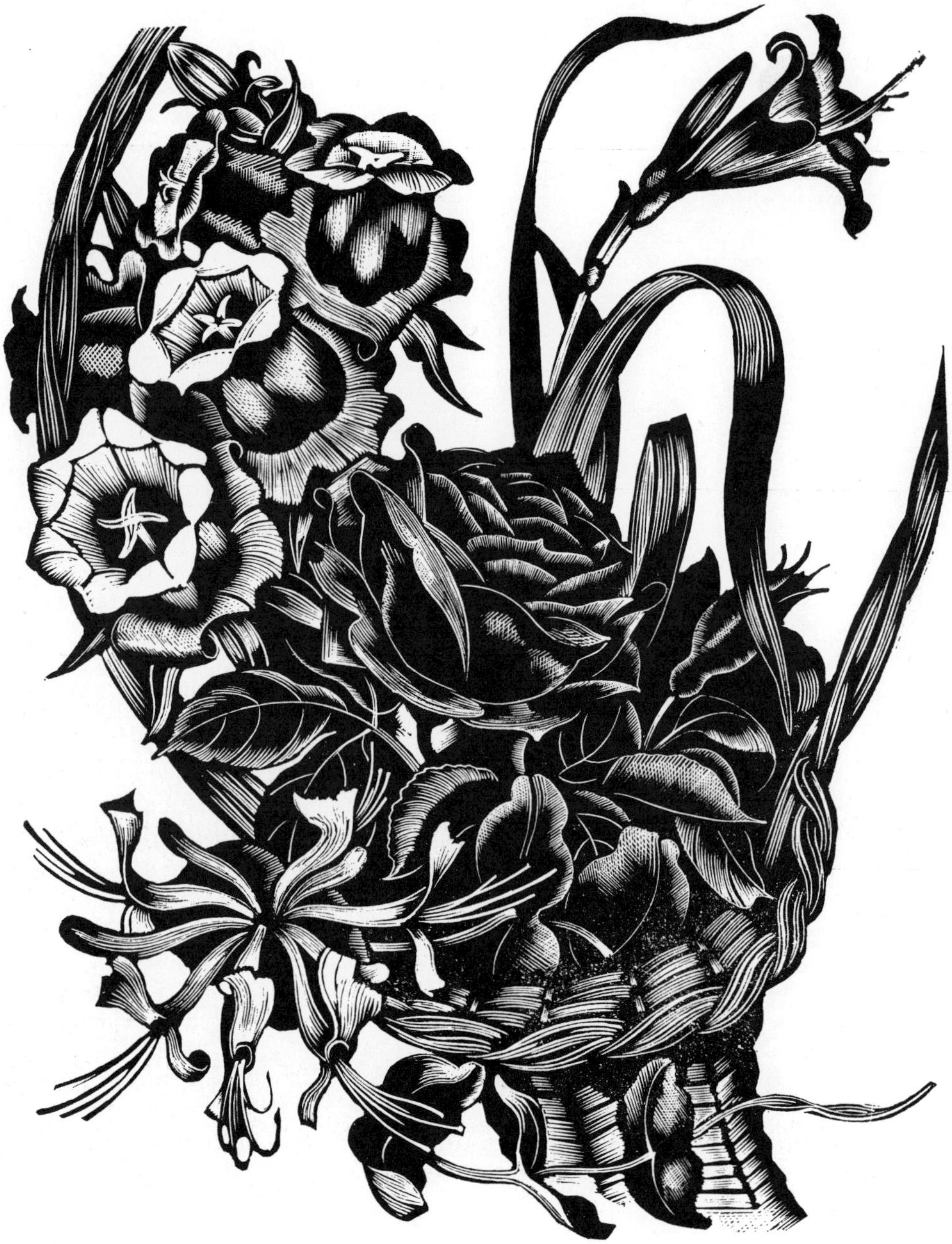

concern for it, concentrating upon the emotion of their subject. The Russians seem able to combine the good executive development with an aliveness that the English lack.' Clare Leighton is equally apt in her comments on the Michael Pikov print *The Actress, M. Babanova in the play Profitable Place*: 'The modern Russian engravers get a silvery quality into their work which is almost unknown in that of the artists of any other country. This is one of the best controlled pieces of tool work in existence.'[9]

The artists of Moscow of the 1930s presented a portfolio of wood engravings to the British Museum Print Department, where Clare Leighton's 'silvery greys' can be seen and the strength of the Russian revival compared with its parallel in London. It is incredible that these two creative national schools have not been exhibited together.

In 1933 Wladimir Favorsky, the great Russian master of wood engraving also

[212] John Nash: *Winter* from *Flowers and Faces*, 1935. 12.7 x 16.5cm

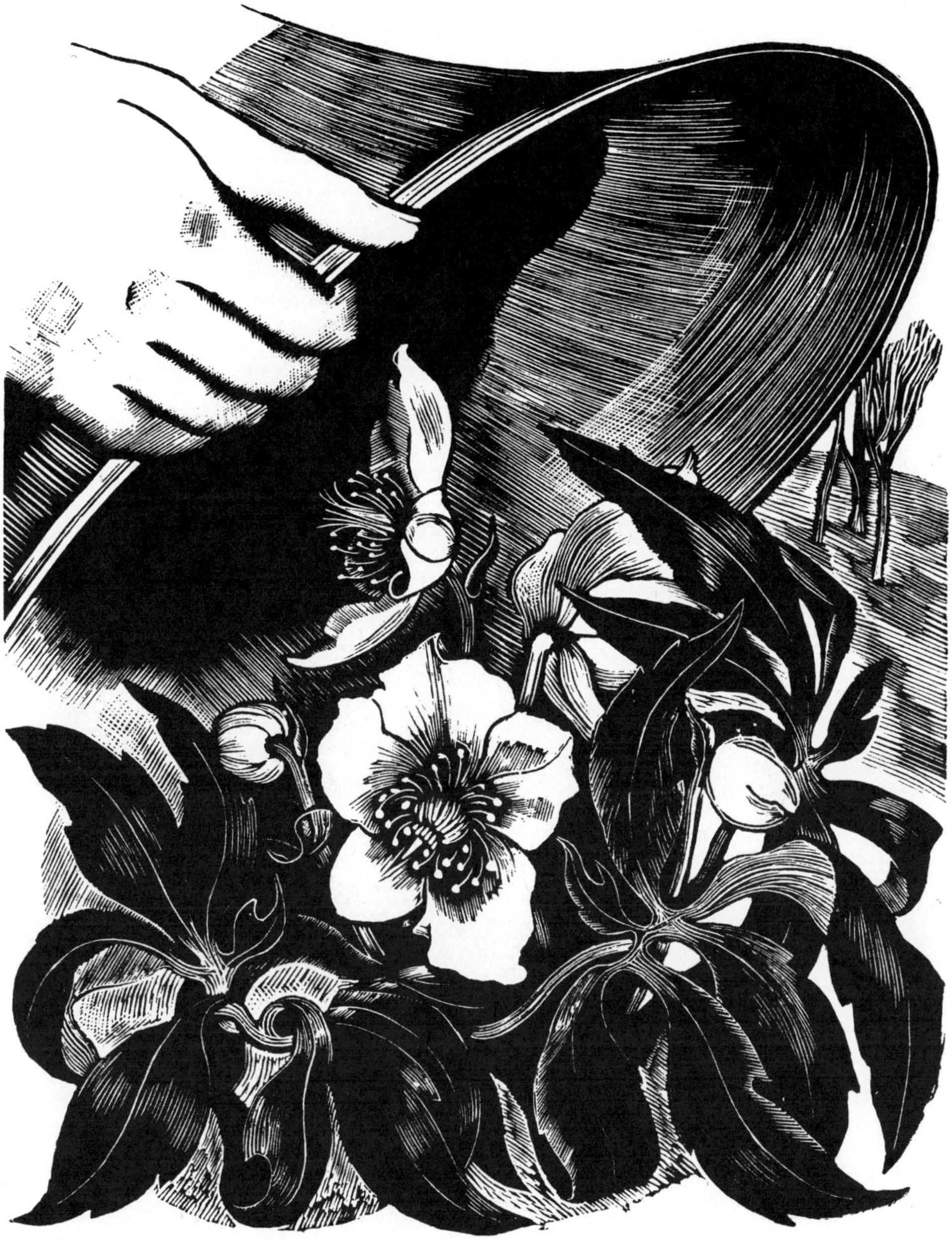

produced a print *Portrait of the Actress Babanova* in the role of a boy in Faiko's play *Chelovek iz Portfellm* [357]. In this print the whole of the background is laid in engraved lines all of the same direction, lying so close together that the eye is unable to focus any dominance over white or black lines; yet the mind receives sufficient physical information to know that every single line is faultlessly engraved. Favorsky's first wood engraving *Madonna in the style of Giotto* was engraved in 1912.

Leighton is the classical line engraver rooted in the Greek and Etruscan tradition as seen in the *Ficoroni Cista.* She practises a strict economy in the use of the burin and in this technique less value is placed on the development of textures. Hermes, on the other hand uses every tool there is in the kit, but she is the first woman to form an original language in a lifetime of continually developing art from the exploitation of the shapes made naturally by the range of tools. Her art is a very personal one but very moving and she designs engraving from the shapes natural to the tools.

Leon Underwood, like Edward Gordon Craig, is a fundamental thinker in art. Both men are oversized personalities through the spreading breadth and timing of their productions. Underwood has not only lived an adventurous life but he is also a very gifted and important artist in sculpture, wood engraving, painting and teaching. He has earned his living as a novelist, poet, scholar, editor and philosopher and in his attitude to art and literature he is very much a man of the Renaissance. In his youth he was fascinated by the emotional impact and the expressiveness of the artists in Roger Fry's Post-Impressionist exhibitions of 1910 and 1912 at the Grafton Galleries.

Underwood started his training at the Regent Street Polytechnic in London in 1907 and studied at the Royal College of Art from 1910 to 1913. While on a visit to Florence in 1925 Underwood read an account in an English newspaper of the caves at Altamira which, although discovered in 1879, were almost unknown to artists in the 1920s. Underwood abandoned his visit to Florence and headed for the caves, completing the last few miles by horse and cart. He had always been aware of an affinity with primitive art and Altamira was a transforming experience.

Underwood is opposed to the widely-held conviction that form is more important than subject, which means he holds no brief for Bell's aesthetic concept of 'significant form'.[10] His lifelong belief is in the superiority of intuition and imagination, which must have a spiritual quality.

Artists must be obsessed with something if they are to see clearly as artists, and following his visit to Altamira, Underwood began to develop an obsession with the beginnings of art. His contribution to the very early history of art consists of three books on African art published in the 1940s.

Underwood's independence of vision stems from his love of Blake and in particular he was deeply affected by Blake's print *Glad Day* from the *Dance of Albion* engraved in 1780. In the same way that Blake sought a new outlook from the engraving of his time and developed new techniques, so did Underwood. As his skill

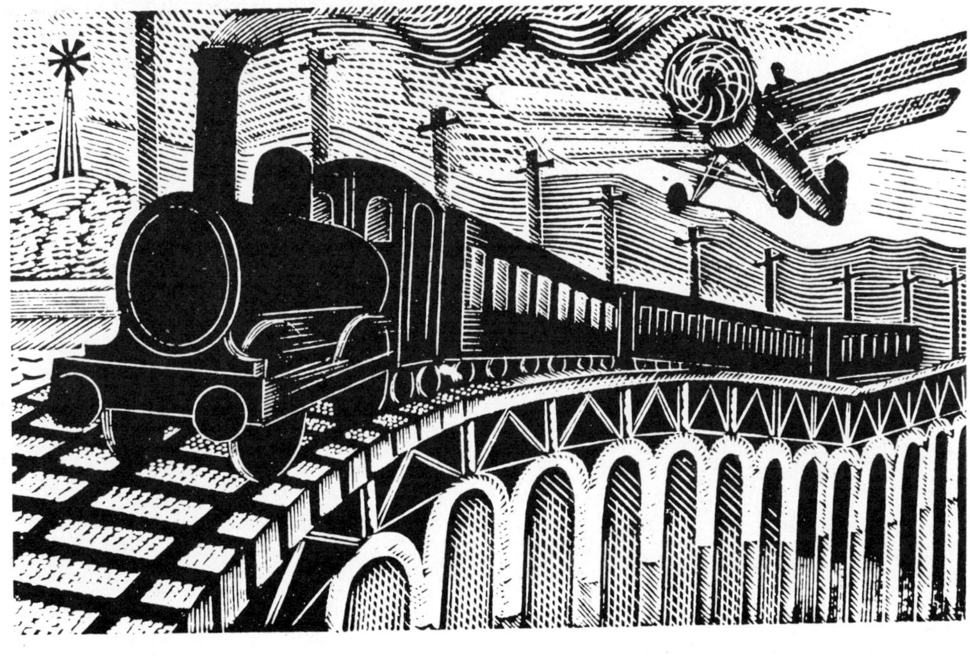

[213] Eric Ravilious: Illustrations from *The Hansom Cab and the Pigeons*, 1935. 10.2 x 16.2cm

[214] Eric Ravilious: Illustrations from *The Hansom Cab and the Pigeons*, 1935. 10.2 x 16.2cm

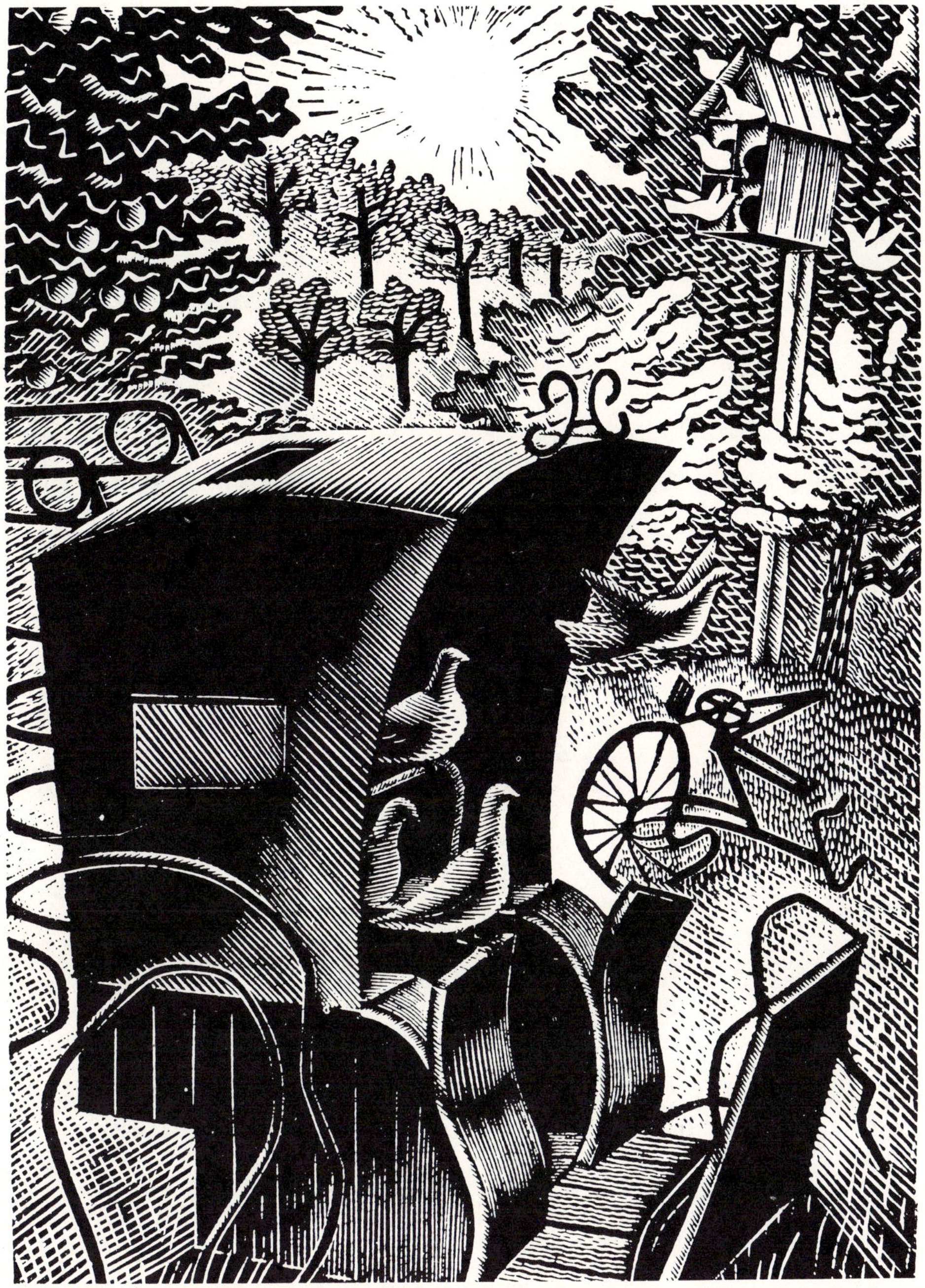

increased, he took wood engraving into softer materials to pioneer the development of the colour print media of lino cut and woodcut.

To see Underwood in his true stature an effort must be made to view his breadth of expression, as is the case with Gordon Craig and David Jones. Subject matter is of import to the engraving profession as a whole, and Underwood believes implicitly in content as distinct from and in opposition to the formal and analytical directions of the European art of his time and the development of abstract theories of form. It is his concern with meaning and the spiritual content of his work that makes him an island in the world of formal revolution and because of this he has been denied the official recognition which is long overdue. Among wood engravers, Underwood is considered something of a hero because of his firmly held concepts and his philosophy as an artist makes very good sense.

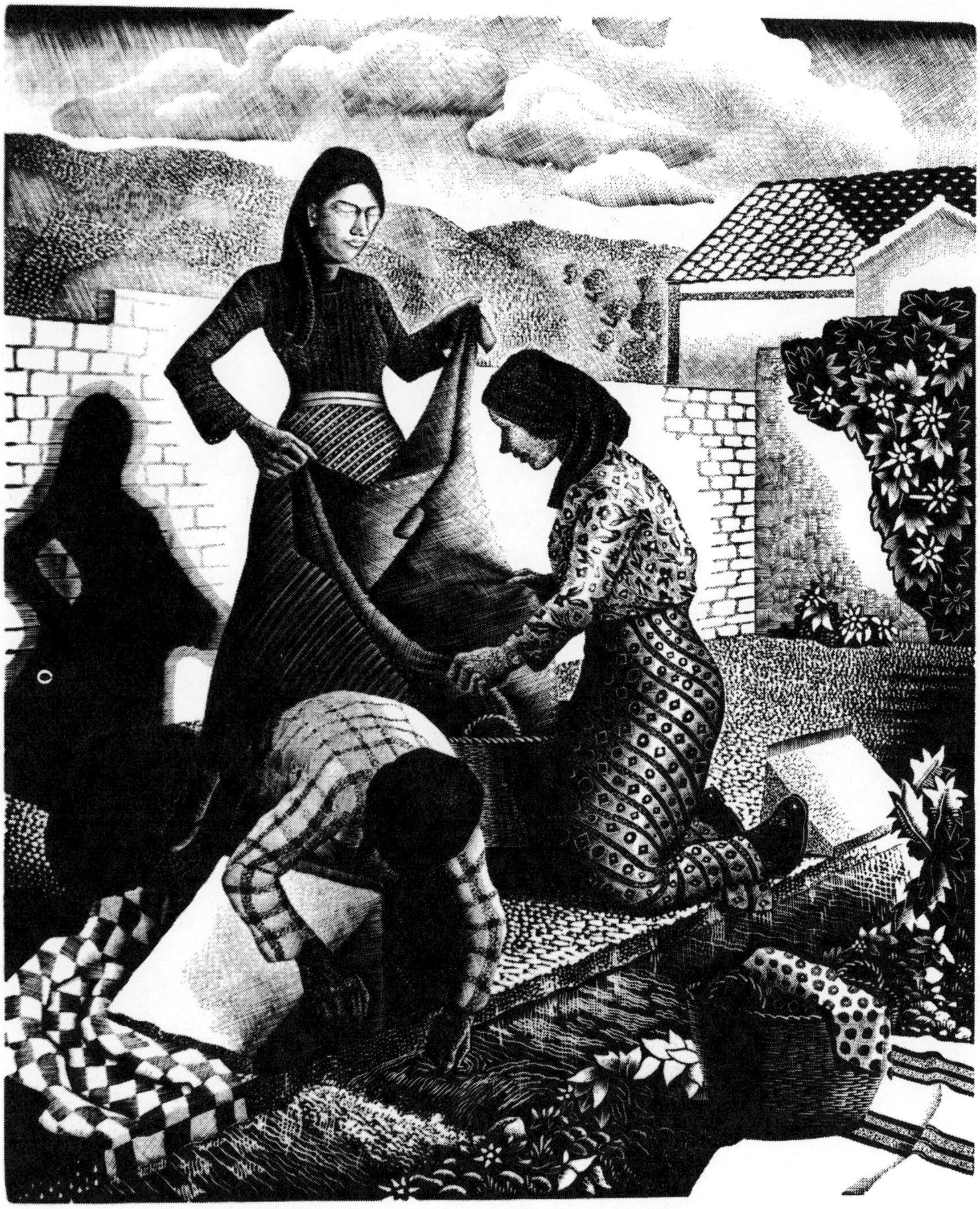

[215] Tom Chadwick: *The Wayside Laundry*, 1935. 20.5 x 25.5cm

In any revolutionary movement, there must be those who march forward and also those who look to the left or to the right or even glance back – and Underwood and his friends Stanley Spencer and Ralph Chubb did just this. They were all revolutionaries in a big enough way to make their own individual contribution to the sphere of art rather than conform to an official line. Spencer had recognition of his ability in his lifetime but Chubb, though a brilliant artist and poet, had none and worked and died in an atmosphere of sheer neglect and indifference.

Underwood has resisted the establishment through his life, yet his formal values and brilliant technical craft are of a very high order and very much of his own time. By looking right and left he and his pupils provided a nucleus of innovators who were to extend the formal range of wood engraving into the world of the colour print, which was to dominate from 1950 onwards.

[216] Clare Leighton: *The Reaper* from *Four Hedges*, 1935. 12.25 x 17.75cm

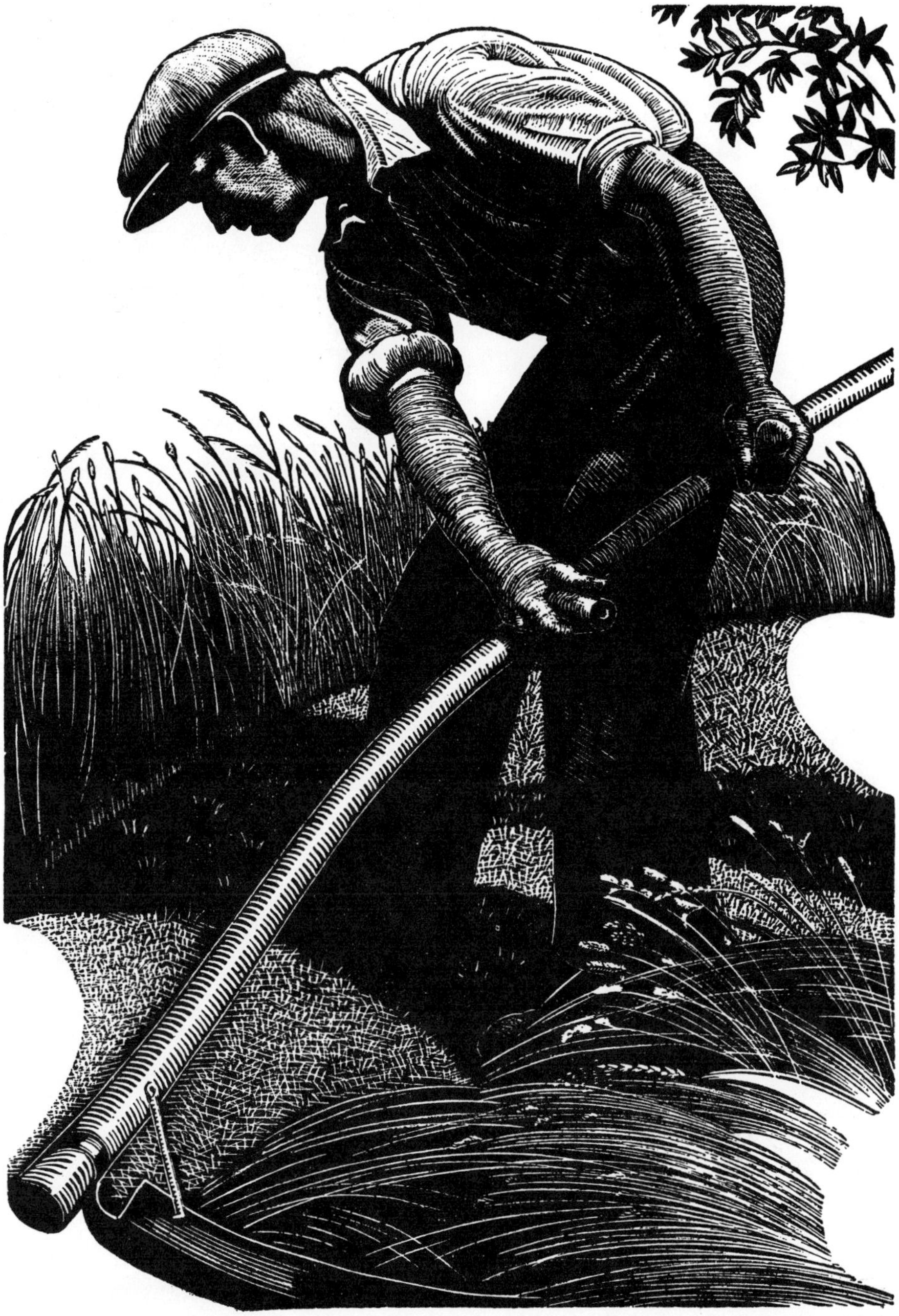

Today in the world of print making nearly all the restrictions on media have gone and the time will arrive when the media are so mixed up and their identity so lost that this will be the target for a future reaction. However, despite the rebel in Underwood, his wood engravings are pure white-line wood engravings, and he has produced more wood engravings than relief colour prints in other media.

Underwood's influence in the development of the modern print is considerable. In January 1921 he opened his own school, known as the Brook Green School, at the western end of Girdlers Road, Hammersmith. He only accepted promising post-graduate students and the first who came to him from the Royal College of Art were Vivian Pitchforth, Henry Moore and Raymond Coxon. They were later joined by Blair Hughes-Stanton, Gertrude Hermes, Nora Unwin, Eard, John

[217] Enid Marx: Cover for a Christmas catalogue, 1935. 7.5 x 11.5cm

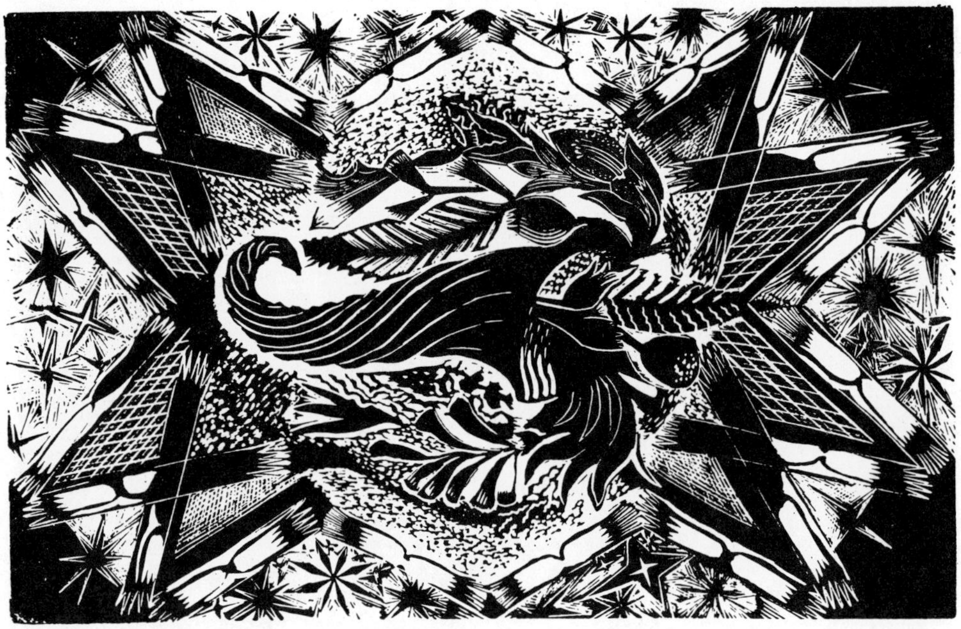

Gould Fletcher, Lawrence Bradshaw, Ralph Chubb, Grace E. Rogers, Eileen Agar and Velona Pilcher.

Underwood and Henry Moore, eight years his junior, together worked out the concepts and language of the new sculpture which was to give rise to the strongest school of sculpture this country has ever known. It is based upon the concept of form purity, truth to materials and meaning. In the Underwood sense, Moore is not an abstract artist and he has said frequently that he is not an abstract sculptor. For both Underwood and Moore, the concepts of Palaeolithic art are very important and fundamental to their form thinking. Moore's abstraction is relative to, and sublimated to his dominant theme of the human figure.

Art with no subject matter was unthinkable for Underwood, as it was for many other artists, regardless of how close some of his studies of form may approach to abstraction. This point was firmly held by the painters and sculptors of Paris who were unable to accept the pure abstraction with no subject matter which was characteristic in the work of the Bauhaus. Underwood's style, which has a syncopated development ranging through sculpture, painting and engraving, has a very consistent evolution in his wood engravings and sculpture. The stylistic unity is in the volumetric expression between these two related media and Underwood uses the burin in the manner of the sculptor.

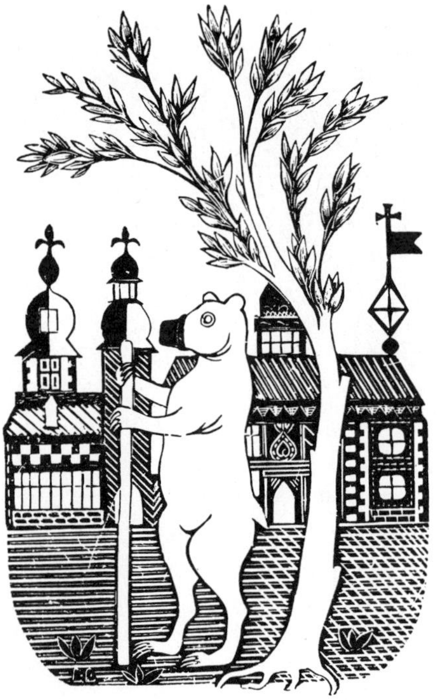

[218] Lynton Lamb: A device for the Nonesuch Press, 1935. 7.75 x 12.5cm

In 1914, Underwood was staying in Poland and was very nearly cut off by the outbreak of war. He left his return to Britain rather late and was forced to make a tortuous journey through Finland and then further north to Tromso on the Norwegian coast before finally reaching Newcastle after a crossing of the North Sea which left a deep impression upon him. In July 1923, he embarked on another strenuous journey but this time he was accompanied by Blair Hughes-Stanton and Rodney Thomas. They sailed to Iceland, landed at Reykjavik and then trekked northwards towards the Arctic Circle. The motivation for the visit to Iceland was the fact that Underwood wished to experience the North Sea again but not to do so in the manner of a conducted tour.

After Iceland Underwood set his sights on Mexico and New York. He arrived in New York in 1926 and went to Palm Beach to paint murals but no commissions were forthcoming. He returned to New York, opened a private school for drawing and wrote a book of verse called *Animalia* and illustrated it with wood engravings [9]. His interpretation of animals is poetic and fanciful rather than scientific. In this book he gives his own identification with the hunter of the bison in the caves at Altamira.[11]

On returning to England Underwood started and edited the magazine *The Island* in the spring of 1931, the articles and illustrations being provided by the students of the Brook Green School. It ran for four issues. The contributors were Henry Moore, Eard, John Gould Fletcher, Lawrence Bradshaw, Ralph Chubb, Grace E. Rogers, Eileen Agar and Velona Pilcher. Underwood's basic philosophy was expressed in *The Island* and the students of his Brook Green School reinforced the belief in the supremacy of the value of imagery and its meaning.

Underwood, Spencer and Chubb were students and friends together at the Slade and Underwood and Chubb became interested in gypsy life. Like Augustus John they spent a lot of time living with the gypsies in the New Forest and drawing them. Chubb dressed as a gypsy and learned the true Romany language and

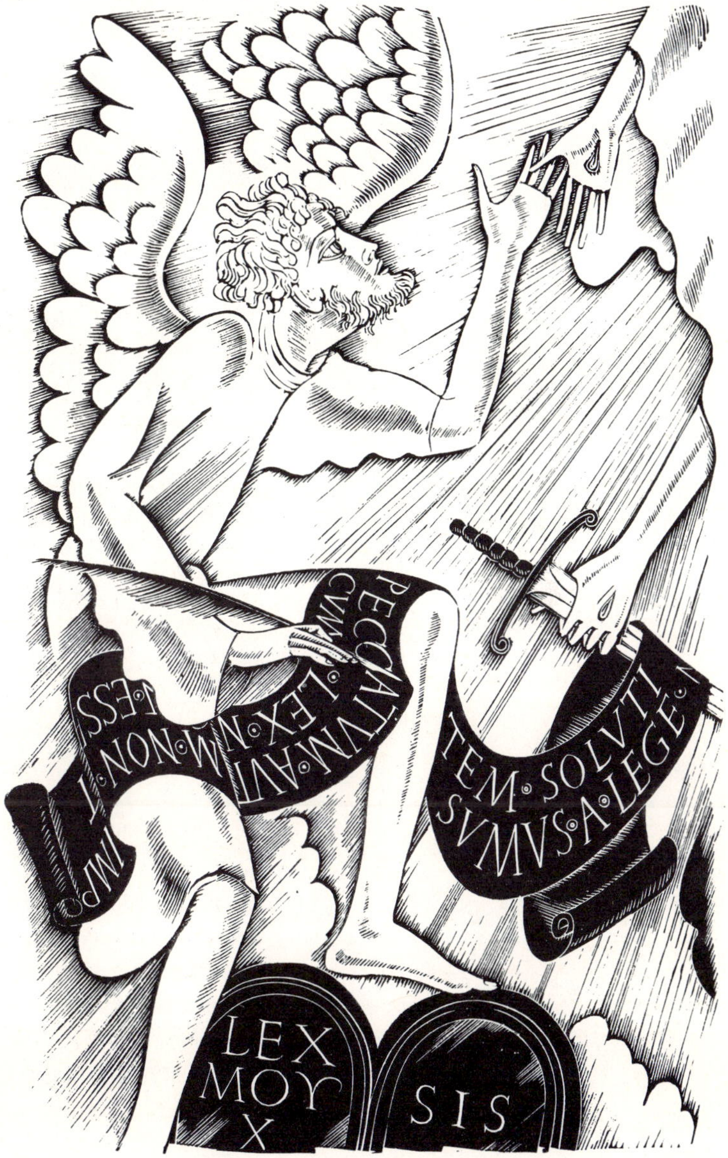

[219] Eric Gill: Illustration from *The Aldine Bible*, 1936. 9.75 x 15.2cm

[220] John Buckland-Wright: *The Model, No 2*, 1936. 11.0 x 17.1cm

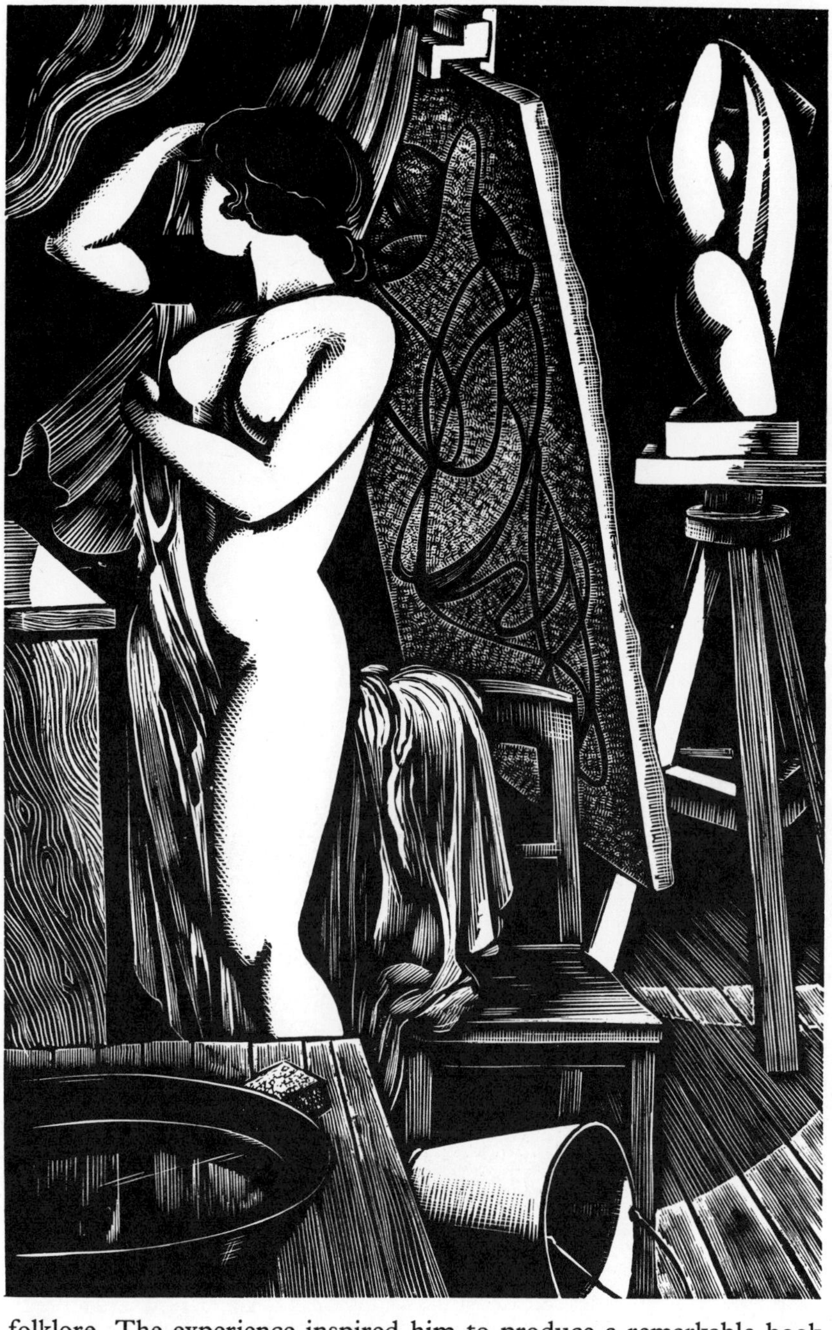

folklore. The experience inspired him to produce a remarkable book called *The Secret Country* in 1939, in which the illustrations and his own handwritten text were reproduced by lithography.

After Ralph Chubb had written *The Secret Country* he developed a semi-calligraphic alphabet and he employed it to produce books in which the text was drawn by hand on hand-made paper with a deckle edge to each page, every volume being bound by hand in leather and black Sundour cloth. Eight such books were produced in editions of twenty to thirty copies, thus demanding several years of intensive work for each book.

Chubb's early books and smaller works were illustrated with wood engravings [182]. In the first instance he took to wood engraving because of its precision, simplicity and minimum cost of equipment. He had the required skills and wanted to get results quickly because he realised the extent of the work he had to do in order to accomplish his ambition before he died. Although his major works were printed by lithography, he hated the method because of the complications of the balance of grease and water. Chubb's books demanded techniques which for him only increased the problem of finance and accentuated the difficulties of production by a hand press, although he accepted this stress for the sake of art.

From the eighteenth century a continuous but limited number of creative engraver draughtsmen, as distinct from the brilliant exponents of nineteenth-century decadence, has evolved, from William Blake, Edward Gordon Craig, Eric Gill, Paul and John Nash and David Jones, all of whom show qualities found only in English art, expressing the true character of the English genius and some, but not all, of its sinews. Creative engraving is a delicate yet tough flower which can be seen blooming twice, each time in the shock wave of the aftermath of two world wars in which most of the major engravers saw active service. While they may not have 'kissed the chains that bound them' to war, they did accept these bonds in the spirit of the self-discipline required of engraving.

[221] Iain Macnab: *Fishermen Portofino*, 1936. 25.4 x 20.2cm

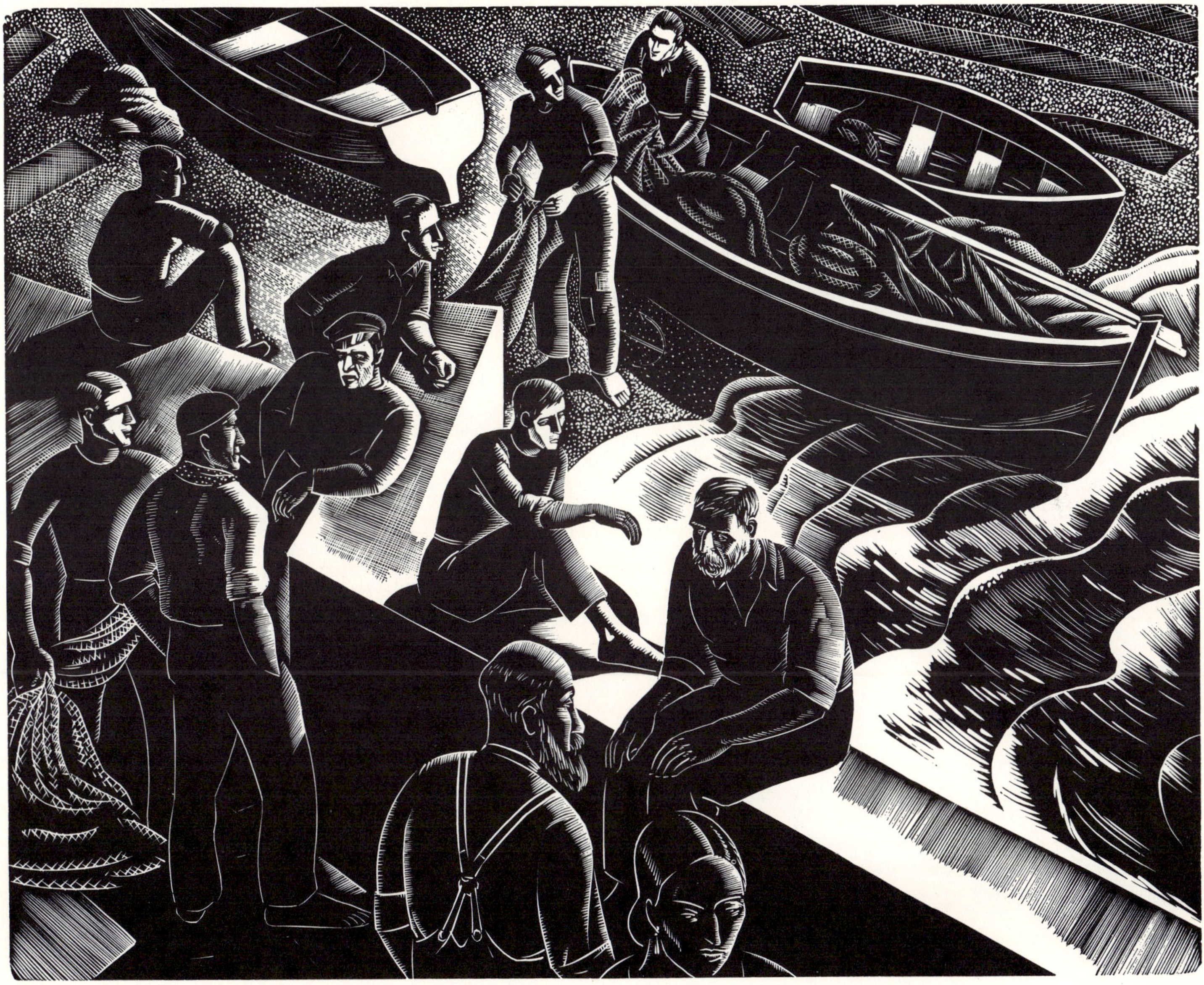

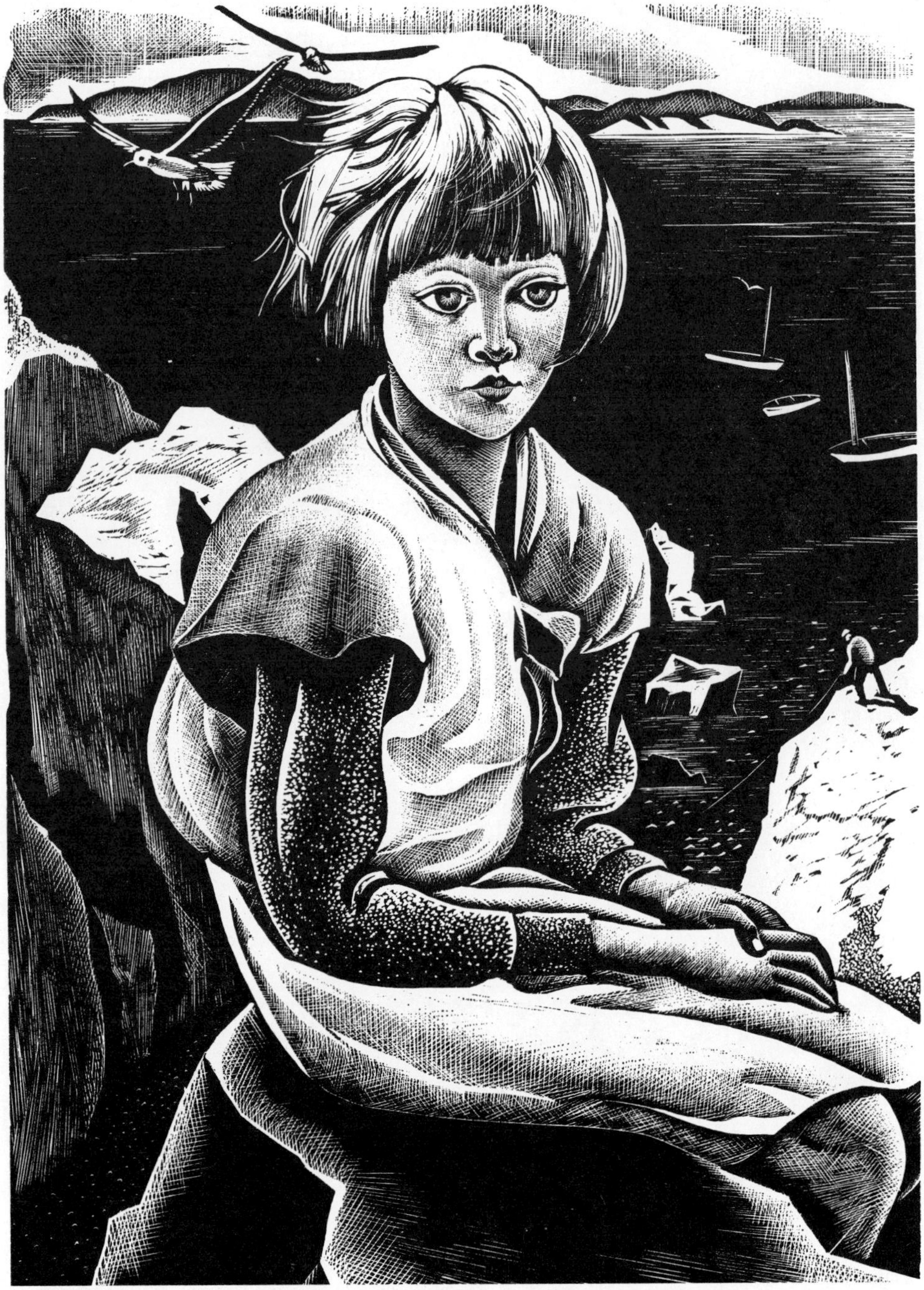

[222] Guy Malet: *Sark Girl*, 1936.
18.0 x 25.5cm

Qualities of linear expression are deeply rooted in Anglo-Saxon and Celtic art. Blake expressed it as 'the bounding line and its infinite inflections and movements'. Paul Nash set out to find this 'Englishness' of English art when he took a leading part in forming the short-lived Unit One group in 1933. In the Unit One magazine he enquired, 'To what extent has contemporary art in England a national character? Can we find in our short history of painting and sculpture qualities so peculiar as to identify their subjects beyond doubt, and, if so, do these qualities persist today? An English genius in the plastic arts has never been allowed, but that it does exist – a distinctive element, traceable through the whole history of our expression – becomes obvious upon any study of the subject beyond surface appearances. It would be ridiculous to claim for it a very powerful personality or a profound influence; that is not its character. It has never possessed the force which created a Shakespeare.'[12]

In his comments Nash distinguished the particular characteristics which recur throughout English art history: ' . . . a pronounced linear method in design, no doubt traceable to sources in Celtic ornament or to a predilection for the Gothic idiom. A peculiar bright delicacy in choice of colours, somewhat cold, but radiant and sharp in key. A concentration, too, in the practice of portraiture; as though everything must be a likeness rather than an equivalent; not only eligible persons and parts of the countryside, but the very dew, the light, the wind as it passed . . .' He then wrote of the imprisoned spirit, the motive power which animates English art: 'If I were asked to describe this spirit I would say it is of the land; "genius loci" is indeed almost its conception. If its expression could be further designated I would say it is almost entirely lyrical.' Then writing as leader of the Unit One group he comments: 'We, today, must find new symbols to express our reaction to environment. In some cases this will take the form of an abstract art, in others we may look for some different nature of imaginative research. But in whatever form, it will be a subjective art.'

It was Nash's friend, the poet and critic Herbert Read, who not only shared with him the horrors of war but made the first real analysis of the art of Nash. Thankfully, Read was not tied to the technical performance of art and this left him free to interpret art and artists as a poet. He stresses that poems are not written for poets and art is not produced for artists, otherwise communication would break down. His views on the importance of the 'Englishness' of English art were close to those of Nash and many others.

In Read's *Philosophy of Modern Art*, he says, 'Blake set himself the task of making vision determinate of giving imagination an outline. His art is an attempt to combine the greatest intensity of subjective thought and feeling with the greatest clarity of objective representation. And that is precisely the character of all great art.'[13]

In Read's final paragraph on Paul Nash he writes: 'One returns, for a final emphasis, to Nash's fidelity to a certain nativeness, a quality representing the historic English tradition in English art . . . it is a quality which we find in the delicate stone tracery of an English cathedral, in the linear lightness and fantasy of English illuminated manuscripts, in the silvery radiance of our stained glass. The same quality is expressed, distinctly, in our poetry and our music. It is not a conscious tradition: it is perhaps an emanation of our soil and our climate, as inevitable and as everlastingly vernal as an English meadow.'

REFERENCES

1 Gill, E. 'The Society of Wood Engravers' from *The Architect*, December 1920
2 *Jewish Guardian*, December 1920
3 Marriott, C. 'Plain and Coloured' from *Outlook*, November 1920
4 *Catalogue for the Second Annual Exhibition of the Society of Wood Engravers*, London 1921
5 *Manchester Guardian*, May 1922
6 Jones, D. *Anathemata*, Faber, London, 1952
7 *Manchester Guardian*, March 1927
8 Leighton, C. *Wood Engraving and Woodcuts*, Studio Publications, London, 1932
9 Leighton *Wood Engraving and Woodcuts*
10 Bell, C. *Art*, Chatto & Windus, London, 1947
11 Underwood, L. *Animalia*, Payson & Clarke, New York, 1926
12 Read, H. (ed) *Unit One: the modern movement in English architecture, painting and sculpture*, Cassell, London 1934
13 Read, H. *Philosophy of Modern Art*, Faber, London, 1952

7 WHITE LIGHT IN FOCUS

The early thirties were eventful years for wood engravers who at this stage had mastered their language and its expression in the hard boxwood and were now turning their attention to softer materials. The links in the chain that were forged were the sublimation of craft to art. The early pioneers knew that it would take time to prove themselves and there were no short cuts to help them. They started experimenting with linoleum to satisfy their curiosity more than anything else just to see what engraving would be like in this soft material. They discovered that the white-line engraving scale had to be much larger than that required in wood, that the grain of the linoleum gave a texture break-up and that the material could be used for colour printing.

The first exhibition of the Society of Wood Engravers that was devoted solely to lino cuts was held in 1929 at the Redfern Gallery and a second one was held in 1930. Ethelbert White was one of the first artists to cut on linoleum but was quickly followed by Leon Underwood, Blair Hughes-Stanton, Gertrude Hermes and Kermode. After the Second World War, exhibitions of lino cuts came from Picasso and Matisse and exhibitions were held in the London dealers' galleries. These exhibitions showed conclusively that linoleum was a satisfactory medium.

The Golden Cockerel Press publication of *The Four Gospels* in 1931 is a work of importance and rare achievement, showing the inspired art of Eric Gill. This masterpiece of book production and design can be grouped alongside the Kelmscott *Chaucer* and the *Doves Bible. The Four Gospels* is a superb example of collaboration between the artist and the typographer. Gill and Gibbings have given expression to Dürer's early concept in his *Apocalypse* of an artist-designed and produced book. The book is set in Gill's Golden Cockerel type and is decorated with forty-one of his engravings; Gibbings considered the Gill engravings for this book to be the finest he had ever produced.

During the early thirties Henry Moore produced a small number of wood engravings [184 and 185]. His interest and experience in a wide range of linear media is now very widely known and appreciated. Moore's wood engravings are powerful statements made by the sculptor with a burin in his hands. He is engraving as freely in wood as in his stone carving. His burin is sensitively exploring the changing shape throughout the entire track of a white line. The shorter lines then develop into textural excursions, obviously leading into stone carving. These wood engravings are studies along the road to the development of final sculptures.

Naum Gabo's sculptural approach to wood engraving is quite different. He has only produced about six blocks [351]. His use of the burin is not at all like Moore's and has something of the linear purity of Gill, but without Gill's technique. Gabo was born in Briansk, Russia, in 1890. Throughout his life he has been a leading

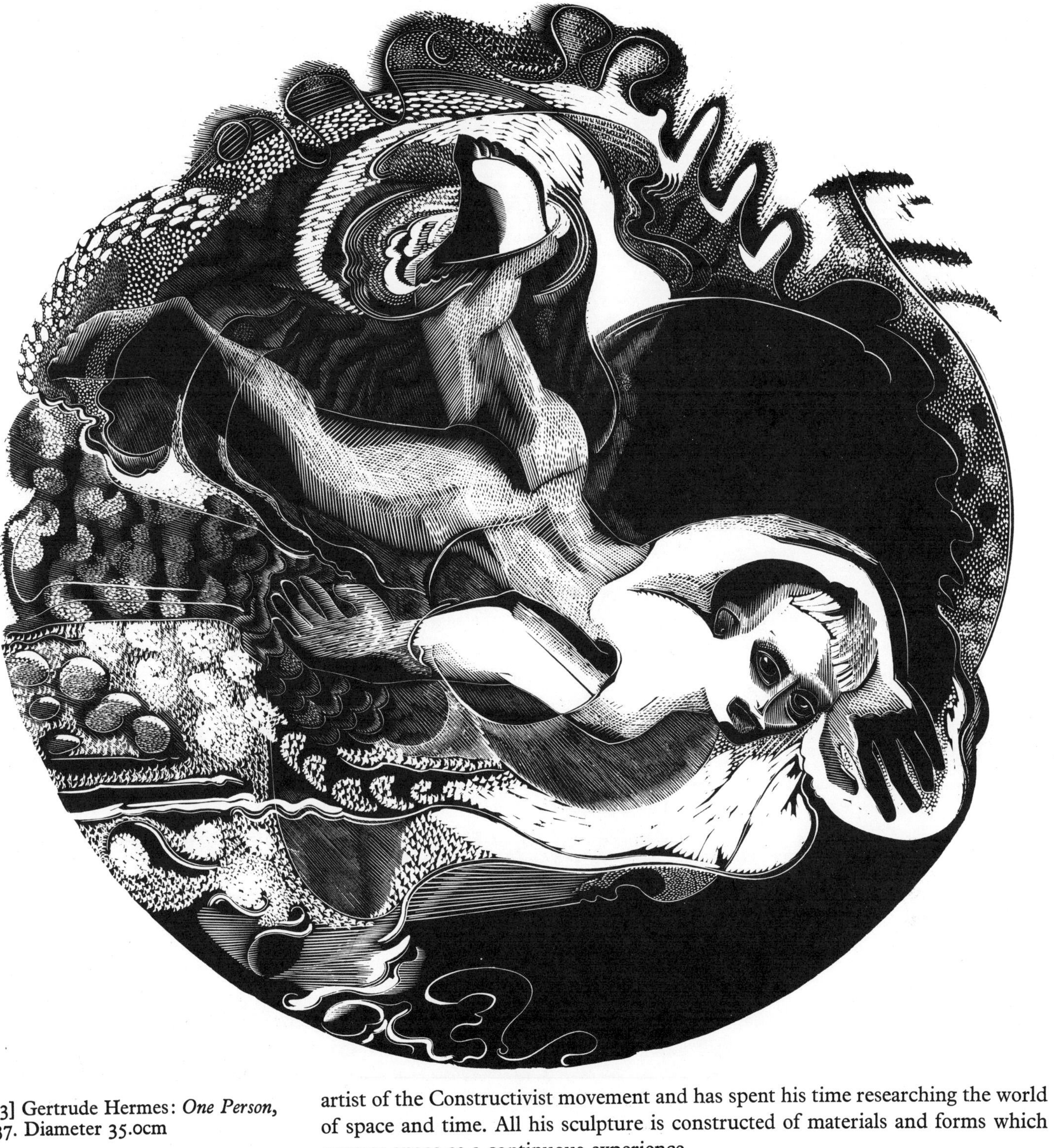

[223] Gertrude Hermes: *One Person*, 1937. Diameter 35.0cm

artist of the Constructivist movement and has spent his time researching the world of space and time. All his sculpture is constructed of materials and forms which express space as a continuous experience.

One of his largest and most famous works is the Rotterdam monument to the people of Holland who suffered in the Second World War. The sculpture project was initiated in 1954 by Dr Van der Wal who saw the monument as part of the architectural environment. Gabo completed the work in 1957. The sculpture rises vertically from the pavement; it is higher than the adjacent Bijenkorf department store building and its construction was made possible by the use of steel and clever engineering.

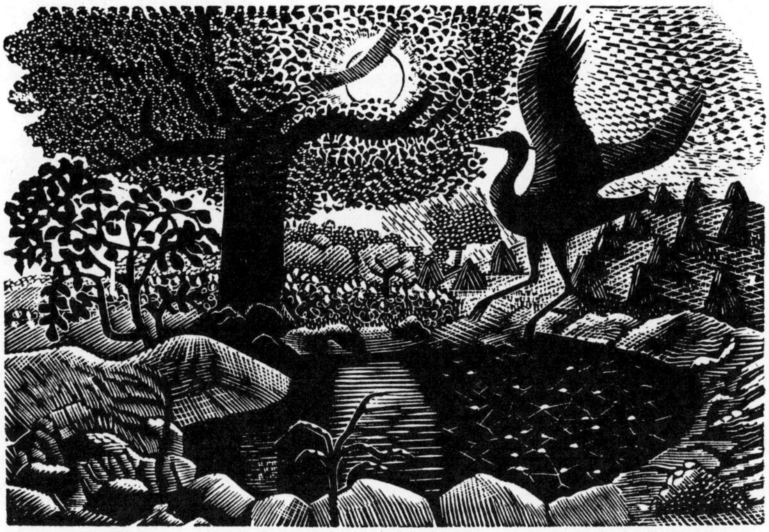

[224] Eric Ravilious: Illustration from *The Natural History of Selborne*, 1937. 10.2 x 7.0cm

During the 1930s wood engraving helped Gabo to research the field of sheet materials of metal and plastics to create the linear definition of space volumes. The Bijenkorf monument is a development from these techniques. In wood engraving he used the pure white line to give light in darkness, to express pure linear space construction themes as studies for the use of transparent plastic sheets. These studies correspond to the perspex sculptures and kinetic space constructions seen from 1930 to 1940. Gabo takes full advantage of the engraving concept of 'a line continuously changing its shape throughout its length'. He used wood engraving just to see him through his sculptural research and this proved vitally important for the development of sculpture. It enabled him to produce linear space volumes, without the need to use the normal materials to form solids. He was not interested in exploiting wood engraving as was Henry Moore and technically Gabo was not a very good engraver, but what he had to say was important.

The Society of Wood Engravers held their second overseas exhibition at the Department of Fine Arts, Carnegie Institute, Pittsburg, in 1931. Of three Mr and Mrs Frank G. Logan awards in the International Exhibition of Lithographs and Wood Engraving, a first prize was given to the wood engraver Muriel Jackson for her print *Wagons on the Heath* and the award carried a bronze medal. A second Logan prize was awarded to the French artist André Derain for his print *Torso*. From 1920 onwards Muriel Jackson has specialised in recording gipsy caravans on Hampstead Heath. She presented the Buckland Caravan to the London County Council in 1948 and it is now on show at Kenwood.

In 1932 the English Wood Engraving Society became defunct and as a result the Society of Wood Engravers gained some new members and regained some old ones. Leon Underwood and Ethelbert White were among those who rejoined and Agnes Miller Parker, Gertrude Hermes and Blair Hughes-Stanton were among the new members.

John Farleigh began to emerge on the London scene about 1932. He was a very expressive engraver, illustrator and designer who trained on the long hard road of experience. At the age of fourteen years he took a job of drawing in the Artists Illustrators Agency and for ten years spent his evenings drawing from life at the School of Photo-engraving at Bolt Court. Unfortunately, his career was to be interrupted by two wars. Farleigh was called up to serve in the Army in June 1918 and he wrote movingly of this experience in his book *Graven Image*. Farleigh

[225] Clifford Webb: *Ana the Runner*, 1937.

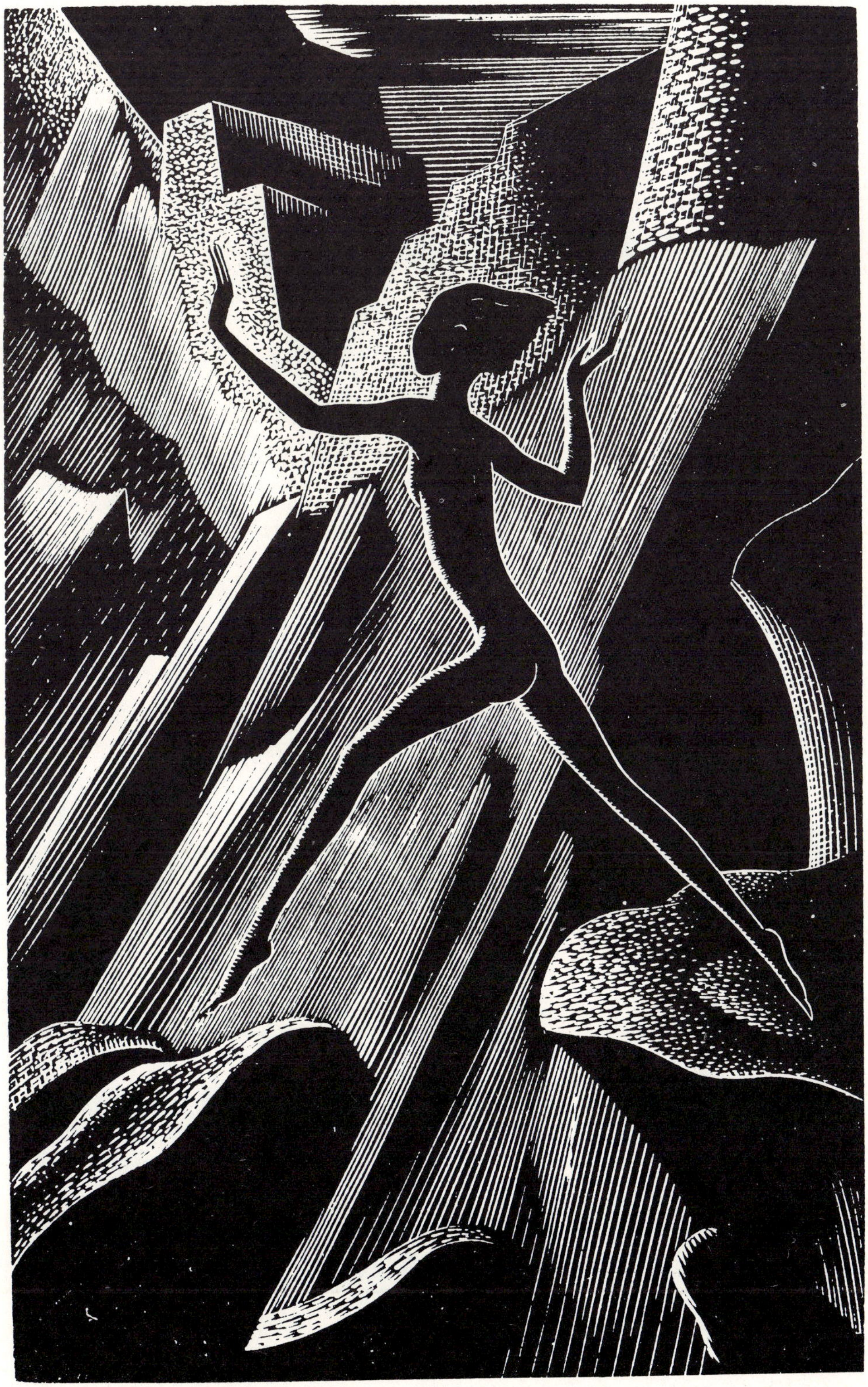

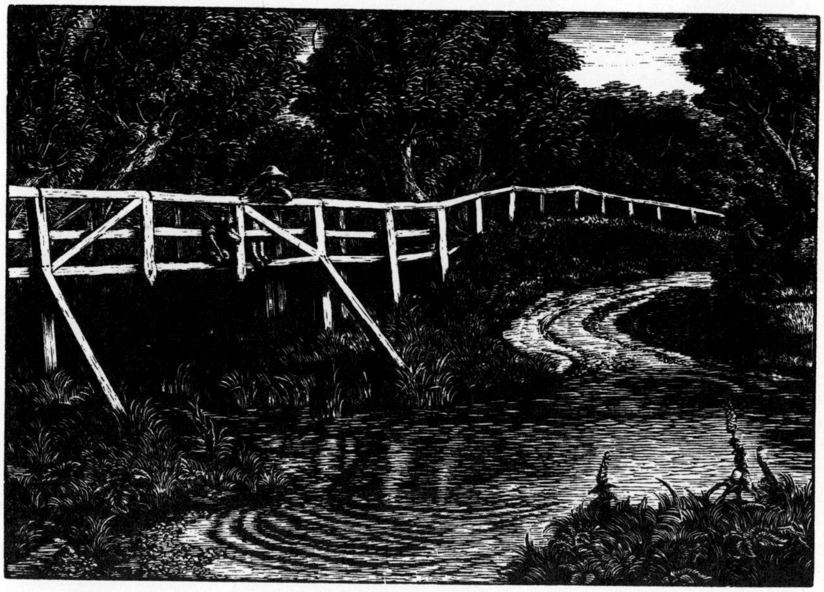

[226] Joan Hassall: *The Water Splash*, 1937. 10.75 x 7.5cm

[227] Agnes Miller Parker: Illustration from *Down the River*, 1937. 12.25 x 12.25cm

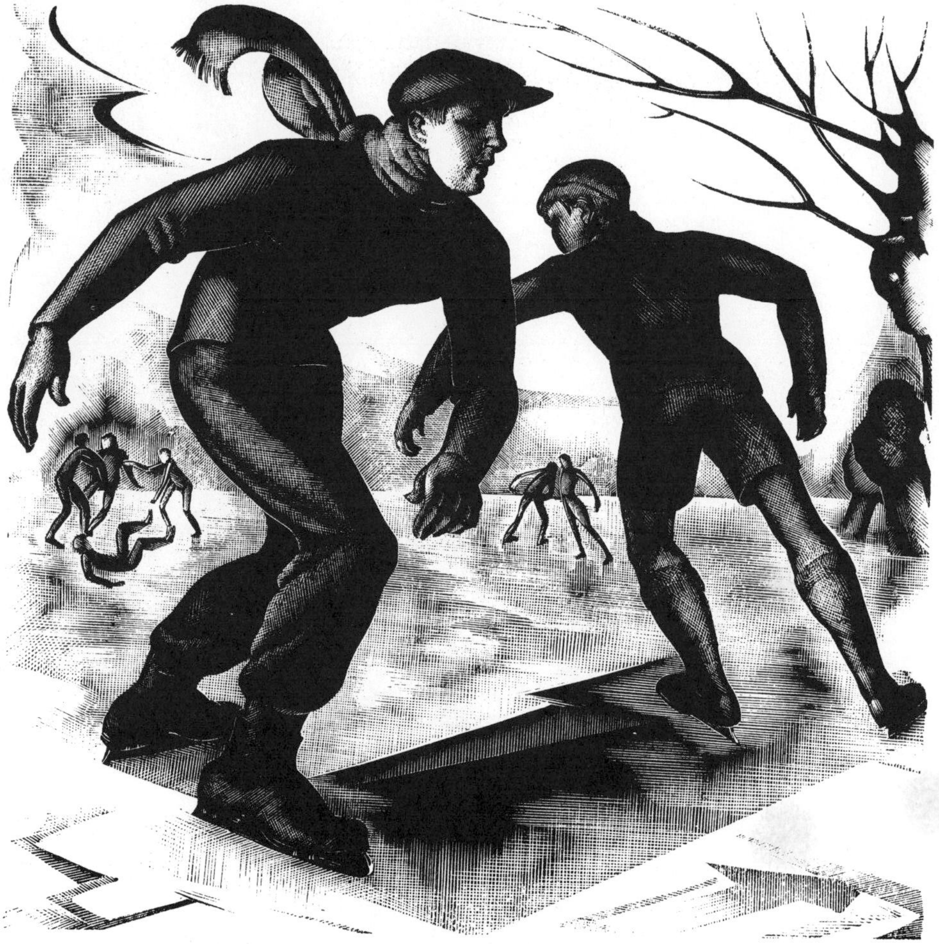

rejoined the Agency for a while and the need to earn a livelihood took him to the provinces as an art teacher in 1922.

In order to complete his training in art John Farleigh enrolled at the Central School where he was trained in wood engraving by Noel Rooke and in draughtsmanship by Bernard Meninsky. The stylistic influence of Meninsky was dominant in Farleigh's drawings. Of Rooke, Farleigh wrote in *Graven Image*: 'I went on to wood engraving – an interest that was partly fostered by the illustrations in old books that I had found, and partly by the atmosphere that Noel Rooke had created at the school and outside it. He had always been convinced of its possibilities as a creative medium, although its long history showed it, with a few exceptions, to be a means of reproducing a drawing in multiple. In spite of opposition, he persisted in teaching what was looked upon as a dead craft and, a pioneer himself, he was

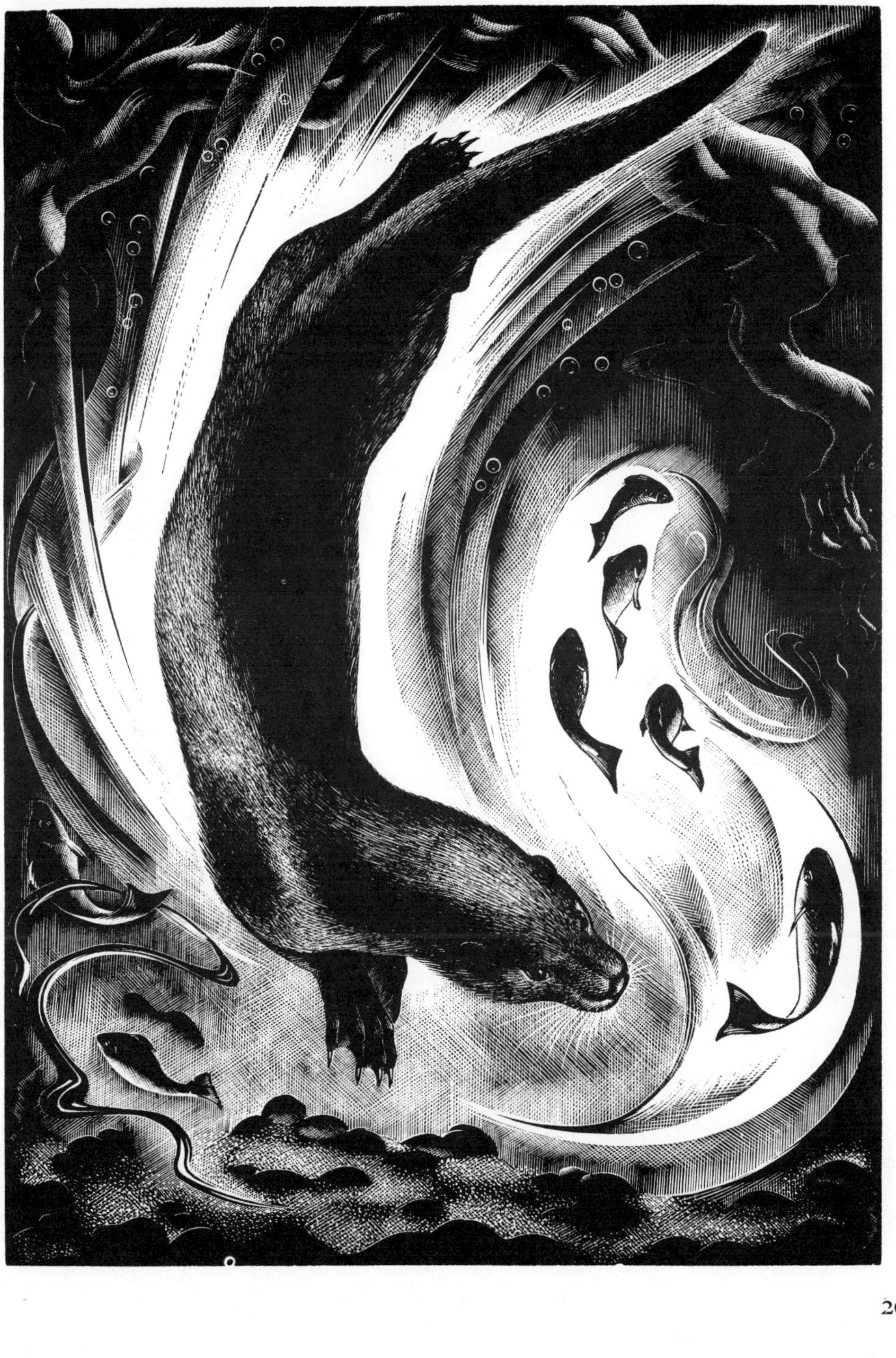

[228] Agnes Miller Parker: Illustration from *Down the River*, 1937. 12.3 x 17.6cm

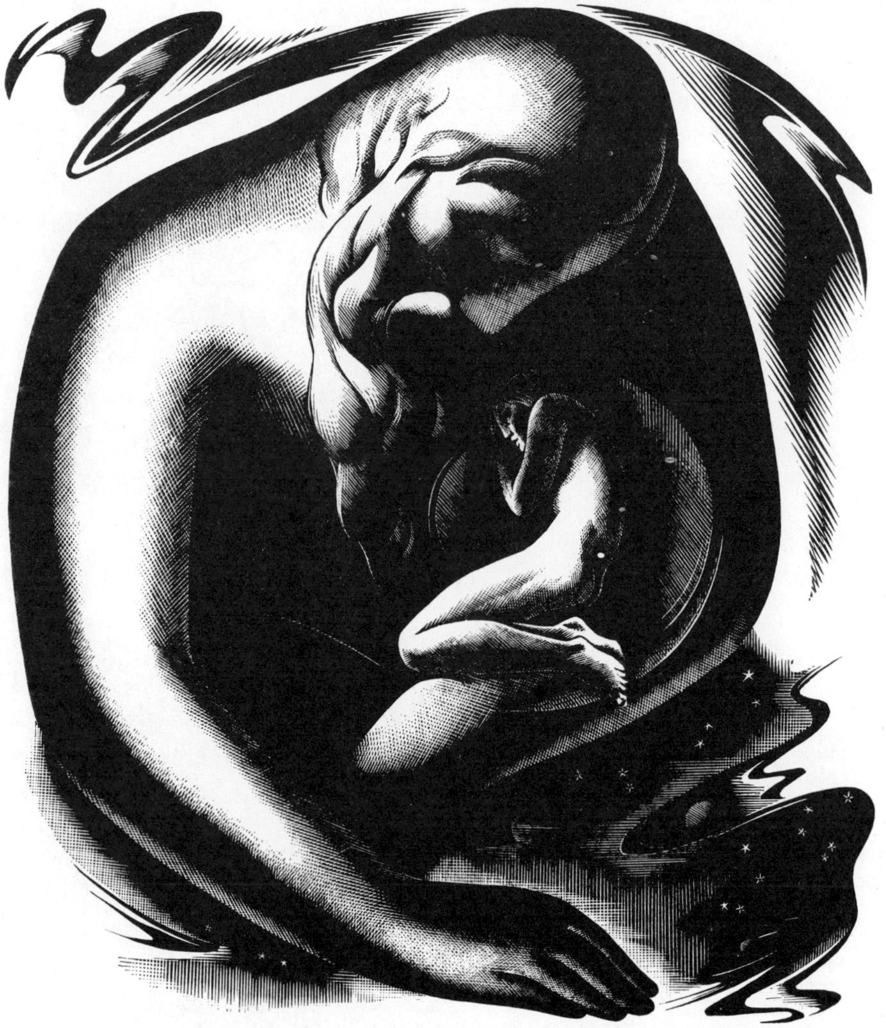

[230] Agnes Miller Parker: Illustration from *Gray's Elegy*, 1938. 11.5 x 13.5cm

convinced of its possibilities and probable revival in a different status. The modern wood engraver owes much to his efforts. There are few who are not his students or students of his students.'

Although Rooke was still active at the Central School, the most important centres of the second generation of teachers and students were Leon Underwood's Brook Green School, Iain Macnab's Grosvenor School of Modern Art, the Royal College of Art, John Buckland-Wright at Camberwell School of Art, the Anglo-French Art Centre and the Slade School of Fine Art.

Farleigh took up a teaching post at the Central School in 1924 and continued the Rooke tradition of technical and experimental development. He began by teaching the antique and still life classes and this started him in his career as a wood engraver. His interests were aroused by unusual objects and by events, scenes, people, antiques and pictures. This was the magpie vision of the born illustrator, in which a number of items could be brought together by craft; it was not the artist's overriding preoccupation of form and space structure and relationships.

He began his wood engraving exhibiting career in 1925 when he joined the English Wood Engraving Society and the Society of Wood Engravers. Farleigh entered the scene when the Society of Wood Engravers introduced Muriel Jackson, Eric Ravilious and David Jones – a vintage year in the development of the British school.

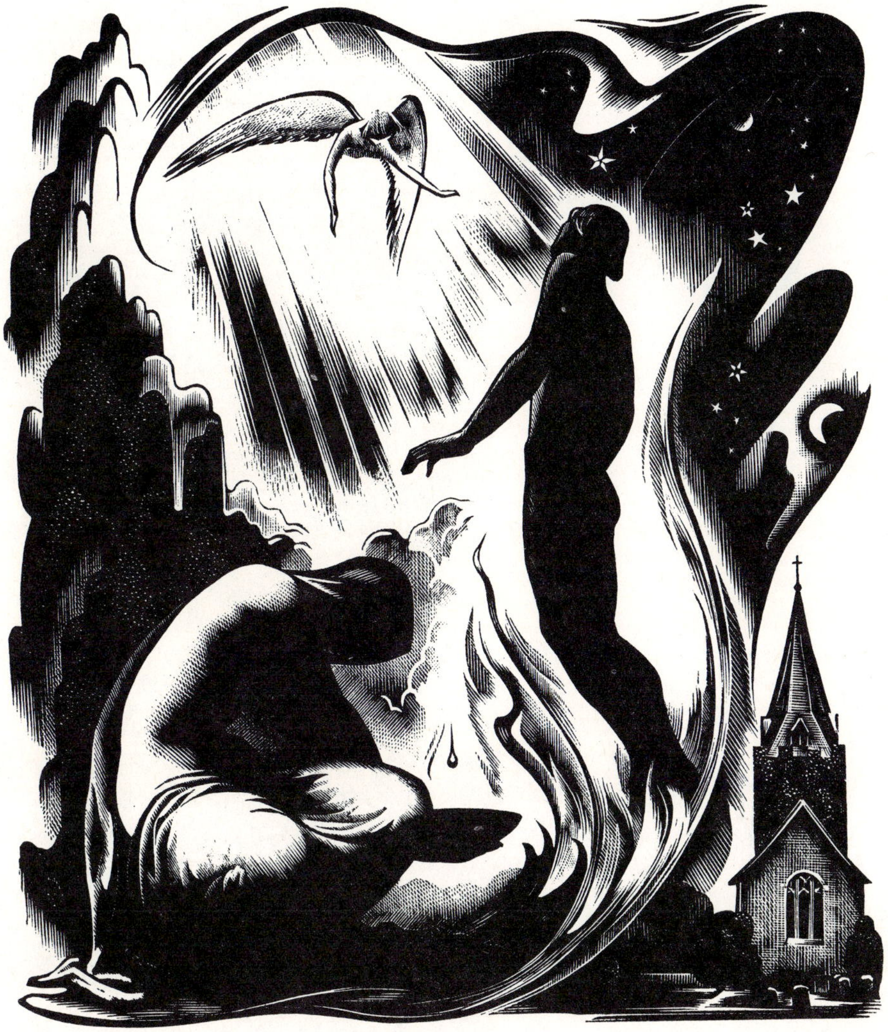

[229] Agnes Miller Parker: Illustration from *Gray's Elegy*, 1938. 11.5 x 13.5cm

Farleigh was to play a major role in engraving and the fine crafts up to the time he died in 1965. His talents were very wide and he succeeded in illustration both in engraving and other media. He was a highly respected teacher and a prolific and successful writer, mostly on engraving and teaching engraving. His approach to art was essentially emotional, intuitive and literary. His skill in engraving was phenomenal and his devotion to the craft considerable. Farleigh the illustrator and designer succeeded brilliantly but when he moved into art and abstraction he was less successful. While at the Central, Noel Rooke introduced him to Robert Gibbings in 1924 and this led to his first Golden Cockerel commission. At first Farleigh wanted to do *Pilgrim's Progress* or *Gulliver's Travels* but both proved unsaleable and *Swift's Essays* was finally agreed. In the final work there are no full-page engravings, the blocks are small, about two inches square. Unfortunately, the venture was a disaster because four hundred copies of the first volume were destroyed by a thunderstorm so the second volume had to be cancelled.

In 1927, Rooke introduced him to another publisher, Basil Blackwell, who wanted engravings for his private press production of *Odes of Pindar* to be printed in two volumes by the Shakespeare Head Press. This work was carried out in the white- and black-line tradition. Farleigh has said that he was always prepared to defend the black-line tradition, but he always preferred to work in white-line. *Odes of Pindar* was followed by the memorable volume of *Homer*.

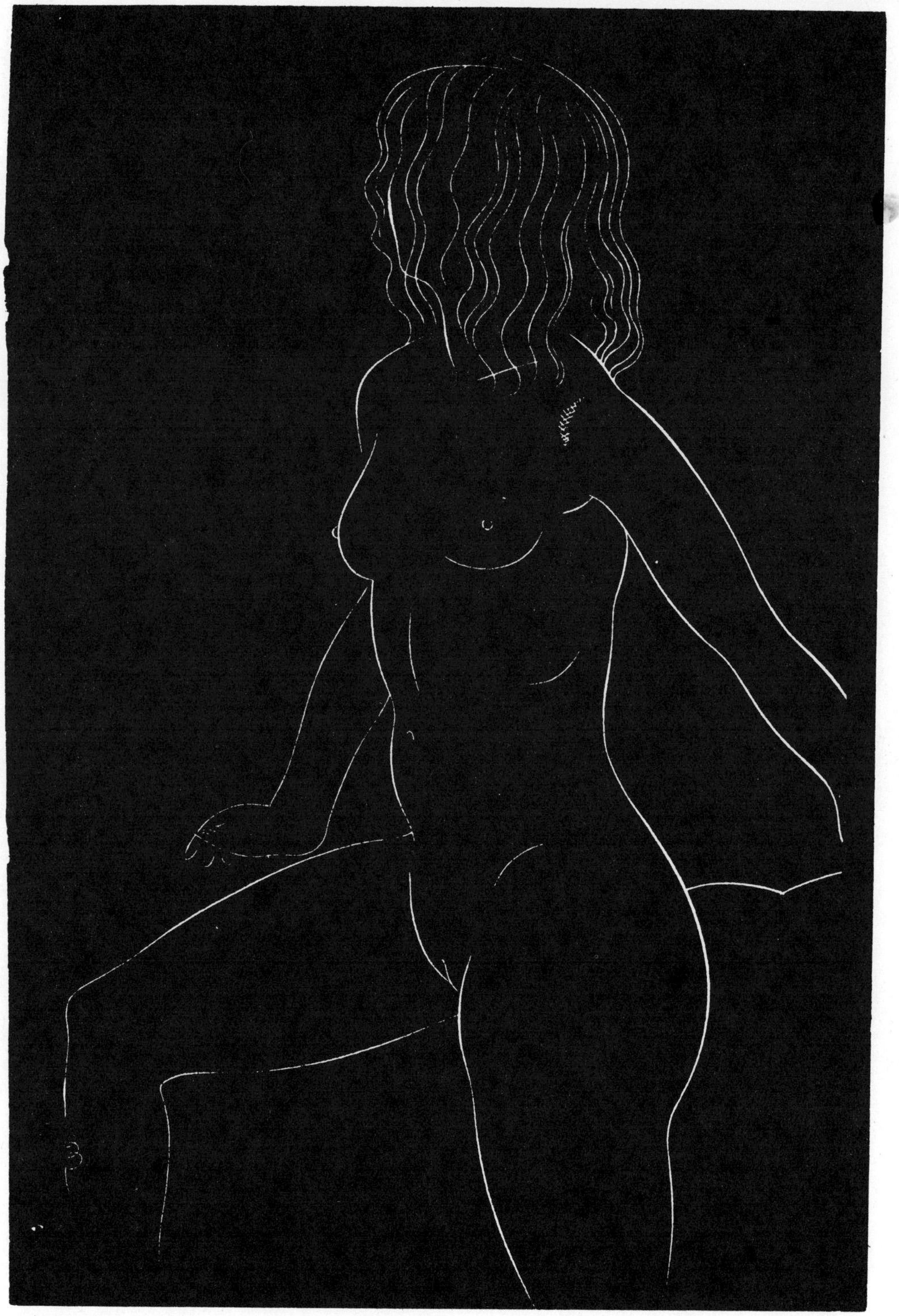

[231, 232] Eric Gill: Illustrations from *25 Nudes*, 1938. 13.0 x 19.5cm

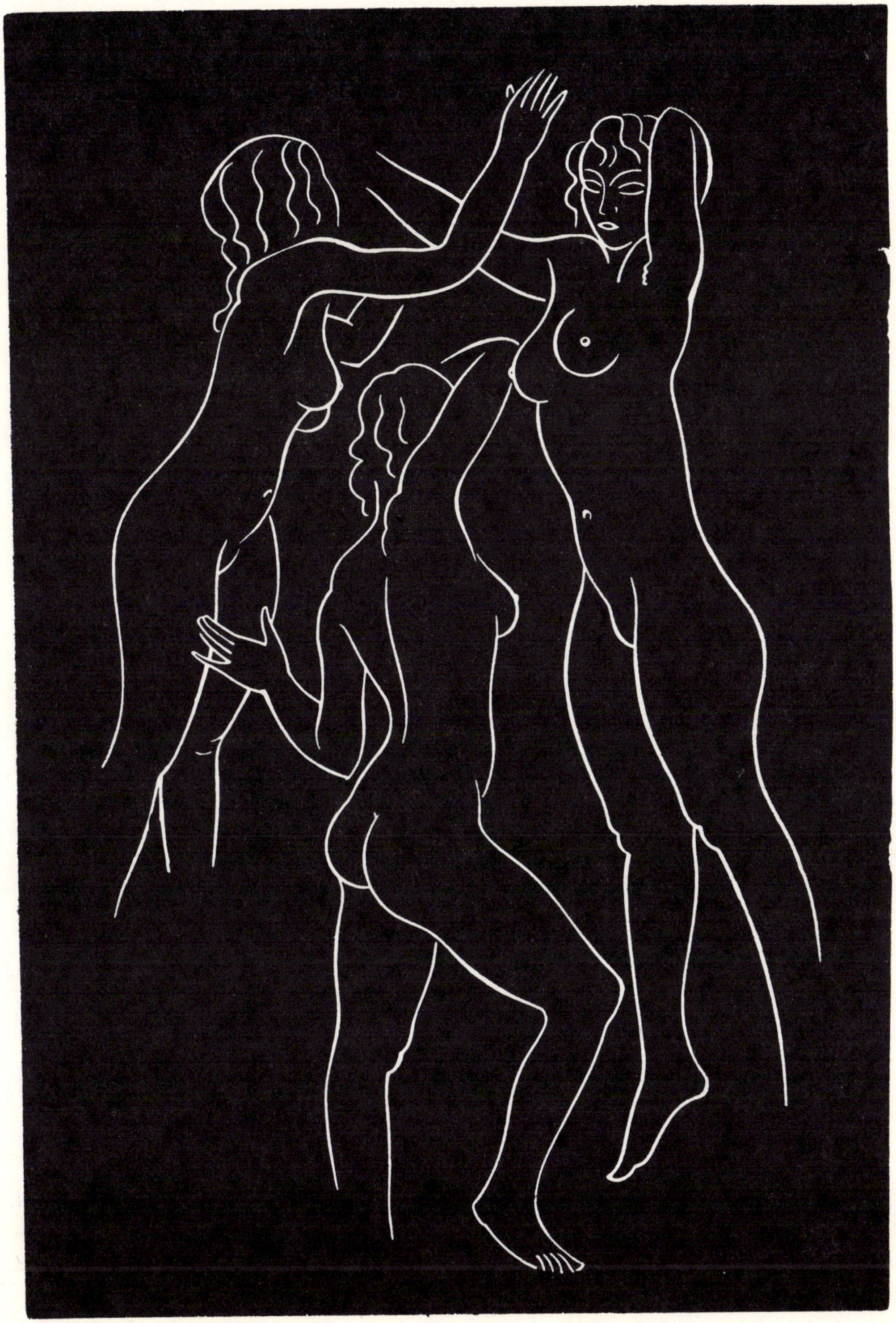

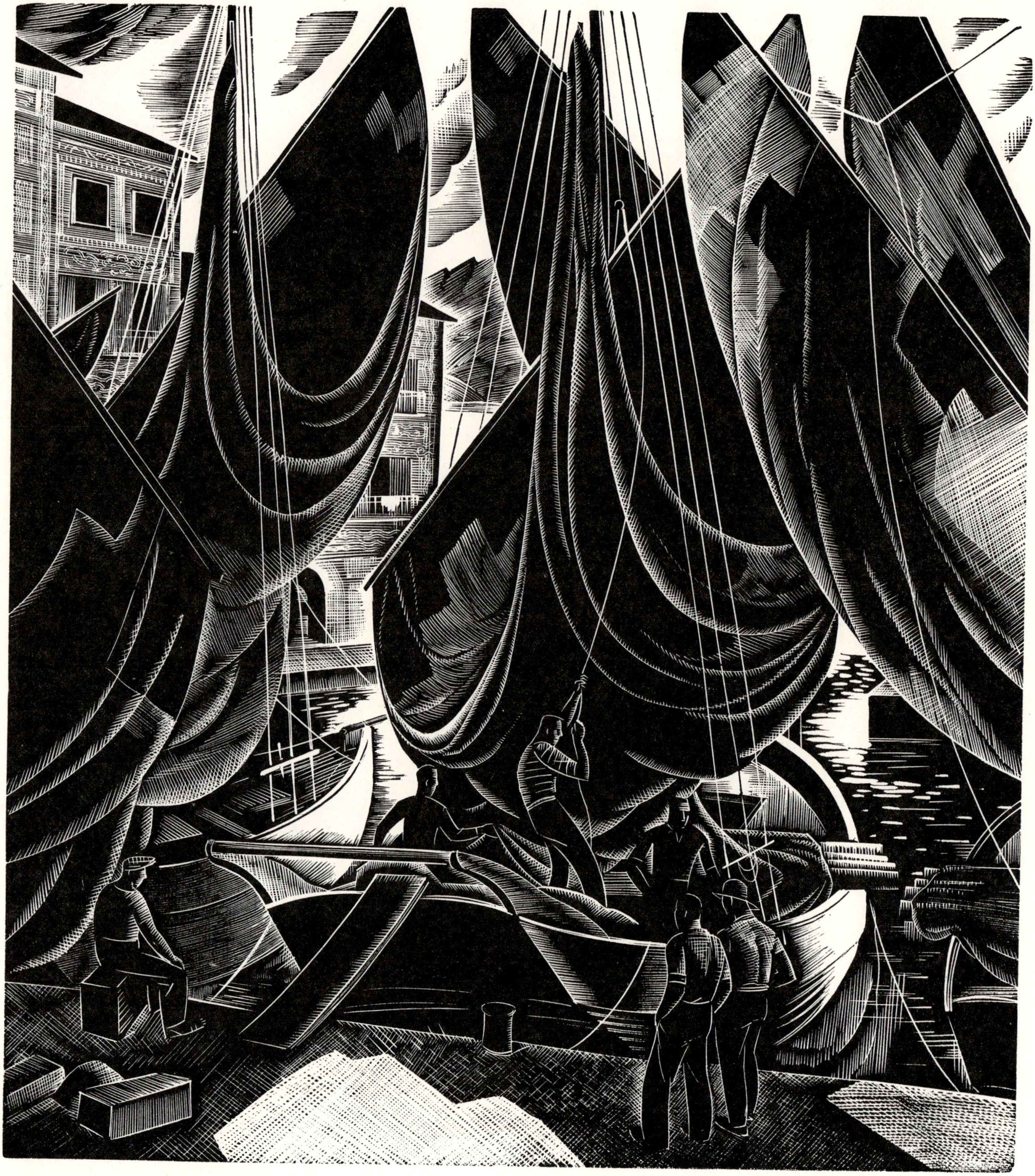

[233] Iain Macnab: *Drying Sails, Lake Garda*, 1938. 19.1 x 21.8cm

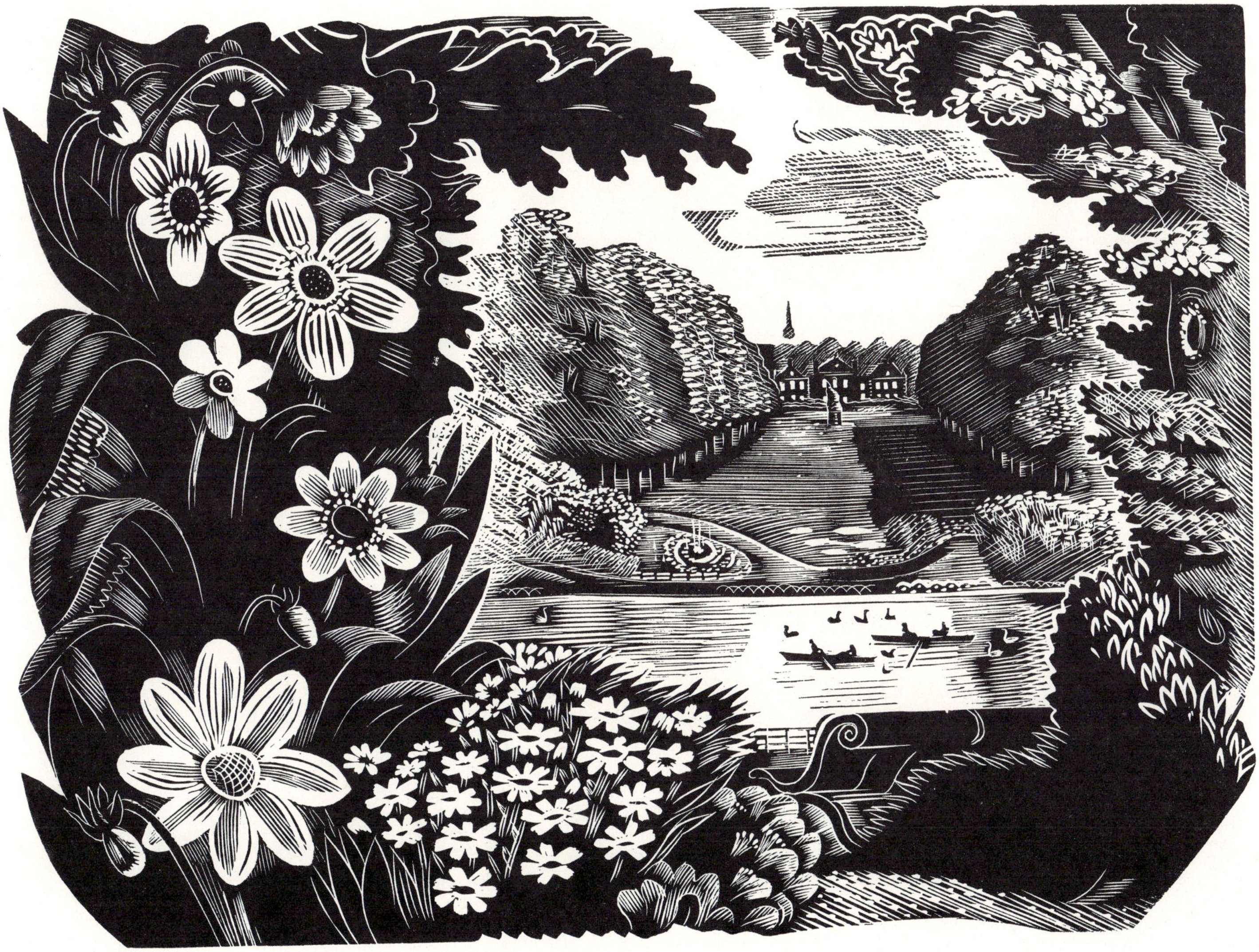

[234] John O'Connor: *Kensington Palace*, 1938. 22.1 x 16.5cm

Farleigh's most outstanding early success was in the field of commercial book production; this was George Bernard Shaw's book *The Adventures of the Black Girl in her Search for God* 1932 [198, 199 and 200].[1] The book ran to six impressions with a first edition of 25,000 copies and also an American edition. His collaboration with Shaw proved lively, imaginative and successful and many of Shaw's ideas, expressed as sketches or correspondence, were used by Farleigh in the book. Farleigh realised that he had a literary masterpiece to illustrate. This was a direct contrast to the two previous books in which Greek legends provided a remote theme. In the *Black Girl* his approach to form is clear and straightforward. The images are based sharply upon visual reality and the three-dimensional solids.

The un-English enjoyment of, and the expression of the sensual aspects of the human form was as brilliantly portrayed by Farleigh as it was by Gill, Buckland-Wright and Macnab. A sense of fun and of the unexpected confrontation was a remarkable achievement in a constricted discipline. The *Black Girl*, because she was engraved, had the outstanding quality of the healthy, young, fun-loving fullness of the quick life so evident in the bursting buds of the chestnut tree. This quickness of life is also a quality found in Gibbings's work.

Although Farleigh's engraving and craft were consistently of a high quality, he was always on the move and continually experimenting. In his two illustrated books *The Man who Died* by D. H. Lawrence, 1935, and *Back to Methuselah* by Shaw, 1938, he left the strictly three-dimensional world of visual fidelity and changed his language, but not his style, entering the field of the artist rather than the illustrator. In these works the separate world of two-dimensional shapes, which run in their own free way, clashes with the form of the solids which is cut up by the former shapes and negates the solids.

During the thirties in Britain, there appears to have been no knowledge of the reconstruction of form which was taking place at Dessau in Germany. If there had been full knowledge and understanding of Bauhaus form, it can be thought certain that Farleigh, being essentially the illustrator and designer, would never have been prepared to accept the discipline, the 'tightrope', required of the artist.

When discussing this aspect of engraving, Iain Macnab (1890 to 1967) said that he likened the artist-engraver to the circus acrobat: 'In some way this is similar to

[235] Alison McKenzie: *The Cod and Lobster Inn*, 1938. 23.0 x 20.0cm

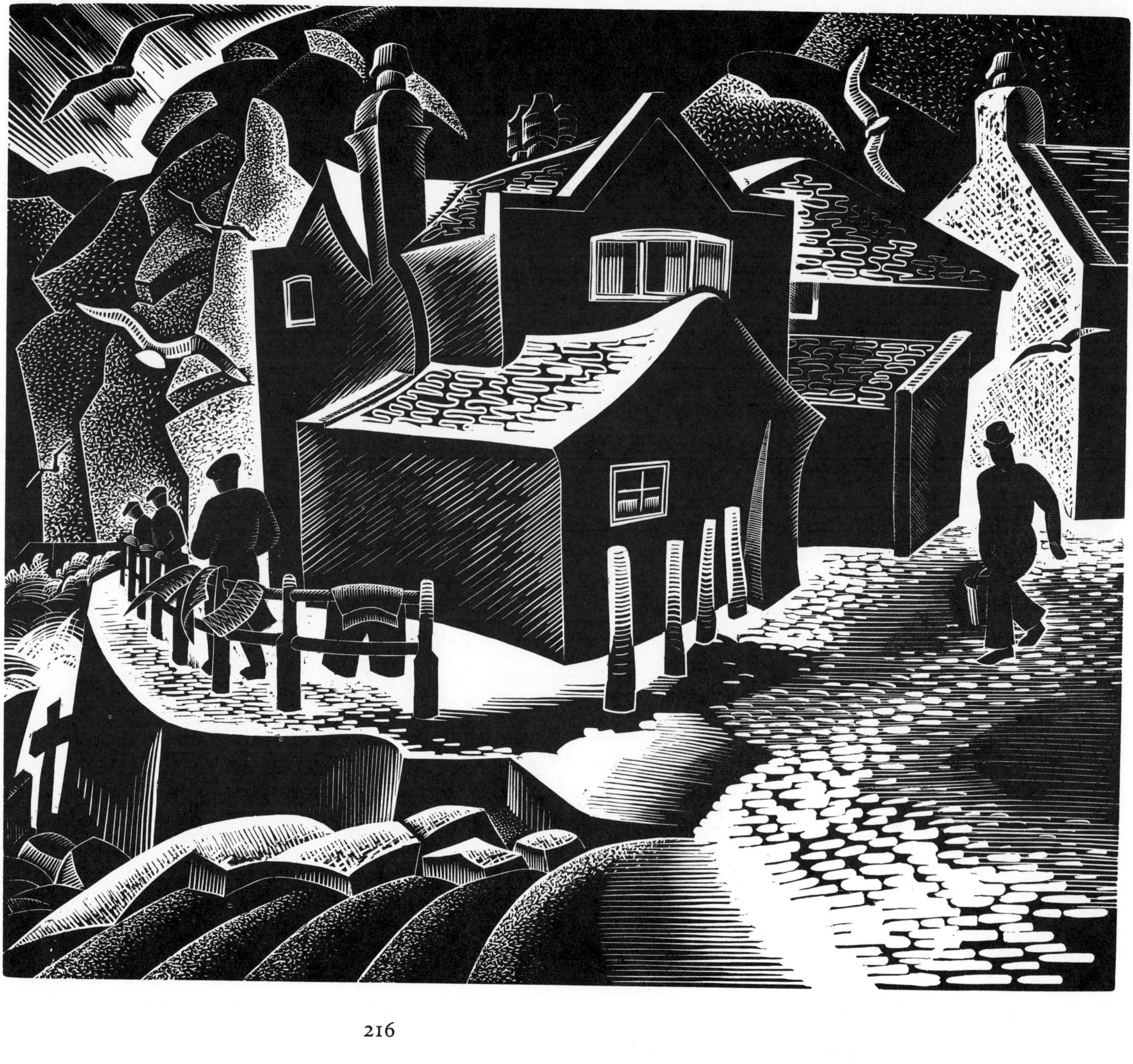

the difference between the athlete and the circus artist or performer. Through training, the athlete will gradually work up to a climax of achieving a record, yet the circus artist must hold this pitch and fine balance in every performance that is undertaken. He is the greater artist because he has the freedom of a restricted discipline which enables him to take over where the athlete may rest content.'[2]

Writing in *Studio* in June 1942 on 'The Future of Wood Engraving', John Farleigh expressed his dilemma as an artist: 'During the past forty years painting has been in revolt. This was first manifest in the return to primitive art and the worship of child art and childish technique. Here is the natural reaction of the technically and mentally over-sophisticated. Painting has in that short space of forty years once more reached complexity and elaboration, except that it is now of a highly intellectual order – the intellectual classicism of the abstractionist and the

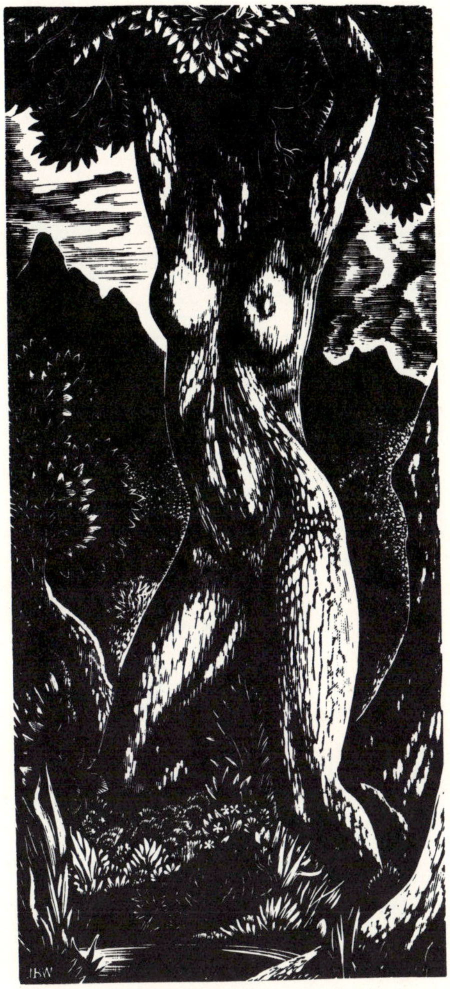

[236] John Buckland-Wright: *Metamorphosis 2*, 1938. 8.75 x 20.0cm

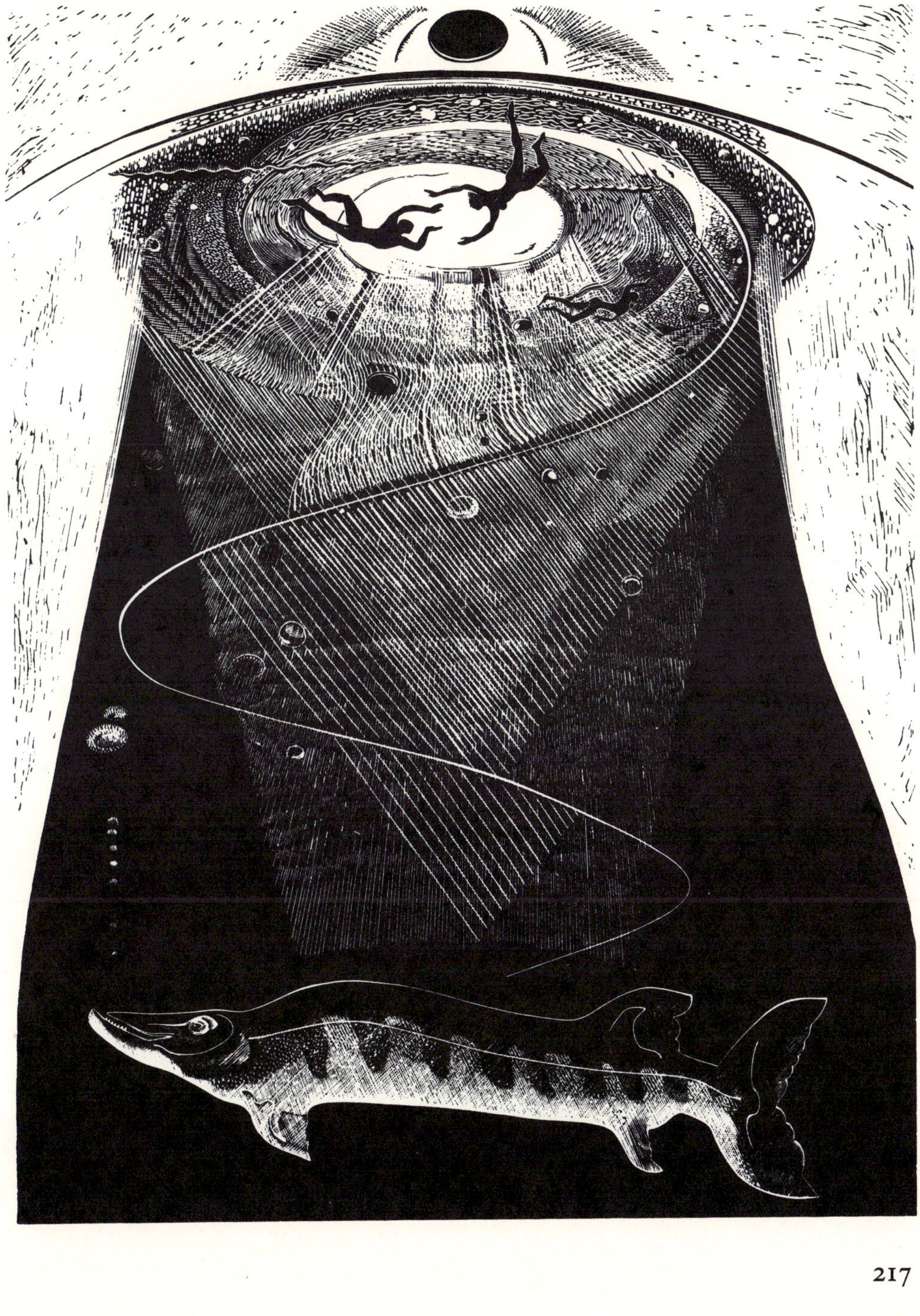

[237] Gertrude Hermes: *Undercurrents*, 1938. 30.4 x 40.6cm

[238] Douglas Percy Bliss: *Fall of the House of Usher*, 1938. 8.25 x 13.3cm

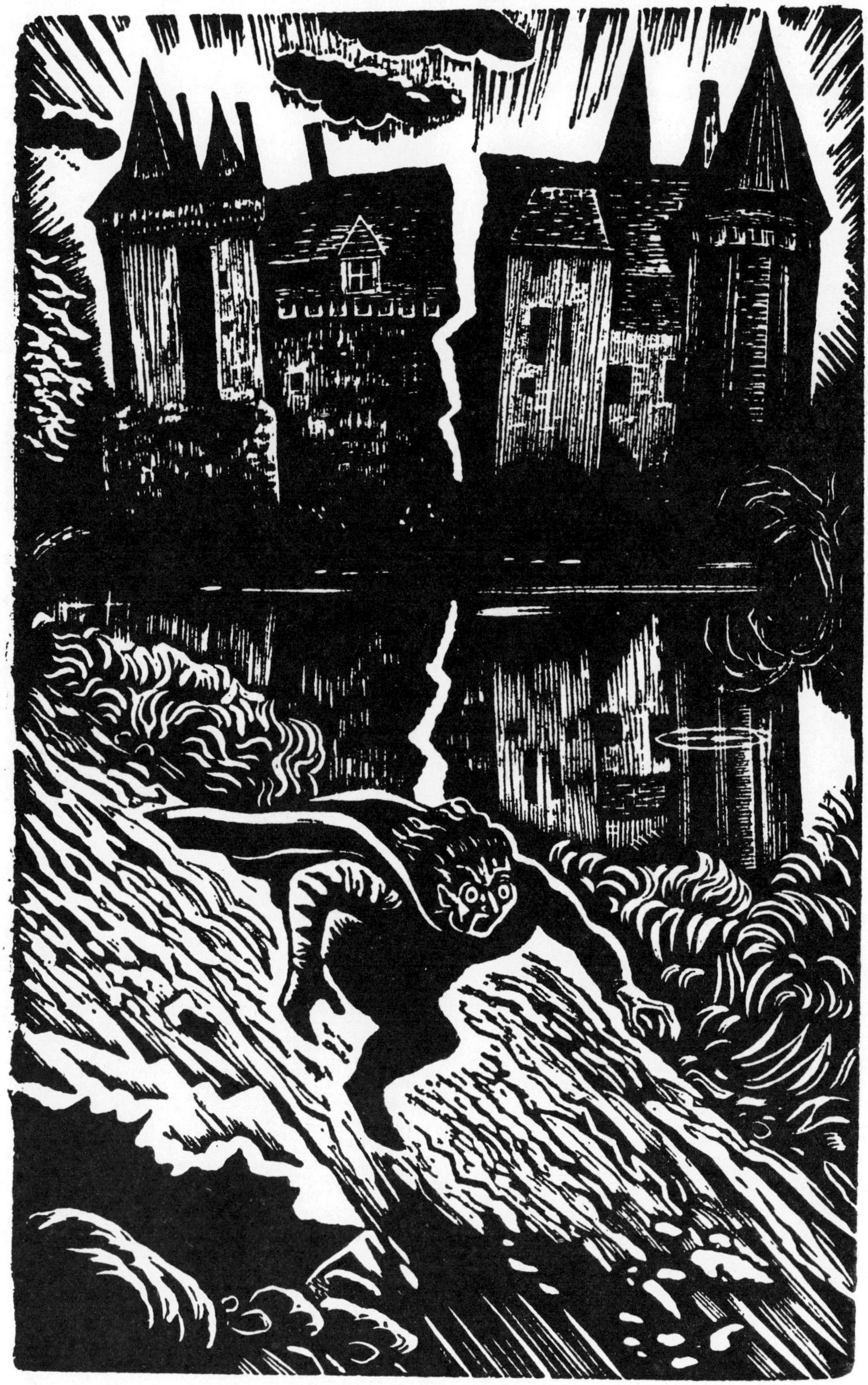

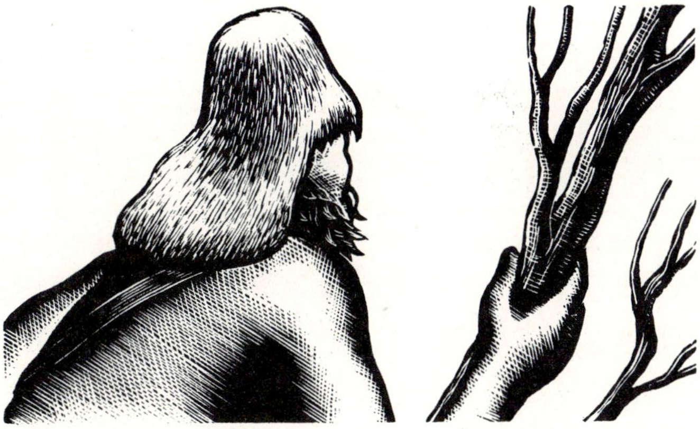 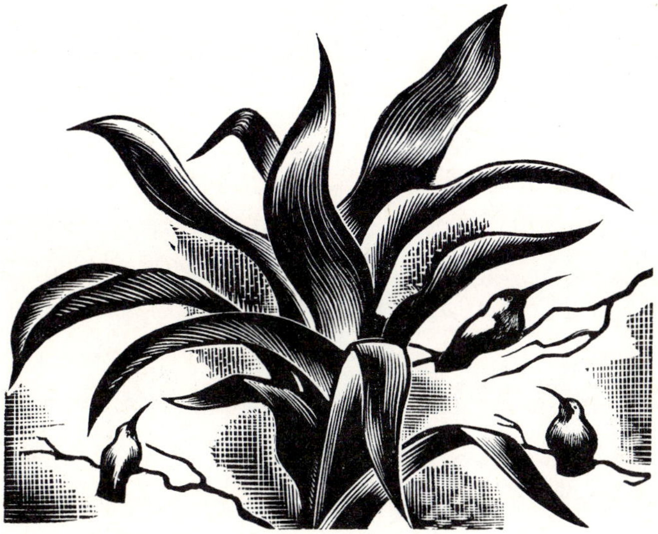

[239, 240] John R. Biggs: Illustrations from *Robinson Crusoe*, 1938.
8.75 x 5.25cm, 8.75 x 7.0cm

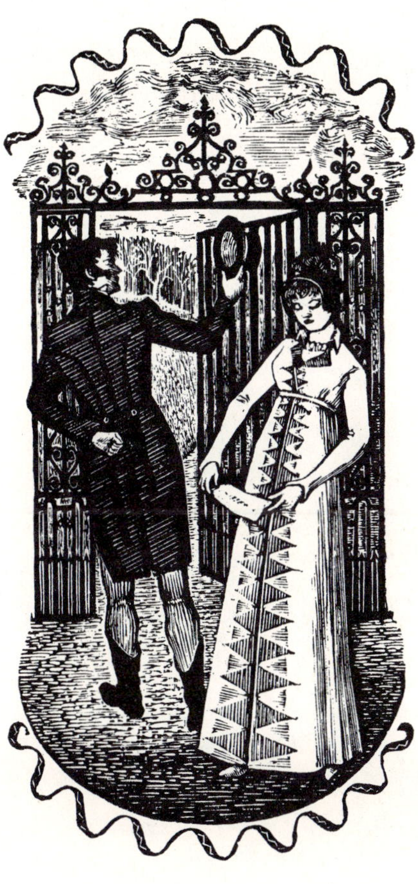

[241] Helen Binyon: Frontispiece from *Pride and Prejudice*, 1938.
7.75 x 14.0cm

intellectual emotionalism of the surrealist. Whether these movements have exhausted themselves it is difficult to say, but there was evidence before the war of a thin stream of good painting flowing between the two extremes that showed a marked tendency to return to more traditional methods.'

Where art is concerned, Farleigh appears ill at ease and his world is divided. Thirty years later, abstraction and expressionism still hold a large slice of the art of our time, it is Surrealism that has receded from the arena at least for the time being, although it is very much alive today in Germany, especially in the world of print.

Farleigh was unable to differentiate between primitive art and Palaeolithic art and a clear understanding of this difference is essential for all creative artists. This is evident with David Jones, Leon Underwood, Iain Macnab, Blair Hughes-Stanton and John Buckland-Wright who all found Palaeolithic art a source of inspiration. Farleigh was also confused in his references to child art and childish techniques. The accepted concept was Matisse's demonstration of a grand and ultimate achievement of a vision as fresh, direct and pure as that of a child, but expressed with the certainty of the child, the content being that of a highly sensitive, experienced and mature adult.

Farleigh at that time, though breaking new ground in illustration, had little meaningful contemporary art as a guide. Everyday Freudian psychology achieves a tremendous popularity when no explanation or facts are required to substantiate statements which are mostly empirical. In the last sentence of his statement in *Studio* he yearns for the flow between the two extremes. Many steered a midstream current, a course from which no art of real value has arisen. The midstream current must end in an all-consuming eddy, circling around its own axis or vortex.

In his teaching he encouraged experiment and change from traditional views in his pupils. He was greatly appreciated as a teacher and made a considerable contribution to British engraving in this capacity. One of the best and most famous of his pupils is Monica Poole. Her engravings are very individual and in most cases almost faultlessly executed. She engraves away most of her blacks, and her near white and light grey prints have the unique quality of the floodlight source illuminating the subject matter.

Monica Poole experimented with engraving in the Farleigh tradition until she arrived at the ultimate in personal expression. A Monica Poole wood engraving is always easily distinguishable.

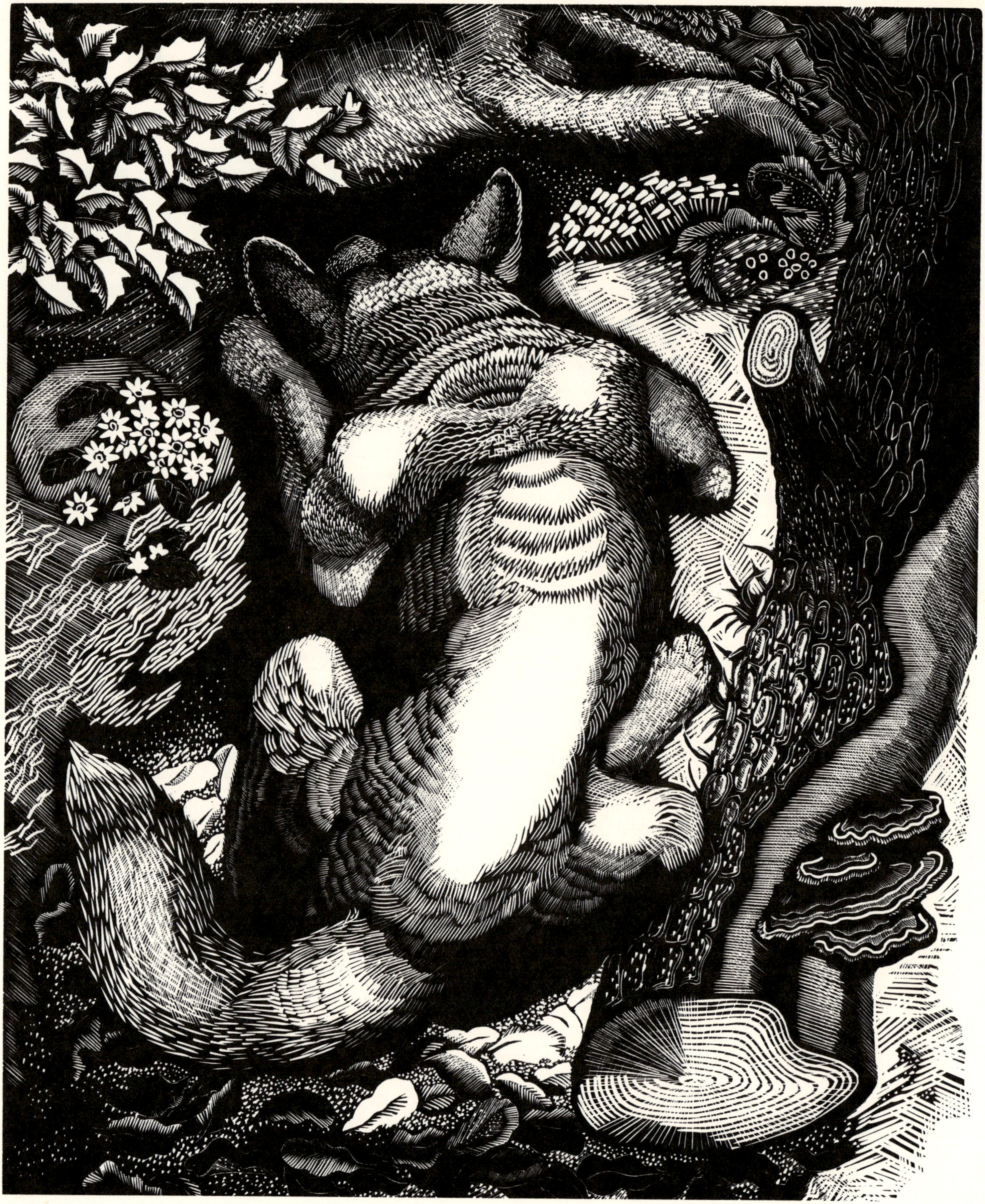

[242] Rachel Reckitt: *Dingo Digging*, 1939. 20.5 x 25.5cm

One of John Farleigh's living creations is the Crafts Centre of Great Britain, which started in Hay Hill, Mayfair, and is now in Earlham Street off Shaftesbury Avenue. His craft movement was based upon 'the fine crafts' and differed in one important aspect from the Ruskin and Morris Aesthetic Movement in that there was no opposition to mechanisation.

The wood engraving of Eric Ravilious is a brilliant example of the articulate designer at work with the burin. He was gifted with an imagination adept at creating memorable images. His volumetric expression is minimal, his language of shape is maximum, and space planes are rendered by graduated grey planes set between the black and white poles. In style his art is illustrative, decorative and dominated by intricate pattern and texture. His textures are quite rightly those cut naturally by the range of engraving tools and not naturalistically representational. The largest single influence upon the style of Ravilious is Dürer.

As a designer of freely-formed images, Ravilious can be seen at his best in his treatment of life or the human being. In his book illustrations the human form is treated as volume working anatomically. However, when he was designing a symbol, device or book plate incorporating lettering, he would throw the volumetric treatment of the human form overboard for a romantic two-dimensional visual sign language. The shapes of this were made to fit an environment of visual images and typography. Here, there is a dimensional switch of firstly a three-dimensional rendering and then a two-dimensional rendering, the language of one differing from the other. Normally, an artist does not work this way. Eric Gill, John Buckland-Wright and Iain Macnab all use the figure as a source of continuous study through which they evolve and perfect a language of form. When this language arrives at a maturity they are able to work on the human form in any dimension without switching from one formal language to another, achieving success by their use of line. For an artist, shape is a part of form; for the book designer shape is a free element to make images fit some other requirement, i.e. the book.

Publishers and typographers rated the talent of Ravilious very highly, and as an illustrator he embodied almost every current requirement of book design; he was excited by the art of the book. In his technique and craft he was a superb performer and throughout his short life was an exponent of the white-line concept. As a designer his precise resolution of complex shapes resulted in the sharp crystallization of images illustrating a theme or commission. He used engraving as a means to an end; he loved engraving but had no interest to exploit it for its own sake. As a designer of shapes his main interest was the further development of engraving pattern textures.

Although primarily a designer, especially for industry, his talent was extensive and included lithography, watercolour painting, mural design, decoration for Wedgwood pottery, furniture, textiles and books. As an engraver who had established an outstanding reputation, his main contribution to wood engraving was that he turned it into a democratic art form once again, in the tradition of the Danube school. He produced very few prints that are autonomous as works of art in their own right.

While Ravilious was a student at the Royal College, Paul Nash was teaching design and he introduced Ravilious to the Society of Wood Engravers. Through this introduction he met Robert Gibbings and received commissions for Golden Cockerel Press books. In 1926 he received two commissions from the Golden Cockerel Press for illustrations to Sir John Suckling's *A Ballad upon a Wedding* and Nicholas Breton's *The Twelve Months*. Both books gave him the opportunity to develop his keen interest in the English countryside and rural colour of life but he had to wait another three years for his third commission from this press in 1929. The next book was Aaron Smith's *The Atrocities of the Pirates*. Two books were commissioned by Gibbings and were never completed or even printed, these were Marlowe's *Faustus* and *Hero and Leander*. Later, in 1933, Christopher Sandford commissioned him to do engravings for the Golden Hours Press of Marlowe's *Tragedy of the Jew of Malta* and this book, with the closely following Shakespeare's *Twelfth Night* from the same press, contained some of his finest work. His rich decoration and pattern remained in direct contrast to the purity and austere linear engraving of Eric Gill. He never quite mastered the relationship of lettering to engraving as it had become known through the work of Gill. *Twelfth Night* was first planned by Gibbings and Ravilious for a Golden Cockerel production in the late twenties.

His complete lack of snobbishness or jealousy, coupled with his gaiety and enthusiasm, made Ravilious a good and respected teacher. His most important teaching post was at the Design School of the Royal College of Art, under Professor Tristram and Sir Frank Short. Through his work and his teaching he became a very real influence both in design and wood engraving. One of his students was John O'Connor. As an engraver O'Connor is an illustrator and very sensitive draughtsman. In style he is influenced by the Ravilious manner, with an emphasis on pattern and book design techniques. He has made a valuable contribution to book design through his technical experiments which include colour. O'Connor has also brought wood engraving and other media together in the same work. These are essentially book designing experiments rather than experiments in engraving as such.

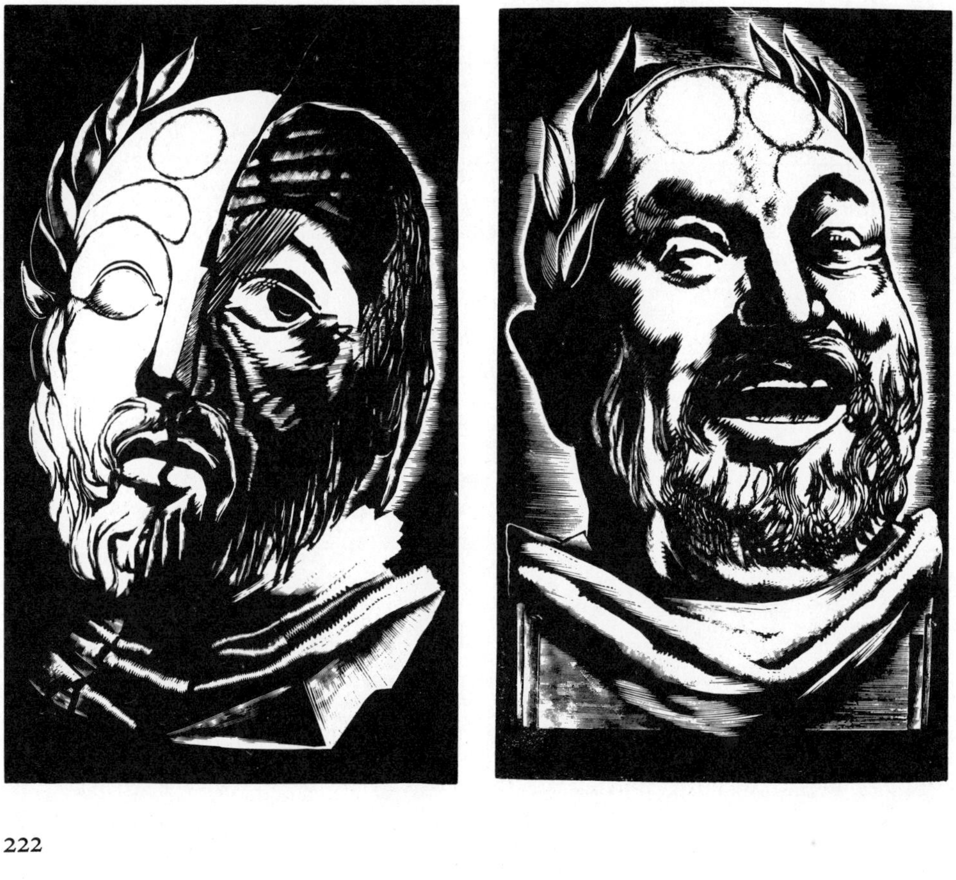

[243] George Buday: *Timon of Athens*, (I, II, III, IV and IX), 1940. 13.5 x 22.75cm

George Mackley is a phenomenon in British engraving. A few square centimetres of Mackley is more highly charged with aesthetic energy, emotion and precision than many artists can muster in a lifetime. In order to accomplish his work, Mackley had to shut his eyes to the changing scene. He can be described as an island, not in the middle of an ocean but just offshore, always in viewing distance of the mainland. His principles are simple – that art is essentially a visual process – and firmly held. He could not tolerate bad or weak craftsmanship under any circumstances; bad draughtsmen met with short shrift from him. He makes no claims to being a creative artist and always stresses that he is primarily a craftsman. Mackley's art will be studied for its mystery, vision and skill well into the future.

Mackley is one of three engravers who have achieved extreme fineness of line and texture and, as with Agnes Miller Parker in particular [186] and Blair Hughes-Stanton, [191], the fineness of linear closeness often confuses the human optical system. The work of artists such as Mackley, Miller Parker and Hughes-Stanton is best seen in prints from the actual wood engraving rather than from mass-produced prints made with the aid of a line block obtained by photography. This emphasises the value of the private press in reproducing artists' work as examples of the art of the engraver.

It is in the work of engravers like Mackley that one can experience the shimmering, silvery greys that are also found in modern Russian engraving. Mackley is possibly our finest exponent of these greys and they are evenly distributed through his compositions. The shimmering greys in Agnes Miller Parker's work are often cut off in development through her uncompromising blacks. Mackley will just skim, very lightly, into a solid black space. Some of the lines on the block are little more than scratches. This can be seen in the most sensitive example of his work *The Lead Mine* [381].

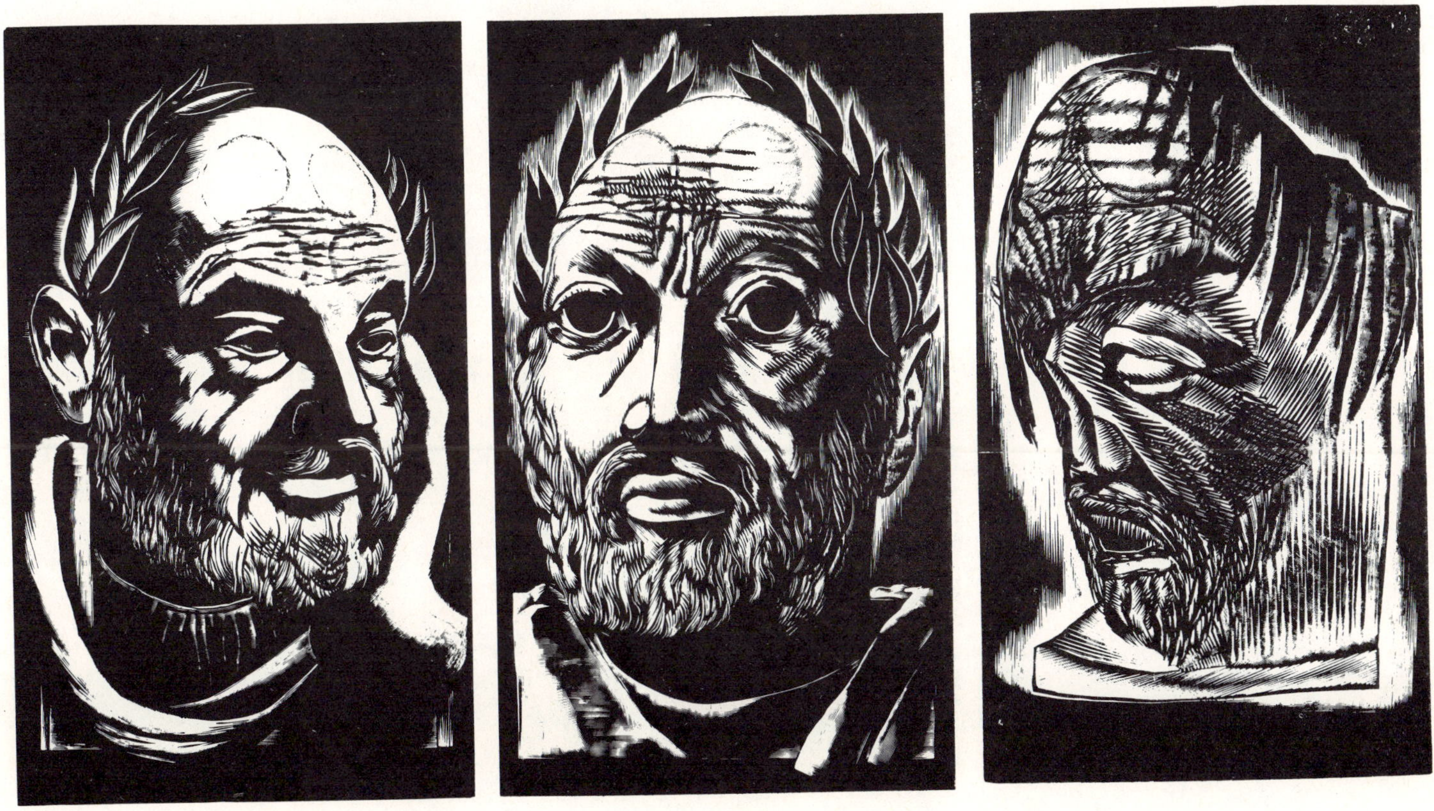

Viewed critically *The Lead Mine* is one of the more significant engraved landscapes of this period and is abstract in form. The spiky areas of flat planes and plants are in clear-cut opposition to the volumetric roundness of the hills and tree foliage. Mackley's simplicity of statement of the structure is masterly. A gabled roof is defined by cast shadows, accurate to within a degree, the curve of the wall is accurately drawn and value change concludes the statement in a manner as crisp as are the angles of ninety degrees of the vertical and horizontal planes. The forms are abstract but are so superbly structured and so visually real that one is first convinced of the reality of the subject and secondly wishes for reality to be so selectively defined. The remarkable effects on space advancement and recession flaunt the orthodox perspective structure. In these terms it just does not work, especially with a solid area of black in the foreground and another solid area of black in the far distance, but it does work optically on the physical visual system in exactly the same manner as a single light in a dark room. Wood engraving involves the manipulation of light; Mackley's single white shape is like the lamp in the dark room, and space recession is registered in the optical system by incident light being selectively reflected on the undulations occurring within the black space. Mackley is very well informed about light and optics.

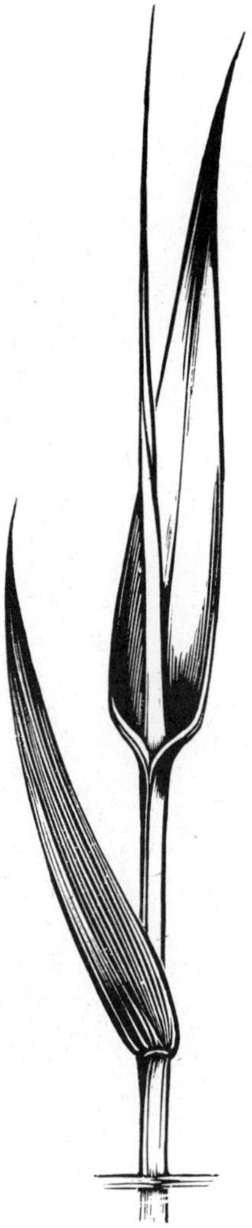

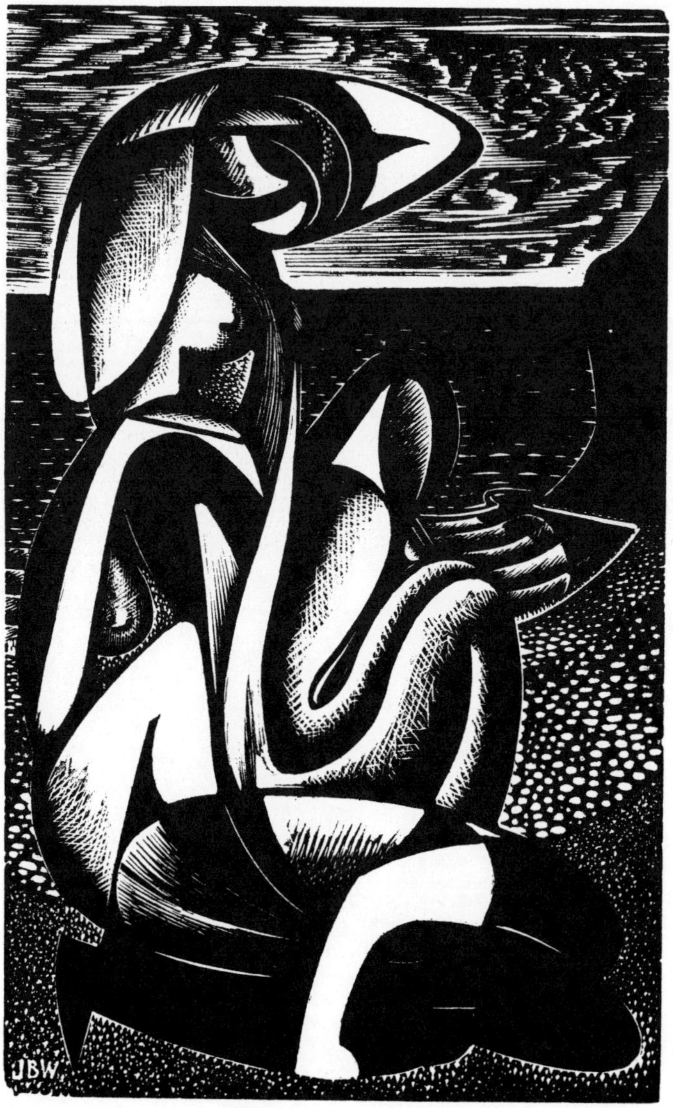

[244] Robert Gibbins: *Reed.* 25.0 x 13.5cm

[245] John Buckland-Wright: *Sibling*, 1940. 8.75 x 14.5cm

[246] Agnes Miller Parker:
Illustration from *Richard II*, 1940.
12.75 x 21.2cm

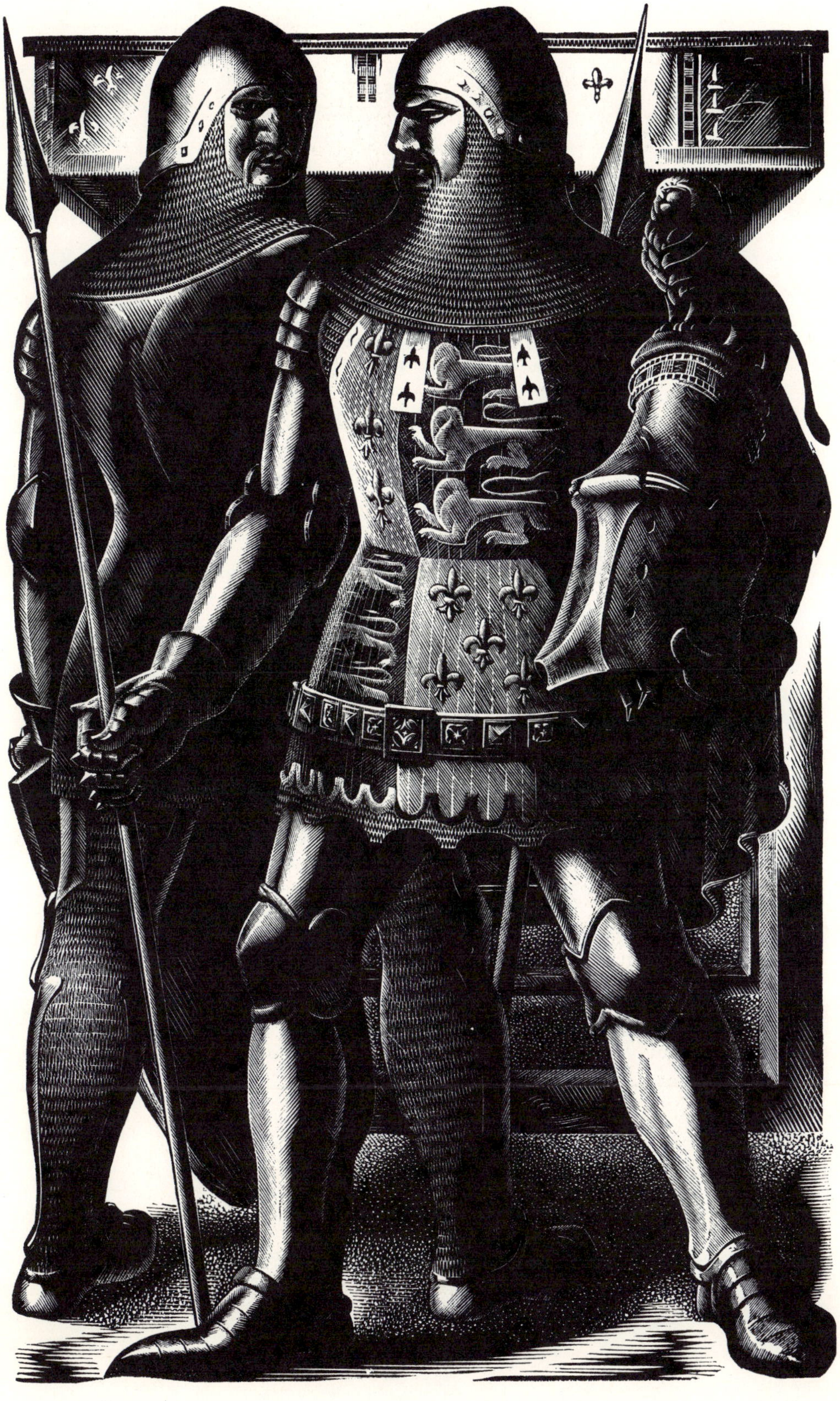

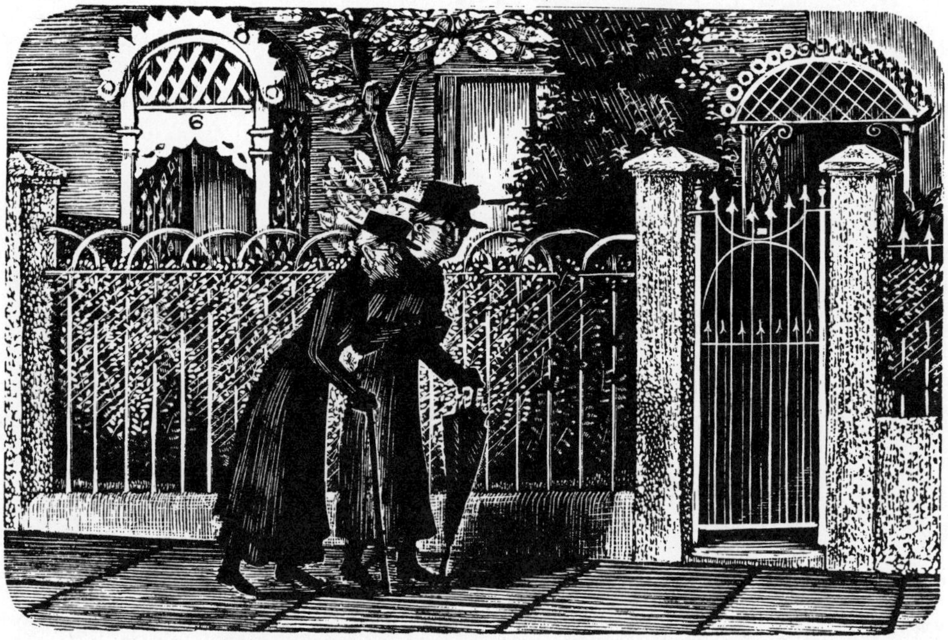

[247] Helen Binyon: *The Old Ladies, Bath*, 1941. 12.5 x 8.35cm

Although the engravers grew in number and achievement after the First World War, the acceptance of their work was not immediate. They were a lively bunch but soon began to find that the prevailing outlook on morals was against them. In 1934 G. K. Chesterton wrote of Gill: 'Belongs to the great company of those who talk too plainly to be understood'.[3] Gill also engraved too plainly to be understood and this led to a misinterpretation of some of his work. Misinterpretation of some drawings nearly cost him the loss of an important client, Count Harry Kessler of Weimar. Gill was a curious mixture of religion and an innocent eye with a deep curiosity about life; it was this innocence which gave rise to works which some considered to be of an erotic nature. However his eroticism expressed in the human figure had a certain coldness about it when compared with the warm, emotional, erotic work of Maillol. He cared very little about the psychology of vision as it applied to interpretation from clerics, counts and politicians.

Gill met Harry Kessler in 1904 and was given his first commission to produce drawn titles and headings for Grossherzog Wilhelm Ernst's edition in twenty-one volumes of the German classics published by Insel Verlag, Leipzig. Gill also engraved on wood the initial letter designed by Maillol for Virgil's *Eclogues* which was printed by Kessler's Cranach Press at Weimar in 1926. In 1910 at Ditchling Gill was engraving for Kessler's edition of *Homer*. Kessler was trying to persuade the German readers to take to a Roman script instead of their traditional Gothic. Kessler invited Gill to work as an apprentice under Maillol for a time, but Gill objected on two points; firstly because Maillol was a modeller and Gill was a stone carver, and secondly because Gill considered himself as superior and senior to Maillol. Thus Kessler's idea of an apprenticeship came to naught, though no one has ever disputed Gill's two claims in sculpture.

Edward Gordon Craig was also involved with Kessler and Craig's masterpiece of book illustration is Kessler's hand-printed edition of *Hamlet* published by the Cranach Press in 1930. A special type was designed by Johnston and cut by Prince in order to give the book an architectural style and suitable typographic background. Craig's achievement of an 'architectural style' can be seen in the dignity of the page layout and the sheer simplicity of the pure white lines giving an overall sensitive

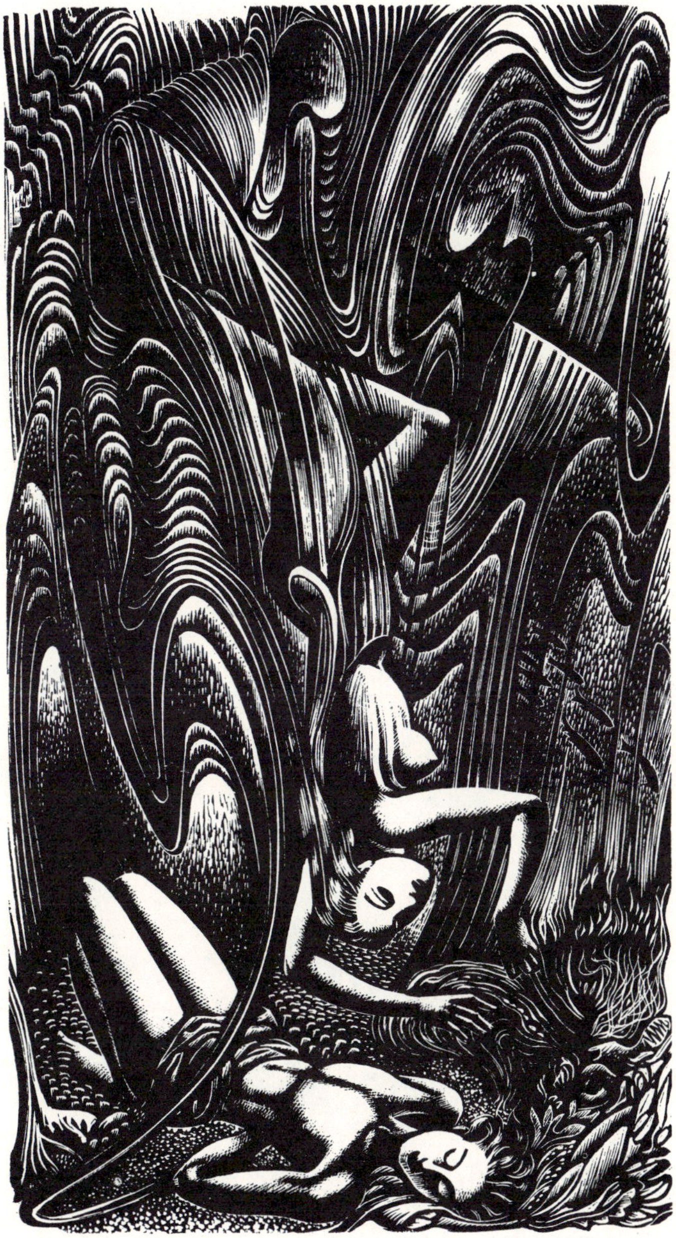

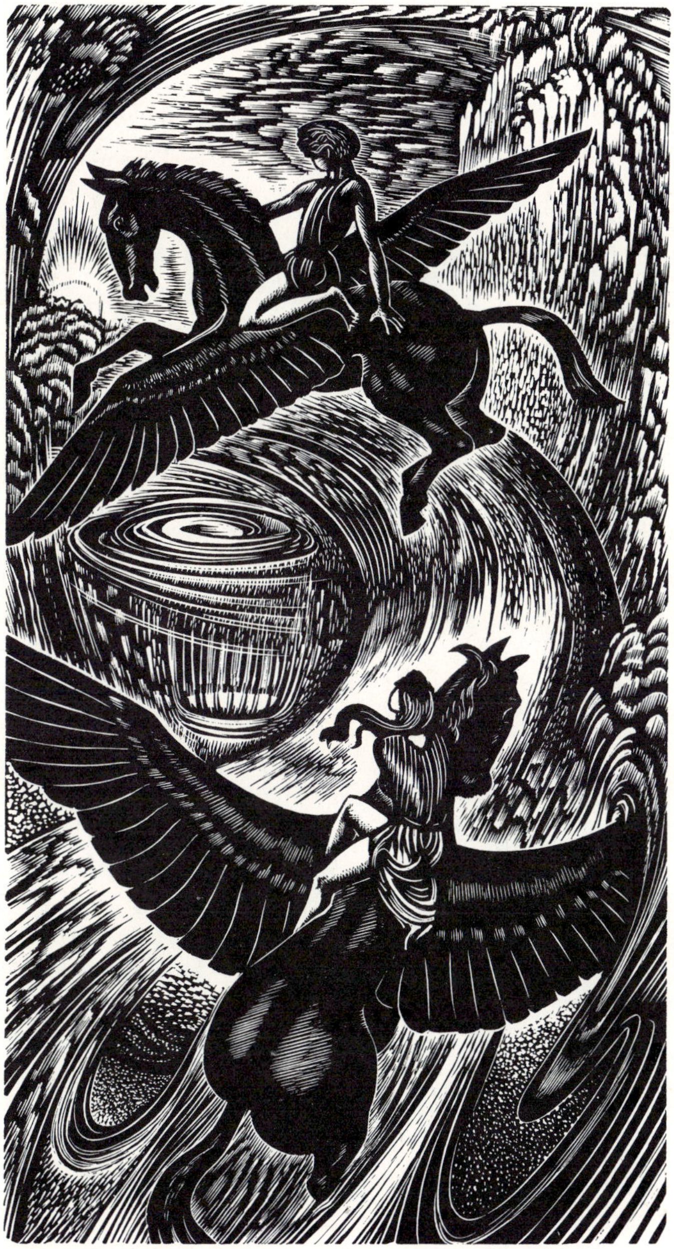

[248, 249] John Buckland-Wright: Two illustrations from *Endymion* by John Keats, 1943. 10.5 x 19.8cm

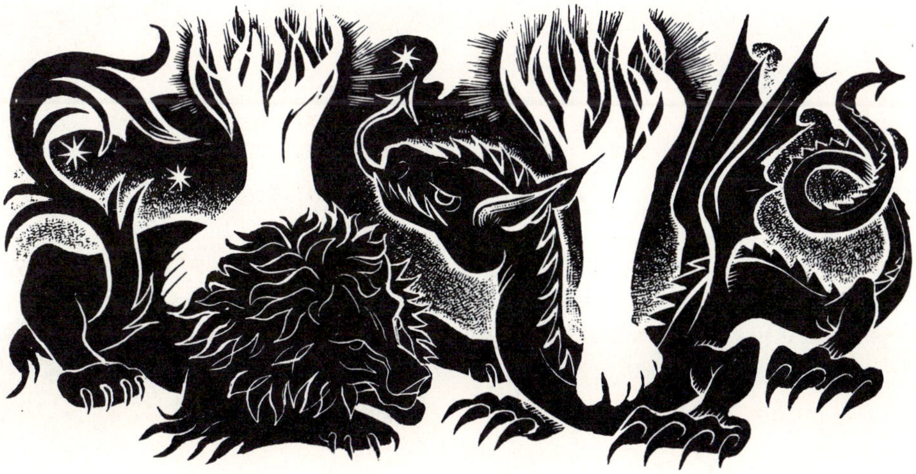

[250] Dorothea Braby: XCIst Psalm tailpiece, 1944. 12.5 x 6.0cm

He cut his blocks with single white lines and a sensitive overall tone effect is given by the printing. The book was initially suggested by Kessler but was not put into production until the 1920s. The work was printed page by page and during the production Craig and the Cranach Press were in constant consultation. A German edition appeared in 1929 and when the English edition appeared in September 1930 every copy was sold. The illustrations from this *Hamlet* still excite the admiration of the younger generation of print makers.

Gordon Craig's works were always small gems, but very big in conception and superb in execution; he was a great artist spanning many fields of expression of his own choice. He had freed himself from the earlier influence of *Art Nouveau* and from being a transitional black-line engraver he had gone over completely to the white-line expression. Like Dürer he was evolving continuously throughout his life. In the two engravings for *Hamlet* can be seen yet a further technical experiment of engraving on the long grain, and incorporating the printed image of the long-grained timber to assist the grey balance he wished to achieve with the type areas. The simplicity and grandeur is pure art. It was Craig's extreme simplicity and sensitivity in engraving which was to inspire another great engraver, John Buckland-Wright.

[251] Dorothea Braby: *The Lottery Ticket*, 1945. 9.5 x 14.0cm

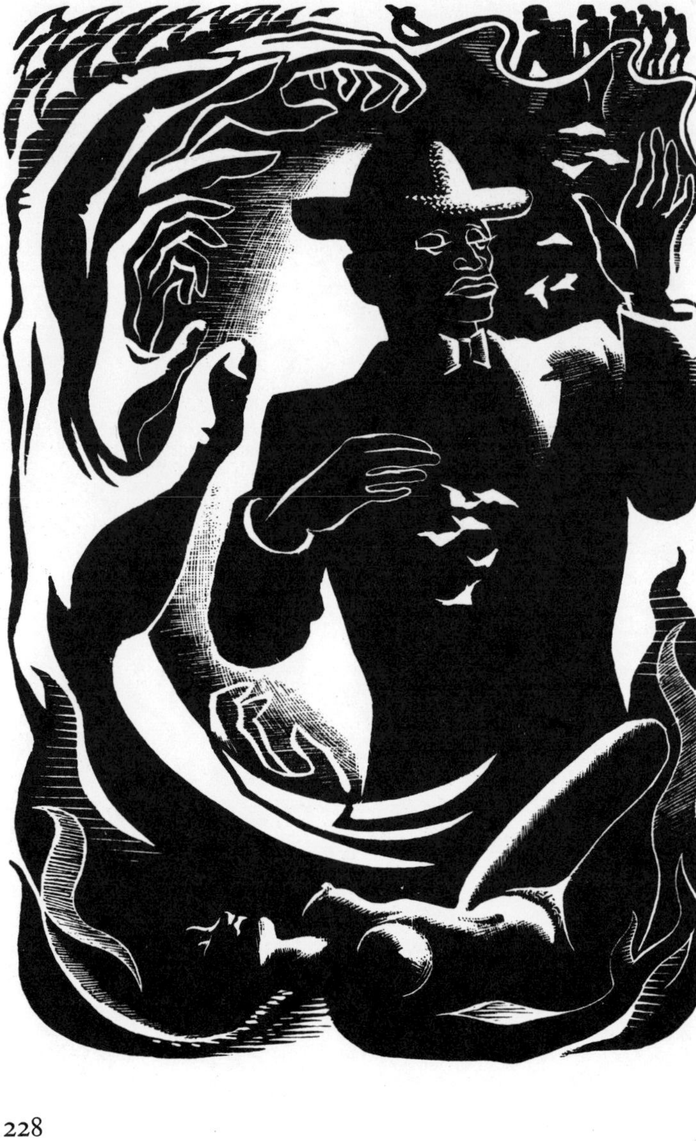

[252] Clifford Webb: Illustration from *The First Crusade*, 1945.

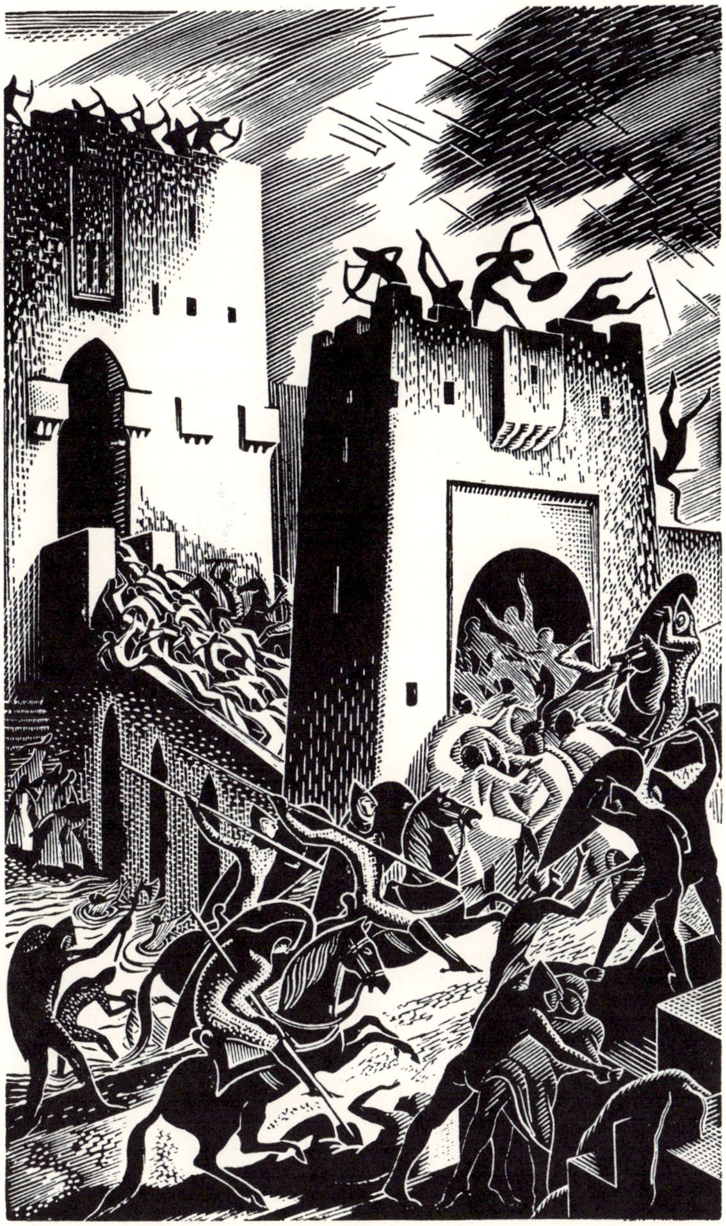

The financial crisis of the thirties did irrevocable harm to the fine book market and in 1933 Gibbings gave up the struggle. On returning from a cruise in 1932 he found the situation very tense with the public being pressed to buy only essential goods and his business suffering. He was forced to sell the Golden Cockerel Press and his house and other possessions were included in the sale.

The Golden Cockerel Press was taken over by Christopher Sandford and his partner Owen Rutter. Sandford was a book designer and printer and Rutter's special functions were to make literary contacts and to find and edit important previously unpublished material. Rutter was also an art critic for the Sunday Times and the Christian Science Monitor. Together the two men continued the fine traditions and standards that had been set by Gibbings at the Press. Sandford learned his printing at the Chiswick Press. He published books under the imprint of the Boar's Head Press, the Golden Hours Press and the Golden Cockerel Press. It was Sandford's wife Lettice, herself a wood engraver, who made him aware of

[253] Clifford Webb: *Roman Wall*, 1945. 18.5 x 15.25cm

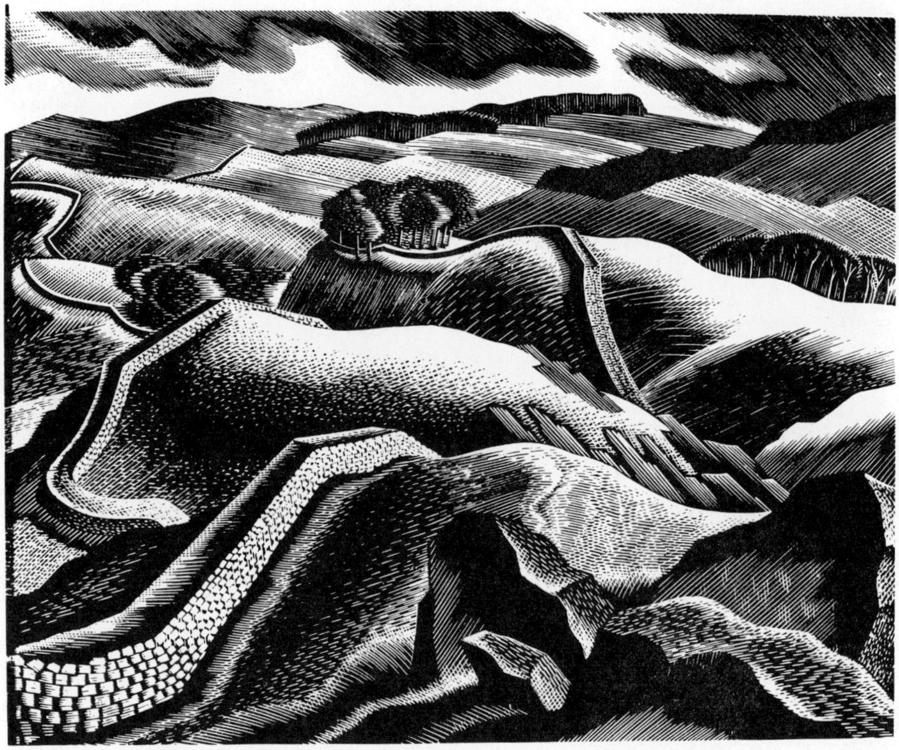

the meaning and value of the wood engravers. Lettice Sandford's wood engravings are very sensitive and practically the whole of her production was for the private press books.

With the sale of his press Gibbings had become a freelance again. He was appointed in 1938 to the art editorship of the new sixpenny venture of the Penguin Illustrated Classics series. He commissioned Helen Binyon, Gwendolen Raverat, Douglas Percy Bliss, Ethelbert White, Iain Macnab, John R. Biggs, Gertrude Hermes and Theodore Naish to illustrate these popular and imaginative paperback books.

From 1936 to 1942 Gibbings was a lecturer in wood engraving with an eye on typography at the University of Reading where Professor Allen W. Seaby had long fostered a virile tradition in wood engraving. In 1936 he was also awarded a medal from the Warsaw International Exhibition. During this period he was engaged on the work of his private press books and on teaching for at least three days a week in term time. He managed to get abroad in the vacations and in 1937 went to Bermuda and in 1938 to the Red Sea. From the Red Sea he obtained the material for his book *Blue Angels and Whales*. The drawings for this book were actually drawn on xylonite at a depth of twenty feet in the sea. Altogether he made about twenty drawings and thirteen sketches of the fish and plants around him.

In 1940 Gibbings wrote 'Having travelled more than 50,000 miles over salt water, and having visited the five continents of the world, it occurred to me that it might be fun to explore the River Thames, in whose valley I had lived for fifteen years.'[4] Following this idea to a practical solution, he designed a flat-bottomed boat. He continued his exploration despite the interruption of the war and in the summer of 1940 he completed the text and fifty engravings for his book *Sweet Thames Run Softly*. In spite of paper restrictions in England the book went through ten large editions in the following seven years.

[254] Clifford Webb: *Cats and Geraniums*, 1945. 23.0 x 28.0cm

Sixty-one books are credited to Gibbings, many of them written and illustrated, designed and printed by him – given the opportunity he might well have considered

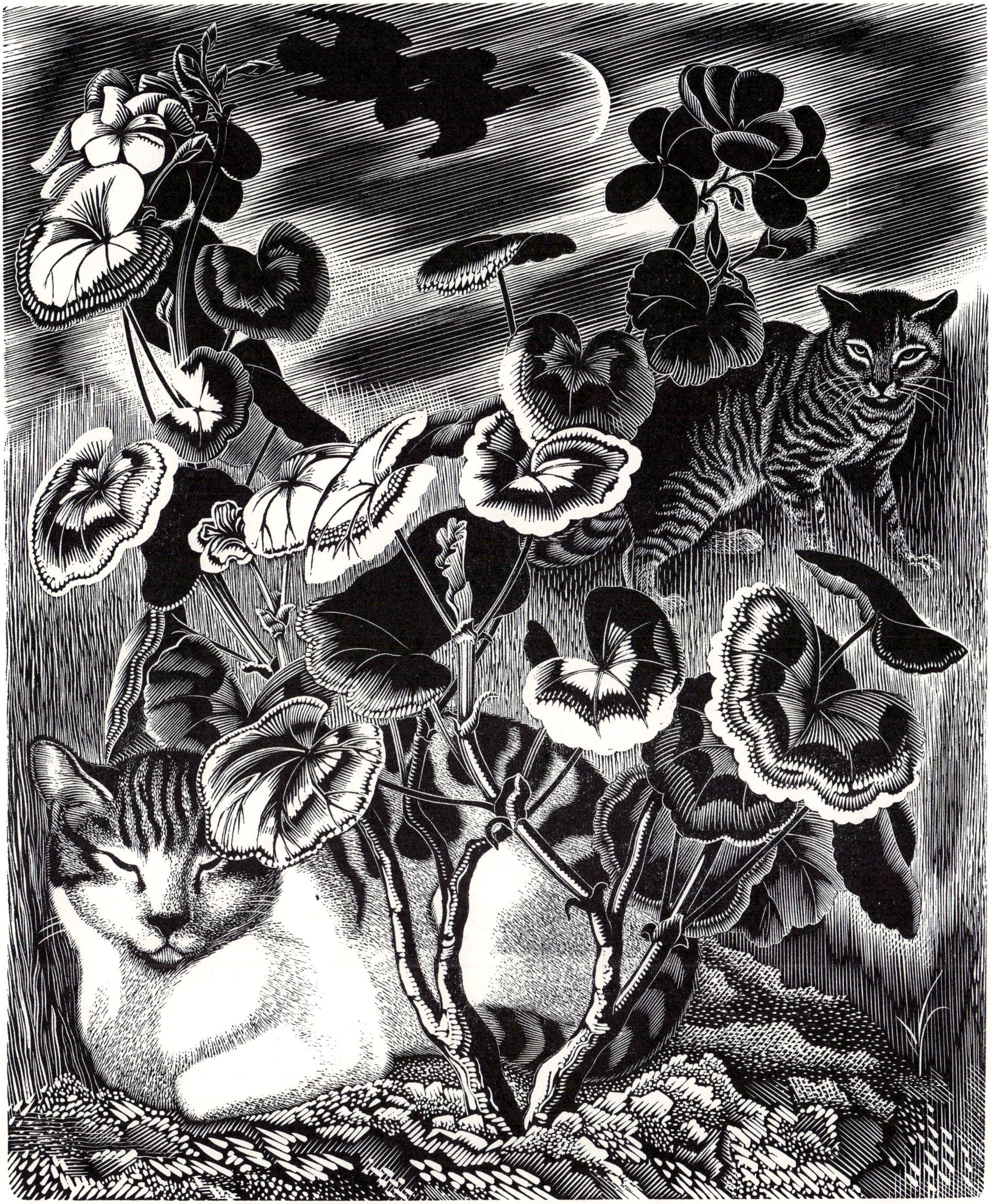

making the paper too. His is an unrepeatable and tremendous output for any one lifetime.

As an illustrator and designer he went from strength to strength and his last works were his best. Towards the end of his career the designer dominated and disciplined the illustrator. Gradually, and it is remarkable how gradually, the influence of his friendship with Eric Gill made itself felt. Gill's tight, austere aesthetics of form became Gibbings's model. During the 1930s Gibbings produced several sculptures carved in stone. In these works the Gill influence is very pronounced. His friendhsip with Gill was very longstanding; another of his friends was Ralph John Beedham who worked on many of his books.

A new artist-engraver emerged on the London scene in 1927. He was a Scotsman and a Highlander. Iain Macnab (1890 to 1967) was a landscape and figure artist in all media and a powerful and dynamic figure draughtsman. However, he was not born in Scotland. His parents had made their living in the Hong Kong and Shanghai Bank and Iain was born on the small island of Iloilo in the Philippines.

Macnab arrived in Scotland in 1894 and settled in Kilmacolm. His language problems eventually resolved themselves into a Scottish Highland accent. Being exiled in London for the greater part of his life made not the slightest difference to his accent or his Scottish cultural background. In fact it became increasingly more important to him. There was sculpture in the family – his uncle was the sculptor Macfarlan Shannon. Macnab's parents said there were already too many artists in the family and he started training as an accountant. He took this training in his stride but had no intention whatever of working as an accountant. The training did help him in his organising of art societies and exhibitions.

His first ambition was to be a cartoonist, as he loved people with all their quirks,

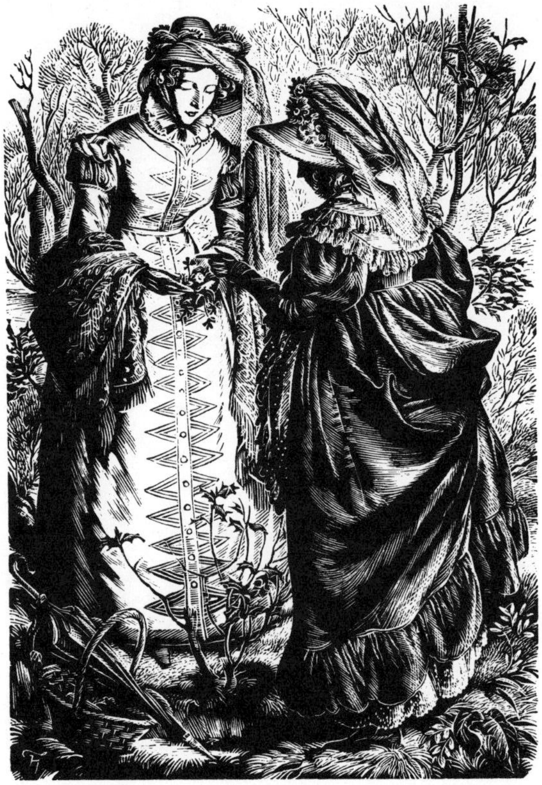

[255] Joan Hassall: *The Wood Sorrel*, 1946. 7.0 x 10.0cm

twists, idiosyncrasies and differences. His second ambition was to be a sculptor but circumstances prevented him realising this aim.

At the outbreak of the First World War Macnab volunteered for active service and joined the Highland Light Infantry. At the battle of Loos he was blown up by shell fire and given up for dead. He was rescued and invalided out of the Army in 1916. From that time onwards until he died he was to spend a lot of time in hospital undergoing numerous operations. It was his war wounds that prevented him from becoming a sculptor but they did not stop him from volunteering again for active service in the Second World War.

It was after 1916 that his thoughts turned to art. In 1917 he started his training at the Glasgow School of Art and in 1918 moved to the Heatherley School of Art in London and then on to Paris in 1919. Then he moved very quickly from being a student of art to becoming joint Principal of Heatherley School of Art. Here his accountancy training proved useful and his powers of draughtsmanship convincing. He became well known as a figure draughtsman and landscape painter well before he found his ultimate *métier* which was wood engraving. He had to experience his

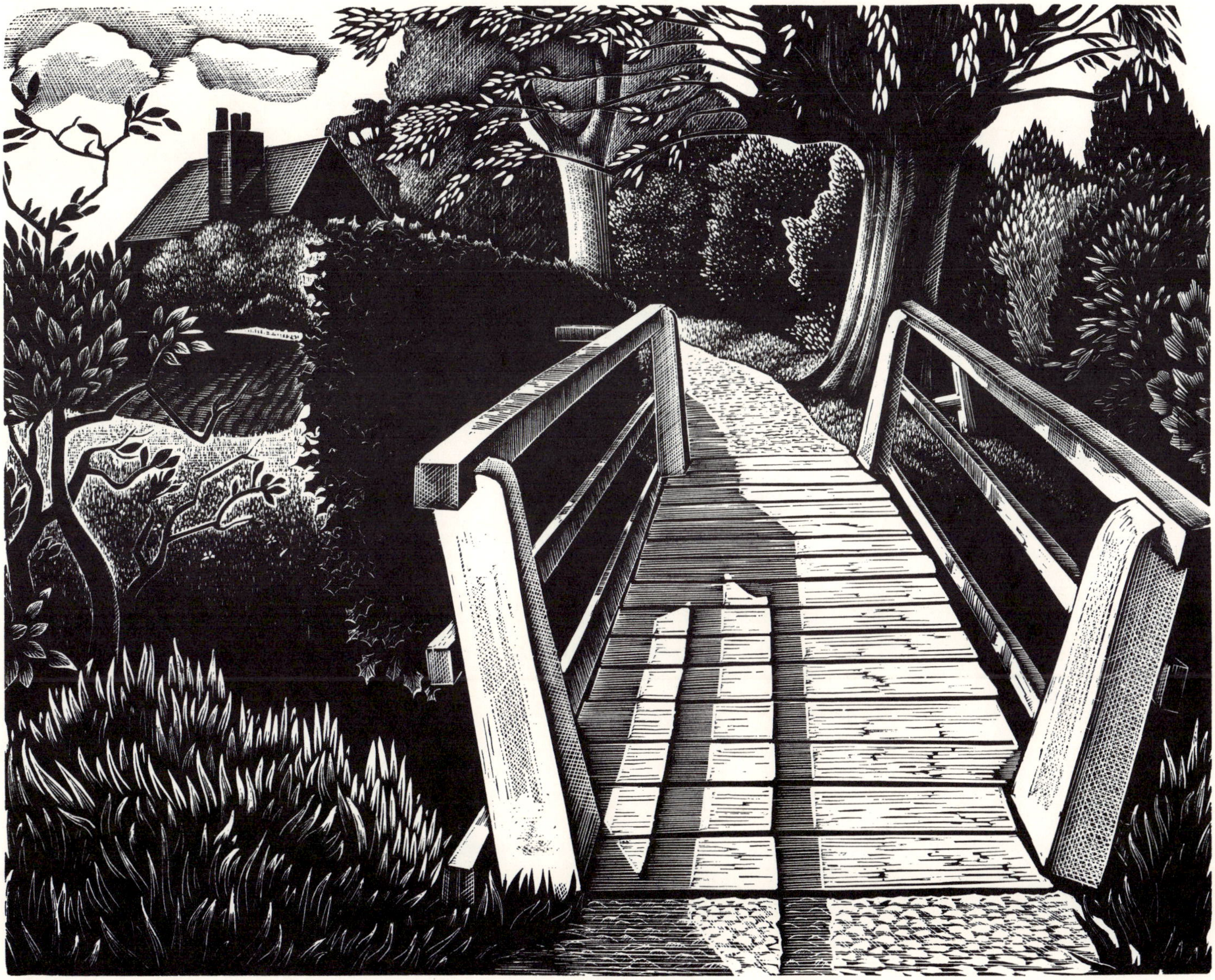

[256] Guy Malet: *The Footbridge*, 1946. 25.5 x 20.5cm

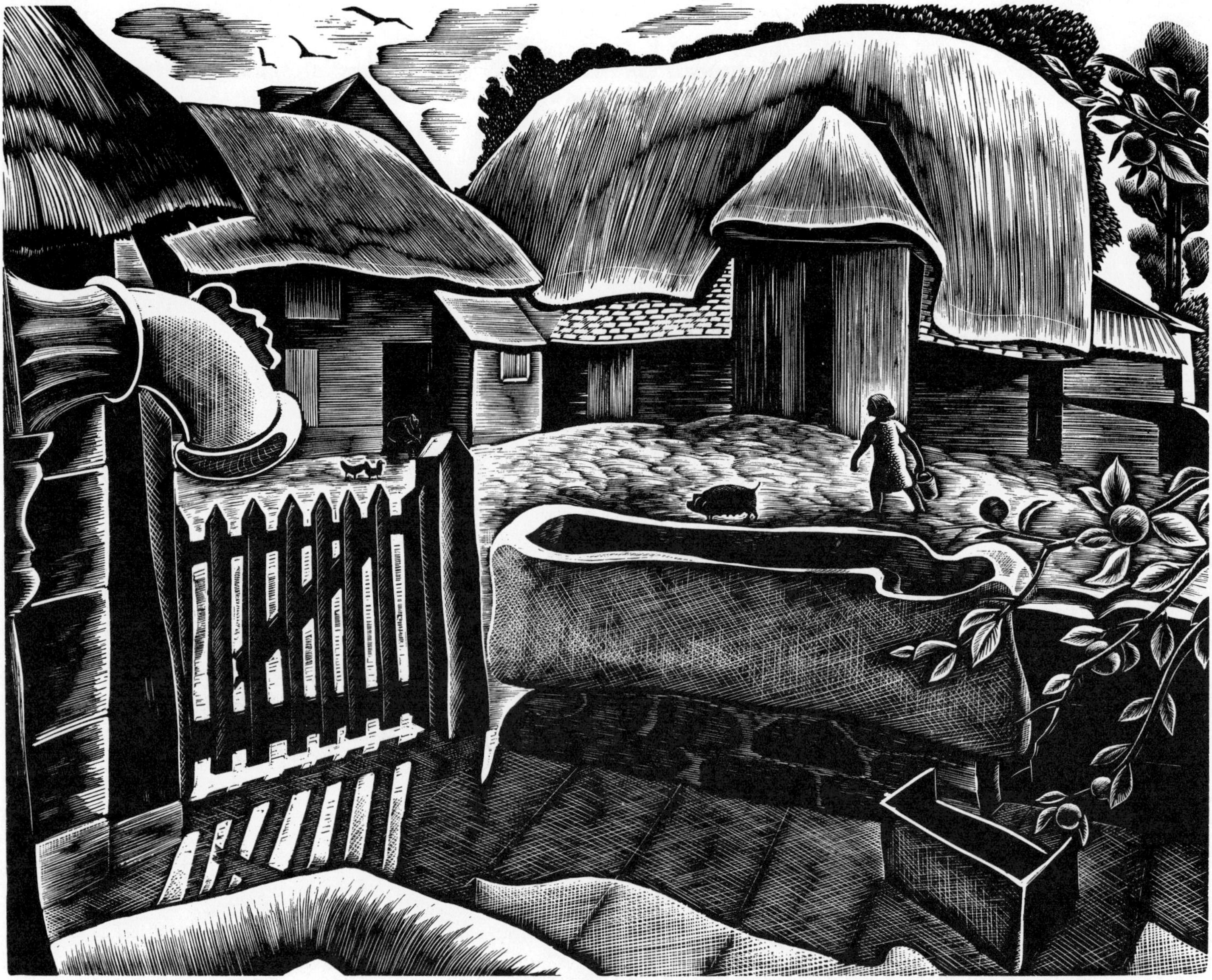

[257] Guy Malet: *A Berkshire Farm*, 1946. 25.5 x 20.5cm

way to it by working through all the other print media, which included etching, dry point, lithography and lino cutting in black and white and in colour.

The history of Scottish firearms and of the workshops making swords and dirks dates back to the sixteenth century when weapons were produced at Doune. Iain had his own collection which included some beautifully engraved Macnab pistols and also a huge double-handed Scottish sword – a heavy and fearsome weapon. The craftsmanship displayed in the making of armour and weapons excited Iain and he had great admiration for the precision that directed the art of the craftsman to its perfection. He was deeply involved in the appreciation of engraving and was concerned with the aspect of man, struggling to express a form of art on a hard material and being chastened by the problems of achieving a suitable form, but ultimately attaining success.

He would delight in discussing the techniques of engraving but even so it took him some little time to discover his own ability. Whilst his war wounds prevented him from developing as a sculptor, the sculptural link with the inherent linear quality of engraving provided a lead into a technique in which he was to make his own masterly contribution to art. In wood engraving, Iain Macnab was able to bring his figure draughtsmanship to bear and evolved a continuity of language which enabled him to relate properly the human figure to a landscape environment.

Macnab was the pure engraver as were Eric Gill, David Jones and John Buckland-Wright; the fundamental discipline of Palaeolithic art and engraving engaged his lifelong interest. Often in conversation he would refer to the caves as 'those underground art galleries where not a single line is wasted'. He regarded the style of engraving which evolved from the nineteenth-century book illustration as a contamination of the arts of design because the designing of books was dealt with as an applied art. In this respect Macnab's approach was in direct contrast to that of Ravilious who virtually adopted all the book design clichés without question and viewed them all as usable techniques – a practice which emphasises the fundamental differences between artists and designers.

The majority of Macnab's engravings are autonomous prints standing in their own right as works of art and as such are a significant contribution to wood engraving. However, he worked on book design when the occasion arose and produced three private press books *Nicht at Eeenie, The Bairns Parnassus* 1932, *Tom O'-Shanter* 1934, both published by the Samson Press, and *The Sculptured Garland* 1948, published by the Dropmore Press.

The pictorial language of Macnab is classical. He could not accept the world as a realist study but had to reconstruct images in his search for perfection of order. He hated the art and philosophy of realism and had the classical concept that man was created in God's image. All Macnab's figures are expressed as being in the full

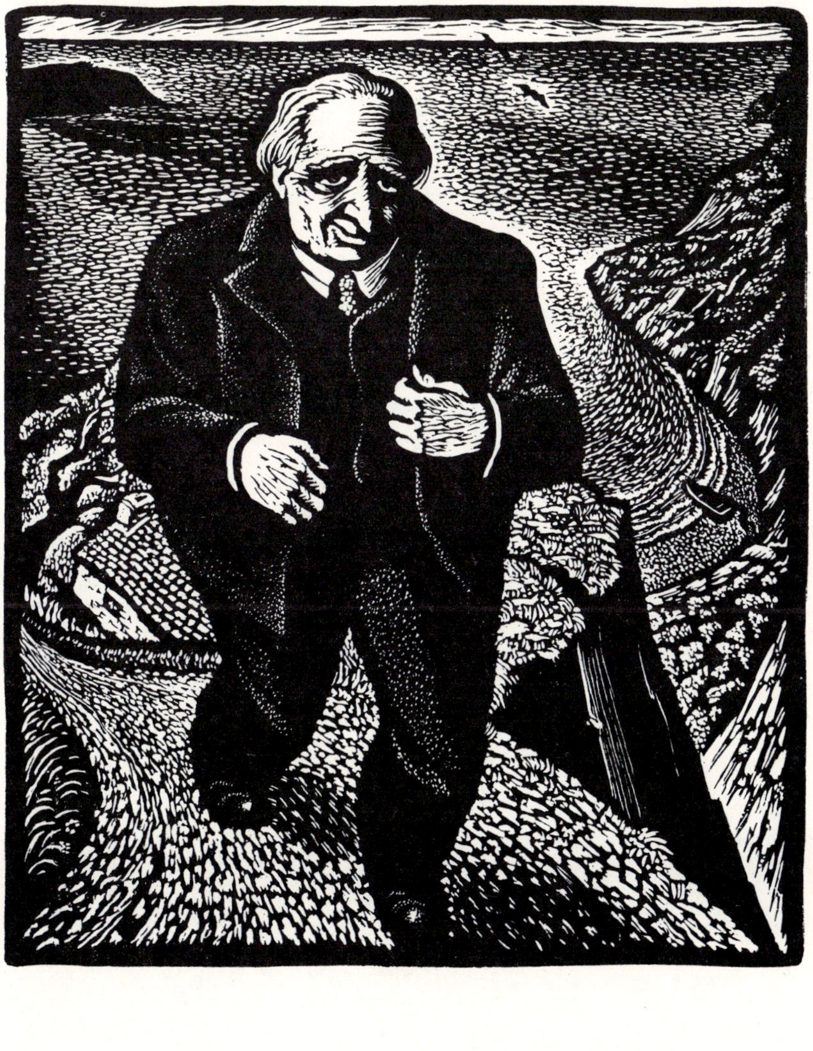

[258] John Petts: *The Soothsayer* from *The Green Island*, 1946. 10.7 x 12.75cm

quickness of life and depicted in an environment of generous proportions which is never cluttered or despoiled. Such an environment is shown as rich in health and purpose, indicating movement and growth; it is the concept of the opposing forms of man and architecture being related to each other with considerable sensitivity.

Macnab's art is an expression of what man could achieve by good sense and by directing his energy to peace rather than to war – which Macnab saw as a dark interlude in his own time and space. He realised that the span of life was short and he wanted to enjoy the fullness of living.

For him every subject must live and be related to the outer boundaries of the engraving. In conversation he said: 'I am primarily interested in form. Everything in a picture must have pictorial significance and there must be a relationship between everything. Otherwise a picture lacks cohesion; it is then a mass of unrelated facts and of no more interest than a catalogue.' In Macnab's composition, the animation unit which articulates throughout the action is the architectural unit of the load-bearing T-joint (an essential feature of Greek architecture). This unit is not only seen in architecture but also in the structure of man, beasts and birds.

His *Fishermen, Portofino* [221] is a good example of the dynamic expressive power of the T-joint principle. It is a rare masterpiece of wood engraving of a crowd of figures in a landscape, which is the Poussin study. Macnab has a number of 'figures in a landscape' to his credit though the subject is one which is avoided by very many engravers. His major motif is a massive inverted 'T' forming the sea wall and every figure except the upper two is used to define the form of that wall. He stresses the fact that the wall stands at ninety degrees and the edges are as sharp as he could make them. The wall and the figures become a solid mass of masterly articulated forms which give the wall its definition.

Such economy of form is rare and remarkable. The inverted 'T' sets the powerful pictorial drama and the artist has driven with astounding clarity and force through the figure group to the boats with the stem of the 'T' joint continued into the picture space using a single relaxed figure to complete the span. The boats, which are engraved with economy and simplicity, then become a parallel to the top bar stroke of the 'T' and the whole of the pictorial force, subject and rhythm are enclosed, equated and expressed. Macnab's statement is an engraving of both power and sensitivity.

The classical structure is very evident in Iain Macnab's famous print *Drying sails, Lake Garda* [233]. A total orchestration is based upon a complex interplay of vertical and horizontal lines, each intersection giving a T-joint counter rhythm. Within this structure the figures as a group draw an upward surging triangle, and the vertical stance of each individual gives yet another series of T-joint counter rhythms. The triangular figure grouping scheme is then inverted high in the composition through the arrangement of the sail lines. These lines set up yet another series of T-joint and triangular counter movements across the skyline.

The total massive movement contained within the four fixed outer lines of the engraving has its vortex focused on the fishermen holding a rope at the top of the triangle figure group. In this engraving every single cut starts in exactly the right point and stops at exactly the right point and between these points each line has delineated the form with accuracy and economy and yet the freedom of the flying bird is implicit in the expression.

The engraver moves with perfect ease between the volumetric and the two-dimensional linear expression, having solved all these problems before the first burin incision is made. Each volume and space plane is illuminated by a thin white-light beam, selectively illuminating the planes, volumes and their sensitive

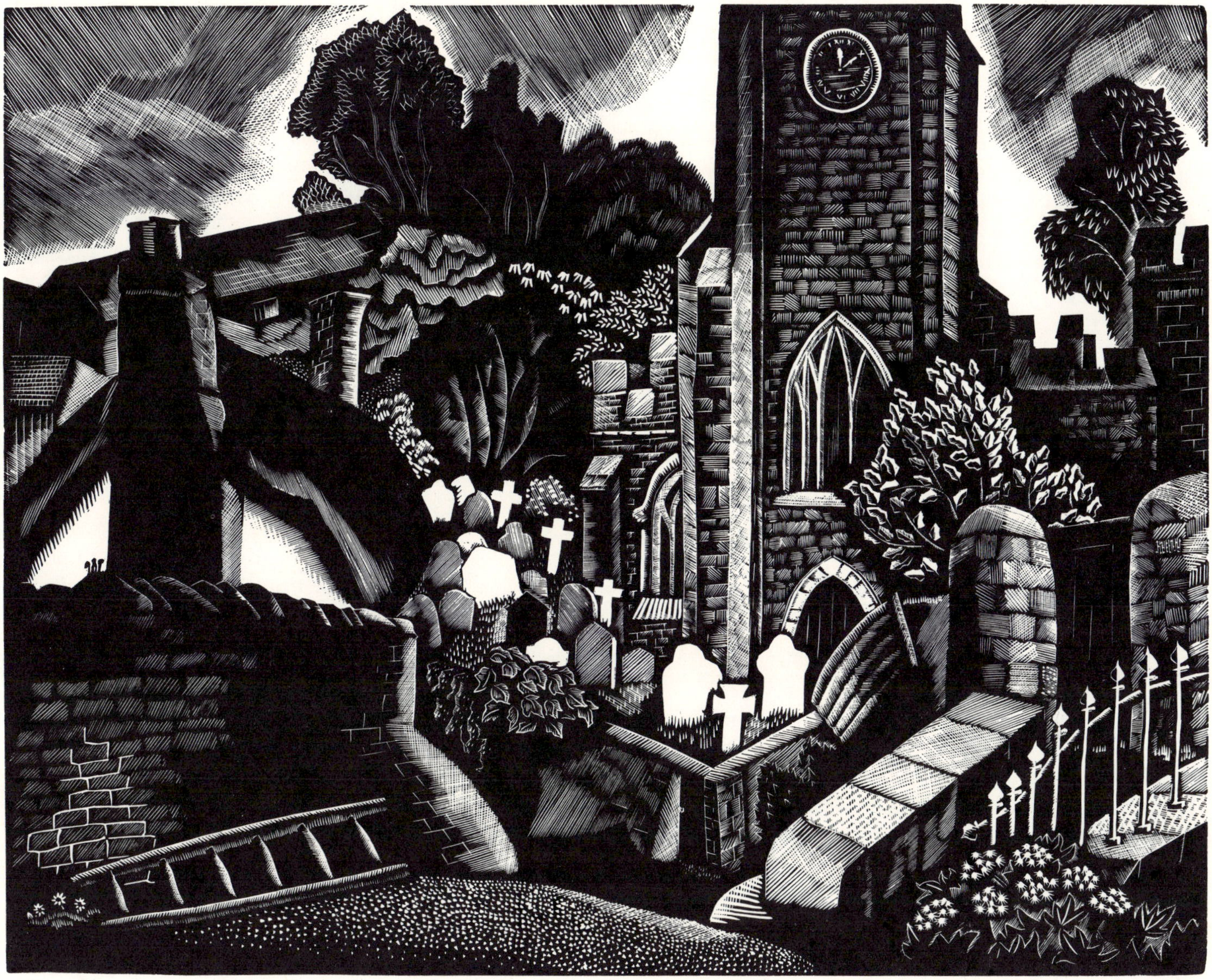

[259] Rachel Reckitt: *Dittisham, Devon*, 1946. 25.25 x 20.25cm

textures. Yet the set of six vertical lines of two sets of three sail ropes are six of the most famous lines known in the history of the British school. As these lines reach the sky plane they change from white to black and the engraver has not wavered in the slightest degree. The white lines are cut below the surface, the black lines are carved, leaving the black part standing on the block. These lines are cut freehand, changing from black to white with amazing precision. Such skill is staggering and phenomenal. Blair Hughes-Stanton also has an outstanding single line of this nature running diagonally through his engraving [202].

Classical art runs very closely to the manner in which nature works, as distinct from what might be seen by the eye, and as such has changed in its form since the Renaissance period when classical art was built on geometrical and arithmetical concepts. Macnab was very interested in the relationship between the concepts of art and science. The order of structure in his *Drying Sails* is not very far removed from the system of life itself, a main difference being in scale and complexity. It is a clear example that today classical art can be said to hold a mirror to nature.

The *Two Fat Ladies, Portofino* [361] is one of the most significant figure compositions in British twentieth-century engraving and its sheer economy of line is without a peer. Macnab's T-joint principle is operating everywhere and fusing all the structural elements which comprise the landscape. Yet the structural element is sublimated to a degree that the aesthetic emotion of relaxation of the lines delineating the two women give by contrast the assurance of security. The softness of the feminine volumes is sharply contrasted by the unrelenting verticals of the architecture. These women are so comfortable and relaxed that they appear to be there for ever. Macnab was a master figure draughtsman and not only knew what he wanted but how to get it.

Macnab was certain that his *Ronda Bridge, Spain* [307] was to be his last engraving. In *Ronda Bridge* the engraving of the two sides of the ravine is extremely fine, ranging from black and white and optical greys, sensitive and creatively meaningful in differentiating the strata and meagre plant life in engraving terms, as one would expect from the eyes of an engraver of thirty or so years' experience. The bridge has to be approached from below and appears to be virtually in the sky out of reach of the traveller who must climb some 183 metres to reach the arch, which joins the Tajo to the almost bottomless pit. The river is as black as the Styx and just drops in a series of cascades and eventually subsides into a gentle stream at the bottom of the ravine, then away out into the light verdurous valley of rich vegetation. Macnab's viewpoint of the bridge is far higher than most other versions of this subject and the river cannot be seen in the engraving; it is well below the second arch. Most artists give up with a viewpoint approximately sixty metres below that of Macnab.

Iain Macnab's life had many outstanding achievements. In 1923 he was elected an associate of the Royal Society of Painter-Etchers and Engravers, and his first wood engraving was exhibited in 1927. It was through the constricting discipline of this medium rather than through the other media with which he had experimented that he found his real freedom. When the English Society of Wood Engravers, of which he was a member, ceased to function, he was invited to membership of the Society of Wood Engravers which he joined in 1932, the year in which he was appointed to the fellowship of the Royal Society of Painter Etchers and Engravers. In subsequent years he was very active in the affairs of this organisation as he was in the Society of Wood Engravers whose informal meetings were frequently held in his studio in Warwick Square. He also took an active part in the early development of the Federation of British Artists at 17 Carlton House Terrace in London, and from 1949 until his death he was President of the Royal Institute of Oil Painters.

REFERENCES

1 Shaw, G. B. *The Adventures of the Black Girl in her Search for God,* Constable, London, 1932
2 Garrett, A. *The Wood Engravings and Drawings of Iain Macnab,* Midas Books, Tunbridge Wells, 1973
3 Speaight, R. *The Life of Eric Gill,* Methuen, London, 1966
4 Gibbings, R. *Blue Angels and Whales,* Penguin Books, London, 1938

8 THE WAR YEARS

The Second World War brought an irreplaceable loss of talent and enforced the closing of many imaginative enterprises and schools, with the private schools becoming early casualties. These private establishments played a very important role in the development of engraving. All of them had a teaching policy based on the professional system of master artist giving individual instruction, a concept vitally important to engraving and one that, regrettably, has not been revived to any major degree in contemporary education.

The Society of Wood Engravers was not inactive in the first years of the war and in 1940 sent a third exhibition, of 180 prints, to the Carnegie Institute in America. Unfortunately, the viciousness of hostilities made further effort impossible and this exhibition was the last one to be held in wartime. With the dispersal of its members because of the war, the Society ceased to hold its annual exhibition.

Leaving the Golden Cockerel Press, Christopher Sandford served in the Army until 1948 when he was invalided out and kept in bed for some weeks. By 1948 the Golden Cockerel had produced 181 books designed by Sandford.

Leon Underwood, an expert on camouflage, served in two wars, thus cutting out a large chunk of his productive life as a wood engraver. During the First World War he served in camouflage from 1916 to 1918 and he met a number of other artists in the Service. At the start of the Second World War Underwood joined the Civil Defence camouflage unit at Leamington Spa, where he began a long series of landscape watercolours.

Sandford's partner at the Golden Cockerel Press, Owen Rutter, joined the Navy. He died in 1944 thus bringing to an end an eleven year collaboration with Sandford. Gertrude Hermes went to Canada and did war work. Douglas Percy Bliss lost his complete stock of prints and blocks when his house in London was bombed and was left with only a record of his engravings which happened to be pasted into a scrap book. William T. Rawlinson served in the Royal Air Force and worked as a war artist mainly for the Signals Section. Much of the work he did during this period provided him with material for engraving many years later.

The most severe loss to wood engraving was Eric Ravilious who was killed in the autumn of 1942 while on active service. He was an official war artist, with the rank of captain in the Royal Marines. He had been posted to Iceland to record the life of the members of the Royal Air Force based there and within a few days of his arrival found himself a passenger in a plane of Coastal Command operating over the approaches to the island. The plane never returned and Ravilious was presumed dead officially in the summer of 1943.

Eric Ravilious had a short but full life of thirty-nine years. It is evident from the quality and consistency of his engraving that his best work was still to come. He was equally talented in watercolour and murals.

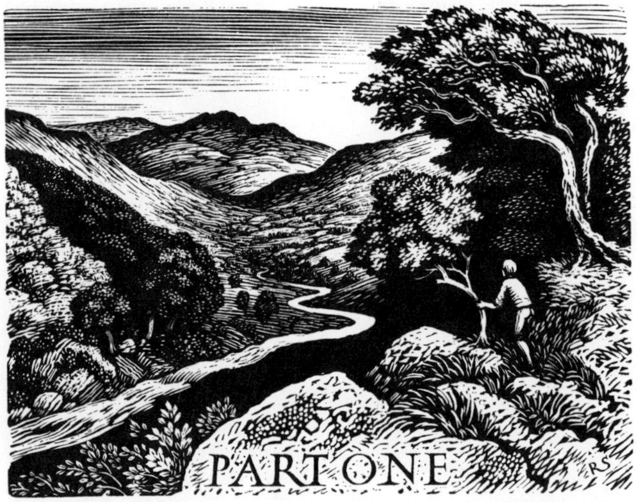

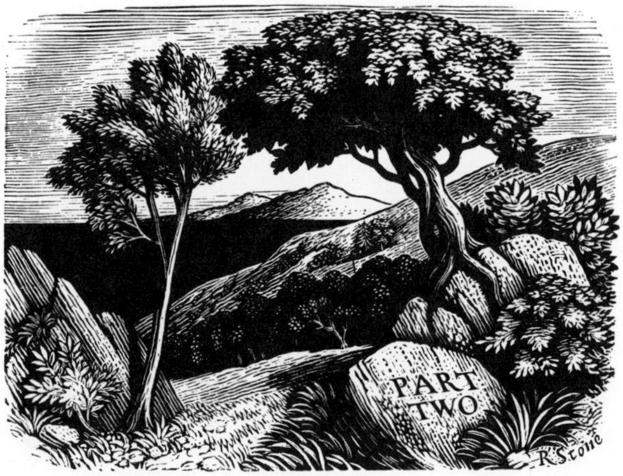

[260, 261] Reynolds Stone: Illustrations from *Apostate*, 1947.

Enid Marx was the first woman engraver to be awarded the designation of Royal Designer for Industry and she has played a significant part in engraving and design. She has also played a leading role in teaching of fabric design. Her engraving is crisp, unexpected in its movement and agile in its creative pattern, and she is like this as a person. Marx cannot tolerate bad craftsmanship in anything an artist and/or designer may produce. Yet she will demand all the freedom in the world if by any chance it will release to some imaginative effort, declaring that this must come first, then if craft kills it, it was not strong enough in the first place.

For Enid Marx, art is not something just to be produced and admired, but a part of everyday life. It was this philosophy that inspired her to adapt engraving to fabric design, in which field she is renowned. Her most outstanding achievement in fabric design was for the wartime Utility Scheme for which she designed the furnishing fabrics used from 1944 onwards. The Marx fabric designs were limited in pattern repeat for minimum wastage of raw material. Despite their simplicity, the fabric designs for the Scheme are as clearly identifiable as the work of Enid Marx as are her engravings.

Much of the success of Enid Marx in fabric design was due to the fact that she was trained as an artist and applied her art through design. This emphasises the need for designers to have training in art because despite the theories of some educationalists, design is art applied to a functional purpose.

Clifford Webb's distinguished contribution to wood engraving is enshrined in an astonishing series of books issued by the Golden Cockerel Press between 1937 and 1954. Webb played an important role in the development of the lino cut as a colour medium. Among the eight books from the Golden Cockerel Press, three contained major works by him: *The First Crusade* 1945, *The Amazons* 1948 and *Caesar's Commentaries* 1948. Thomas Balston wrote of them as 'works of great distinction'. Never one to do things in a small way, Webb had one of the largest flatbed presses ever made; the platen was approximately 125cm in its length measurement.

As a person Clifford Webb was strong, authoritative, yet sensitive. As a young man he was described by Sandford as 'tall, ruddy, grizzled and hail-fellow-well-met'. Webb had the air of the old campaigner and in order to record the natural life around him, he used to tour the country in a very commodious vintage car. He liked to work in solitude and would pitch a tent, lay down some sacks then sit at the entrance of the tent with his easel before him. He had the wisdom to keep his art running along a straight and well-defined course, having a strong dislike of abstraction. The abstract qualities of his art were, however, derived from the reduction of the form, and the formal simplifications of classical composition arising from the demands and strictures imposed by the wood and/or lino and the act of engraving. This quality makes Webb's work easily identifiable. His sheer technical brilliance illuminated everything he engraved within his course boundaries. There are no bad Webb engravings and his work is a superb example of art sublimating craft, rather than craft simulating art.

Clifford Webb was a master at expressing aesthetic emotion. Using only the expedient of a multiplicity of parallel lines he could throw the viewer crashing over a mountain side, or cast an imposing figure calmly behind a linear screen, yet using the same means establish a sense of peace and repose, similar to the great calm of Raphael.

He was a soldier before he became an artist. He started as a guardsman and carried himself like a guardsman on all occasions. From 1914 to 1919 he served in the Grenadier Guards and was later commissioned in the Wiltshire Regiment. He fought in the major battles of Mons, Gallipoli and Mesopotamia and was wounded four times. Later he served with his regiment in India where he held the rank of

[262] John O'Connor: *Little Garden in the Evening*, 1947. 17.5 x 12.75cm

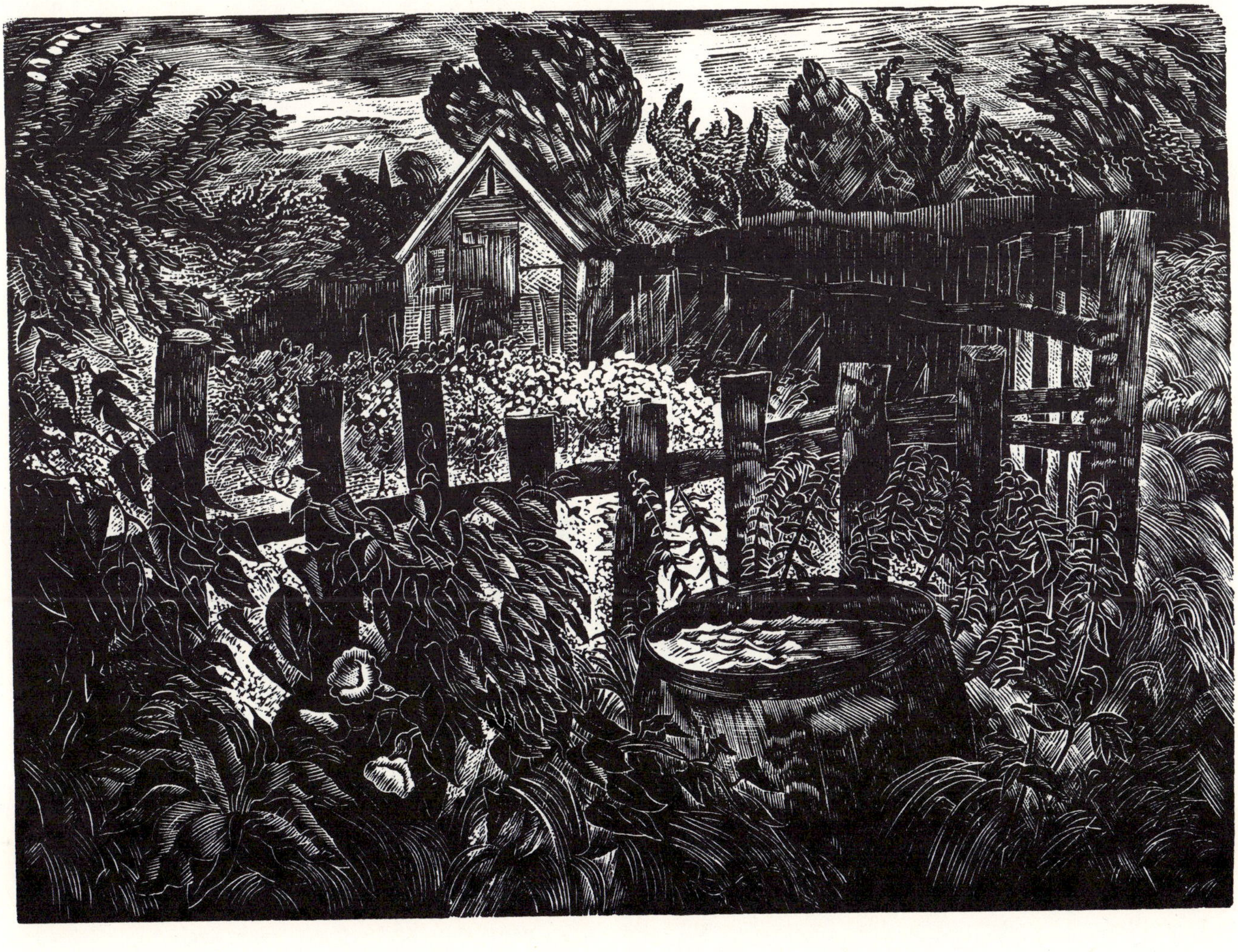

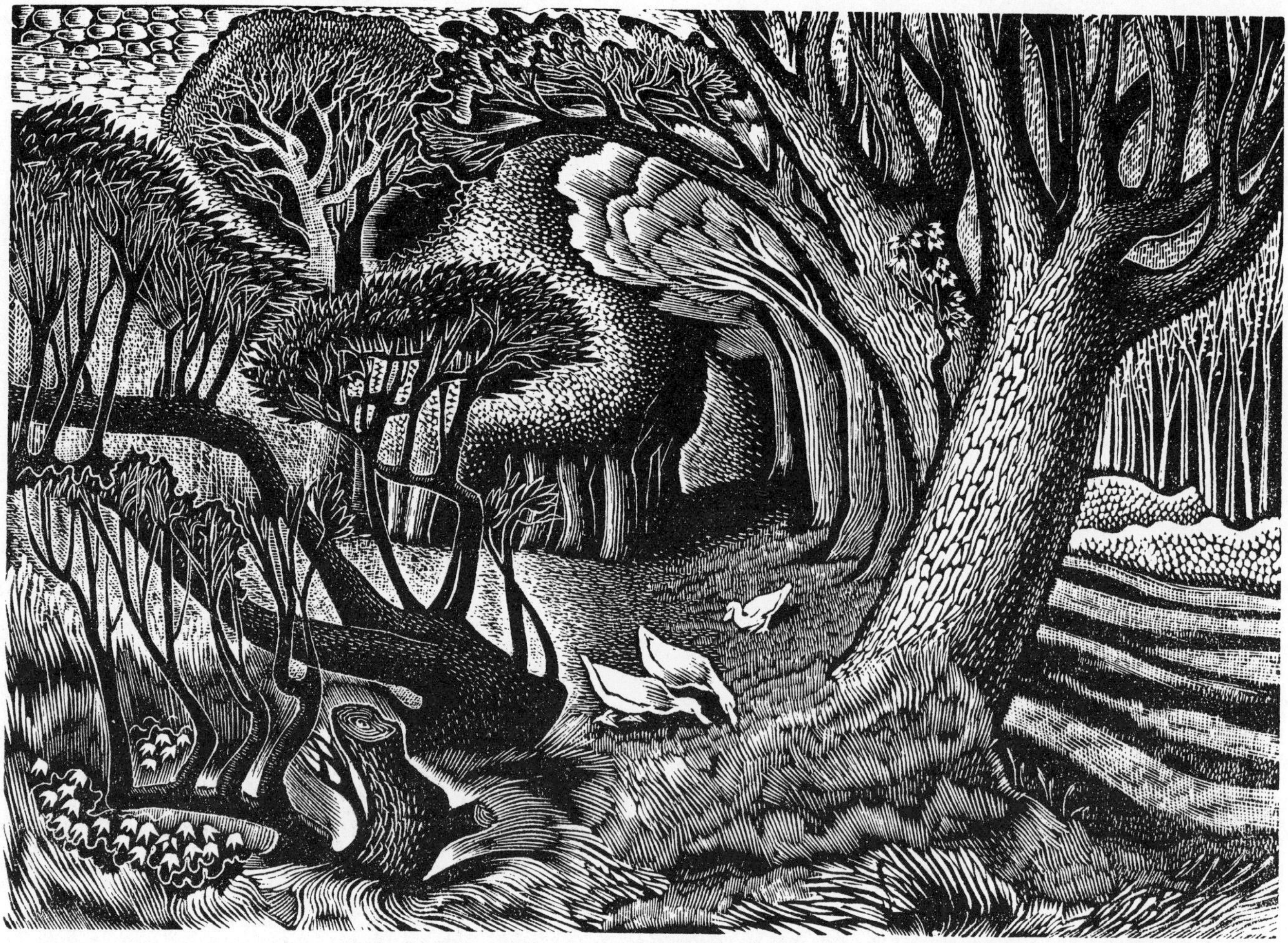

[263] James Bostock: *Ducks in the Wood*, 1947. 17.5 x 12.5cm

captain. In the Second World War he held the unusual appointment (for an artist) of Controller of Petrol for the North of England. In this capacity he was stationed in Newcastle from 1939 to 1945.

John Nash who, like his brother, served in the First World War, was to volunteer for service again in the Second World War. At the outbreak of war he joined the Observer Corps. In 1940 he became an official war artist to the Admiralty but in November of that year opted for a more active role and joined the Royal Marines. He started as a captain and eventually became a major on the staff of the commander-in-chief at Rosyth and later in Portsmouth.

Having served in the First World War, Iain Macnab volunteered for the conflict of 1939. This deprived the world of wood engraving of one of its most successful teachers who was highly regarded by his pupils. He had founded the Grosvenor School of Modern Art at Warwick Square in London in 1925 and this establishment, like other private schools, played an important part in the history of British wood engraving. Among its pupils were Tom Chadwick, Gwenda Morgan, Guy Malet, Rachel Reckitt, the sisters Alison and Winifred McKenzie, Peter Barker Mill, Julia Mavrogordato, Pauline Logan and William Kermode.

The Grosvenor School became a casualty of war in 1940 when it was forced to close, the building having become an air raid warden post. Without his teaching activities, Macnab became restless and joined the Royal Air Force in 1941. As

[264] Clifford Webb: *The Amazons* from *Garden of the Hesperides*, 1948. 12.75 x 18.5cm

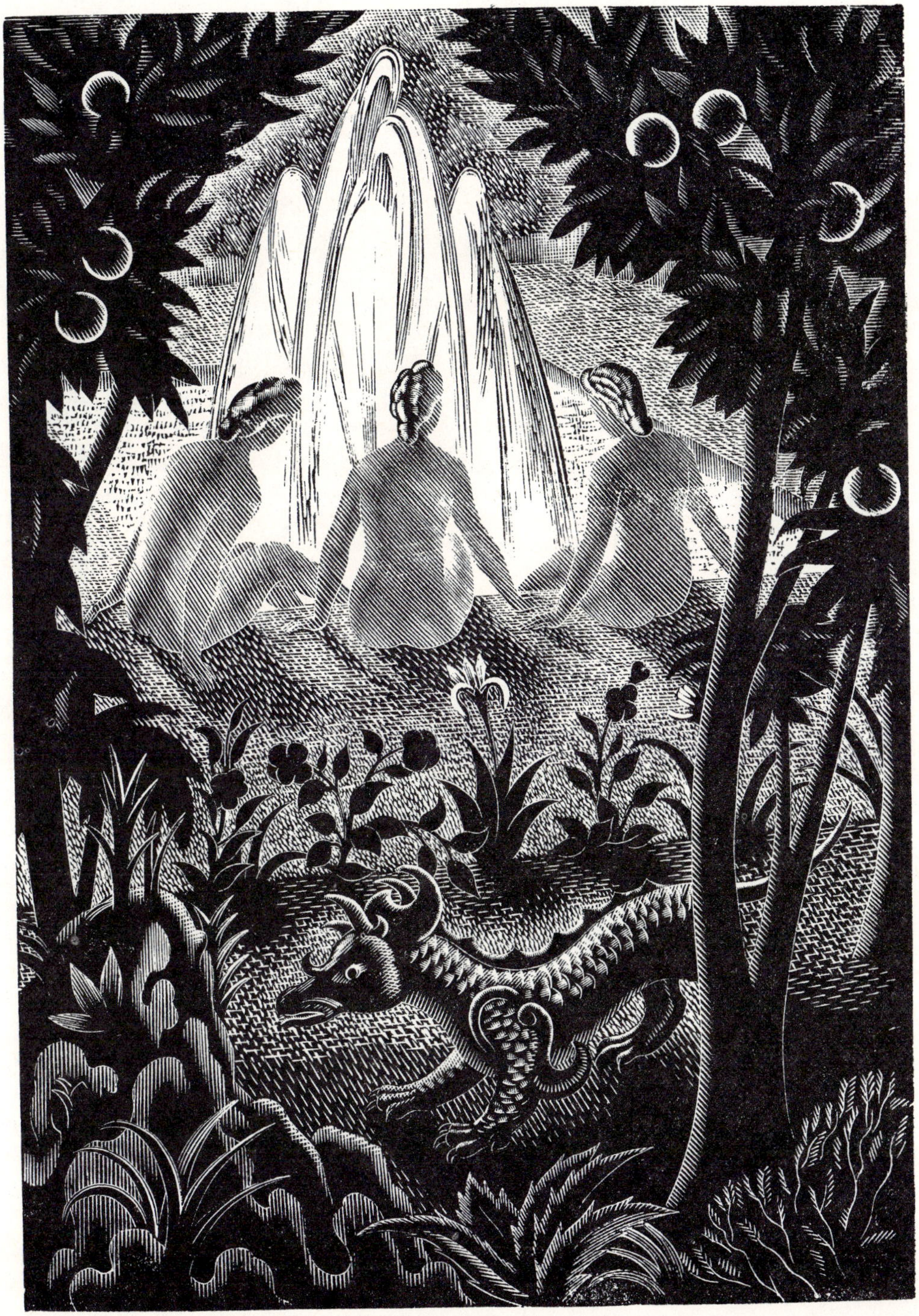

in the First World War, he was wounded and in 1942 was invalided out of the service, spending a whole year in Middlesex Hospital. However, despite this experience he rejoined the Air Force in 1943 and served as an adjutant in various establishments until he was again invalided out in 1945. He resumed his work in wood engraving in which he was to make such an outstanding contribution.

Tom Chadwick (1915 to 1942) was trained by Iain Macnab at the Grosvenor School and became a brilliant wood engraver, though his life was cut short by the Second World War. Iain Macnab always spoke of him as an outstanding artist engraver and his most brilliant student. Guy Malet and Ernest Fedarb have also said that they rated him very high. An examination of Chadwick's work confirms

[265] John Farleigh: *Dahlia*, 1948.
31.7 x 22.8cm

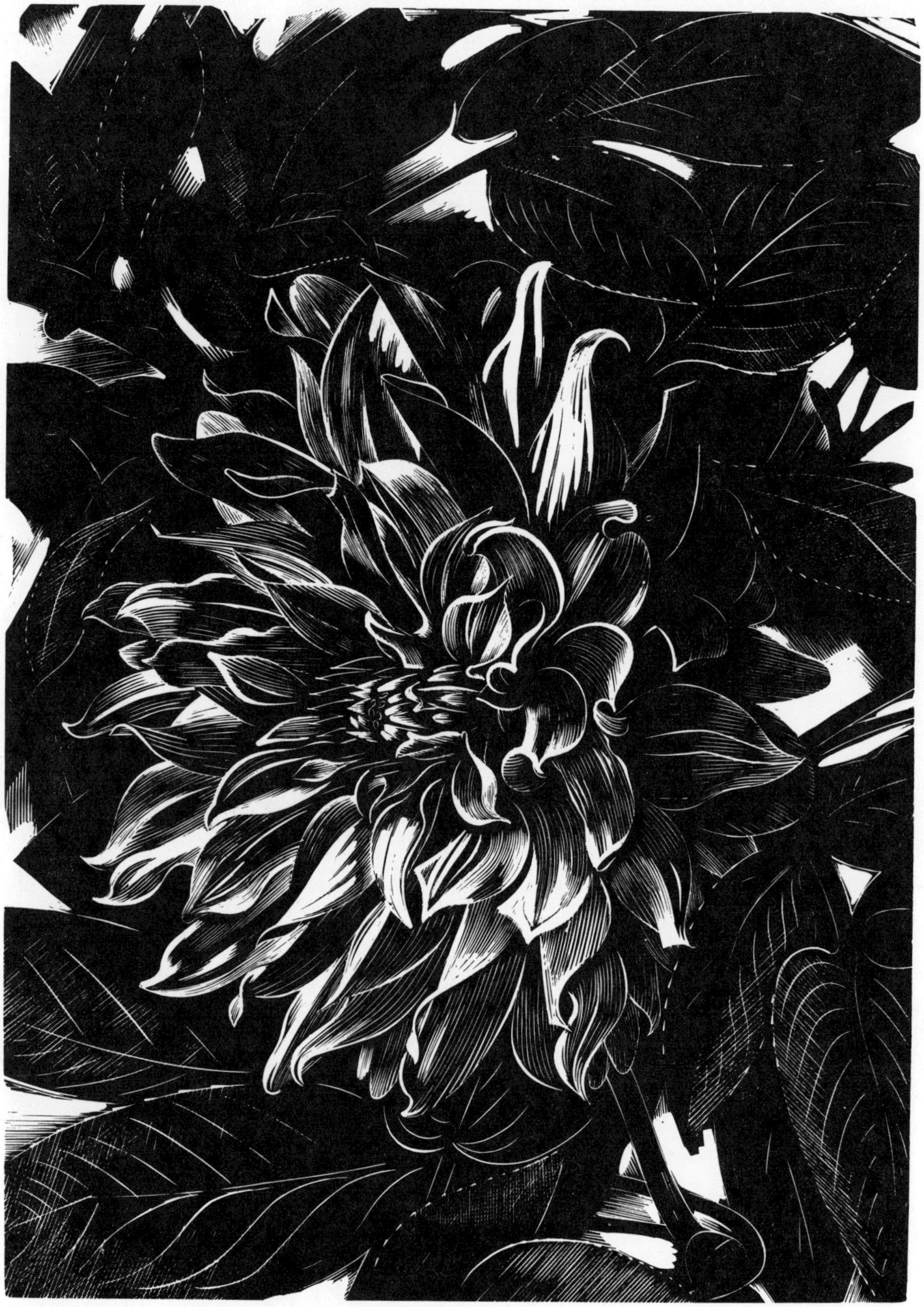

the high opinions that have been expressed. His potential for the future, so tragically cut off, was a sad loss to British wood engraving [215].

Chadwick's first teaching post was at the Westminster School of Art; he was very young for such a position. Under the dynamic principal Kirkland Jamieson, the Westminster School was one of the first of the London County Council schools to teach abstract art during the 1930s. Kirkland Jamieson gathered around him a talented and progressive staff comprising such artists of vision as Bernard Meninsky, Mark Gertler, Blair Hughes-Stanton, Ernest Fedarb, Clifford Webb and Chadwick. Jamieson at that time accepted the changing future as inevitable and began the study of art as an abstract creative thought process.

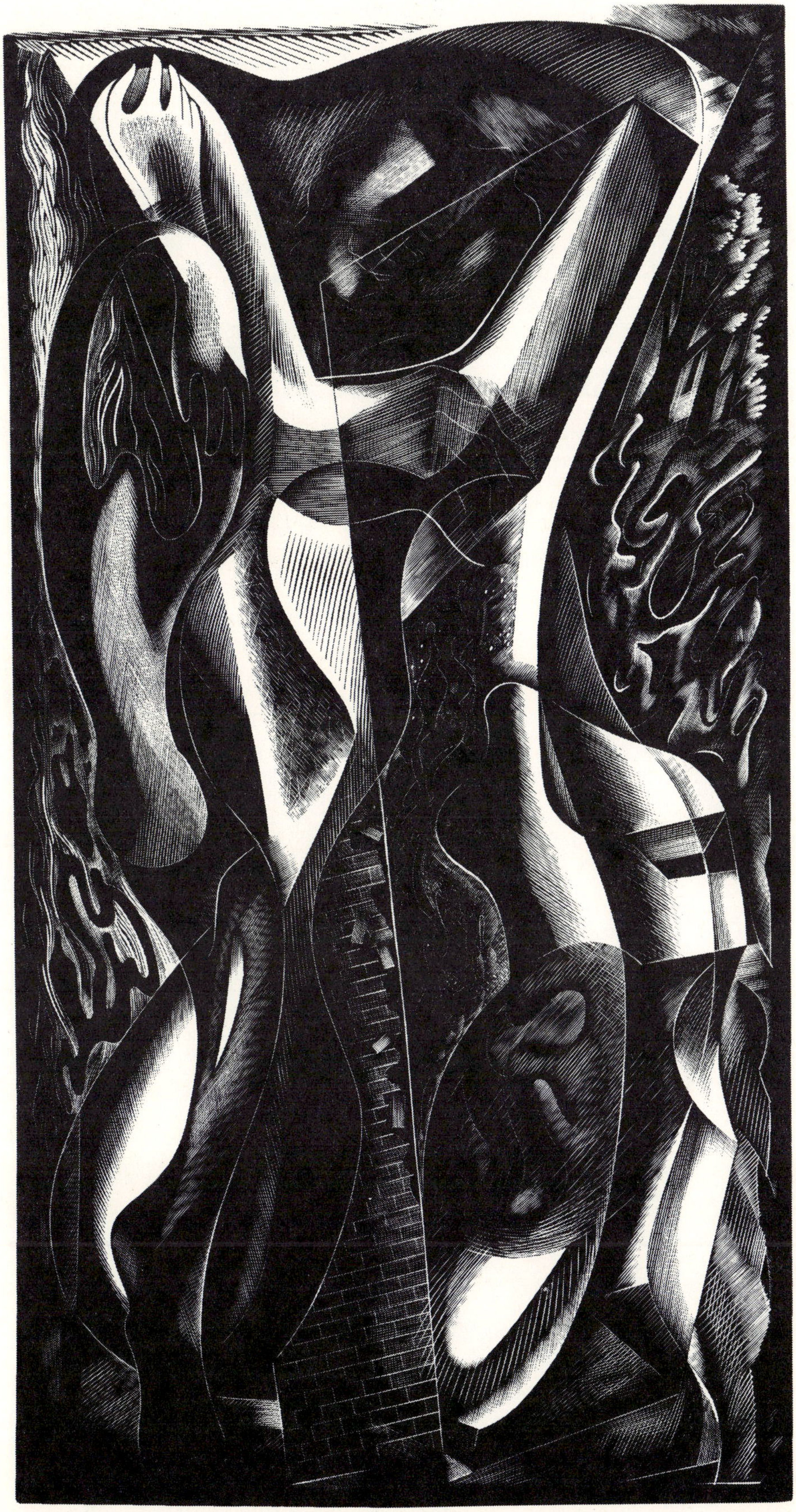

[266] John Farleigh: *Lilith*, 1948.
23.0 x 43.0cm

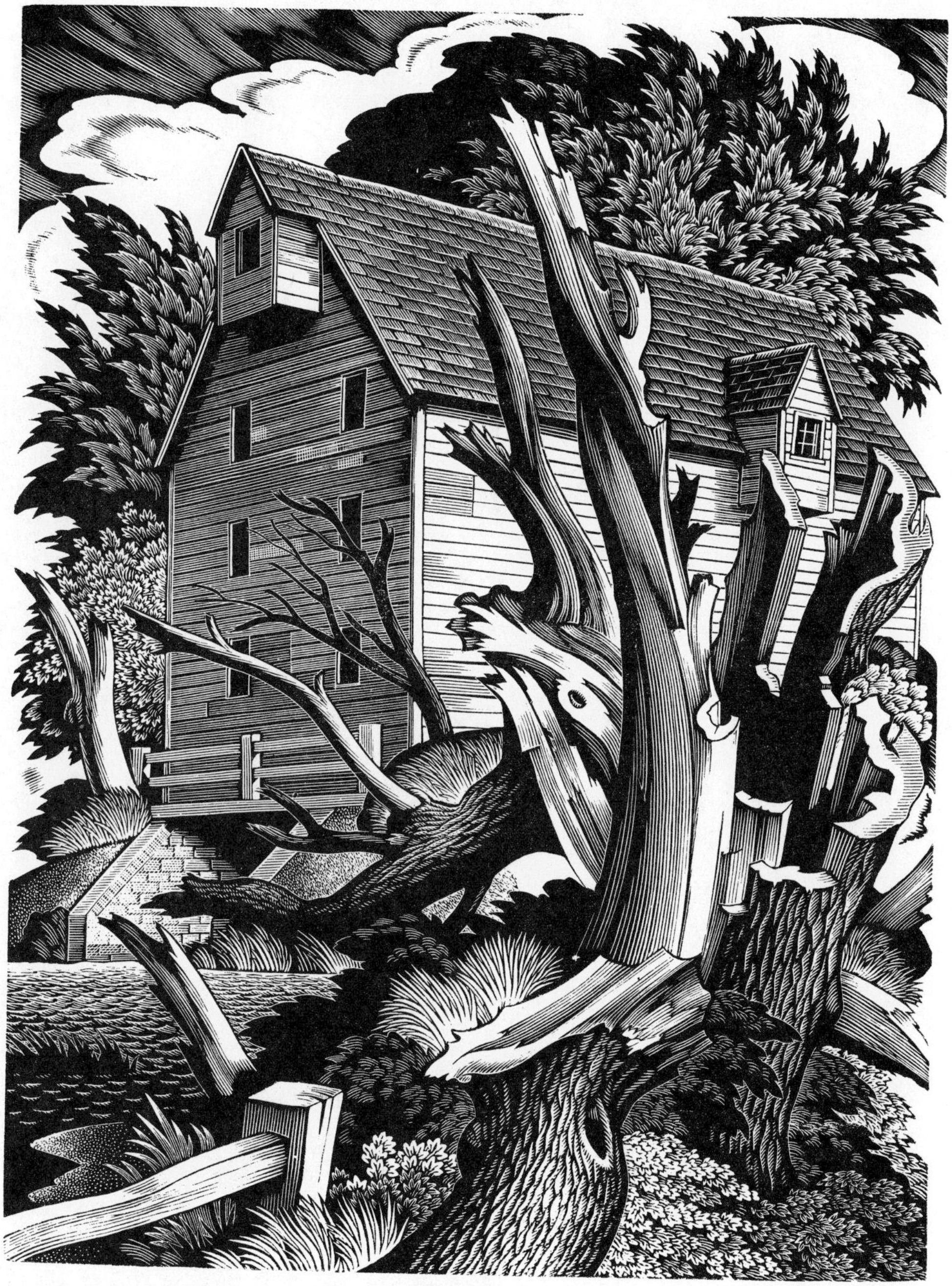

[267] George Mackley: *The Broken Willow*, 1948. 14.0 x 19.0cm

Because Chadwick was only twenty-seven when he died there is only a small number of engravings available for study, although he also worked in other media which do not come within the scope of this history. For a short period a few works were published in magazines and exhibition reviews, but because of the limited quantity of the total output there is a danger that Chadwick's work could be lost. This would be deplorable in view of the brilliance of his work.

Chadwick visited the Costa Brava and Barcelona in 1933 and produced several wood engravings which expressed the Catalonian industriousness, sense of order and national pride. These landscapes are sensitive to the sudden and extreme temperature changes and the heaviness of the abundant foliage in a situation where every inch of soil is under cultivation. In 1934 he went to Italy to extend his horizons still further.

[268] Winifred M. McKenzie: *House over the Canal*, Bath, 1948. 17.2 x 23.75cm

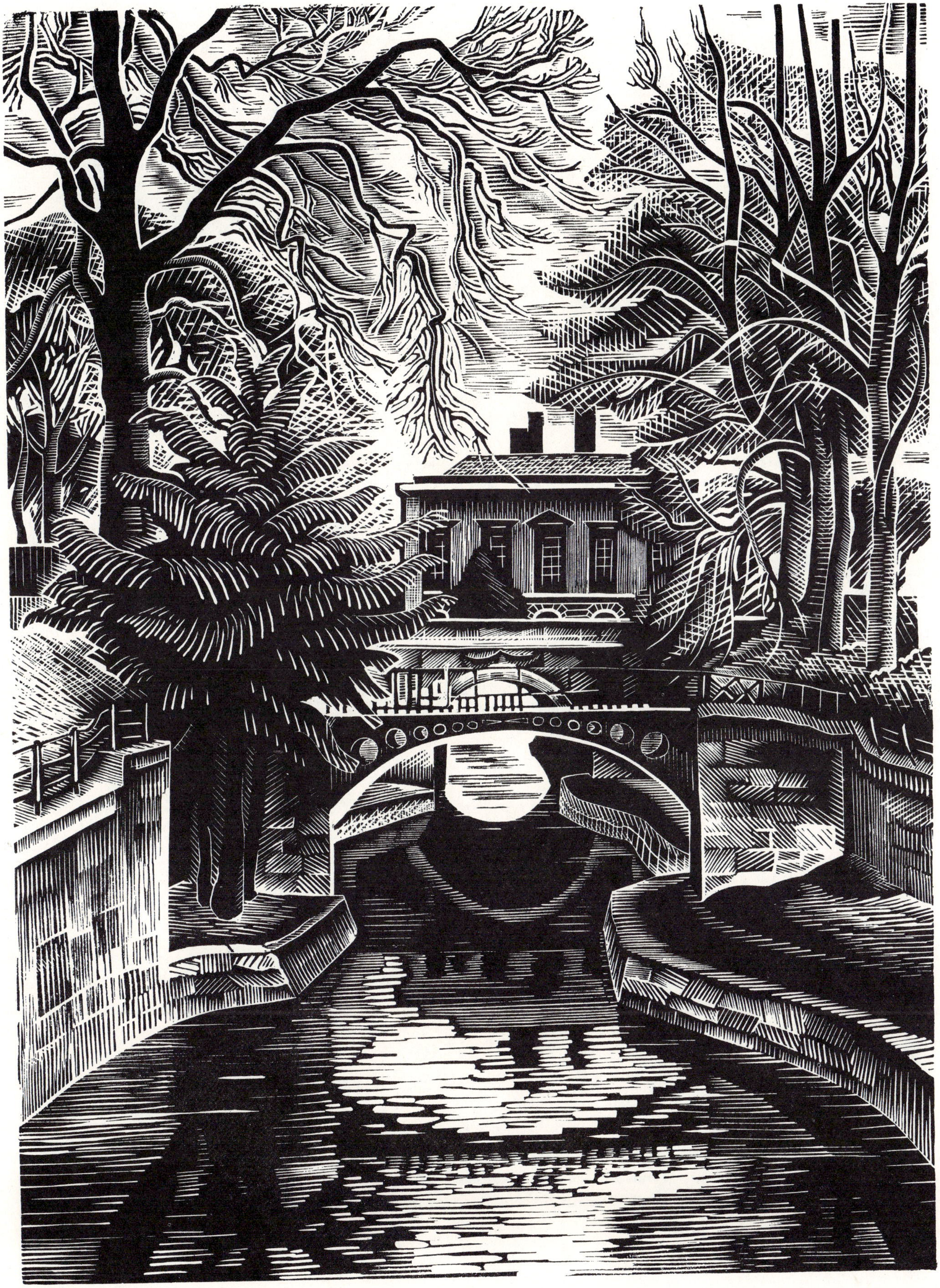

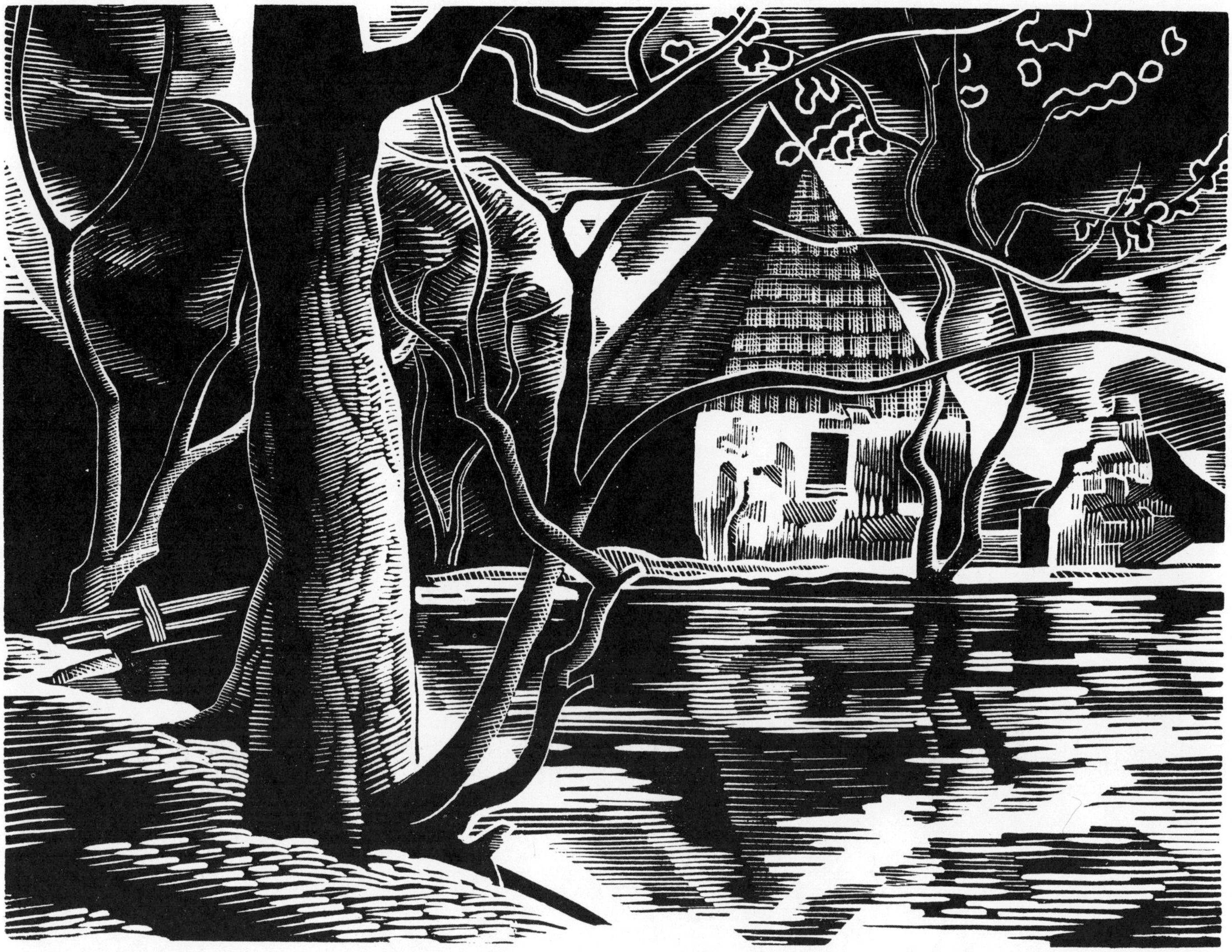

He exhibited with the Society of Wood Engravers from 1932 to 1939. The seven works recorded in the catalogues are *Lorton, Cumberland* 1932 [194]; *Derby Day* 1933; *Cadaques, Spain* 1934; *Wayside Laundry* 1935 [215]; *The Introduction* 1935; *When Fishes Flew and Forests Walked* 1936 and *Who is Worthy to Open the Book* 1939. In addition to these titles Iain Macnab's collection of prints contained *The Fan Dance, On the Costa Brava, Snow in the Village, Look not in My Eyes* and *Sasso, Italy*.

Chadwick's engraving *Wayside Laundry* was issued as an edition of sixty prints and the illustration was reproduced in Iain Macnab's book *The Student's Book of Wood Engraving* published in 1938.[1] This engraving is a remarkable feat of design, texture and volumetric expression, beautifully fused. An outstanding feature is the rendering of the penumbra of the girls' shadow on the wall and it displays an unusual and quite objective understanding of light.

Guy Malet (1900 to 1973) was trained as an engraver by Iain Macnab at the Grosvenor School of Modern Art in 1927. Malet was a painter; he did not intend taking up wood engraving, but was persuaded to do so by Macnab and this led to their lifelong friendship. During the thirties Malet spent much of his time between London and Sark in the Channel Isles. His best-known works are his *Sark Girl* 1936, *The Footbridge* 1946 [256] and *A Berkshire Farm* 1946 [257]. His technique,

[269] Winifred M. McKenzie: *The Law Mill, St Andrews*, 1949. 19.5 x 15.0cm

[270] Jozef Sekalski: *The Three Shepherds*, 1950. 13.0 x 18.5cm

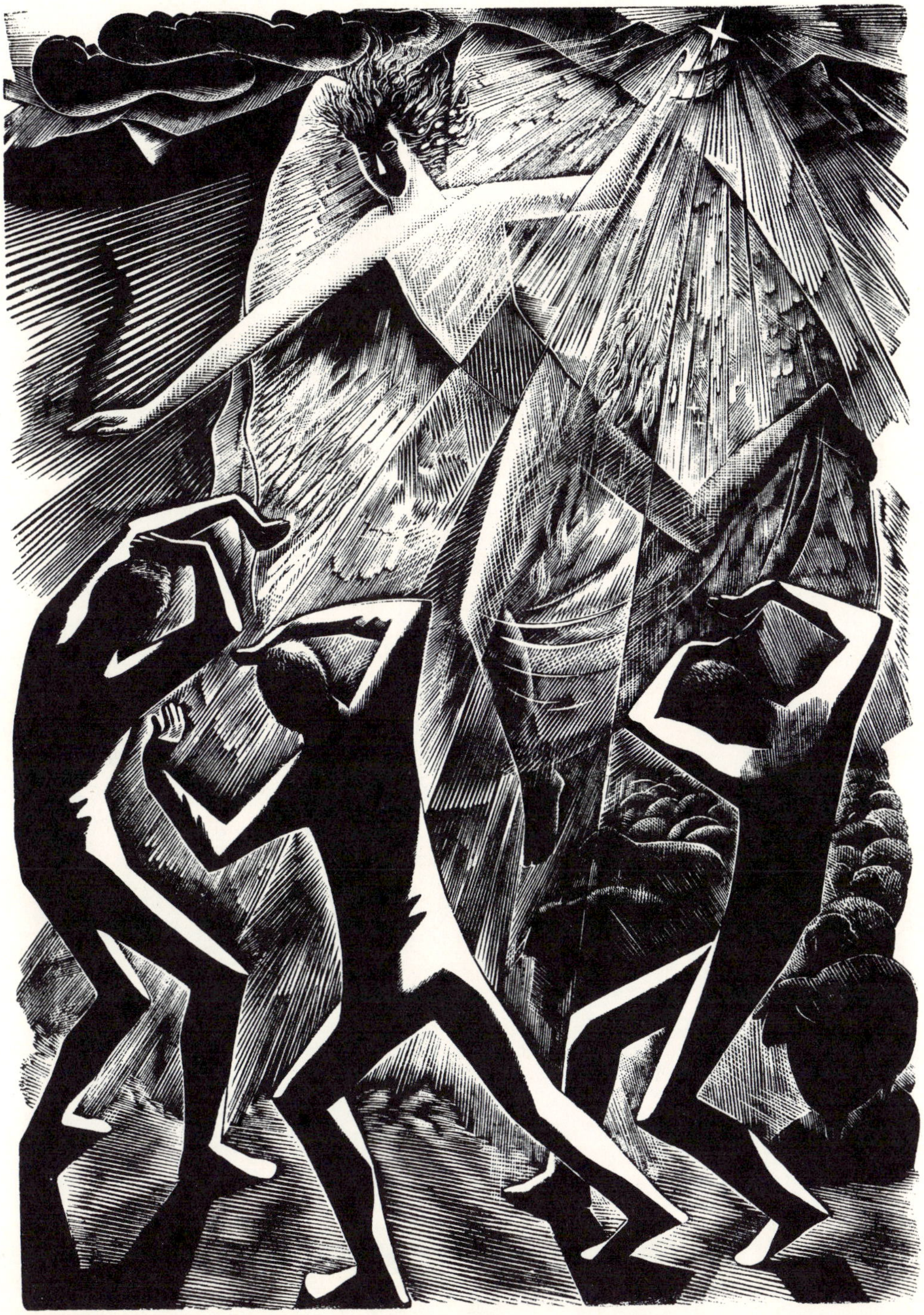

[271] Jozef Sekalski: Device for Michael Oliver printing press, 1949. 3.75 x 3.5cm

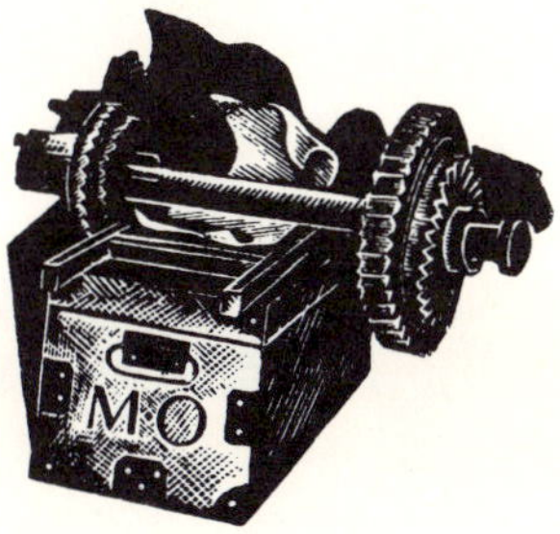

always important to engravers, was sensitive and of a high order, and his engraving units of form and space were fused into powerful compositions. All his wood engravings were produced as autonomous prints. For the latter part of his life he lived in the village of Ditchling where artists continued to gather long after Gill's Community had collapsed.

On the north-east coast of Scotland an isolated pocket of important wood engravers came together during the Second World War and set to work. The St Andrews Group included the sisters Alison and Winifred McKenzie, Annabel Kidston and Jozef Sekalski.

The two McKenzie sisters have lived close together throughout their lives, and as engravers each has a remarkable quality though in matters of individuality they are surprisingly different. The handling of light in Winifred's engraving is the flood source, breaking through the arboreal colander [268]. Her engraving technique is that of the painter. Alison's handling of light is the beam source, illuminating a world of solids, a sculptural concept expressing solidity, security and order. Her engraving is remarkable for its economy and precision. This difference of outlook in terms of style and content is very evident in the comparison of their signatures. The sculptural roundness can be seen in Alison's signature whereas in Winifred's the letter forms are closer together and are more even and pointed. The sisters have shared a studio for nearly fifty years and are the best of friends, the relationship exerting no undue influence on style. Their engraving quality is of a very high order. They studied at Iain Macnab's Grosvenor School during the early thirties and returned home at the outbreak of war. Alison served in the ATS and Winifred took up teaching.

Annabel Kidston also studied wood engraving in London, at the Slade School of Fine Art under Thomas Smith. Stylistically, her form is earthy, emotionally charged and sensitive. She has a strong sense of pattern which is rendered in

[272] Joan Hassall: *The Old Tree*, 1950. 9.5 x 14.5cm

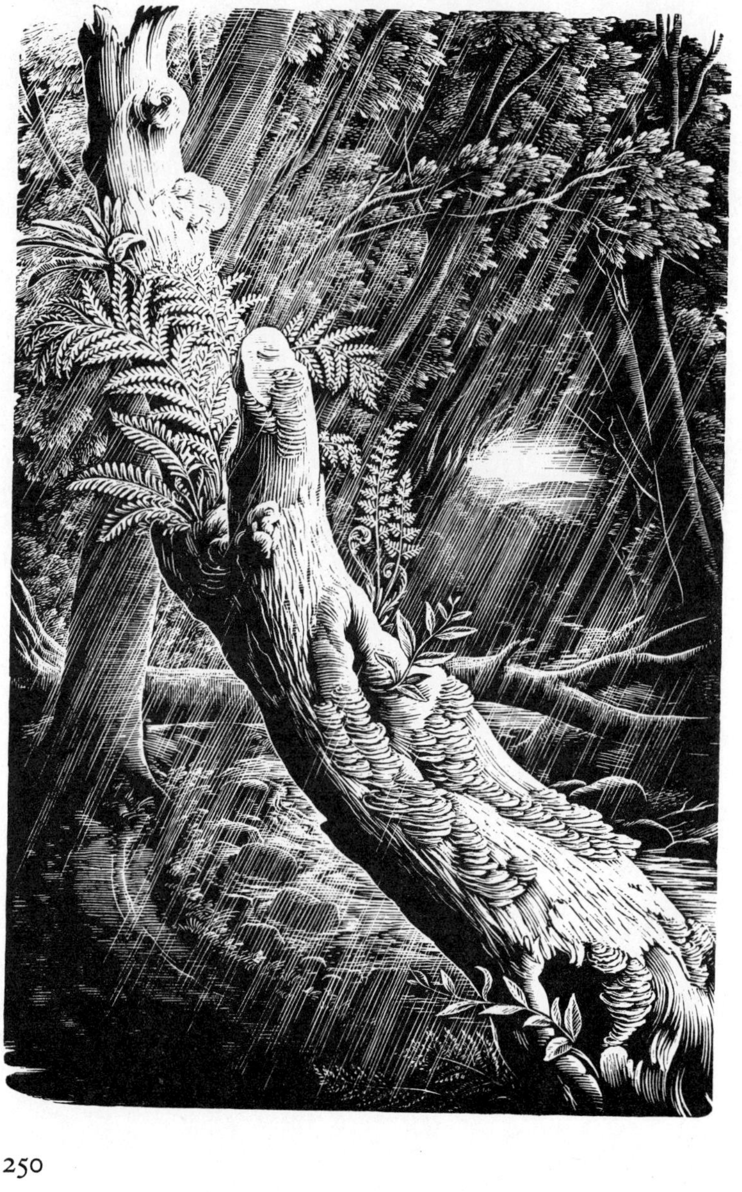

engraving terms and she ranges through from the fine to the heavy white line. During the war years she was an instructor of drawing and wood engraving for the Committee for Education for the Forces and with Winifred McKenzie she started wood engraving classes for the Forces at St Andrews University. These classes were run on a voluntary basis of three nights a week and were attended by airmen and soldiers but were most appreciated by the Polish contingent stationed in the town. This teaching resulted in an exhibition of Polish wood engraving being held at the National Gallery of Scotland in Edinburgh in 1944. The engraving tradition in Poland is in the white-line technique. In the autumn of 1944 Winifred McKenzie started a wood engraving class for Diploma students at the Dundee College of Art and Alison joined her in 1946.

When Winifred McKenzie retired from the Dundee College of Art in 1958, her post was taken over by the Polish artist and wood engraver Jozef Sekalski (1904 to 1973). He had qualified in wood engraving after studying medicine at Wilno University. His engraving instructor was Jerzy Hoppen. When war broke out Sekalski was resident in Lodz and in charge of an art and design studio. Jozef Sekalski, whose works were exhibited regularly in London at the Royal Society of Painter-Etchers and Engravers exhibitions, introduced new elements into British

[273] James Dolby: *Away Lifeboat's Crew*, 1951. 15.3 x 17.7cm

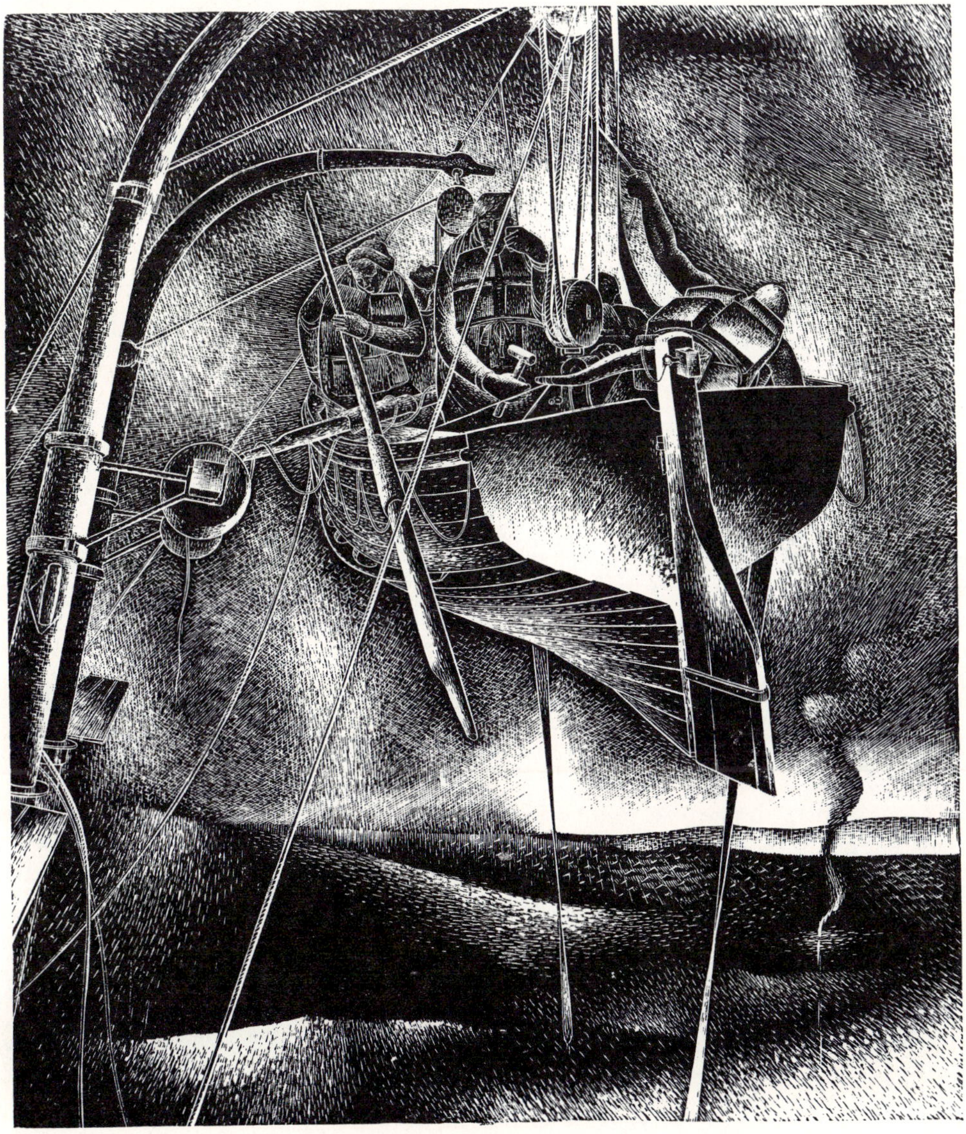

wood engraving. These were the Polish sense of engraving drama and the expressionist emotion which accompanies it. A feature of the expressionist emotion is the javelin thrusts piercing a composition structure as in *Starburst.* The javelin thrust is also a dominant feature of Spanish art and it persisted in Picasso's work throughout his life.

Life did not treat Sekalski kindly. When the Germans invaded Poland and overran Lodz, he was captured and suffered great privation which was to undermine his health and shorten his life. He escaped from captivity with one companion, took all the prints he could find from the studio in Lodz and carried them with some burins in his pack.

He went to Warsaw, which was under German occupation, and while hiding in an alleyway drew the smouldering ruins of Warsaw Castle, He was able to transfer the drawing to a block and added it to the contents of his pack. In January 1940, in falling snow, he crossed Slovakia with the help of smugglers and reached Budapest. He was able to complete his engraving of Warsaw Castle while in Budapest and, with the help of the Red Cross, held a one-day exhibition. This event was remarkably successful, all exhibits being sold, including more than 120 prints of Warsaw Castle and many other works in black and in colour.

The proceeds of the exhibition enabled Sekalski and his companion to remain in Budapest for one week before continuing their journey through France to Marseilles and from there to Gibraltar and Britain. Unhappily, when he reached the Vosges he was again taken prisoner by the Germans but he was able to escape and reached Britain in 1942.

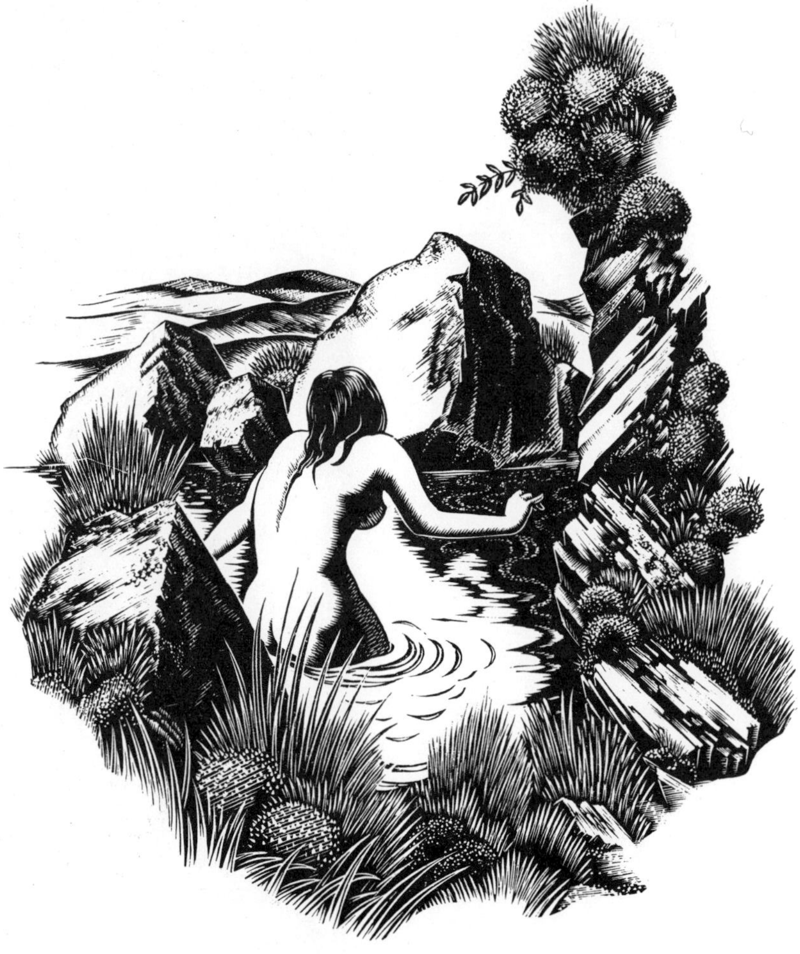

[274] Robert Gibbings: *Illustration from Sweet Cork to Thee*, 1951.

Between 1944 and 1945 he worked as an illustrator and designer for the Polish Library and Publishing Company in Glasgow. In 1957 he obtained the teaching post in the Duncan of Jordanston College of Art in Dundee on the retirement of Winifred McKenzie and was engaged in print making.

Sekalski was a very successful teacher and in his engraving his craft is superb. His engraving technique, which is the white line, is closely akin to Russian engraving. In *Starburst* [285] the long lines giving rise to the shimmering greys are fabulous for their precision and call to mind the engraving of the Russian Alexis Kravchenko. Sekalski's wife Roberta, who is an artist trained at the Slade under Tonks, says, 'In the case of the engraving *Starburst* my husband started with the barest sketch in ink line and wash and no tracing on to the block. He then, while working and on completing the block, knew what he really wanted to do and started right away on a second block. To the casual glance they look very similar, but to the expert eye the improvement is quite clear and I think this point is a good example of his perfectionism.' The illustration shown in [285] is reproduced from the second block.

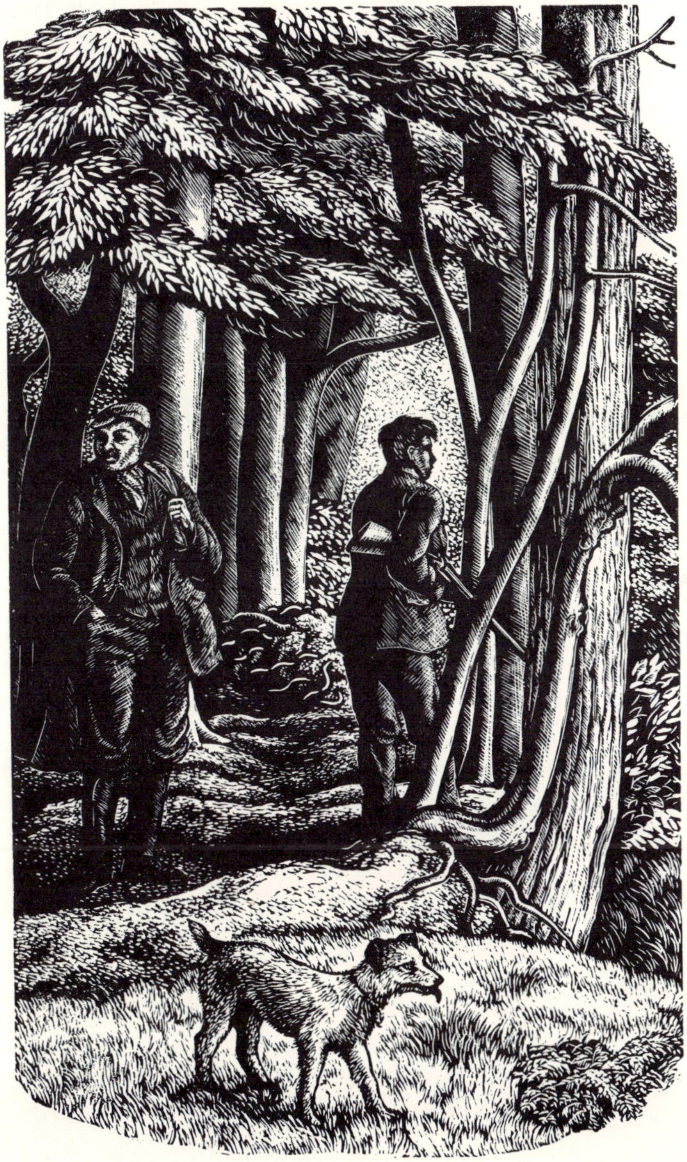

[275] Barbara Greg: Illustration from *The Poacher's Handbook*, 1951. 9.0 x 15.2cm

[276] Roderic Barrett: *Ass and Man*, 1951. 17.0 x 18.5cm

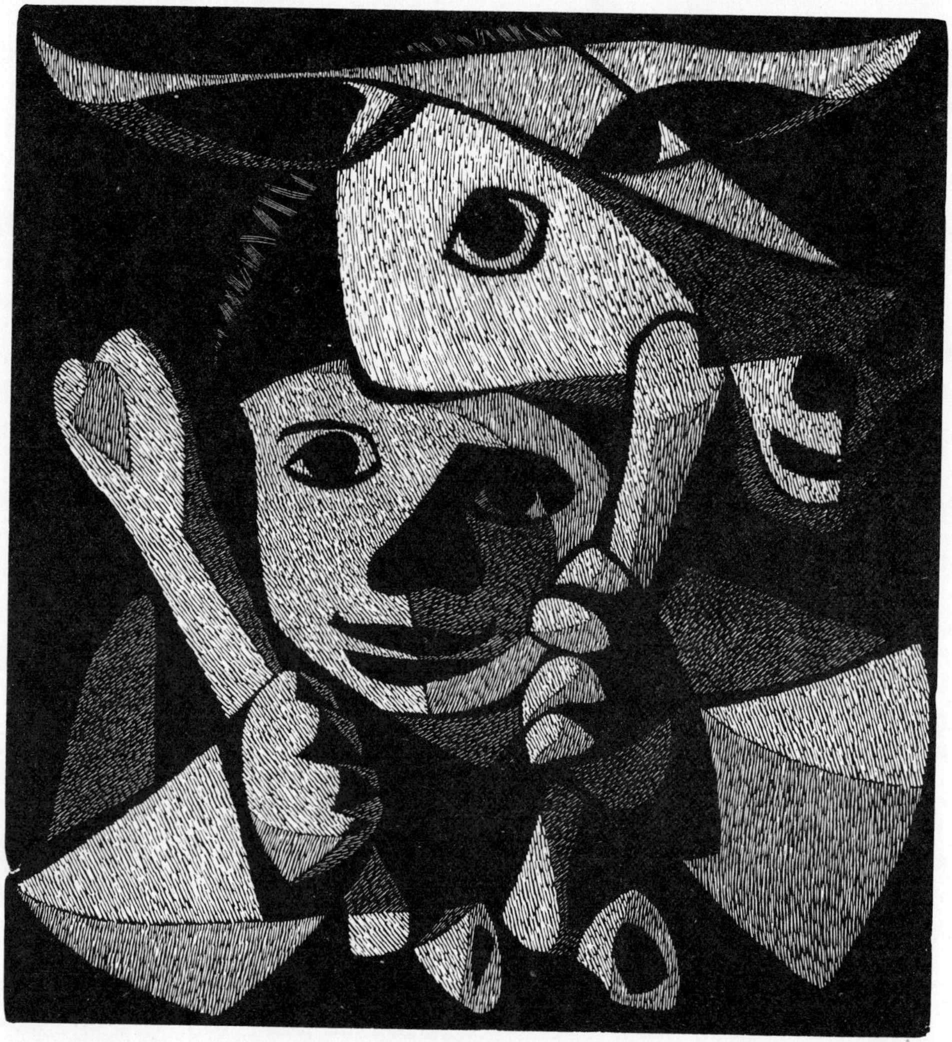

Sekalski's most endearing symbol of his individuality is his engraving of a printing press – probably one of the smallest engravings of this piece of machinery ever made [271]. The first book produced on the press shown in Sekalski's engraving was *Twelve Poems* by Alastair Reid published at St Andrews in 1949. The edition was limited to fifty signed copies and was printed by hand. Sekalski constructed the press from the back axle of a car, a tuck box and odd items, and built the machine on the floor of his apartment at 29 North Street, St Andrews.

The art of John Petts is known to a wide public through the two BBC documentary films *Out of the Rock* made by Derek Trimby, for BBC Wales and BBC-1, and the television feature film *The Art of John Petts* made by Nan Davies, for BBC Wales. Much of Petts's work is sited in the churches of Wales; he is a sculptor, engraver and stained glass artist. His art is a finely distilled essence of vision, with a sharp understanding of the physical stimulus of light and the part played by its psychological interpretation. This statement could not be more clearly illustrated than by the engraving of Petts *The Soothsayer* [258], the model being described by the artist as 'a canny old devil'. It is an outstanding achievement of economic volumetric structure which is made even more difficult by the foreshortening of the bird's-eye viewpoint, while the engraving of the figure is disarmingly simple; despite the economy of detail, the information is brought together in the mind of the observer to give a very complete impression.

[277] Roderic Barrett: *Fallen Chair*, 1952. 26.0 x 20.5cm

In art Petts is very different from his friend David Jones, but being a sculptor, his work, like Gill's is very compressed in form content. He has extended his engraving range by engraving on lead-crystal glass with a diamond point, a taxing technique which is tense and exciting; it is a world of maximums and minimums.

The one work which sums up everything that Petts is in engraving is *Coire Mhic Fhearchair Ross* [379] and for sheer economy it is an astounding work. Although the light on the eroded, contorted rock strata appears powdered, an important aesthetic quality in the engraving discipline is established in this work. He makes no attempt to initiate natural appearances and everything is executed throughout with lines, long, short, narrow and thick. The shape of the tool that cut each stroke is sharply imprinted on the work.

In 1945, Petts enlisted in the 6th Airborne Division and served in the Middle East, Israel, Greece and Egypt. While he was serving in the Negev Desert, south of Gaza in Israel, he was commissioned by Christopher Sandford to illustrate *The Green Island* by Gwyn Jones for the Golden Cockerel Press. He engraved a set of eleven blocks for that book, crouched over a card table in a tent in the desert.

John Buckland-Wright was a New Zealander, born in Dunedin in 1897. His father died when he was only five years old and about three years later the Wright

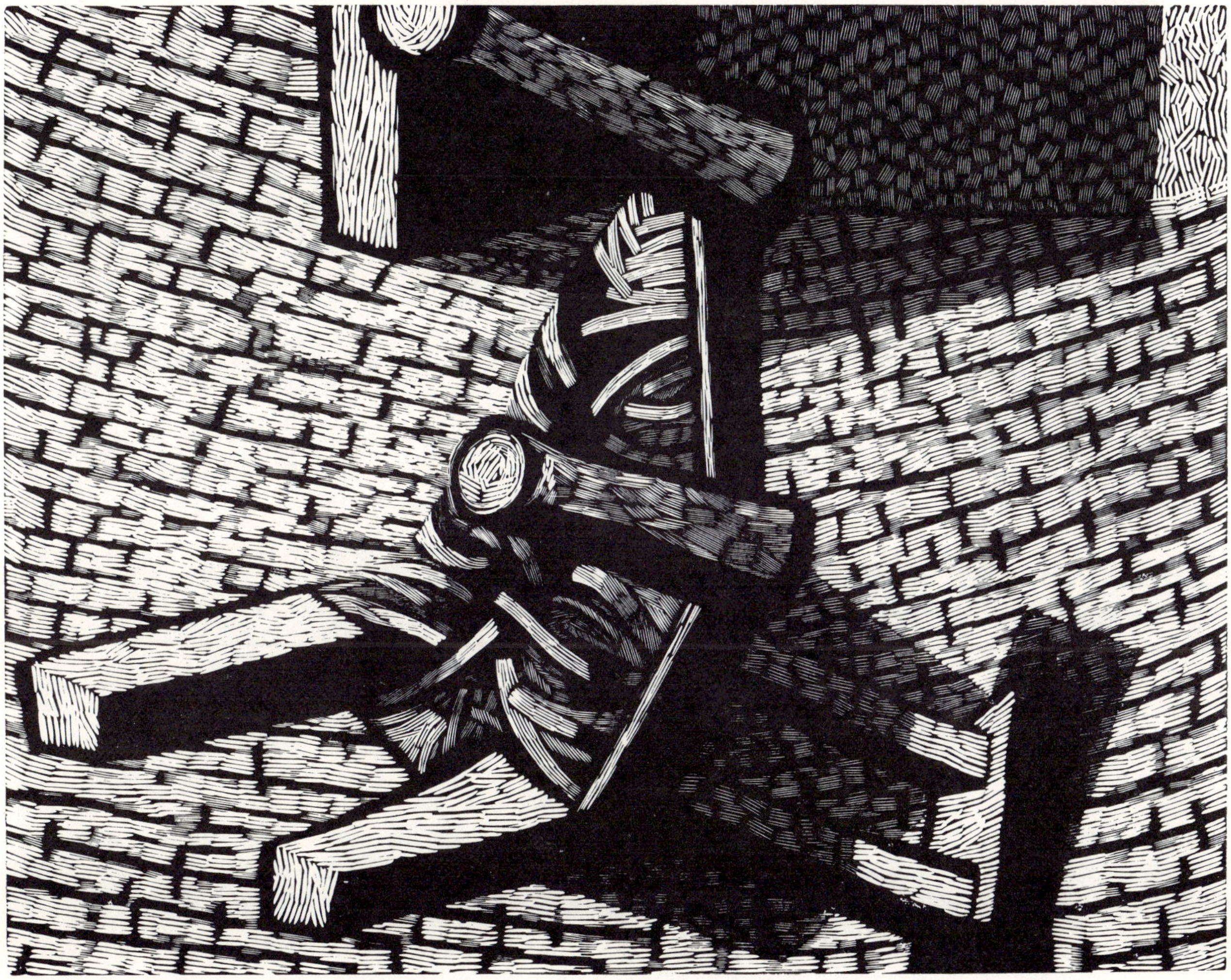

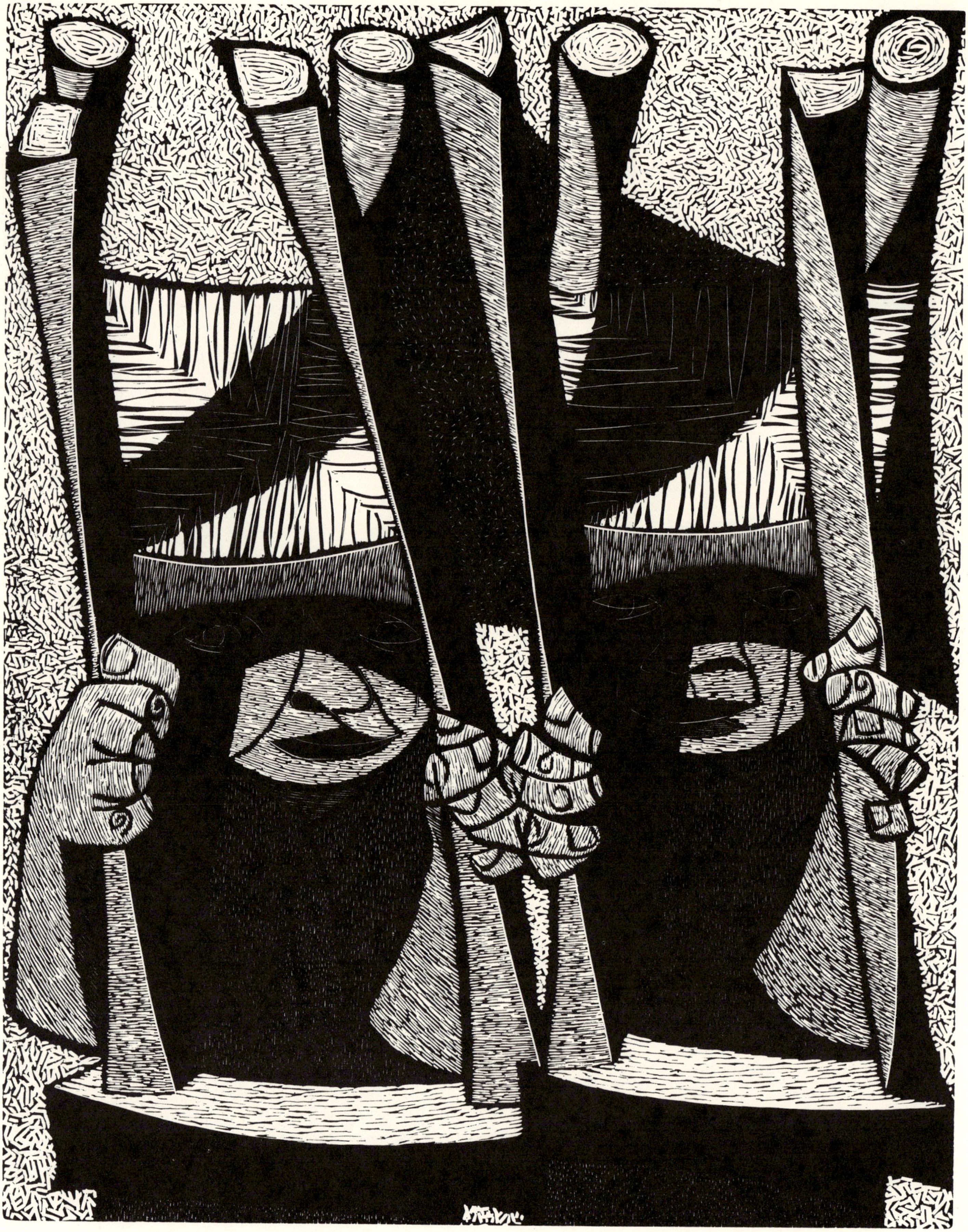

[278] Roderic Barrett: *Chairs and Men*, 1952. 21.0 x 26.25cm

family left the country. Later they came to England. In 1914 Buckland-Wright volunteered for active service but the Army discovered that he spoke with a severe stammer and he was turned down. In 1916 he joined a Scottish ambulance unit attached to the French Army. His war record was distinguished and he was awarded the Croix de Guerre for gallantry in rescuing French civilians from burning buildings.

At the end of the war in 1918 John Buckland-Wright went to Oxford where he took a degree in history. After the degree course he studied architecture and graduated in that subject at the Bartlett School of Architecture next door to the Slade School of Fine Art in London, where eventually he was to teach engraving and etching. When asked why he gave up architecture he said, 'At the time I qualified the prospect of ever achieving a building of my own before the age of sixty was so remote it was a prospect I could not accept.' He turned to engraving after a visit to the Victoria and Albert Museum, where he saw engravings and a book by Edward Gordon Craig on the subject of engraving. Here he also saw engraving tools and blocks. He was very impressed with the precision of the steel point which he felt 'would either give you everything or nothing'. He was also impressed with Craig's extreme sensitivity and subtlety of expression. From the time of his visit to the Museum, drawing and engraving in wood and copper became his life's work. He taught himself engraving but had already received an

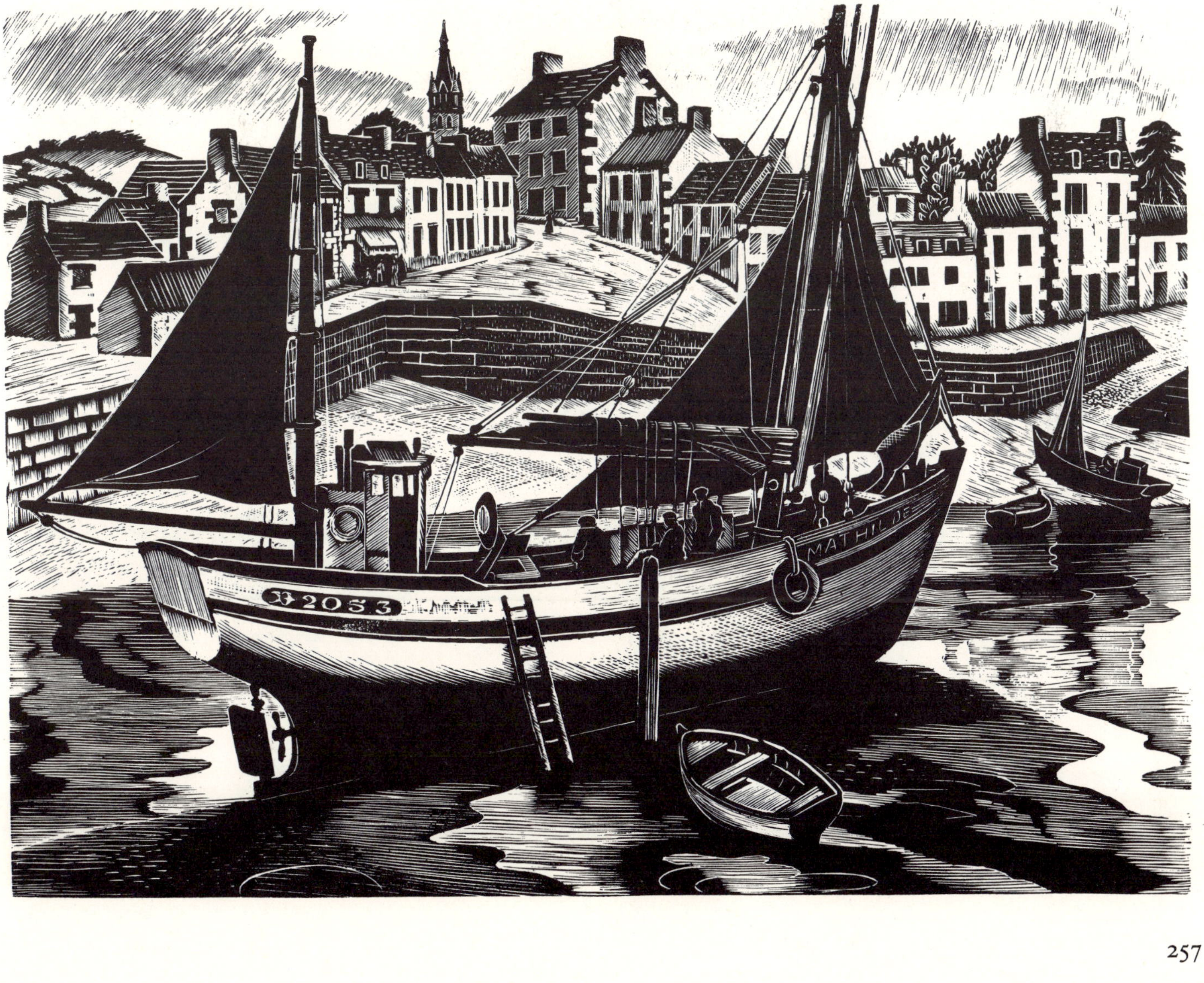

[279] Norman Janes: *Tunny Boat*, Brittany, 1952. 22.0 x 16.4cm

[280] Clare Leighton: *The Cotton Pickers*, 1952.

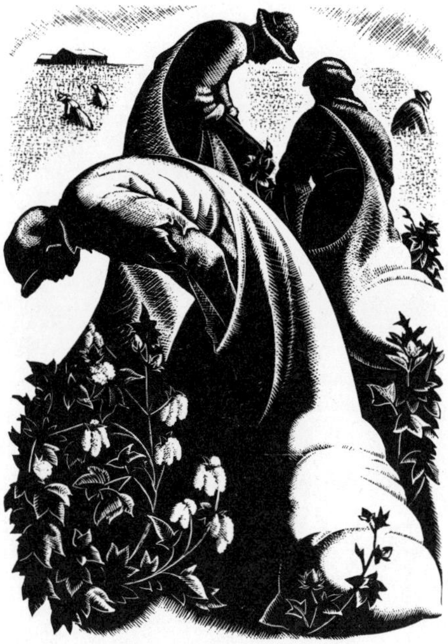

extensive training in forming and designing space structures at the Bartlett School of Architecture. This ability to form and develop meaningful structures was to give his art and its language its authority.

Salome [154] is one of Buckland-Wright's first wood engravings, produced in 1926 soon after the decisive visit to the Victoria and Albert Museum and it has not been reproduced or exhibited before. It shows the direct influence of Gordon Craig. Like Craig, Buckland-Wright uses both the black-line and white-line engraving techniques. After *Salome* two or three small engravings appeared in which he used both techniques. He went very quickly into the white-line development. In 1927 he left Britain and went to Belgium and later to France. The Belgian writer Jan Greshoff was the first to notice the young engraver and introduced him to A. A. M. Stols, the Director of the Halcyon Press. Though Buckland-Wright had only a few small engravings Stols gave him his first commission to illustrate Keat's *Sonnets* published by the Halcyon Press in 1930 [178]. This introduction from Greshoff started him off on a lifetime of work for the various private presses.

In his early work the architect in John Buckland-Wright can be seen as dominant. There is no language confusion; confronted with this new world of expression he went back to basic design and employed it with a strong orientation to architecture. However, at that time he was in Belgium and was unaware that the young Gill and Gibbings were also working in simple basic design terms. A new language must always start that way and from these two early works and the other engravings

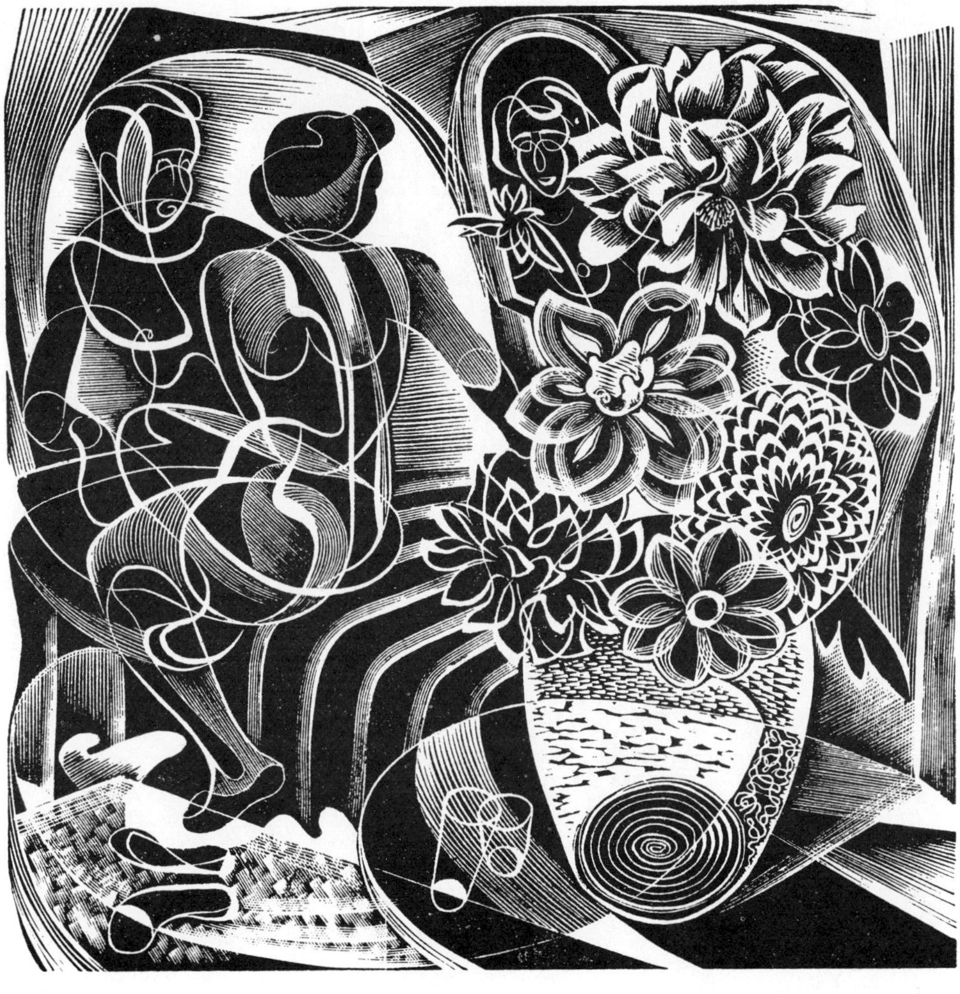

[281] James Bostock: *The Mirror*, 1952. 15.3 x 15.3cm

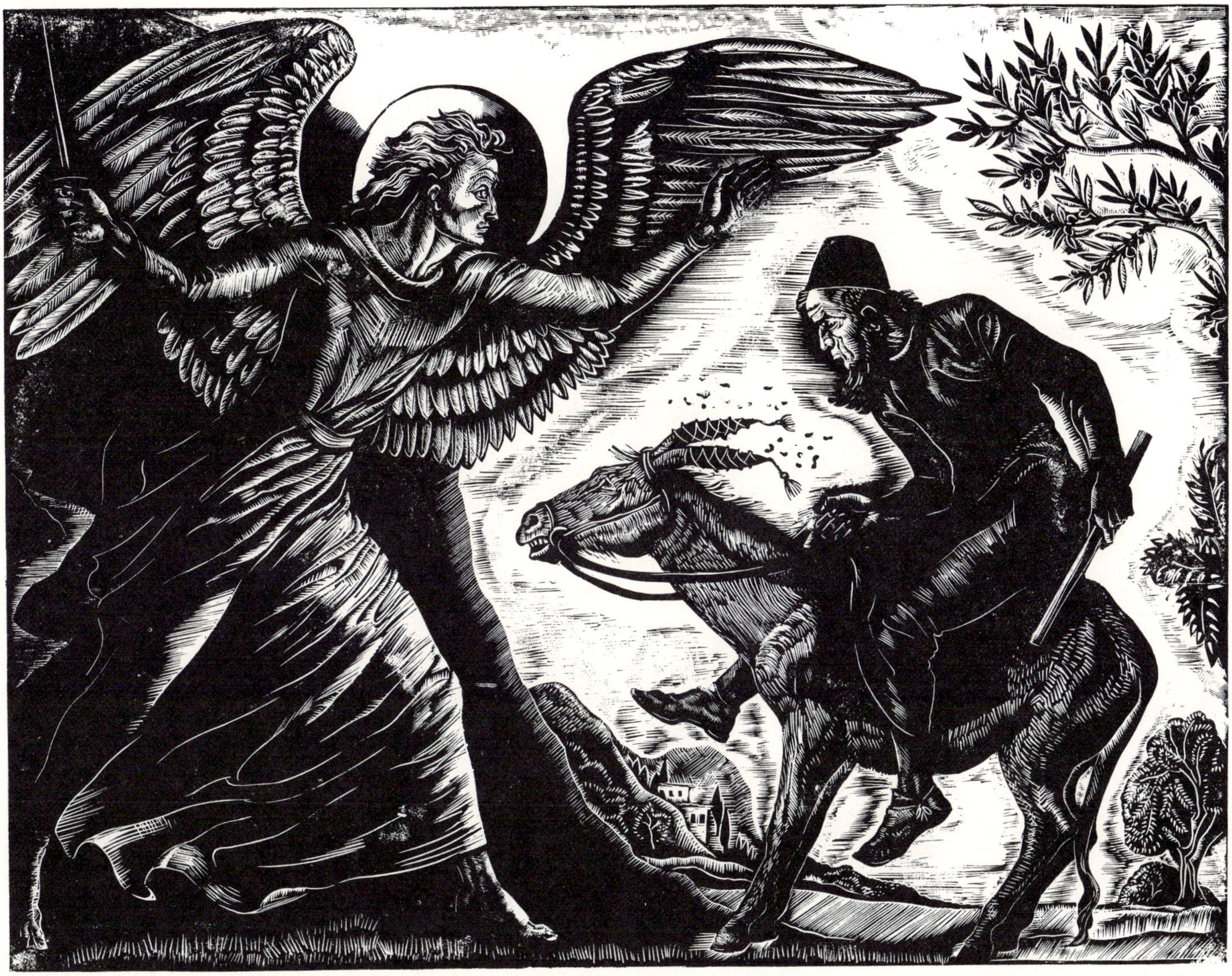

[282] Muriel Jackson: *Balaam's Ass*, 1953. 28.25 x 22.0cm

shown in this book, his creative language as an artist can be seen developing logically and progressively to the final engraving of pure expression [248, 249].

While in Paris Buckland-Wright came under the influence of Jean Laboureur, an important engraver who rated him very highly. This was the last influence on him before he attained maturity. Laboureur was black-line orientated and Buckland-Wright was to find his black-line medium in copper engraving and in this form of expression he has no peers; he is the English Schongauer.

He remained in Paris until the outbreak of war in 1939, when he and his wife Mary left the Continent and returned to Britain. At that time he was unknown in this country except to those in the profession but on the Continent he was famous as an artist with a considerable production to his credit. He was elected a member of the Xylographes Belges and the Société de la Gravure Originale Belge. Most of his earlier works were shown in the exhibitions of these societies. While still on the Continent his work was shown for many years at the exhibitions of the Society of Wood Engravers. In 1938 he organised an exhibition in Lyons in which the work of English engravers from the Society was shown alongside that of French engravers.

John Buckland-Wright was the creative artist; his craft is spellbinding. The engraving flowing from his burin was in the same pedigree as that of the engravers

[283] Reynolds Stone: Coat of Arms for the Coronation service of HM Queen Elizabeth II, 1953. 14.6 x 18.0cm

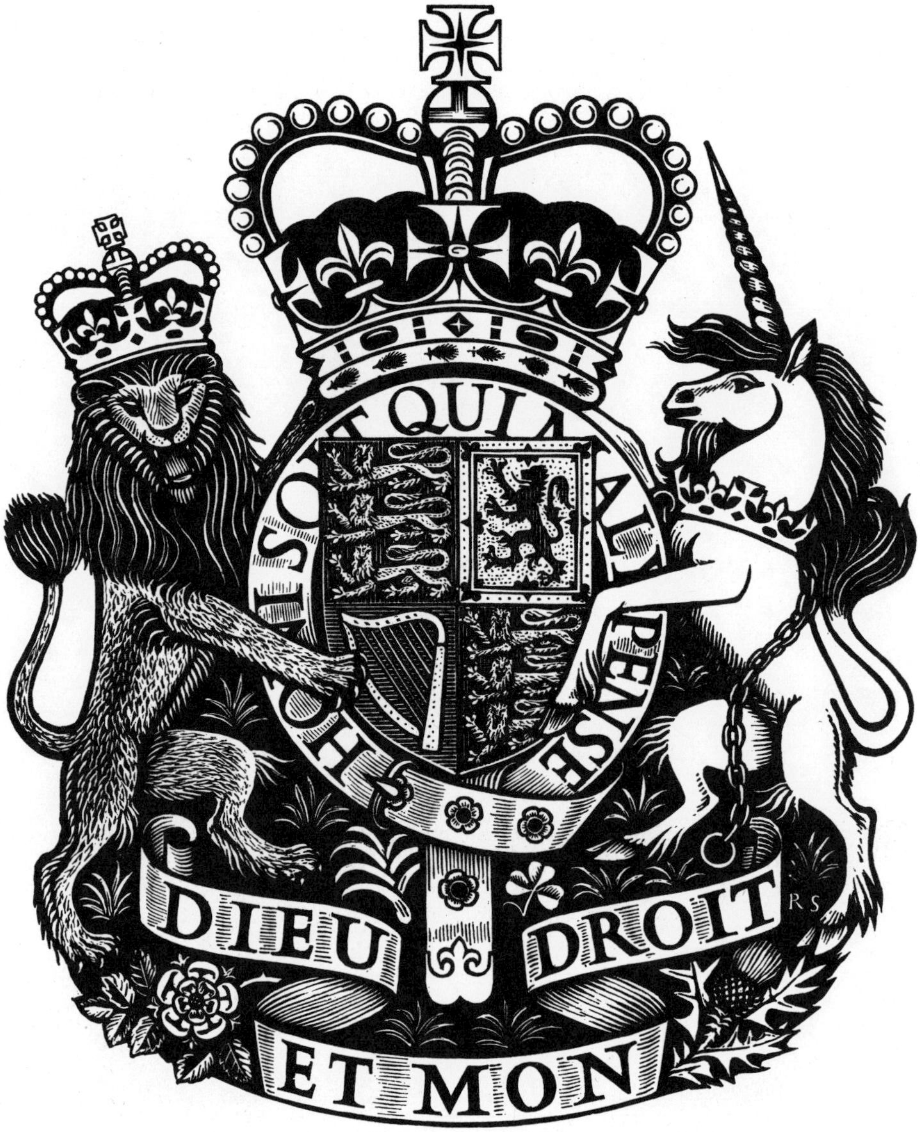

he admired so much, Antonio Pollaiuolo, Andrea Mantegna and Martin Schongauer. His art is rich, emotional in its aesthetic quality and at times esoteric. Throughout his life his art was unified in expression and vision by an underlying abstract structure to which every detail is formally related. He helped to establish the true nature of engraving and the autonomous print independent of book illustration.

He could never tolerate the dimensional confusion that Ravilious the designer accepted to achieve an image. Dimensional confusion also entered John Farleigh's later adventures in abstract art. Equally Buckland-Wright would not tolerate dimensional confusion in the work of students and this was because of his inherent interest in architecture – a quality that has been missed by most observers.

In character, he was simple, direct, quietly extroverted, but always accurate and very articulate in English or French. He was completely unpretentious, always natural and very even tempered, but if roused he could be very indignant. He had little to say on rules and regulations, and even less on politics. His authority arose from his achievement, and in this there was nothing superficial.

[284] Dorothea Braby: *Some Sleep* from *The Way of Wood Engraving*, 1953. 14.0 x 19.0cm

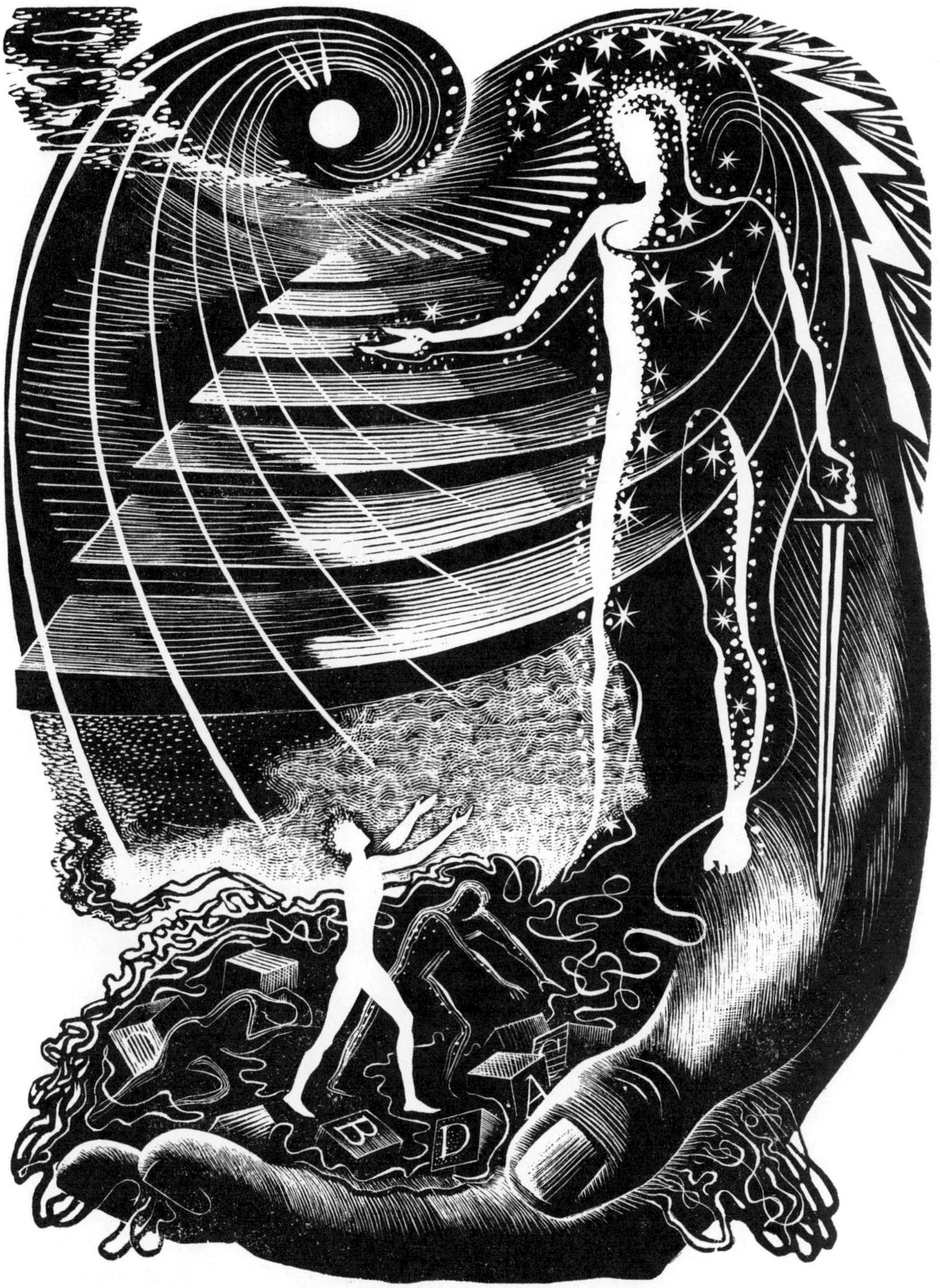

John Buckland-Wright was a great and respected teacher and was revered as a man and as an artist. In appearance he was tall, upright, balding with some white hair and had a kind and handsome, finely chiselled face. His voice was quiet, his diction was always perfect and he treated everyone as an individual. In his teaching he would tell the student how to work and would demonstrate and explain, but he would never touch a student's work. He explained this attitude by saying 'A student must always do the production and not be misled.' This was a mark of his honesty.

He taught his students the qualities of a good artist, to be professional in behaviour and explained the meaning of the commitment that art demanded. In this respect a chance remark of his at an exhibition is pertinent. He said 'The figure draughtsman is still a mark of the professional' and he also stated 'If a work is good, it will always be good, there will always be someone who will appreciate it regardless of changing fashions.'

In Brussels and Paris he had achieved a grand production. He worked in Stanley William Hayter's Atelier 17 in Paris. Here during the thirties he had met Brancusi, Miró, Picasso, Orovida Pissarro, Matisse, Lacourière, Anthony Gross, Dolf Rieser, Julian Trevelyan and Leon Underwood. He had worked with the painters of the Ecole de Paris at the peak of their great period. He was one of the very few artists at Camberwell or the Slade who could give students first-hand information and experience of how these important artists felt, thought, worked and played. He summed up London and Paris with the statement: 'In Paris the world's best and worst are produced; in London the best and worst are missing'.

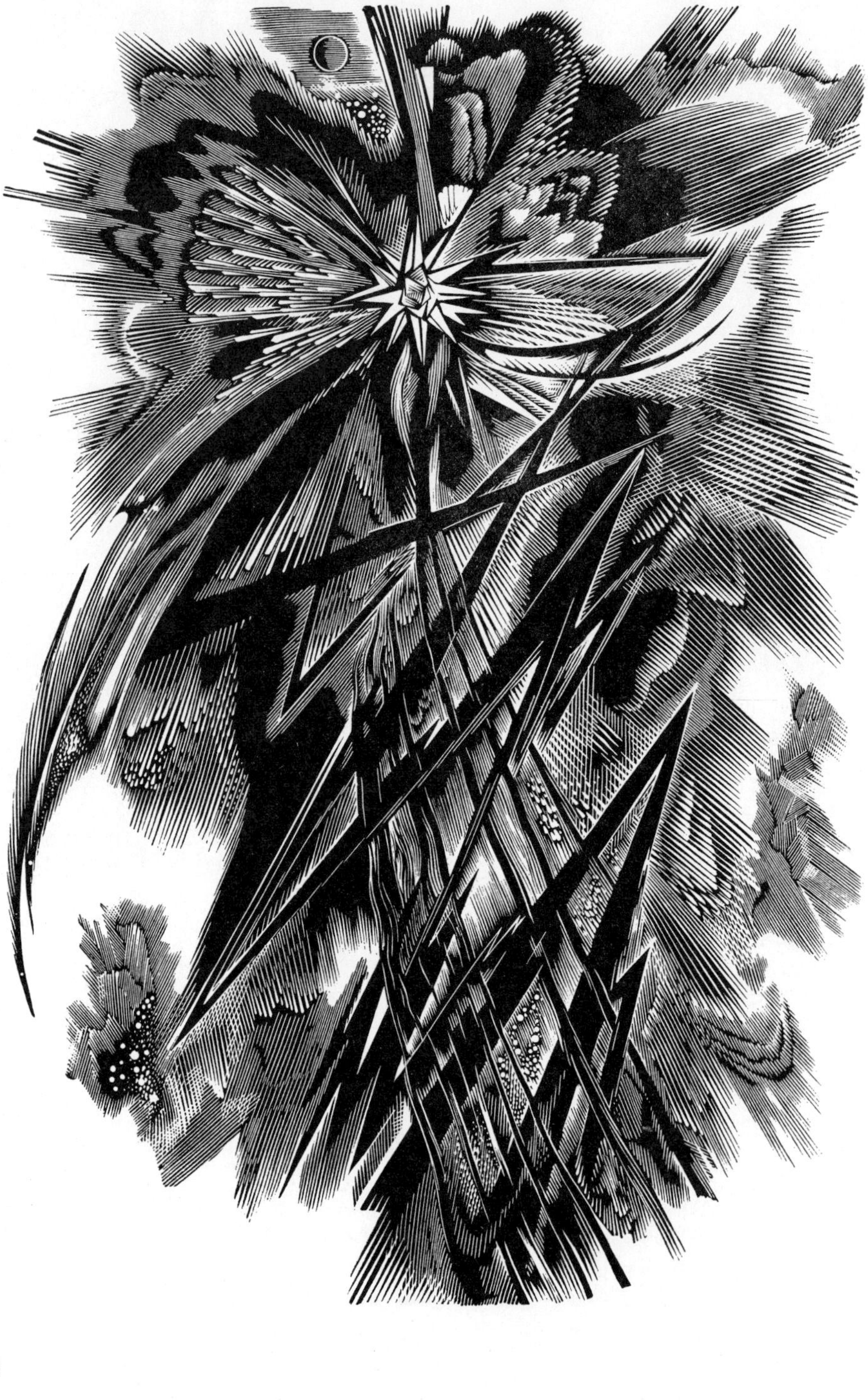

[285] Jozef Sekalski: *Starburst*, 1953.
11.75 x 17.6cm

His domestic situation demanded that John Buckland-Wright maintained an intensity of production. He not only had to live but had to provide for a family, and, in consequence, was forced to accept virtually every commission that came his way. He always worked very hard indeed but seldom had money to spare. Moreover, payment for book illustrations has alway been very low in Britain and hardly worth the materials and creative effort involved.

Most of his work appeared in books published by the private presses. These volumes not only change hands for very high prices but remain in the possession of private collectors, thus depriving students of wood engraving and the art-loving public in general of normal access to the work. Similarly these engravings have no permanent exhibition.

As a student at Camberwell I remember the hot and protracted arguments that used to arise between John Buckland-Wright and Edward Ardizzone on their attitude to the work of the private presses. At that time Ardizzone would in no circumstances, and partly for political reasons, allow any of his production to go into a publication where the edition was limited. His work was for the people, and to be seen by the people. Accordingly he developed a style of illustration that could be satisfactorily reproduced in magazines and books using the technique of rotary printing on cheap paper. This attitude arose because Ardizzone was an illustrator and not an artist engraver.

Unlike Ardizzone, John Buckland-Wright was primarily an engraver and he naturally wanted to work as an engraver. In discussing the situation, he would make the important point that there was no way of knowing what a book could be like as finished product, even given sensitivity and superb craftsmanship in all

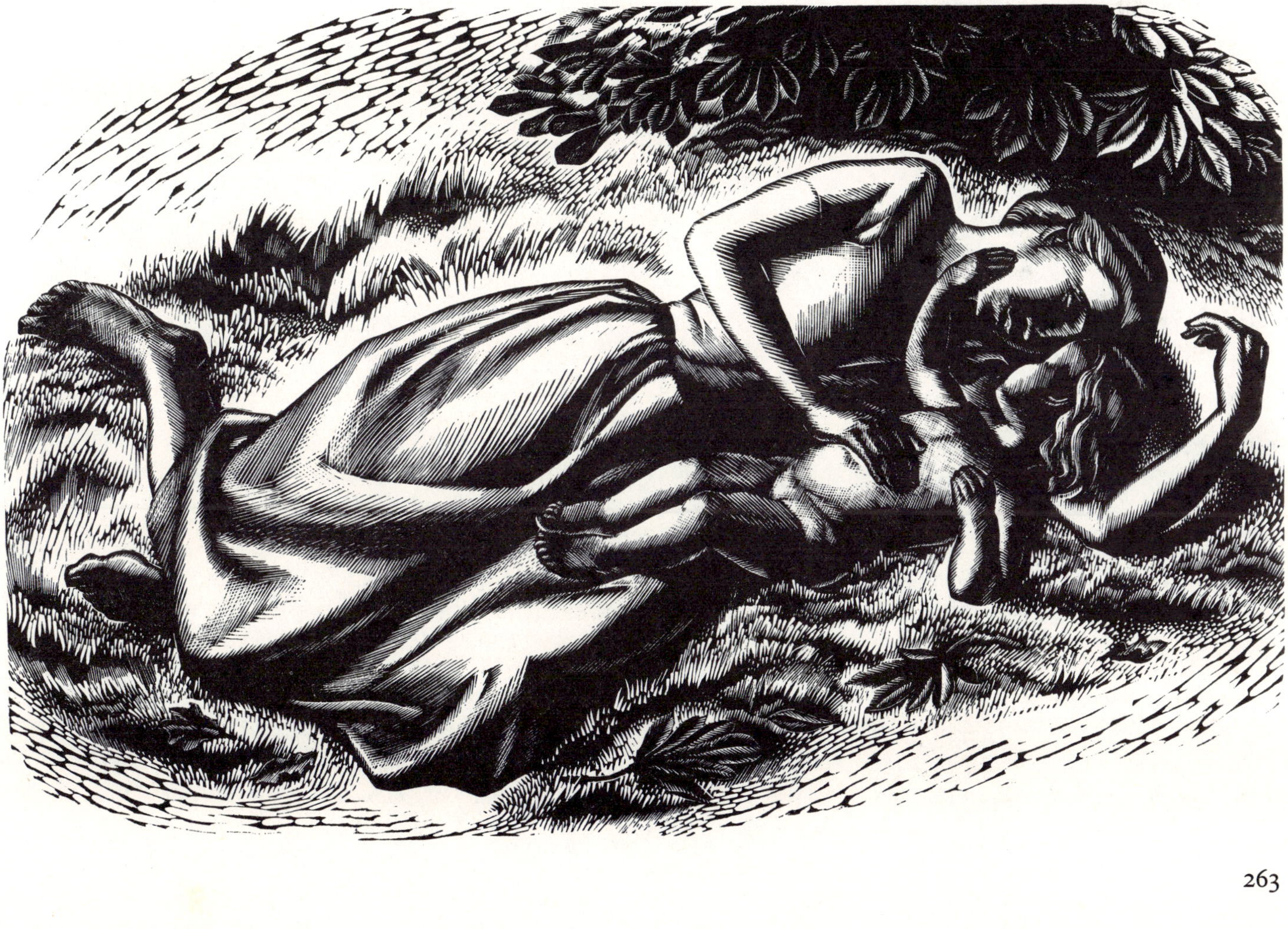

[286] Nora S. Unwin: *Warm Afternoon*, 1953. 19.5 x 12.75cm

[287] Nora S. Unwin: *Shadows in a Winter Wood*, 1953. 12.0 x 17.25cm

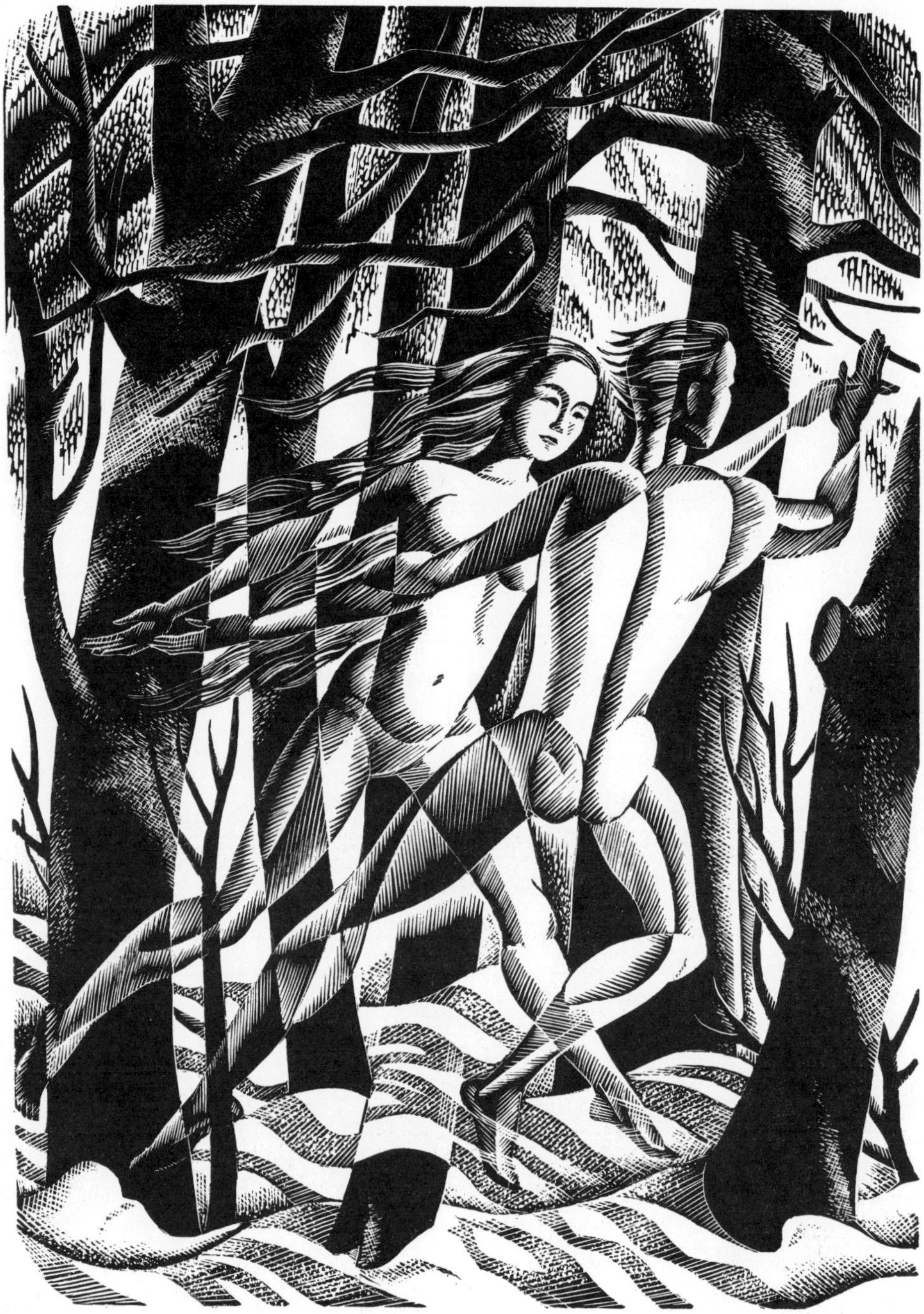

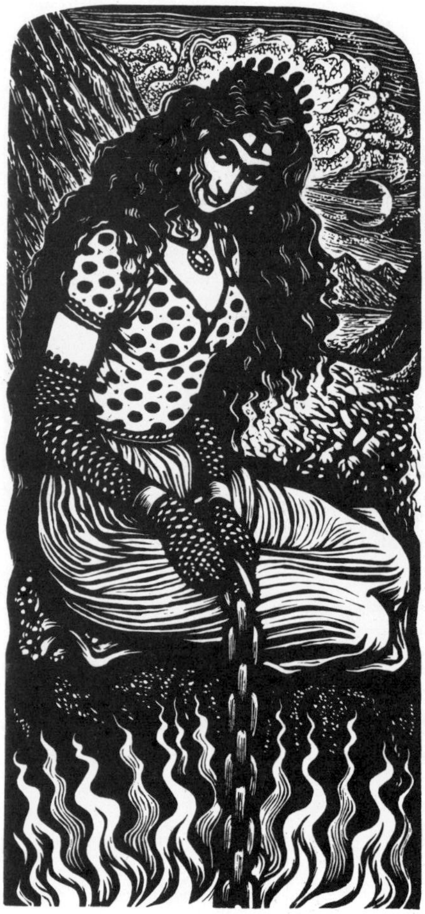

[288] John Petts: *Proserpina* from *Against Women*, 1953. 7.0 x 15.0cm

those engaged in production, and involving hand printing, the use of damped hand-made paper and hand binding. Further, though wood engraving is able to be reproduced on newsprint, copper engraving cannot and must be reproduced in a sensitive manner using the best quality paper. It was because he was a superb engraver on copper that Buckland-Wright took the opposite view to Ardizzone.

The presence of private presses with their particular qualities and concepts of production gave John Buckland-Wright his range of expression in wood engraving. Because his major contributions were made in the field of privately produced books, he has suffered an eclipse in the last decade, partly because he has been labelled an illustrator. In fact, he was, a very distinguished artist, most of whose work went into books. In engraving the influence of John Buckland-Wright will be alive for many generations to come.

Dr George Buday was born in Kolozsvir, Transylvania of Hungary in 1907 and has made a memorable contribution to the British school of wood engraving, bringing to it the European Expressionist art in an individual manner. Buday's style of expression is virtually the opposite to the archetypal Eric Gill. The technique of Eric Gill was, of course, erudite and puritanical; whereas Buday uses freely and eloquently both the white- and black-line principles, the bold juxtaposition of solid blacks against white, the cut and thrust of the very long against the very short line, including the use of the single burin contracted with the multiple tool.

Possibly Buday's most original contribution to the art of engraving arises from his persistent and technically amazing contrasts of the scale range within a single work, from areas almost savagely engraved in large, sharp and deep strokes driven home like a rapier to an acute degree of sensitivity. His art is charged with energy and in a good Buday engraving all forces are equated. His is an emotionally orientated art from which Expressionism arises. To select engraving as the vehicle of Expressionism is to present the ultimate contrast, accepted by the performer of the most strictured tightrope walk.

As a boy of thirteen Buday began to study painting as an apprentice in the

[289] George Mackley: *Fenland River*, 1954. 20.3 x 15.0cm

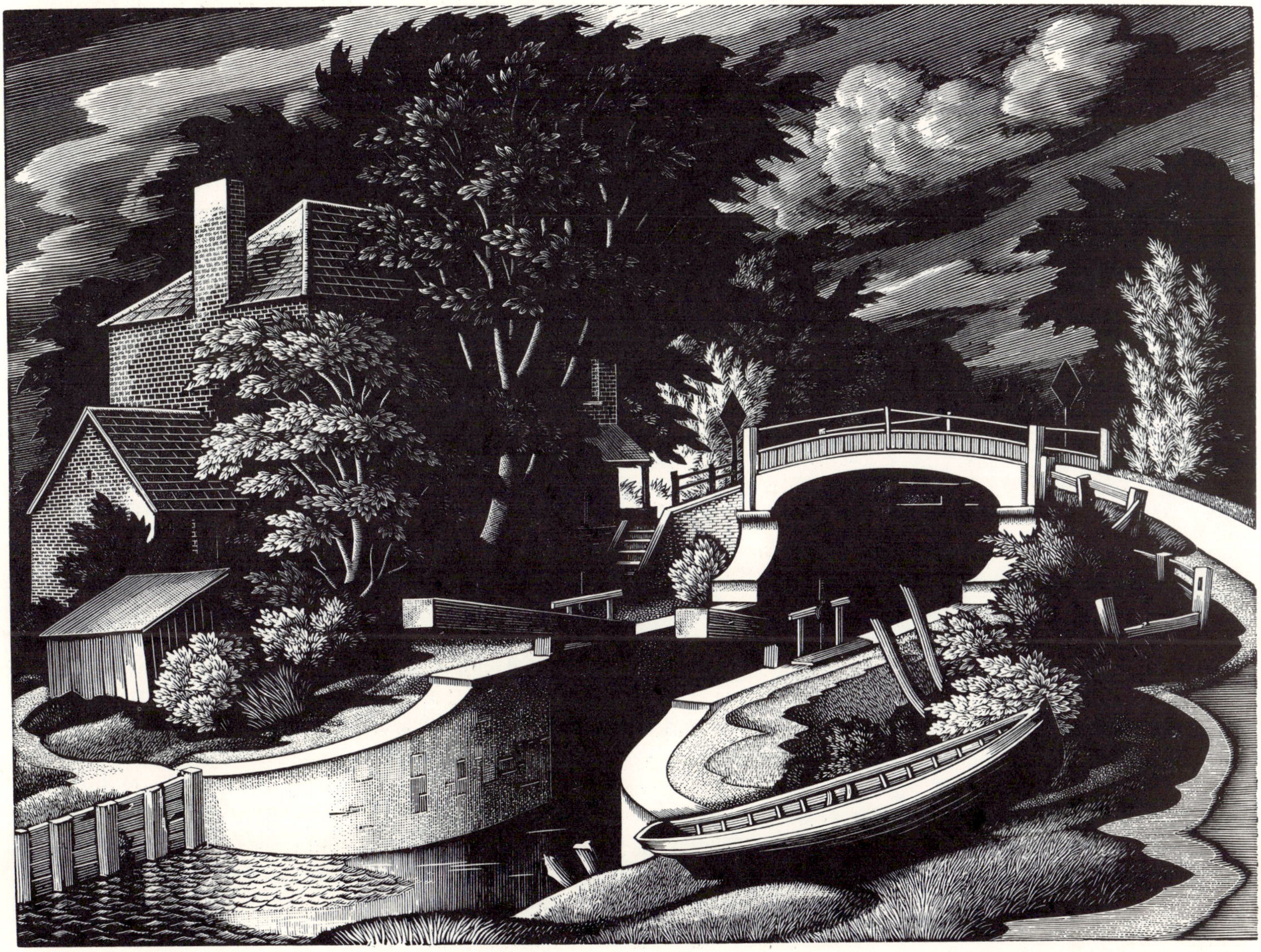

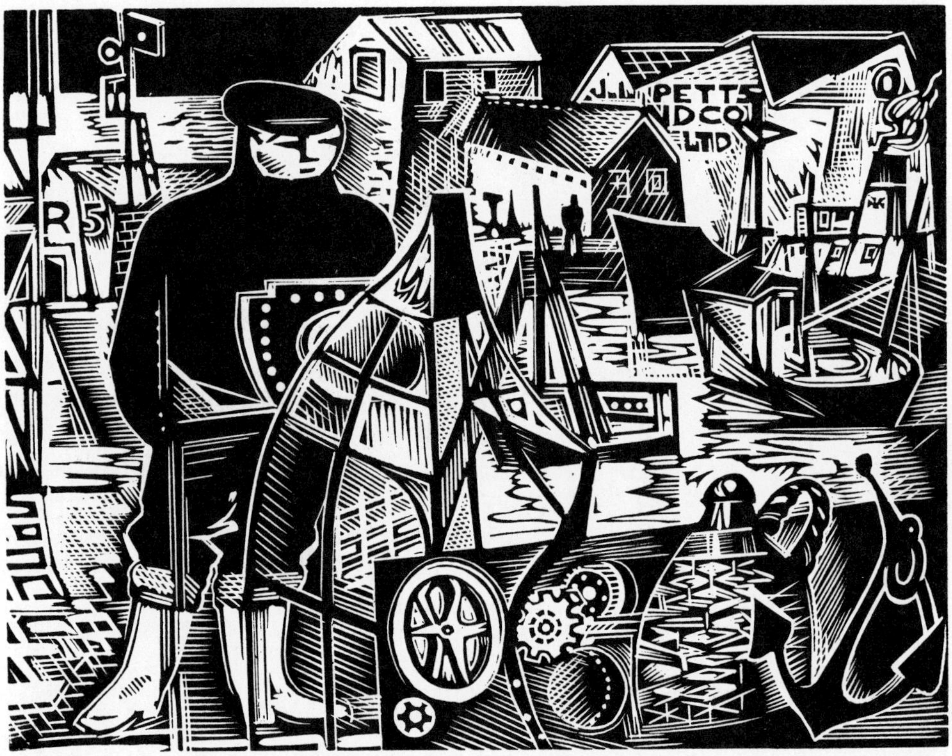

[290] Geoffrey Wales: *Man on the Quay*, 1955. 14.0 x 11.0cm

studios of Louis Meczner and G. Daday where, as he writes: 'While cleaning brushes and varnishing canvases and similar apprentice work, I learnt much of the principles and language of the art of the period in the 1920s. In their studios I first came across numbers of the *Blaue Reiter* with reproductions of the works of Kandinsky and the others.'[2] No doubt at that time he was not able to anticipate the *Blaue Reiter* artists moving into the Bauhaus and the development of pure abstraction, but he did have the advantage of finding himself as an Expressionist very early in his art career. The *Blaue Reiter* group and the Bauhaus was to have an effect upon English artists at least fifteen to twenty years later.

Buday was taught black and white art by Cavalier Albert Manz who was also his first private teacher in English. At his first one man show in 1924 at the age of seventeen years, Buday began to indicate his strength in the field of black and white art. He had no specific teacher in wood engraving and his introduction to the art was through working with the apprentices at the museum in Szeged where his father was Professor of Roman Archaeology and later a Director. He also studied art at the Kolozsvar Presbyterian College under the watercolourist Steven Deak. Of this period Buday said, 'I'd fallen in love with wood engraving for the rest of my life and felt proud of the fact that Albrecht Dürer's father was also born in Hungary.' Buday turned to wood engraving on becoming acquainted with the early works of the young engravers of the British school of wood engraving. His first visit to Britain was in the winter of 1928/9.

While in Britain he visited the very important Dutch exhibitions. The other decisive influence was seeing British graphic art in its context. Previously the only examples he had seen in Hungary came from magazines like *Studio*.

The landscape of his early youth has had a lasting influence on Buday's work. He spent days of lonely wanderings in the mountains and forests, the green fields and villages of the lovely countryside of Transylvania and continued his excursions into the great plains of the Hungarian *pusztas*. Buday was a great walker and explored the fine mountains of Austria. Many of these rambles were sketching expeditions which brought him into contact with the country folk, mostly peasants, their social conditions, their work and their poetry and art.

His Hungarian engraving consists of Transylvanian landscapes, buildings and still life. In Hungary proper his landscapes suddenly became richly populated. It was there that he illustrated representative collections of ancient Transylvanian (and other) folk-ballads and folk tales, besides some contemporary writers, some classics, and records of the collective feelings and acts of the people. The wood engravings of his 'Hungarian period' are now appreciated as a part of the deeply-rooted romantic Hungarian visual tradition, as are the compositions of Bartók and Kodály in music.

In 1970 Buday collaborated with Gynla Ortutay the distinguished Hungarian folklorist who edited *Acta Ethnographica* Volume 19 published by the Academial Scientiarum Hungaricae and containing Hungarian and Szekler folk-ballads and folk tales. Buday also did the wood engravings for this work and he commented 'I thought the best way I could contribute to the celebration of my old friend was to make an engraving illustrating a traditional story preserved by the peoples of the British Isles. Going through all that I have learnt during my thirty years' stay in London of the ancient English and Scottish ballads, Welsh and Irish folk tales and legends, I came to the conclusion that the most suitable subject for this occasion

[291] Cecil Keeling: *Illustration from Eastrozzi*, 1955. 10.5 x 14.0cm

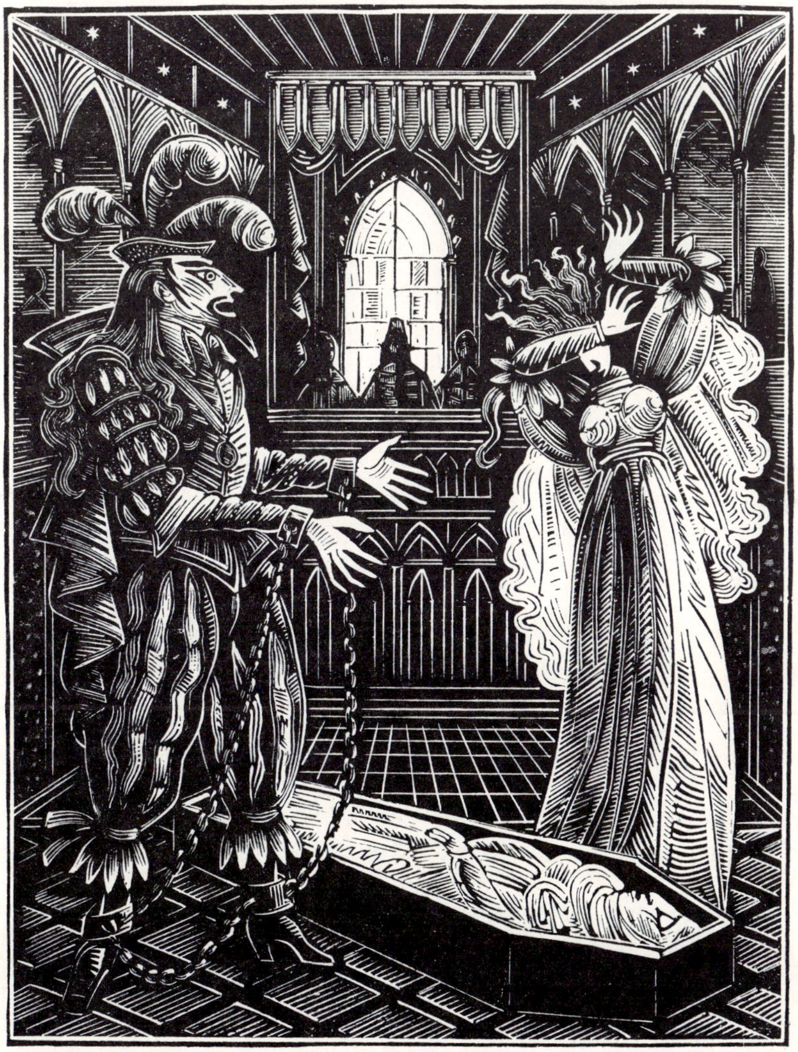

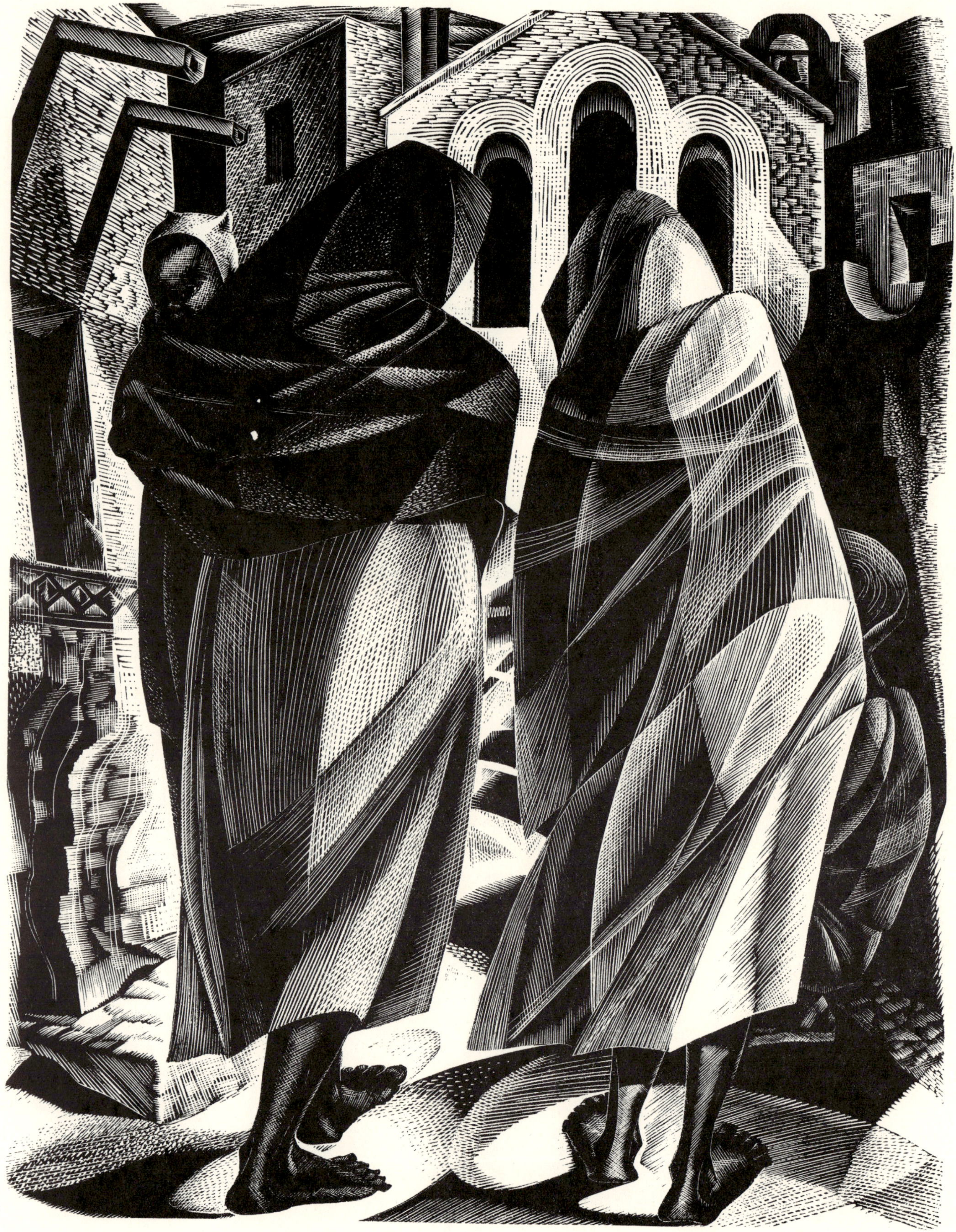

[292] Nora S. Unwin: *Mexican Women*, 1956. 17.75 x 22.5cm

[293] Donald Plenderleith: *Reclining Cat*, 1956. 23.0 x 15.5cm

was *Oisin I Dtir na N-og*, an Irish Fenian Saga, The title brought up to date means *Oisin in the land of the ever young*.'

In 1936/7 Buday applied for a travelling scholarship to Britain but was awarded the Rome scholarship instead. He now has no regrets on the way things worked out for him and, in any case, it has always been an honour and distinction to be selected as a Rome Scholar, an annual award usually made to an architect, painter, engraver and sculptor from each nominated country. The students selected are based at the School of Rome where they can both work and travel. Although Buday had made two previous visits to Italy, the longer stay, which included excursions to other parts of Italy, had a decisive influence on his creative work and, unknown to him at the time, was to prepare the way for his masterpiece *Timon of Athens* engraved in 1940 [243].

Buday arrived in Rome with no preconceived plan and but a half-hearted wish to go there, which may have been the reason why he was so receptive to the subtle, yet powerful, influence of a city where one not only studies art, but also lives and breathes art. Before he went to Rome the emphasis of his work had been on national motives, ways and means; but once there, he experienced the simple reality of the classic attitude and manifestation of the human spirit, the emotion it aroused in him dwarfing his earlier enthusiasm for the particular. Of course, he had known of classicism on previous visits to Italy and had given it some little attention, but it was not until he lived in the country that he became deeply involved. He became a devotee of the classical in the sense of appreciation of it; not the restricted Greek-

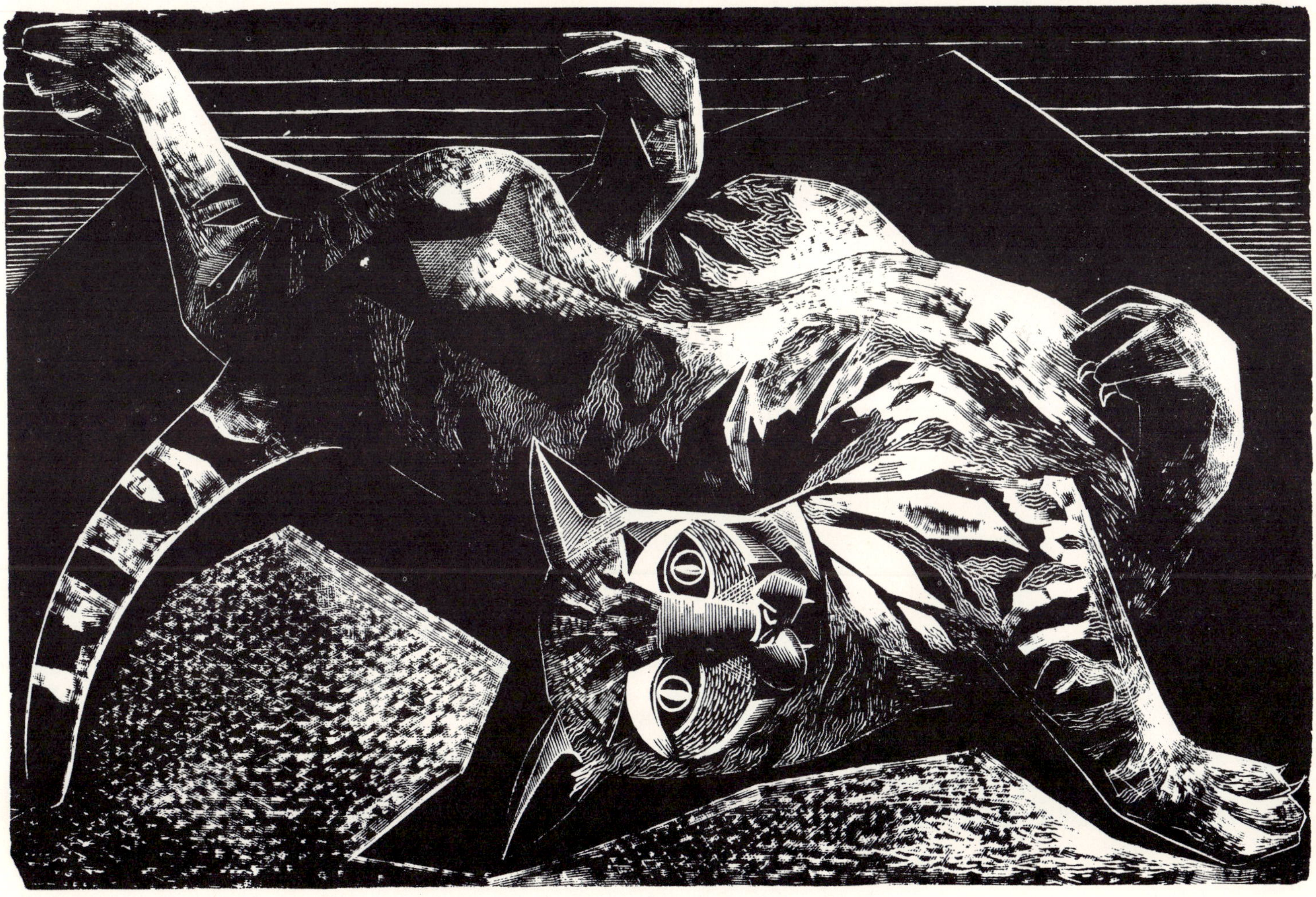

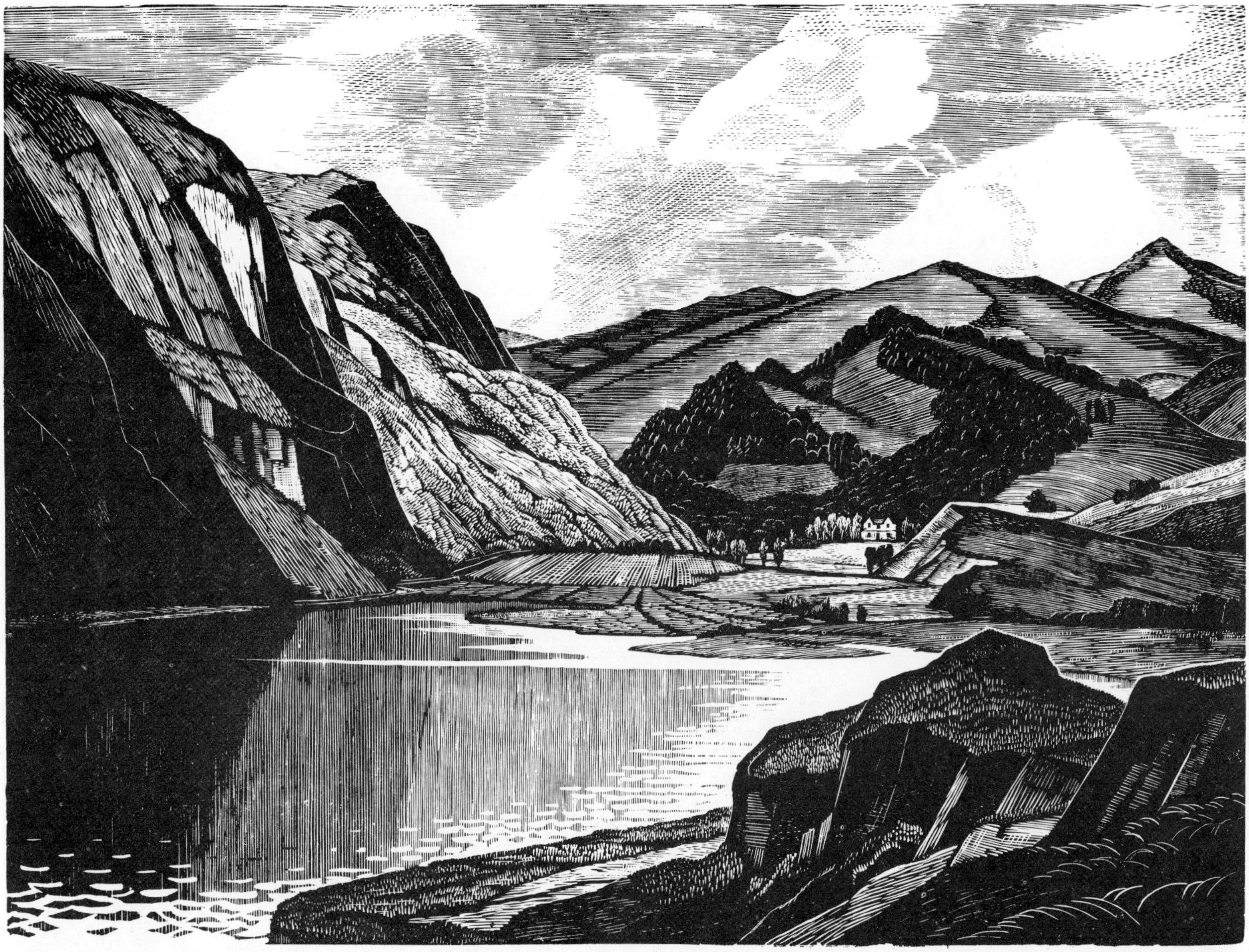

[294] Norman Janes: *Llyn Dinas*, 1956. 30.5 x 23.0cm

Roman usage, nor the 'Latinity' alone, but in its wide sense as a visual philosophy. While he was in Rome he made fifty-five wood engravings for François Mauriac's *Life of Jesus* as well as other works.

On the completion of his Rome scholarship in 1937 George Buday came to live in Britain. In the following year he was elected an associate of the Royal Society of Painter-Etchers and Engravers. The two years in Rome had greatly expanded his thematic and formal characters and of these two years he said: 'These couple of years "qualified" me not only in the eyes of members of the Council who awarded the Rome scholarship, but in a deeper and personal sense, to come to England next. The first months in London I spent in the Prints and Drawings Department of the British Museum, where besides the innumerable treasures I diligently went through all the etchings, engravings etc. of the British school. It was a great experience and I still have many of the paper slips on which I recorded my reactions to the work of the various artists, some of whose work I was seeing for the first time. But where I think the British school inspired me most was the – until recently quite unconscious – emphasis on portraiture in my output during recent decades. It is true that British portraitists were mostly painters and not really engravers, but it must be more than a coincidence that I developed new possibilities in the usage of images when in the land of some of the greatest portraitists of art history.'

George Macy, Director of the Limited Editions Club in New York, commissioned Buday to provide illustrations for the volume of Shakespeare's *Timon of Athens.* The complete set ran to thirty-seven volumes and as such was a great challenge to to any engraver. In this work Buday has made a major contribution to the British school, even though the work was an American publication. Of this project Buday says, 'It seemed to be a sudden inspiration to illustrate the tragedy with a sequence of imagined portraits of the principal character Timon, showing him as the original, rather jovial, idealistic patrician turned into an anti-social, disillusioned and bitter man-hater as the Bard created him. . . . As far as I know this was the first time a story was illustrated not by depicting episodes but simply by a number of portraits of the hero of it.'

In December 1939 George Macy wrote to Buday: 'I have carefully gone over the new engravings . . . I congratulate you upon them, I feel that you have made your whole idea explicit. From the jovial Timon of the first act, all the way to the engravings for the last act, with the calm serenity of Timon in death behind his mask, the story of your engravings becomes both interesting and well told. I think now that you have made a wonderful series of blocks, possibly the best in our whole Shakespeare . . . I even congratulate myself upon having told you to go ahead with this idea after you outlined it for me.'

John Buckland-Wright reproduced *Timon* IX in his book *Etching and Engraving*[3] and it was he who first introduced this profound work to students at the Camberwell School. He told us about the total work but we could not see it as the book was so expensive only the wealthy could afford to buy it. Without seeing it we were unable to comprehend or appreciate the scale of conception. It is especially pleasing to be able to reproduce five of the portraits from *Timon of Athens* in this book and their appearance raises the pertinent question of whether the complete set of nine engravings, together with large numbers of other masterpieces, will ever be seen on the walls of a public gallery.

Buday expresses a complete range of engraving emotions in this visual drama; it embodies the unquestioning spontaneity of the Palaeolithic artist but sets it in a very sophisticated twentieth-century classical structure. Buday's engravings are clear-cut examples of autonomous works of art which are entirely free from the *clichés* of illustration as applied to book design. He is an artist who brings tradition forward and adds to it, in the manner of the Chinese philosophy. Although stylistically Buday's engraving is quite different from that of David Jones, they both research deeply into the past. The academic life of these two artists is as important as is their aesthetic performance and production. The British school of wood engraving which initially attracted Buday to live in this country, can now justly claim him as one of its masters.

REFERENCES

1 Macnab, I. *The Student's Book of Wood Engraving*, Pitman, London, 1938
2 Kandinsky & Marc (eds) *Der Blaue Reiter*, Munich, 1912
3 Buckland-Wright, J. *Etching and Engraving*, Studio Publications, London, 1953

9 THE WAVE BREAKS

After the Second World War, the wood engravers found that they had lost the support of publishers and new commissions were not forthcoming. The change in the economic situation gave a slowly increasing opportunity for expansion in commercial book production but offered no incentive to the book that could be produced privately as a work of art. Publishers declared that public taste had changed and there seems to be some truth in this. The general public showed little interest in the private press books, and many owners of large private libraries were disinclined to give financial support to limited editions of works in which the wood engraver might have had an outlet for his talent.

Despite the publishers' claims that they could no longer afford to market the *de luxe* volume produced as a work of art, there was no shortage of engravers of quality, nor did the lack of opportunity of publication daunt the younger generation from developing its abilities.

Margaret Pilkington (1891 to 1974) reformed the Society of Wood Engravers and it held its first post-war exhibition in 1949 at Heal's Gallery. She had been invited to membership of the Society in 1922 and her engravings were hung in the first exhibition of 1920. She trained at the Slade, studied wood engraving with Lucien Pissarro and then with Noel Rooke at the Central School. In 1924 she became the Secretary of the Society and in 1952 was elected its Chairman until she retired in 1967. Margaret Pilkington was a very active personality and played a major role in the forming of the Red Rose Guild of Craftsmen in Manchester, of which she was a founder member. Later in 1925 she became a Governor of the Whitworth Art Gallery, Manchester, and here she built up a collection of the Society's prints. Another collection of the Society's prints up to the Second World War has been formed at the Portsmouth Art Gallery. These public collections supplement the larger collections of wood engravings at the British Museum, Victoria and Albert Museum and the Ashmolean Museum at Oxford.

As an engraver Margaret Pilkington had a calm and relaxed personality. In engraving she had the ability to release tension and her burin flowed rhythmically. Most of her prints are landscape and her approach to engraving is akin to the simplicity of Gwendolen Raverat. Margaret Pilkington's style is linear in emphasis, her lines are dominantly parallel and a little coarse in texture, which gave her prints their distinctive crisp quality. Her intellectual integrity as an engraver and her consistent objective values follow from her training with Lucien Pissarro. However, she did not take to Lucien's black-line engraving but went solidly over into the white-line school. She was a severe critic of engraving values and was apprehensive of formal experiment beyond visual reality.

[295] Clifford Webb: *The Alarm.*
14.0 x 12.0cm

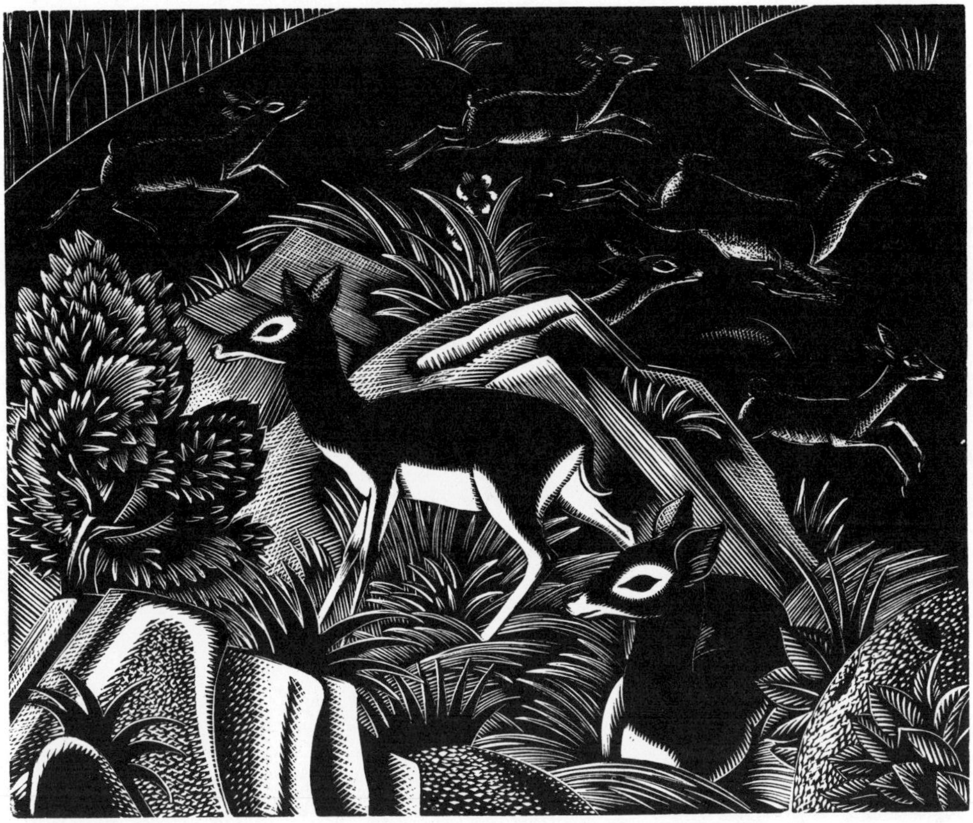

Reynolds Stone, a remarkable engraver and designer, carried out a memorable experiment in 1968 when he produced illustrations in wood engraving interpreting the drawings by John Piper and executed in line, wash and watercolour for the book *The Mountain* by the Reverend R. S. Thomas [321]. The book was a private press production by the Chilmark Press, New York and fine results were achieved. Reynolds Stone spent some time in North Wales with John Piper and the result is a very sensitive engraving dialogue between Piper and Stone. This must be one of a very few books of this century where a creative white-line engraver has interpreted the work of another artist. Evidently Piper considered *The Mountain* a worthwhile venture and no protests have been heard that his individuality was ravaged at the hands and burin of the engraver.

In terms of wood engraving, Stone is very close in technique to Thomas Bewick. Stone is a master designer in the heraldic field and in the combining of lettering with pictorial matter. He has many government and official commissions to his credit, including bank notes. When these two qualities are combined in the same person with the necessary technical skill, then creativity and authority can live together. His production of illustrations for books is enormous; his work has appeared in more than a hundred. His major production has been for the commercial press though he has engraved for some private press books. He engraves deeply enough for everything in the block to be reproduced adequately on the type of paper normally used in commerce.

Not all artists engrave very deeply. Christopher Sandford writing in his book *Cockalorum* stated: 'I have included the two engravings by David Jones only because I have a passionate admiration for the conceptions of this great artist. Owing to his shallow engraving of the wood, these blocks are virtually unprintable. Artists please mark my words – when engraving for publishers, scrap your thinnest

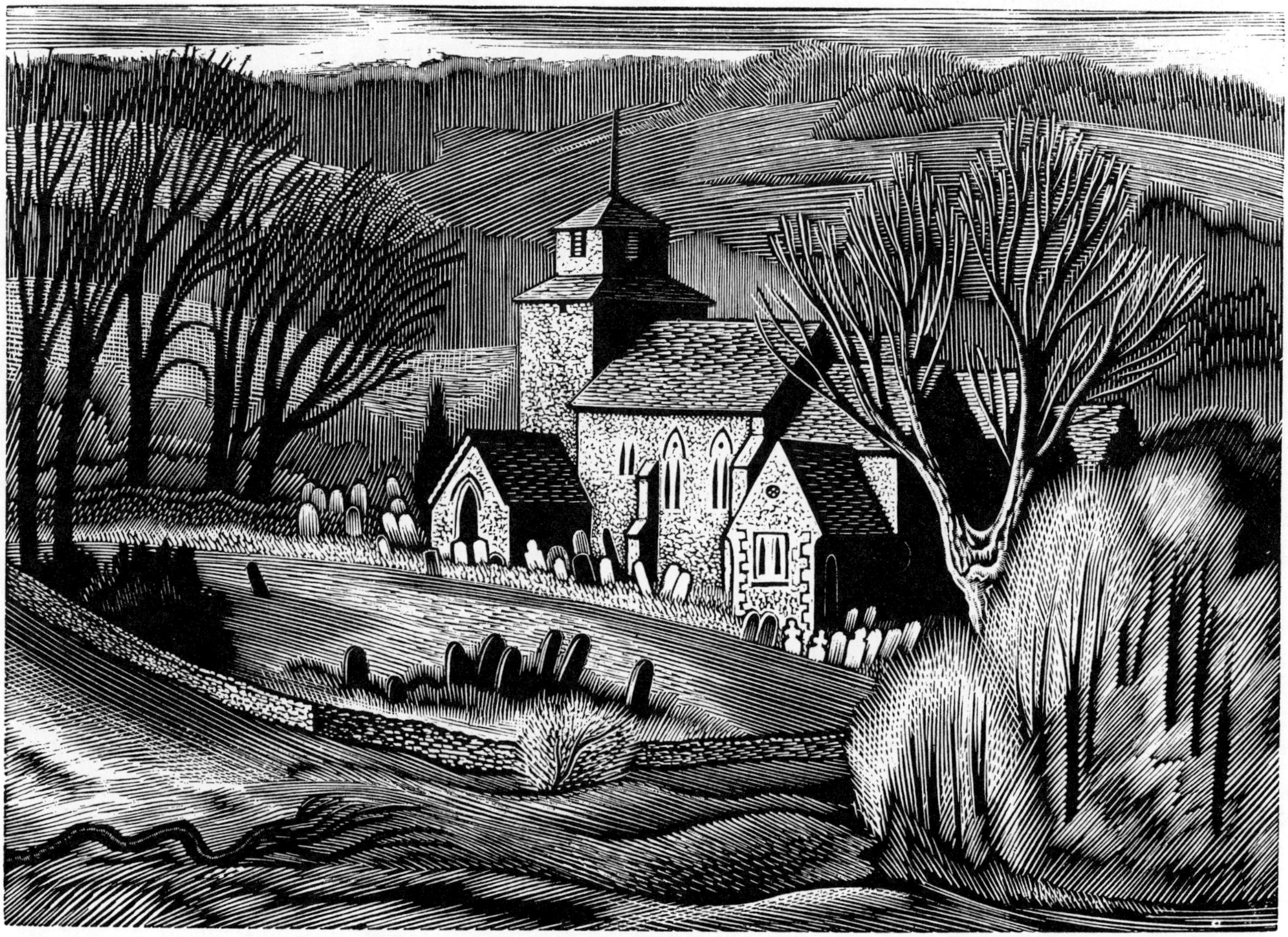

[296] Clifford Webb: *Wootton Church*. 17.5 x 12.75cm

tools and cut deep.' He might also have said this of the work of Blair Hughes-Stanton and Agnes Miller Parker; John Buckland-Wright's blocks were also finely engraved. Sandford's understandable plea makes a sharp point: that we can only have art of this sensitivity in books produced in limited editions by the private presses.

The art of David Jones (1895 to 1974) is that of the pure poet who fuses all images and symbols in an environment in which they alone can live. As a writer he is equally independent and unclassifiable. His book *In Parenthesis*, published by Faber in 1937, was awarded the Hawthornden Prize in 1938. The work distils a most intense personal experience arising from the stress of modern war. He gives expression to the emotions of fear, nostalgic tenderness, religious sacrifice and the polarities of physical and spiritual reality. James Agate wrote in the *Daily Express*: 'David Jones handles action as Virginia Woolf handles stillness . . . The book is written as Picasso paints, and if literary models must be sought for, one would suggest Malory rewritten by Joyce, but whatever the model, I say that David Jones is a magnificent writer, and that this book is the best fresco of the war conceived in terms of pure art. . . . This book will last because its painter author has used words like paint.'

The other piece of major writing by David Jones is *The Anathemata: Fragments of an Attempted Writing* published by Faber in 1952. In this work he provides a key to the understanding of man and his work. As author of this book he was awarded the Russell Loines Award for Poetry from the National Institute of Arts

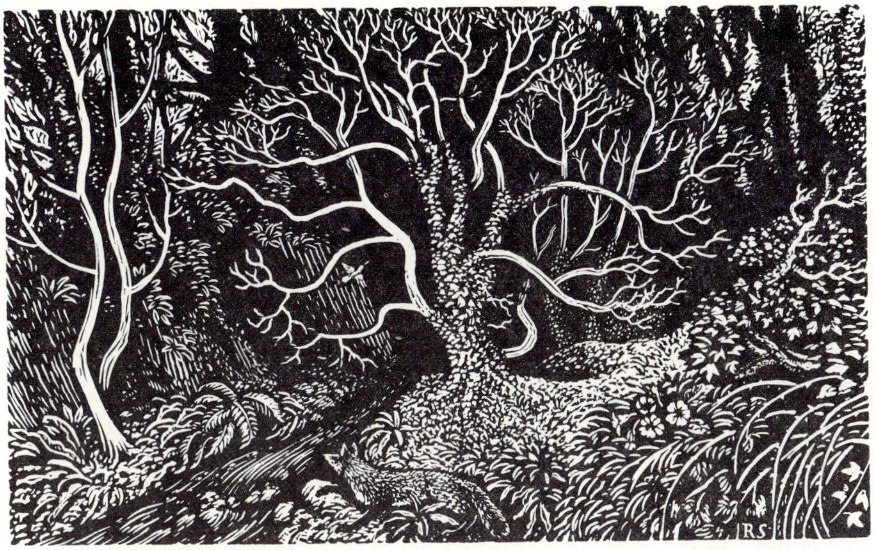

[297] Reynolds Stone: *The Fox.* 11.5 x 7.0cm

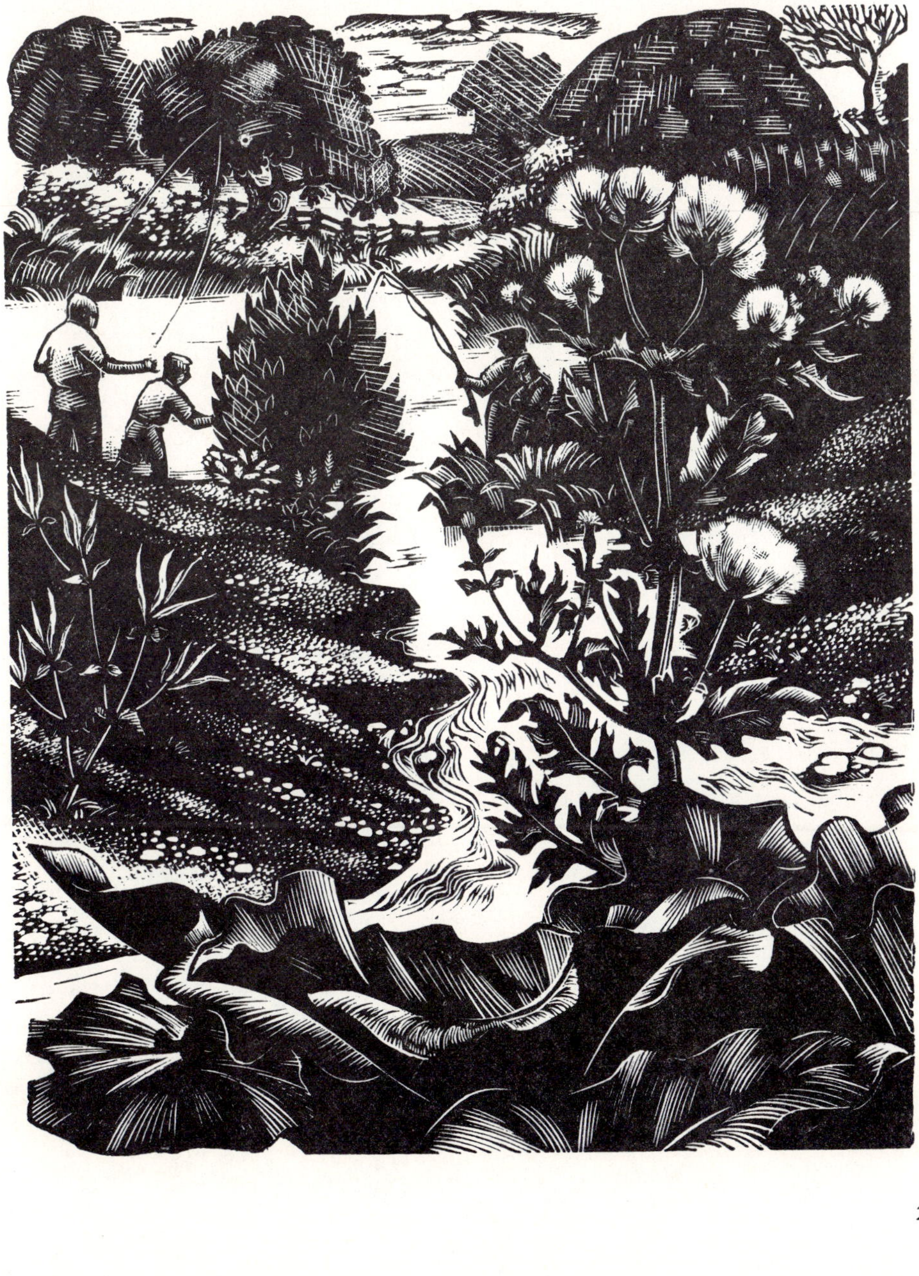

[298] John R. Biggs: *Fishing at Rickmansworth.* 12.0 x 15.0cm

and Letters, USA. He is the first European to receive the award since its inception. *Anathemata* presents the reader with an almost endless sequence of poetic and prose images, spanning man's history and achievement, moulding the past with the present, giving simultaneity to the expression of time. On reading the *Anathemata* I was reminded of the kinetic sequences of images in Dylan Thomas's *Under Milk Wood.* Jones expresses the simultaneity of time in his wood and copper engraving compositions, but his time spectrum has a wider span than that of Dylan Thomas. In this respect Jones the writer and Jones the engraver are one. However, Sandford's plea for deeper engraving had no effect upon Jones and, like other engravers, he was intent on exploiting the subtlety of engraving still further. Extreme sensitivity in wood engraving had to be fully exploited if for no other reason than to find out just how sensitive a medium it really was. However, this sensitivity to engraving was by no means confined to Jones's generation and his influence is still alive and meaningful to some of the younger generation of wood engravers, and in particular to Richard Shirley Smith.

Shirley Smith was a pupil at Harrow School, and first met Jones there in about 1958. Their friendship extended over a long period.

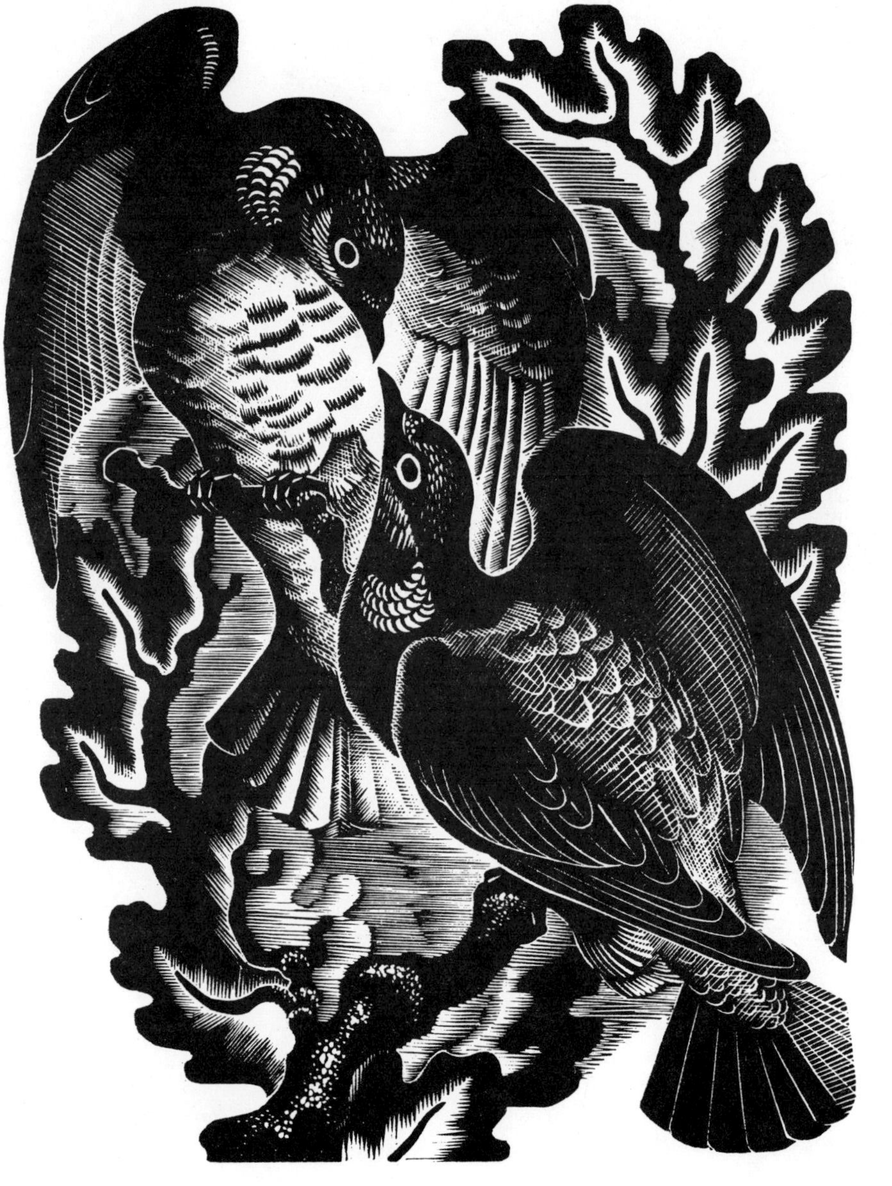

[299] Eileen Mayo: *Two Doves*, 1958. 11.5 x 15.5cm

[300] Zelma Blakely: Illustration from *El Larco the Bandit*, 1957. 8.2 x 14.4cm

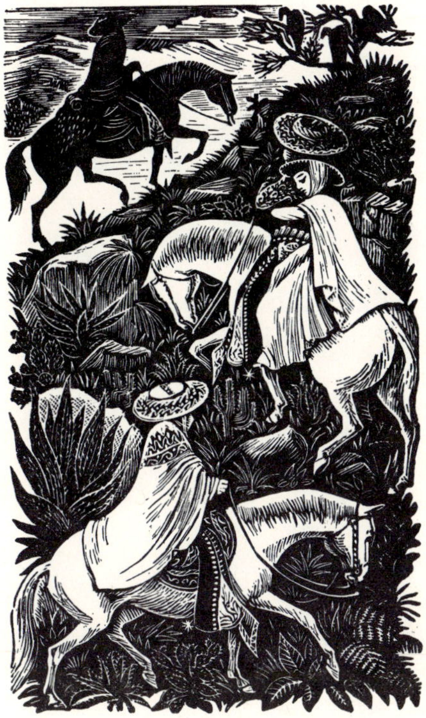

Jones lived at Northwick Lodge, a porticoed, grey brick Victorian mansion in Harrow, his room at the back overlooking London and the steep gardens and nearby trees which are to be seen in his works. During Jones's Harrow period little is known or was written about him. He was dogged by illness and went into almost complete retirement, albeit not a very comfortable one. In a letter to Shirley Smith in 1961 Jones wrote 'This house is like an ice-box because the fools won't light the furnace, in consequence of which I've no hot water except what I boil in kettles.'

Shirley Smith taught himself wood engraving in Rome during 1961. Jones not only sponsored him for the Slade School, but helped him with wood engraving by criticising his prints. Writing to his protégé in Rome in February 1961, he comments of Bewick's work 'Yes, in wood engravings in general, the most satisfactory kind are those where the blacks and the whites and the greys are so "organised" or managed as to give this unity. In one way old Bewick has never been surpassed in knowing how to get the best advantage out of the greys and whites very subtly set off against very small areas of solid black.' While Jones's wood engravings are very solid in the black, his greys are very evenly distributed. In some of his wood engravings, his greys skim through the composition as lightly as windswept cirrus clouds. They were equally lightly engraved, some lines little more than a scratch, and one can only sympathize with Sandford's plea for deeper engraving, at least for the fine productions of the Golden Cockerel Press books.

The influence of David Jones in Richard Shirley Smith's work can be seen in the content of his art rather than as a stylistic influence [340]. Both engravers are very English in content; Shirley Smith has visual poetry in common with Jones and like Jones he can distil the Englishness of English art. Literary values also have an important role to play in much the same measure as in Leon Underwood's school. In Shirley Smith's engraving *The Periodical* [330] the interplay of fantasy is counterpointed by wit, and the sharp, precise burin has engraved the realist form of a lovely innocent young girl that gives the answer to Kenneth Clark's question of the difference between the nude and nakedness. He stated that the nude can be partially draped and still be a nude, and equally nakedness can be partially draped.[1] Clark is obviously dealing with judgement of a qualitative difference because the model can be the same one in each case. The situation here is not unlike that of the physical processes of vision common to every individual where the differences in quantitative stimulus received by the brain will result in a variation according to the psychological outlook of the individual. However, in *The Periodical* Shirley Smith has predetermined the issue because his highly-charged field surround, loaded with fantasy, leads the viewer to the unmistakable interpretation of nakedness, which is another way of saying that form without meaning can be cold. It is fortunate that Britain can still produce draughtsmen of such expressive power and subtlety.

Richard Shirley Smith has developed quickly. Already he has to his credit illustrations to Shelley's *Poems* selected by Stephen Spender and published by the Limited Editions Club of New York, containing forty-two wood engravings. These engravings create their own poetry; looking at them it is a simple matter to appreciate how the friendship grew between David Jones and the young engraver. Like Jones's, Shirley Smith's images grow in profusion and take flight in their content, both elements being fused by a remarkably precise burin.

As far as creative engraving is concerned the Victorian period had little creative engraving life to offer but demanded fabulous commercial engraving skills. Most

[301] Gwenda Morgan: Cover design for *Petworth Deanery Review*, 1960. 15.25 x 19.0cm

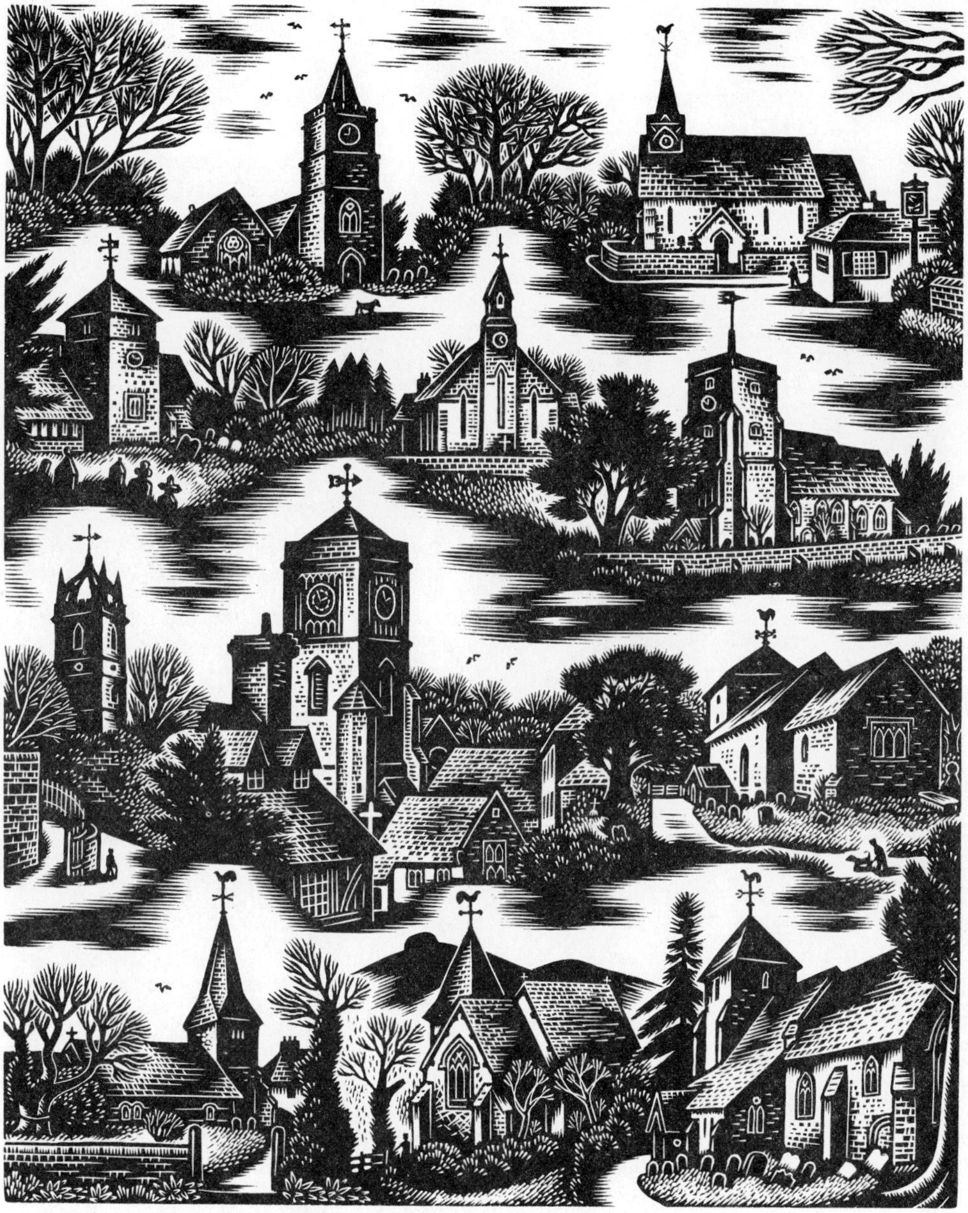

of the wood engravers in London at that time were those trained by Bewick, and they were relying very heavily upon the inspiration of the creative engraving of their master but lacked that spark of creative ability themselves. It is not surprising that these engravers reverted to the transitional black-line technique. As for the lady wood engravers of the period, there appears to be none on record. Kate Greenaway (1846 to 1901) the Victorian book illustrator became known in the latter part of the nineteenth century but it is not until the twentieth century that the first women artist engravers come on the scene.

By the end of the Second World War Hermes, Miller Parker, Hassall, Leighton and Raverat had arrived in wood engraving and Hepworth and Frink in sculpture. Men have been marvelling at women's performance in art ever since. In the history of engraving there is no precedent for such a talented group of females. It is strange that these women artists broke through and established themselves in the two most difficult disciplines of wood engraving and sculpture rather than in the easier field of painting.

[302] Gwenda Morgan: *The Seasons*, 1964. 13.5 x 10.0cm

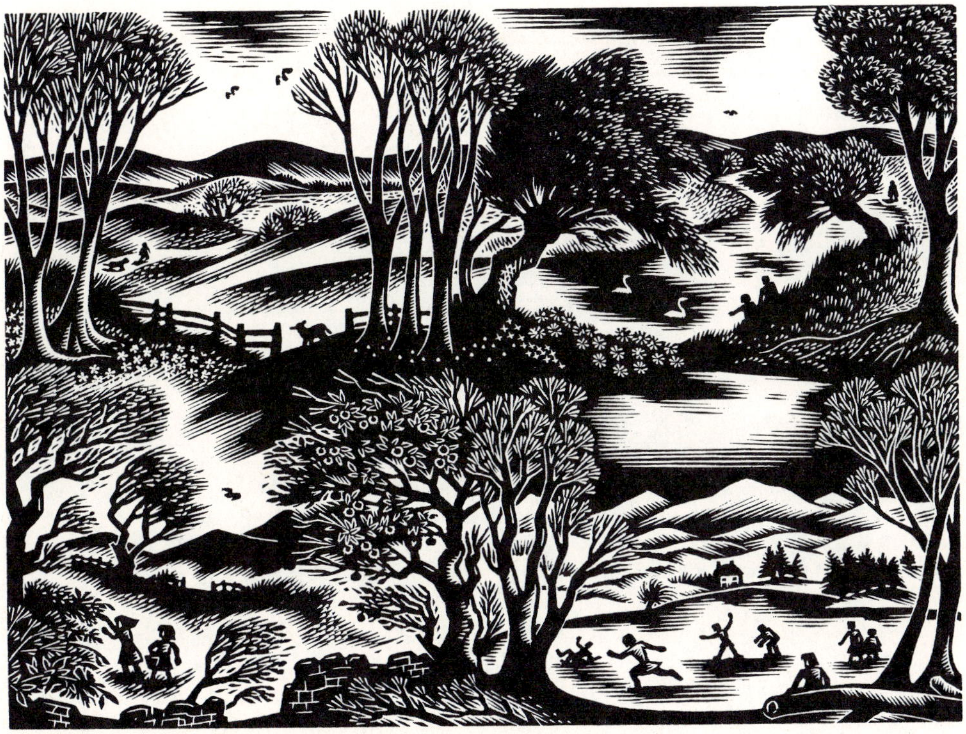

Gertrude Hermes was elected to the Royal Academy in 1963 and is also a sculptress. Joan Hassall is a book illustrator with a massive output to date of fifty books illustrated with wood engravings. Agnes Miller Parker is an engraving phenomenon who worked almost solely for private press productions.

Of the three women, Gertrude Hermes has made the most important creative contribution to the British school and has played a major role in the development of other relief media and also the colour print. She is an engraver who went into the lino cut and the woodcut as an experiment in softer material. She was born in 1901 in Kent of Anglo-German parents. She married the artist Blair Hughes-Stanton in 1926 and has two children. In 1921 she joined the Leon Underwood school where she came into contact with the new school of wood engraving. As an artist she often employed her children as models. During the Second World War she was in Canada doing war work.

Gertrude Hermes, more than any other women, has exploited the art of engraving. Hermes in engraving is what Hepworth is in sculpture. Of all the wood engravers of either sex, possibly Hermes alone has given full expression to Noel Rooke's original concept of a 'new designed engraving' and this has resulted in a lifetime of glorious production which has shown a state of continuous creative development over the years. She has exploited the concept of the engraved line as 'continually changing its shape throughout its length' and her language of engraving runs in close parallel to the four *Tripitaka* landscapes. This means that line and shape are not separate elements as is the case with the work of Ravilious.

Hermes has a masterly control of the dispensation of light, which is adequate to realise the form but no more. This measurement described as 'adequate but no more' is a very fine standard for an engraver such as Hermes. The work of Gill and Gibbings is dominated by this technique of freely cutting away wood to express light as a contained force – as can be seen in Mackley's *Rocks* [380] and *Coire Mhic Fhearchair* by Petts [379].

The engraving creativity of Hermes and her lyrically free line are more closely

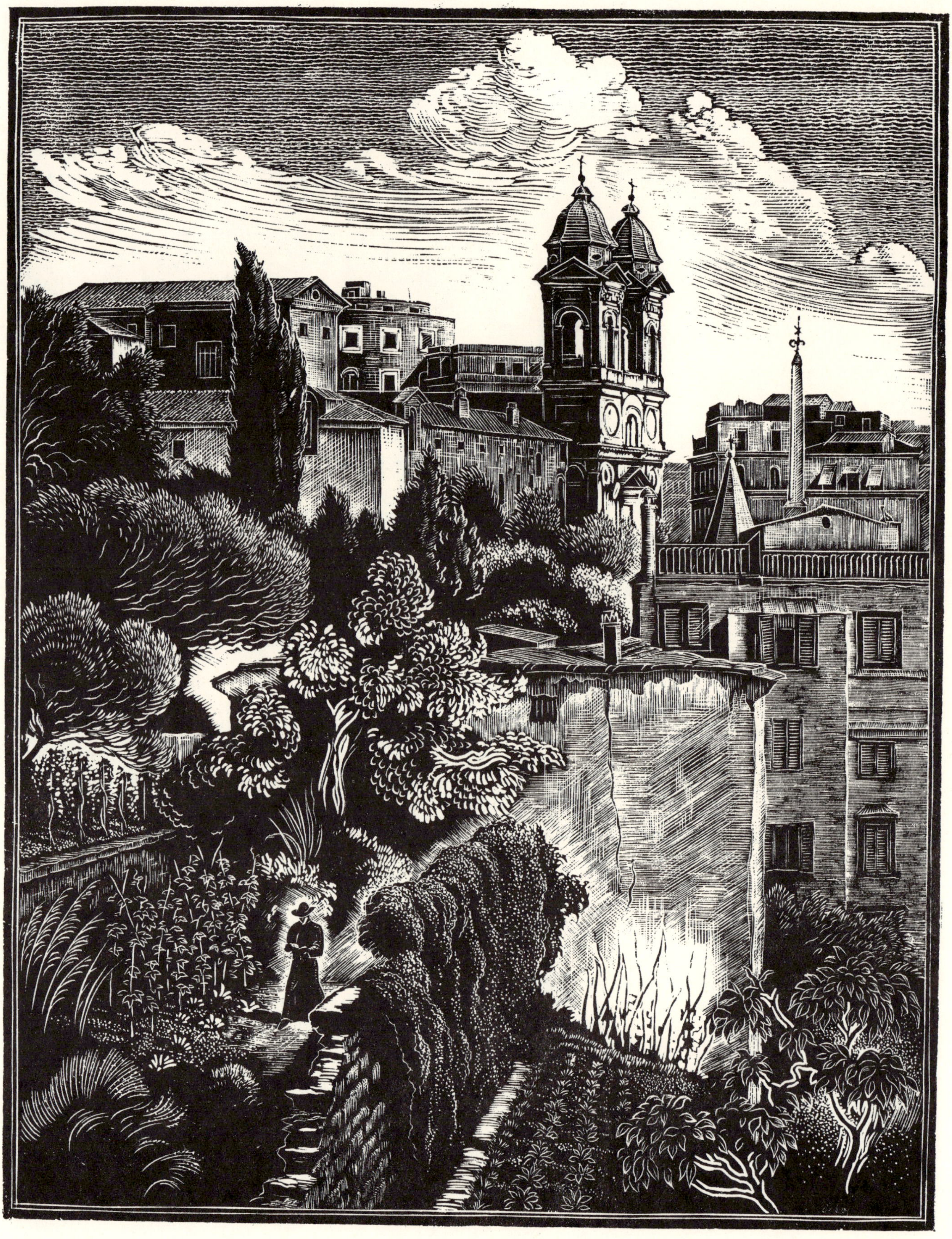

[303] William T. Rawlinson: *Trinita dei Monti*, 1960. 17.8 x 22.85cm

allied to Holbein than to Dürer. A Holbein engraving (black-line technique) fully demonstrates the sensitivity of the line continuously changing its shape throughout its length. To demonstrate this concept on a block demands a very high degree of creative thinking and sensitivity. Hermes finds the engraving equivalent to the part and then to the whole, so that a Hermes mushroom is an engraving construction which not only looks like a mushroom but is so personal that another engraver could not copy it. Gertrude Hermes is a much-loved teacher. Because she lives and breathes engraving, she can not only talk about it but can demonstrate the solutions. Recently I visited her at the Royal Academy Schools where she teaches engraving. Whilst instructing one of her students she was not telling him what strokes to make but advising in terms of the balance of light throughout the subject, thus leaving the student free to cut in the way that was his personal manner.

During the 1950s the work of Hermes developed into a much larger scale to include woodcuts and lino cuts. In 1953 she engraved her masterpiece *Stonehenge* [312] and, unfortunately, this was to be her last wood engraving. *Stonehenge* marked a departure from the restrictions of book illustration, and the development of her woodcuts and lino cuts gave a tremendous boost to the British colour print. Eventually, this development led to the mixed media printing upon which so much of the present print making is based.

In Hermes's engraving *Waterlilies* [177], she has solved in her own terms the language for engraving a large circular plane that has gentle undulations. For most

[304] David Gentleman: *Breton Farmyard*, 1960. 25.5 x 17.5cm

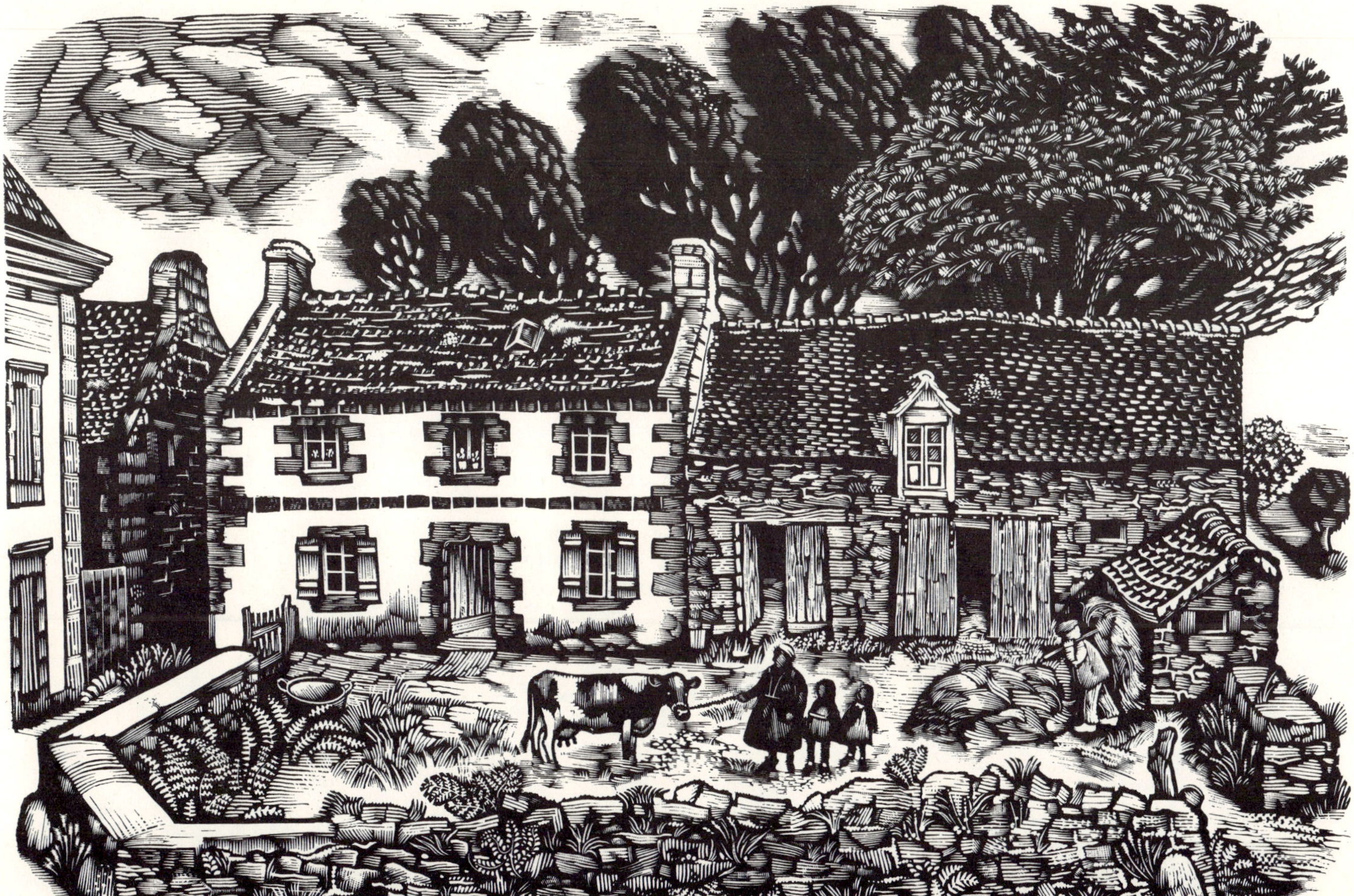

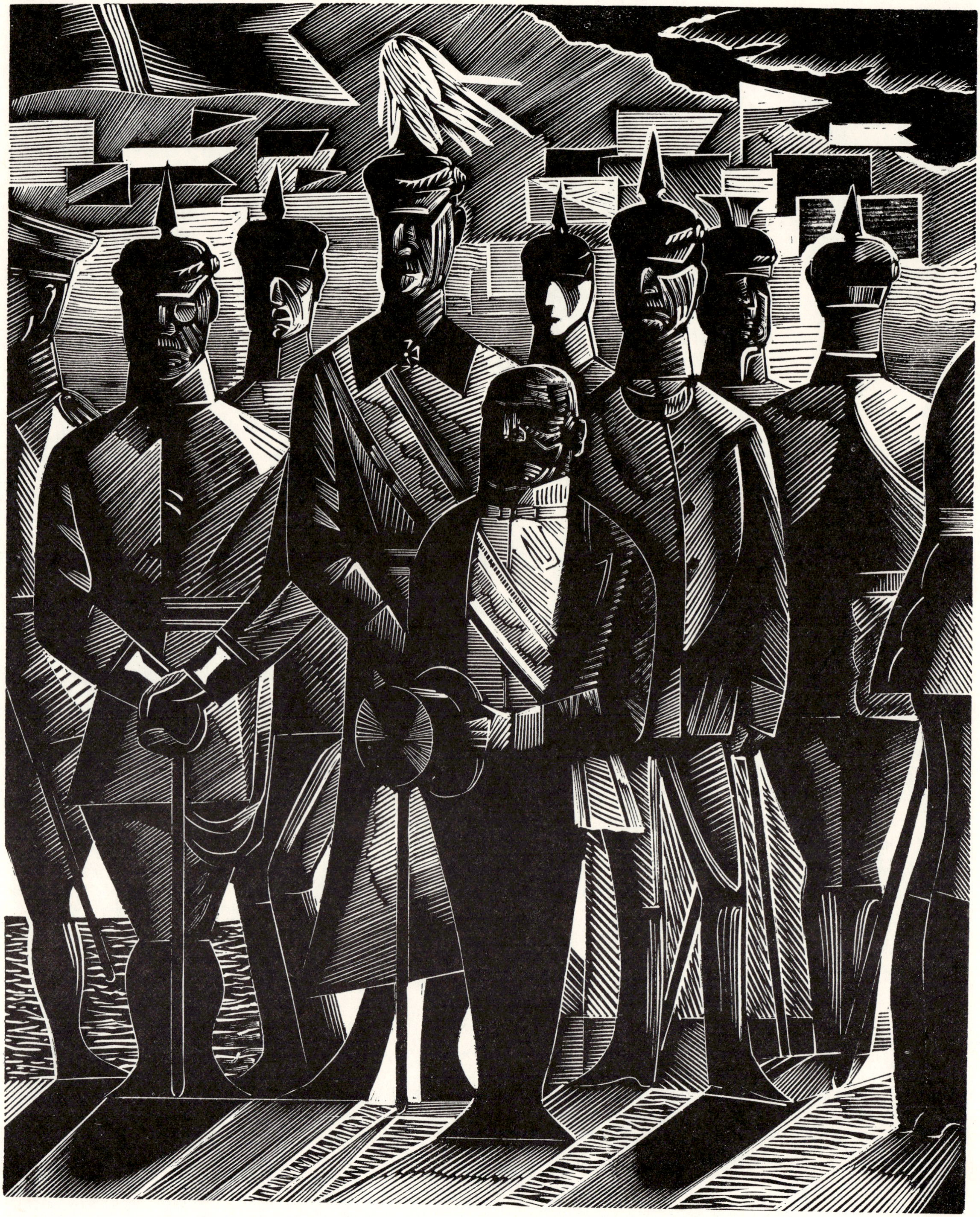

[305] Cecil Keeling: *Twilight of the Gods*, 1961. 20.5 x 25.5cm

people, a waterlily leaf is a solid plane but in this engraving Hermes sees it as a space plane solution. Similarly, the leaf as a space plane can be seen in her engraving *Undercurrents* [237] and is also present in the central form of her powerful *Fathomless Sounding* [190]. In the engraving *Waterlilies* the leaf acts as a tightly-wound spring (serving a similar function to the pin of a hand grenade). This is a whiplash potential which is released with a sudden force that can be anticipated in the long lines of sprung curvature seen in her later works *Undercurrents* and *Fathomless Sounding*.

Asked how far she was aware that the shape of the light beams entering the water in depth in *Undercurrents* was scientifically correct (because as the beam penetrates deeper, so there is a progressive loss of width arising from the cut-off of both short and long waves) Gertrude gave a knowing look, laughed, and said 'I felt it was right!' This was the reaction of a philosopher who had done more research than most and who had closely observed the behaviour of light in water and had worked out the reasons for such behaviour, thus discovering the engraving solution which permitted the block to be produced – yet had forgotten about the investigation. In fact, the solution to the form of space-solids first shows itself in her earlier engraving *The Slough of Despond* cut in 1928 when she was a student at Leon Underwood's school.

Hermes found her scale in the toughest medium of all – wood engraving – and she proved equally creative in her large engraving as in her smaller work. *More People* engraved in 1935 is her greatest work in the Palaeolithic style. The idea of the 'oneness' of man and woman was attractive to her and she included it in several engravings. This theme was inspired by the layered Palaeolithic engravings [4] and she understood the conception of fluid non-geometric space better than any other engraver.

Referring to *More People* she said 'It was Leon Underwood who made us aware of the importance of Palaeolithic art. He was a good teacher and a very fine man.' In this engraving and also in *One Person* [223], the sculptress and the engraver are fused. The sculptural gravity of the muscular and skeletal strength stands comparison with the *Bulls of Lascaux* and the *Bisons of Altamira*.

Hermes lays great stress on the need for creative engravers to be either painters or sculptors. In this she is close to Haden's concept of the painter-engraver or painter-etcher which gave the cumbersome title of the Royal Society of Painter Etchers and Engravers and echoes Vollard's insistence that all his books had to be illustrated by painter-gravers.

The last work done by Hermes is very pure engraving. It has an overall savage quality yet in the bottom right-hand corner there is the calm of Salisbury Plain and the sensitive lyrical line wandering gently as in the aftermath of the storm above. The audacity of the cloud engraving, slashed with chisel engraving, is the most memorable sky engraving solution in the whole of the British school. *Stonehenge* is a brooding, tense and forceful masterpiece; in this work Hermes sums up everything she is in engraving in the same way as did Iain Macnab in his final engraving *Ronda Bridge*.

Joan Hassall was born in the house in Kensington where she has lived ever since. Her life has been fully occupied as a wood engraver for both commercial and private press books and a large part of her work has been in natural history illustration. Her eyesight has always been phenomenal and she was engraving in very fine work well on into her seventies. In all these years her technique has never faltered. In 1972 she had the unusual honour of being appointed as the first woman master of that very mature institution the Art Workers' Guild. In 1973 she was awarded the bronze medal for engraving in Paris. Joan Hassall has been a personality of Kensington and Chelsea for close on three quarters of a century.

Agnes Miller Parker was born in Irvine in Ayrshire and trained at the Glasgow School of Art but also studied engraving with Gertrude Hermes and Blair Hughes-Stanton. In style her work is strange, intensely personal but memorable. Her images are engraved shapes, unified by the body curve, which sets up a strong aesthetic emotion to the form. She is a remarkable artist but because her engraving is for the private press books, the general art public rarely sees it and many people may not even know of her existence. While her work can be seen in the big national libraries, students rarely make the effort to see it.

Her technique is unusually simple and it has the simplicity of the copper engraving technique of Martin Schongauer, comprising the basic line and the dot. This use of line follows directly from Leon Underwood and Blair Hughes-Stanton. She is creative within these exceptionally narrow boundaries but her volumetric and sculptural expression of forms looks as if it were burnished. The polish and freshness of her vision are remarkable, as is her characterization and flawless craftsmanship.

Agness Miller Parker married the sculptor and typographer William MacCance and they worked together on *Aesop's Fables* for the Gregynog Press in 1931 [186 and 192]. MacCance designed the typography and cut the letters for the frontispiece whilst Miller Parker fitted the illustration to the typographic structure and produced one of the finest pieces of book design in the British school. In technique, Miller Parker appears never to have been interested in exploiting engraving as a white line continually changing its shape; in this respect she is at the opposite end of the pole to Gertrude Hermes.

Although the majority of Agnes Miller Parker's engravings were for books, there are in existence some prints standing as autonomous works of art and she also engraved some colour blocks. A remarkable feature of her *oeuvre* is the apparent lack of early works that show how her technique evolved. It seems as if her very individual style developed quickly and without the usual experiments that most artists have to go through to find themselves, though in fact she must have worked experimentally at the beginning.

In 1962 she and her husband, William MacCance, left Glasgow and sought peace and tranquillity in the Isle of Arran. At this date Agnes was made an honorary member of the Society of Wood Engravers and 1962 marks the close of her main engraving production because she then turned to painting, perhaps because her eyesight was no longer adequate for engraving.

Agnes Miller Parker's engraving style is very closely related to that of Blair Hughes-Stanton. It is basically linear, and pattern and texture development becomes a development of linear activity as, for example, in cross-hatching at various angles – a technique that is not as simple as it looks. There is much that can be written about her *Richard II* engraved for the Limited Editions Club, New York [246]. It is remarkable for its steel-like and burnished sculptural quality and the engraving is amazingly simple: just the line of varying length and the dot.

Miller Parker is a superb exponent of the shimmering silver greys of which the Russian engravers are masters. These greys can only arise from very fine engraving and the effect is caused by optical confusion. Such greys are evident in the engraving of the ice in [227] and the water in [228]. Both were produced as illustrations

[306] Cecil Keeling: *God of War*, 1961. 20.5 x 25.0cm

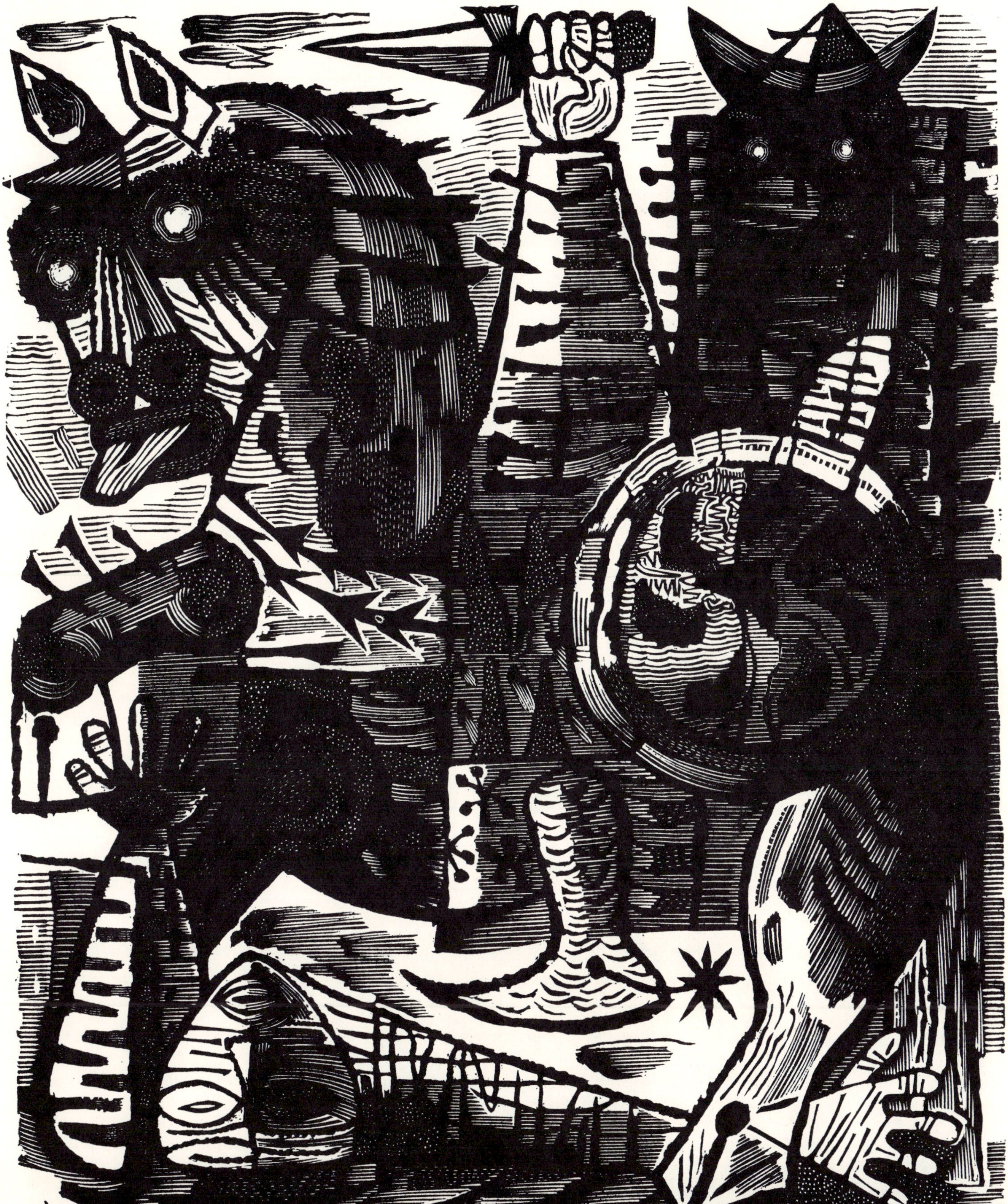
CK

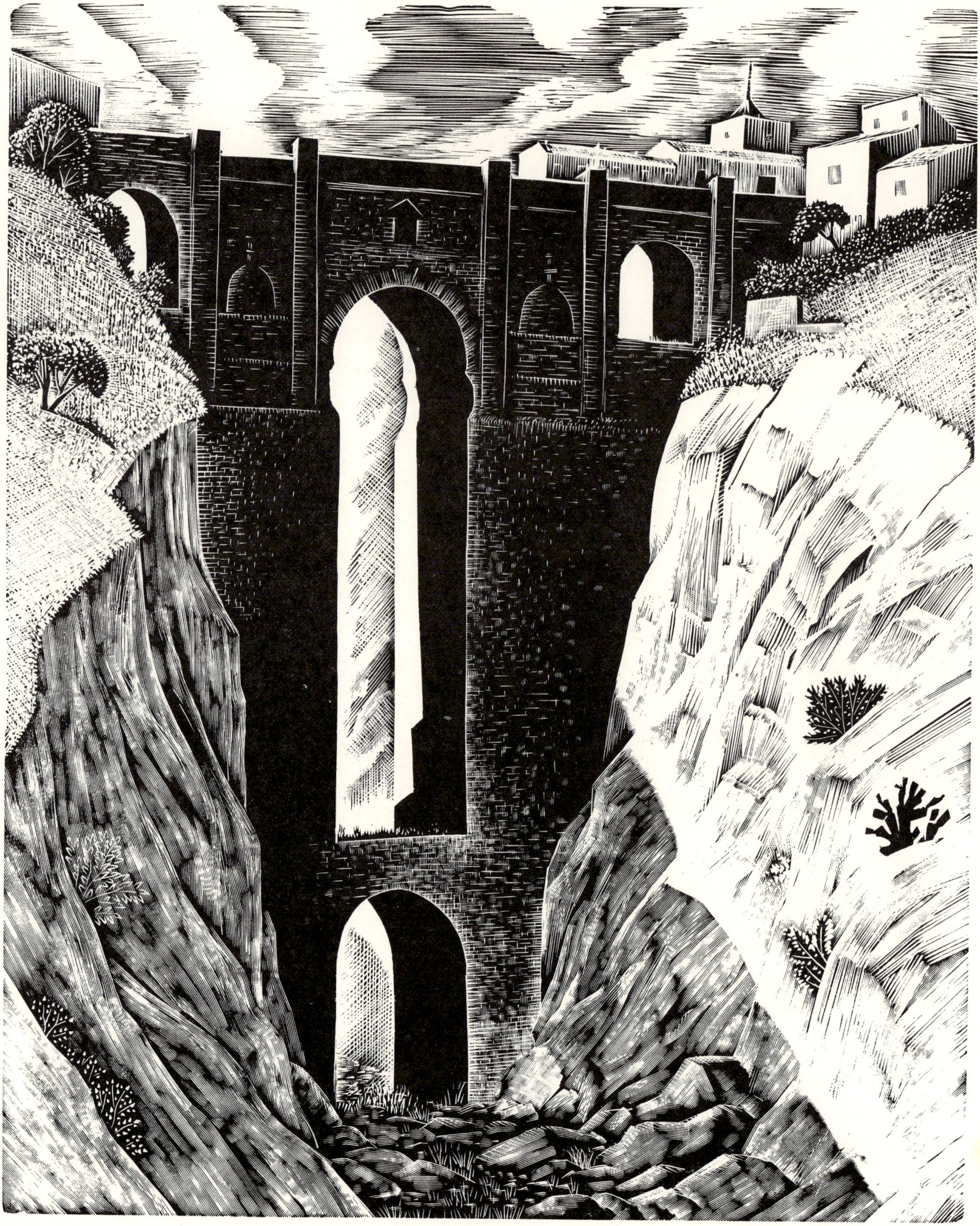

[307] Iain Macnab: *Ronda Bridge, Spain*, 1961. 20.3 x 25.4cm

for the book *Down the River* published by Gollancz in 1937. The rhythms and the austere control of black and white are so individual that they can never be confused with any other artist.

The Limited Editions Club of New York, for which Agnes Miller Parker engraved *Richard II*, was founded in 1929 by George Macy. Its membership grew to one thousand five hundred and in its first twenty-five years it published 250 books for its members. Macy also commissioned the famous artists from France and it was a mark of distinction for any engraver in any country to receive a commission from him. A check through the list of books illustrated by wood engravings will disclose the strength of the British contribution to this fine enterprise. The Limited Editions Club aimed to make fine books available at comparatively reasonable prices, but mechanical means of production were used, as distinct from the English private presses whose books were based upon hand production. The English Nonesuch Press was a similar enterprise to the Limited Editions Club and was founded in 1923 by Francis Meynell. He made full use of the printing machine and was thus able to issue much larger editions than the usual three hundred or so copies common to the editions from hand presses. Meynell believed that mechanical printing could be controlled to serve the ends of fine production.

Nora Unwin is a sensitive artist and wood engraver and her technique is in the tradition of Leon Underwood, Blair Hughes-Stanton and Agnes Miller Parker. She studied wood engraving at Leon Underwood's school, whose engravers have always stressed form development and simple sculptural qualities, never allowing volume to be broken into by pattern; this style is the very antithesis of the Ravilious following of pattern makers. All the engravings arising from Underwood's school have a marked cleanness and a flowing rhythmical quality. Their technique is classical and closely allied to that of copper engraving.

The work of Nora Unwin has been seen over a long period at both the Royal Society of Painter-Etchers and Engravers' and the Society of Wood Engravers' exhibitions. She has been resident in the United States since 1946 and is usually claimed as an American artist though she is English born. The woodcut is another of her media and in the States she was one of the early pioneers of the new medium of colograph prints. Her first colograph was exhibited by the Society of Wood Engravers in 1966 and many have been exhibited since. Some of these colographs were also exhibited at the Royal Society of Painter Etchers and Engravers but were not listed as colographs because the Society does not recognise the medium.

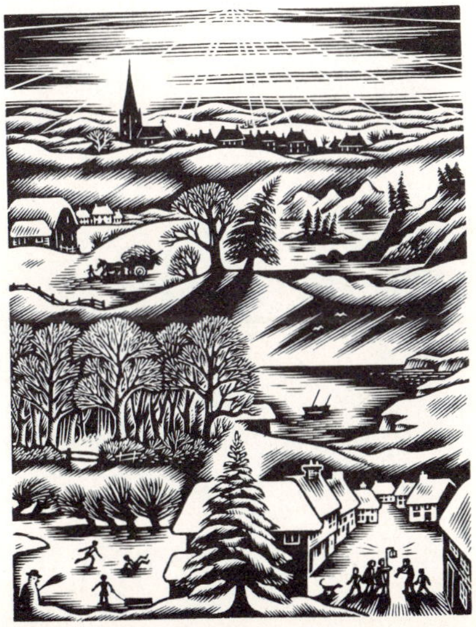

[308] Gwenda Morgan: *Midwinter*, 1962. 9.5 x 12.5cm

Blair Hughes-Stanton (son of Sir Robert Hughes-Stanton, President of the Royal Society of Painters in Watercolour) is an artist and an engraver who, in 1937, was awarded the International Prize for Engraving at the Venice Biennale. He studied art at the Byam Shaw School and at the Royal Academy Schools and completed his formal art education at the Leon Underwood school. After three years as a book designer and wood engraver at the Gregynog Press at Newton in Montgomeryshire, he started a career as a teacher.

Hughes-Stanton's first teaching appointment was at the Westminster School of Art in 1934 and from 1945 to 1947 he was at the Colchester School of Art teaching drawing and wood engraving, following that with a year at St Martin's School of Art. In 1948 he began a distinguished career at the Central School of Art and Design. Despite the fact that at the time of writing he is seventy-three years of age, his advice is still sought by students.

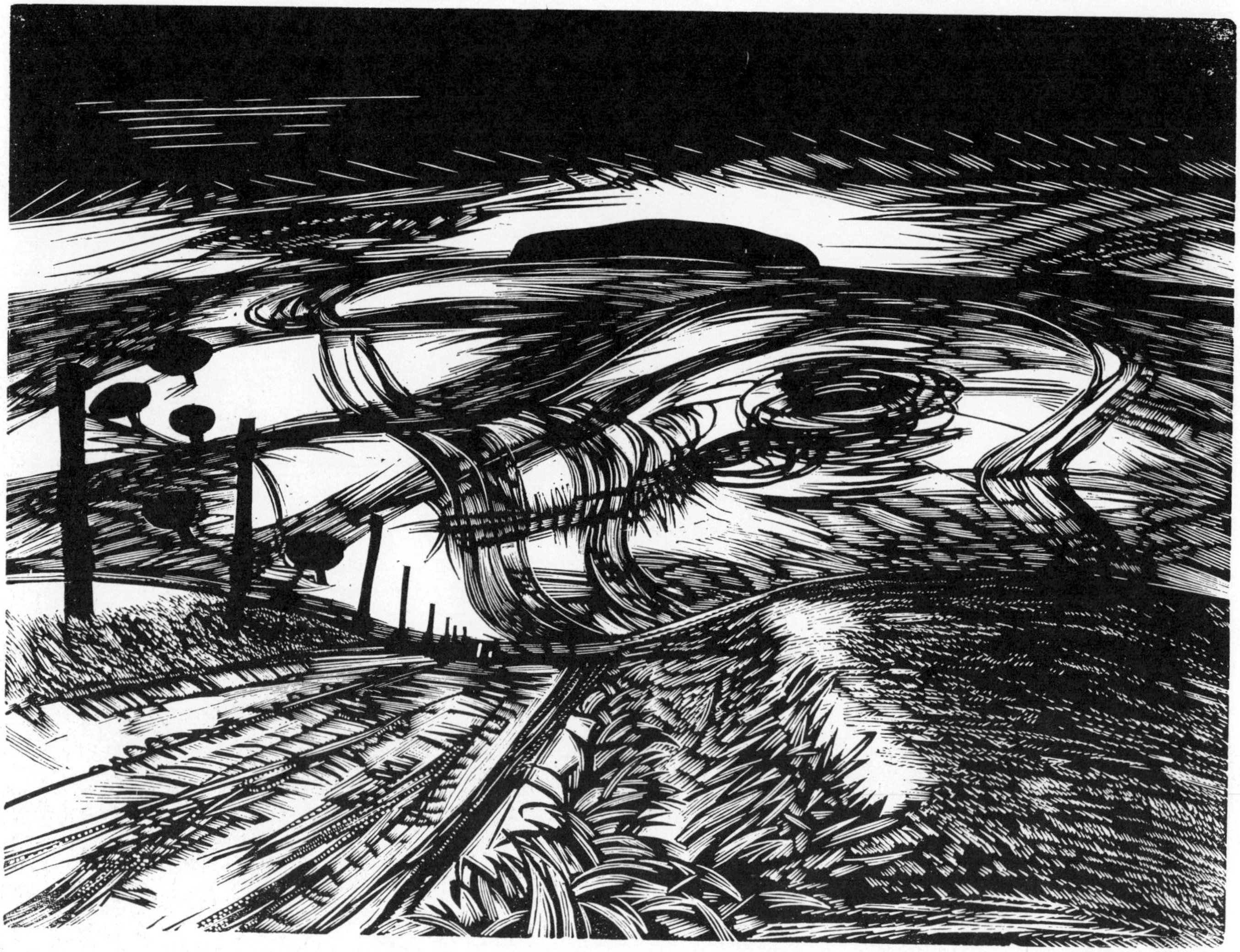

[309] Kenneth Lindley: *The Road to 4 mile Clump*, 1962. 17.75 x 13.5cm

Hughes-Stanton's prints are of superlative quality. Initially, his printing problem was to find the equation that would give him an ink film of the correct density yet being able to reproduce the finest and closest lines; to apply the right degree of pressure so that the solid areas appear dense, yet not to impart so much pressure that the finer detail is distorted – and to employ a paper with a surface that will accept the thin film of ink and absorb the oil which acts as a vehicle for the ink pigment. His success in solving this problem is demonstrated adequately by his products.

He has been a contributor to some very fine private press books, starting with ten wood engravings in T. E. Lawrence's *Seven Pillars of Wisdom* in 1926. In all, his production spans twenty-five books containing over three hundred wood engravings. Where book design and production are concerned, he has set the type, designed the typography and in some cases actually done the printing. In other cases he even designed and cut by hand his own type and did his own binding, in a variety of leathers.

Like Underwood, Hughes-Stanton attached a high importance to Blake and to subject and meaning in art. There are two strong elements evident in his style: the nervous, emotional and spiritual rhythms and counterpoint of El Greco and the superimposition of images from the engraving of the Palaeolithic artists of the Dordogne. His is a dramatic world and the opposite to that of John Nash and

William T. Rawlinson, yet it is a world in which pictorial drama would be as nothing were it not animated by the dominant aesthetics of form, which are rhythms, proportions, structure, volume and counterpoint.

During their younger days, Fry and Bell were formulating the aesthetic theories of 'Significant Form' and 'Form before content' but both Underwood and Hughes-Stanton were in opposition to it as a concept. The 'Significant Form' theory contained the dictum that a work of art need not have a subject. Moore was also opposed to pure abstraction, which was to flower at the Bauhaus. He has always observed 'truth to materials' and has shown clearly the value he has placed on subject matter. The human figure and biological forms have always been his vehicle of expression. No matter how abstract his sculpture may appear to be, Moore has always claimed that he is not an abstract artist and this concept has held in the work of Underwood and Hughes-Stanton.

In engraving Hughes-Stanton is a superb craftsman. His engraving scale is very fine, in fact so fine that much of his best work could not be reproduced effectively in commercial printing. Hughes-Stanton, like David Jones, took full advantage of the private press as a means of eliminating the intervention of the camera to translate the engraving into the printed page, and technically both artists push the extreme fineness of boxwood engraving to the limit. Unfortunately, books do

[310] Kenneth Lindley: *Langdean and Cow Dow*, 1962. 18.1 x 14.2cm

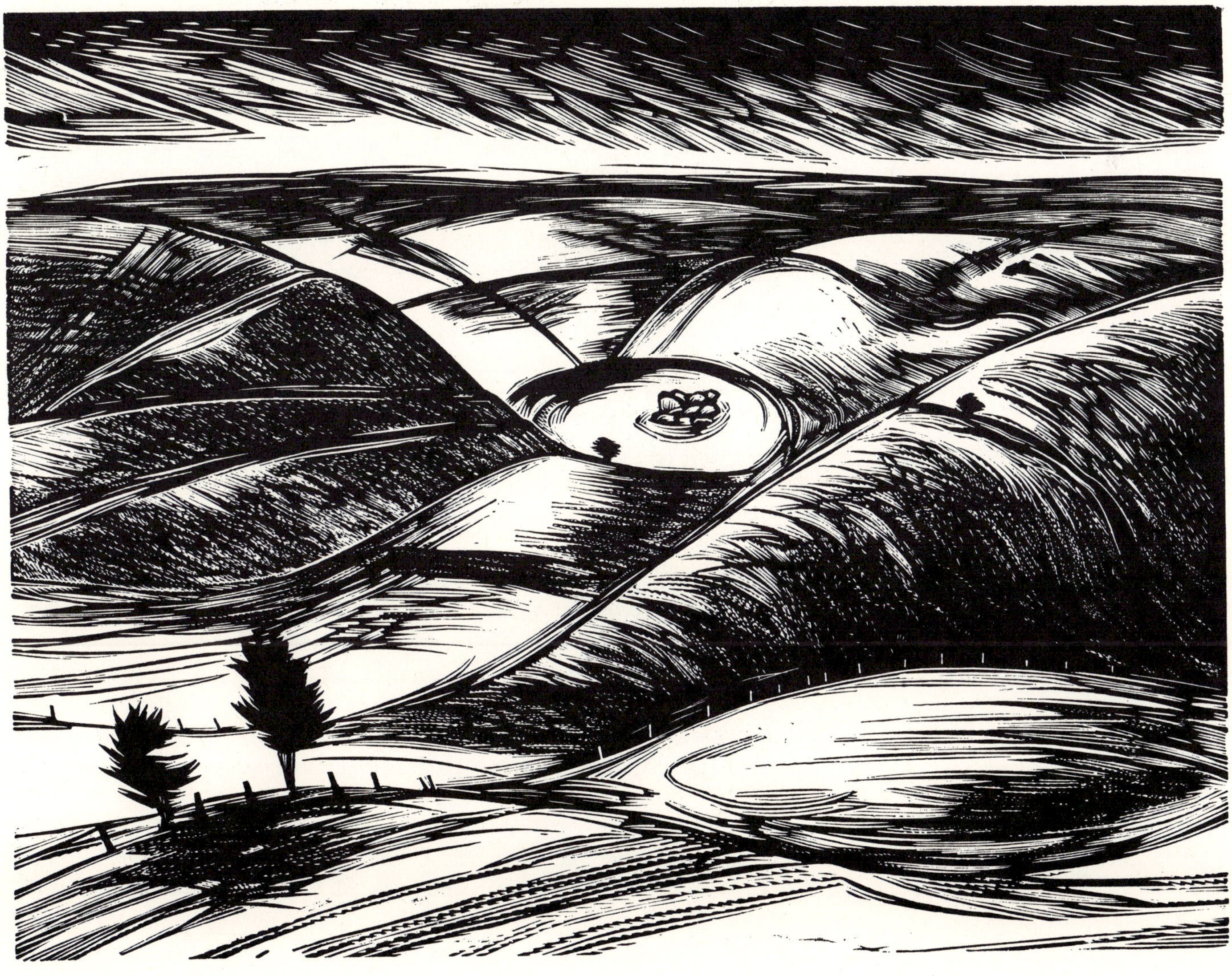

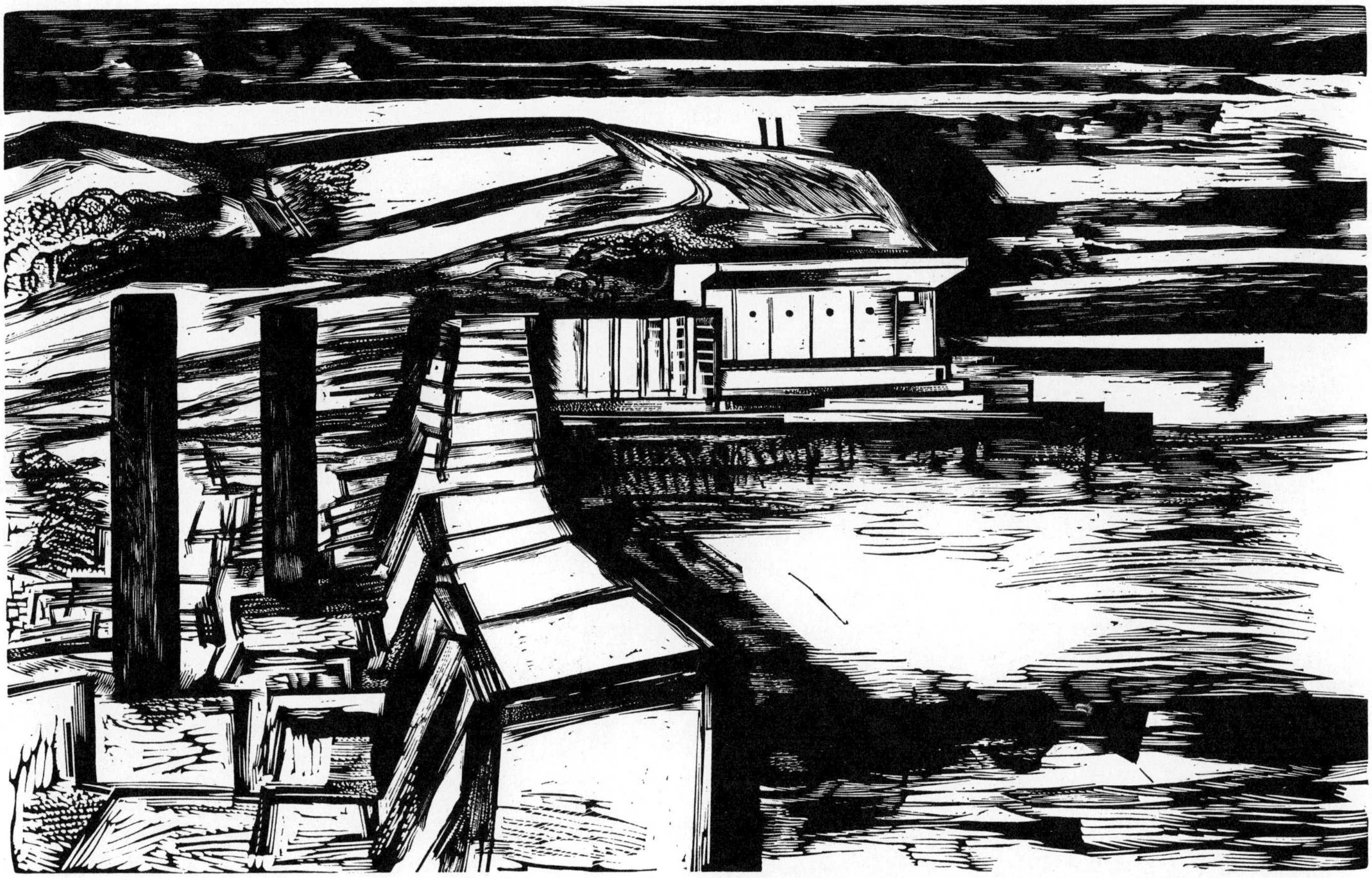

[311] Kenneth Lindley: *Broken Sea Wall, Essex,* 1964. 28.0 x 17.75cm

not show the full engraving spectrum of Hughes-Stanton because he moved into the world of relative abstraction, despite the fact that he and his friends were against it. The world of relative abstraction pursued by Hughes-Stanton was that of the underground caves and not that of the Bauhaus, and this led to some of his most durable works [191 and 210]. The simple grandeur, clear diction and superb engraving in these works give them their uniqueness as works of art in their own right. Even the textures are derived from the linear development of the total theme. In these engravings, Hughes-Stanton has to leave his dramatic situation behind him but he loses nothing from the exercise. From one point of view, these abstract works are tantalizing and they suggest that Hughes-Stanton might well have made a greater contribution to art had he pursued it further. Yet here again he was in a similar position to John Buckland-Wright who also produced works of pure abstraction; both were pulled to and fro by the representational demands of book illustration which had to provide them with the means to live.

Hughes-Stanton has carried the fineness of wood engraving to greater extremes than any other engraver. He is a great exponent of the silvery shimmering greys which are unique to twentieth-century wood engraving in the white-line technique. Examined under a magnifying glass, Hughes-Stanton's engraving *The Woman in Heaven* which appeared in the private press book *Revelation of St John the Divine* published in 1933, shows in the circle tone of the bottom left-hand corner which forms the crescent moon and encloses the woman's feet, one hundred white lines and the same number of black lines to the inch. These lines are equally spaced and no single line is broken. The plate shown in [202] does not reproduce this texture adequately because it has been obtained from a photograph. The illustration as

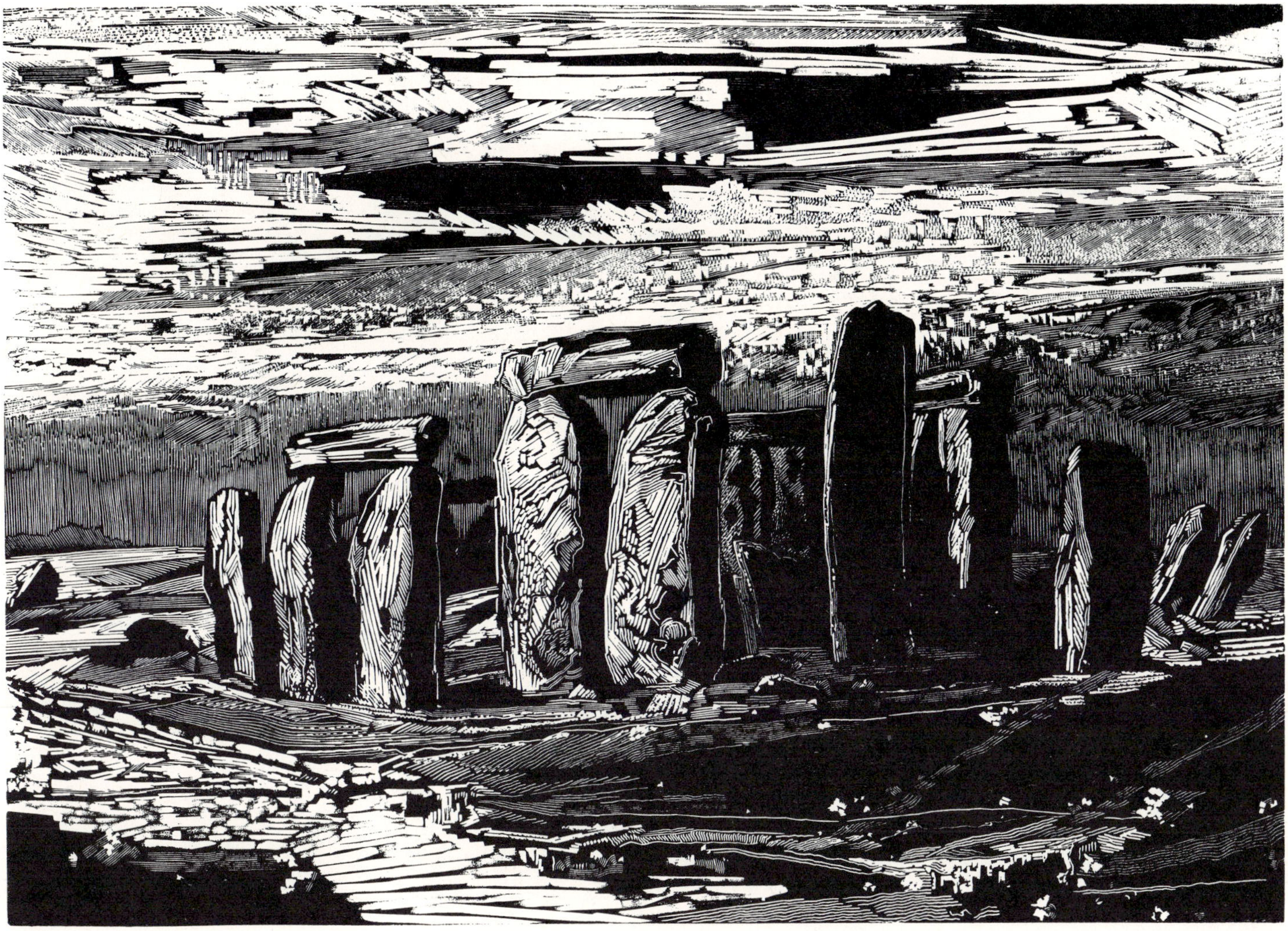

[312] Gertrude Hermes: *Stonehenge*, 1963. 35.3 x 25.5cm

published in the book was printed direct from the engraving and the lines can be identified clearly. In *The Woman in Heaven*, the masterly subtle line running from the bottom of the crescent moon through the centre of the figure to the star in the top right-hand corner changes from black to white several times in its length, in a similar manner to the six lines in Iain Macnab's *Drying Sails, Lake Garda* [233].

Hughes-Stanton became involved in an international movement which has since become important. As a representative of the Society of Wood Engravers he attended a meeting of a group of people interested in promoting wood engraving on an international basis. It was agreed that an international exhibition of wood engraving should be organised and the event took place in September 1953 at the Kunsthaus in Zürich. The exhibition was called Xylon and was under the presidency of Frans Masereel (1889 to 1972). The success of the first exhibition, now called Xylon I, led the Swiss delegates of the organising committee to propose that a society be formed to promote the art of wood engraving in other countries and to continue to arrange annual international exhibitions. The International Society of Wood Engravers was formed and its organisation was the work of Dr R. Wehrli, the director of the Kunsthaus, and Hans Bollinger also of the Kunsthaus.

The aim of the Xylon exhibition was to receive and show the great range of the medium, after the neglect it suffered through the war. It aimed to create a large international body of life lay members interested in engraving and cutting. Some of the major aims and objects of Xylon were short lived. Today it bears no relation to its original intentions and has gone the way of most international print exhibitions, which now aim to show the great breadth of relief printing together with all the gimmicks implied in mixed media.

The object of holding an international exhibition every two years has been maintained but an engraving in wood is now very rare in Xylon, though engravings are still exhibited in other international exhibitions. In the first Xylon exhibition 327 prints were shown from thirteen countries and they were arranged as exhibits of the work of groups or of individuals from the different countries. The work of twenty members of the British Society of Wood Engravers was shown at this exhibition and in Xylon II the work of fifteen members appeared.

At Xylon I the Belgian room was dominated by the work of the President, Frans Masereel, whose pictorial philosophy had not changed since he produced his first book entirely in woodcuts in the twenties. His style was always deceptively simple, highly objective, with a certain Belgian quaintness which gave his work its charm. He was an artist with an enormous output and the energy and economic technique with which he put across his ideas kept him in the forefront of the medium.

Hughes-Stanton's international interests continued and he worked on the document *The definition of an Original Print* agreed at the Third International Congress of Arts, Vienna, in September 1960. The work was published by the International Association of Art (affiliated to UNESCO) in 1963. The Print Council of America also published a similar document *What is an Original Print?* in 1961. By 1960 it had become necessary to clarify what constituted an artist's original print for the purposes of international customs authorities, to counter the heavy trade in spurious prints and to call the artists' attention to the need to observe the original print identification system of very long tradition. The definitions of an original print are set out in the Appendix.

Kenneth Lindley is an engraver of the post-war generation who has made a considerable contribution to the art of wood engraving. He is successfully exploiting a black-line wood engraving concept more consistently than any other engraver. The individual aesthetic ryhthms and emphasis are emotionally orientated but as an engraver he is clearly an 'expressionist'.

Lindley has thrown off the tendency to be a designer and pattern maker and has become a highly meaningful artist flowing on the wave of emotion. He has developed a form language that carries him freely through the world of the figure and landscape; in this respect he is an artist engraver. From his work [309], [310] and [311] have been chosen to show the progress of his development in what was to him an unexploited field of creative engraving.

Whatever the future may hold for Lindley and his Pointing Finger Press books, one thing is certain: he will be unable to come to the same 'black-line conclusion' as obtained for W. J. Linton. The full meaning of the word 'creative' in the Rooke sense comes between Linton and Lindley. Lindley is also an author and some of his books have been published by the Pointing Finger Press which he founded. Whilst these books are of a modest literary scale, they are expansive in design, engraving and production.

Of his first ventures into the black-line world Lindley has the following to say: 'The recent print *The Road to Four Mile Clump* [309] shows an intricate pattern of black and white expression with the sky an almost untouched black slab, an essential feature of calm. Here I began consciously to exploit the full range of the engraved line, black on white and white on black. The pursuit of this has led me to extremes on occasion, as with several black-line nudes used in my book *Nostalgic*.'

In the print *Shimabara* [364] the black line can be seen running in free exchange with the white. The black line assumes all widths from the graduation of fine to the eventual bulk of shape. Here Lindley's success lies in the fact that the white line graduates from fine to the extension of the line itself being lost into that of shape. So far he is achieving a very fine synthesis of these elements and observing that creative engraving is a line moving forward and continually changing its shape. He is also demonstrating that the line can either be white or black or both in unison.

Kenneth Lindley's black-line print *Dorset Coast* is one of the best examples in recent work illustrating the difference between the *formschneider* interpretative concept, the conception of the Linton artist-interpreter, and the Lindley development of the *formschneider* technique into a creative concept [49]. The engravings printed in the Chinese Northern Sung dynasty from the *Sung Imperial Commentary on the Chinese Tripitaka* [16 to 18] have only recently become available for study in this country but they are very reassuring for Lindley's black-line creative concept. The critical factor involved in the *Dorset Coast* is the development of a linear black quality which cannot be produced by any other means. This landscape is as extreme in its aesthetic structure and abstract language as is the Mackley print *Rocks*. Although it is as yet a little early, the *Dorset Coast* could well become a precursor work, if the black-line concept should inspire other engravers strongly. Lindley became a teacher of some renown and is principal of the Hereford College of Art.

Frank Vernon Martin is also an artist of the post-war generation and is a teacher. He is a distinguished engraver and figure draughtsman and like Lindley has experimented successfully with black-line wood engraving [314 and 315]. Most of his wood engravings have found their way into books as illustrations and his

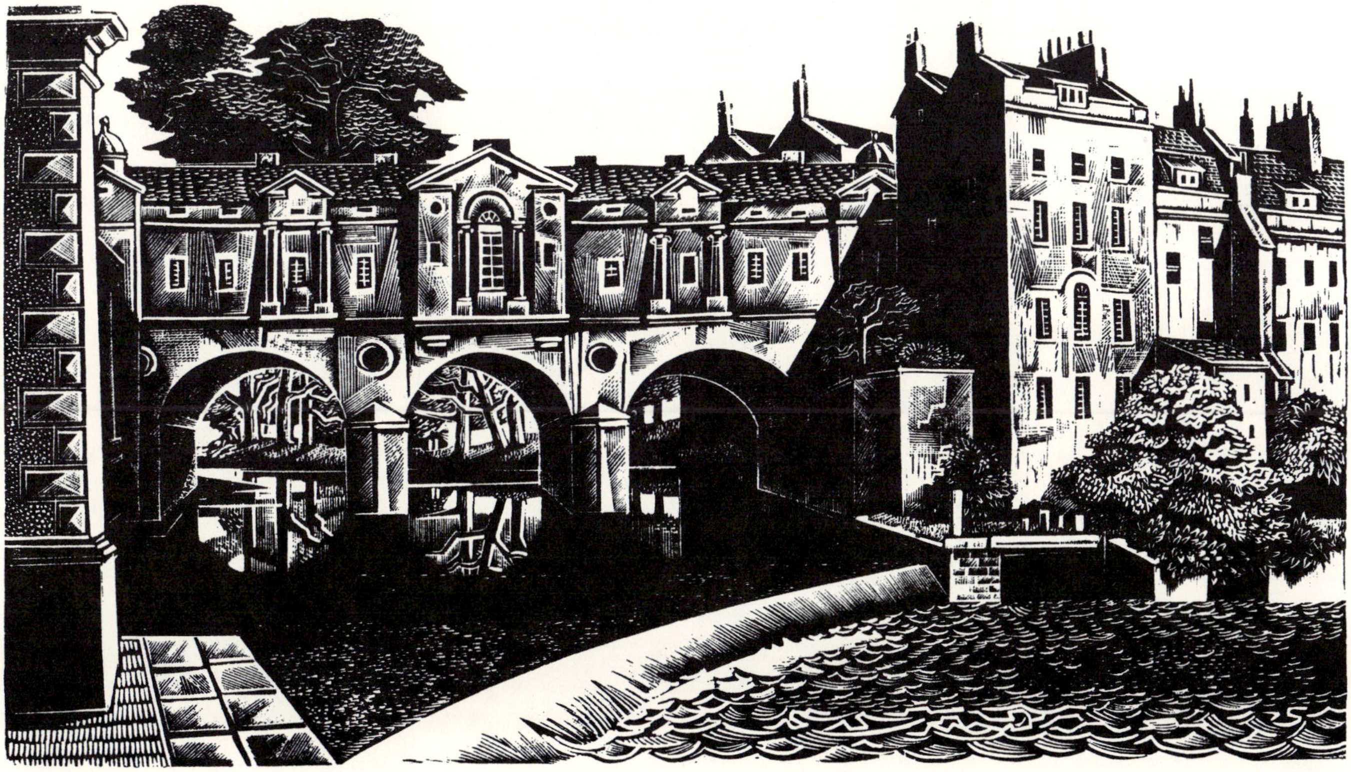

[313] Donald Plenderleith: *Pulteney Bridge, Bath*, 1964. 21.5 x 12.0cm

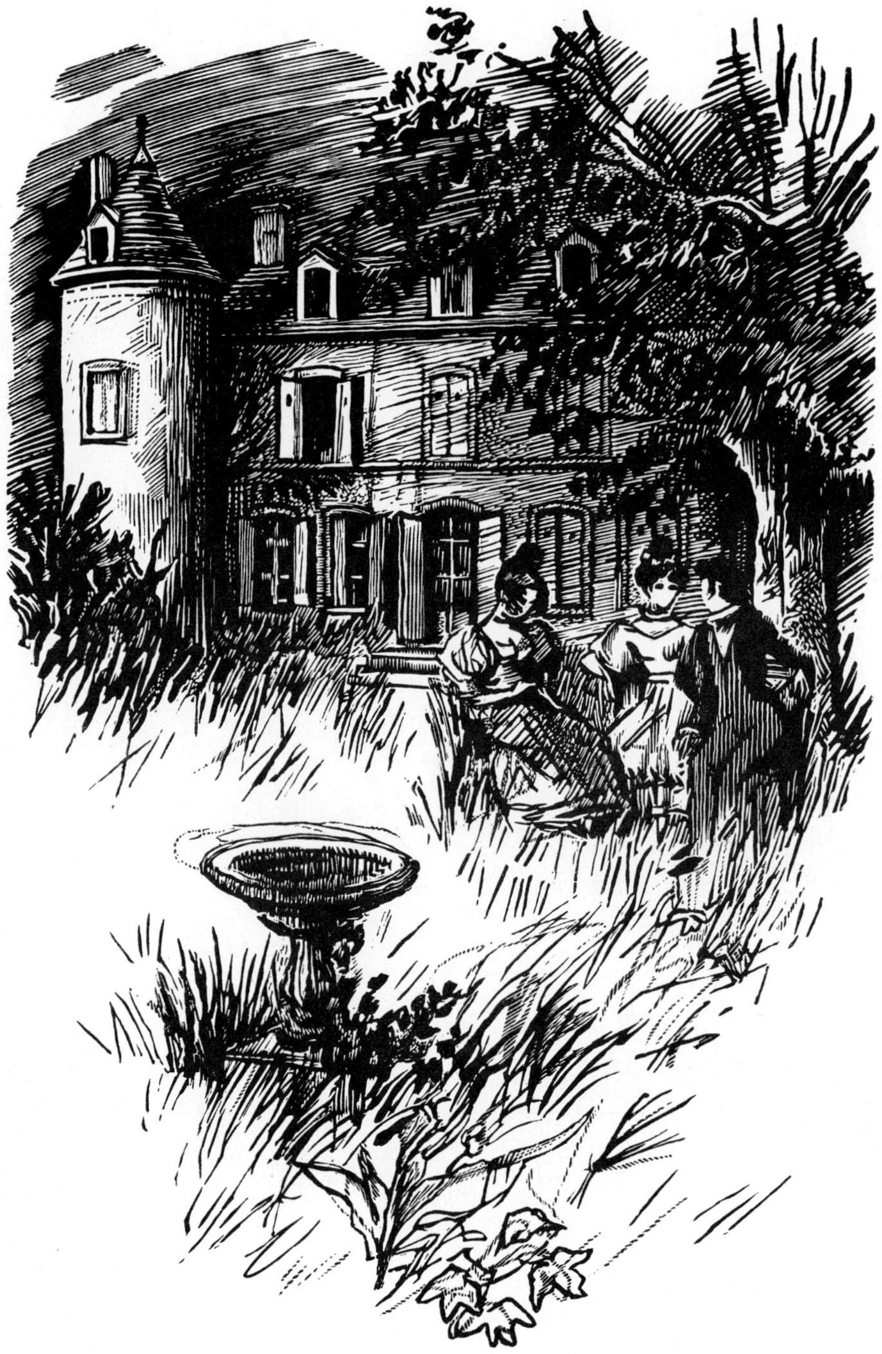

largest contribution to the development of the autonomous print is in the media of woodcut and etching. Throughout his production he displays a very marked sense of period. No matter in what period he elects to work, he always manages to create a distinct personal flavour.

Martin's draughtsmanship is superb and his engraved black line is remarkably sensitive, changing its shape throughout its course, the motivation for such changes being likely to be a muscle, joint, texture, space or solid; though whatever the reason it always arises from very acute observation. In Martin's engraving no line is ever repeated as a formula. Every move through the length of a line is recording visual experience. Martin is highly competent in anatomy but this extensive knowledge is sublimated.

[314, 315] Frank Martin: Illustrations from *Le Rouge et Le Noir*, 1965. 11.5 x 17.8cm

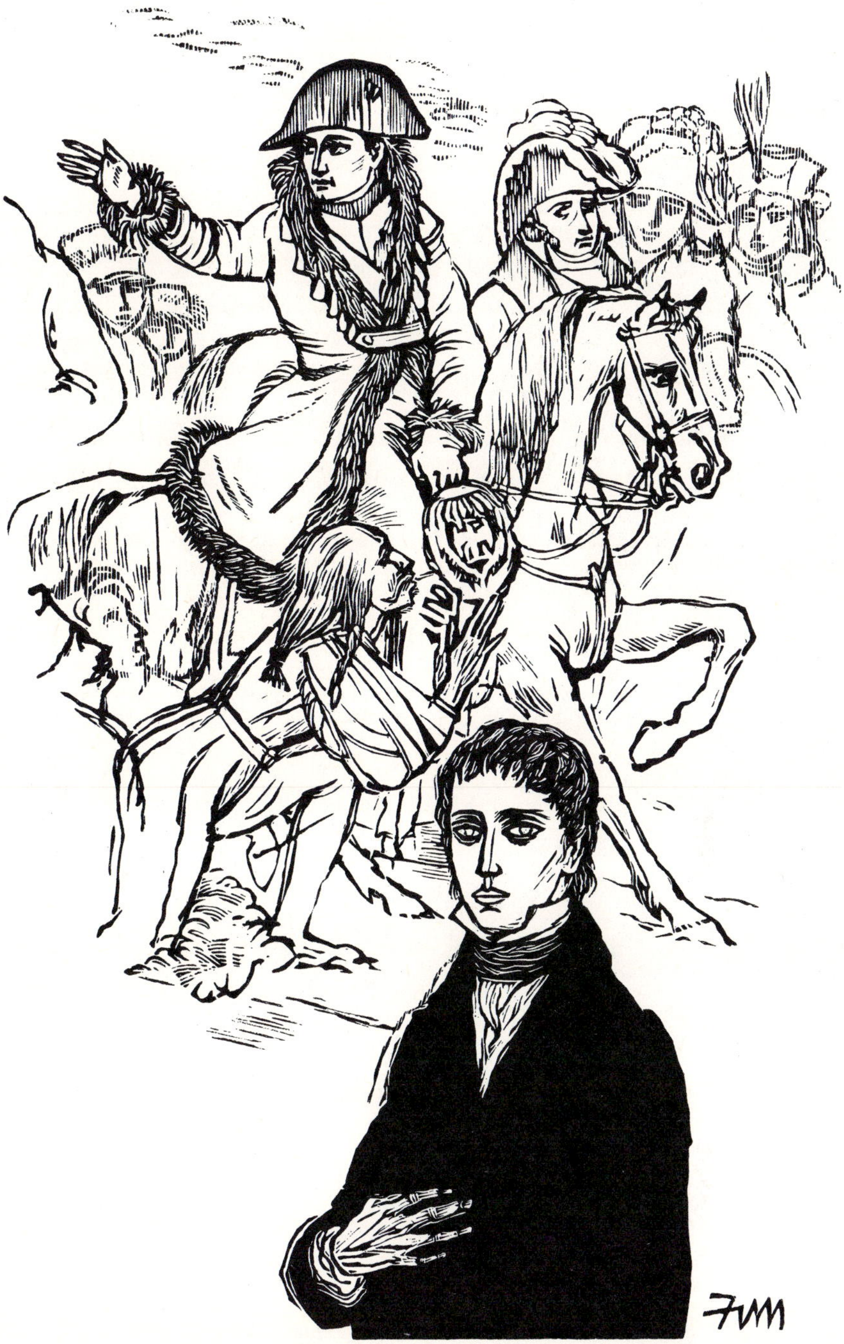

[316] Diana Bloomfield: Illustration from *The Green Road*, 1965. 6.0 x 6.5cm

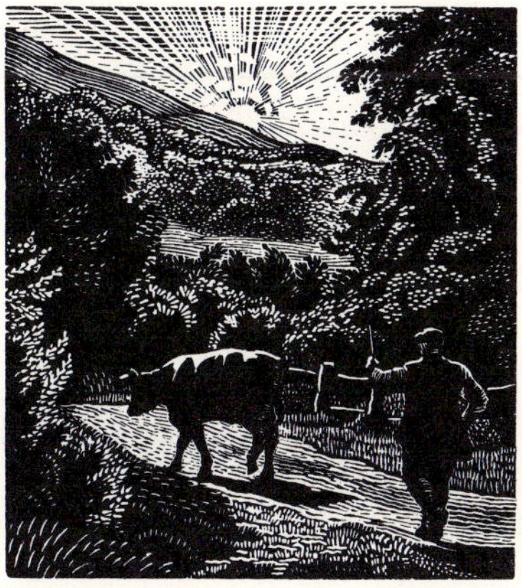

When it is successful, the teaching of wood engraving should result in what David Jones called *sub specie aeternitatis* or 'a rose grower developing a new species'. Martin was a student at the Camberwell School of Arts and Crafts and Gertrude Hermes was his teacher. Hermes builds her forms in terms of the tools and their individual cutting shapes and the amount of light needed for their development. She is a white-line engraver but Martin, as a *sub-specie* reverses the engraving technique to that of black line. When he had completed his studies at the Camberwell School, Frank Martin continued to attend but as a teacher.

John Lawrence is also a teacher at the Camberwell School and like Martin he is a sensitive wood engraver who was taught by Gertrude Hermes. The David Jones dictum of *sub specie aeternitatis* holds good for Lawrence too. Both Martin and

[317] John Lees: Illustration from *L'Allegro*. 8.6 x 18.0cm

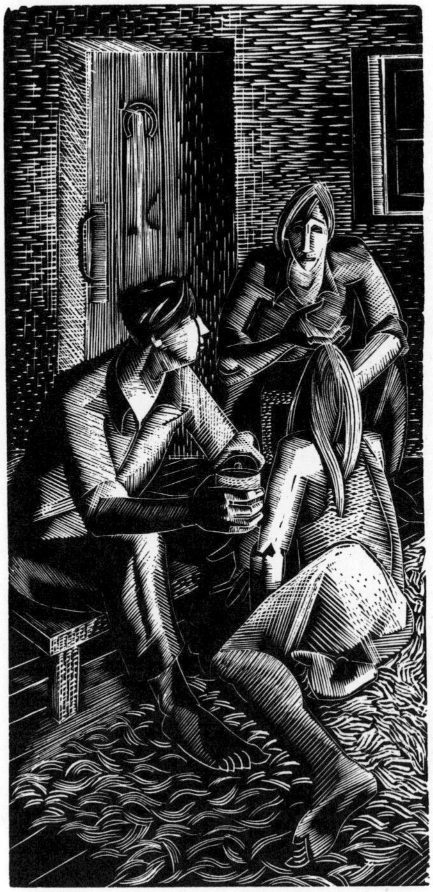

Lawrence are sufficiently strong in engraving to have easily identifiable personalities. Lawrence's engravings are very busy and his wit and humour are essentially English. In some respects he is the Rowlandson of the twentieth-century engraving school. His engravings are tightly packed, highly charged and with the exact number of burin thrusts to make a salient form. It is in the burin thrusts where, when he so chooses, he splits the form through from the black to white poles.

In draughtsmanship Lawrence is confident enough to enable him to sublimate it to the point of implying a form where it is most telling. The Lawrence figure [320] is not only reminiscent of the strutting cock turkey, but is engraved with a remarkable, bristling, cutting energy. He cuts shapes with his tools and each one is clearly defined but only the form is implied, yet the viewer receives just enough visual information to cause him or her to complete the form mentally.

Sarah van Niekerk is a younger generation engraver who was trained at the Central School by Gertrude Hermes, and at the Slade by the etcher Anthony Gross and the engraver Lynton Lamb. Her print *Jacobins in a Bay Tree* [349] has the engraving quality of woven silk illuminated by two white light beams, and the very sensitive half-tone grey of the leaves appears to be reflecting the light from these two beams. The light is in the picture, just as it is in Rembrandt's *Anatomy Lesson*. Gertrude Hermes teaches in terms of light and as her student Sarah van Niekerk fully understood the message. This same message is seen in George Mackley's *Rocks* [380] and John Petts's *Coire Mhic Fhearchair. Ross* [379]. The composition of *Jacobins in a Bay Tree* is simple and a classical one of the horizontal and vertical line avoiding an obvious centre. Her engraving is also sensitive, switching from white to black line at will. She defines the forms, planes and shapes and never initiates the detailed character of feathers and leaves. The print is a work of art; it happens to be about two birds though it is not an illustration but an interpretation, which illustration should be but rarely is. Like Martin and Lawrence she gives just sufficient information of visual form for the viewer to be able to complete the form mentally.

Roderic Barrett is a very individual artist who moved into wood engraving during the 1950s. He has made a significant contribution in painting and although he has not produced very many wood engravings, his work in this field is distinguished. The engravings that he has produced are intensely individual; his visual images are mysterious in character and enact a theatre of domestic life. His world is very still and darkness is gently relieved with images just adequately illuminated. Technically his prints and craftsmanship are impeccable.

Barrett has brought to wood engraving the emotion he feels as a painter. He ignores the fundamental linear character of the engraving discipline, and sublimates line to the delineation of shape and compositional structure only. In many aspects of his work he sees line only as a difference between changing areas. This is a painting concept where all the elements are required to be fused within a form. By ignoring volume and expressing space as colour, he then comes into engraving; likewise ignoring volume and line and, picking up the engraver's white-light pencil beam, he then graduates and illuminates his space planes which are differentiated by burin textures. Roderic Barrett is a good example of Haden's interpretation of the French concept of a *peintre-graveur*. The language between the two means of expression is creative and identical.

[318] Simon Brett: *Westminster Abbey*, 1965. 21.5 x 25.5cm

An outstanding example of abstract art using single squares, circles and triangles can be seen in the wood engravings of Josef Albers who was born in 1888. His

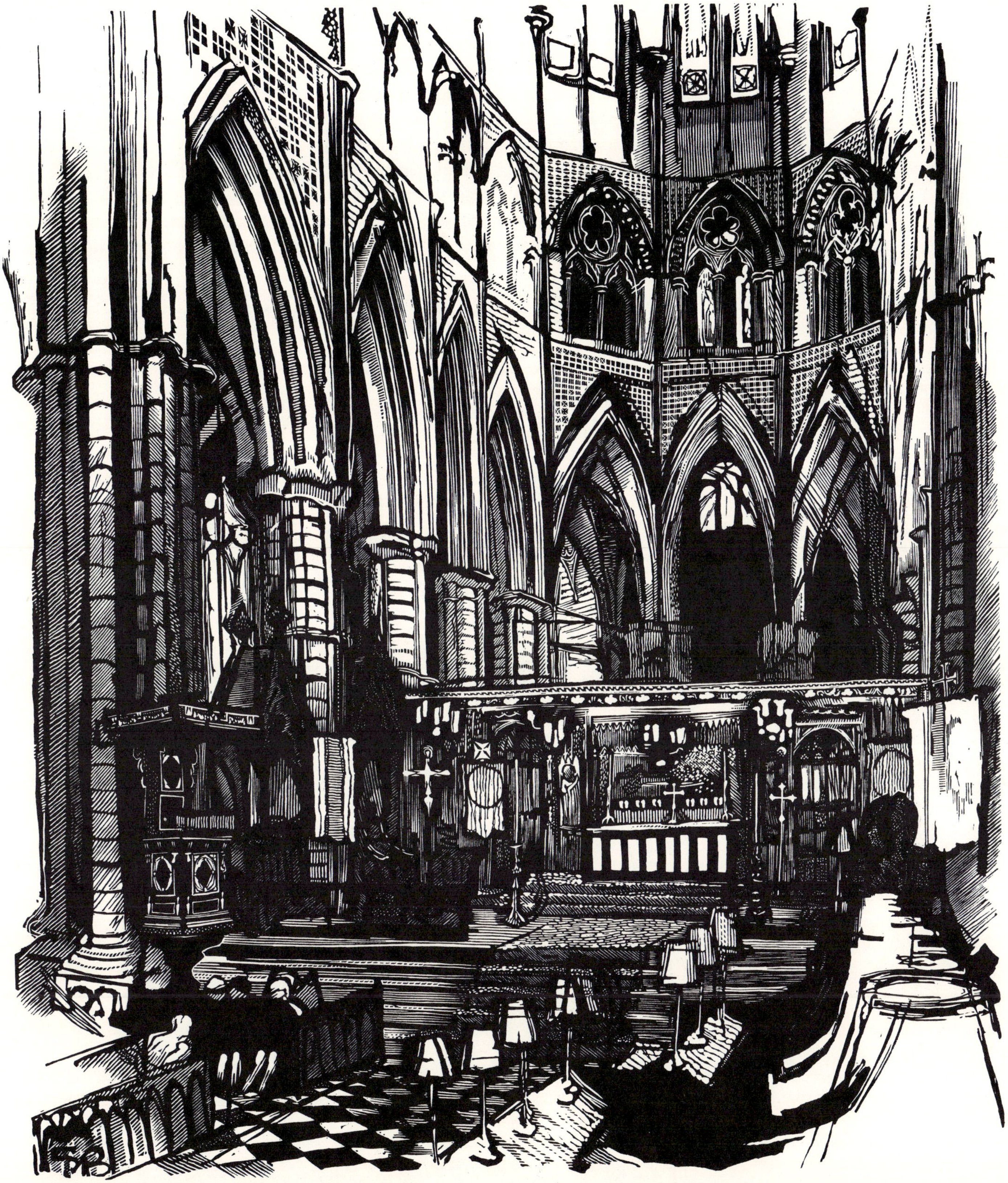

engravings are technically exciting and his craft is superb but his language is Bauhausian and the content of his work is virtually little more than the juggling of simple geometry. As art, his engravings represent a highly sophisticated boredom. Such themes of abstraction have their place and their value, and make some contribution to art, but they are of little use in engraving as a lifetime's commitment.

Albers was a student at the Bauhaus in Weimar from 1920 to 1923 and was a teacher there from 1925 until Hitler closed the Bauhaus in 1933. From Germany he went to the United States and there he realised that it was boring to continue to explore abstraction and moved out of wood engraving into other fields of expression. From an engraving point of view this can only be of particular interest because the question implied is, where would Albers have gone had he elected to spend his

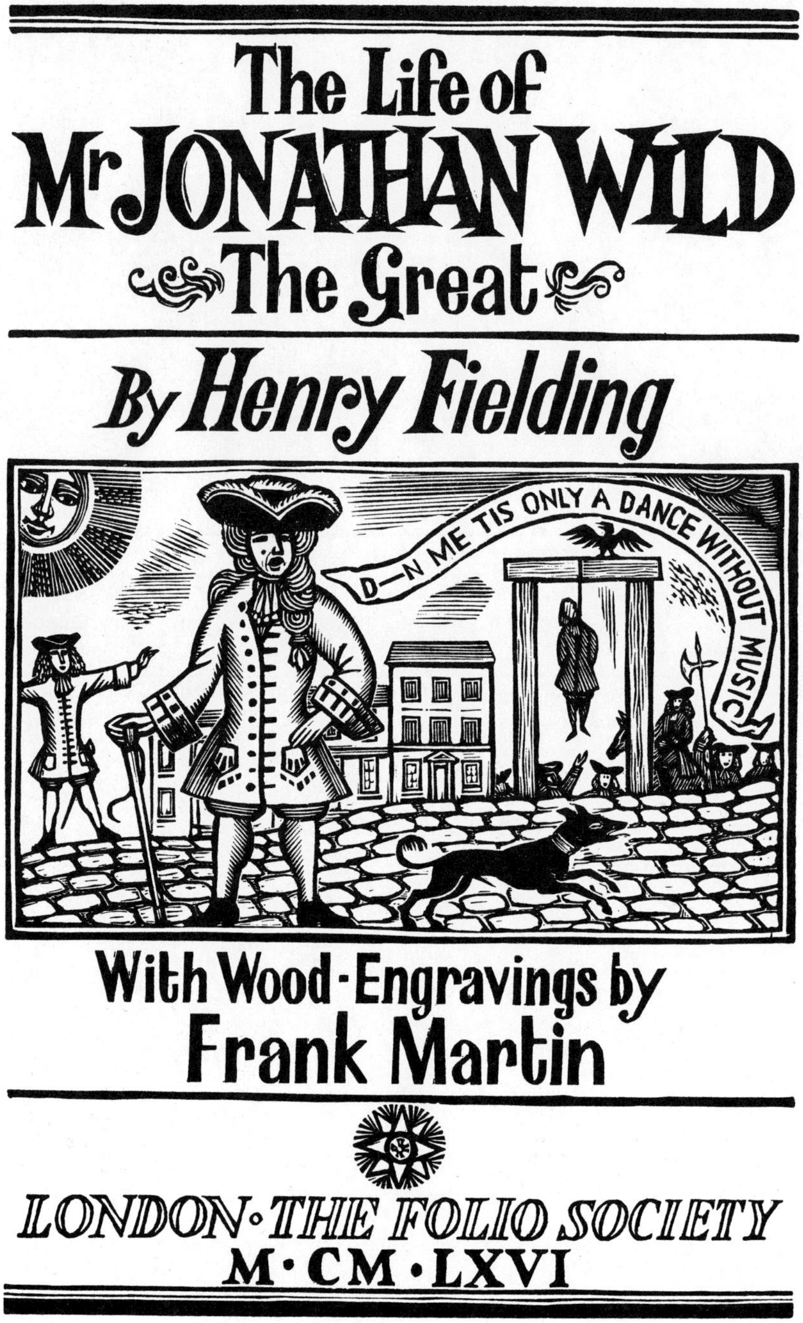

[319] Frank Martin: Frontispiece from *Jonathan Wild*, 1966. Page size 10.5 x 17.5cm

life as an engraver? He used engraving to serve his purposes of transition from one medium to another.

From the Bauhaus and its important reforming concepts, engraving was the one fundamental discipline which Paul Klee (1879 to 1940) failed to take into account. Theoretically he should have taken his analysis of the properties of the line into a medium where it is a final statement. In his lectures on modern art which he delivered at Jena in 1924, he analysed the aspects of form, space, tone and line and this analysis had a profound influence on art. He defined all the expressive properties of line as drawing which is the initial image-forming process and not the final

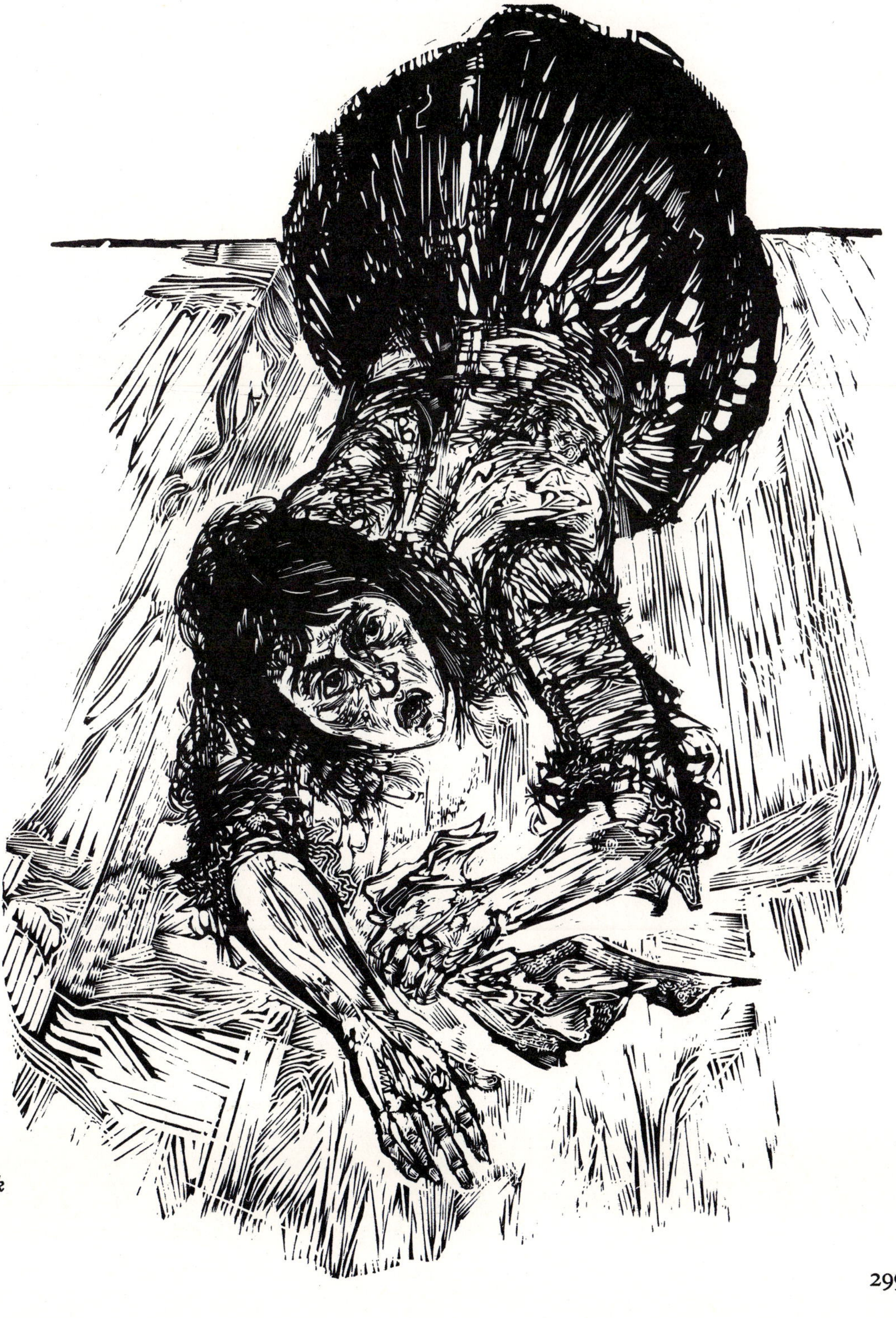

[320] John Lawrence: *Colonel Jack* from *Daniel Defoe*, 1967. 13.5 x 19.0cm

statement, and made the following statement on line: 'Line is the most limited, being solely a matter of simple measure. Its properties are length (long or short), angles (obtuse or acute), length of radius and focal distance. All are quantities subject to measure. Measurement is the character of this element. Where the possibility of measurement is in doubt, line cannot have been handled with absolute purity.'[2]

The lecture at Jena in 1924 marked the historical point where for the first time line as drawing did not require a representational subject for its use. The aesthetics of abstract drawing had been defined. Most people at that time thought that the last bulwark of sanity had broken down and with no subject to worry about, then everybody could do just as they wished. Little did they realise that it was to make art still more difficult and that there are in fact only a very small number of artists who will ever need an abstract language to say what they wish. John Buckland-Wright, whose art was of an abstract nature, said that for him abstraction was like a tunnel, 'You have to go in, but God help you if you don't come out at the other end'.

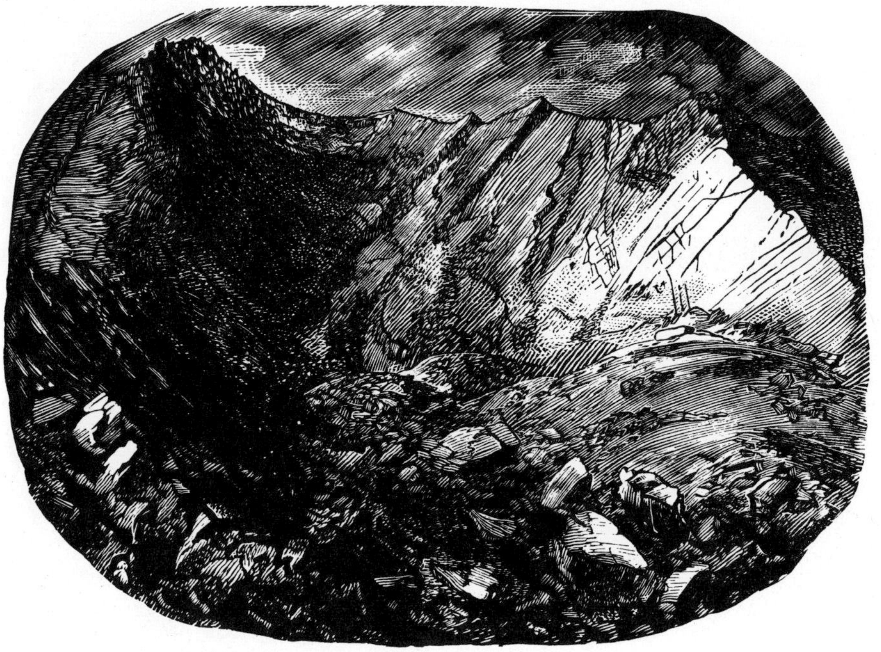

[321] Reynolds Stone: *Cwm Graianog from the Mountains.* Drawing by John Piper, 1968. 11.3 x 8.5cm

Geoffrey Wales was a student at the Royal College of Art when engraving was an important subject. He was trained under Malcolm Osborne, Robert Austin, John Nash, Eric Ravilious and Edward Bawden. The talents of Wales were strong enough to make him develop as an individual and he is an artist who has evolved through engraving and has found that the aesthetics of form and the disciplines of engraving run in parallel. Wales has evolved gradually, solving one set of form and space problems before extending his range. Because of this he is the rare artist who through research evolves logically and progressively. His earlier work can be seen in his print *Man on the Quay* [290]. The structure evolves from the images regardless of the degree of abstraction and is not superimposed upon it. This principle is the basis of the school of Paris concepts from Cézanne and the Impressionists.

Wales has accepted a further restriction by being creative in pure line. In his later works *The Waves* [324] and *Shells and Rock Form* [323], two brilliant wood engravings, he brings all elements of form together in an impressive economy of structure, line, texture, tone and shape. There are no inside or outside shapes; they are equated and every form and shape is sensitively related to the four outer and binding lines.

Like Wales, Raymond H. M. Hawthorn is a fine engraver who is now confidently on the road to the establishment of an individual personality. His technique is superb and like Wales he has many form problems to solve, given the time. Although he is very abstract in expression, his art is very differently orientated from that of Wales. Hawthorn's art arises from a world of symbols all of which are given a visual image whether or not they possess such an identity. In his remarkable *Noumenal Phenomenal* [336] we see him interpreting pure philosophy as a decorative diagram for Kant's *Critique of Pure Reason.* In respect of visual symbols he is, of course, close to William Blake, but so far he has substituted science for religion. His scientific image is very much of today where an extensive interest is directed to environmental science. In these terms the engraving makes exciting reading. From left to right, the first section of the engraving makes a lot of sense for the neurophysicist; the second section would be understood by optical physicists; the third section is well known to the biologist; the fourth section expresses the world of space and astronomy. Formally, the first and fourth sections are beautifully counterpointed. It is the resolution of all the symbols within one work which is remarkable.

Hawthorn must at some time or other have been aware of Aldous Huxley's poetic image 'A thousand thousand spermatoza all of them alive'. He must have seen Edward Munch's woodcut print of man, woman and the tadpoles representing spermatoza. Hawthorn comes up with an image of embryonic life which is both human and tadpole, and within the narrow biological strip there is a flowing graduation from the spermatoza to the full-grown human being. He also sets this section of the drama, which is extremely important, properly sited in the narrow belt of atmosphere between the earth's surface and the sun. It is not too difficult to view the black dividing line between the third and fourth sections as the protective cloud and particle belt. The simple, economical and beautiful engraving solution of the sun, earth and the moon in eclipse relationship makes the total image memorable.

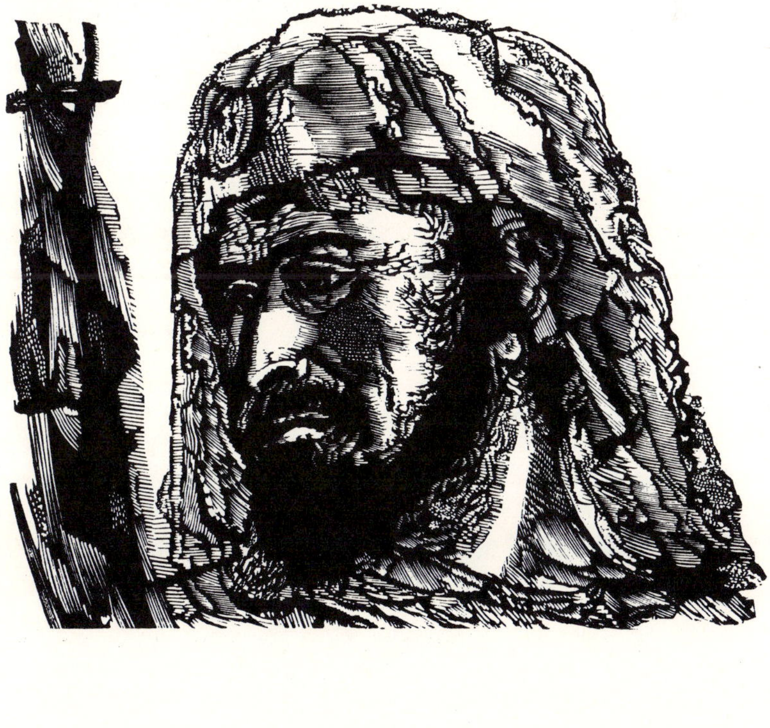

[322] Peter Reddick: *Saul* from *The Poems of Robert Browning*, 1969. 10.0 x 8.3cm

[323] Geoffrey Wales: *Shells and Rock Form*, 1969. 11.5 x 13.25cm

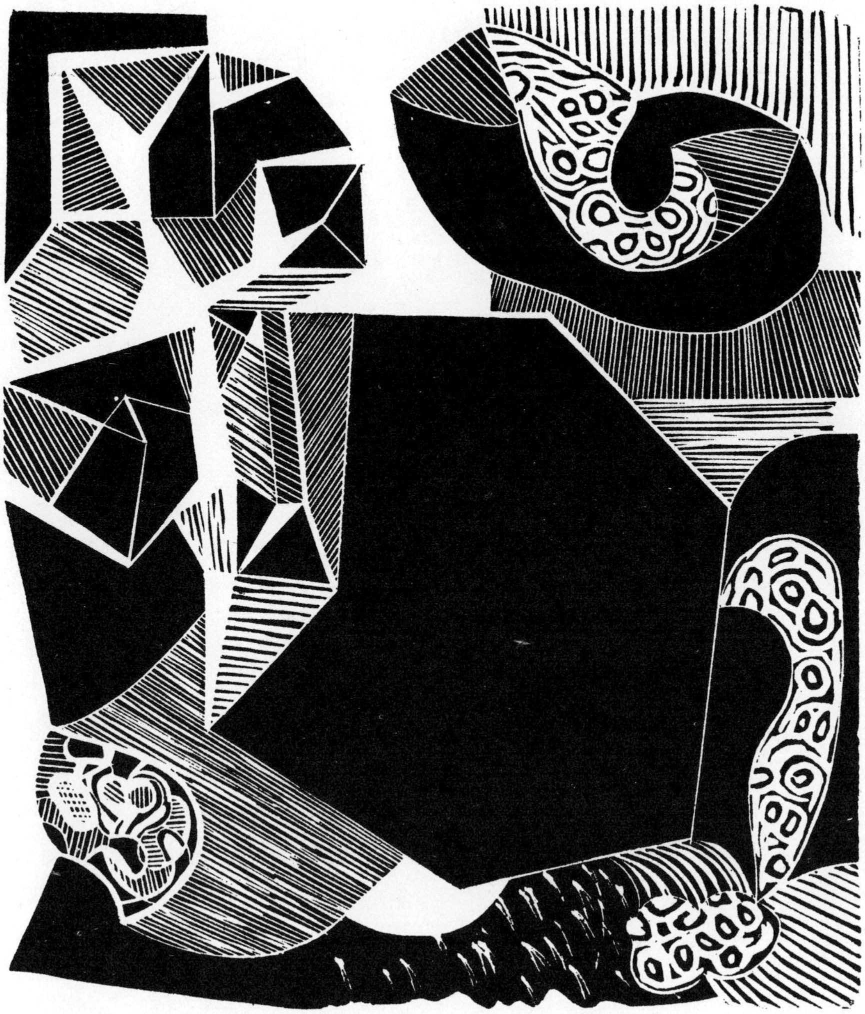

In the engraving *Estuary* [335] Hawthorn is seen performing on straight landscape and he has kept the three-dimensional space concept intact. The lighthouse on the horizon is a very concise engraving statement; it is the only vertical line on the block, its height and width have been calculated to a very fine degree. Hawthorn's sky is very expressive of wind forces and on the ground plane he brings his strongest light into the foreground. The light in the sky is achieved by pure line throughout and it also establishes the sky plane, but the ground plane is really stated by the weight of white shapes. The white ground shapes are dramatic, hard and insensitive. The shape is a straightforward two-dimensional pattern, superimposed on the ground plane rather than being engraved. The starkness of this cut-out is emphasized by the brilliant sensitivity of the engraving solution of the plane of the sky, and the sense of isolation and the impending storm is very real.

An essential part of the British art scene are those artists of independent character who spring up from time to time in various parts of the country. The contributions of some of these people are of a unique nature. William T. Rawlinson and James Bostock are two such artists. Rawlinson is an independent wood engraver who had no early contact with those who adhered slavishly to the white-line technique. In fact for a long time he met only rejection from them, although he is basically a

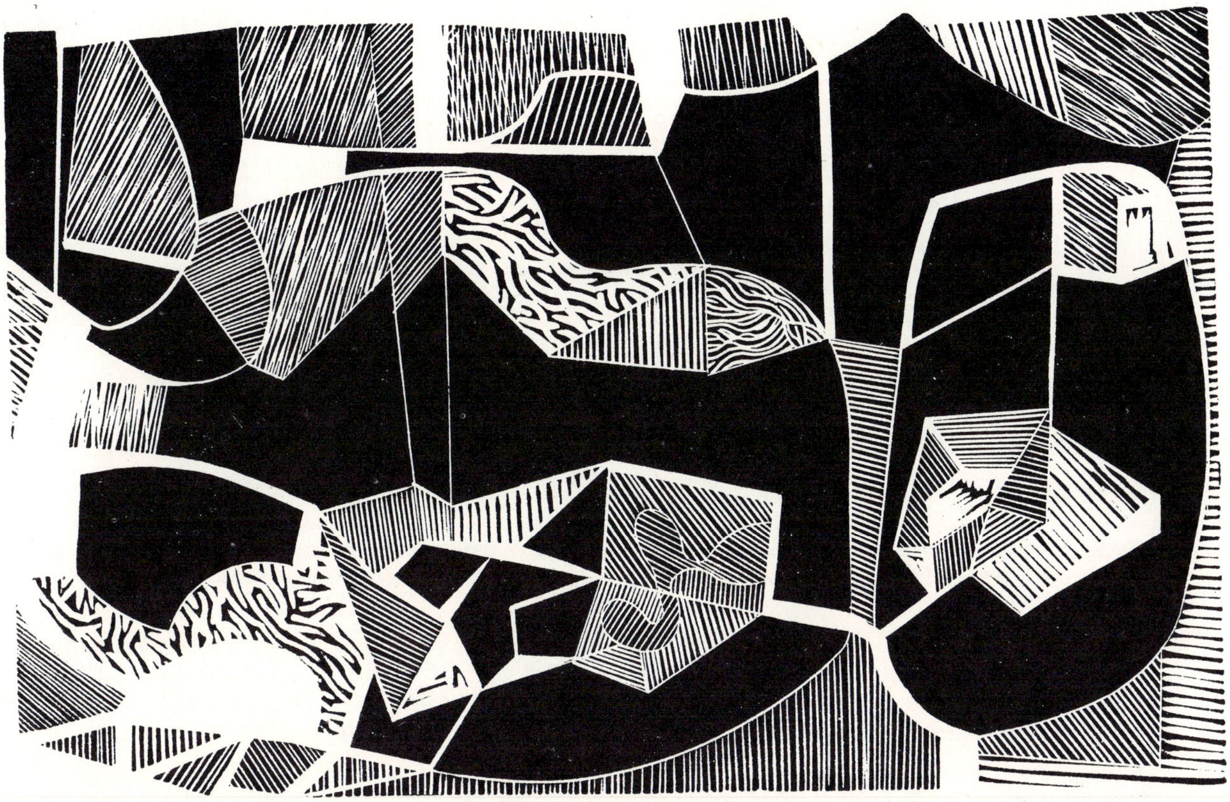

[324] Geoffrey Wales: *The Waves,* 1969. 16.0 x 10.35

white-line engraver but not in a puritanical way. He considers the white line as the natural way to engrave but would also use the black line should he need it. Rawlinson has a great admiration for Dürer, the Danube school and Holbein. This influence can best be seen in the brilliant cloud and sky scene in his *The Graveyard of the Giants* [frontispiece]. Rawlinson is the English master of the overall half-tone optical grey of engraving; only rarely does he have a solid black. The half-tone between the black and white poles is a point of arrival in the forming process and not a point of departure. It is the point of development of full form and it is quite scientific, accounting for Rawlinson's refusal to decorate with shape or imposed pattern.

Rawlinson was trained at Liverpool College of Art from 1929 to 1935; very few engravers seem to have emerged from this area. Except for a considerable amount of travel overseas, he has spent most of his life in the Midlands. He remains completely untouched by the dominating influences of such artists as Rooke, Gill, Gibbings, Ravilious and others. Rawlinson has a sympathy with John F. Greenwood [157] and C. W. Taylor and he has brought their concepts to fruition. Equally, he is untouched by the many aesthetic theories which have characterized this century's art. Throughout Rawlinson's entire production there is no evidence of his having emerged from a tradition of book design and illustration; he has developed as a free agent. Neither has he ever allowed shape and pattern to dominate his search for form. His shapes evolve, fused from the evolution of the forming process. For him shape has no separate existence whereas Ravilious, the supreme pattern maker, consciously cuts and fits together a complex of small shapes to make a large one. On one of my visits to Rawlinson's home he called my attention to the fascinating forms of the seeded clematis in his garden. Holding the geometrically spiralled seed head, comprising coiled and feathered stems, he said 'Look at this wonderful form; for years I have been trying to find the engraving solution.' There is one of course, and there is little doubt that eventually Rawlinson will discover it.

In orientation Rawlinson is a true landscape artist in the English tradition. Like Mackley, he does not engrave until he has firstly fallen in love with his subject and secondly thoroughly understood it. In some instances the engraving has appeared as long as six years after the initial studies were made. Rawlinson solves a new problem in every engraving and rarely produces a new work without there being a new problem to solve. He imbues his subjects with a cool, generous and distilled nobility which is a classical nobility of sensitivity arising out of strength, understanding and a clear vision.

In his earlier days Rawlinson was rejected for membership by both the Royal Society of Painter Etchers and Engravers and the Society of Wood Engravers, yet he was a Gold Medallist in engraving at the 1935 Paris Salon. He started exhibiting with the Society of Wood Engravers and in 1972 the Society honoured him by inviting him to full membership.

The attitude of the two societies towards Rawlinson indicates a situation which existed at one time when, despite an enthusiasm for a particular creed and strong

[325] Garrick Palmer: *Circular Forms*, 1969. 23.0 x 17.75cm

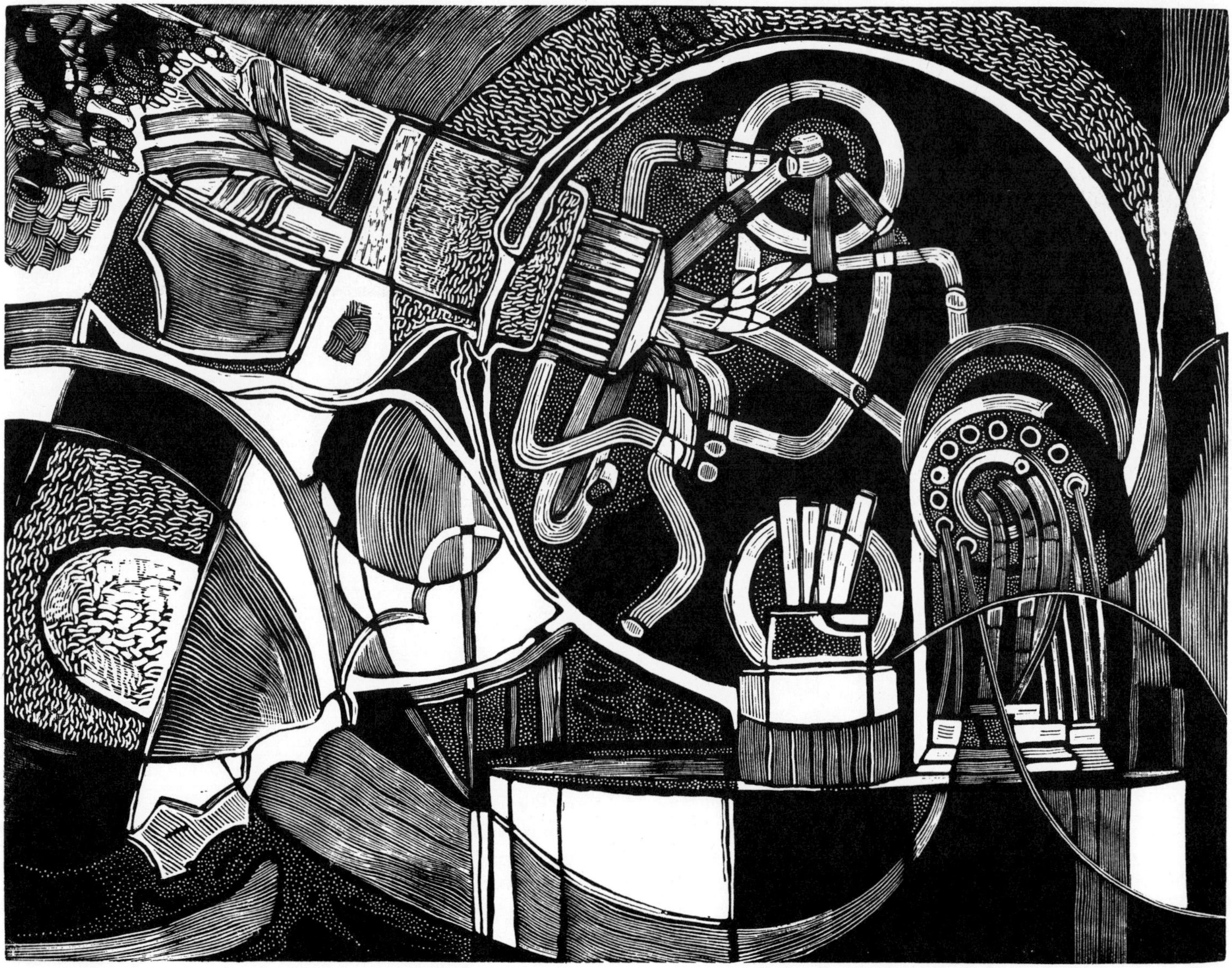

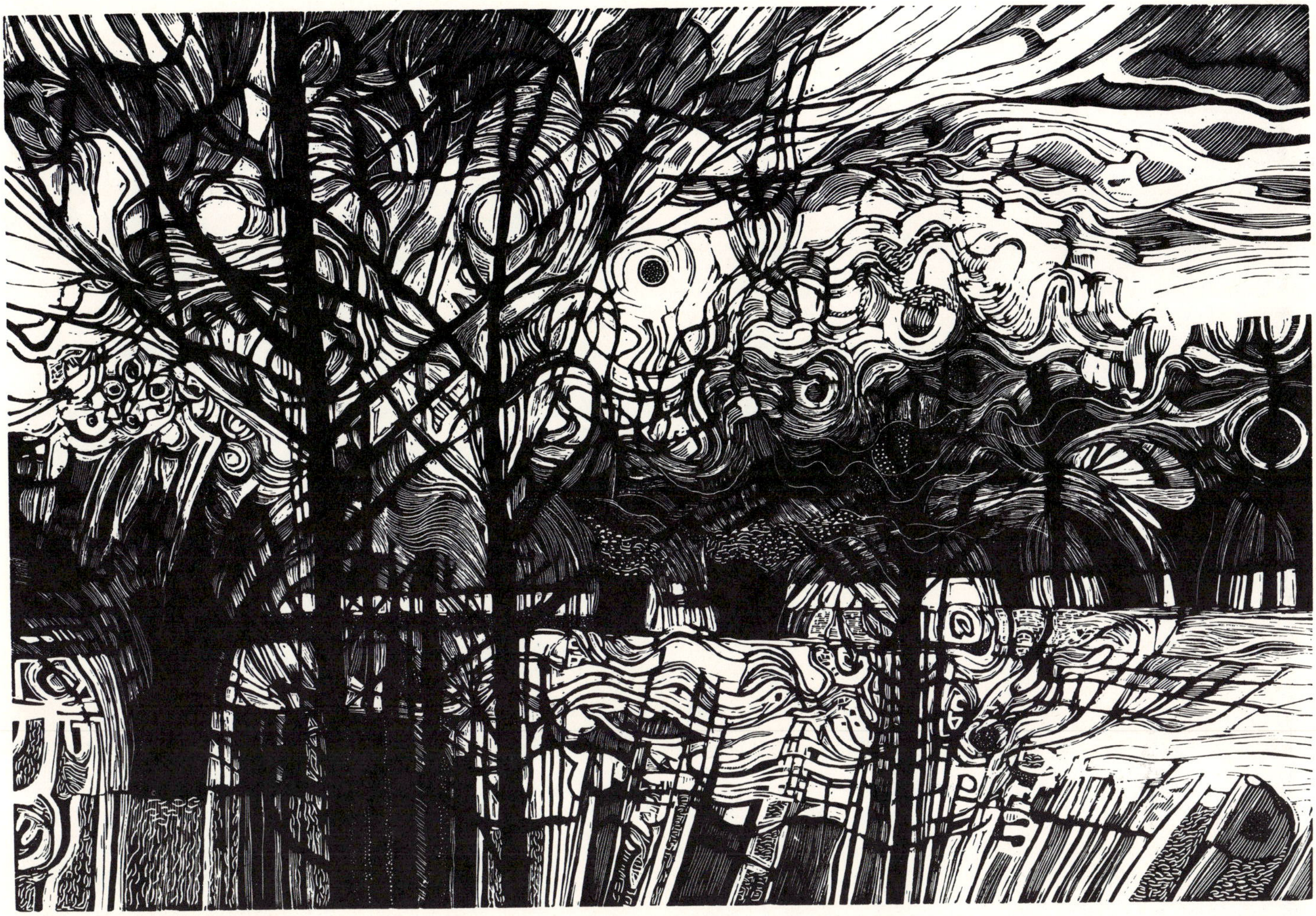

[326] Garrick Palmer: *Summer Trees*, 1971. 28.8 x 19.8cm

convictions, the individual was not given the recognition that talent warranted. It has been suggested that this was particularly true in the case of artists whose ideas did not conform to the accepted views of the establishment, and the resulting lack of professional recognition undoubtedly made the artist feel insecure. Fortunately, the liberal views of Iain Macnab and John Buckland-Wright prevailed and the Society of Wood Engravers adopted a more enlightened attitude towards membership and a generous policy continues to be followed.

James Bostock is a remarkable wood engraver, an artist and a superb craftsman in technique. His engraving of cacti [374] shows classical form interpretations of pure engraving. Of his art he has written: 'I have always had a kind of puritanical ideal in wood engraving. I mean that as the act of engraving is to create positively the white areas of a design, I have tried to draw with the white line, instead of drawing on the block with a pen or brush and then merely engraving away the background white. This I feel creates a black image which has the qualities resulting from a pen drawing and not the essential quality of wood engraving. It is extraordinarily difficult to do it my way and involves a sort of mental readjustment so that one becomes aware of the light in a subject as being the positive factor and the darkness as an absence of light. Thus one draws with the burin, as the converse of

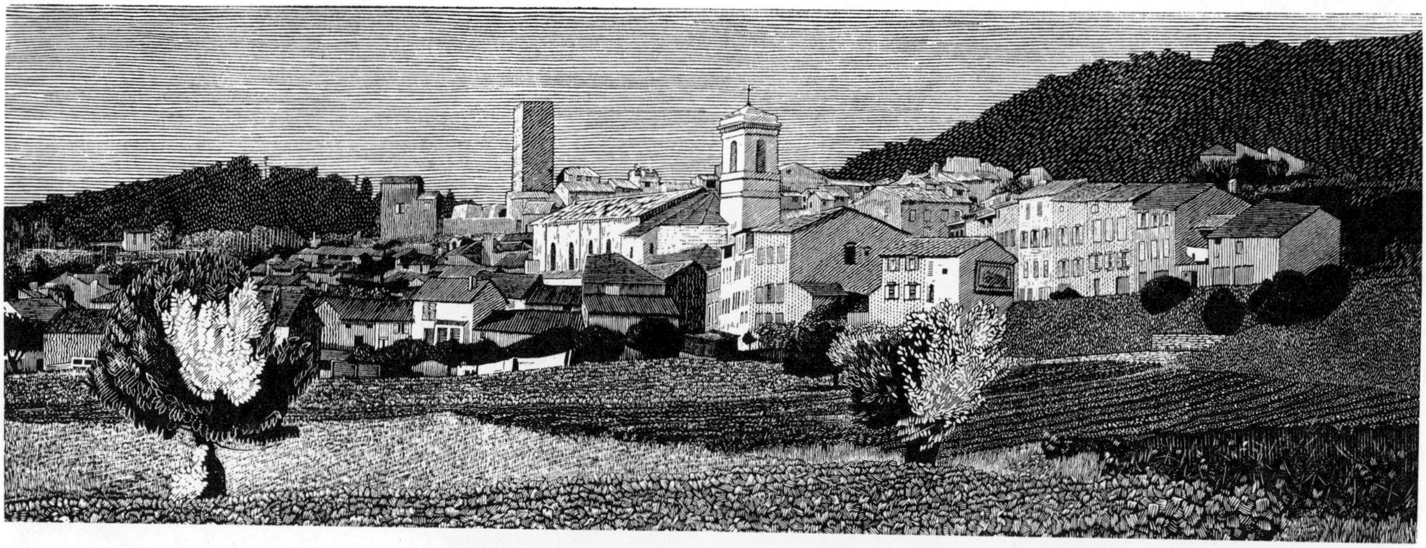

[327] Simon Brett: *L'Automne en Provence*, 1970. 25.3 x 10.0cm

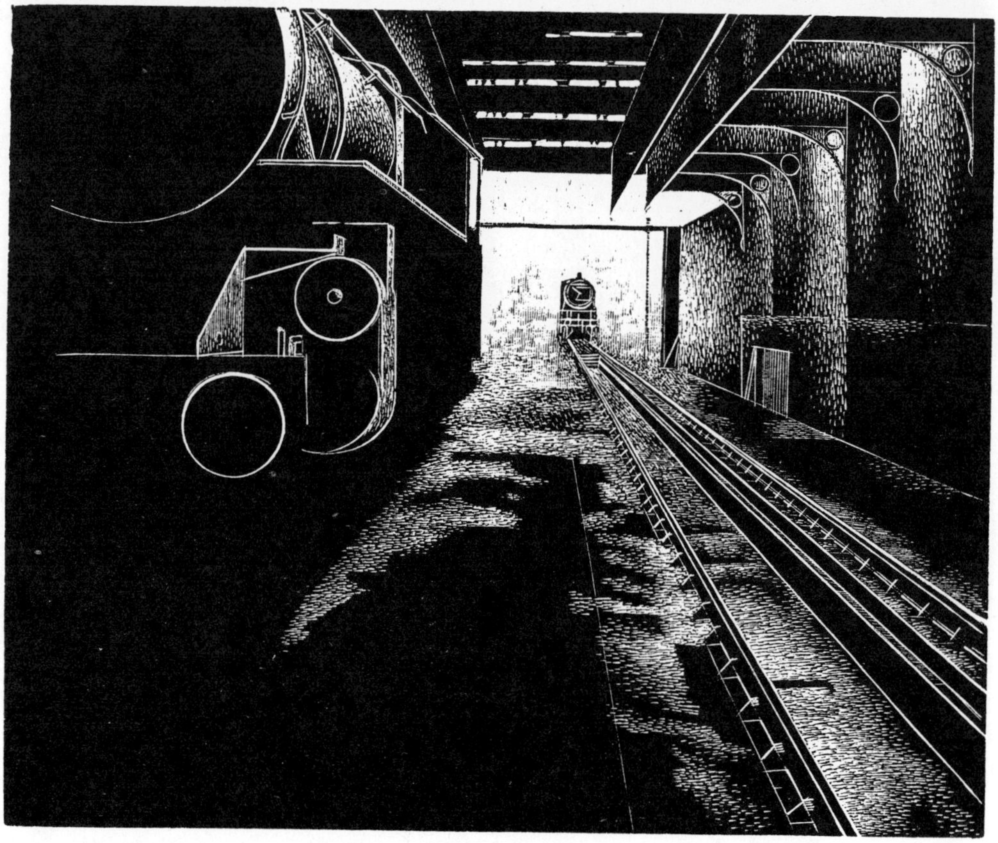

[328] James Dolby: *Troglodyte*, 1970. 14.5 x 12.0cm

[329] Shirley Mungapen: *Stonehenge*, 1970. 21.75 x 24.5cm

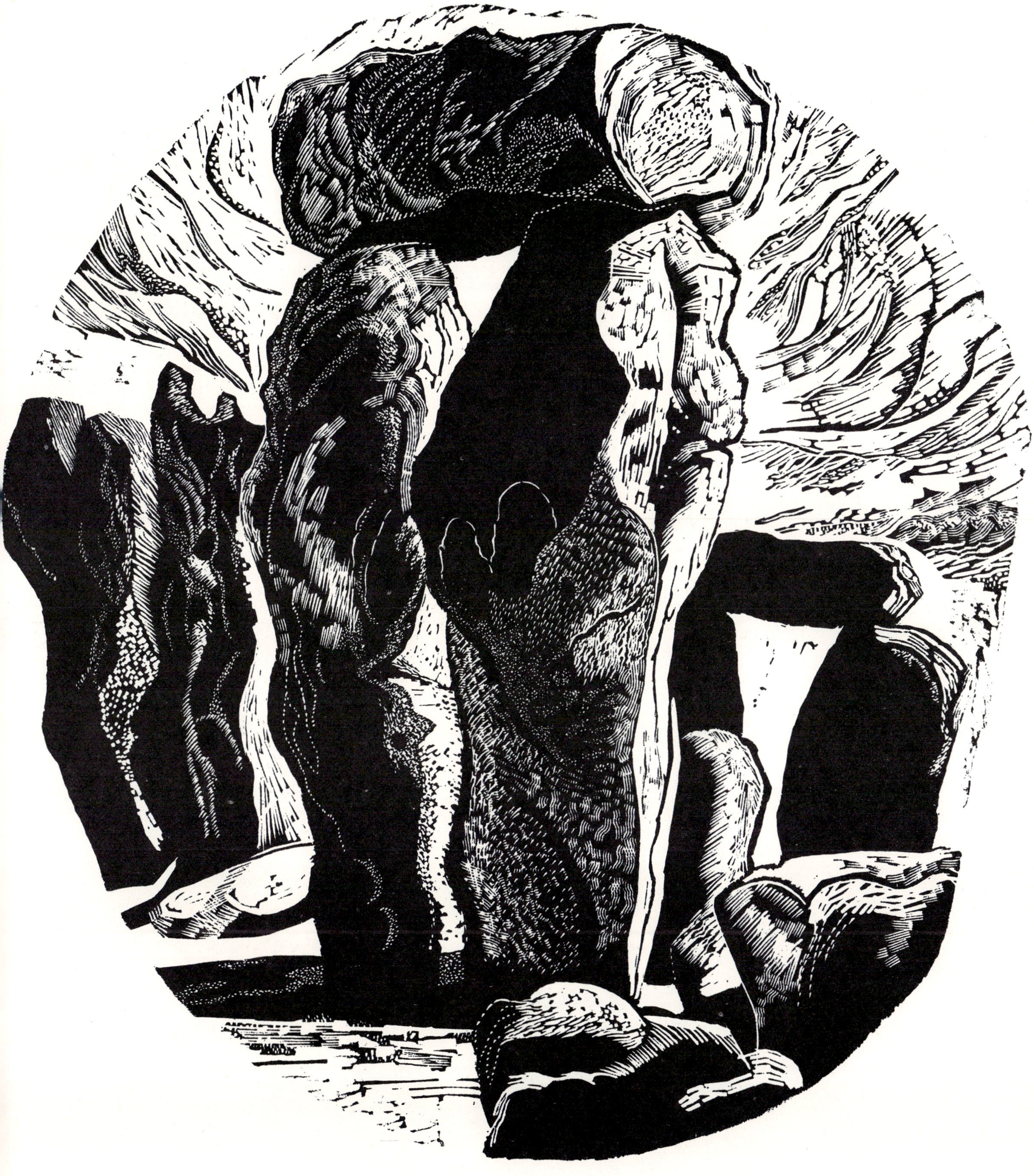

drawing with a pen or pencil. Thomas Bewick did it most of the time, so did Eric Ravilious. Blair Hughes-Stanton did it quite often. Most engravers, however, seem to draw on the block and they whittle away the background. The wood makes its presence felt, of course, but I feel almost accidentally. However, my way makes life difficult and might amount to a kind of masochism. Any print from a wood block has a unique beauty which comes from no other method. "Bostock's puritanical ideal" and "a kind of masochism" is the artist with a dynamo charged to create pure form, which comes from no other method.'

Bostock nearly gave up wood engraving when he found the sale of prints diminishing and had no requests for book illustration to stimulate his interests. No artist of this calibre will prostitute his art for commercial purposes, so he went into education. Like Rawlinson, he could have lifted the whole world of natural science illustration to a higher level, had he been given the opportunity. Both Rawlinson and Bostock are masters at volume expression and could be regarded as distinguished individualists in any school of engraving. Bostock's eye and burin can sharpen a form and make it too easy to see, beautiful to read and a memorable encounter. He has the ability to compress the form to square inches.

Pauline Clark was trained at Luton. She loves engraving, speaks like an engraver and has the talent to be able to make her statements very clear on the block. Her chief interests are the theatre and the opera, and most of her engravings are portraits of opera singers dressed for their stage roles [337]. She is happily tackling the very difficult and exacting task of portrait engraving to which is added the further difficulty of interpreting the massive detail of period costume. Ultimately she will not be judged by the rendering of the period costume, nor of the portrait but on her figure drawing. Peter Reddick was one of the first wood engravers to exploit

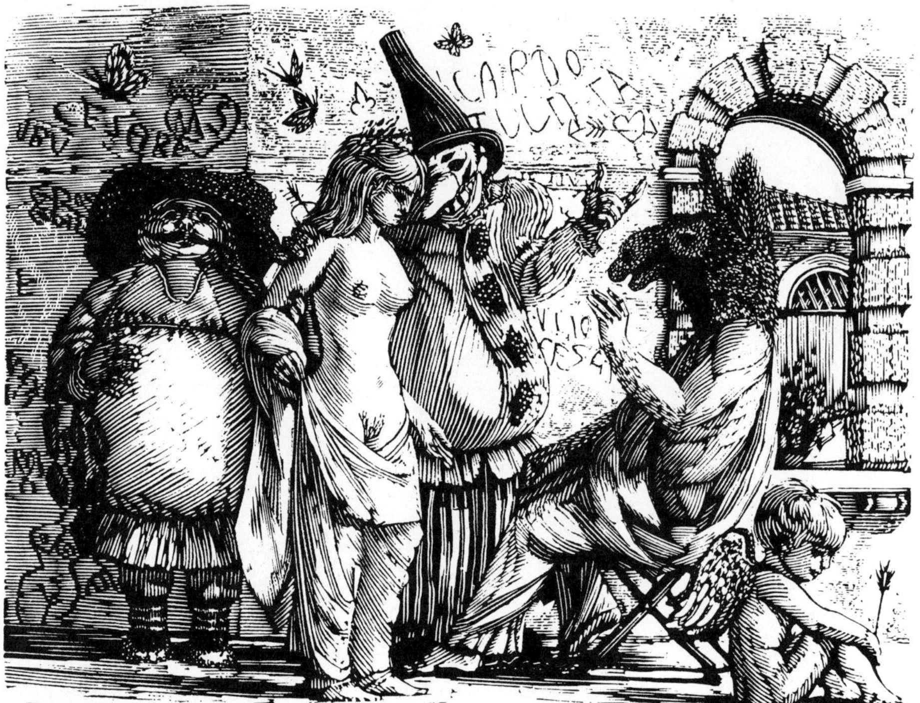

[330] Richard Shirley Smith: Cover for *The Periodical*, 1970. 12.0 x 9.5cm

the portrait, but most of his subjects are historical [342]. In depicting a living person, Pauline Clark is embarking on a new development.

Between 1955 and 1964 a new school of wood engravers came into being at the Portsmouth College of Art under the very respected tutorship of the Yorkshire-born Gerry Tucker. His main contribution to wood engraving would appear to be that of teaching the four leading wood engravers from this college: Garrick Palmer, Yvonne Elston, Hilary Paynter and Shirley Mungapen. The work of these engravers is characterized by a very sharp eye and enjoyment of visual reality, leading them to use engraving patterns to simulate the natural textures of objects. In respect of their use of engraving pattern, they are more closely aligned to the Ravilious technique than to the Hermes tradition of reality being represented by the engraving pattern equivalent. If uncontrolled, the Ravilious technique of simulating engraving pattern can quickly run to seed, and the Hermes technique of equivalent

[331] George Buday: *Osin I Dtir Na N-Og*, 1970. 9.7 x 15.25cm

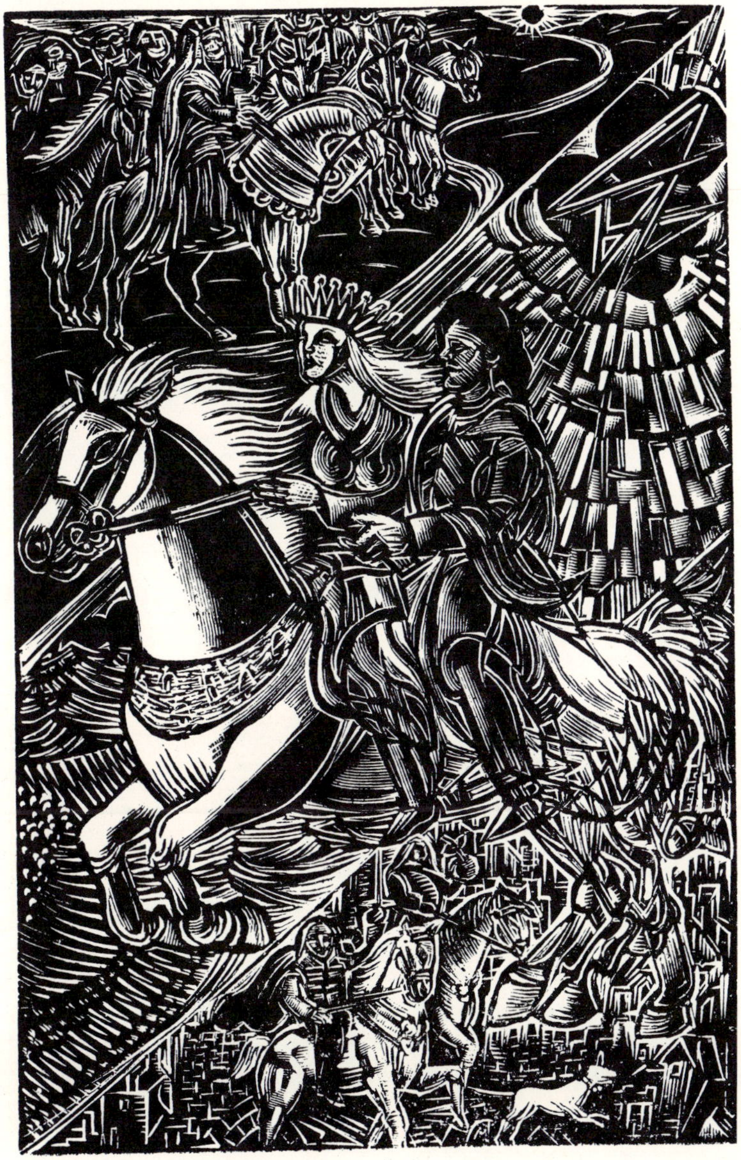

[332] Hilary Paynter: *Airspace*, 1971.
10.6 x 16.0cm

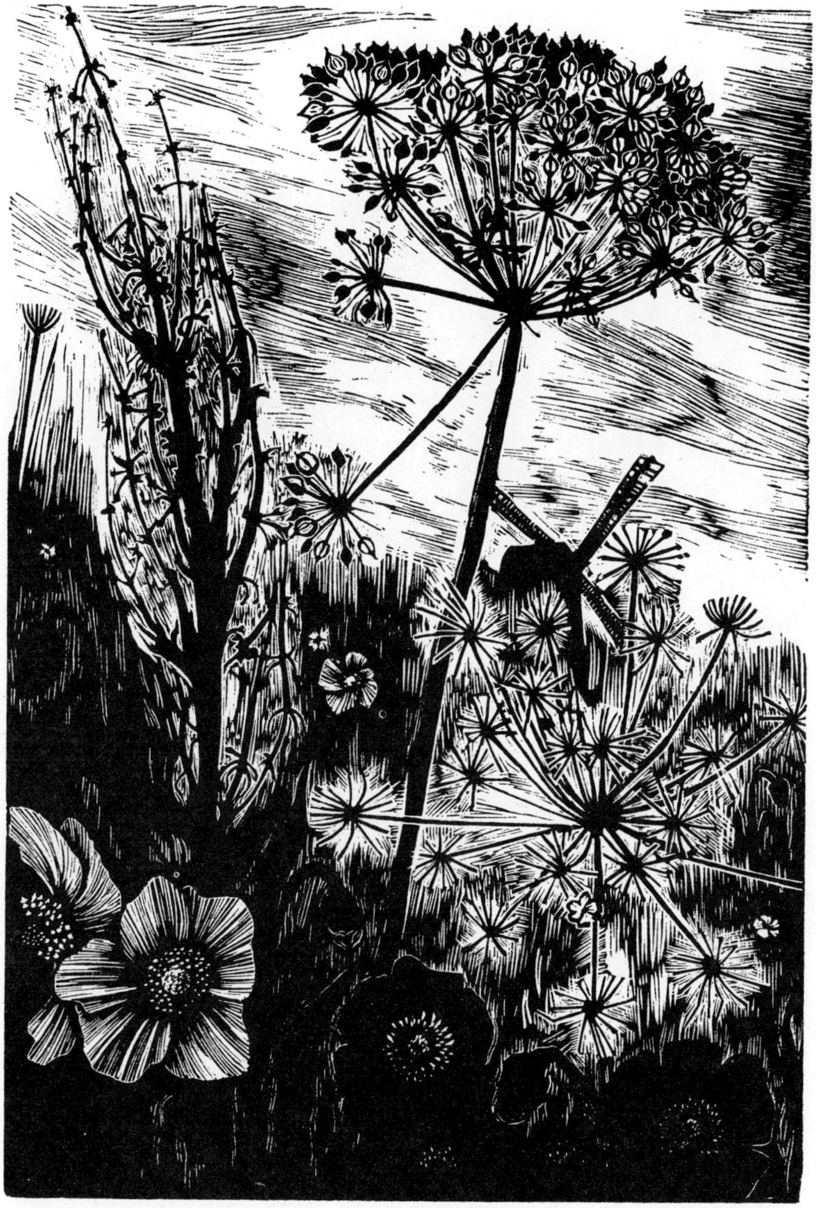

pattern, which is the other reforming side of visual reality, relies for its success upon the recreation of form in its own terms.

Garrick Palmer to date has illustrated three books for the Folio Society and two for the Imprint Society of Massa. In his engraving, Palmer is an imaginative composer and his technique is highly developed. His compositions are usually based upon an abstract structure or framework. In his most successful works the abstract compositional structure is fused with the subject in general. Some of his engravings lack the sublimation required of these two major elements in order that the work can appear as of one voice. His engraving shown in [326] is an excellent example of the abstract structure being used within the subject matter.

In general, the post-war engravers have concentrated on pure engraving and the autonomous print because there is very little interest shown by publishers or by commercial users of illustration. Whilst it is recognised that publishers must embark upon projects that are economically viable, they also have some responsibility for stimulating public interest and imagination.

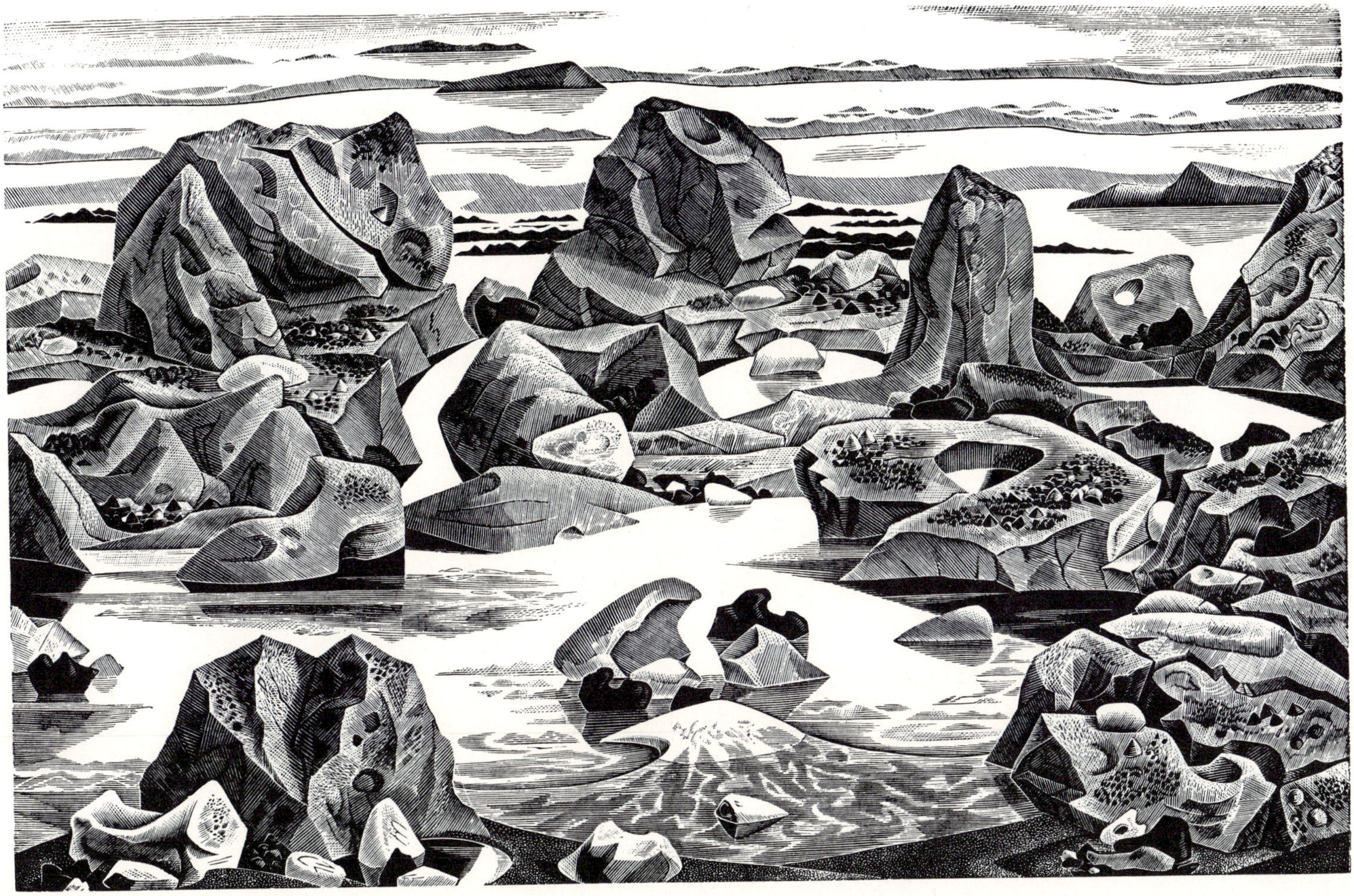

[333] Monica Poole: *Edge of the Sea*, 1972. 24.0 x 15.5cm

It is thought that the work of artists like Gill, Gibbings, Buckland-Wright, Webb and Hughes-Stanton can be regarded as 'safe bets' for the publisher. In their book illustration, these artists are all representational and interpretative in style. Nevertheless, many artists become more abstract and interpretative in maturity, as shown in [210] and [14], and this is not a matter of stylistic change but rather a continuation, purification and concentration of artistic language.

This mature work is rarely seen in books and it might be argued that the publishers and the book reading public are showing some intellectual laziness in relying on the photograph for visual information.

REFERENCES

1 Clark, K. *The Nude, a Study of Ideal Art*, John Murray, London, 1956
2 Read, H. (introduction by) *Paul Klee on Modern Art*, Faber, London, 1948

10 FUNDAMENTAL DISCIPLINE

The full spectrum of visual art consists of three fundamental disciplines, painting, sculpture and engraving. Each has its own end product that is unique to that particular discipline. All three disciplines appeared at the birth of art in the caves used by Upper Palaeolithic man, and these three basic forms of expression comprise the language structure of art which enables the aesthetic forming experiences to be communicated between individuals.

For man to develop as a complete being, the context of his aesthetic forming experiences is vital, and a study of the achievement of great artists shows this to be true. It is equally true that man must appreciate both science and art as being inseparable parts of a whole and both should be seen as complementary to each other.

Science is objective in its general character but the aesthetics of art are very subjective and because of this art demands individuality from its exponents. The greater the masterpiece of art, the more sensitive are the aesthetics of the artist. It is for this reason that appreciation of the great achievements in art continues for centuries, though in each period the analysis of the work is different. It is evident that for continuity of understanding, a work of art must firstly have meaning for its own time.

The noblest attainments of art and the greatest developments of society are seen in periods when art and science are parallel in communication with each other. Such a situation was seen in ancient Greece and in the Renaissance and there is some ground for believing that a similar development may take place in the present century.

The nature of painting lies in its fluid breadth, the nature of sculpture is in the flow of volume and space, and the nature of engraving is the linear precision statement arising from strictures of a steel point cutting through some hard material.

Engraving is an image-forming process which is a means for developing a final statement. Drawing, its near relation, is not a fundamental discipline but is a process of developing intermediary statements. The earliest work of art produced by man was an engraving; he could equally well have drawn the subject but chose not to do so. Engraving as an art discipline is based upon a line which is in a state of continuous change throughout its entire length. It can also be defined as a small shape elongated into a line which is continuously changing.

It is common to view an engraving through the medium of a print but the print itself is nothing more than a bonus arising from the invention and development of paper. Engraving is not dependent upon the print; it was a major art form long before paper was thought of.

Engraving has a unique end product in some hard and tough material, and the final results of copper or wood engraving are often works of art in their own right. If the production of a print from an engraving is ignored, the plate or block remains

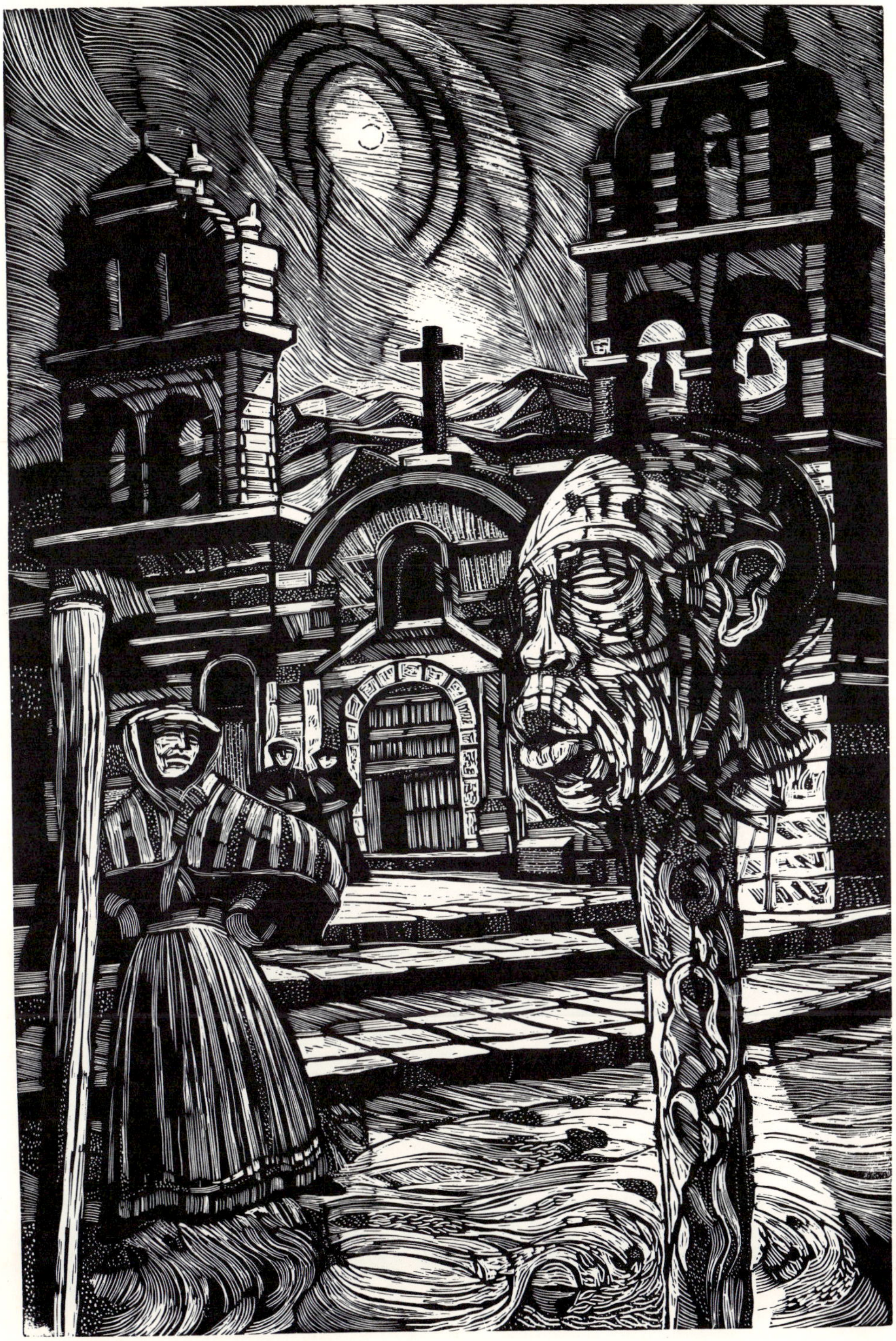

[334] Garrick Palmer: *Benito Cereno*, 1972. 15.0 x 22.75cm

as a three-dimensional work of art – unlike other print media. Unfortunately, the habit of taking prints from an engraving and then assuming that they represent the end product has led to the destruction of many plates and blocks after printing. This wasteful action is deplorable, and it is reassuring to know that the Victoria and Albert Museum in London, like many other museums, has collections of plates and blocks for the benefit of posterity.

However, there is an important difference between a one-off engraving on hard material like rock, metal, wood or stone (e.g. Chinese calligraphy on stone) and a print of an engraving. For viewing purposes the engraving itself is a three-dimensional experience, similar in many respects to viewing a bas-relief in reverse, but the print of an engraving on paper is a two-dimensional viewing experience. A three-dimensional aspect has been given to the copper engraved print during this century through the work and experiments of Stanley William Hayter. In his technique the plate is etched very deeply by acid, the image being preserved by the skilful application of acid resist, and the paper is pressed into the etched cavity, thereby obtaining the effect of embossing. The technique is limited in its range of expression and it has also proved to be restricted in its scope of development. In the world of applied art, the engraved embossing of, for instance, a coat of arms or an heraldic symbol is not as limited as it might at first appear. This kind of embossing is sculptural volume in reverse and the engraver cuts the depth of the form and image in reverse into the metal as a continuation of engraving.

Embossed engraving is a similar development to that of the embossed letterheading, although the cost of engraving the dies from which this type of stationery is printed is high; thus for economic reasons the technique is now considerably restricted in its use. An alternative to the embossed letterheading is the cheaper thermo-plastic technique which, whilst being clever technically, does not equal the effect obtained from an engraved metal plate.

In many countries engraving is often neglected. The reasons for this are twofold: firstly, in any one country at any time there are only a few students of engraving, and, secondly, the wastage rate in training is always very high because of the stringent craft requirement involved.

Each of the disciplines of painting, sculpture and engraving provides a means of expression for different types of personality. There are also many cases where artists of the calibre required will span two disciplines with equal success, but an artist spanning all three equally is unusual. Picasso and Klee come to mind in this respect, but neither of them engraved in wood or copper, although both worked

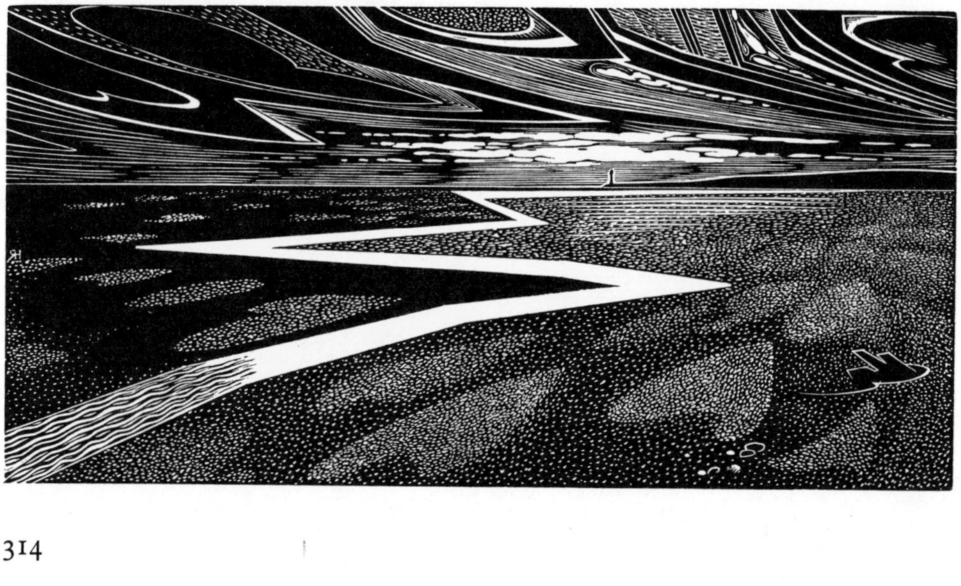

[335] Raymond H. N. Hawthorn: *Estuary*, 1972. 14.8 x 7.5cm

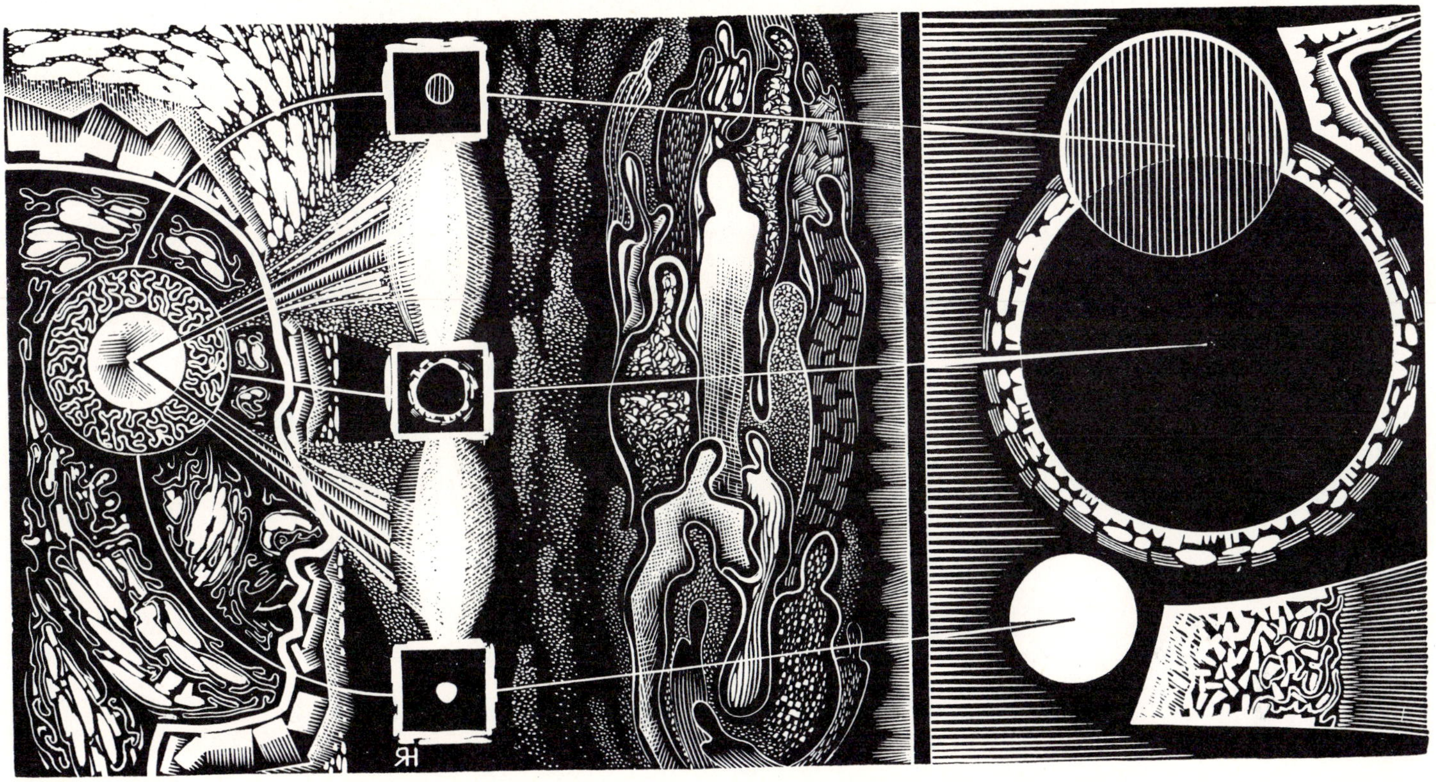

[336] Raymond H. N. Hawthorn:
Noumenal Phenomenal, 1972.
18.9 x 10.0cm

freely in the intaglio etching process, which offers an unlimited freedom of expression. Among many exponents of engraving a number of painter-engravers and sculptor-engravers are to be found. In the British school, John Buckland-Wright was probably the most complete and pure engraver. He worked freely and equally between both wood engraving and copper engraving. He also painted, as did Iain Macnab and Lucien Pissarro. Eric Gill and Leon Underwood were sculptors as is Gertrude Hermes. John Petts is another sculptor. Paul Nash was a painter who moved into and out of engraving, which helped him to formulate his language. Throughout history the commonest fusion of dual-disciplined artists has been engraving linked with sculpture or with painting.

[337] Pauline Clark: *Jon Vickers in Verdi's Otello*, 1972. 8.0 x 9.5cm

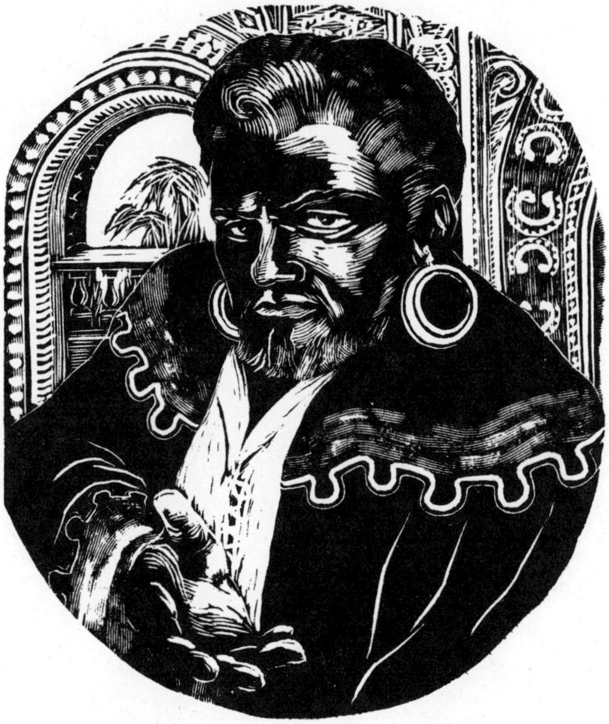

The freedom of artistic expression can be a death trap for a poor or indifferent artist. Painting offers the maximum freedom, including effects obtained accidentally, in oil or watercolour; engraving however offers maximum restriction and has no margins for error. A mistake in engraving as in sculpture becomes palpably obvious but this is not the case in painting. The painters need engraving to crystallize and sharpen their images, structure and imagination. It would be difficult to imagine both Dürer and Holbein the younger without their drawings for engravings or their engravings reproduced by the fabulously skilful *formschneiders*.

A good and more recent example is Paul Nash, the painter-engraver and designer. He can only be fully appreciated in the complete aspect of a painter-engraver. His first engravings were clumsy and awkward; they consisted of cut-out shapes only and the quality of the cutting was, in some cases, rough. His errors were worked in as part of the general composition. On gaining confidence he developed structure and, in particular, the kind of structure for which he was searching in his painting. He was also working in the unrestricted medium of lithography but in structure it gave him nothing. His lithographs are limpid and watercolour in character, but in his wood engraving we can see the painter, working himself out completely in the most restricting of all media. In his *Genesis* series [137, 138, 139] we can say, failing all other production, that we have the essence of Paul Nash.

Nash crystallized his language in wood engraving. It can be said of Nash that his engraving could only have been done by a painter and not by a sculptor. His engraved lines are short, whereas those of Eric Gill the sculptor are long. Long lines in engraving are a special feature of the twentieth-century revival. Nash was short in his brush strokes, to give him the control of space, structure and solids. In painting, elements of line and shape need to be fused to the total aspect of form; this is evident in Nash's engraving. His complete forming process is at all times under his intellectual control. Because of this there is little evidence of the body

[338] Yvonne Elston: *View from a Balcony*, 1973. 13.5 x 19.0cm

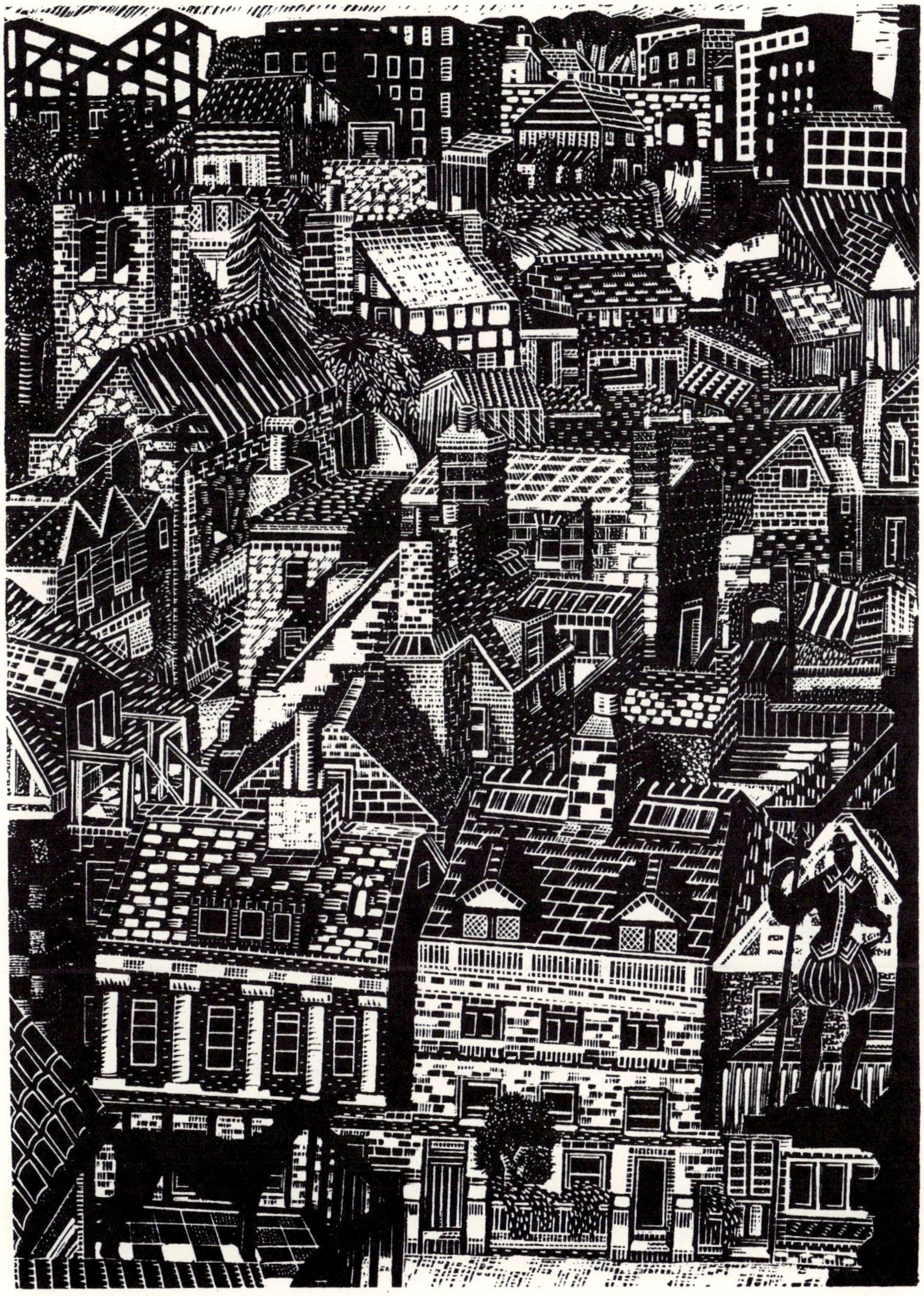

[339] Donald Plenderleith: *Signs of the Zodiac*, 1973. 22.75 x 45.75cm

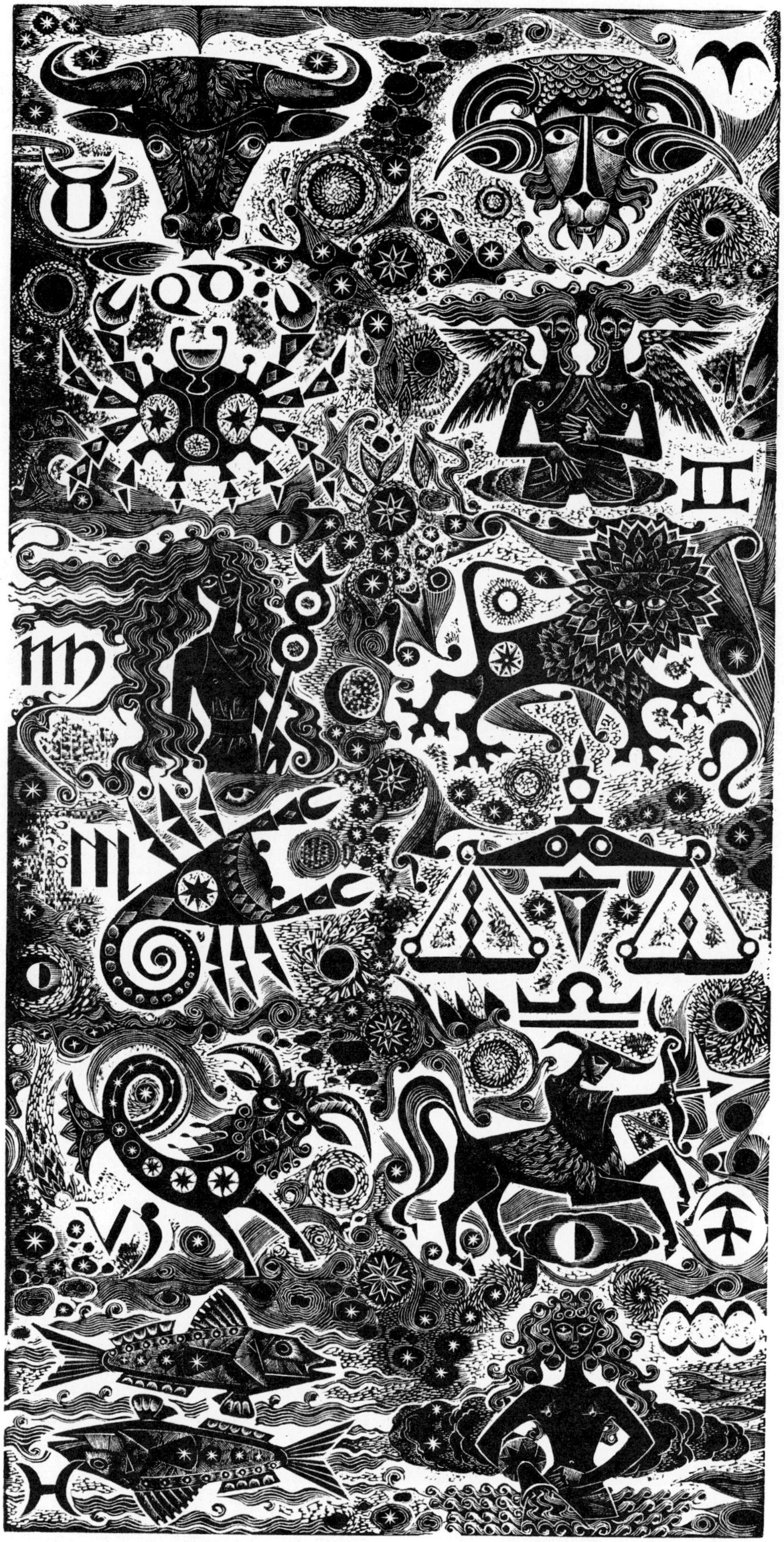

[340] Richard Shirley Smith: Illustration from *Lord Chesterfield's Letters to his Son*, 1973. 10.0 x 12.75cm

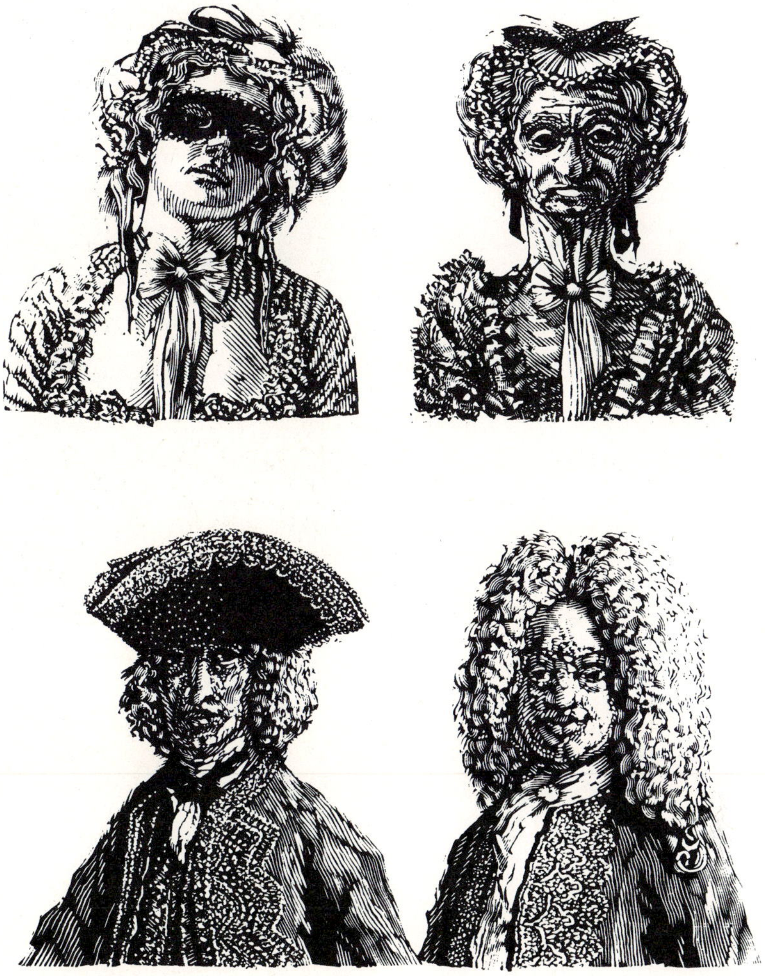

curve. Obviously he liked engraving but did not enjoy the physical process. This aspect remained constant throughout his engraving period. Nash's engraving is not essentially linear; the form arising from the structure of solids and space definition caused him to shorten and sublimate his line. He is a good example of the French concept of *peintre-graveur*.

In his sculpture Alberto Giacometti sublimated volume and the effect was to emphasize shape. Shape in the sculptural world of volume cannot be sublimated. The sculptor uses engraving expression to explore and develop forms, shapes, movements, concepts and themes. In engraving the sculptor finds the most sculptural of all the forms of linear expression. The engraved line can be continually changing in its depth, throughout its length, which gives a changing width of the line, very suggestive of depth, gravity and volume. Both engraving and sculpture are directly concerned with the resistance to hard materials but for the sculptor the relationship is much more direct. Outstanding examples of the sculptor engraving creatively are the few wood engravings produced by Henry Moore [184, 185] and Naum Gabo [351]. The wood engravings of both men were produced in the early stages of their language development.

Body curvature, as expressed by the sculptor or the engraver, conveys such

[341] Peter Reddick: *The Legend of Black Shnuck*, 1973. 13.5 x 9.0cm

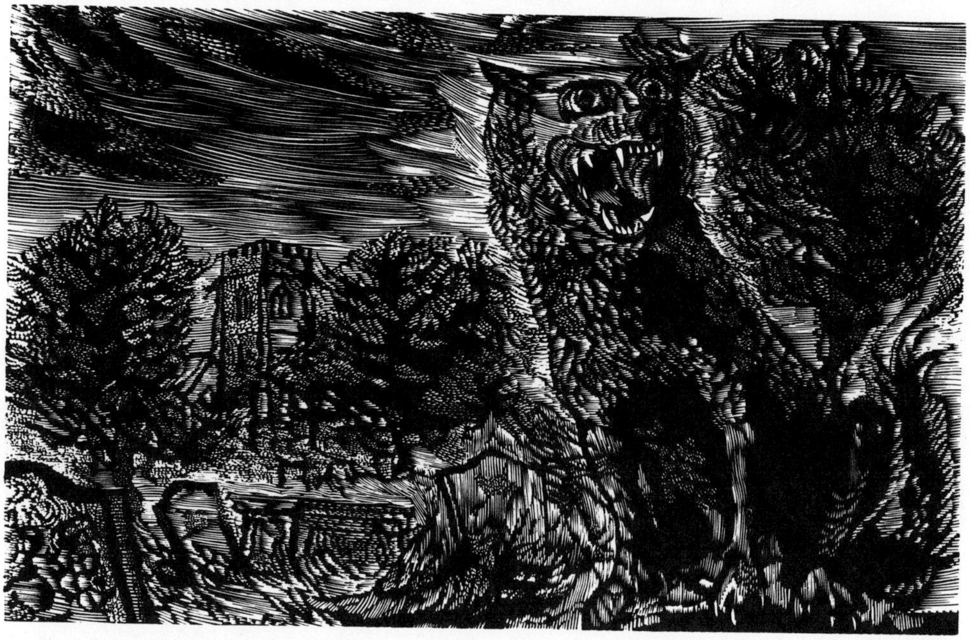

sensitivity that these artists, like the potter and the musician, can impart into their creative work a flow of life that becomes an essential part of the structure. Curvature essentially expresses the life flow; the straight line cannot fulfil this function.

An ability to make the whole body sensitive to the action of engraving is the supreme quality which John Buckland-Wright considered vital for an engraver. He thought that unifying curvature was essential to the nature of engraving. It was this very quality which Mantegna, Pollaiuolo and Schongauer had in abundance in their engraving. Dürer lacked it. He would persistently allow his superb intellect to interrupt the flow of engraving, break into developing curvature and distort the flow of growth for the sake of the repetition of conventions well known to him.

[342] Peter Reddick: *The Fairy Boy Leith*, 1973. 13.5 x 9.0cm

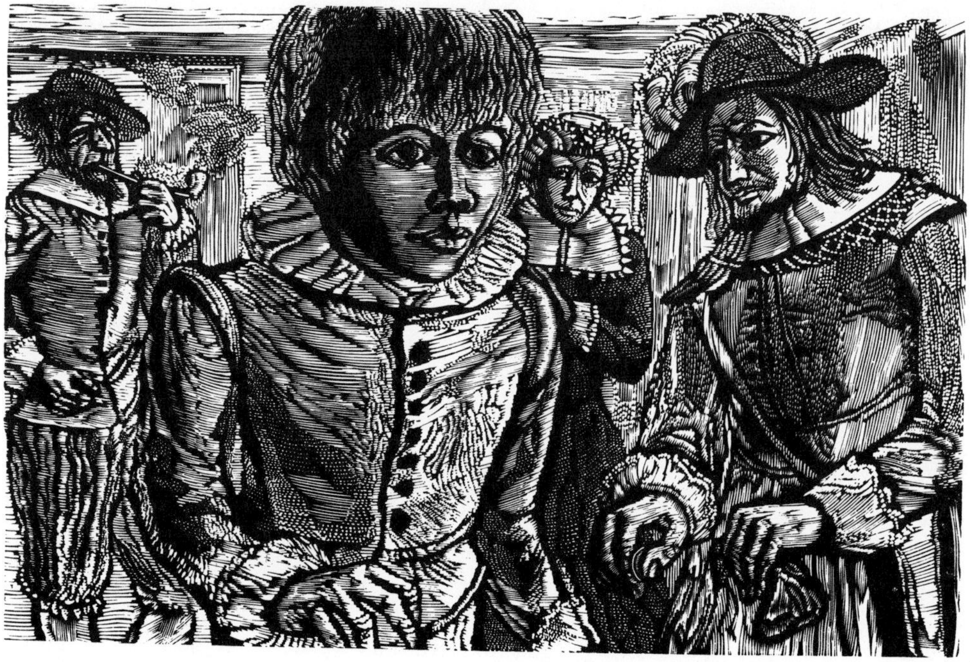

Control of light is a fundamental aspect of the discipline of wood engraving. To the engraver, the virgin block presents an area of 'black' space in which all light is absorbed. Immediately the burin makes an incision, light has entered the black area. The development of a theme in wood engraving is accomplished by the addition of more white lines or by deepening existing ones.

Maurits Cornelis Escher's wood engraving *Three Spheres I* [352] is an excellent example of simplicity and illustrates light control in a superb way. It has simple form, the engraving is economic and the aim of three-dimensional illusion has been achieved. The middle and bottom spheres were developed progressively. The artist engraved the top sphere and took a print, then cut out the spherical image and folded it and engraved the second sphere, the third sphere being engraved on the block as viewed from the flat print seen in perspective. Incidentally, this

[343] Peter Reddick: *The Death of William Rufus*, 1973. 13.5 x 17.75cm

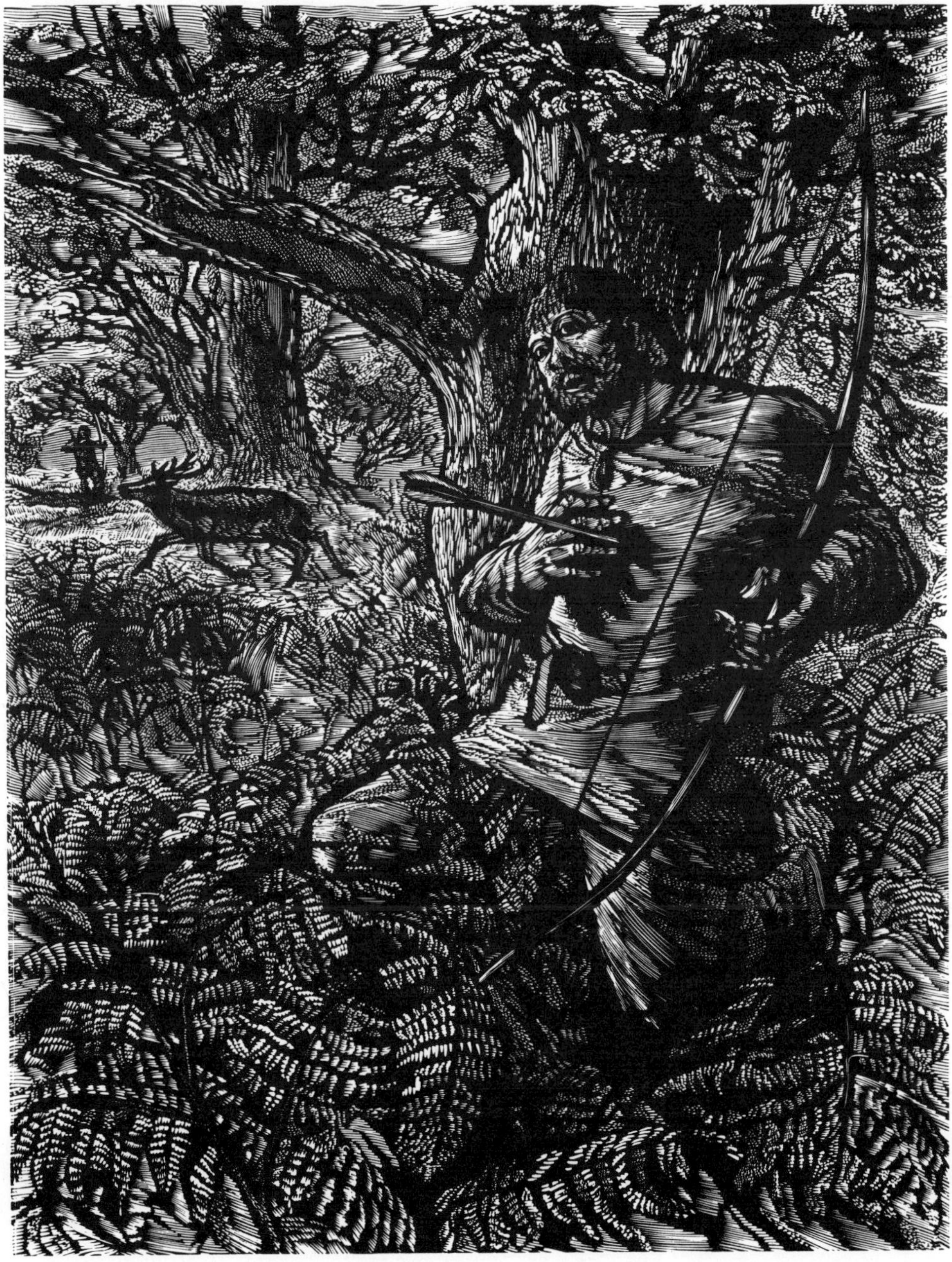

[344] George Tute: *Caitor Virgins*, 1973. 13.5 x 17.5cm

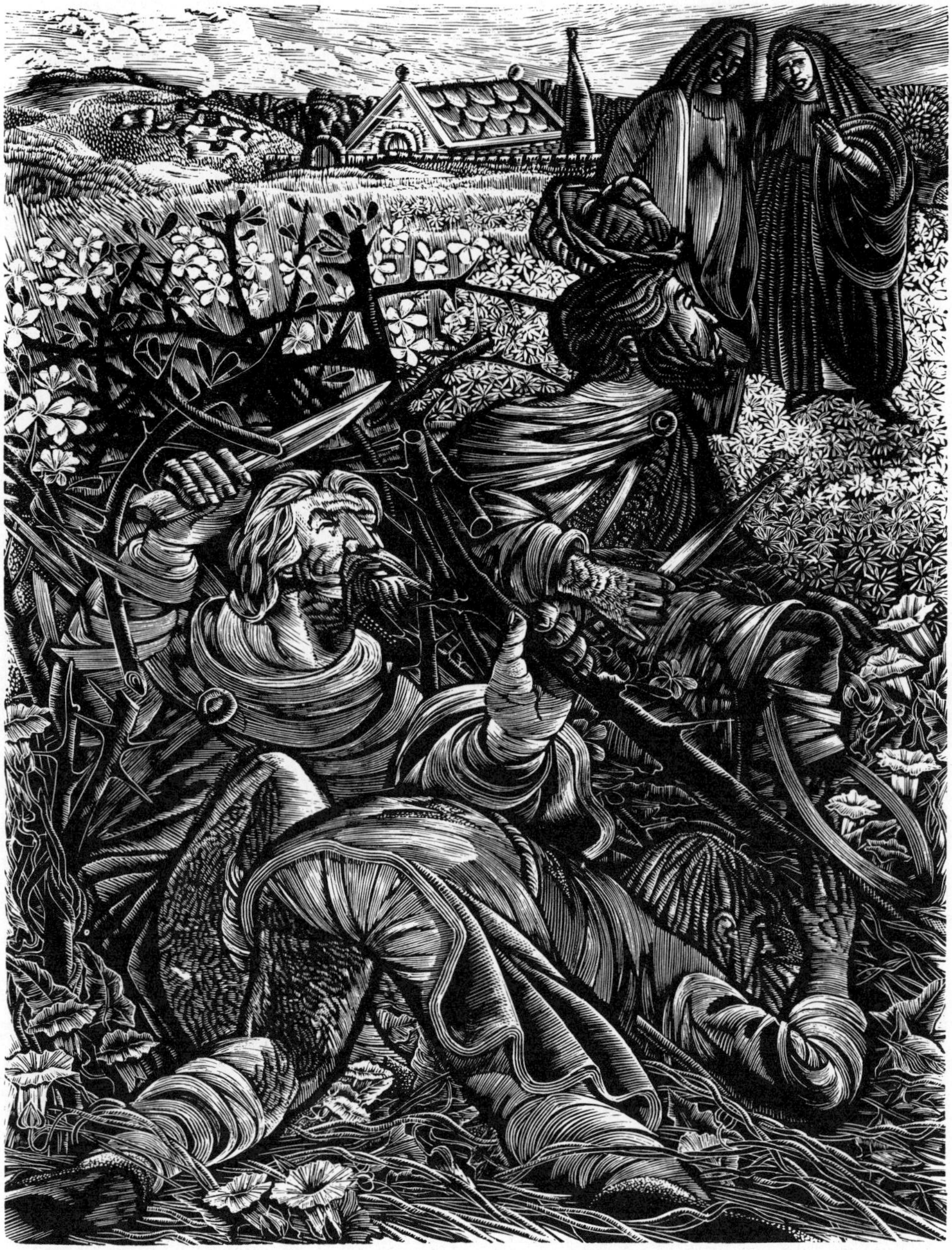

engraving serves as a prime example to settle the difference between an engraving and a woodcut; it is as far removed from a woodcut as is an engraved banknote.

Escher was born in Leeuwarden, Holland in 1898 and his professional training was undertaken from 1919 to 1922 at the School of Architecture and Ornamental Design in Haarlem. His master there, and first strong influence, was S. Jessurun de Mesquita (1868 to 1944) who was deported with his wife and son by the Germans in 1944. Escher has made his own contribution to the changing world of space-time form though his expression is basically philosophical. His prints are a strange mixture of visual images changing through sophisticated formal juxtapositions into a fantasy and in some engravings he even reverses the process. The graphic puzzles have a strange logic of their own, being cunning studies in black and white counterpoint, juxtapositions of perspective systems and unusual transitions from two to three dimensions and vice versa. Many of his prints are made up

[345] George Tute: *Sunflower*, 1973. 9.85 x 12.75cm

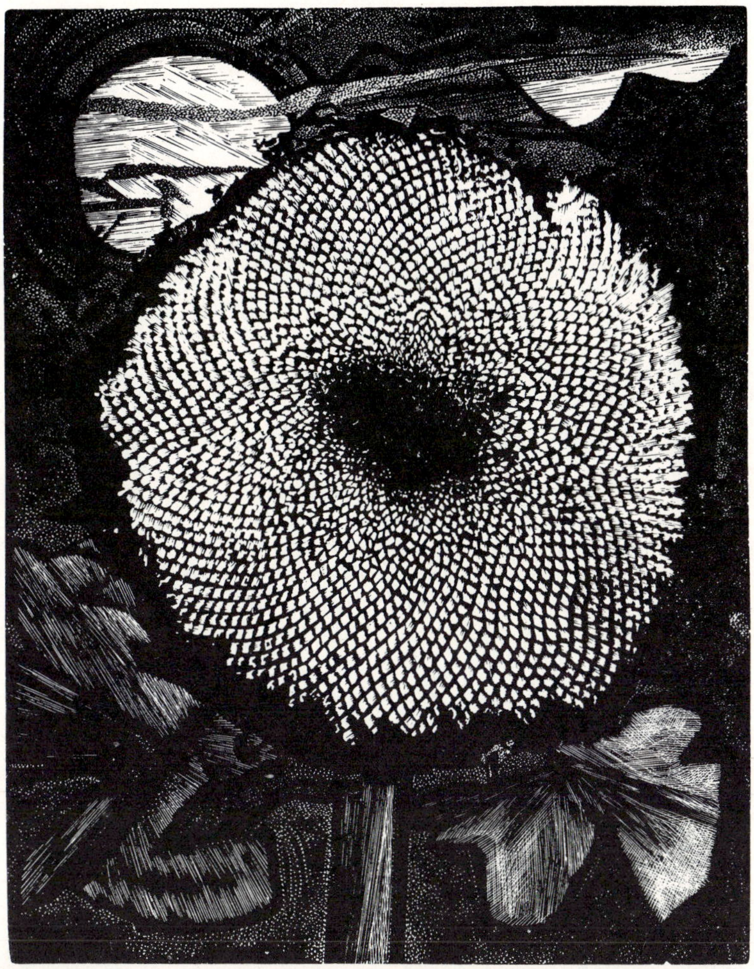

[346] George Tute: *Dandelion Storm*, 1974. 15.25 x 10.1cm

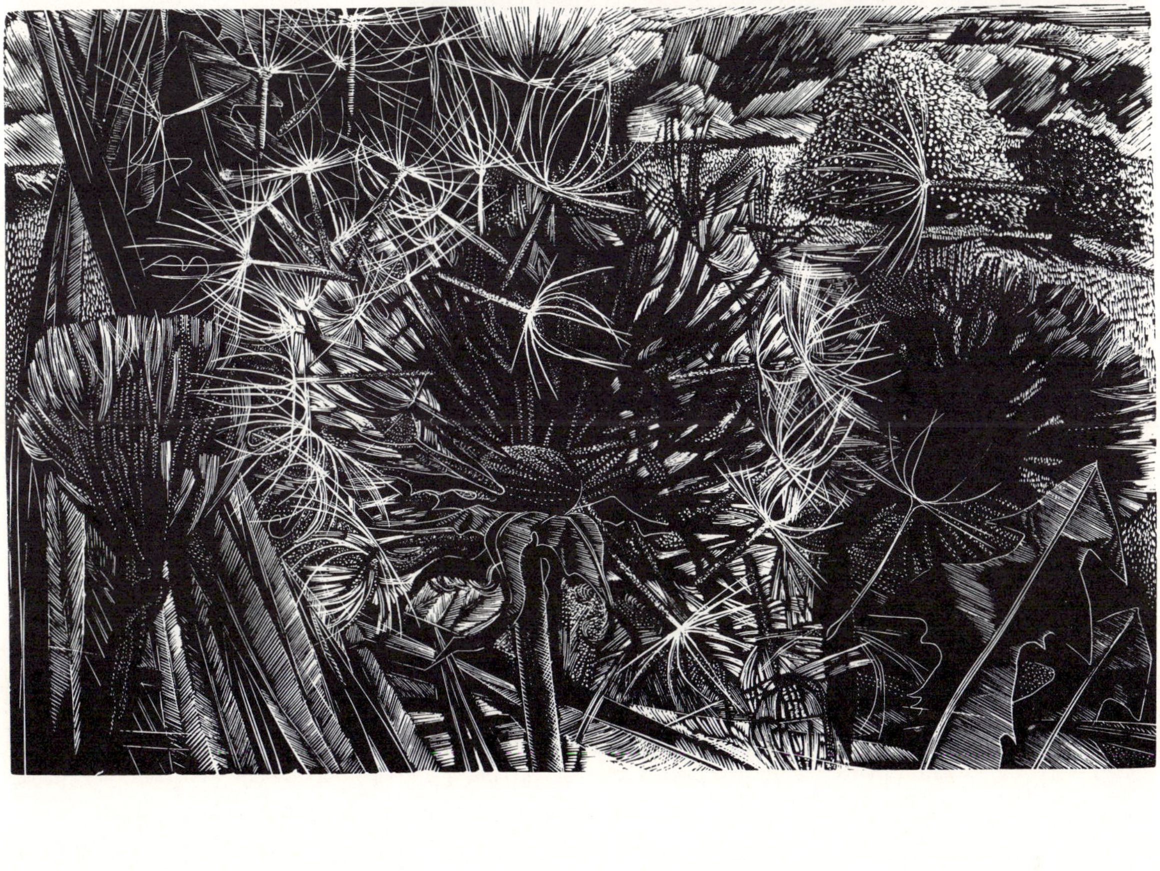

[347, 348] John Lawrence:
Illustrations from *Rabbit and Pork*,
1974. 14.5 x 11.2cm

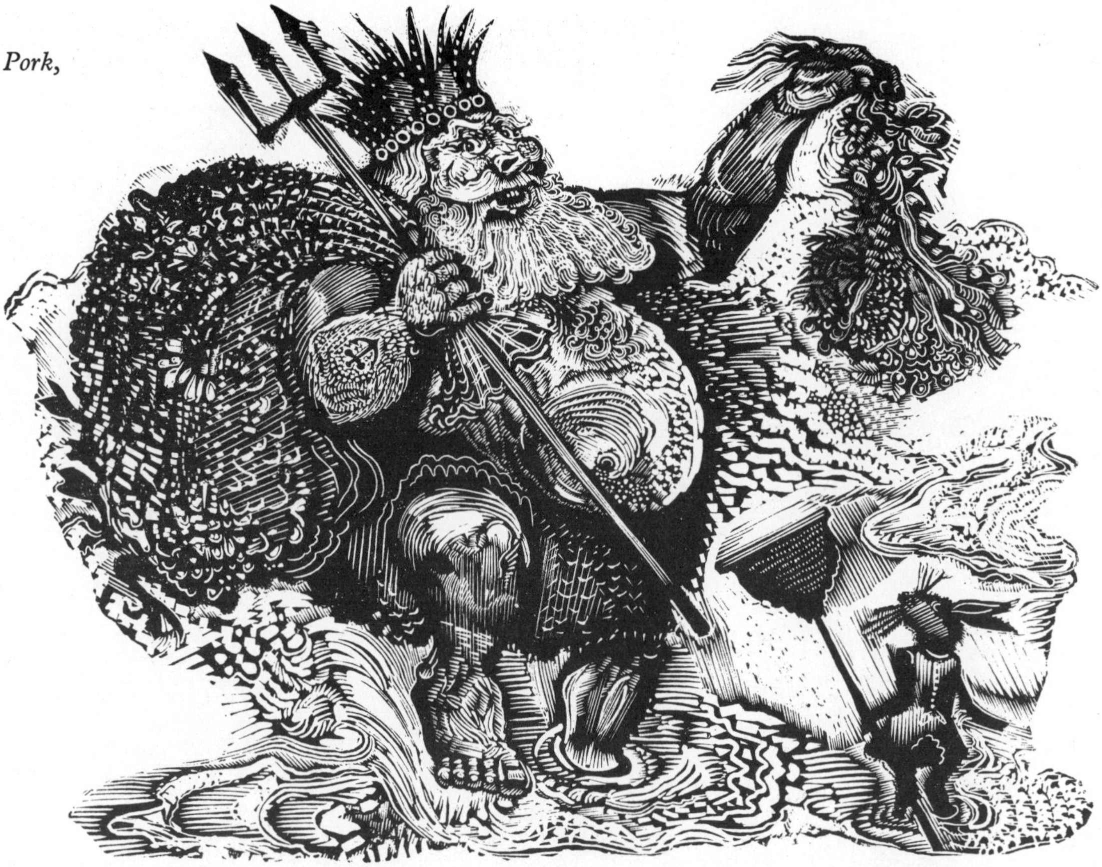

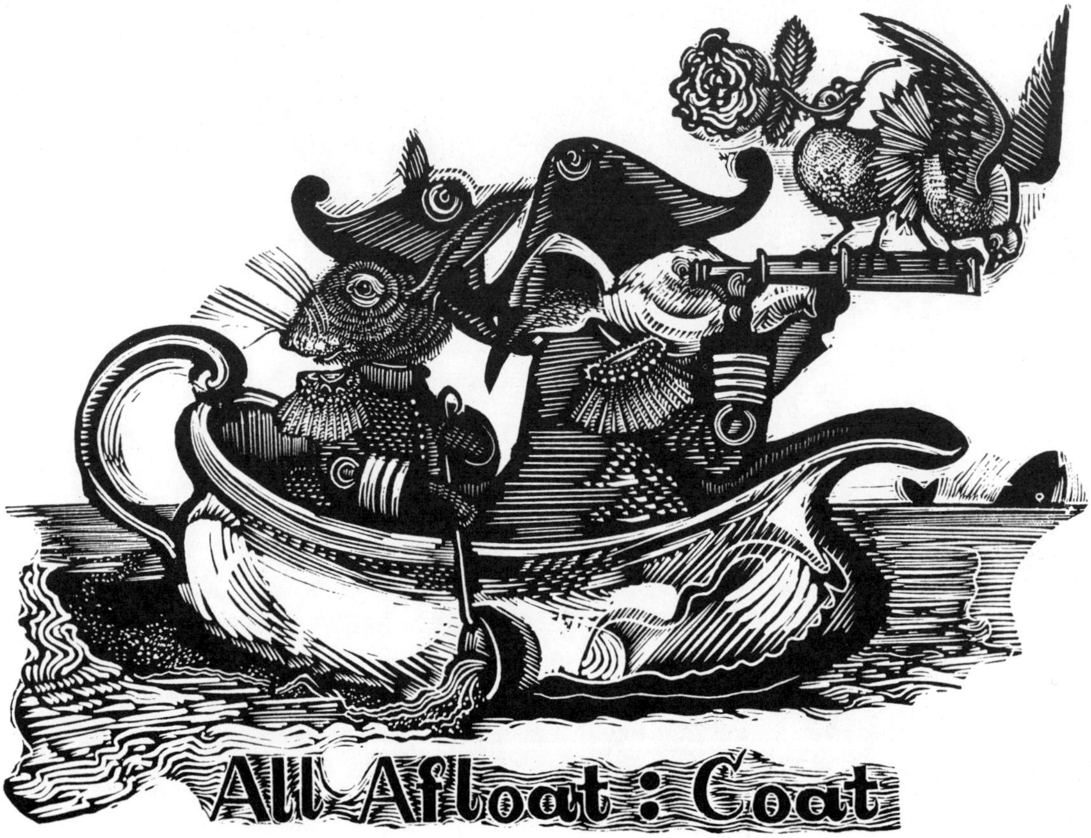

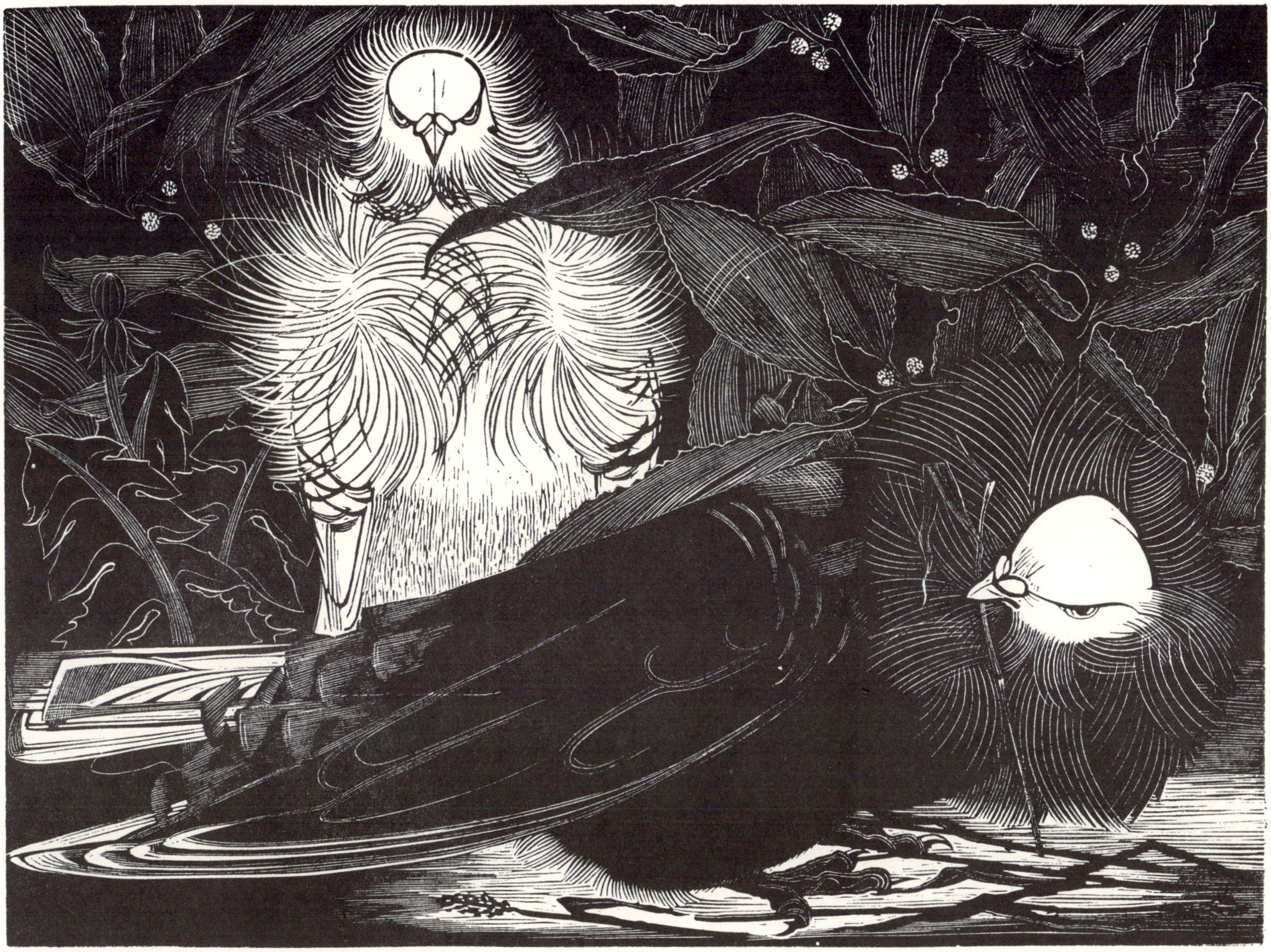

[349] Sarah van Niekerk: *Jacobins in a Bay Tree*, 1973. 20.0 x 14.8cm

of three and sometimes four blocks. Escher's woodcut *Metamorphosis* engraved in 1939-40, was printed from twenty-nine blocks and is 700cm in length. Throughout its length the transformation of images is continuous and time is expressed in the changing formal matrix.

In the *10th Space-Time Form* series by the author [382] the amount of available light had to be carefully calculated to divide equally between four prints, which in this case had to come from the same block. Any further development of the space-time theme is prevented as there is insufficient light left on the block. Theoretically, an engraver can give away approximately 85% of all the light potential of the complete block. Monica Poole closely approaches this point in her *Magnolia* [353]. A parallel exercise in paint would be Malavitch's *White Squares on White*. This kind of aesthetic exercise, important in itself to make a point, needs to be done only once. In itself, it becomes a point of no return for the artist and it is that which is to follow that is more significant.

The white-line concept in wood engraving not only led to the flowering of wood engraving and design but also embodied the concept of light. This light concept is as fundamental to wood engraving as was the study of light to the French Impressionists, though the Impressionists based their growth and development upon the defracted beam. In controlling the amount of white light expended, the wood

[350] Guy Worsdell: *Two Tunnels*, 1975. 17.75 x 12.75cm

engraver can employ beams of light that are sharply pointed, parallel or steraidian, according to the effect required. The delineation of form using a minimum of light – a pointed beam – can be seen superbly expressed in Iain Macnab's *Two Fat Ladies. Portofino* [361]. Form volumetrically developed by a parallel or a steraidian beam can be studied in George Mackley's masterpiece *Rocks* [380]. The full white light – the flood source – developing an environment around the form can be seen in the astonishingly cool and sensitive *Magnolia* by Monica Poole [353]. These three works establish the principles of application of the basic types of light beam expression used by the British school.

It is obvious that students have to give very careful attention to the use of light and their work has to be guided with discretion. Gertrude Hermes does this excellently in coaching her students at the Royal Academy Schools where she will encourage them to let a little more light into their work, though advising caution in the degree of illumination. She does not tell her students what tools to use or how to cut the block; she directs the control of light and its distribution.

The exploitation of the white light beam is probably the most important of the contributions made by the wood engravers of this century. Whilst the work of the transitional engravers is both fine and sensitive, it shows no evidence of the presence of the white light beam. The work remains what it is, engraved drawings and the poetry of their art expression did not extend to this world of light. The transitional engravers worked in a relaxed situation and, quite naturally, they resisted the

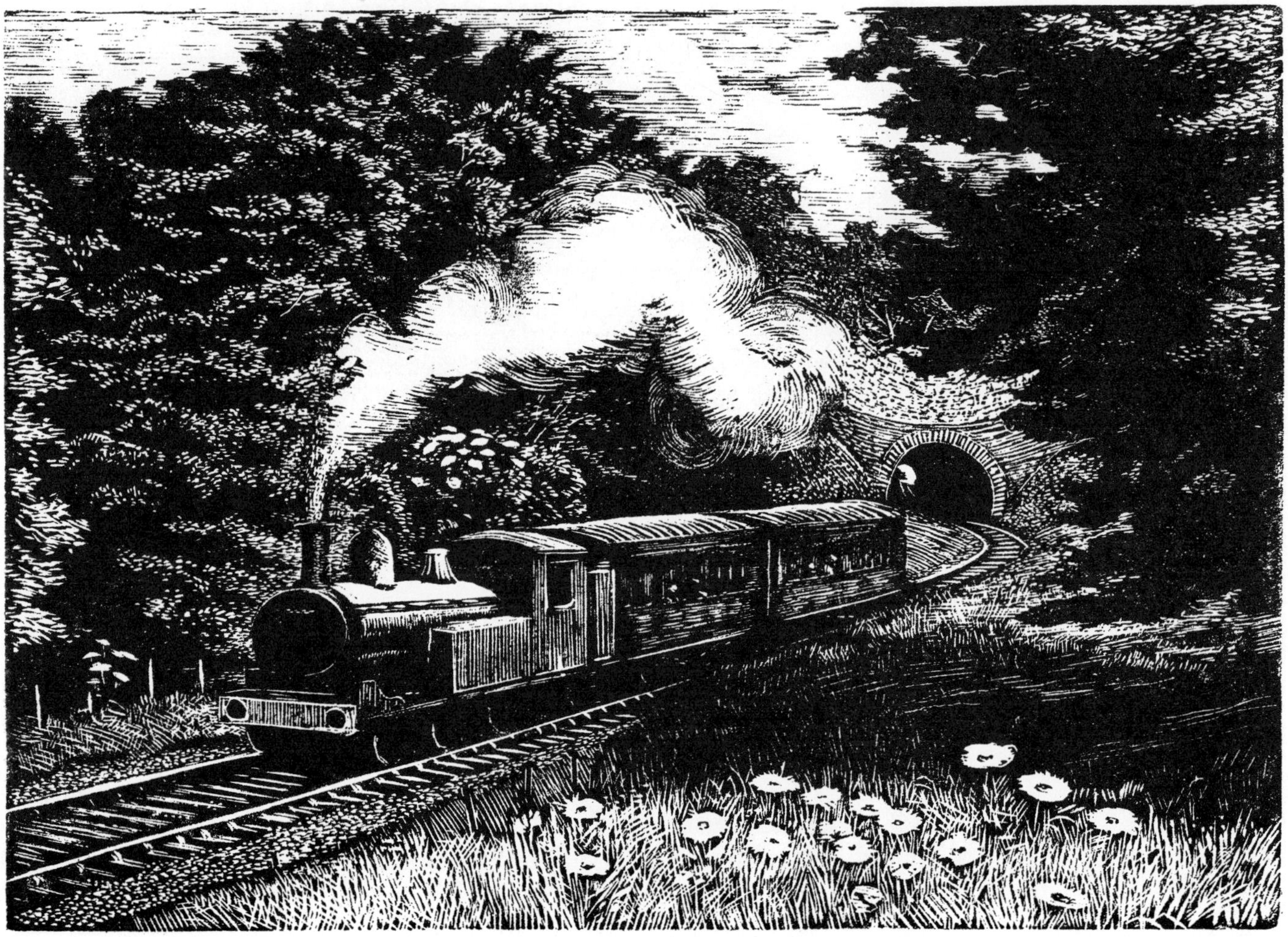

changes promised by the younger generation whose new disciplines imposed restrictions which the older engraver could not accept.

Mark F. Severin the illustrious Belgian wood engraver, whose engraving *Yalk* is shown in [354], described his experience of engraving in his small and lively book *Your Wood Engraving* published in 1953. He wrote: 'Engraving, like art in general, is very illusive, very disheartening and discouraging; indubitably it is the most demanding and unrelenting mistress; she offers the greatest thrills and satisfaction, but allows no one to come before her. Wood engraving consists in removing all that is not needed – thus more intriguing.'[1] The challenge of engraving is to win freedom from the maximum restriction.

While the wood engraver blossoms when given complete freedom to express his individuality, there are occasions when he can employ his art to fulfil a commercial need with all its limitations. An excellent example of this application is to be found in security engraving. The engraved banknote is highly regarded by banks as a safeguard against forgery. Until recently, all postage stamps were engraved and many philatelists will identify an engraved stamp as a collector's item. The final statement of engraving also gave an air of authority to such as degrees, diplomas, legal and government documents and many other items in official paraphernalia. The later nineteenth and early twentieth centuries are rich in examples of this official engraving.

In engraving, the quality of the performance plays a more important role than in painting or sculpture. Whilst in painting and sculpture it is not unusual for an indifferent performance to be excused on the plea of genius, with engraving, however brilliant the genius, the public and critic alike always demand a brilliant performance. Eric Gill would express concern about the aspect of perfection in engraving; because of his modesty this would have been an understandable worry for him. The same might be said of the work of his close companion Robert Gibbings. At first sight this worry might be thought of as a fear of a mechanical perfection setting in and implying an impending sterility, but this was not the substance of Gill's apprehension. He was concerned with the relationship of engraving to the subject matter which he loved, the human figure. His objective realist approach to his subject matter was preconditioned by the burin and the craft. Gibbings had similar feelings and apprehensions. His subject matter was always biological forms of one kind or another and, like Gill, his vision was sharply objective and realist in approach.

In considering the engraving perfection of Gill and Gibbings, it has to be realised that each was a separate biological entity despite the fact that in sitting down and grasping a burin each was employing a similar set of muscular actions. The body attitude in relationship to the block being engraved is a curvature which is not mechanically regular in its movement but is continuously changing, forming a rhythm which affects the course of the line. This body curve process has the effect of unifying all the elements of the engraving and had Gill and Gibbings been concerned about the unity instead of the perfection of their work, they would probably have been nearer the truth because the quality of unity is evident in the work of all eminent engravers whose work is essentially linear, using long lines.

However, Gill and Gibbings are not alone in this. Italy has produced a Tranquillo Marangoni [356]. His aesthetic and technical perfection is as constant as that of Gill and Gibbings and this is equally true in the work of John Buckland-Wright. The unity of curvature predominating in Marangoni's engraving of abstract structure is nearly all based upon the body curve. Such is the reason for the superb consistency throughout his work.

[351] Naum Gabo: Opus 3 and Opus 4.

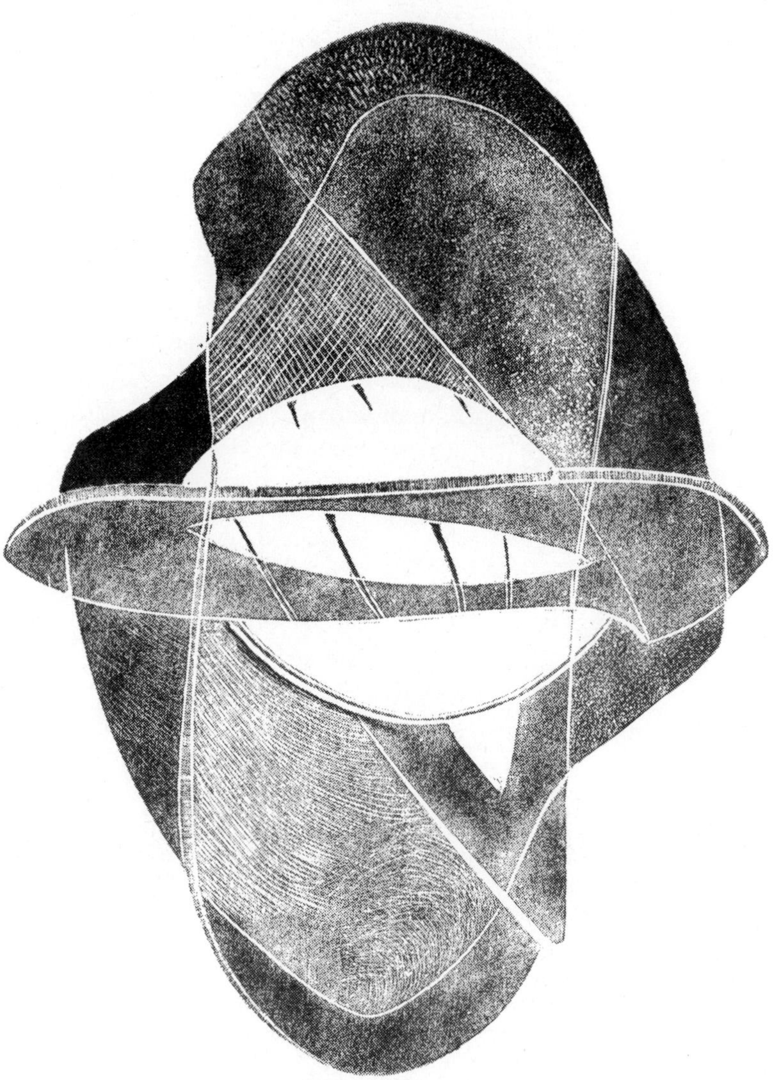

Tranquillo Marangoni is the master Italian wood engraver. He was born in the northern Italian village of Pozzuolo in 1912. He began wood engraving about 1942 and his first commission was for a book plate. He made all his own tools and blocks but this was not particularly surprising as he had been a carpenter and later worked in naval architecture at Monfalcone.

To celebrate the seventy-fifth anniversary of its foundation in 1952, the Casa di Risparmio, a savings bank of Udine, published *Fruili*, a magnificent volume of Marangoni's wood engravings on special hand-made paper. The twenty-five engravings illustrate scenes of the ancient town, villages and churches of the region and a text was written to fit the engravings. Marangoni was honoured by the Society of Wood Engravers in 1956 and he held a one-man show of his wood engravings at the Artists International Association, Lyle Street, London in June of that year. In the same year he was selected to contribute works to be shown at the Venice Biennial Exhibition and twenty engravings were displayed. In 1973 he was made an honorary member of the Royal Society of Painter Etchers and Engravers.

His subject matter is closely related to architecture and expounds the theme of men at work. In this respect it is as monumental as Stanley Spencer's wartime masterpieces of men at work in the shipyards at Glasgow, but whereas Spencer's

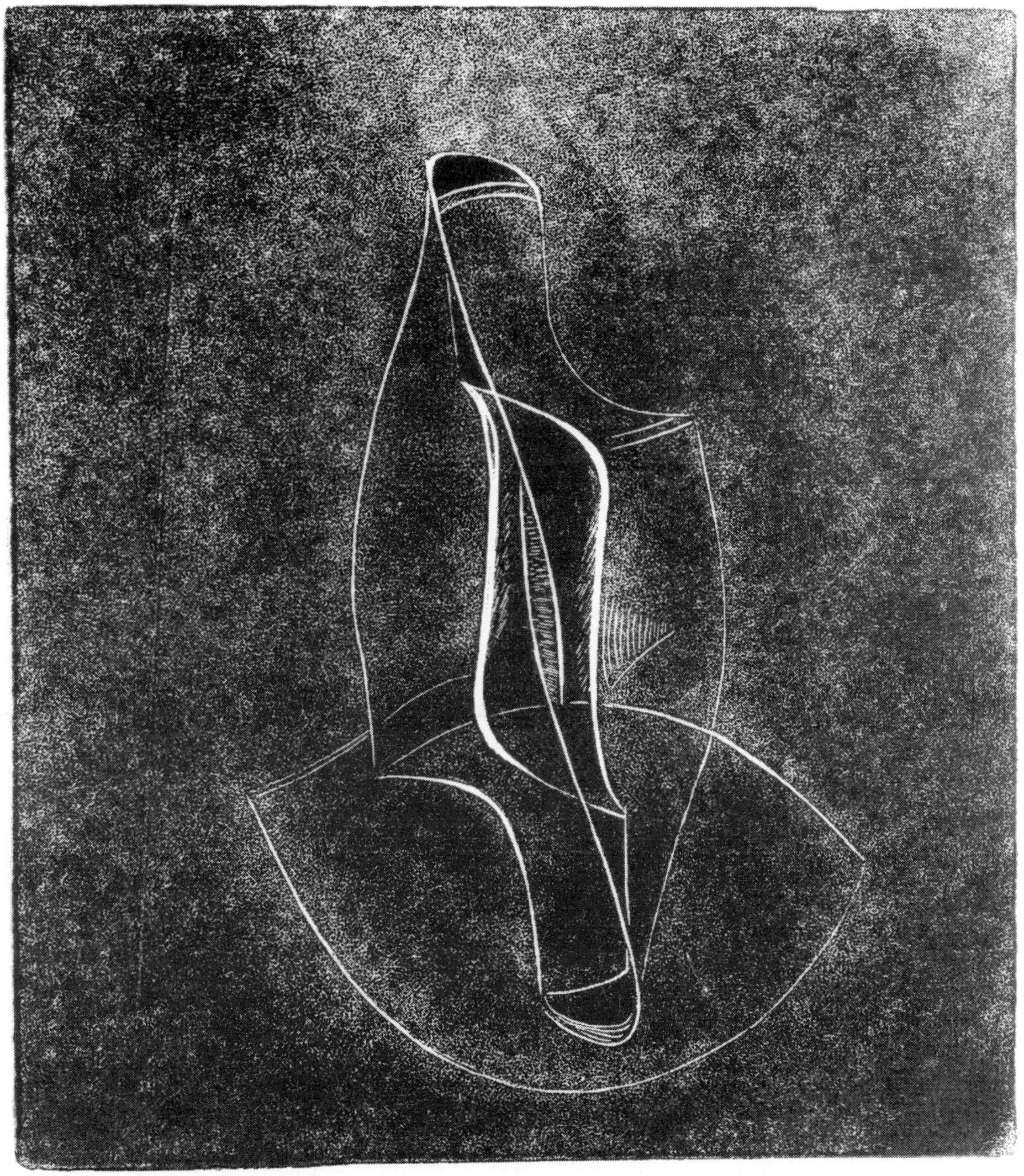

work is very large, that of Marangoni is small. No other contemporary wood engraver has developed the medium as an architectural expression quite like Marangoni. To do this the engraver must have a deep understanding and know it as structure, and feel it. His expression of the structural stresses are superb and astonishingly economical and well understood. In the craft and art of engraving he stands unique to his country of origin, as are Favorsky (Russia), Escher (Holland), Lepère (France) and Gill (Great Britain).

Marangoni's style of engraving is based upon the body curve, the white line changing continually throughout its course. The shape of each line forms his unit and controls the dispensation of light. A large number of units, laid side by side, finally produces the architectural image; the subject is sublimated to his engraved image and his craft. Another superb example of complex curvature unified through the body curvature can be seen in Iain Macnab's *Drying Sails, Lake Garda* [233].

[352] Maurits Cornelis Escher:
Three Spheres I, 1945. 17.0 x 28.0cm

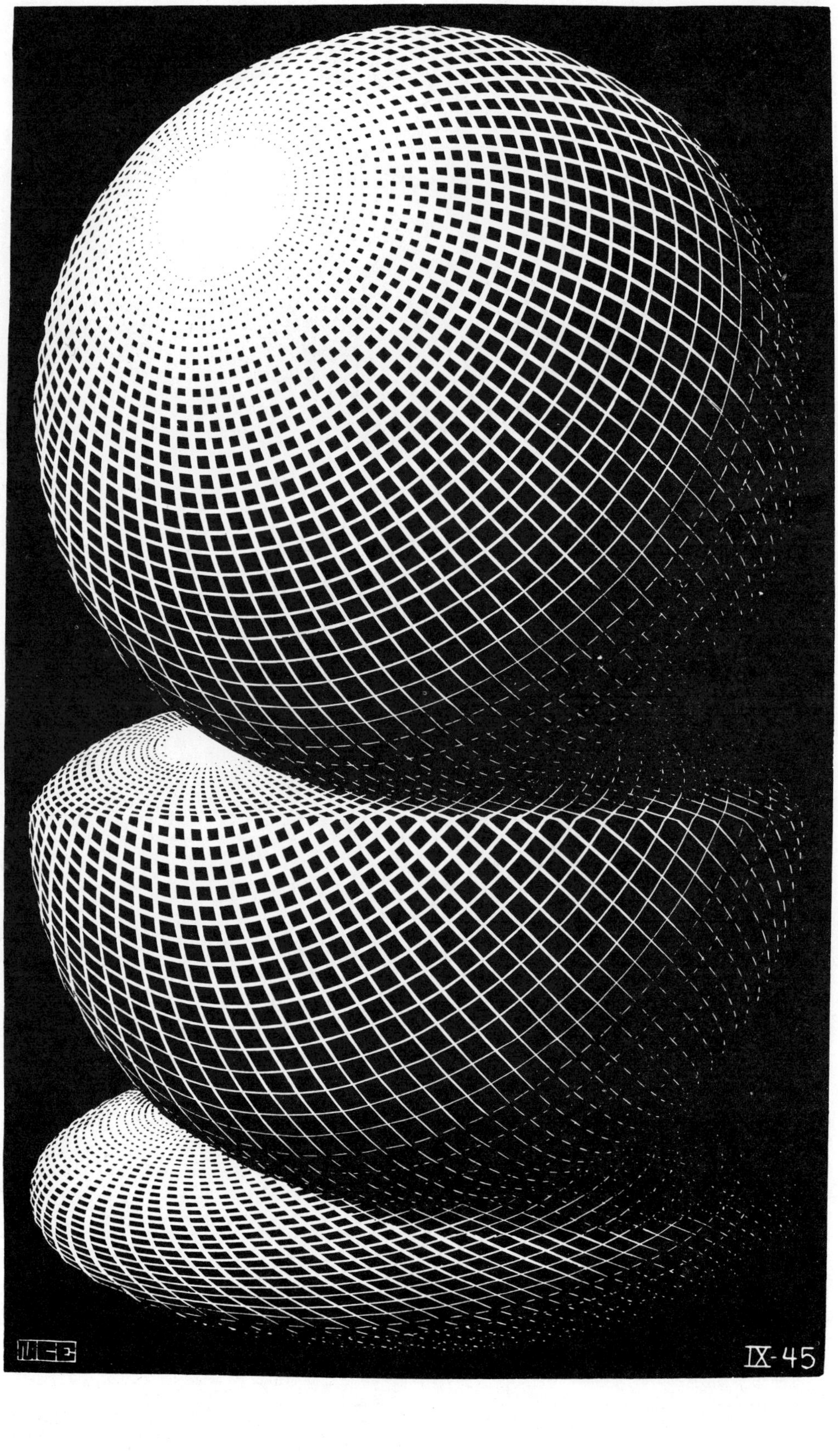

[353] Monica Poole: *Magnolia*, 1971.
16.0 x 18.5cm

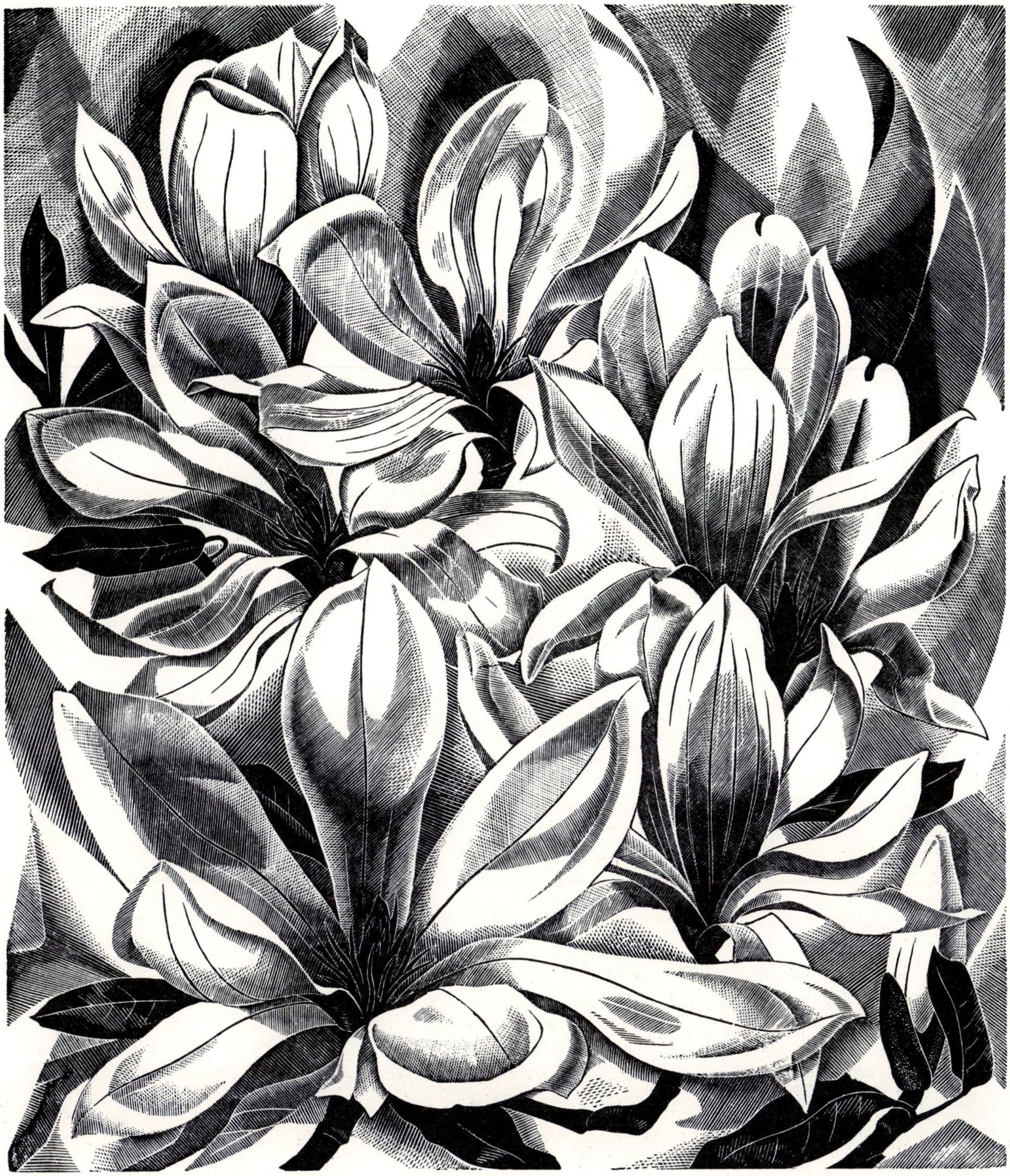

The body curve influence is strongly evident in the work of John Buckland-Wright, regardless of his subject or material, and it was this influence of which he was aware when discussing feeling and emotion. He described engraving as the fingers of the lover moving over and around the form of his partner; through the flow the form was defined. The line being a non-visual line is pure in feeling, its track is emotionally orientated, capturing the volume as in a wire-taut cage. This quality of the flow of line and volume is what Dürer lacked and Mantegna had in such abundance. Paul Nash never got through to this flow in engraving, but he did in his later paintings. Henry Moore is another such supreme example of the flow of line and volume.

In the world of print making the Japanese artists produce works which make some European productions appear clumsy, vulgar and inarticulate. There is no comparison to make with engraving, because there is very little produced in Japan where there is little history of engraving. Engraving in Japan appears most frequently not as a fundamental discipline but as a part of the woodcut technique. During the seventeenth, eighteenth and nineteenth centuries wood engraving in

[354] Mark Severin: *Yalk.* 19.1 x 14.25cm

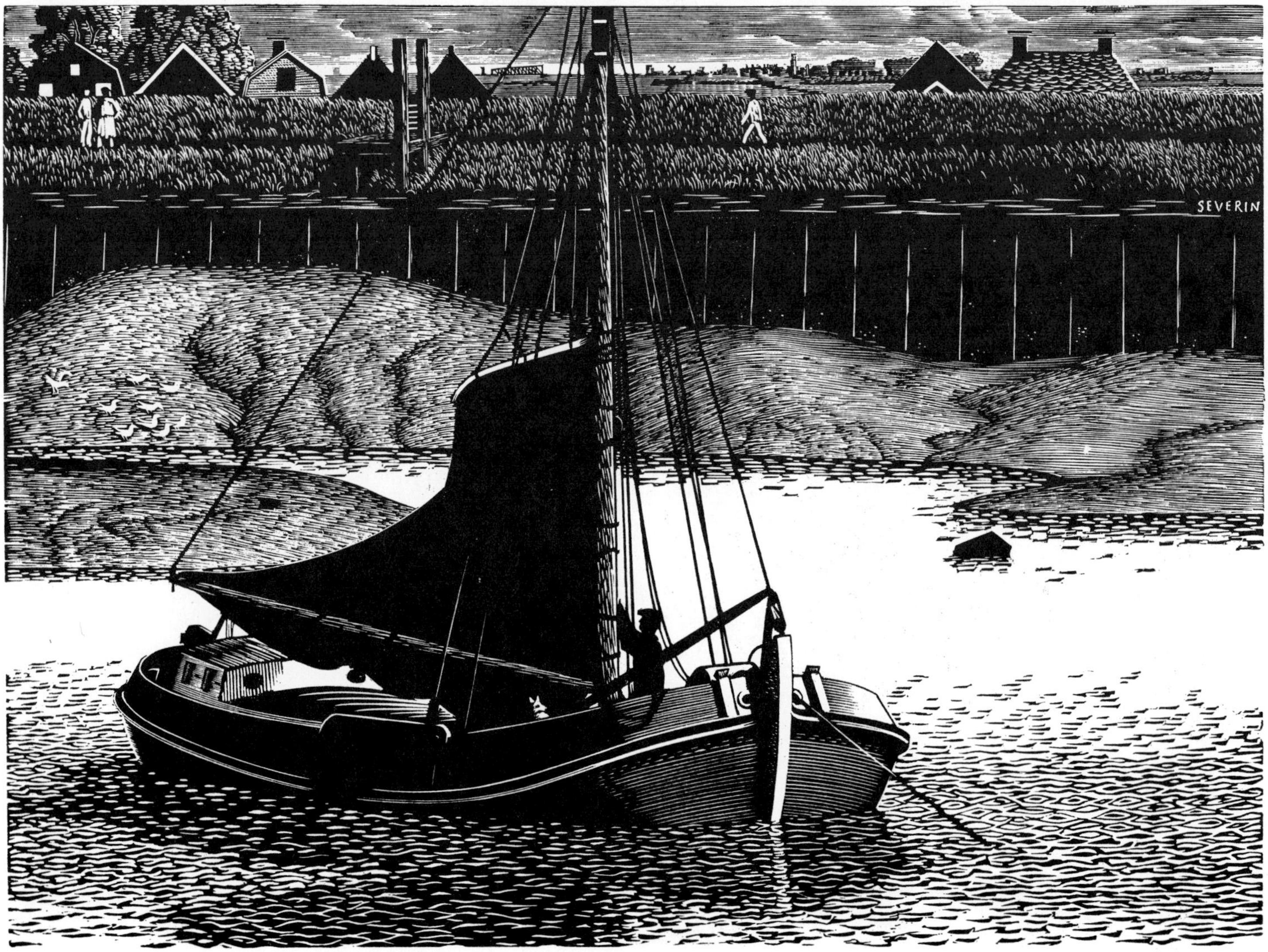

[355] Tranquillo Marangoni: *Crypt of the Basilica of Aquileia*, 1950. 14.8 x 20.0cm

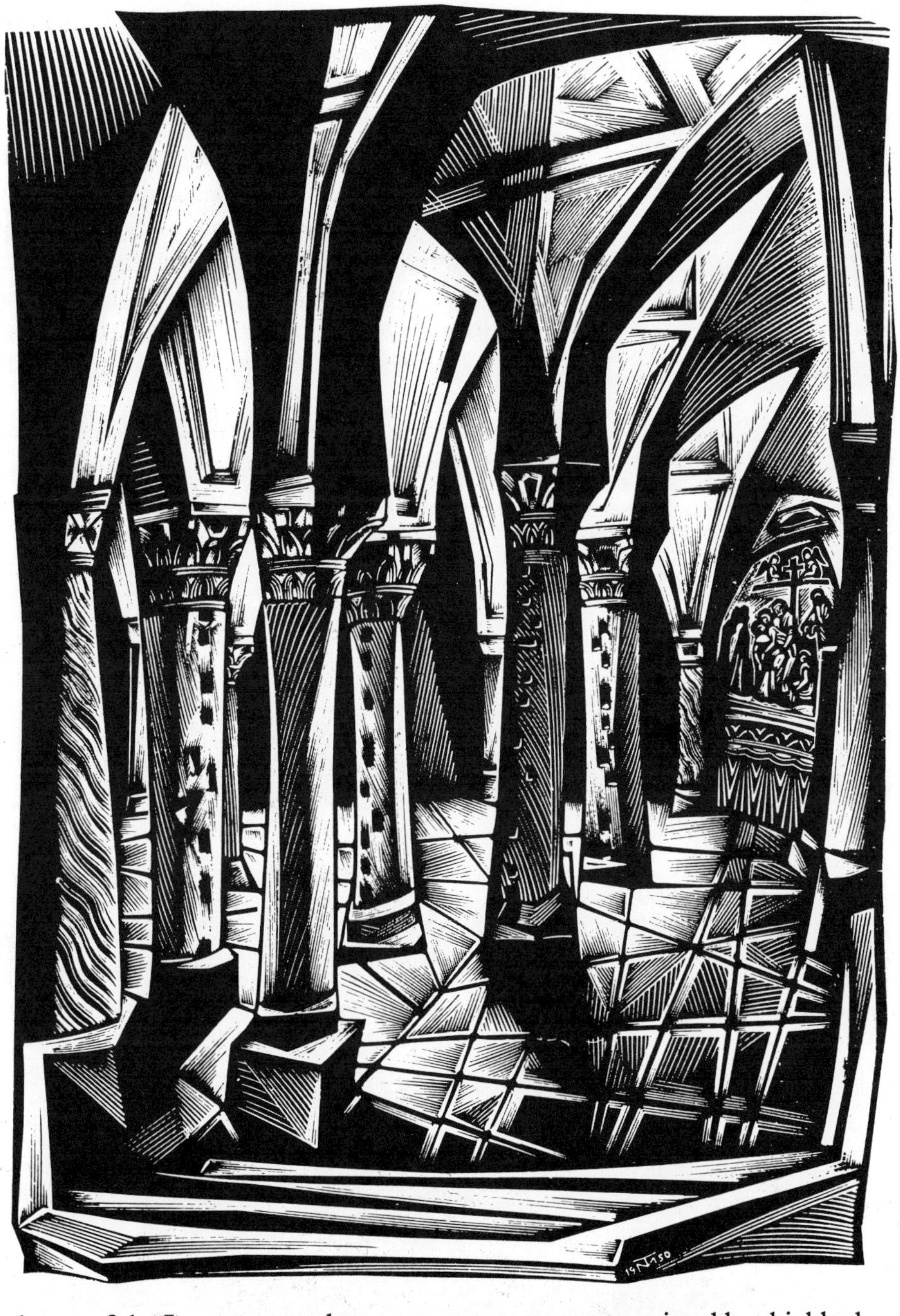

the art of the Japanese woodcut appears as a strange, restricted but highly developed convention confined to the rendering of the hair on the human face and head. This very restricted application of engraving was done on the long-grained wood. The choice of timber was critical for the combination of knife cut and engraving; it had to be fairly soft and fast growing in order to produce a very even grain with the minimum difference between summer and winter growth.

Engraving is an art expression almost confined to Europe, Russia and North America. The tradition of engraving is much more constant than in the sister arts of painting and sculpture, which both undergo violent metamorphic changes in time. Engraving ebbs and flows in a lost and found pattern. In different periods concepts change matters of style and content, but not the essential character of the medium. There is a very close relationship between a good contemporary engraving in wood or copper and the work of any other period or, for that matter, engraving on an early piece of armour or cave rock. Wood engraving is a very sensitive technique and because of this individual and national characteristics can be expected to be clearly marked.

Restriction of the medium, i.e. wood, metal, etc. is responsible for the continuity of the engraving tradition. Because of the nature of the burin and the cut it makes, the engraver must be conscious of the limitations and allow a personal technique to evolve. If the engraver is good, his personality and style will be established naturally rather than contrived. The continuity of the engraving tradition is also strongly supported by the fact that it arises from the combination of physical and visual elements in which thinking and planning must be done before engraving begins.

Whilst there are no engraving sketches in the same sense that there are sketches and studies in painting and sculpture, there is a relationship between drawing and engraving: both are built upon a set of conventions, though these are used to achieve different results.

Iain Macnab's statement that 'Drawing is design' is still true and alive. It is designing within the form. Not only was he a very expressive draughtsman, he also produced some good draughtsmen and engravers through his teaching at the Grosvenor School of Modern Art. Contemporary with Macnab was the draughtsman and painter Bernard Meninsky. Students queued to be taught drawing by him. During the main formative period of the British school of engraving, there were a number of schools of drawing and two of the best known were the Bloomsbury school dominated by Roger Fry, which was not a school for teaching students but a school of criticism and of influence, and the Euston Road School led by the draughtsman and painter William Coldstream, now Sir William Coldstream.

The teaching of students originally in the Euston Road later formed the main teaching influence at the Camberwell School of Art in Peckham Road during the post-war years. The concepts taught at the Roger Fry school were based on Cézanne and his cube, cone and cylinder, which were pertinent for Fry's period of influence and necessary to boost his unhealthy critical power and the grip he exercised on

[356] Tranquillo Marangoni: *Carretera a Milagros*, 1961. 49.5 x 20.0cm

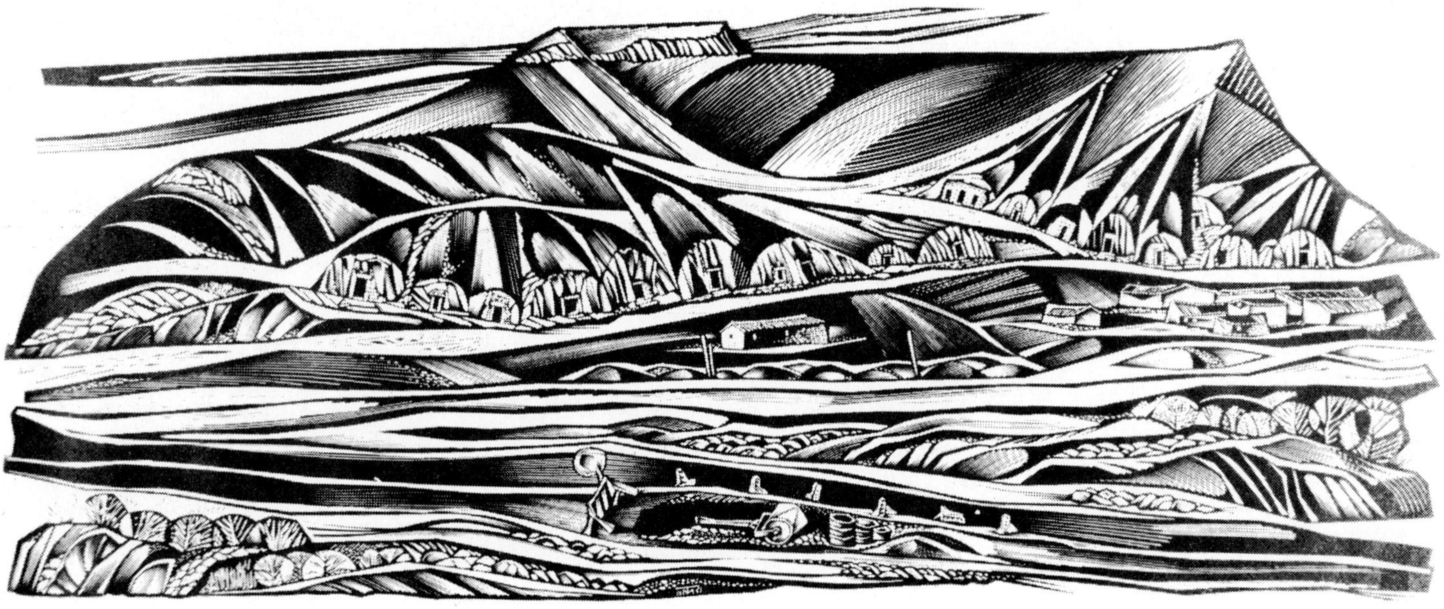

London's art life. In the early days of Paul Nash, Roger Fry wrote well of him until he discovered that Nash was developing in another direction, which he, Fry, had not sanctioned. Thereafter he did not rest content just to write disparagingly about Nash, but actively tried to block the channels open to him. In his critical evaluation of Cézanne, Fry was brilliant, but in dealing with the production of works of art his counsel was not well directed. His good but limited concepts were to be completely shattered when Paul Klee came on the scene.

The Euston Road School also made a very important contribution to drawing and draughtsmanship. This too has now proved to be good of its time, even if only to point out that there existed points of departure different from those of Fry. Its concepts in no way anticipated the fundamental changes required to express form

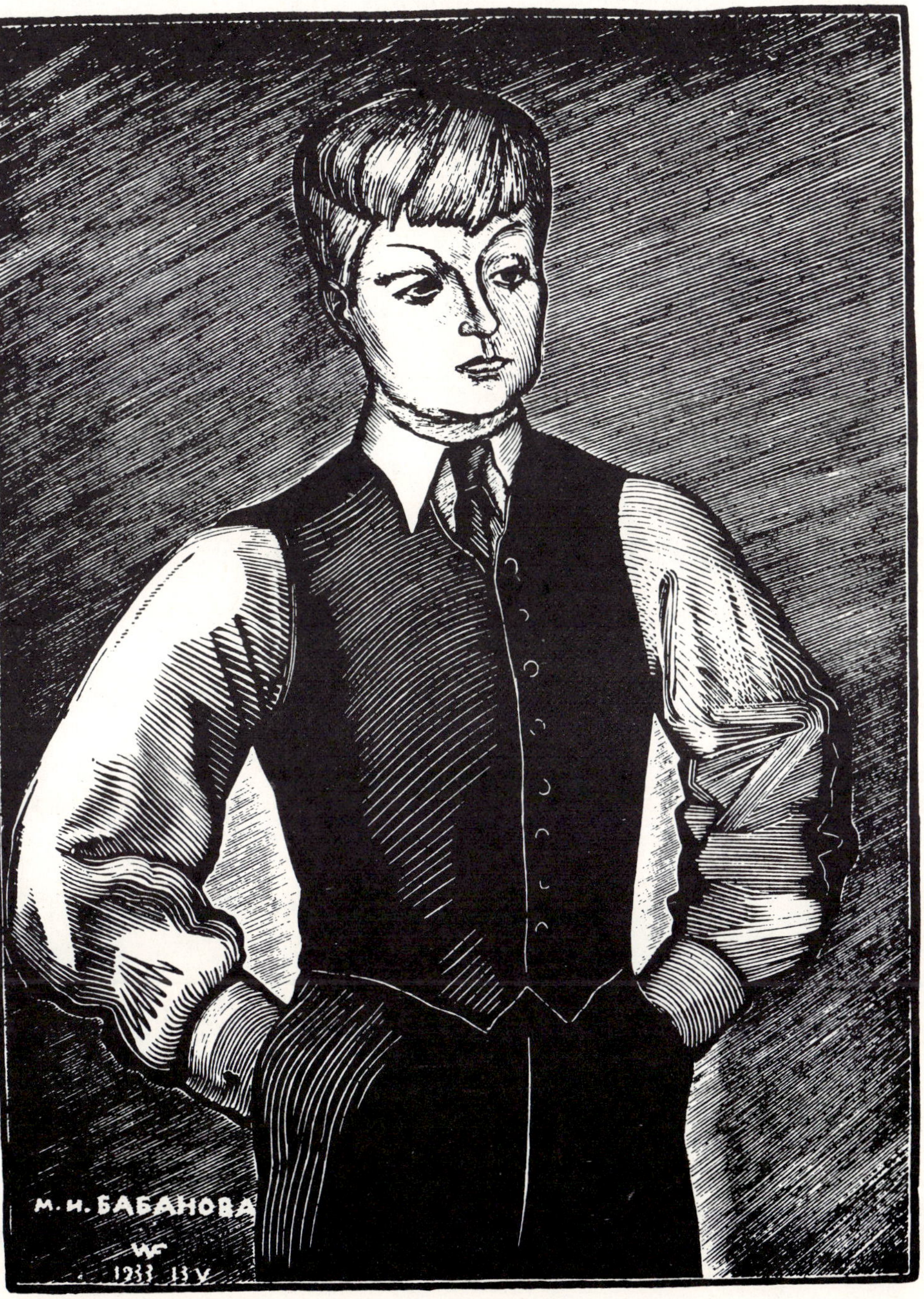

[357] Wladimir Favorsky: *Portrait of the actress Babanova*, 1933.

[358] Bernard Rice: *Bridge of Titograd*, 1926. 42.0 x 36.25cm

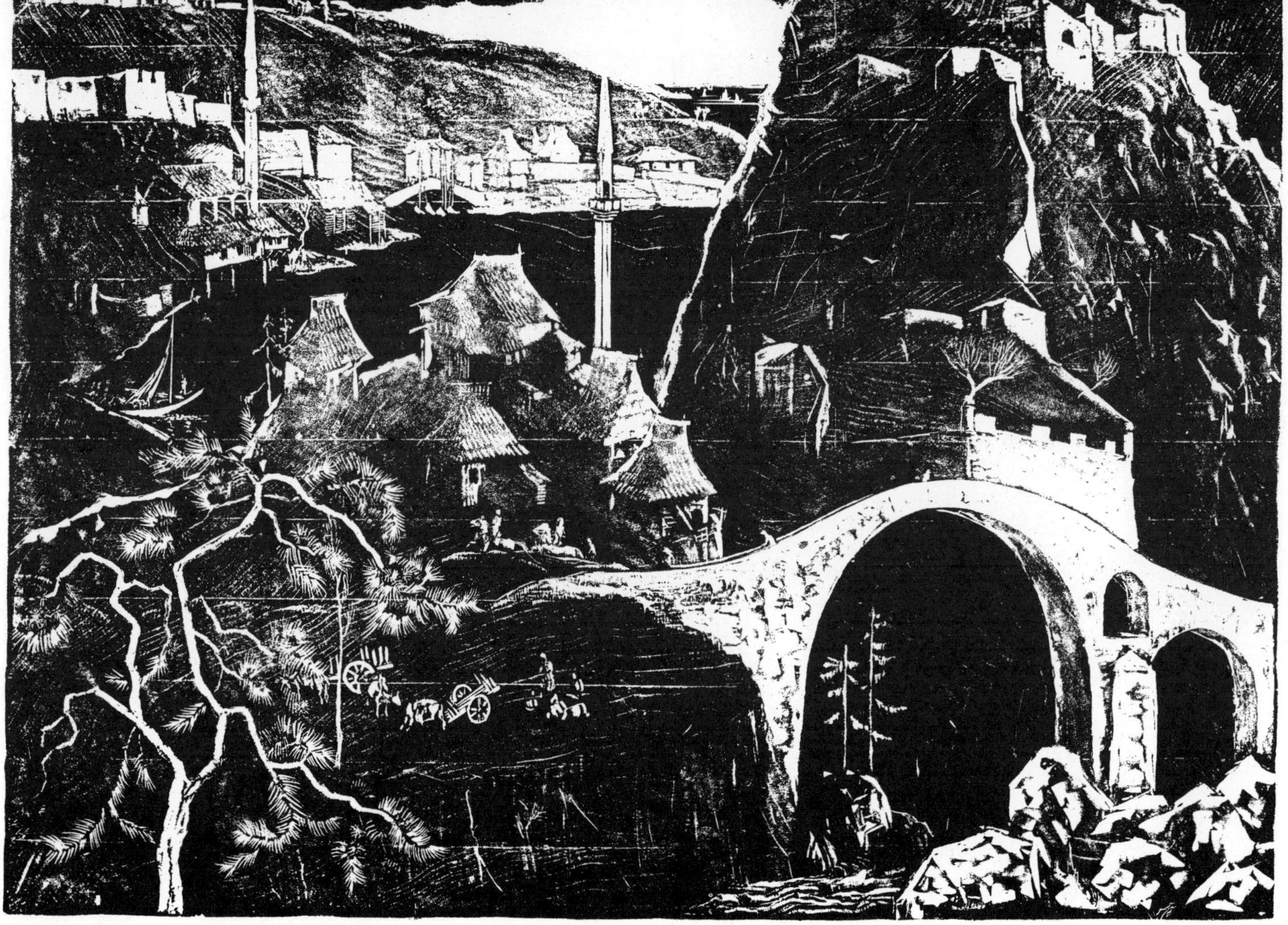

[359] Eric Gill: Illustration from *25 Nudes*, 1938. 13.0 x 19.5cm

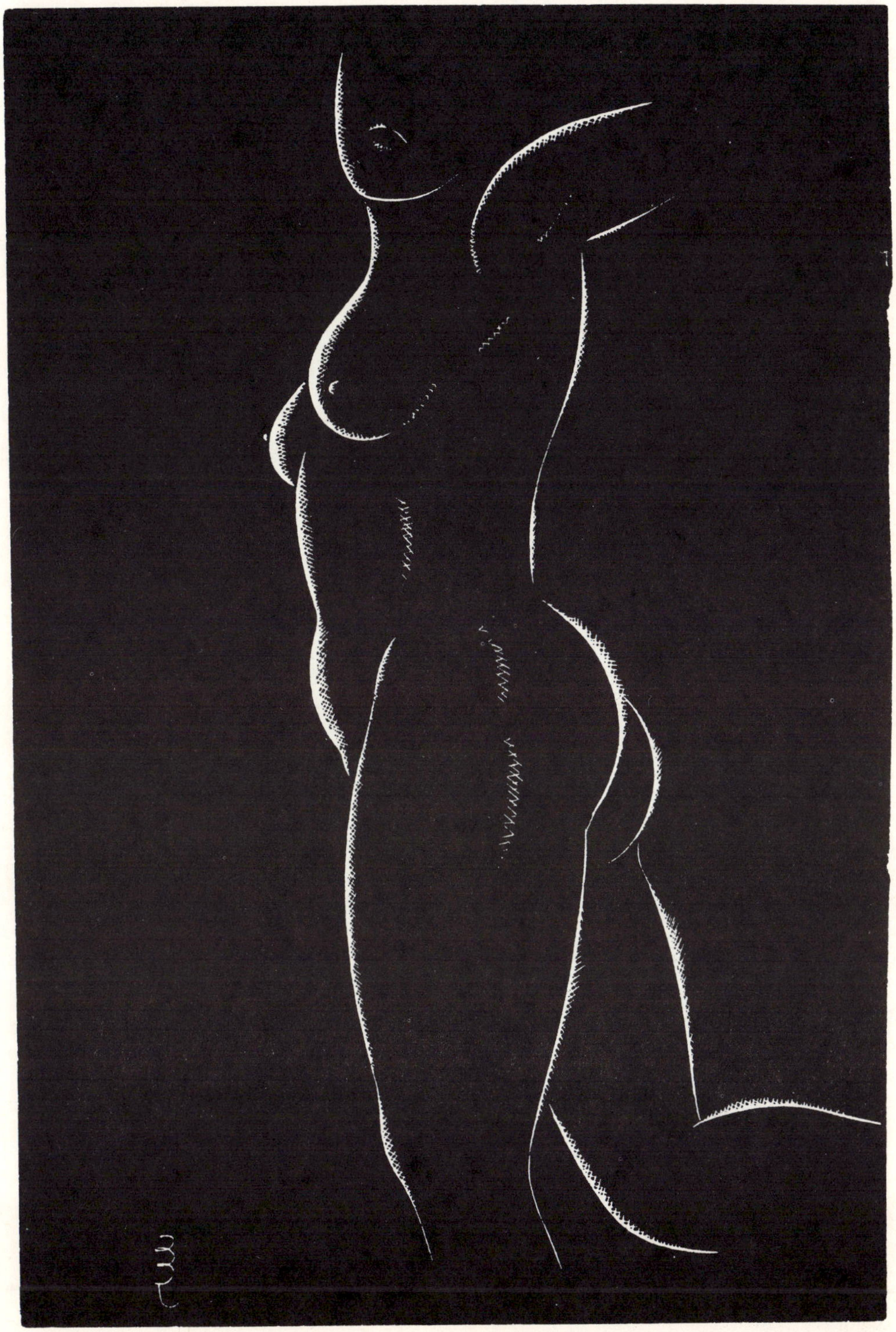

[360] John Buckland-Wright: *Nu*, 1929. 5.4 x 13.3cm

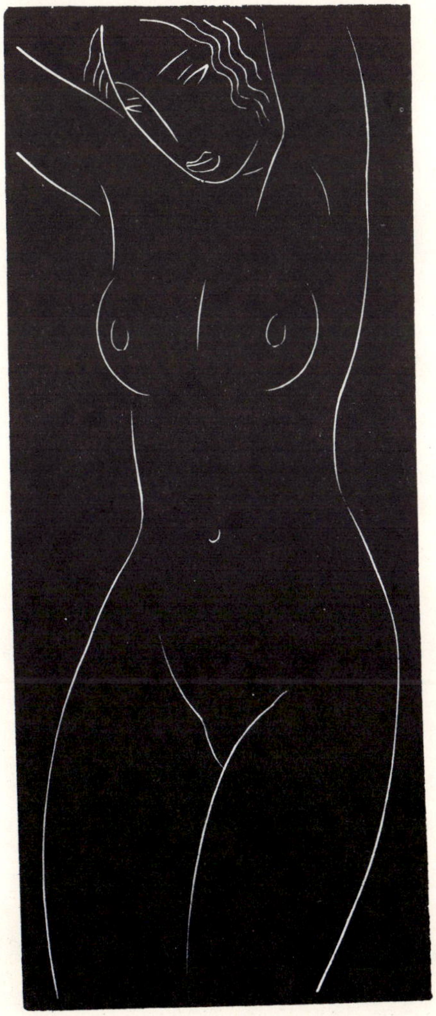

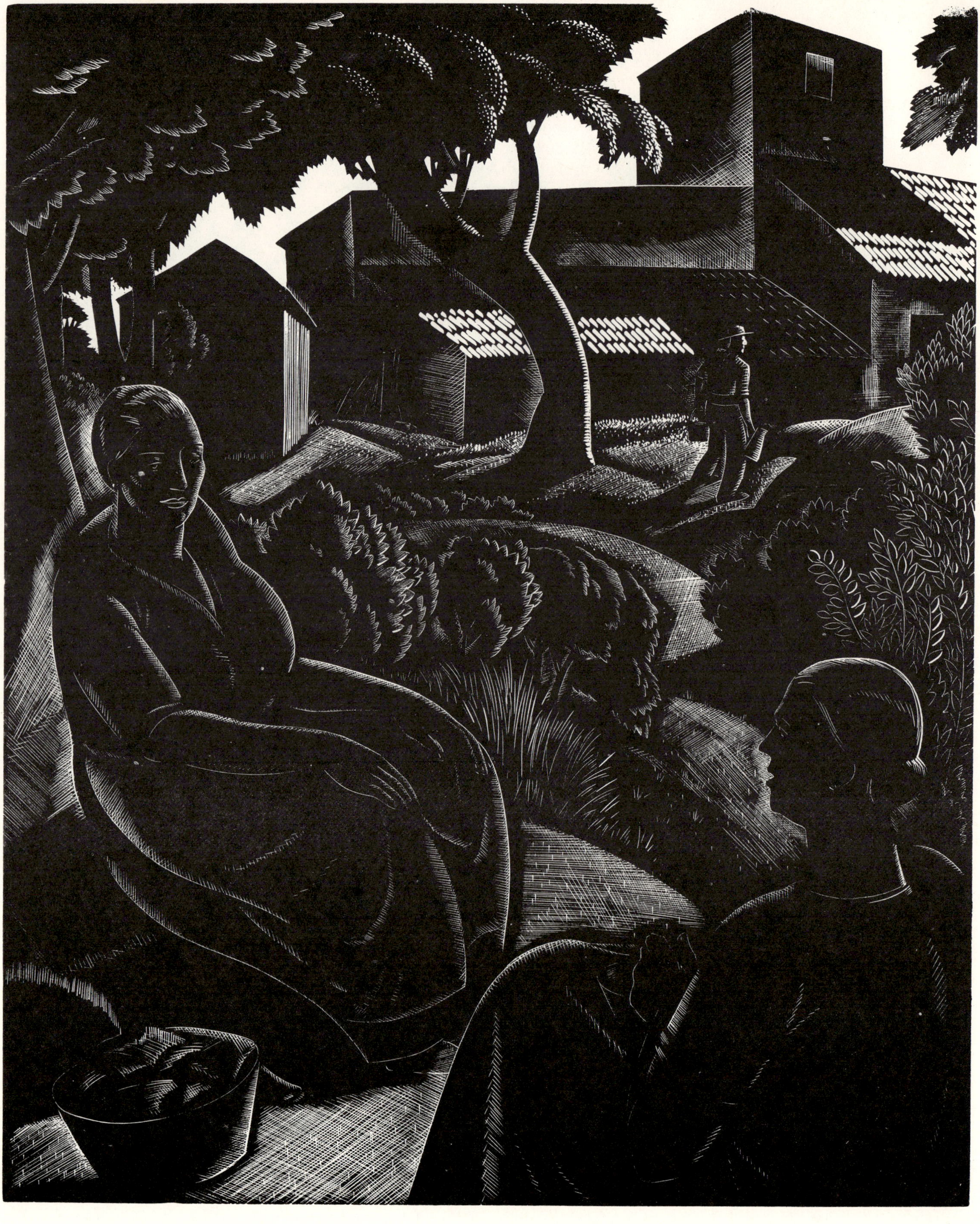

[361] Iain Macnab: *Two Fat Ladies, Portofino*, 1936. 20.5 x 25.25cm

after the Second World War. The Euston Road School and Sir William Coldstream are unique in that the philosophy expounded was based upon realist, clinical examination of form. Their aim was to view form and its structure objectively, and to record their findings as accurately as possible. To do this, romantic, classical and emotional concepts had to be excluded. It is possibly the only 'realist' manifestation there is in our very recent art history.

Leon Underwood's school of drawing, engraving and sculpture made a considerable contribution to the development of wood engraving and draughtsmanship. The school was run in Underwood's studio at Girdlers Road, Gunnersbury. In character Underwood's school was possibly the most English of all the schools and independent in its approach. Underwood, a renowned sculptor, engraver and writer, had very clearly defined concepts as to what art is or is not. For him it is certainly not the end product of an intellectual process.

Underwood always placed emphasis on subject matter. It follows from this that content is of great importance in expressing buoyancy and optimism. Such a concept cuts clean across Bell's critical theory of 'significant form'; in fact it cuts across all the main theories of the time. Underwood is very close to the spirit of William Blake in this respect. He was also one of the first serious artists to understand and appreciate Palaeolithic art after he visited Altamira in 1926. It was not until December 1948 that London received the impact of the art of primitive man when the exhibition *Forty Thousand Years of Modern Art* opened at the Academy Hall, Oxford Street under the sponsorship of the Institute of Contemporary Arts.

The modern technique of advertising presents the public with visual information of very large dimensions and it appears that it is not fashionable to give attention to art that occupies only a small space, although in engraving, very small work is often both important and subtle. Nevertheless, there are engravers who work on a large scale and one such artist is Bernard Rice.

Bernard Rice's first engravings were exhibited at the St George's Gallery in

[362] John Nash: *Two Bathers in a Landscape*, 1930. 7.75 x 8.4cm

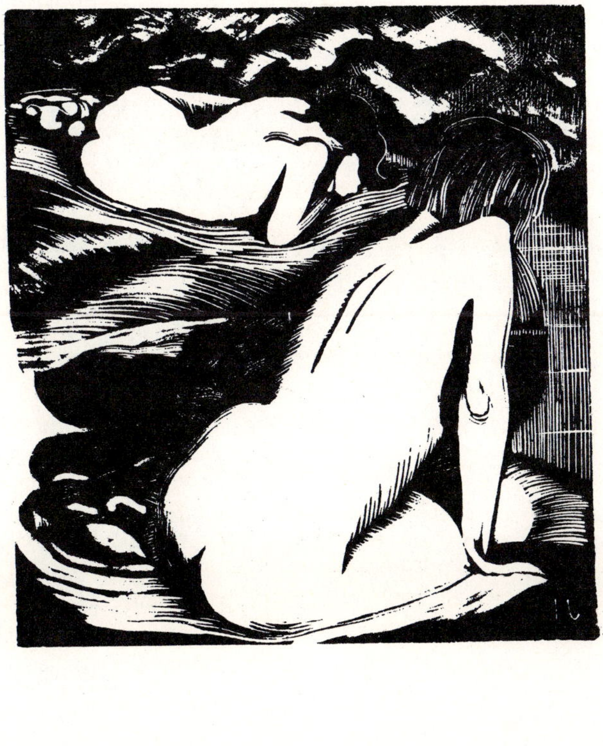

[363] James Dolby: *Life Study*, 1967. 10.2 x 17.75cm

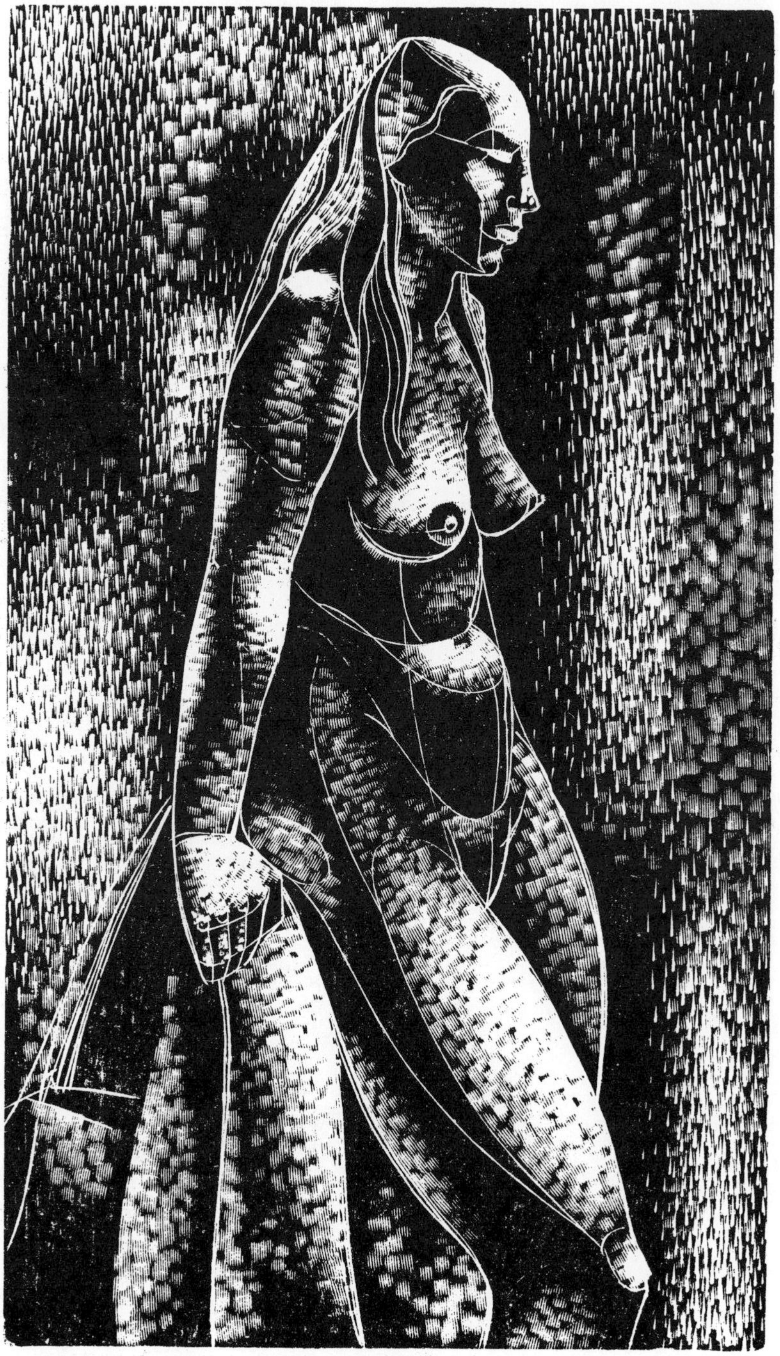

[364] Kenneth Lindley: *Shimabara I*, 1971. 10.25 x 13.0cm

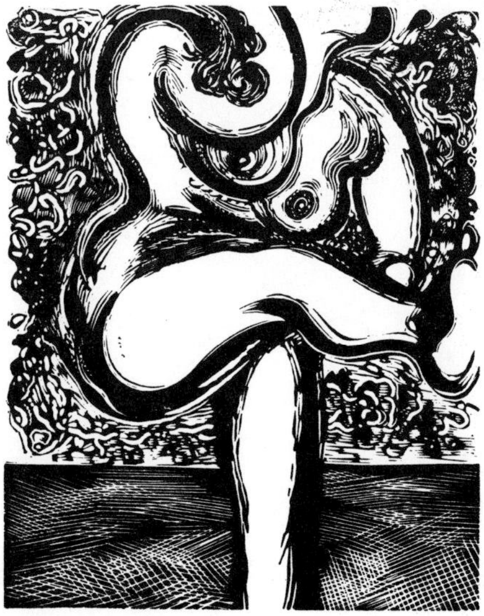

1926 in the English Wood Engraving Society exhibition; though barely past his student days, he sold about ten prints. In the profession, Rice has been recognised for a long time as a brilliant, sensitive engraver and woodcut artist. In some of his prints both crafts are used. He had very little in common with the hard white-line exponents who were so dominant between the two wars. He is the one engraver in the British school who has broken most of the rules.

However, John Buckland-Wright had his students studying Rice's engraving and woodcuts. In his book *Etching and Engraving*, Buckland-Wright says of Rice's *Rammuda* print, measuring 152cm wide by 97cm high: 'Of Bernard Rice's magnificent *Rammuda*, cut on plywood and printed on cotton cloth, there is little

[365] Clare Leighton: *Field Mice*, 1931. 8.5 x 5.75cm

[366] Joan Hassall: *Harvest Mice*, 1959. 6.5 x 8.75cm

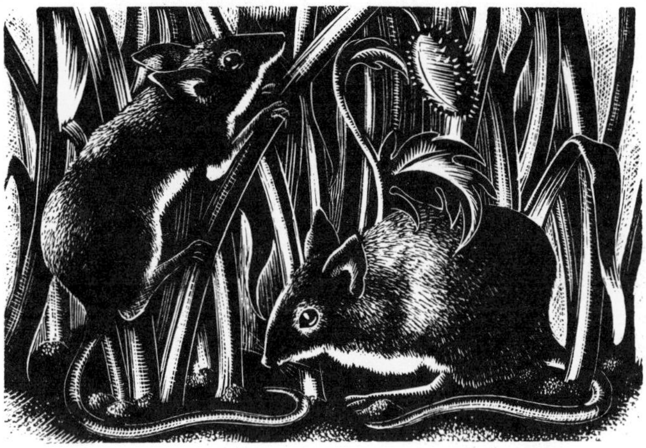

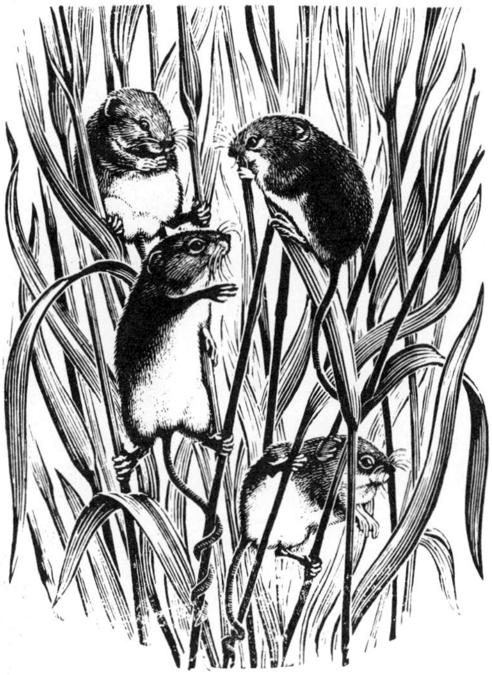

to equal this rhythmic flow of line, the overall pattern and the effect of light he obtains with under-printing. He has combined eastern and western techniques and has still managed to retain a unity of expression.' Many of Rice's prints have a Chinese character [358] yet he is not a student of Chinese art as such, but like the Chinese he distils the essence of his subject, philosophically rather than visually, so that each print becomes a new experience and a new discovery. He is an adventurer and explorer of aesthetics.

Rice's parents were stained glass designers and hailed from Birmingham. They migrated to Germany and Bernard was trained by his father in stained glass. He has lived in Austria, Yugoslavia and Egypt. His work in engraving, stained glass and painting is scattered through these countries. Rice's sensitivity to light as an expressive element arises from the family experience in glass.

Bernard Rice loves materials and has a special regard for wood. He made his own blocks because he wanted to exploit not only the hard woods of box and holly, but lime, laurel and cherry. What attracted him was the changing rhythms of the annular rings of the alternating hard and soft layers. He found that he could scrape the soft rings and by lowering these parts he could obtain a mezzotint effect which was printable. When asked why he rejected the professional blockmaker who is the mainstay of the British school, he replied; 'My ideas start from the wood itself – the particular kind of wood – some are more absorbent of ink than others; and most of all I get a variety of wood grains from which I can choose.' He does not

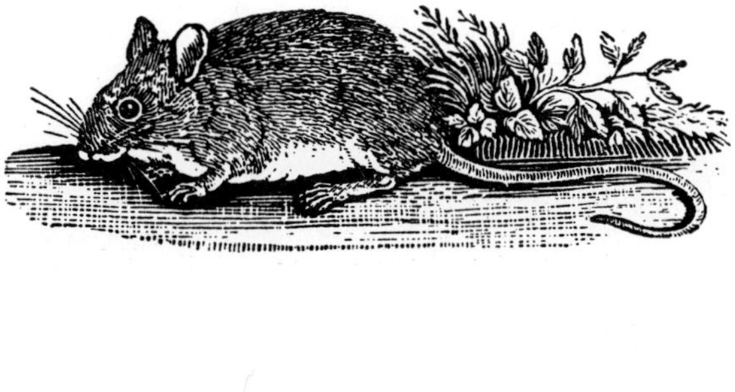

[367] Thomas Bewick: *The Long-tailed Field Mouse*, 1790. 7.25 x 2.4cm

[368] Eric Gill: *Self-Portrait*, 1927.
12.5 x 15.2cm

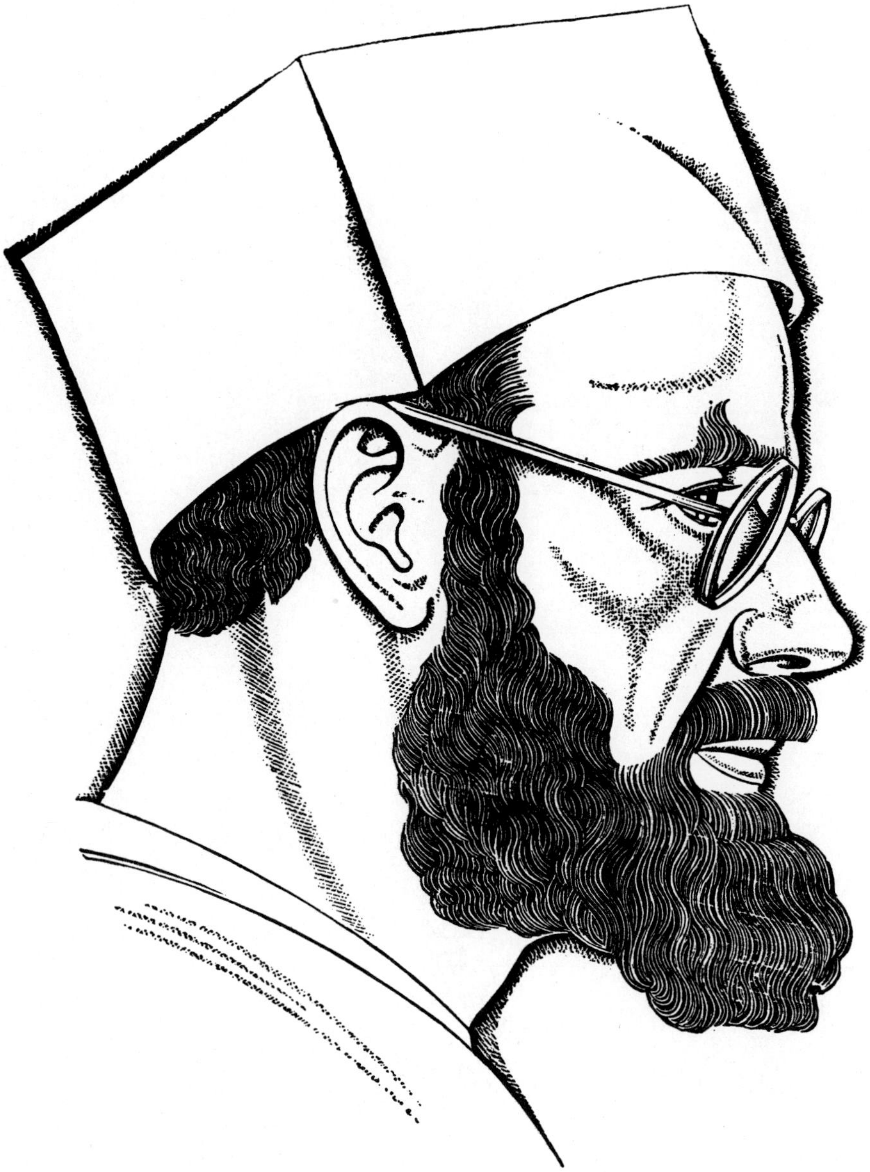

place a high value on dense black as such, for this reason he is able to use the softer woods that are incapable of competing with the dense surface of boxwood which can be printed as a solid black.

The annular rings of limewood give a hard winter and softer summer growth and Rice uses this feature of the timber. The grey-tone effect is achieved by scraping timber and lowering the surface, which then takes less ink from the roller. Bewick did this on occasion to achieve effects of grey, and it has been continued since. Gertrude Hermes expressed strong views on this aspect of engraving, telling her students: 'Everything in the print must be on the block, otherwise trick printing is involved which in most cases gives bad repeatability in the edition.' The important point about the Rice tone effect is that it is only Rice who has developed the lowered surface as an integral part of his technical expression.

His approach to engraving is that of a painter. Rice is the painter-graver of the French tradition who has virtually taken the discipline of engraving into painting.

[369] Paul Nash: *Portrait of proud Paul*, 1922-23. 12.0 x 17.75cm

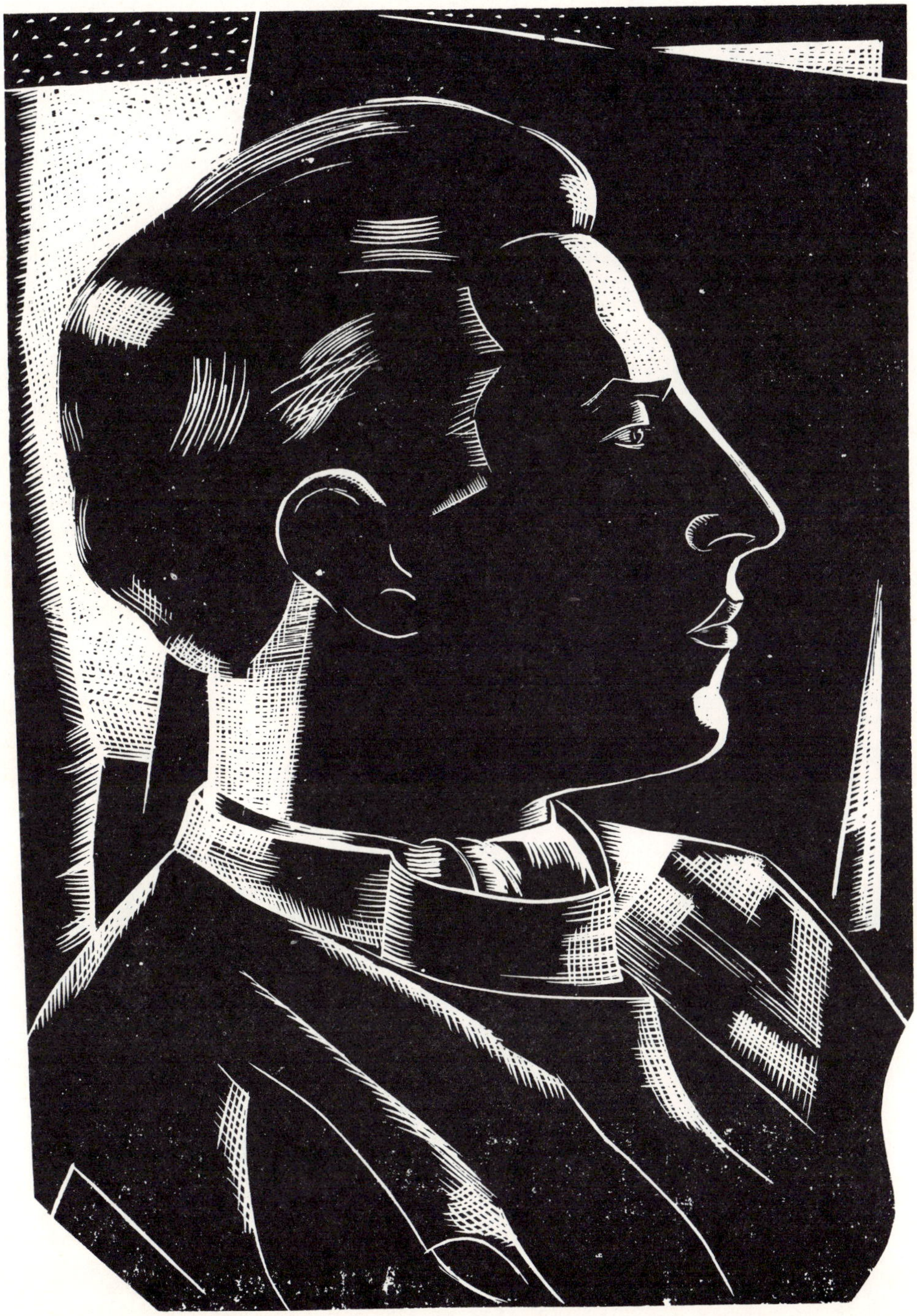

He even uses the burin as a paint brush. His burin is used sparingly, as a notation in defining a form or image. In pure engraving everything is linear and Rice subjugates the line and makes it share a role with the half-tone work. He has succeeded in this magnificently. It is too early to say yet whether his way is a purely personal manifestation only or whether it will lead to a more general application in the future.

Examination of the six wood engravings [359 to 364] will dispel the popular critical argument that the creative wood engraver artists are to be limited in the

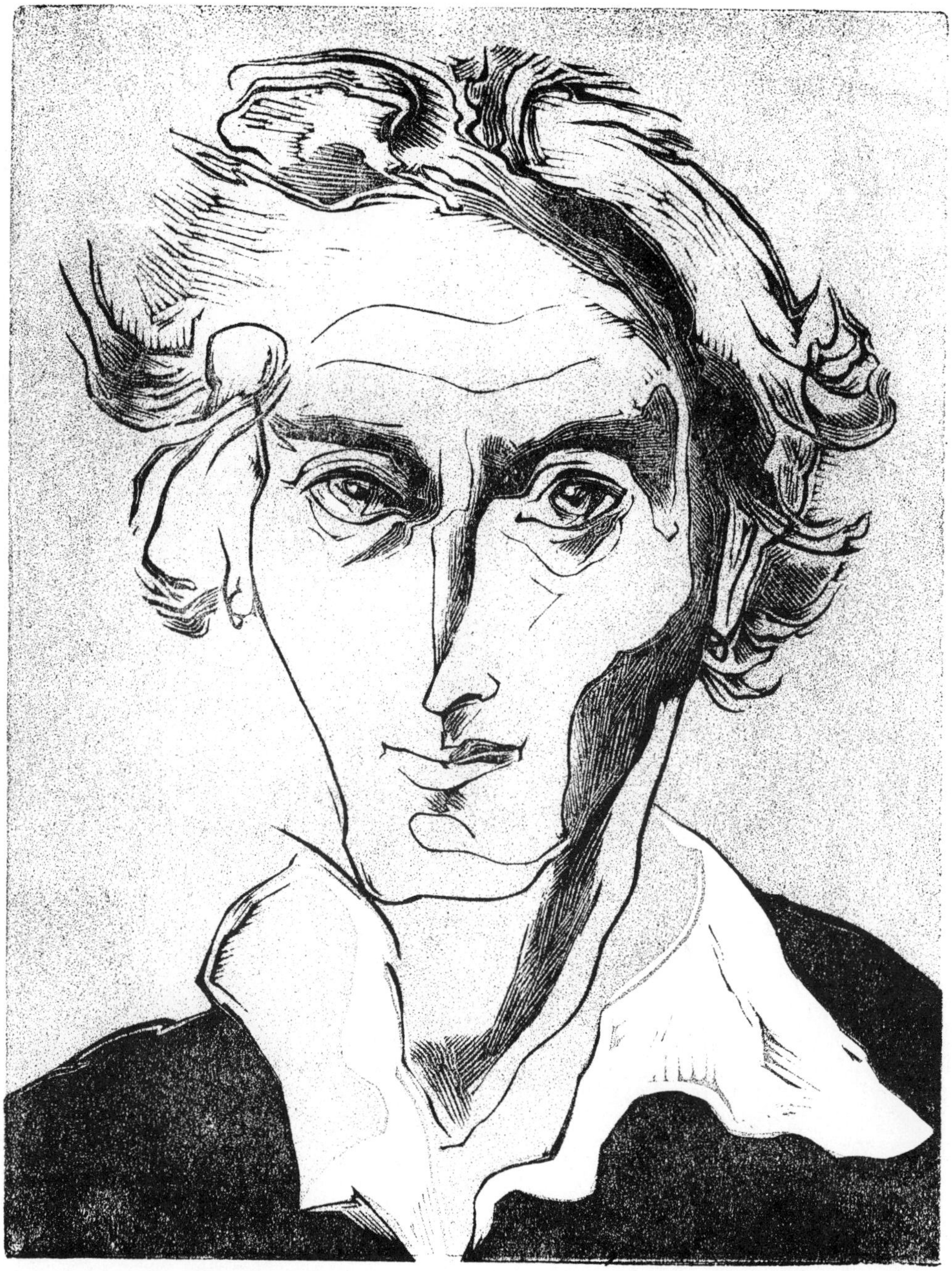

[370] Gertrude Hermes: *Self-Portrait*, 1949. 15.2 x 20.45cm

expression of aesthetic emotion through the human form. Also, critics generally find it difficult to visualize works of art arising from a medium offering such craft restrictions. All these engravers have not only accepted the challenge, but obviously have enjoyed doing it. This is the first aesthetic quality communicated through the line and form to those sensitive enough to feel it. The group of six examples should be viewed with a seventh, Gertrude Hermes's masterpiece *More People* [1]. These engravings show the work of seven artists who are remarkably even in quality.

The second aesthetic quality is stylistic identity which must be obvious to those used to viewing art, even if they have not met these artists before. Then thirdly, a common aesthetic quality is the authority arising from the erudition of the forms and their relationships. Much of this aesthetic quality comes from the emotional rhythms arising from the forms, and the seven engravings are designed as final statements, each having arisen from a number of drawings done previously.

It is this aesthetic emotional quality which accounts for the difference of line quality and image emphasis between the two sculptors Eric Gill and Gertrude Hermes and the five painters, John Buckland-Wright, John Nash, Iain Macnab, James Dolby and Kenneth Lindley. These five painters display their own sharp aesthetic form differences in the way their images are formed. John Buckland-Wright and Iain Macnab are classical artists in vision, John Nash is their opposite,

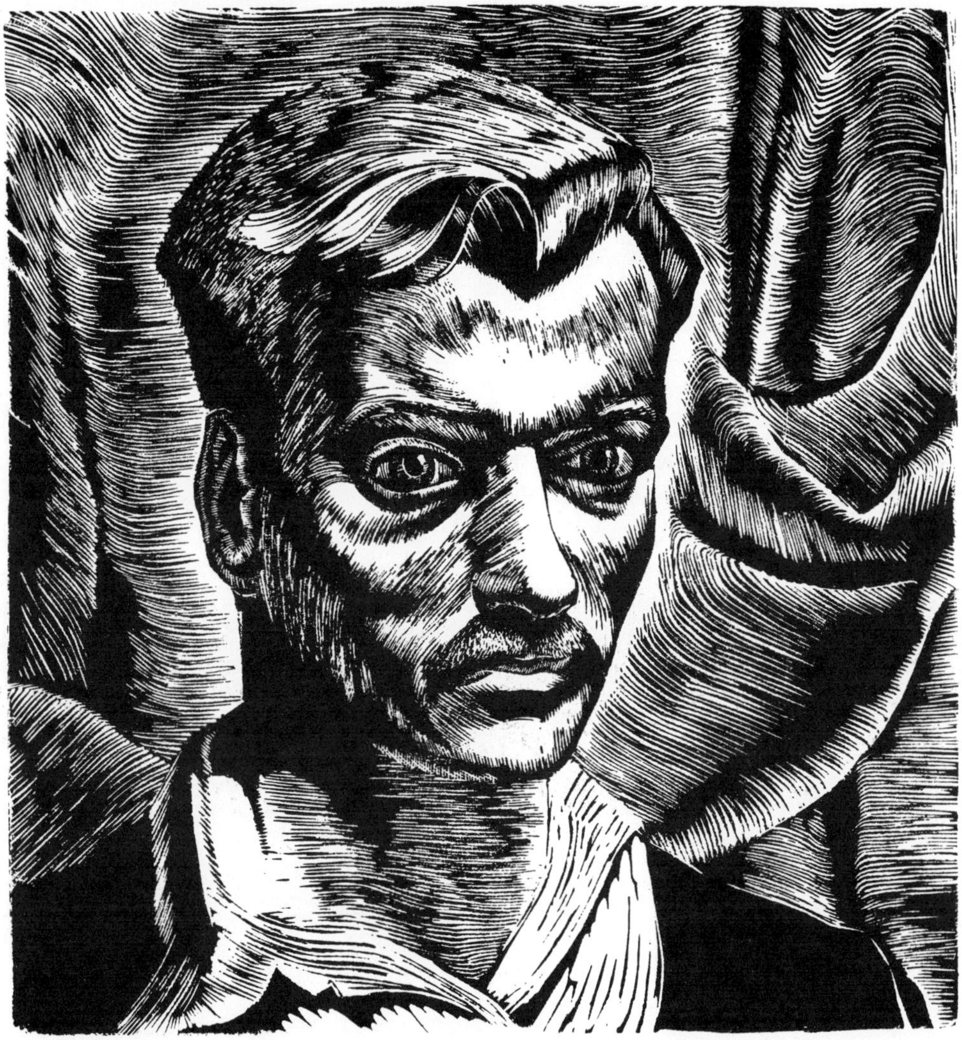

[371] James Bostock: *Self-Portrait*, 1948. 15.0 x 16.25cm

he is the sharp visual realist in the French tradition of Camille and Lucien Pissarro. Kenneth Lindley and James Dolby are Expressionists. As such they form a point of view which is therefore basically a commentary.

The aesthetic emotion of the flow of each form is different. That of Gertrude Hermes is both lyrical and sculpturally massive, volumetrically. Eric Gill's figure is 'as quick as a horse chestnut bud' yet remote, god-like and not to be touched. John Buckland-Wright's line and form expresses warmth and relaxation. Even more relaxed are Iain Macnab's figures; even the line is reclining, yet through the composition there is the arresting, emotional aesthetic impact of the syncopated architectural counterpoint. The counterpoint is based on the architectural principle of the T-joint or the 'column and lintel' method of construction.

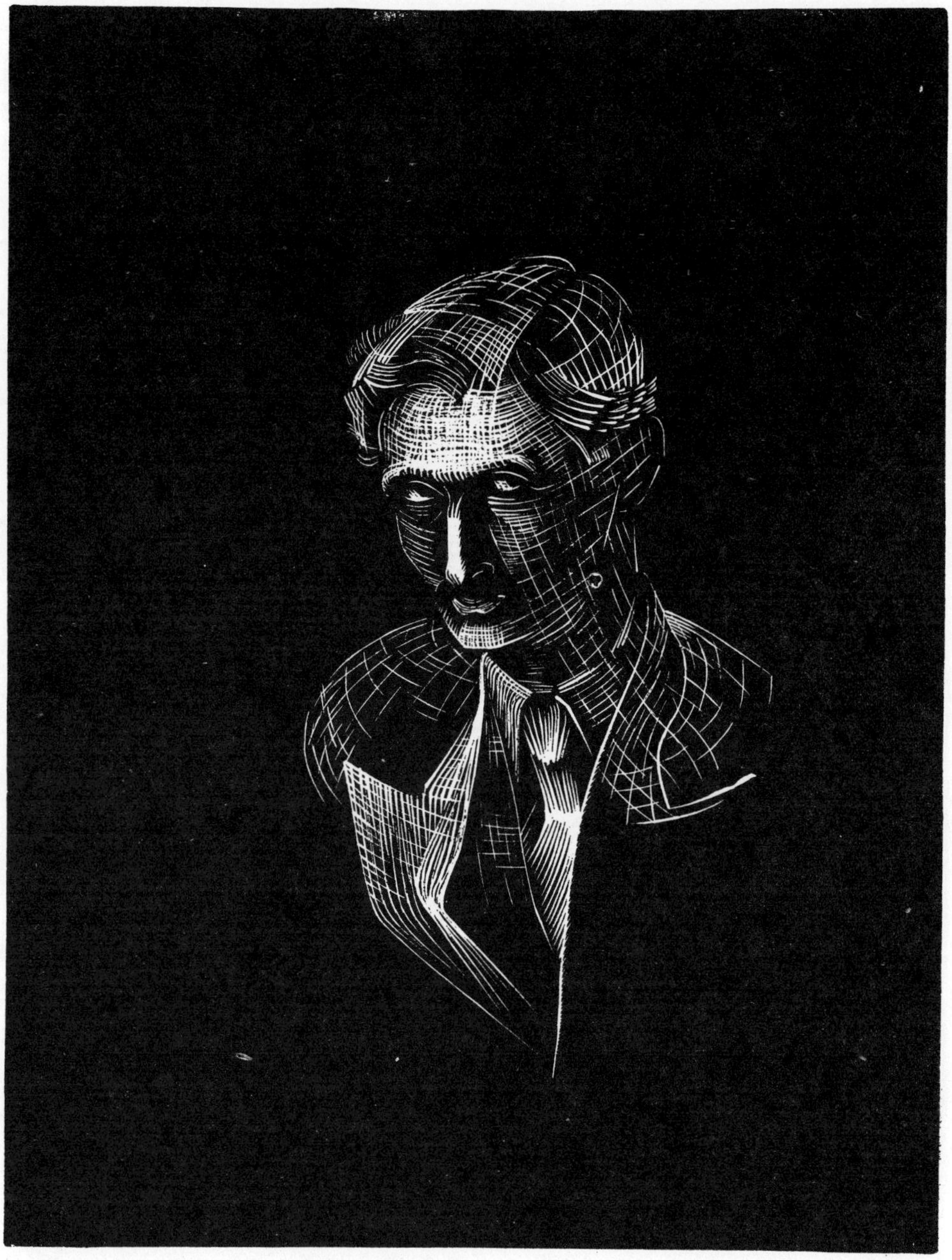

[372] Albert Garrett: *Self-Portrait*, 1961. 15.0 x 20.0cm

[373] William T. Rawlinson: *Cactus*, 1970. 23.0 x 28.0cm

John Nash uses the sharp counterpoint of the two figures and the solid black and white shapes to emphasize his objective realism; so sharply engraved with no sign of a single flourish. How different is the aesthetic emotion in the massive flow of Kenneth Lindley's *Shimabara* [364]. The flow is that of a river torrent and does not the white line even flow into the black line? Only an artist of his quality could get away with the visual pun of the left foreleg in the foreground deflecting the flowing current at the knee joint of the right leg. This counterpointed thrust gives quite an emotional force to the composition. The aesthetic emotion in this engraving is not typical of English engraving – but he is English. *Shimabara* is a print from his Pointing Finger Press book of that title, with the poem written by David Burnett. In this book the voluptuous swirl of form virtually makes Lindley the Matthew Smith of engraving.

In the past and present mice and butterflies have been used as artists' signatures.

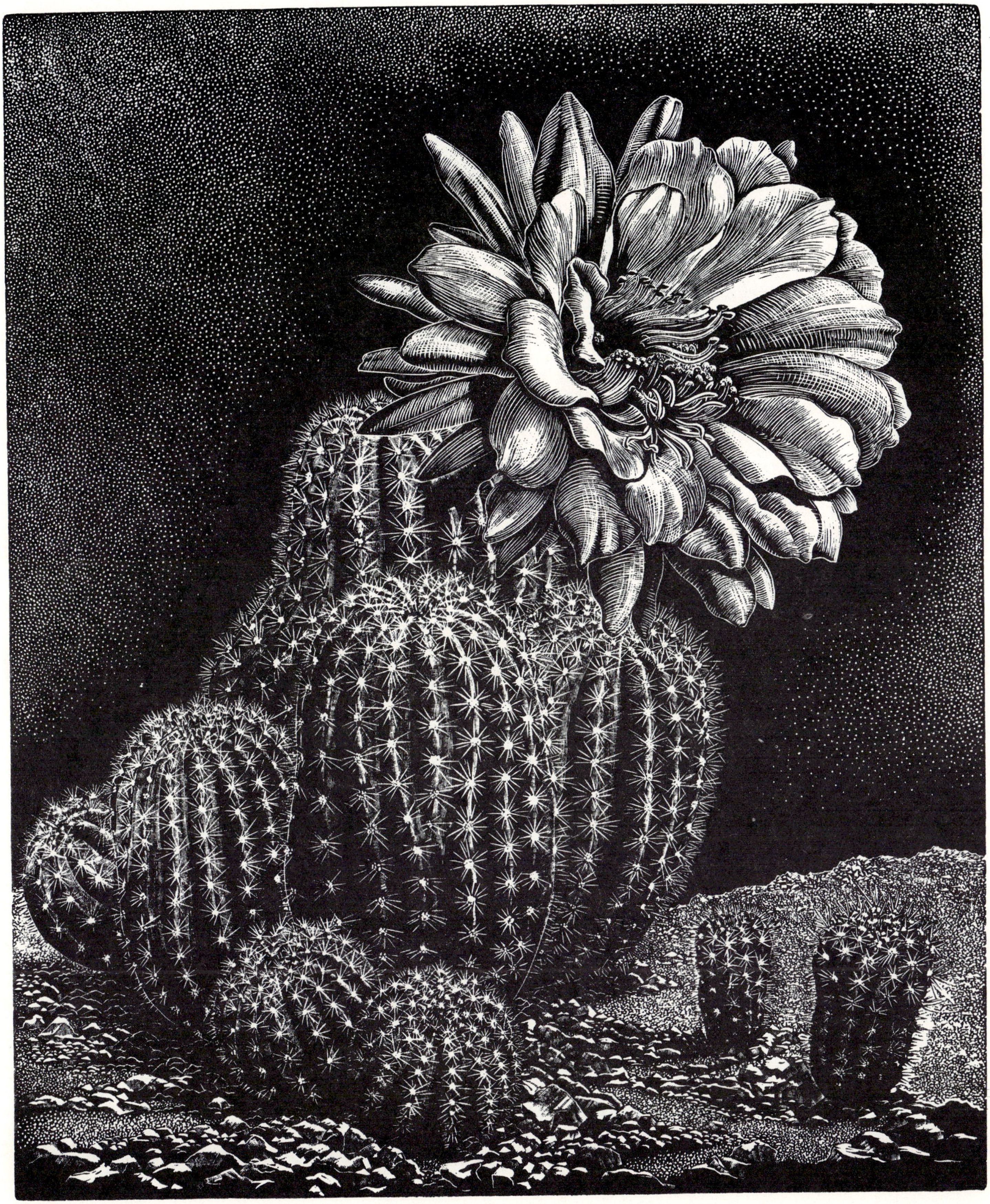

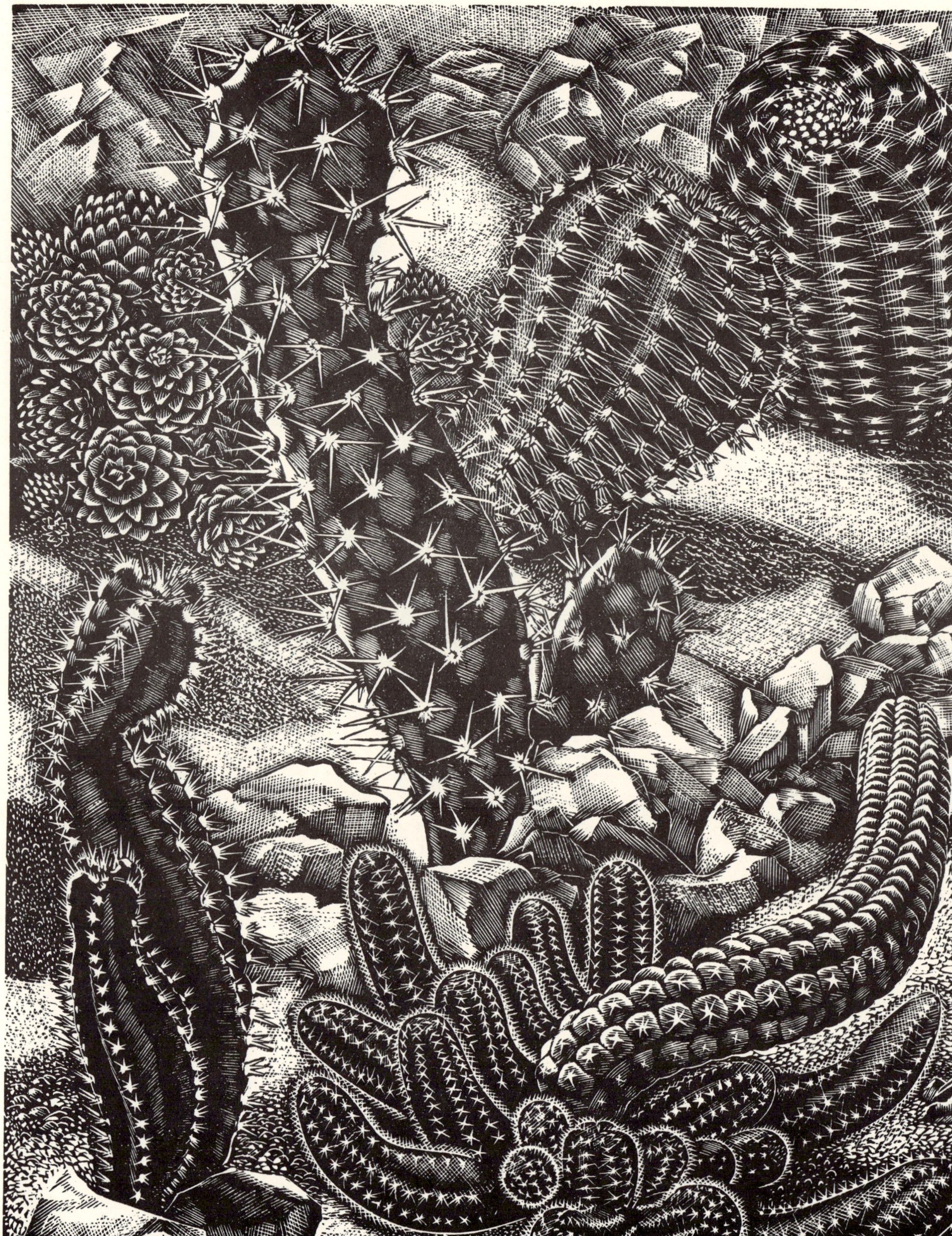
J.E.B

[374] James Bostock: *Cactus Garden*, 1955. 18.0 x 23.0cm

Other than that, mice generally may not play a very important role in art, but there are three wood engravings of mice that have a significant part to play in the British school of wood engraving. A first one produced by Thomas Bewick for his book *Quadrupeds* is *The long-tailed field mouse* [367]; the second is Clare Leighton's *Field Mice* for her book *Selborne* [365] and the third by Joan Hassall *Harvest Mice* [366]. All three engravings are similar in size and all three were produced specifically as natural history book illustrations for the commercial press.

If the subject of natural history is disregarded and the engravings viewed as forms and volumes with a fur-like texture, then these elements are remarkable for the sheer economy of use. Even the eyes of such small creatures as mice are balls in sockets, and in all three engravings it is obvious that each artist worked with a magnifying glass, inserting the volumetric lines which give these minute forms their individual life and expression.

When these three engravings are considered technically under a magnifying glass then Joan Hassall's is the most remarkable. Her *Harvest Mice* [366] are approximately half the size of the mice engraved by Bewick and Leighton. The sheer skill in Hassall's engraving is fabulous. Even the black lines in the left-hand group of five whiskers in the lower harvest mouse are split, confidently and without a single waver. The fat, happy and contented form of the upper harvest mouse

[375] James Dolby: *Shunters*, 1965. 18.5 x 14.0cm

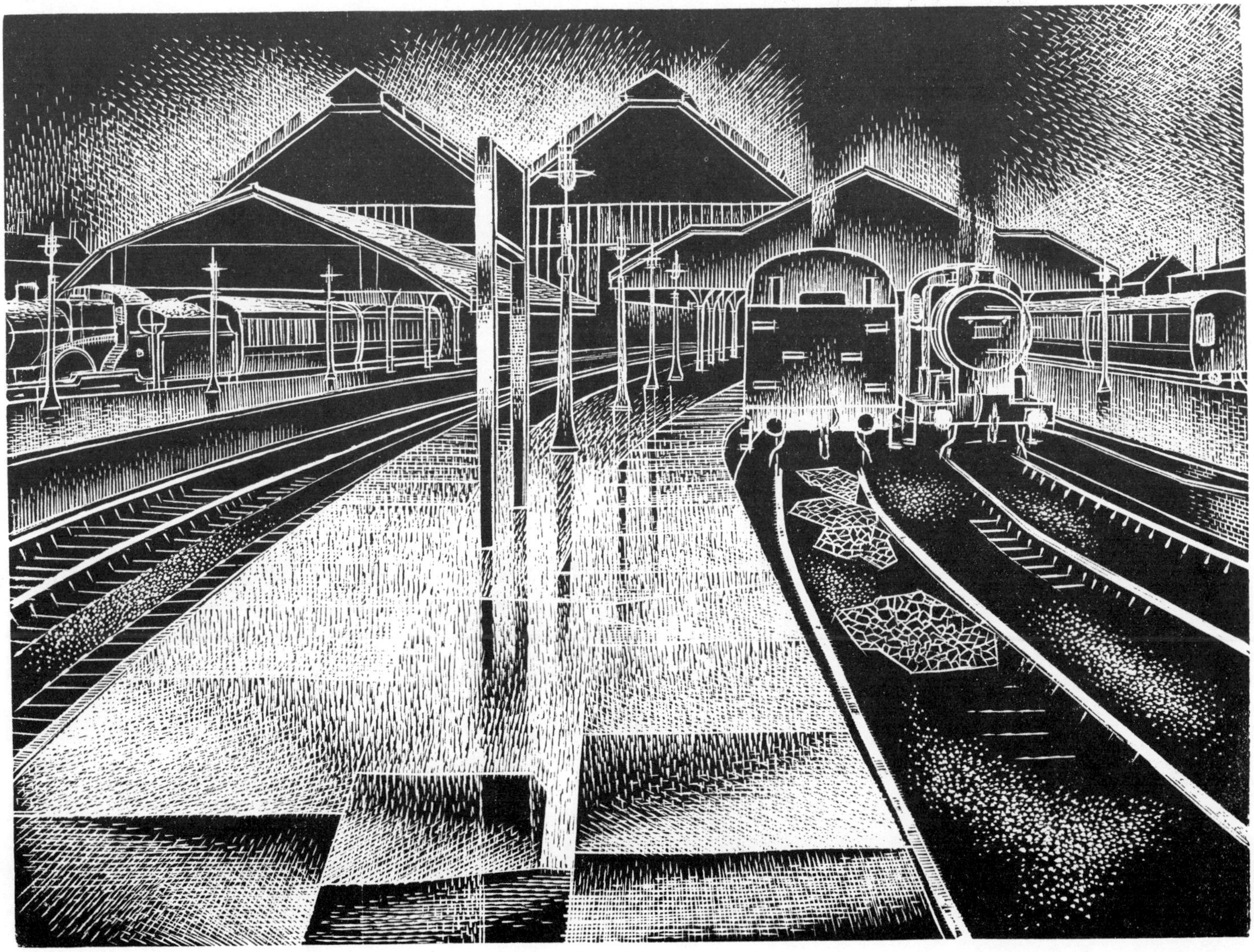

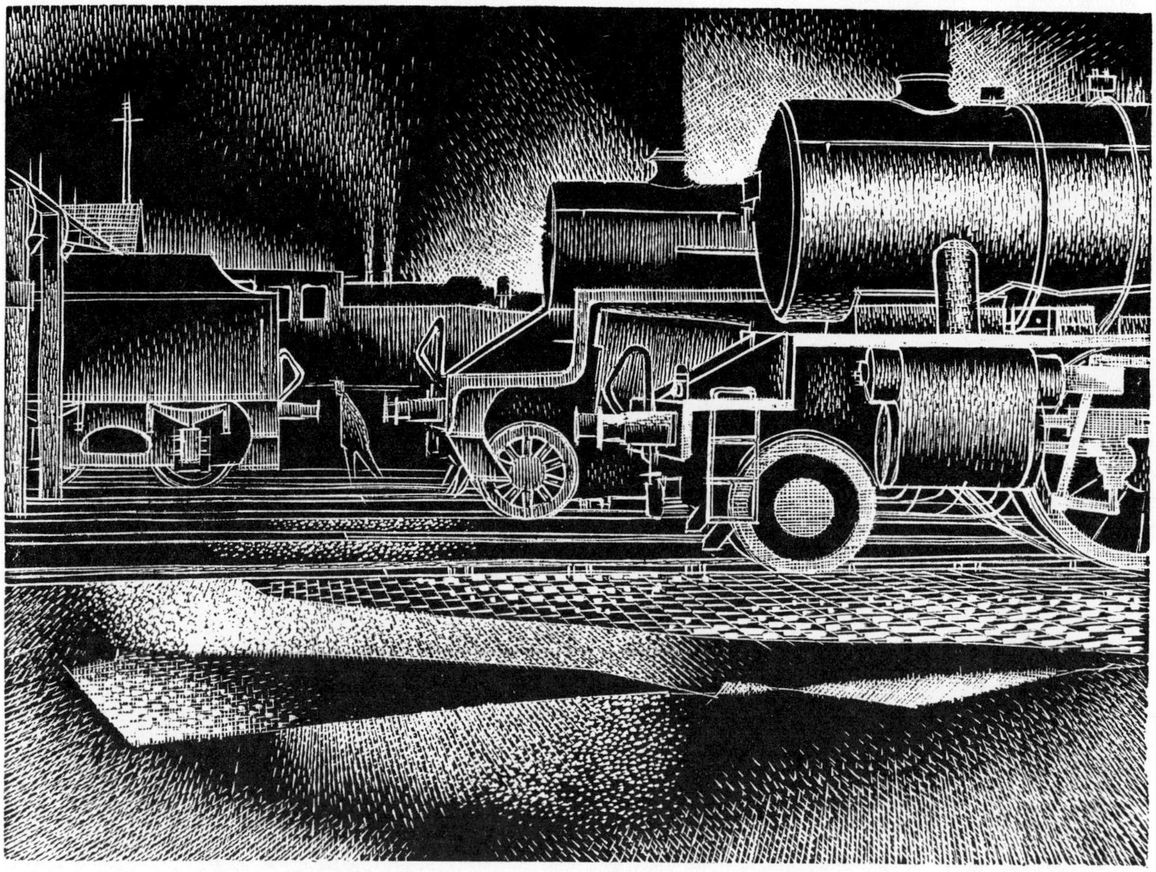

[376] James Dolby: *End of the Line*, 1964, 15.25 x 11.25cm

[377] Engraving of the John Fowler steam ploughing engine, 1871.

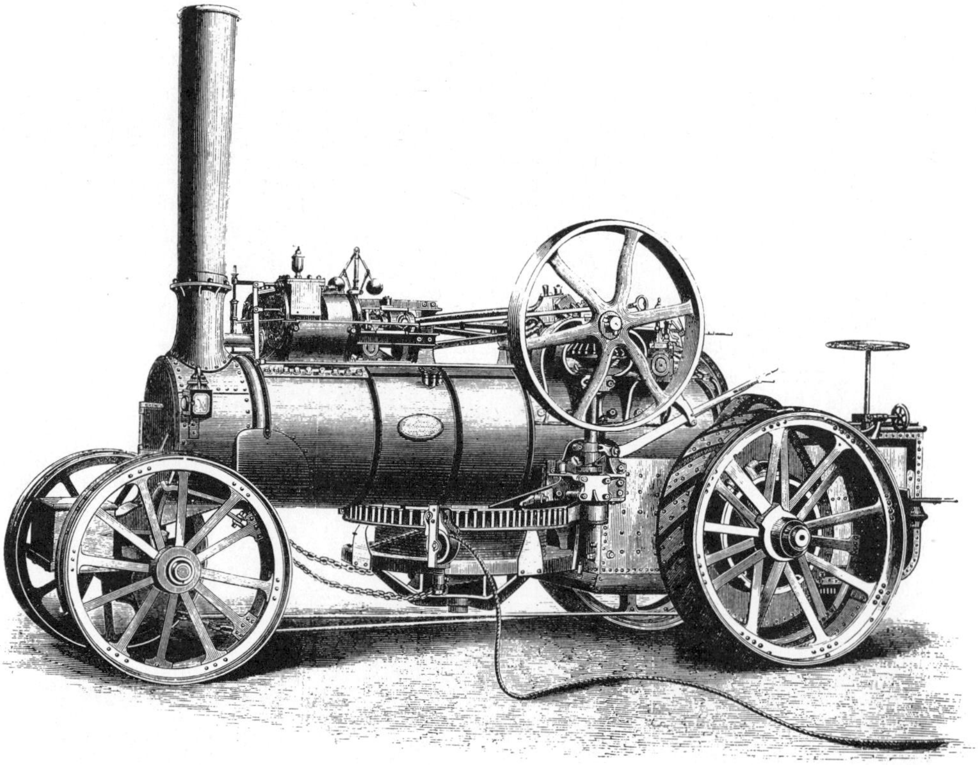

[378] William T. Rawlinson: *The End of the Road*, 1968. 28.0 x 20.25cm

could be better appreciated if it was enlarged photographically to several feet in height. On this scale, this image would be very impressive.

In considering the engraving by Joan Hassall and that by Clare Leighton, it must be concluded that the control of form, the composition and the remarkable unity between animals and plants have been achieved with no evidence of distortion. The skill of the individual engraver has made the tails of the mice tube-like, tough and prehensile, and with considerable subtlety has employed them to provide a connecting link between animals and plants so as to bind the compositions into significant structures. Hassall's *Harvest Mice* is a black-line engraving and Leighton's *Field Mice* is a white-line engraving, but despite their size these diminutive blocks establish different aesthetic qualities that identify the artists as two separate personalities.

In using the medium of wood engraving for self-portraiture, the engraver encounters certain problems because the human head is a complex form when viewed objectively. Overall, it is egg-shaped, with eyes, mouth, nose and ears being minor forms. To the casual observer of a portrait, the head expresses the personality of the sitter with the colour of the hair and of the skin being noticed, but rarely the volume of the head as a whole or the cylindrical volume of the neck supporting it. Should the engraver fail to set the volume of the head securely upon the neck, no amount of detail in the minor shapes can remedy the catastrophe.

Self-portraiture is a very challenging and objective study, demanding not only

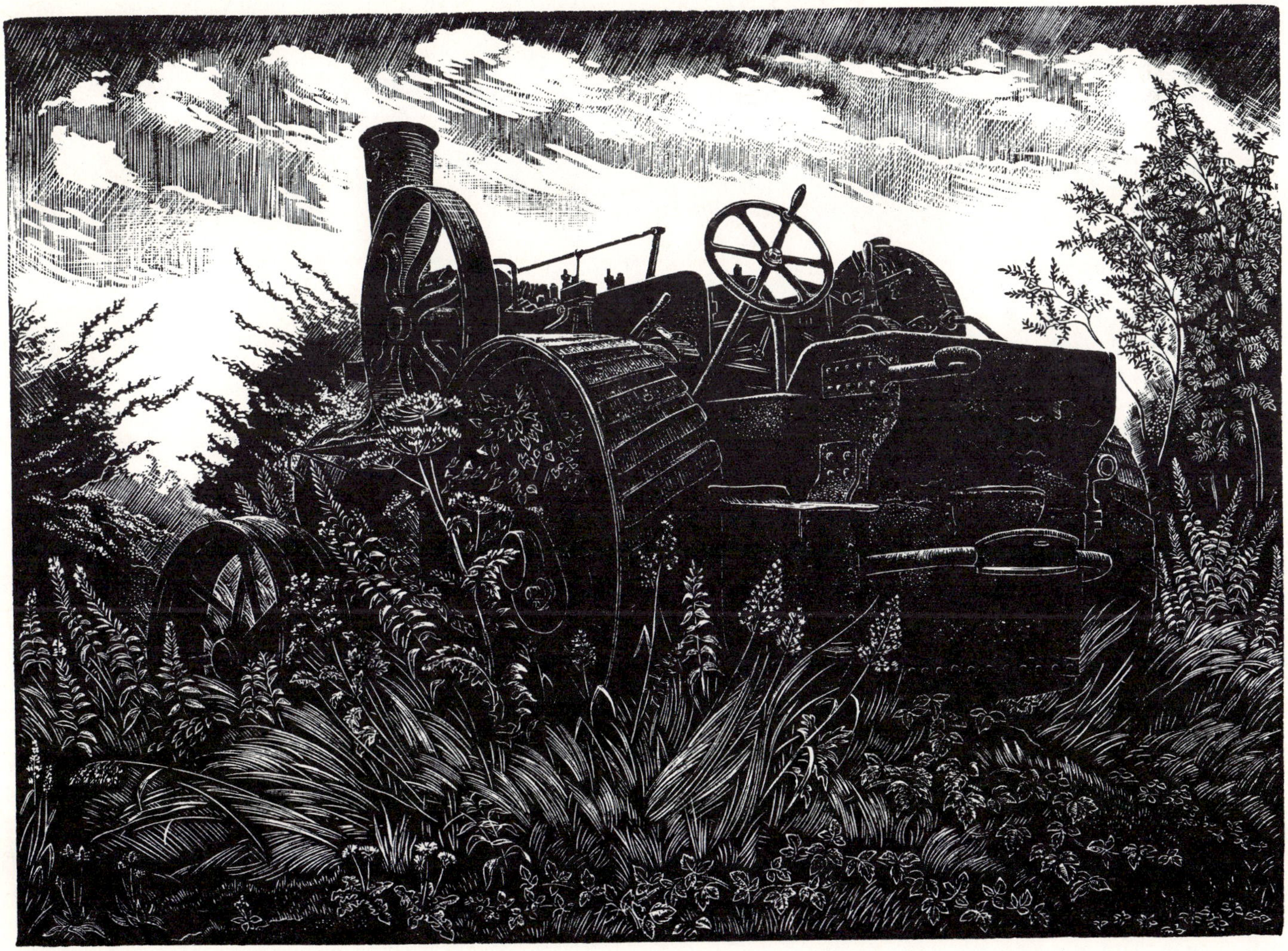

[379] John Petts: *Coire Mhic Fhearchair, Ross*, 1939.
12.8 x 10.25cm

[380] George Mackley: *Rocks*, 1967.
23.5 x 16.0cm

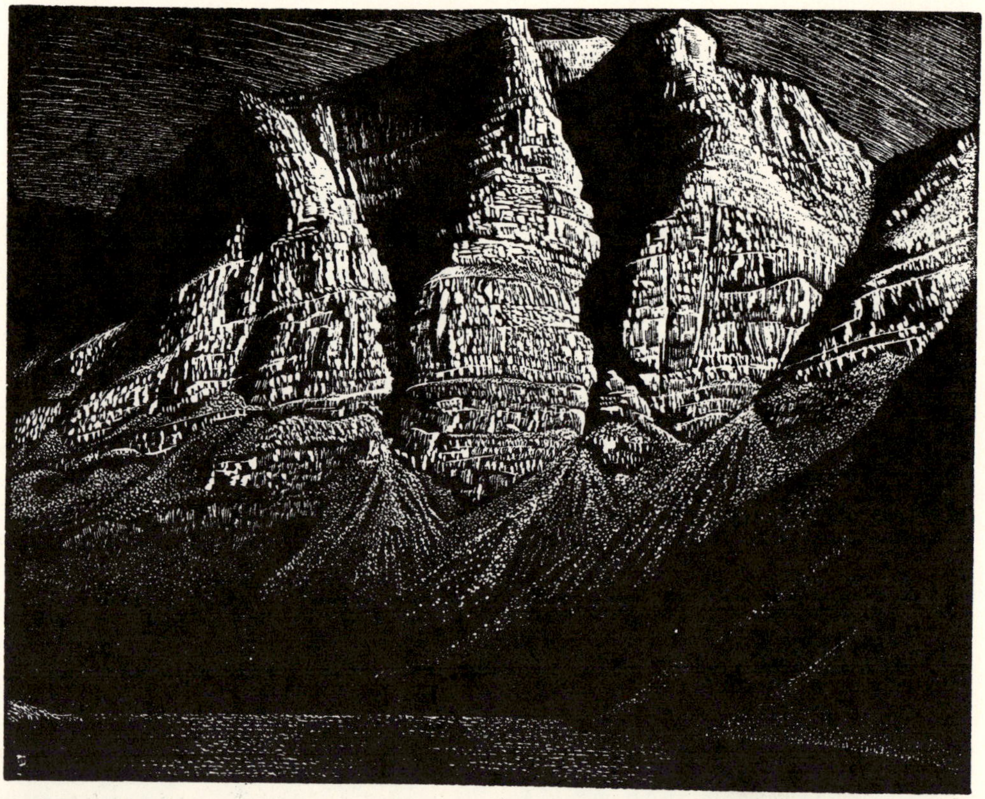

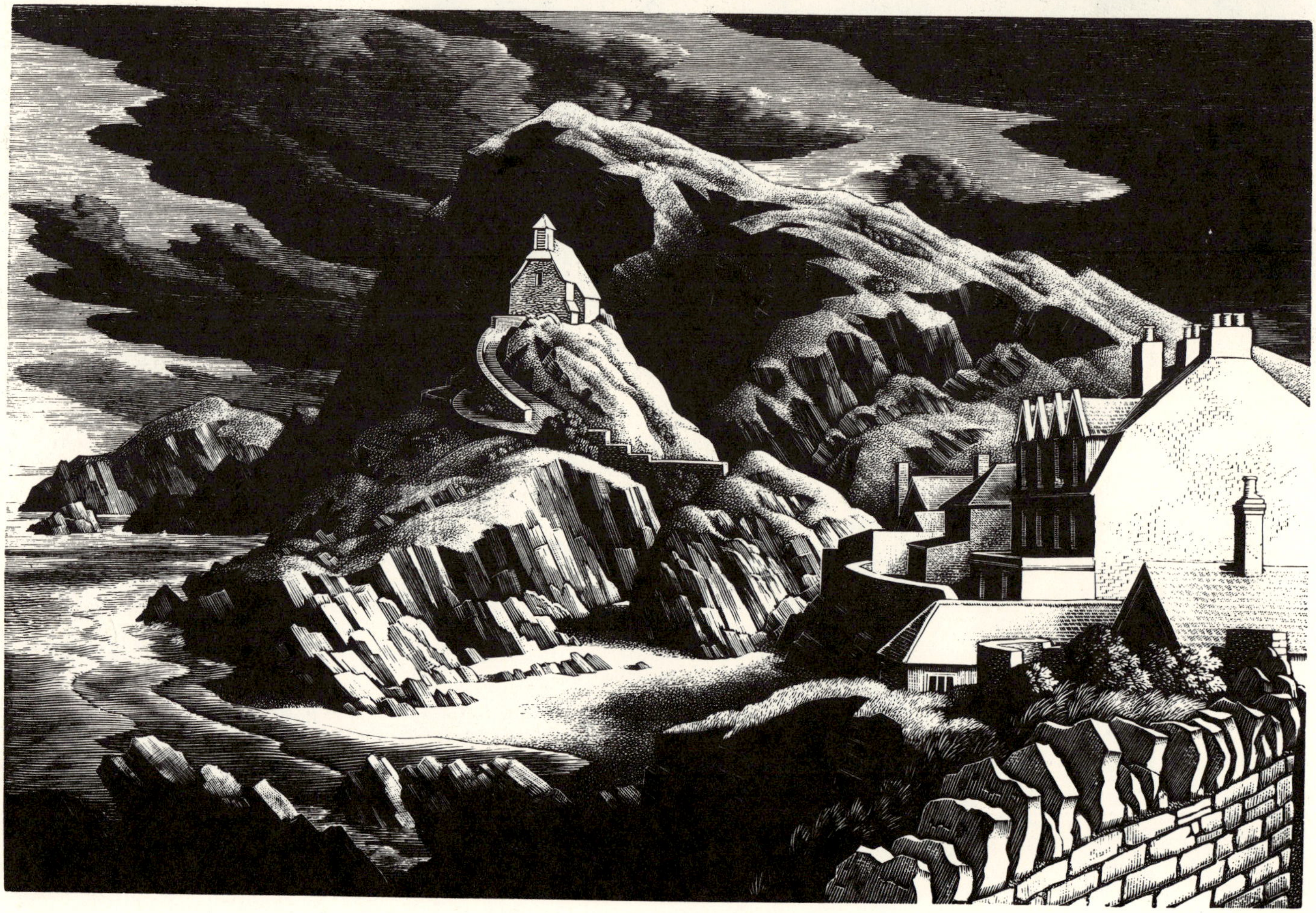

[381] George Mackley: *Lead Mine*, 1960. 15.25 x 12.5cm

competent draughtsmanship but considerable self-confidence. It can be claimed that self-portraiture is attempted to test the engraver's self-confidence and that such a test is often a necessary part of the artist's development. In engraving, the end product must appear as if it came about without effort and in a self-portrait this demands that the whole being is tensioned intellectually, emotionally, and physically. To maintain an observation of one's own face without relaxing the tension throughout the engraving process is usually a convincing reason for the engraver to decide not to attempt a self-portrait.

In examining the self-portraits of five artists, it is seen that in that of Nash [369] the designer is dominant whereas in Gill's portrait [368] the dominant quality is the clear, idealized but unrelenting line of the stone sculptor. The enigmatic portrait of Gertrude Hermes [370] is sensitive, lyrical and wayward, yet tough, whilst that of Bostock [371] is painted with a burin, achieving the volumetric egg from rendering a light beam hitting a solid object. The main interest shown in the portrait of the author [372] is the pure volumetric expression with the minimum number of lines, conveying a taut, wire-like quality.

Nash and Gill are the first generation of white-line engravers and form their blacks and whites into shapes. Hermes is second generation and has broken away from the dominance of shapes and developed the autonomous print. Bostock and the author are of the third generation, learning the lessons from the previous two generations and sublimating technique and craft.

Each of the five portraits discloses a completely different language and manner

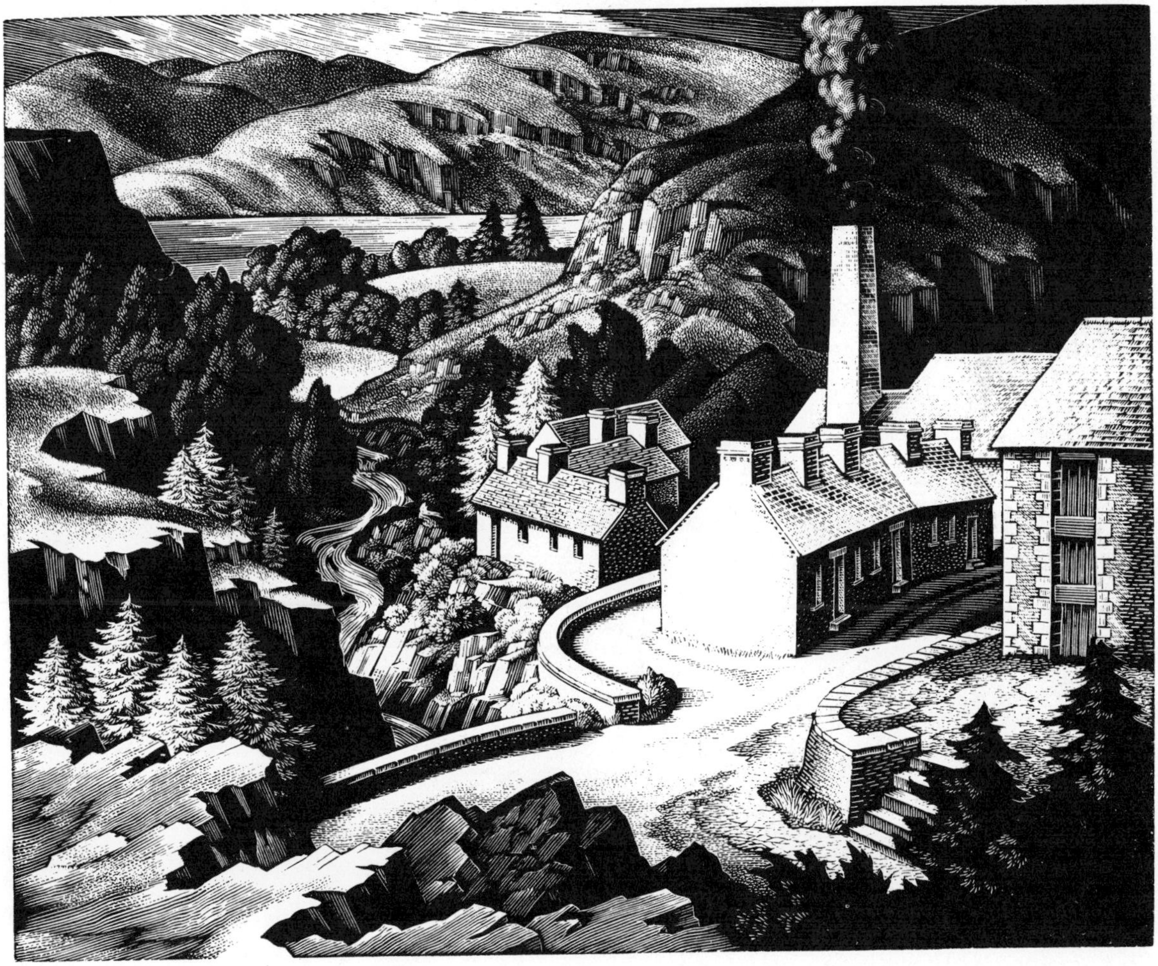

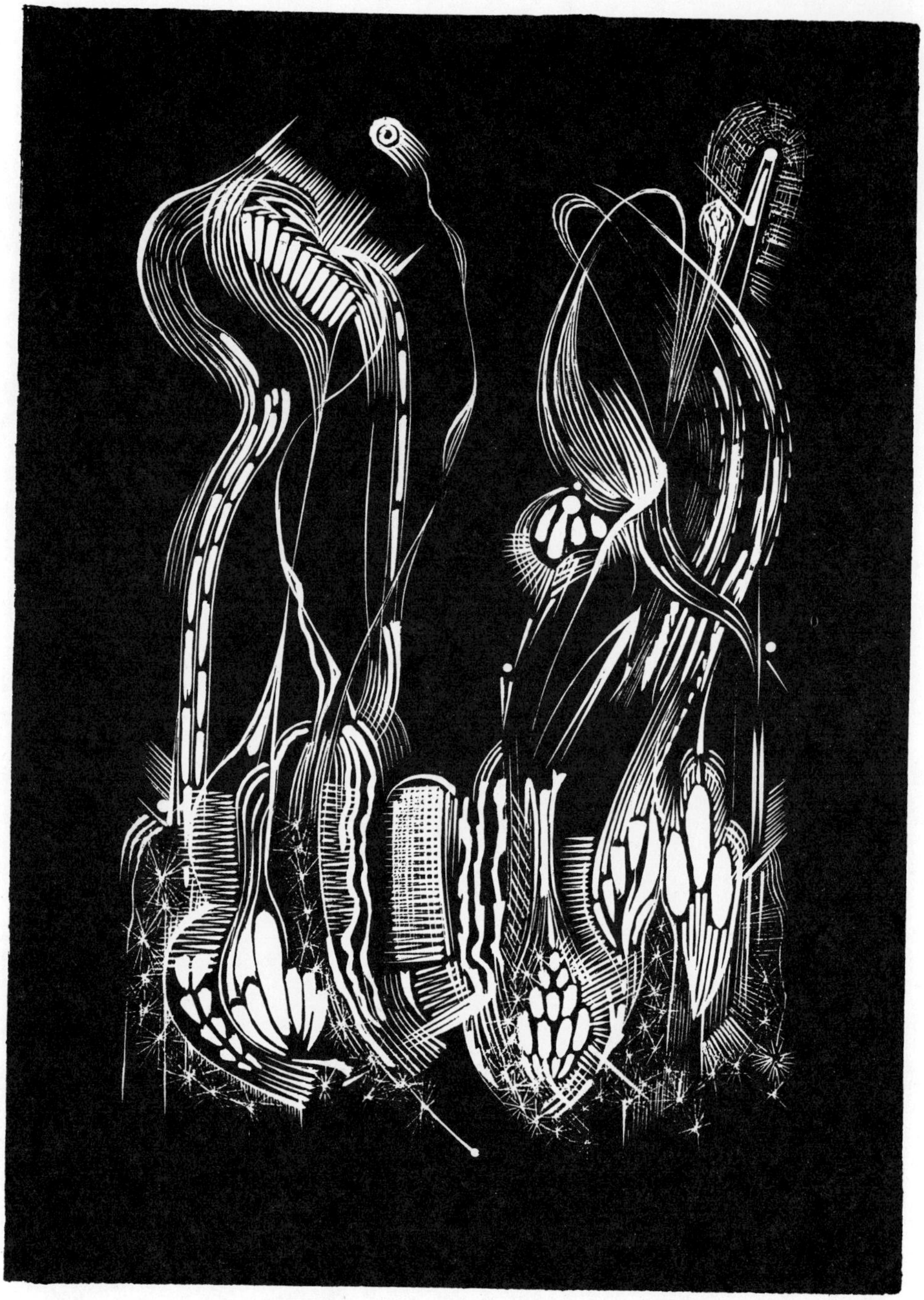

[382] Albert Garrett: *10th Space-time form No 1*, 1967. 14.5 x 20.5cm

in which volumes are expressed. The Gill portrait is an archetypal construction, that of Nash is designed objectively, whilst the portrait of Hermes is pure philosophy and poetry. Bostock's portrait is plastic fluidity and the author's is the volumetric bird caught in a cage. The differences in the language of form are such that one engraver can be of little use to another, neither is it possible for one to copy the language of another. The major object in showing the five heads is to demonstrate by visual comparison the differences in language.

It will be seen that Gill and Nash present a profile whilst the other three attempt the frontal view. The profile view with its plainer volumes lends itself more naturally to a treatment of shape that is linearly dominant. Both Gill and Nash avoid the full volumetric development but take full advantage of shape and line. Both

[383] Albert Garrett: *10th Space-time form No 2*, 1967. 24.5 x 20.5cm

portraits have grandeur and dignity and they were the first self-portraits to be produced as creative engraving, Nash in 1922 and Gill in 1927.

The portrait of Hermes is completely different to the other four. In this engraving she even unwinds through her form and comes up with the apparently wandering, relaxed but delicately controlled lyrical and flowing line. Alongside the other four portraits, she shows just how tightly wound up they are, especially in Gill's case.

John Farleigh's very early self-portrait which he published in his *Graven Image* is very confused in language. It requires a certain kind of abandonment to a particular kind of madness to attempt such a thing and there appears to be no instance of an engraver producing a second engraving of this type.

Peter Reddick has produced more objective studies of heads of historical personalities than any other engraver of the twentieth century. In all examples of his work – and there are very many small items – he always holds his form. Possibly his best-known work in portraiture is the group of Past Presidents of the Royal Society. Pauline Clark's portrait of Jon Vickers in Verdi's *Otello* [337] is a confident and lively work of one of the younger generation of wood engravers.

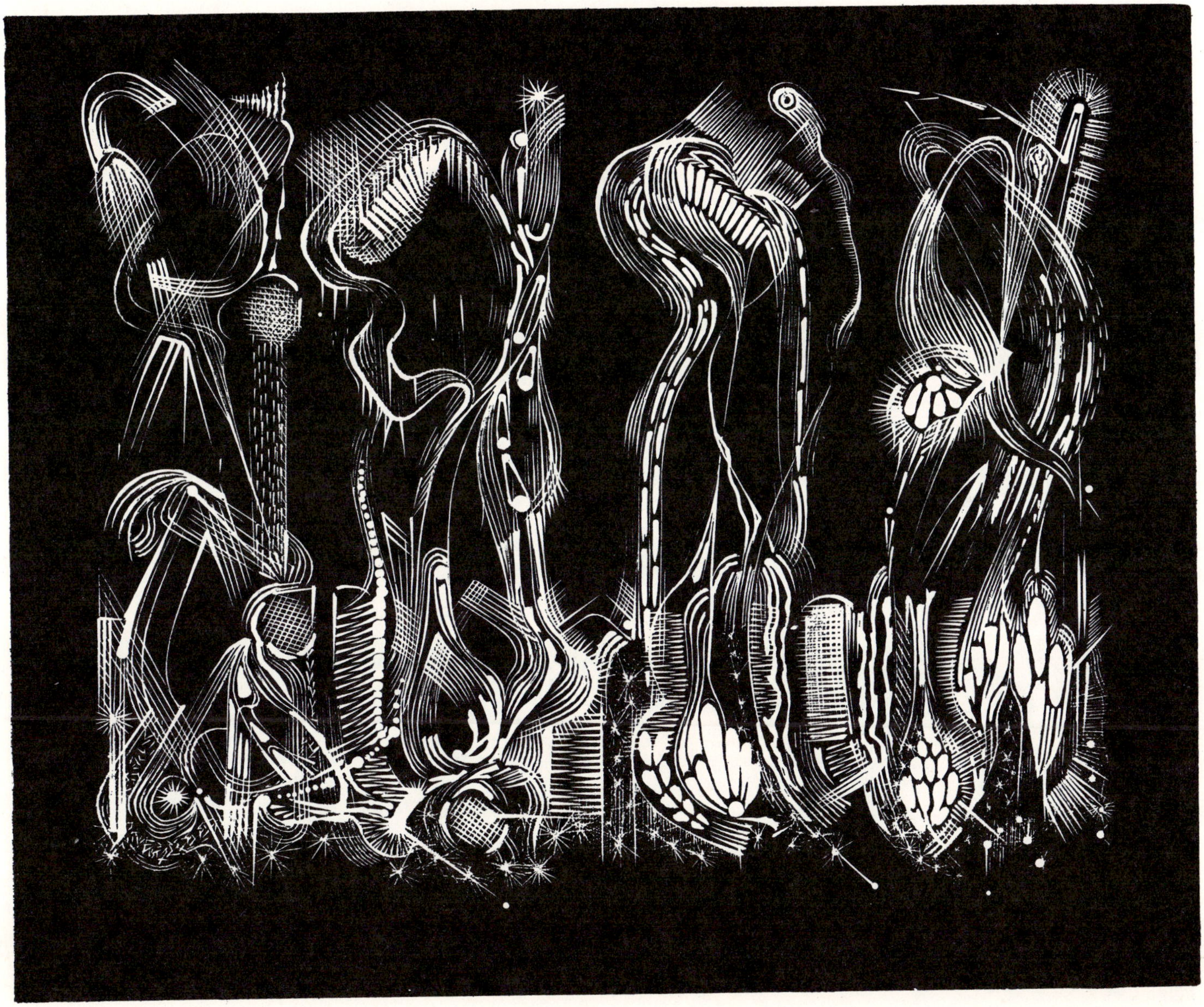

The wood engraver must find and create his own equivalent to any form in strictly engraving terms. Common form solutions can be compared in William T. Rawlinson's *Cactus* [373] and in James Bostock's *Cactus Garden* [374]. These cacti are not drawn in the usual sense of the term, they are constructed with a series of minimum burin incisions. Each would fail if a single spine was mis-stated. The intensity of volumetric expression and sensation in both engravings is an optical illusion. These forms are deeply corrugated and near circular volumes, and if they were drawings and not engravings the corrugations would need to be defined by shading to give their recession. However, in parts of these cacti the corrugations are not even indicated as such. The burin action of the radial spines converging at a point on the corrugation ridge culminates in a white spot, similar to a sharply focused set of light beams. When viewing beyond two spotlights reasonably close together, it will be noted that the darkness behind the lights appears as a converging but dark depth and recession is due to a very small amount of specular light spilling over the edge and partially softening the effect. In the engravings of the cacti, the sharp, clean-cut white spine lines crossing the dark depth behind create the illusion that the corrugations are drawn in section. The corrugations can be seen to be sparsely drawn in those parts which meet the stronger light definition. This phenomenon of engraving could only occur in white-line engraving.

The difference in the sharpness of the white spine lines is due to the difference in the timbers used to make the blocks. A softer quality is evident in William T. Rawlinson's *Cactus* because the block is made of end-grained pearwood, and the extreme spine sharpness in James Bostock's *Cactus Garden* is due to the extra hardness of the end-grained boxwood block. It would be difficult to find a better pair of engravings to demonstrate as clearly the differences arising from the two different timbers.

[384] Albert Garrett: *10th Space-time form No 3*, 1967. 46.0 x 20.5cm

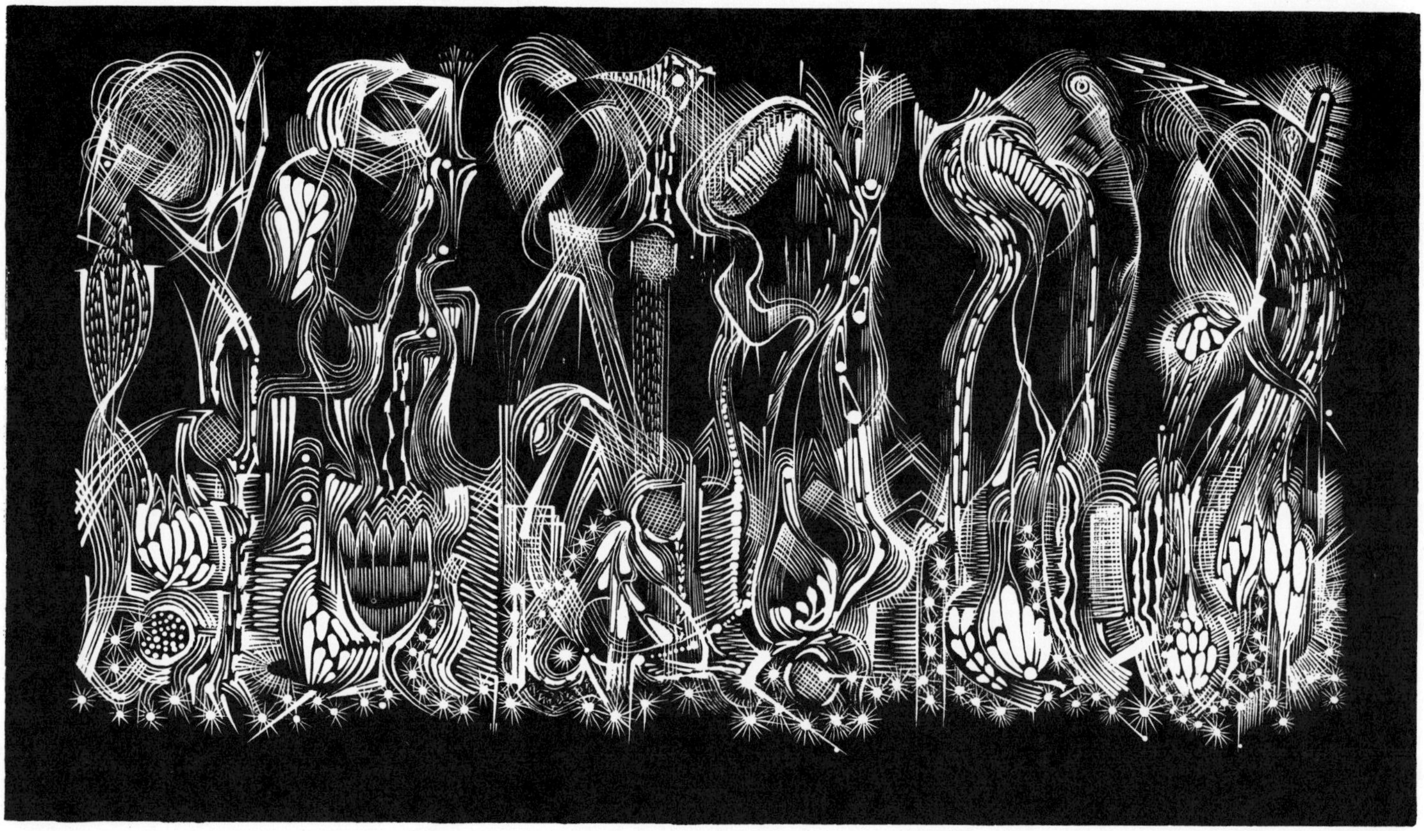

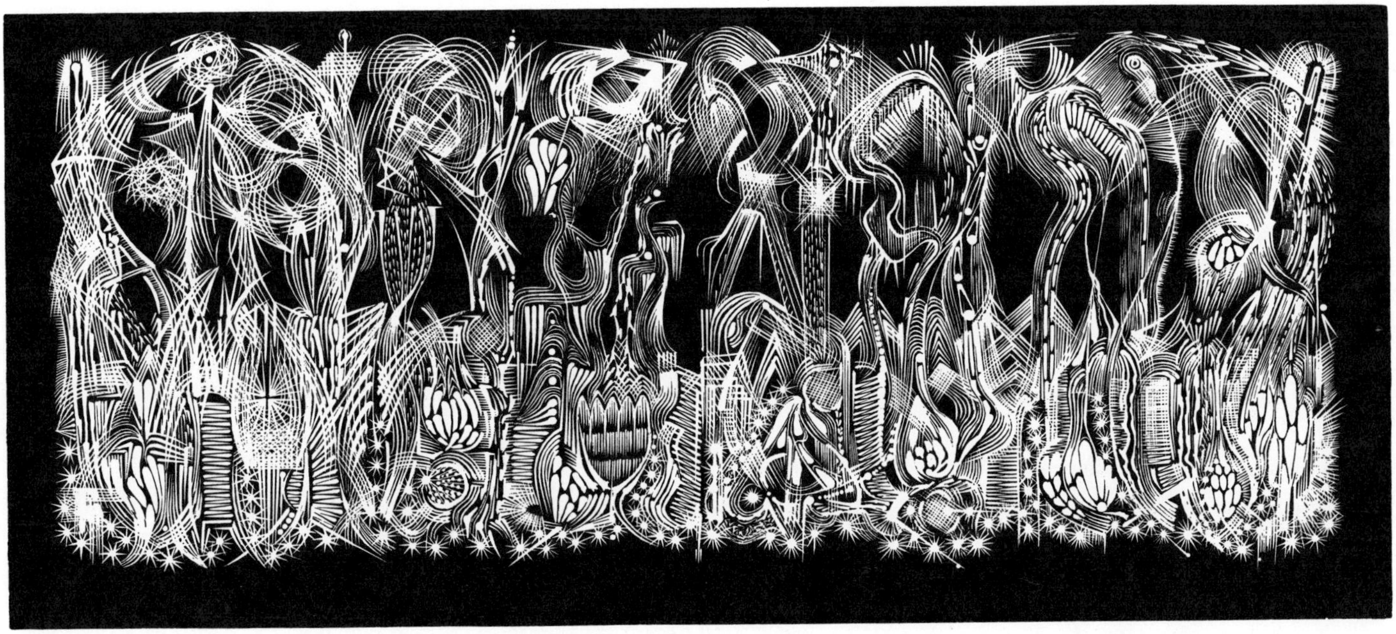

[385] Albert Garrett: *10th Space-time form No 4*, 1967. 46.0 x 20.5cm

Approximately a century separates John Swain's engraving of the ploughing engine [377], which appeared in an issue of *The Engineer* in 1871 as the very latest model of applied steam power, from the railway engine white-line engravings by James Dolby [375 and 376] and the pair of ploughing engines by William Rawlinson [frontispiece and 378]. Such a group of engravings of a common subject offers significant aesthetic and technical engraving comparisons. Rawlinson's engines were engraved on the end-grained pearwood blocks giving a slightly softer effect. Dolby's engines were engraved on end-grained boxwood blocks producing a sharper line image. To be able to make such a comparison is a rare experience. In the commercial black-line engraving on boxwood, the engine is shown in mint condition ready for sale, with every nut and bolt clearly defined, and much of its dignity arises from the fabulous craftsmanship bestowed upon it by the engraver.

Dolby is a seaman with a love of sailing who had a wartime naval career as a captain. He loves order, control and discipline and this is evident from the manner in which he bestows dignity and appreciation on the engines in their premature and enforced retirement. The sympathetic design, order, measured rhythm and the fullness of volumetric expression are achieved in pure line only. One senses that he regrets the passing of the steam locomotive with its individuality of design, smell and sound, and that there is sadness in the change from steam to diesel. In this white-line engraving, sadness is conveyed in the slow pictorial ryhthms of the night and the wet platform, and he expresses loneliness by placing his engines in the middle distance.

Rawlinson places his engines in the foreground, for close scrutiny. He studied these engines for a long time at the spot where they were abandoned on rough ground close to his home in Evesham. He stresses the rusting and corroding sores of his giants, once loved and cared for and now forlorn in their helplessness under the wild skies, moving into the oblivion of the cold night. Yet Rawlinson bestows a serene dignity on these engines.

In what might seem an unusual opinion for an artist, John Petts claims that parachuting in and out of aeroplanes gave him an unusual point of view of most

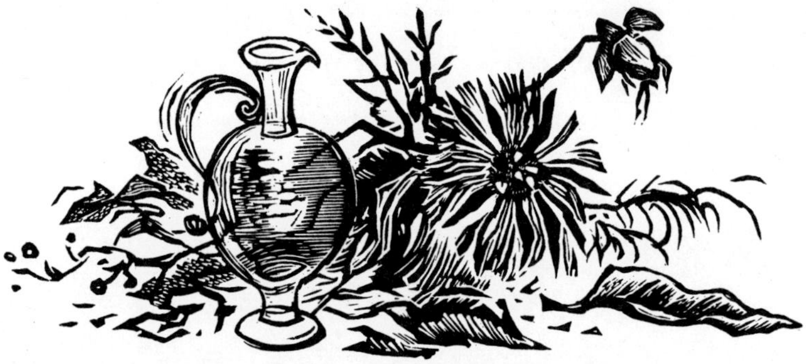

[386] Frank Martin: Endpiece from Charles Lamb *Essays*, 1963. 10.0 x 4.5cm

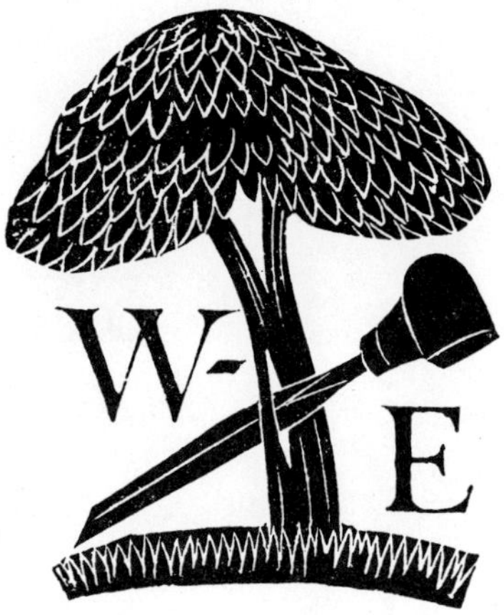

[387] Eric Gill: Symbol (first version) for the Society of Wood Engravers, 1921, 4.4 x 5.4cm

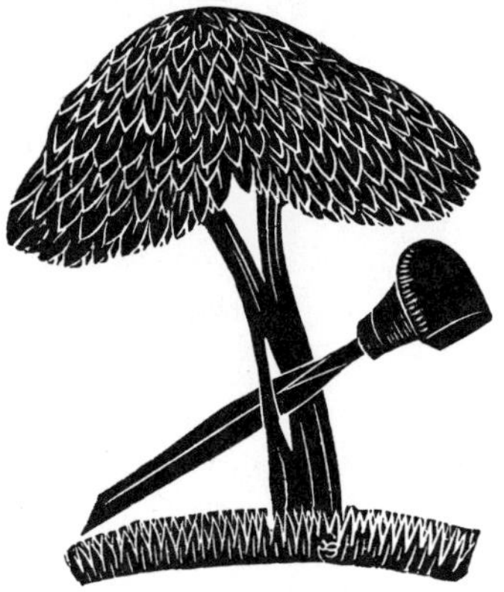

[388] Eric Gill: Symbol (final version) for the Society of Wood Engravers, 1921. 4.2 x 5.0cm

things and of people. It might well be said also, that spending so much time in parachuting gave him more experience than most of being in light which had not yet been absorbed and reflected at ground level. The difference here is that above the clouds the light is unidirectional and on the ground plane it is multi-directional. Therefore, visibility above the ground plane is very much sharper.

The unusual viewpoint of Petts can be appreciated in his engraving *Coire Mhic Fhearchair, Ross* [379]. Petts usually refers to this work as *The Three Crags* though the Gaelic title means 'the corrie of the son of Farchar'. This engraving should also be seen in relation to Mackley's *Rocks* [380]. Together they are a unique pair in subject but opposite in their expression and use of the medium. Yet each engraving is an eloquent commemoration of a beam of light. The intensity of the landscape depicted by Petts arises from the skilful use of a minimum number of short, powdery white lines and the rocks have a hardness with no parallel in British wood engraving.

Mackley's engraving *Rocks* and Petts' *Coire Mhic Fhearchair* are two of the most singularly important landscapes of the whole of the British school but neither of them would have achieved their success without Bewick's white-line concept and Rook's designed engraving concept. Both works are expressing light with a scientific appreciation of the subject as distinct from a purely aesthetic understanding.

In 1962, the Society of Wood Engravers sent an exhibition of wood engravings for exhibition in Leiden, Utrecht and Amsterdam. Three works by Mackley were soon sold and he wrote: 'I will add the Dutch to my list of high-minded and righteous people, now that you tell me that they are buying three of my prints. I thought that in Holland they were all very advanced and that they were very unlikely to buy old-fashioned work like mine. I am glad to learn that there are some who have lagged behind as I have. There is one trouble. I did not print the full edition and I have by me only one print. I am not entirely satisfied that this print is on a sympathetic paper.' Mackley's dissatisfaction with the paper means that the quality of light was not reproduced to his standard. He is very conscientious in maintaining the standards he sets himself and he has clear personal ideas about art and himself. If he fails to attain his objective he rejects the work. He is aware, as are many others, that art at some time or other must become more objective in its aim if not interpretation. In this respect he is the philosophical realist of the British school. The clinical observation of the artist, his power of execution that is surgically accurate, the subtle difference between the light values bouncing off the several planes of sky and rocks, can only be described as a 'Mackley phenomenon'.

The landscape *Lead Mine* [377] is well known in wood engraving. Mackley wrote of it: 'It is so old-fashioned that it might well have been left over from the time of the Prince Consort. But it is the only kind of engraving that I know how

[389] Iain Macnab: The end-grained block for *Snow*, 1927. 10.3 x 15.4cm

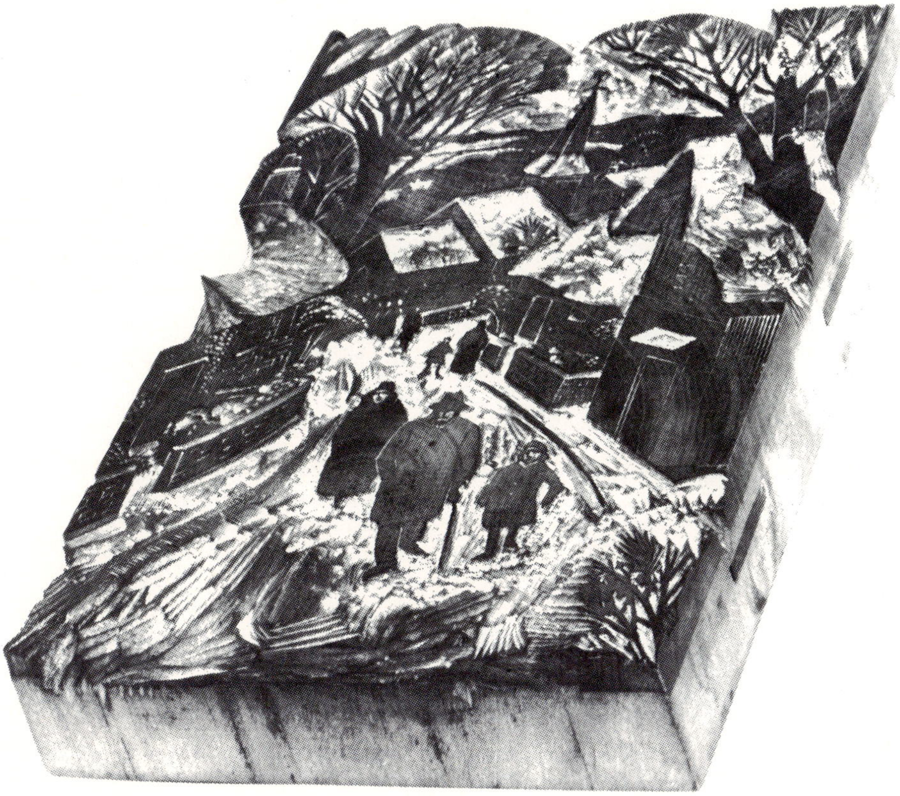

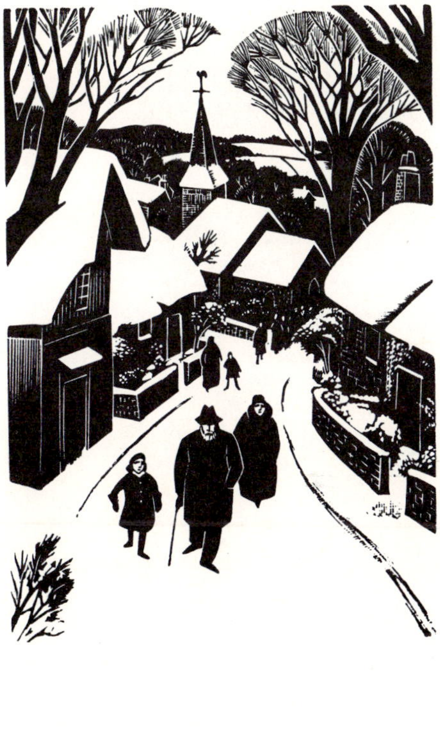

[390] Iain Macnab: *Snow*, 1927. 10.3 x 15.4cm

to do. I like doing it, anyway, and am unlikely to do anything very different at my time of life.' Mackley is a very clear-sighted man with a great love of the craft of engraving but he is too modest as an artist to acknowledge that he has sublimated the craft and turned his work into art, and art of a very high and rare order.

After Newton diffracted a beam of light through a prism in the seventeenth century, a new conception of solids and space was evolved but these new ideas did not begin to be seen effectively in the world of art until Cézanne began to paint. His use of colour expressed spatial measurement and the evolution of solids in space. In art, this development was a point of no return, and in wood engraving the concepts of light and the forms evolved in white light are strongly influenced by Cézanne's treatment of the diffracted beam. The engravings of Mackley and Petts show this influence clearly.

Cézanne's images are particular and each has its individual characteristics. He reduced images by abstraction but no matter how far that process was developed, the basic form of the image remains, thus enabling its nature to be recognised. Cézanne arrested time; in painting a subject he depicted it as it appeared before him in space and time. It was Paul Klee who first expressed the simultaneous aspects of space; he would paint the exterior and the interior of a house in the same picture to embody in the images a conception of the whole.

The Taoist philosophy of China included time in its point of view and could regard an image as expressing the essence of all images contained in the whole and thus could accept a simultaneous view of the exterior and the interior. From the first century AD, Chinese artists accepted the desirability of expressing simultaneous vision of separate situations; whereas western culture demands that only the image that can be seen should be depicted, the Chinese have always found nothing incongruous in showing a person in front of a wall and on the other side of it another individual who in reality would be out of view.

In their art, the Chinese place little value on three-dimensional perspective and their expression of depth is a matter of representing space planes. The philosophy behind this art expression owes much to the fact that vision is a physical stimulus which is interpreted by the brain as a three-dimensional image but at the same time the interpretation is affected by certain psychological aspects of the individual person. This situation gives rise to interpretation which is at variance with the exact replica of the initial physical stimulus.

In the more recent consideration of wood engraving, attention has been paid to conceptions that are not confined to the traditional three-dimensional view. The aspect of working in space-time form is that of experimenting into the unknown in order to experience a range of imaginative images and to bring this experience to fruition in the final work. This experience can be referred to as the 'point of view' of the artist wherein he has been released from the confinement of a situation to take flight into free space and time. His point of view in the confined situation will be different to that in free imaginative flight and as such is an example of the separate relationship of space and time.

Growth is the theme development in the series of wood engravings by the author called *10th Space-Time Form* [382-385]. The series is preceded by nine other sequential engravings in the space-time context. *4D Globular* was the first such production to be widely exhibited from 1958 and represents a simple everyday globular form in a state of continuous change in the six versions. It is important

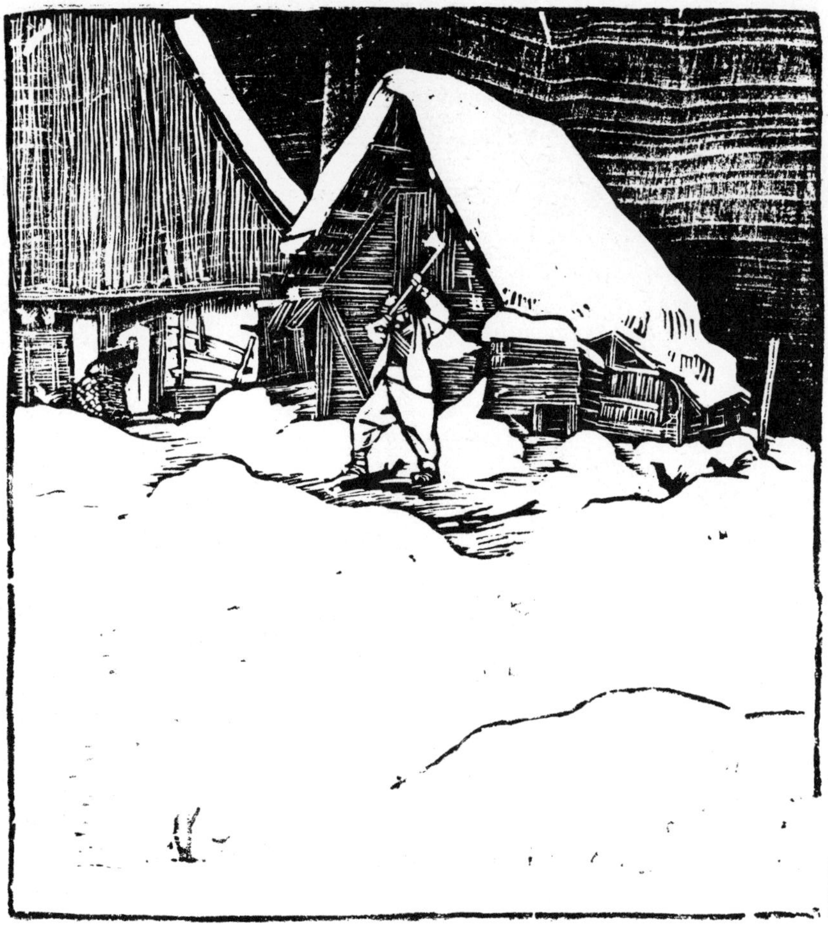

[391] Bernard Rice: *A Peasant's House in Bosnia*, 1924. 11.0 x 12.0cm

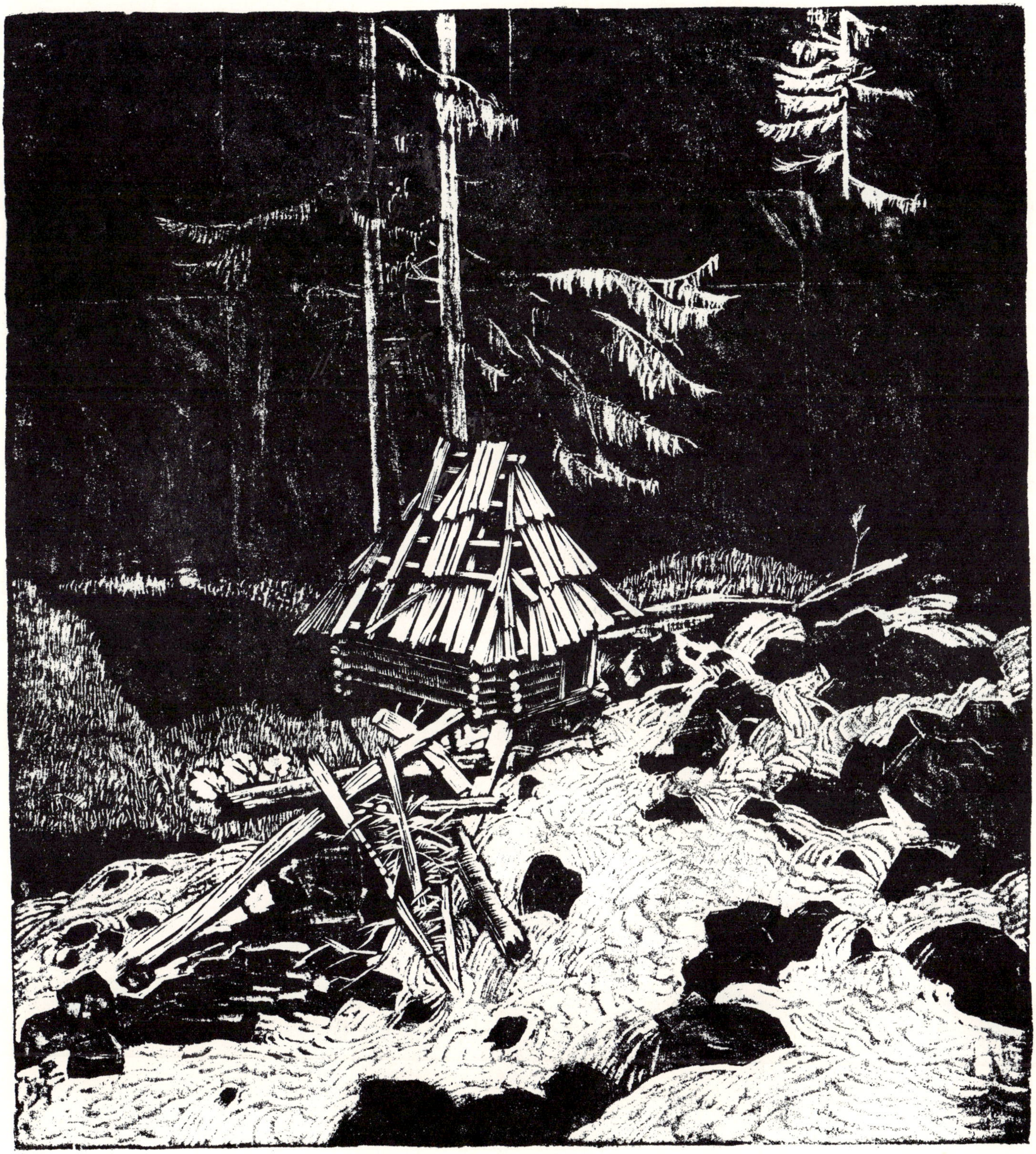

[392] Bernard Rice: *Ruined old Water Mill, on the River Ugar*, 1924.
21.7 x 24.2cm

that when a series of engravings is being developed each print must stand in its own right as a complete aesthetic statement. The lines of the first engraving are retained and brought forward into the block successively through to the last one. In this concept of the changing of growth forms, one form or part of a form is able to move through another and thus it is an essential feature of growth.

Inspiration can come from unusual sources and an artist must be aware of the environment. It was the window cleaner, working on the smeared pane of glass, who gave me the ideas in 1958 which resulted in the series *4D Globular*. The window cleaner's textured cloth makes sweeping lines of an engraved character on the window pane. His curvature was a direct expression of the body curve which started from the feet. He repeated the gestural performance in the same place several times and each set of marks, although obliterating the previous set, was similar yet different. In translating this inspiration to the engraving on the end-grained boxwood block, the first set of marks was retained and carried into the second print.

The problem in engraving a series to express a particular theme is to decide the amount of engraving to be allocated to each print and to decide on the amount of light to be spread over more than one print. The engraving itself had to be developed in much the same way as a cellular structure in a growing biological or botanical form. A micro-unit structure was conceived as the continually changing line dispensing its quota of light into the black space. Its length and width determines the rate at which the light is dispensed. The work exercising the main influence on the micro-structure concept was D'Arcy Wentworth Thompson's *On Growth and Form*, though this was not written with art in view.[2] In *10th Space-Time Form* No. 1 [382], the first print had to evolve economically with a minimum amount of light expended. More lines were engraved for the second print [383] to develop the image a stage further and consequently there was a higher degree of illumination. Prints No. 3 and No. 4 [384 and 385] could only be developed provided that sufficient light was held in reserve on the uncut parts of the block, and the percentage of unexpended light had to be equally divided. The lines engraved in the single block are contained in each successive print.

The developments in space-time indicate that the British school of wood engraving is maintaining an attitude that seeks to retain all that is good in past achievements yet continually search for new means of expression. In order to consolidate their position and retain an awareness of the need to explore new concepts, the artists of the British school have had to extend their studies over a wide range so as to be able to express the full sweep of aesthetic emotion of which wood engraving is comprised. Thus study has ranged from the Dordogne to the present day because it has been necessary to go back into history to understand the true character of creative engraving and project a new art, attaining considerable achievement, in which craft technique are sublimated.

It is only through the Dordogne that one can explain the art of Henry Moore, Leon Underwood, Gertrude Hermes, Blair Hughes-Stanton and those who were students with them at Underwood's school. Likewise, the roots of John Buckland-Wright, John Farleigh and Agnes Miller Parker reach back to the Ficoroni Coffer. Then there is the rare example of Bernard Rice whose roots are to be found in early Chinese wood engraving. The widest influence of all was that of the Danube school which affected such brilliant talents as Ricketts, Shannon, Gordon Craig, Ravilious and Lucien Pissarro.

To be continuously creative in engraving over a lifetime of production in a linear discipline, and thereby to contribute to a meaningful language of form, and to increase our understanding of the world about us, requires a massive clear-sighted effort. A creative engraver must also be either a painter or sculptor and those who are engravers only are usually brilliant exponents of technique rather than of art. In Europe this concept starts with Dürer, one of the greatest of artists, and in Britain with Blake. The French still hold the *peintre-graveur* tradition in high esteem and can claim Camille Pissarro as an example, as Britain can claim Lucien Pissarro, and there are many others.

The leading creative engravers of the British school are either sculptor- or painter-engravers, beginning with the sculptor Gill and the living sculptors Petts and Hermes. Hermes has said that creative engravers must be either sculptors or painters, otherwise they are likely to lose inspiration. John Buckland-Wright has said the same thing to his students many times. The Nash brothers are painter-engravers and it is important that this fact is taken into account if a real understanding of their development is the objective. Macnab and others like Chadwick, the McKenzie sisters, Rachel Reckitt, all of whom are painters, have the roots of their engraving in the classical tradition of the Renaissance.

Some of the younger generation of engravers have evolved an abstract language based upon the Bauhaus concepts of form. The school of Paris has a few exponents in the younger generation though the influence is not strong. The linear aspects of form were more clearly researched at the Bauhaus than was the case with the Paris school. However, in their own way the younger engravers are adding to our experience of engraving. Engraving must always be dependent upon the draughtsmanship and the quality of the practitioners of the time.

Campbell Dodgson, a great expert on engraving, summed up his faith in the pioneers of the revival of wood engraving and his hope for its future in a statement in the catalogue of the 1920 Exhibition of the Society of Wood Engravers. He wrote: 'Let them be themselves, frankly of their own time, and develop a modern style. If it is good it will make its impression, tomorrow if not today. If it is not good there's an end of it. In art everything is worth doing; the great requisite is that it must be well done.'

REFERENCES

1 Severin, M. F. *Your Wood Engraving*, Sylvan Press, London, 1953
2 Thompson, D'A. W. *On Growth and Form*, Cambridge University Press, London, 1966

11 BOXWOOD

The box tree has played such an important part in the history of wood engraving that it is no exaggeration to suggest that the wood engraver regards the tree as sacred. Eric Gill chose the box tree as the symbol of the Society of Wood Engravers when he cut the block in 1921 [387 and 388].

The box is a member of the family Buxaceae; it is known as the Common Box or Buxus Sempervirens and some people believe it to be indigenous to Britain. The tree is an evergreen and has thick foliage. It reaches to an average height of five or six metres. There are about thirty species of the box tree throughout the world and it seems that the tree will succeed in almost any soil, though perhaps preferring a limestone formation when growing in the wild.

Box trees with straight trunks are very rare and most twist in a snake-like manner. A box tree in the Royal Botanical Gardens at Kew started its growth with a clear sky overhead and, in consequence, the first section of the trunk is vertical but an adjacent tree outgrew the box and obscured the light. This resulted in a curved section in the second part of the trunk of the box. Eventually the neighbouring tree died and the trunk of the box again twisted to take advantage of the now clear sky above. This ability to change the course of its growth to avoid a deficiency in ultra-violet light accounts for the survival of the box in situations in which other trees would die.

In England the box tree is found in parks, in ornamental grounds and also growing wild. Box Hill, a famous vantage point near Dorking in Surrey, provides the site for a number of box trees – as the name suggests – and has done so for many years. It is recorded that in 1815 box timber to the value of ten thousand pounds was taken from Box Hill.[1]

Because the growth of the box tree is slow, the grain is very hard and the wood is so heavy that of all native British timber it is the only one that will not float in water. In colour it ranges from a yellow-gold to a red-gold, depending upon the species and the country of origin. Throughout the wood, the colour is remarkably even and closely graduated in hue, with the variations occurring within a very narrow band of wavelength. The timber appears to contain no pigment; the exceptionally stable colour arises from the action of light rays upon the wood – the interaction of absorption, reflection and diffraction.

Because of its fine grain and hardness, box timber is in demand commercially as well as for wood engraving and sculpture. It has remarkable lasting qualities and the examples of boxwood sculpture from the German school of 1500 to 1800 that are in the Victoria and Albert Museum in London are in a perfect state of preservation despite a slight darkening of the colour of the wood.

The sculpture *The Virgin and Child*, cut in boxwood about 1500 in the medieval

[393] A proof from an engraved end-grained boxwood block, used by nineteenth-century salesmen. 14.25 x 17.0cm

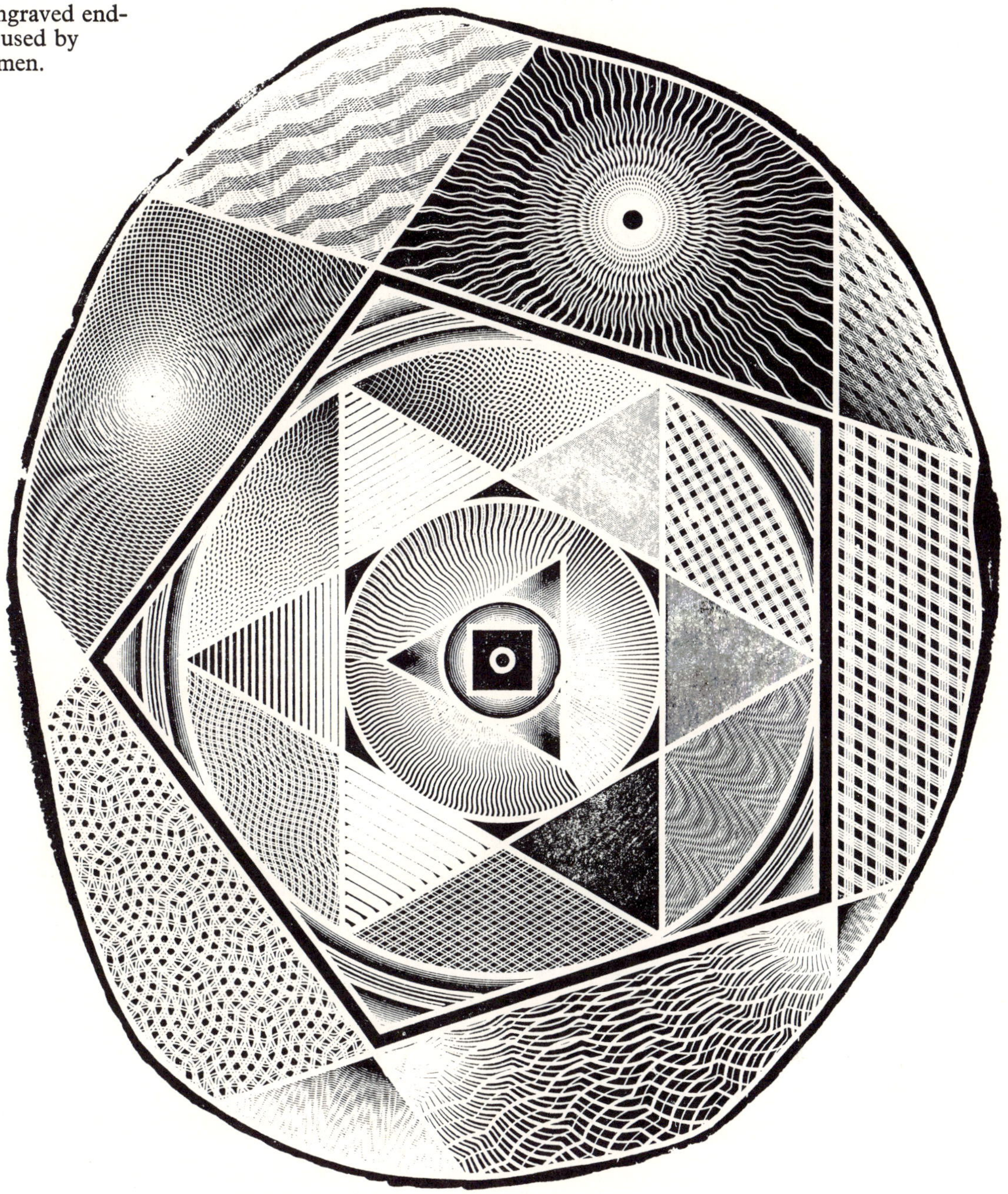

style by Veit Stoss (1447-1533) of the Nuremberg school, is the only known example of a statuette by this sculptor and is in the Wallace Collection in London. The sculptor, like an engraver, has used the consistency, closeness and density of the wood grain to move freely and three-dimensionally, drawing the drapery arcs and angles of the folds wherever he wishes them to go. This sculpture displays a similar freedom of crossing the grain as does Iain Macnab in the engraving of his block *Snow* [389 and 390]. Boxwood sculpture was also produced in Italy and Belgium.

[393] shows an example of a sophisticated form of selling in the nineteenth century. The engraving was used by a traveller to sell boxwood to the trade block-makers and it was engraved entirely by a ruling machine. There are no joins in the

block: it is a complete slice across a trunk. Even today there are no signs of star or radial shakes; the bark is still intact and can be seen as the black outer and bounding line. The triangles comprising the six-pointed star are demonstrating the range of linear tones from near white to near black.

If the separate lines of the lower dark right-hand triangle in the illustration are viewed through a magnifying glass, they are seen to be broken into minute short lines. When the engraving was completed the printing was done direct from the block and each impression could be termed 'original'. The advertisement is a tribute to the methods of seasoning such hard timber. There is a good account of the blockmaking industry of the nineteenth century in Kenneth Lindley's book *The Woodblock Engravers.*[2]

Most of the timber used in the last half of the nineteenth century and in the early part of the twentieth century came from the Caucasian mountain region, noted for its very large box trees. The export from that area was stopped in 1935. The sources of boxwood today vary; Venezuelan box has been used a great deal but the species is becoming scarce due to over-exploitation and much is now imported from Asia Minor, in particular from Turkey and Persia.

In engraving, English boxwood is the most highly favoured for its evenness of grain, hardness and consistency across the annular rings; but it is also the most expensive. Some of the very fine engravings reproduced in this book could only have been executed on English end-grained boxwood. Other timbers, though softer, have been, and are still, used successfully in wood engraving, including holly, lime and pear end-grained blocks. All these timbers are much cheaper but

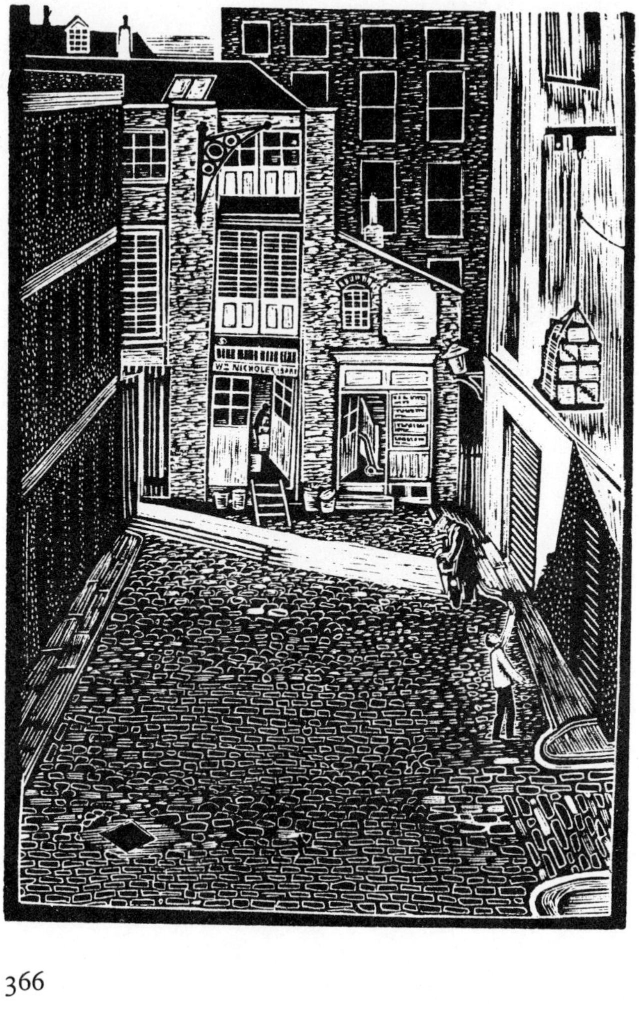

[394] Hilary Paynter: *Bleeding Heart Yard*, 1972. 8.25 x 12.25cm

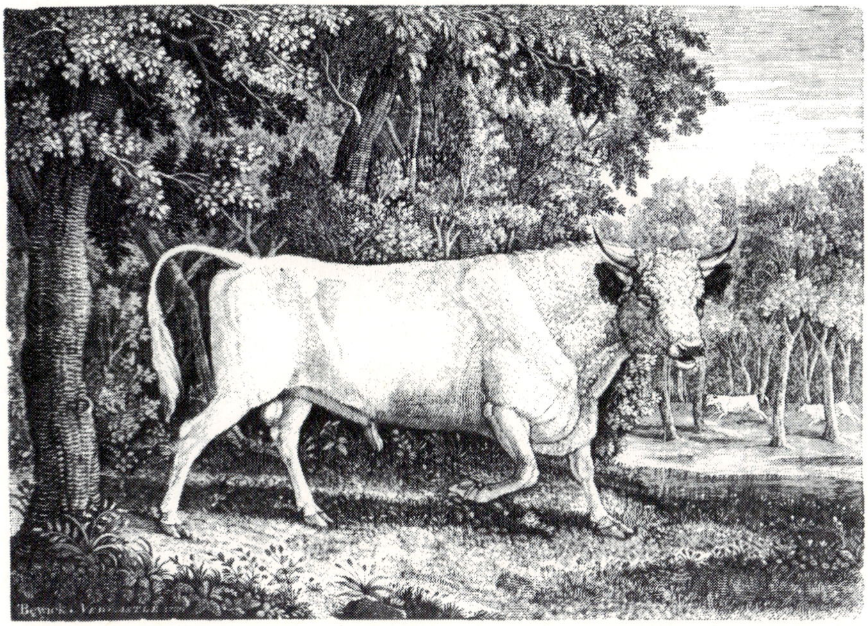

[395] Thomas Bewick: *The Wild Bull at Chillingham Castle Park*, 1789. 19.5 x 14.0cm

they cannot give such a high precision of fine line and print quality. William T. Rawlinson has exploited the properties of pearwood in his two prints *The End of the Road* [378] and *The Graveyard of the Giants* [frontispiece]. For the engraving shown in [391] Bernard Rice used limewood to enable him to scrape into the soft annular rings to obtain the mezzotint effect.

It is essential for boxwood to be properly seasoned in order to be suitable for engraving. A traditional method of seasoning the wood required that a trench be cut in the ground. The bottom of the trench was lined with brushwood and the pieces of boxwood were then placed on top and left for a long period. This method slowed down the rate at which the wood lost moisture: an important factor in the case-hardening of the block. The method also reduced the extreme parameters of heat gain and heat loss occurring between day and night, and the variation of temperature from summer to winter.

Below-ground seasoning considerably reduces the total number of hours in which the wood is exposed to ultra-violet radiation. This radiation effects a colour change in the surface of the timber by a photochemical process.

Because of the high cost of production, the traditional method has given way to a seasoning process above ground or by drying in a kiln until the wood has the correct moisture content. However, the modern method of seasoning appears to increase timber wastage because in kiln drying, the boxwood shows radial star shakes which have to be cut away before the block is ready for engraving.

The boxwood engraving from which the print shown in [393] was taken recently is over a hundred years old, but the wood has not a single shake in it and even the bark is intact. The block shows remarkable stability and its colour is evenly distributed; it is an excellent example of the effective nature of seasoning below ground.

A block for wood engraving must be end-grained in order that the burin can glide freely in any direction. The completed block is finished to a height of 23.317mm from base to printing surface, and in this condition the block is said to be 'type high' because in Britain this measurement is normally the height of type and other printing surfaces. The height of type to paper is an illogical measurement and appears to have been established as a matter of tradition of usage. Even today the height of type to paper is not uniform internationally.

[396] George Mackley: *Vonders at Giethoorn.* 12.75 x 10.0cm

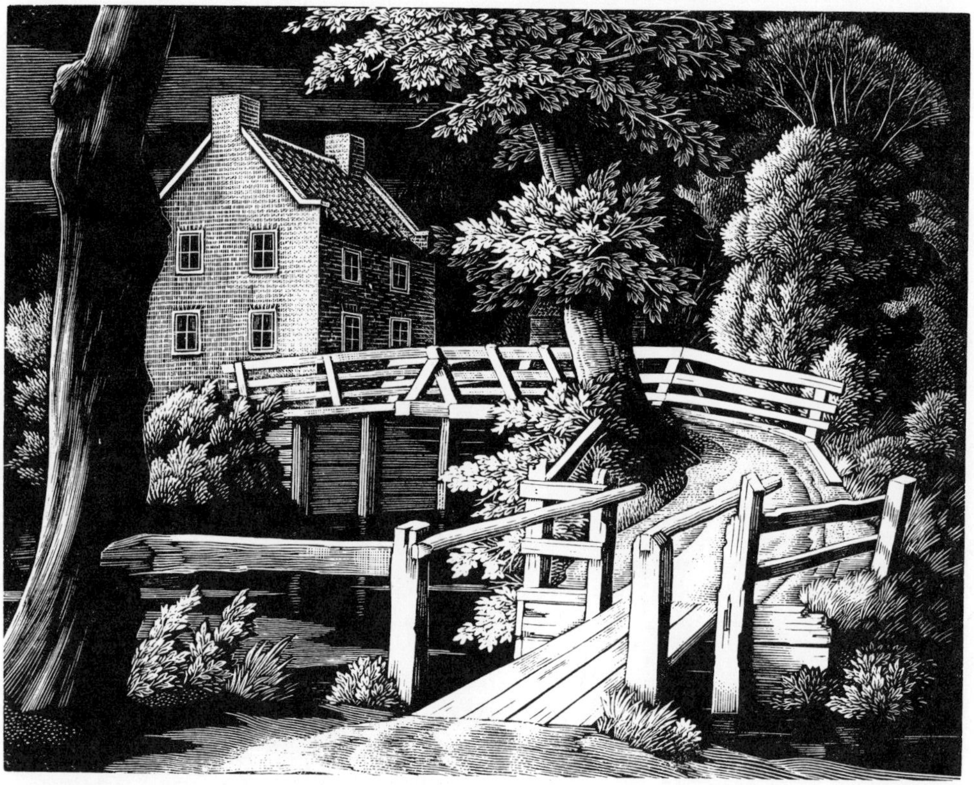

[397] Agnes Miller Parker: *The Fiery Dragon* from *Welsh Gypsy Folk Tales*, 1933. 12.5 x 11.8cm

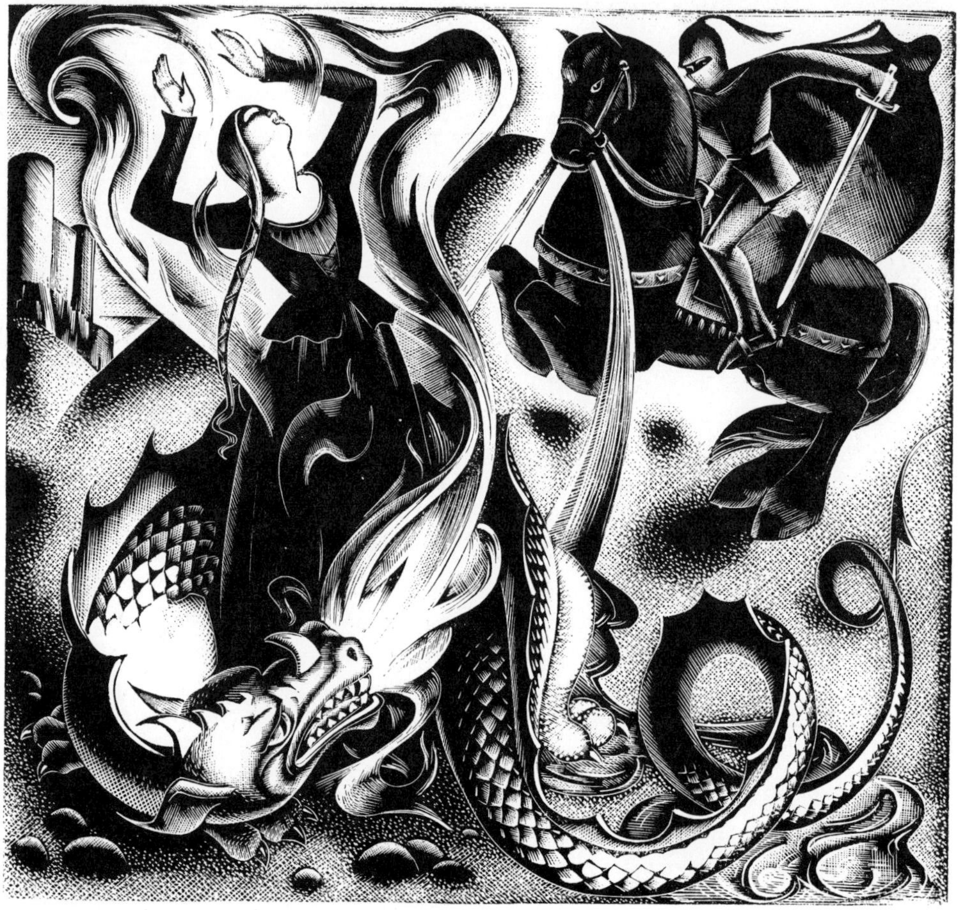

In the eighteenth century the making of end-grained boxwood blocks began to develop considerably in England and by the nineteenth century had expanded to become a very large business, supplying an increasing demand for illustrations in the form of wood engravings. Today this tremendous output is reduced to such an extent that the demand is almost met by the products of only one man. Most of the blocks used by the British school of wood engraving have been made by Stanley T. E. Lawrence who has also supplied blocks to engravers in other countries. His workshop at the picturesque address of Bleeding Heart Yard in London's Hatton Garden is a meeting place for engravers from all parts of the world. The premises are shown in Hilary Paynter's engraving [394]. The Victorian hoist is still used to lift supplies to the workshop on the top floor. Stanley Lawrence's family have been blockmaking since his grandfather started work in 1859.

Of the three disciplines of engraving, painting and sculpture, engraving is the smallest in scale. As is evident from the details given in this book, the majority of blocks are of modest dimensions. Nevertheless, there have been occasions when large engravings have been attempted. Lawrence preserves in his workshop a very small block made for George Mackley. Mackley had started engraving on the block and completed a few square centimetres at the top when a joint opened very slightly, but just sufficiently to print a white line so he rejected it. Lawrence gladly replaced the block but retained the original.

The effect of temperature change on a piece of hard wood can be dramatic. In the summer months when there is a sharp variation of temperature between night and day, the wood can split with a crack that is similar to a rifle shot. In boxwood, these small explosions can take place inside the block with no visible trace on the surface; though in one or two years, short hairline cracks will appear.

Lawrence has a block illustrating the London Lord Mayor's Show of 1847 which is made up of small sections bolted together. This block shows that although the invention of joining small blocks together to form a large illustration is credited to Charles Wells in 1860 (see Chaper 5), earlier attempts at this technique were made.

In 1885, Lawrence's grandfather, Thomas J. Lawrence, made a block measuring 20.0cm by 22.0cm for an edition of the newspaper *The Christian Herald* [102 and 103]. The illustration of the back of the block shows dark markings on the divisions

[398] James Bostock: *Black Park*, 1960. 32.0 x 13.0cm

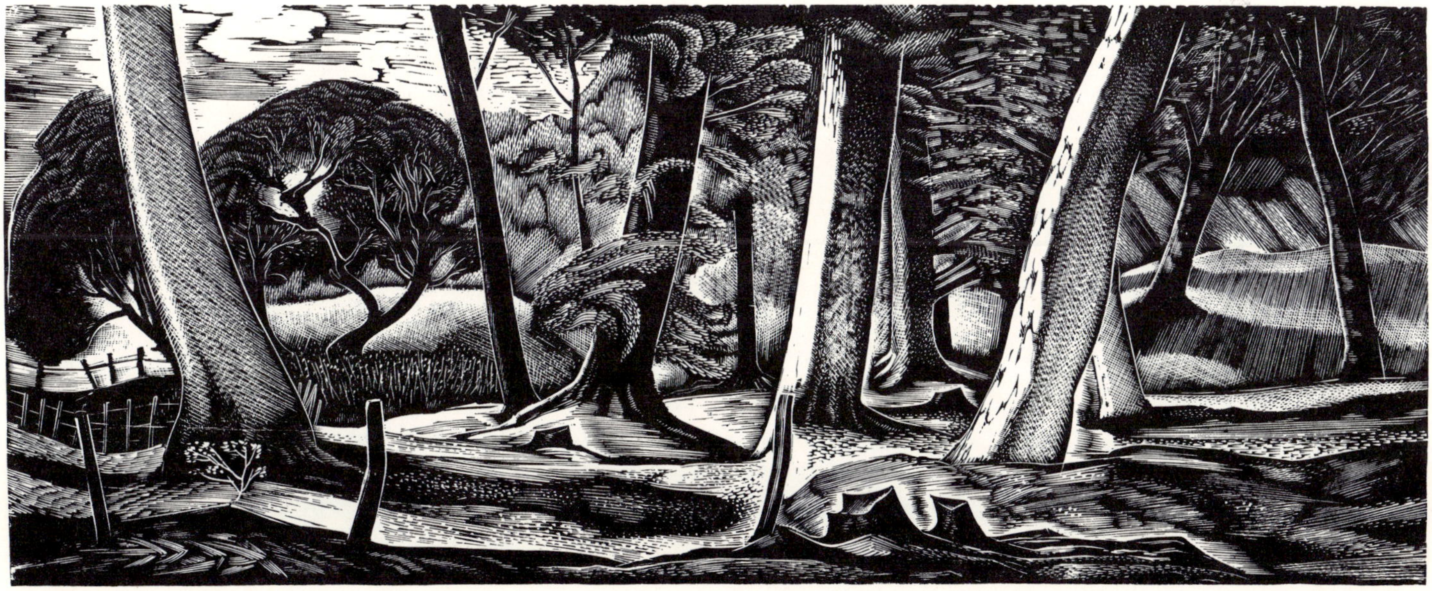

[399] A wood engraver at work

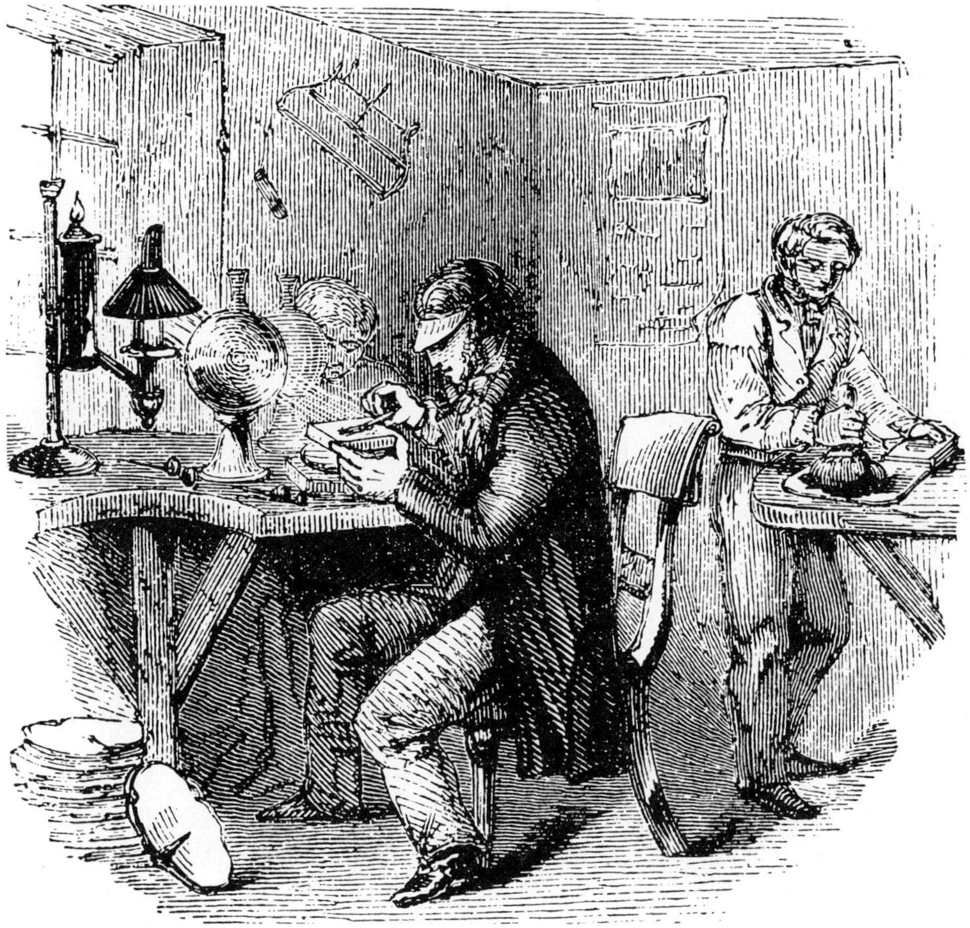

into smaller sections; these indicate where paper packing was applied to adjust the printing pressure.

A print taken from this block recently can be seen in [101]. It will be noted that the joins remain perfect. Before the engraving was begun, the image would have been transferred photographically to the surface of the block after it had been made sensitive to light. The print shows a typical example of a news illustration of the period and the black shape at the top centre was probably removed when the metal duplicate plate was made, to allow for the insertion of type matter.

The delicate nature of the surface of wood engravings necessitated that a metal duplicate be made in cases where a large number of copies were required to be printed and where a multi-image technique would be employed in the printing process; only very occasionally was the actual wood block used, for printing short runs.

The method of preparing a duplicate was to secure an electrotype and this would give an exact duplicate of the engraving. The technique used in the nineteenth century was to take an impression of the engraving in wax to form a mould which, after suitable preparation, would be placed in a special bath so that a thin shell of copper could be formed by electric deposition. This shell would then be backed with lead to form a printing plate which would be mounted on wood to make it type high. Early in the twentieth century other materials of a special nature were used to make an electrotype mould, though by that time the normal method of reproducing a wood engraving was by photo-engraving.

Engravers have experimented with materials other than boxwood. John Buckland-Wright tried several types of plastic but found the material unsatisfactory, being either too brittle or too tough and making the burin travel unwillingly in depth. James Bostock has produced engravings on perspex, vulcanite and xylonite [398].

The criterion of a good print from a wood engraving is its blackness. This is achieved by using an oil-based ink in which the pigment particles are in close association to provide the required density. The nature of boxwood provides a surface that will carry a film of ink and permit it to be transferred to the paper cleanly. Material softer than boxwood tends to retain part of the film of ink, which results in a print lacking density.

In examining a black surface, the viewer is looking at an area from which very little light is returned. True black means the absorption of all visible rays; but inadequacies in ink pigment and irregularities of paper surface mean that whilst a large quantity of light rays is absorbed, some light must be reflected.

Whilst the early practitioners of wood engraving had hand-made paper, the quality of the ink that was available did not equal the modern range of inks in density, covering power and drying qualities. It is paradoxical that during the eighteenth century wood engravers lacked the refinement of inks and a variety in choice of paper, yet advances in technology which presented the engravers with improved material also decreased the scope in the use of wood engraving in favour of the photographic methods of reproduction.

The engraving shown in [399] is typical of the commercial use of boxwood in the nineteenth century. However, not only does the illustration show the situation in which engraving was carried out; in itself the wood engraving is a very good example

[400] Hans Holbein the Younger: *Two Art Critics* from *The Praise of Folly*. 3.6 x 3.0cm

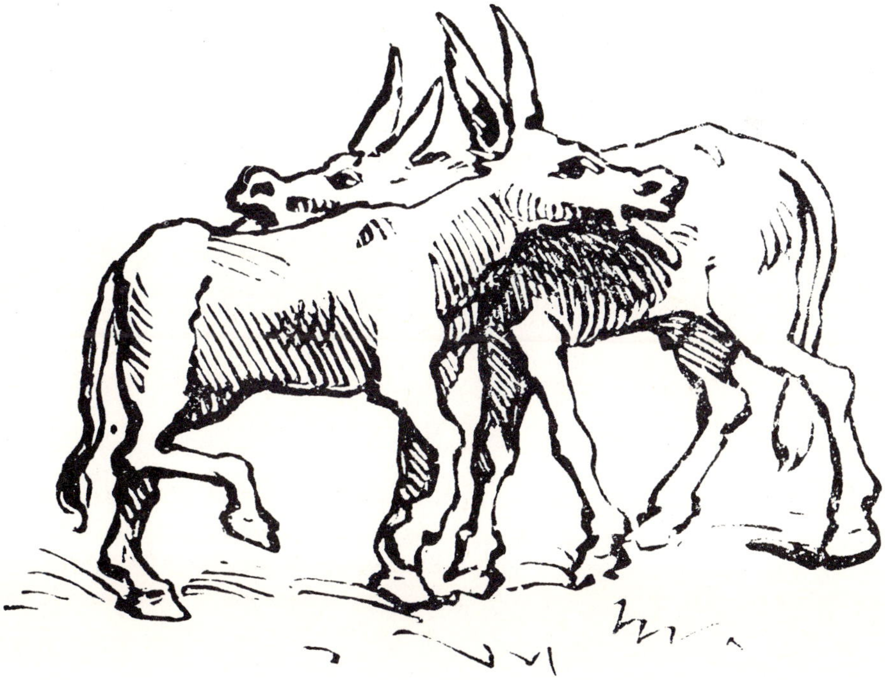

of the craft skill of the reproductive engravers and evidence of their lack of artistic ability and understanding.

It is thought that at least two engravers would have worked on the block. The engraving suggests that it might be an interpretation of a photograph. Whilst the engraving is an interesting statement of an industrial situation, as an illustration it is full of errors. Yet the figure of the man who is standing and taking proofs on the right is brilliantly engraved and sensitively rendered anatomically.

In the bottom left-hand corner of the picture can be seen slices of oval end-grained boxwood showing the inevitable star shakes. The regularity of the stock suggest that the slices were all cut from the same tree. These pieces of boxwood are approximately forty-five centimetres in diameter and because of their exceptional size are most unlikely to be English; boxwood grown in England rarely produces trunks exceeding thirty-five centimetres in diameter. The lamp is of special interest; it is adjustable and portable. In front of the lamp is seen a clear glass sphere filled with water. When the lamp was lit, the light passed through the glass and the water, the angles of refraction being changed twice by the two different materials, thus enabling the sphere to act as a lens. This water lens had the effect of concentrating the beam of light and compensated for the low energy of the light source.

The angles of refraction of the glass and the water removed the glare effect, which would be very disturbing to the engraver, and the direct reflection of the source of the illumination was not seen through the sphere. It will be noted that the lamp is placed in front of the window. The water sphere, being larger than the lamp, would have received daylight energy as part of the whole illumination available, thus drawing the maximum light direct on to the block.

The concentrated beam of light from the water lens produced a clearly defined shadow on one wall of the V-shaped groove made by the engraver's burin – the light energy being sharply reflected on the other wall of the groove. Because the flat surface of the boxwood would have been dark, the illumination of the V-shaped grooves produced an optical contrast which aided the engraver when cutting very fine lines.

The engraving in [399] was probably made in the later eighteen hundreds. It was probably produced with the aid of a new process introduced in that period wherein the surface of the wood block was covered with a light-sensitive emulsion and the drawing transferred to the block photographically in order to produce the image for engraving. When completed, the engraved block would not be used for printing but instead an electrotype would have been made.

The technique of transferring an image photographically on to boxwood for subsequent engraving has now disappeared. John Farleigh was probably the last creative engraver to use the method in this country. It has remained in continuous use in America.

REFERENCES

1 Bean, W. J. *Trees and Shrubs Hardy in the British Isles, Vol I*, John Murray
2 Lindley, K. *The Woodblock Engravers*, David & Charles, Newton Abbot, 1970

APPENDIX: THE DEFINITION OF AN ORIGINAL PRINT

The following definition was agreed at the Third International Congress of Arts, held in Vienna in September 1960. The definition was published by the International Association of Art in 1963 and a version was issued by The Print Council of America in 1961.

THE DEFINITION

(1) It is the exclusive right of the artist-printmaker to fix the definitive number of each of his graphic works in the different techniques; engraving, lithography, etc.
(2) Each print, in order to be considered an original, must bear not only the signature of the artist, but also an indication of the total edition and the serial number of the print.
The artist may also indicate that he himself is the printer.
(3) Once the edition has been made, it is desirable that the original plate, stone, wood block, or what ever material was used in pulling the print edition, should be defaced or should bear a distinctive mark indicating that the edition has been completed.
(4) The above principles apply to graphic works which can be considered originals, that is to say to prints for which the artist made the original plate, cut the wood block, worked on the stone or on any other material. Works which do not fulfil these conditions must be considered 'reproductions'.
(5) For reproductions no regulations are possible. However it is desirable that reproductions should be acknowledged as such, and so distinguished beyond question from the original graphic work. This is particularly so when reproductions are of such outstanding quality that the artist, wishing to acknowledge the work materially executed by the printer, feels justified in signing them.

The version of The Print Council of America is similar in its requirements and states:
An original print is a work of graphic art, the general requirements of which are
(1) The artist alone has made the image in or upon the plate, stone, wood block, or other material for the purpose of creating a work of graphic art.
(2) The impression is made directly from that original material by the artist or pursuant to his directions.
(3) The finished print is approved by the artist.

BIOGRAPHICAL NOTES

ANNESLEY, LADY MABEL

b 1881 at Annesley Lodge, London, NW1, died in New Zealand.
Wood engraver.

1895	Studied art at the Frank Calderon School of Animal Painting.
1920 – 1921	Studied engraving at the Central School of Art and Design under Noel Rooke.
1924	Elected member of the Society of Wood Engravers. Went to live in Co Down, Ireland.
1928 – 1929	Lost the use of her right hand. Interpreter of the Mourne Mountains and lives of the people of Ulster.
1933	One-man show at Batsford Gallery, London.
1933	One-man show at Stephen's Green Gallery, Dublin.
1950	Went to live in Nelson, South Island, New Zealand. One-man show at Wellington.
1951	One-man show at Nelson.

BARRETT, RODERIC

b 1920 in Colchester.
Painter and wood engraver.

1936 – 1940	Studied art at the Central School of Art and Design under John Farleigh.
1947 – 1957	Visiting instructor of drawing and design at the Central School of Art and Design.
1952	Elected a member of the Society of Wood Engravers.
1957 – 1958	Invited to be guest lecturer at Phillips Exeter Academy New Hampshire, USA.
1958 – 1968	Visiting instructor at Central School of Art and Design.
1968	Drawing and painting tutor at the Royal Academy Schools.

BEEDHAM, RALPH JOHN

b 1879 in Whitecross Street, Cripplegate, London. d 1975.
Probably the last professional reproductive engraver.

1893	Apprenticed for six years, commencing at thirteen and a half years of age, to an old-established firm of wood engravers, Hare and Co, Essex Street, Strand. At the end of his apprenticeship he found wood engraving had been superseded by the photographic half-tone blocks etched on to copper. Instructor of engraving at the LCC School of Photo-engraving and Lithography. Two of his students were Joan Hassall and Mabel Alleyne. Instructed in lettering by Eric Gill at Ditchling and became his assistant in lettering for the rest of Gill's life.
1956	Worked on Robert Gibbings's blocks for the Limited Editions Club, New York production of *Voyage of HMS Beagle* by Charles Darwin. He also engraved eight facsimiles of Gibbings's original illustrations for this edition.
1962	Engraved his last block at the age of eighty-three.
1974	In a letter to the author he apologised for the nervous character of his handwriting. His doctor had informed him that it was a sign of his age.

BIGGS, JOHN R. SIAD, ATD, FRSA

b 1909 in Derby.

Wood engraver, designer and typographer.

1931	Studied at Derby School of Art.
1931 – 1933	Studied engraving at the Central School of Art and Design. His tutor was Noel Rooke.
1933 – 1938	Studied evenings at the Central School of Art and Design.
Pre-war years	Taught engraving at the Chelsea School of Art and the Gravesend School of Art. Travelled to Russia, Norway, Sweden, Denmark and Finland.
1936	Member of the Art Workers' Guild.
War years	Taught at the London College of Printing.
Post-war years	Taught at the Norwich School of Art. Travelled to Germany, Holland, France, Italy, Spain, Russia, Ukraine and America.
	Head of the Graphic Design Department at Brighton Polytechnic (now retired).

BINYON, HELEN. ARCA

b 1904 in Chelsea.

Wood engraver, book illustrator and puppetry.

Educated at St Paul's Girls School.

1922 – 1926	Studied art at the Royal College of Art under E. W. Tristram and Paul Nash.
1927	Studied art at Académie de La Grande Chaumière Studio, Montparnasse.
1928	Studied engraving at the Central School of Art and Design under W. P. Robins.
1931 – 1938	Taught at the Eastbourne College of Art and the North London Collegiate School, Camden Town.
1940 – 1942	Drew charts for the Hydrographic Dept of the Admiralty and worked for the Ministry of Information.
1945	Taught at the Willesden School of Art.
1946	Elected a member of the Society of Wood Engravers.
1950	Taught at the Bath Academy of Art, Corsham Court, puppetry, design, drawing and engraving.

BLAKELY, ZELMA. RE

b 1927 in London.

Wood engraver and teacher.

1939 – 1942	Studied art at Kingston School of Art under Wilfred Fairclough.
1945 – 1948	Studied art at the Slade School of Fine Art under Norman Janes and John Buckland-Wright. Awarded Wilson Steer Gold Medal.
1955	Elected associate of the Royal Society of Painter-Etchers and Engravers.
1966	Fellow of the Royal Society of Painter-Etchers and Engravers.
1970	Taught at the Heatherley School of Fine Art.

BLISS, DOUGLAS PERCY. ARCA, MA

b 1900 in Karachi.

Wood engraver, painter, illustrator and writer.

1912 – 1918	Educated at Watson's College, Edinburgh.
1918 – 1922	Edinburgh University where he obtained M A (Hons.)
1922 – 1925	Studied painting at the Royal College of Art under Sir William Rothenstein and started wood engraving with Eric Ravilious.
1928	Published his *History of Wood Engraving*.
1932 – 1940	Part-time teacher at Hornsey School of Art.
1934	Elected a member of the Society of Wood Engravers.
1934 – 1940	Part-time teacher at the Blackheath School of Art.
1941	Joined RAF Fighter Command at Stanmore and met Iain Macnab.
1945 – 1946	Part-time teacher at Harrow School of Art.
1946 – 1964	Director of the Glasgow School of Art. Five visits to Ghana as adjudicator at the School of Art at Kuman University. Frequent visits to Italy, Denmark, Sweden, Germany, France and Russia.

BLOOMFIELD, DIANA

b 1916 in Harrow.

Wood engraver, book illustrator and fabric designer.

1923 – 1925 Studied art at Harrow School of Art.

1966 – 1969 Taught wood engraving at the City Literary Institute.

1971 – 1976 Taught at Education Development Studies Centre and the Gardner Centre for the Arts, University of Sussex.

BOSTOCK, JAMES. RE, ARCA

b 1917 in Etruria, (part of Hanley), Staffordshire.

Wood engraver, painter and education organiser.

1928 – 1933 Educated at Borden Grammer School, Sittingbourne.

1933 – 1936 Studied art at the Medway School of Art, Rochester, under Harold Shimmell.

1936 – 1939 Studied at the Royal College of Art and influenced by Paul and John Nash and Eric Ravilious. Awarded associateship of the RCA.

1940 Joined the Kings Shropshire Light Infantry and later transferred to the 9th Battalion Durham Light Infantry.

1941 Left England for Port Tewfik, Egypt and for service in Cyprus, Iraq and the Western Desert.

1942 Transferred to Royal Corps of Signals (Ciphers) for service at GHQ Middle East. Spent two years in Turkey as Sergeant.

1946 Demobilized.

1946 – 1958 Senior Lecturer in art at the Ealing School of Art.

1947 Elected associate of the Royal Society of Painter-Etchers and Engravers.

1949 – 1955 Worked freelance, drawing and engraving for advertising.

1952 Elected a member of the Society of Wood Engravers. Awarded third prize in the Giles Bequest Competition.

1961 Elected fellow of the Royal Society of Painter-Etchers and Engravers.

1962 – 1965 Deputy Principal and Head of Diploma Studies at Stoke-on-Trent College of Art.

1965 – 1970 Vice-Principal of the West of England College of Art.

1970 Academic Development Officer at the Bristol Polytechnic.

BRABY, DOROTHEA

b 1909 in London.

Wood engraver, portrait painter and book illustrator.

1926 Studied art at the Central School of Art and Design under John Farleigh.

1927 Studied art at Florence under Mafori-Savini.

1928 – 1930 Studied at Heatherley School of Fine Art.

1930 Studied art at Académie de la Grande Chaumière Paris.

1931 Studied at the Central School of Art and Design under Noel Rooke.

BRETT, SIMON

b 1943 in Windsor.

Wood engraver and painter.

Educated at Ampleforth College.

1960 – 1964 Studied art at St Martin's School of Art. Obtained NDD in painting. Taught wood engraving by Clifford Webb.

1965 – 1967 Awarded the Helene Worlitzer Foundation grant to study in New Mexico.

1969 – 1970 Worked at Les Arcs in Provence.

1971 Taught at the Art School, Marlborough College.

BUCKLAND-WRIGHT, JOHN. BA, RE, SIAD

b 1897 in Dunedin, New Zealand. d 1954.

Wood and copper engraver, etcher and painter.

1905 Family left New Zealand.

Educated at Clifton and Rugby.

1914 Volunteered for active service but was rejected by the British Army because of a severe stammer.

1916	Volunteered into a Scottish ambulance unit attached to the French Army. Awarded the Croix de Guerre for rescuing French civilians from burning buildings.
1918	Entered Oxford and studied history at Magdalen College gaining a BA.
1920	Graduated in Architecture at the Bartlet School of Architecture, London University.
1924	Settled in Brussels. Visited France and Italy.
1925	Founder member of Gravure Originale Belge.
1929	Elected a member of Xylographes Belgium, the London Group, London, and the Salon des Surindependants, Paris. He became President of the Society of Anglo-American Artists in Paris. Settled in Paris for ten years. Worked with Stanley William Hayter in 'Atelier. 17'.
1930	Married Mary Anderson and lived in the Latin Quarter in Paris.
1936 – 1939	Taught at 'Atelier. 17.'
1939	Returned to England.
1940	Chosen as one of seven wood engravers to represent British Engraving at the Venice Biennial International Exhibition. Elected a member of the Society of Wood Engravers.
1948	Taught at Camberwell School of Art and the Anglo-French Art Centre, St John's Wood.
1952	Appointed instructor at the Slade School of Fine Art.
1973 – 1974	Survey Exhibition of wood and copper engravings toured New Zealand Art Galleries.

BUDAY, GEORGE. RE

b 1907 in Kolozsvár, Transylvania.
Wood engraver, painter and writer.
Father was a Professor of Roman Archaeology.

1920	Studied painting as an apprentice in the studios of Louis Meczner and G. Dadey. Trained in black and white by Cavalier Albert Manz. Introduced to the *Blaue Reiter* Group and in particular to Kandinsky. Studied art at the Kolozsvár Presbyterian College under the water colourist Steven Deak.
1924	First one-man show.
1928 – 1934	Graduated to Doctorship at Szeged University.
1928 – 1929	One of five delegates representing Hungarian University students at the triennial SCM Conference at Liverpool. Attended Dutch Art Exhibition in London. Made and published his first wood engravings.
1930 – 1939	'The Settlement' established under his Presidency, of young artists and writers at Szeged College of Art.
1934 – 1941	Lecturer on graphic arts at the Royal Hungarian Franz Joseph University, Szeged.
1936 – 1937	Awarded Rome Scholarship.
1937	Began living and working in Great Britain.
1938	Elected associate of the Royal Society of Painter-Etchers and Engravers.
1941	Member of the Art Workers' Guild.
1953	Elected fellow of the Royal Society of Painter-Etchers and Engravers.
1954	Elected a member of the Society of Wood Engravers.

CHADWICK, TOM

b 1915 in Yorkshire. d 1942.
Wood engraver, water colourist and teacher.
Studied art at the Grosvenor School of Modern Art under Iain Macnab and William Kermode.

1932 – 1936	Exhibited six wood engravings with the Society of Wood Engravers. Art Lecturer at the Westminster School of Art.
1936	Awarded medal and prize by the Art Institute of Chicago for his wood engraving *The Introduction*.
1937	Short article published on his work in the July issue of *Studio*. Enlisted in the 3rd Hussars.
1942	Killed at the Battle of El Alamein.

CHUBB, RALPH, N.

b 1892 in Harpenden Common. d 1960.

Poet, artist and writer.

1910	Won an open scholarship to Selwyn College, Cambridge.
1913	Moved to Curridge, near Newbury, Berks, with his sister Emily.
1913 – 1914	Studied art at the London School of Art.
1915	Enlisted in the Army and served in France; was in the Battle of Loos. Later commissioned and attained the rank of Captain.
1918	Invalided out of the Army.
1919 – 1922	Studied art at the Slade School of Fine Art.
1921	Set up his own private press at Curridge.
1924	Post of part-time art master at Bradfield College.
1927	Family moved to Fair Oak Cottage, Kingsclere Woodlands, near Newbury, Berks.
1933 – 1960	Chubb's major lithographed books were produced in this period at Fair Oak Cottage.
1940	Chubb's first meeting with the author in the fields of Harridens Farm, Kingsclere, Hants.

CLARK, PAULINE. NDD, NTD

b 1944 in Luton.

Wood engraver and stage designer.

1961 – 1963	Studied art at the Luton School of Art.
1963 – 1965	Studied at St Martin's School of Art where she obtained the National Diploma in Art and Design. Studied wood engraving under John O'Connor.
1965 – 1966	Studied for the Art Teacher's Diploma at the Leicester College of Art, Department of Education.
1966 – 1969	Art teacher at Beckenham Grammar School for Girls.
1969	Freelance restoration, engraving and stage design.
1974	Elected a member of the Society of Wood Engravers and Relief Printers.

CRAIG, EDWARD GORDON. CH, RDI

b 1872 in Stevenage, Herts. d 1966.

Wood engraver, etcher, writer, actor, theatrical designer and producer.

1893	Moved to Uxbridge.
1895	Began to produce little blocks using woodcut.
1897	Gave up acting. Left Henry Irving's Company.
1899	Met William Nicholson and James Pryde at Denham. Nicholson taught him wood engraving. Craig published his woodcuts in his periodical *The Page*.
1903	His mother Ellen Terry and sister Edith joined him and commenced theatrical management in the Imperial Theatre at Westminster.
1905	Met Isadora Duncan in Germany and evolved his new concept of kinetic theatre. Published his first book *The Art of the Theatre* when in Germany.
1906	Daughter Deirdre born in Holland.
1907	Stanislavsky invited Craig to Moscow. Successful designs and production of *Hamlet* at the Moscow Arts Theatre. End of theatre partnership with Isadora Duncan.
1908	Published his periodical *The Mask* which continued until 1929. Commenced frequently-held exhibitions of his prints throughout Europe.
1910	Made four drawings for W. B. Yeats's *Plays for an Irish Theatre*. (Yeats and Lady Gregory were the first to make practical use of Craig's work.)
1913	His school for theatre was eventually established through Lord Howard De Walden. Brought to a premature end by the outbreak of the First World War.
1914	A large international exhibition of theatre work held in Zurich.
1915	Continued to publish *The Mask*.
1917	Moved to Rapallo near Genoa.
1919	Founder member of the Society of Wood Engravers.
1947	Wrote *The Theatre Advancing*, published by Benjamin Blom Inc., New York.

DICKEY, EDWARD MONTGOMERY O'RORKE

b 1894.

Painter and wood engraver.

1920 Founder member of the Society of Wood Engravers of which two meetings were held in his studio in London.

Drawing Master at Oundle School.

Director of the King Edward VII School of Art, Armstrong College, Newcastle.

DOLBY, JAMES TAYLOR. RE, ARCA

b 1909 in Oxenhope, Nr Haworth, Yorks. d 1975.

Wood engraver, etcher and teacher.

1920 – 1925 Educated at Keighley Boys Grammar School.

1925 – 1929 Studied art at Keighley School of Art.

1929 – 1933 Studied engraving and etching at the Royal College of Art. Etching under Malcolm Osborne RA, metal engraving under Robert Austin RA and H. H. Wolfenden, lithography under F. H. Spear, figure drawing under Rodney J. Burn and Penny Horton and lettering under Edward Johnston. Awarded the ARCA (etching). Studied for and awarded the Board of Trade Yacht Master's Certificate (Ocean).

1933 – 1936 Member of the Senefelder Group.

1934 – 1938 Taught illustration and stage design at the Bournemouth School of Art.

1936 Began to engrave on wood. First wood engraving exhibited at the Society of Wood Engravers.

1938 Joined the Royal Naval Volunteer Reserve.

1940 Commissioned in the RNVR for the duration of the war.

1946 Demobilized with the rank of Captain.

Visited Iceland and met the Icelandic sculptor Einar Jorson.

1946 – 1947 Taught illustration at the Portsmouth School of Art.

1947 – 1969 Head of the Blackburn School of Art.

1949 First wood engraving exhibited at the Royal Academy. Elected associate of the Royal Society of Painter-Etchers and Engravers. Elected a member of the Society of Wood Engravers.

1970 Elected a fellow of the Royal Society of Painter-Etchers and Engravers.

ELSTON, YVONNE

b 1935 in Southsea.

Wood engraver.

1940 – 1941 Educated at Woodford House School.

1942 – 1953 Upper Mount School, Waterlooville.

1954 – 1955 Studied kennel management at Nunsoe Kennels, Hever, Kent.

1956 – 1961 Studied illustration, engraving and typography at the Portsmouth College of Art under Gerry Tucker, ARCA.

1958 Awarded the Southern College of Art major travelling scholarship.

1966 Awarded first prize for drawing arranged by John Lewis Partnership.

1974 Elected a member of the Society of Wood Engravers and Relief Printers.

FARLEIGH, JOHN FREDERICK WILLIAM CHARLES. CBE, RE, RBA

b 1900 in London. d 1965.

Wood engraver, painter, illustrator, writer, and teacher.

Educated at St Mary Abbots, Kensington.

1914 Articled as apprentice for five years to the Artists Illustrators Agency. Commenced a ten-year period of study at evening classes at the Bolt Court School Life Classes.

1918 Called up for service in the Army but was discharged after a few months.

1919 Studied art at the Central School of Art and Design under Bernard Meninsky, James Grant and Noel Rooke.

1922 – 1924 His first post, appointed art master at Rugby School, Rugby.

1925 Appointed teacher of the antique and still-life at the Central School of Art and Design. Elected a member of the Society of Wood Engravers and associate of the Royal Society of Painter-Etchers and Engravers.

1940 President for six years of the Arts and Crafts Exhibition Society.

1947 – 1948 Head of the Book Illustration Department at the Central School of Art and Design.

1950 – 1964 Honorary Chairman of the Crafts Centre of Great Britain, Hay Hill.

GARRETT, ALBERT. ROI, FRSA

b 1915 at Harridens Farm, Kingsclere, Hants.

Wood engraver, painter and writer.

1944 – 1947 Enlisted in the Northants Regiment and was later transferred to the Royal Army Educational Corps.

1947 – 1949 Studied art at Camberwell School of Art and engraving under Gertrude Hermes and John Buckland-Wright.

1949 – 1950 Studied art at the Anglo-French Art Centre, St John's Wood and engraving under John Buckland-Wright.

1950 – 1951 Studied art at the Slade School of Fine Art, London University and engraving under John Buckland-Wright.

1958 Elected a member of the Society of Wood Engravers.

1960 Elected a member of the Royal Institute of Oil Painters.

1963 Appointed Art Lecturer at the Polytechnic of North London, in the School of Architecture.

1965 Became the Honorary Secretary of the Society of Wood Engravers.

1967 Elected President of the Society of Wood Engravers on the retirement of Margaret Pilkington.

1971 Invited to Fellowship of the Royal Society of Arts. Became Chairman of Mall Prints Annual Exhibitions of the Federation of British Artists.

1973 Wrote *The Wood Engravings and Drawings of Iain Macnab of Barachastlain* published by Midas. Organised the John Buckland-Wright exhibition of wood and copper engravings touring New Zealand art galleries, with Campbell Smith, wood engraver and director of the Waikato Art Gallery and Mrs John Buckland-Wright.

1974 – 1975 Awarded two silver medals for wood engraving at the Grand Concours International by the Académie Internationale de Lutèce, Paris. Appointed Senior Lecturer in the School of Architecture at the Polytechnic of North London,

1976 Awarded the silver medal of the Société des Artistes Français.

GENTLEMAN, DAVID. RDI, FSIAD, AGI, ARCA

b 1930 in London.

Wood engraver, graphic designer and illustrator.

1947 – 1948 Studied art at St Albans School of Art.

1950 – 1953 Studied art and engraving at the Royal College of Art under John Nash, RA.

1953 – 1955 Taught at the Royal College of Art. Many short periods in Europe, India and United States of America.

1969 One-man exhibition of stamp designs at the National Postal Museum.

1970 Awarded ARCA Gold Medal for stamp designing. Appointed Royal Designer for Industry. Elected a fellow of the Royal Society of Arts.

1972 Publication of his book *Design in Miniature*.

GIBBINGS, ROBERT

b 1889 in Cork, Eire. d 1958.

Wood engraver, writer and typographer.

1912 Studied art at the Slade School of Fine Art, London University, and joined Noel Rooke's engraving classes at the Central School of Art and Design.

1913 Produced his first white-line wood engravings.

1914 Enlisted with the Royal Munster Fusiliers and served at Gallipoli.

1918 Invalided out of the Army suffering from a serious wound in the neck. Became a freelance engraver.

1919 Formed the Society of Wood Engravers.

1920 Exhibited twelve wood engravings at the first show of the Society of Wood Engravers.

1921	Produced his first book at his own expense entitled *Twelve Wood Engravers.*
1924 – 1933	Became Director of the Golden Cockerel Press. Lived at Waltham St Lawrence, Berkshire.
1929	Visited Tahiti and was inspired to write and illustrate the book *Iorana.*
1930	Commenced work as a sculptor.
1932	Cruise to the West Indies.
1933	Sold the Golden Cockerel Press. Retired to Cornwall to complete *Glory of Life* and *Beasts and Saints.*
1936 – 1940	Appointed lecturer in Book Production at Reading University under Professor Allen W. Seaby. Awarded medal from Warsaw International Exhibition.
1937	Visited Bermuda.
1938	Went to the Red Sea to draw underwater.
1939 – 1940	Explored the Thames in a flat-bottomed boat and produced fifty wood engravings for *Sweet Thames Run Softly.*

GILL, ARTHUR ERIC ROWTON. RDI, ARA

b 1882 in Brighton. d 1940.

Sculptor, wood engraver, writer and typographic designer.

1897	Studied at the Chichester Theological College.
1898	Studied at the Technical and Art School, Chichester.
1899	Joined Edward Johnston's lettering class at the Central School of Art and Design.
1900	Worked in the offices of the architect of the Ecclesiastical Commissioners.
1904	Taught gilding at the Central School of Art and Design. First daughter born (Elizabeth). Moved from Battersea to Hammersmith.
1905	Taught lettering for stonemasons at LCC Paddington Institute.
1906	Second daughter born (Petra).
1907	Moved from Hammersmith to Ditchling to a house called 'Sopers'. A community of artists and craftsmen began to develop around him.
1910	Third daughter born (Joanna).
1912	Visited Gwendolen Raverat at Royston. Edward Johnston settled at Ditchling.
1913	Moved from 'Sopers' to Hopkins Crank at Ditchling.
1914	Enrolled in the Home Defence Brigade.
1915	Met Hilary Pepler who then started the Ditchling Press.
1917	Gill, Pepler and Father Vincent McNabb conceived a religious order of artists.
1918	Met Desmond Macready Chute at Ditchling. Eric and Mary Gill, Hilary Pepler and Desmond Chute made novices of the Third Order of St Dominic. Gill called up for service in the Army but served for a few months and was discharged in November.
1920	Founder member of the newly formed Society of Wood Engravers. David Jones arrived at Ditchling and stayed with the community.
1921	Members of the Ditchling Community formed themselves into the Guild of St Joseph and St Dominic. Philip Hagreen joined the Ditchling Community.
1924	The Ditchling Community affairs wound up. Gill took up residence at Capel-y-ffin, Abergavenny where he was joined by Philip Hagreen and Joseph Cribb.
1925	Visited Rome, Rapallo and Paris. The Hagreen family left Capel-y-ffin.
1926	Visited Paris with Robert Gibbings and met Zadkine and Maillol.
1928	Gill left Capel-y-ffin and took up residence at 'Pigots', High Wycombe, where Laurie Cribb joined him.
1930	Visited Count Kessler at Weimar.
1933	Visited Palestine.
1935	Awarded honorary associateship of the Royal Institute of British Architects.
1936	Appointed as a Royal Designer for Industry. Visited Desmond Chute at the Villa Rallaele in Rapallo.

1937 Elected associate of the Royal Academy. Visited Palestine. Awarded honorary associateship of the Royal Society of British Sculptors.
1938 Awarded honorary Doctorate of Laws at Edinburgh University.

GINNER, CHARLES. CBE, ARA
b 1878 in Cannes. d 1952.
Painter and engraver.
Educated at the College Stanislas of Cannes.
1904 Studied art at the Académie Vitti, Paris under Anglada y. Camaraga.
1905 Studied at the Ecole de Beaux-Arts.
1906 Returned to Académie and left in 1908.
1910 Came to London. Visited Paris with Harold Gilman.
1911 Helped to found the Camden Town Group. First Group Exhibition.
1914 Exhibited with Harold Gilman at the Goupil Gallery.
1915 Taught at the Westminster School of Art.
1916 Served in the Royal Army Ordnance Corps and later transferred to the Intelligence Corps.
1922 Invited and elected a member of the Society of Wood Engravers.

GREG, BARBARA. RE, MMAFA
b 1900 in Styal, Cheshire.
Wood engraver and illustrator.
Educated at Bedales School.
1919 – 1923 Studied art at the Slade School of Fine Art under Norman Janes.
1921 – 1923 Studied art at the Central School of Art and Design.
1926 – 1927 Studied art at the Westminster School of Art.
1952 Elected a member of the Society of Wood Engravers. Elected a fellow of the Royal Society of Painter-Etchers and Engravers. Elected member of the Manchester Academy of Fine Art.

GREENWOOD, JOHN F. RE
b 1885 in Rochdale. d 1953.
Wood engraver and designer.
Studied art at the Bradford School of Art.
Studied engraving at the Royal College of Art.
1921 First wood engraving exhibited with the Society of Wood Engravers.
1922 Elected associate of the Royal Society of Painter-Etchers and Engravers, and a fellow in 1939.
1928 – 1942 Taught at the College of Art, Bradford, Yorks.
1940 Exhibited three engravings with the Society of Wood Engravers at the Department of Fine Arts, Carnegie Institute, USA.

HASSALL, JOAN. RE, FSIAD
b 1906 in Notting Hill, London.
Wood engraver, book illustrator and typographer.
1928 – 1933 Studied art at the Royal Academy Schools.
Studied wood engraving under Ralph John Beedham at LCC School of Photo-engraving and Lithography, Bolt Court, London.
1938 Elected associate of the Royal Society of Painter-Etchers and Engravers.
1940 – 1947 Taught book production at the Edinburgh College of Art.
1947 Elected a member of the Society of Wood Engravers.
1948 Elected a fellow of the Royal Society of Painter-Etchers and Engravers.
1953 Commissioned to design and engrave the official invitation card for the Coronation of HM Queen Elizabeth II.
1964 One of the first three women to be elected a member of the Art Workers' Guild.
1972 First woman Master of the Art Workers' Guild.
1973 Awarded bronze medal for engraving at the 1973 Paris Salon.

HAWTHORN, RAYMOND HUMPHREY MILLAS. ATD, ARE

b 1917 in Poole, Dorset.
Wood engraver and teacher.

1935 – 1939 Studied art at Coventry School of Art.
1939 – 1940 Studied engraving at Hornsey School of Art and Crafts under Norman Janes and engraving history with Douglas Percy Bliss. Secured Art Teacher's Diploma.
1940 – 1946 Served in the Army and on being demobilized secured his first teaching post at Coventry School of Art.
1946 – 1947 Taught at the Medway School of Art. Acquired his air pilot's licence.
1947 Appointed to a teaching post at the Laird School of Art, Birkenhead.
1960 Elected associate of the Royal Society of Painter-Etchers and Engravers.

HERMES, GERTRUDE. RA, RE

b 1901 in Bromley, Kent.
Wood engraver, stained glass designer and sculptor.
Educated at Belmont Private School, Bickley, Kent.

1920 – 1921 Studied art at the Beckenham School of Art.
1921 – 1925 Studied art at Leon Underwood School of Painting and Sculpture.
1922 Began to engrave on wood.
1925 Awarded Prix de Rome for engraving.
1926 Married Blair Hughes-Stanton and collaborated with him producing *The Pilgrim's Progress* for the Cresset Press.
1927 Daughter born (Judith).
1928 Son born (Simon). Her prints and blocks destroyed by the Thames flood in her basement home in Hammersmith.
1929 Moved to Hatcheson, Suffolk.
1931 Moved to Gregynog in Wales.
1932 Invited to membership of the Society of Wood Engravers.
1934 Exhibited for the first time at the Royal Academy.
1935 Elected a member of the London Group.
1937 Designed the thirty foot sculptured glass Britannia window for the British Pavilion at the International Exhibition of Arts and Industry, Paris.
1939 Selected as one of seven wood engravers to represent Britain at the Venice Biennial International Exhibition. Designed three glass panels for the British Pavilion, Worlds Fair, New York. Appointed visiting teacher at the Westminster School of Art. Taught wood engraving at the St Martin's School of Art, and life drawing at Camberwell School of Art.
1940 – 1945 Lived in Canada with her children, and did war work.
1945 – 1960 Returned to London and lived in Chelsea. Taught wood engraving at Camberwell School of Art, St Martin's School of Art and later at the Central School of Art and Design.
1946 Started the wood and lino cut colour printing.
1949 Elected associate of the Royal Society of Painter-Etchers and Engravers.
1951 Elected a fellow of the Royal Society of Painter-Etchers and Engravers.
1961 Awarded first prize in the Giles Bequest competition (organised by the Victoria and Albert Museum) for the lino cut *Stonehenge*.
1963 Elected an associate of the Royal Academy. Visited Greece.
1966 Retired from teaching at the Central School of Art and Design. Visited Italy. Taught engraving at the Royal Academy Schools.
1967 Awarded the Jean Masson Davidson Medal for sculpture by the Society of Portrait Sculptors. Retrospective exhibition at the Whitechapel Art Gallery, London.
1973 Retrospective exhibition of engravings at the Print Makers Council, Ely House, Dover Street.

HUGHES-STANTON, BLAIR ROWLANDS

b 1902 in London.
Painter and engraver.

1919 – 1922 Studied art at the Byam Shaw School of Art.

1922 – 1923 Continued his studies at the Royal Academy Schools.
1923 Frequent visits to France and Italy.
1923 – 1925 Studied at Leon Underwood School of Painting and Sculpture.
1924 Visited Iceland with Leon Underwood.
1925 Visited Jugoslavia.
1929 – 1932 Book designer and wood engraver at the Gregynog Press.
1932 Invited to membership of the Society of Wood Engravers.
1934 – 1939 Lecturer in drawing at the Westminster School of Art.
1937 Winner of the international prize for engraving at the Venice Biennale.
1945 – 1947 Lecturer in drawing and wood engraving at the Colchester School of Art.
1947 – 1948 Lecturer in wood engraving at St Martin's School of Art.
1948 Lecturer in drawing and printmaking at the Central School of Art and Design (to date).

JACKSON, MURIEL BLOMFIELD

b 1901 at a house in Mecklenburg Square, London.
Wood engraver and portrait painter.
Educated at Ruskin House School, Hampstead.
1917 – 1922 Studied art at the Central School of Art and Design under Noel Rooke for engraving and F. Ernest Jackson for tempera painting.
1920 Specialised in study of gypsy caravans on Hampstead Heath. Presented the Buckland Caravan to the London County Council in 1948.
1925 Elected a member of the Society of Wood Engravers.
1931 Awarded first prize Logan Medal, Art Institute of Chicago.

JANES, NORMAN. RWS, RE, RSMA

b 1892 in Egham, Surrey.
Wood engraver, etcher and painter.
Studied art at the Slade School of Fine Art. Studied engraving under W. Thomas Smith.
1915 – 1917 Served in the Army.
1926 – 1930 Made the first use of wood engraving to illustrate pianola rolls for Aeolian Company. Elected associate and later a fellow of the Royal Society of Painter-Etchers and Engravers.
1942 – 1945 Served in the Royal Air Force. Elected a member of the Royal Society of Marine Artists.
1952 Elected a member of the Society of Wood Engravers.
Elected a member of the Royal Watercolour Society.
1969 Visited Australia.
1970 – 1973 Conducted painting tours in Italy.

JONES, DAVID

b 1895 in Brockley, Kent. d 1974.
Painter, wood and copper engraver and author.
1909 Studied art at Camberwell School of Art.
1915 Joined the Royal Welch Fusiliers and served in France until 1918.
1919 Studied at the Westminster School of Art under Walter Bayes and Bernard Meninsky. Awarded a scholarship.
1922 Joined Eric Gill's Guild of St Joseph and St Dominic at Ditchling, Sussex, where he was taught the art of engraving by Father Desmond Chute.
1925 Joined Eric Gill at his workshop at Capel-y-ffin, Abergavenny.
1927 Returned to live with his parents at Brockley. Welsh drawings exhibited at the St George's Gallery. Invited to join the Society of Wood Engravers.
1928 Started engraving on copper and became a member of the Seven and Five Group.
1929 First one-man show in London.
1930 – 1933 Exhibited as a member of the Seven and Five Society. Began to suffer successive periods of ill health. Lived at 3 Glebe Place, Chelsea, SW3.
1933 Work shown in Chicago.
1934 Venice Biennial Exhibition British Pavilion.

1937	Won the Hawthornden Prize for literature with his book *In Parenthesis.*
1940 – 1941	Made two large drawings for *Onenever and the four Queens.*

KEELING, CECIL. FSIAD

b 1912 in Teddington, Middlesex.

Wood engraver, illustrator, book designer and writer.

1930 – 1934	Studied art at the Putney School of Art.
1935 – 1936	Studied life drawing at Chelsea School of Art.
1945	Member of the Art Workers' Guild.
1951	Elected a member of the Society of Industrial Artists and Designers.
1953	Elected a member of the Society of Wood Engravers.
1956	Elected a fellow of the Society of Industrial Artists and Designers.

KIDSTON, ANNABEL. DA (Glasgow).

b 1896 in Hilthead, Glasgow.

Wood engraver and painter.

1918 – 1921	Studied art at the Glasgow School of Art under Maurice Greiffenhergen and Forester Wilson. Awarded the Diploma of Art.
1922	Studied painting in L'Hôte's Studio at La Grande Chaumière.
1922 – 1925	Worked as Head of Art Department, Laurel Bank School, Glasgow, and also as teacher of art and drama at its primary school, Beauden.
1926	Studied engraving under Thomas Smith at the Slade School of Fine Art and painting under Henry Tonks and Wilson Steer.
1941 – 1946	Instructor of drawing and wood engraving for the Committee for Education for the Forces.
1946	Elected first Chairman of the Art Committee of St Andrews.
1947 – 1950	Part-time instructor on painting at Duncan and Jordanston School of Art, Dundee.
1972	Elected President of the Art Committee of St Andrews.

LAMB, LYNTON. RDI, FSIAD, FRSA

b 1907 in India.

Wood engraver, painter, designer and illustrator.

Educated at Kingswood School, Bath.

Studied art at the Central School of Art and Design and later joined the staff at the Slade School of Fine Art.

1939	Elected a member of the London Group.
1949	Elected a fellow of the Society of Industrial Artists and Designers.
1951 – 1952	President of the Society of Industrial Artists and Designers.
1951 – 1954	Member of the art panel of the Arts Council.
1952 – 1955	Member of the Design Council.
1953	Elected a fellow of the Royal Society of Arts.
1953 – 1958	Member of the National Advisory Committee on Art Examinations and the external examining boards for the University of Reading and the Liverpool College of Art.
1956 – 1970	Part-time lecturer at the Painting School of the Royal College of Arts.
1960	Won the International Philatelic Art Society Award for stamp design.
1974	Appointed a Royal Designer for Industry.

LAWRENCE, JOHN

b 1933 in Hastings.

Wood engraver and teacher.

1951 – 1953	Studied art at the Hastings School of Art.
1954 – 1955	National Service in Ghana, West Africa.
1955 – 1957	Studied engraving under Gertrude Hermes at the Central School of Art and Design.
1958 – 1960	Part-time lecturer at the Maidstone College of Art.
1960 – 1968	Part-time lecturer at the Brighton College of Art.
1960	Appointed part-time lecturer at the Camberwell School of Art.
1972	Won second prize in the Francis Williams Book Illustration Award.

LEIGHTON, CLARE. RE, Hon. DFA (Colby College, Maine).
b 1901 in London.
Wood engraver, stained glass designer and writer.
Educated privately and studied art at Brighton School of Art.
Studied art at the Slade School of Fine Art and engraving under Noel Rooke at the Central School of Art and Design.

1932 Elected associate of the Royal Society of Painter-Etchers and Engravers. Wrote *Wood Engraving and woodcuts* published by Studio, London in four editions.

1934 Elected a fellow of the Royal Society of Painter-Etchers and Engravers. Wrote *The Wood Engravings of the 1930s* published by Studio, London.

1939 Went to the United States with her parents (both writers) and lived in Baltimore for nine years.

1945 Became a US citizen. Lectured at the Duke University until 1947.

1951 Went to live in New England. Designed set of twelve engravings for Wedgwood plates. Took up residence in a contemporary house designed and built for her in Woodbury.

1954 Obtained the New England Society of New York award for greatest contribution to New England culture.
Member and Past Vice-President of the National Institute of Arts and Letters. Awarded gold medal.
Past Vice-President of the Society of American Graphic Art.
Fellow of the National Academy of Design, New York.
Represented Great Britain in Venice Biennale.
First prize and Logan medal, Art Institute of Chicago.
Second prize, International Engraving Exhibition, Art Institute of Chicago.
Awarded the Pennell prize, Philadelphia.
Awarded the Eyre Medal, Philadelphia.
Awarded the gold medal by the American Academy of Arts and Letters.

LINDLEY, KENNETH ARTHUR. ARE, NDD, ATD, MSIAD
b 1928 in Shepherds Bush, London.
Wood engraver, painter, writer and teacher.

1938 – 1943 Educated at St Clement Danes Grammar School.

1943 – 1949 Studied art at Ealing School of Art under James Bostock.

1949 – 1950 Studied art at Hornsey School of Art and Crafts under Arthur S. Mills and Norman Janes. Elected a member of the Society of Industrial Artists and Designers.

1950 – 1957 Art Lecturer at Loughborough College of Art.

1957 – 1965 Art Lecturer at Swindon School of Art.

1959 Elected associate of the Royal Society of Painter-Etchers and Engravers.

1960 Elected a member of the Society of Wood Engravers and Relief Printers.

1966 Appointed Head of Wakefield School of Art, and served until 1971.

1971 Appointed Principal of Herefordshire College of Art.

MACNAB OF BARACHASTLAIN, IAIN. PROI, RE
b 1890 in Iloilo, Philippines. d 1967.
Wood engraver, etcher, lithographer and painter.

1894 Arrived in Scotland from Iloilo and resided in Kilmacolm.

1911 Studied accountancy in Glasgow.

1914 Volunteered for the Highland Light Infantry.

1915 Commissioned in France and gazetted 2nd Battalion The Argyll and Sutherland Highlanders as Divisional Machine Gun Officer.

1917 Studied art at the Glasgow School of Art.

1918 Studied art at the Heatherley School of Fine Art.

1919 Studied art in Paris. Became Joint Principal of Heatherley School of Fine Art.

1923 Elected associate of the Royal Society of Painter-Etchers and Engravers.

1925 Founded The Grosvenor School of Modern Art in London.

1928 Visited Paris. Studied at Académie Julian.

1932	Married Helen Mary Tench, well known in the dancing profession as Helen Wingrave. Invited to membership of the Society of Wood Engravers and fellowship of the Royal Society of Arts.
1935	Elected fellow of the Royal Society of Painter-Etchers and Engravers.
1941	Joined the Royal Air Force. Met Douglas Percy Bliss at Fighter Command, Stanmore.
1953	Relinquished post as Director of Art Studies at Heatherley School of Art.
1959	Elected President of the Royal Institute of Oil Painters. Became a governor of the Federation of British Artists.
1961	Produced his last wood engraving *Ronda Bridge, Spain.*
1962	Elected Chairman of the Imperial Arts League.

MACKLEY, GEORGE. RE
b 1900 in Tonbridge, Kent.
Wood engraver and water colourist.
Educated at the Judd School, Tonbridge.
Studied wood engraving under Noel Rooke.

1948	Wrote and illustrated book *Wood Engraving.*
1950	Elected associate of the Royal Society of Painter-Etchers and Engravers.
1952	Elected a member of the Society of Wood Engravers.
1959	Member of the Art Workers' Guild.
1961	Elected a fellow of the Royal Society of Painter-Etchers and Engravers.

MALET, GUY SEYMOUR WARRE. RBA
b 1900 in Southsea, Hants. d 1973.
Wood engraver and painter.
Educated at Downside School.

1918	Educated at the Royal Military College, Sandhurst.
1920	Commenced work in an insurance office at his father's instigation.
1924 – 1926	Studied art at the London School of Art under Frank Eastman.
1926 – 1927	Studied art at the Polytechnic Regent Street, London.
1927	Studied wood engraving under Iain Macnab at the Grosvenor School of Art.
1931	Work accepted at the Royal Academy.
1935	Elected a member of the Royal Society of British Artists.
1947	Elected a member of the Society of Wood Engravers.

MCKENZIE, ALISON. DA (Glasgow)
b 1907 in Bombay.
Wood engraver and painter.

1921 – 1925	Educated at the Prior's Field School.
1925	Began to study art at the Glasgow School of Art.
1929	Awarded the Diploma of Art and the Fra Newbery medal at the Glasgow School of Art.
1932 – 1933	Studied wood engraving at the Grosvenor School of Modern Art under Iain Macnab.
1943 – 1946	Served in the Auxiliary Territorial Service.
1946 – 1958	Taught life drawing at the Dundee College of Art.
1952	Elected a member of the Royal Society of Painters in Watercolour.

MCKENZIE, WINIFRED M. DA (Glasgow)
b 1905 in Bombay.
Wood engraver and painter.

1921 – 1923	Educated at the Prior's Field School.
1923	Began to study drawing and painting at Glasgow School of Art.
1927	Awarded the diploma and teacher's certificate.
1932 – 1933	Studied wood engraving at the Grosvenor School of Modern Art under Iain Macnab.
1940 – 1945	Held wood engraving classes for the Services at St Andrews University.
1944 – 1958	Taught wood engraving, life drawing and composition at the Dundee College of Art.

MARTIN, FRANK V. MA, RE, MSIAD

b 1921 in Dulwich, London.

Wood engraver, woodcut, etcher and teacher.

Educated at Uppingham School and Hertford College, Oxford where he obtained the degree of Master of Arts (History).

Studied art at St Martin's School of Art under Gertrude Hermes.

1941 – 1946 Served in the Army.

1946 – 1949 Freelance illustrator and wood engraver.

1952 – 1967 Elected a member of the Society of Wood Engravers. Served as Honorary Secretary from 1952 to 1959.

1953 Teacher of etching and engraving at the Camberwell School of Art. At present Senior Lecturer in Graphic Design.

1955 – 1971 Member of the Society of Industrial Artists and Designers.

1955 Elected a fellow of the Royal Society of Painter-Etchers and Engravers.

1965 Elected Honorary Academician of the Academia della arti del Disegno, Florence.

MARX, ENID. RDI, FSIAD, FRSA

b 1902 in London.

Wood engraver, fabric designer and writer.

Educated at Roedean School, Brighton.

Studied art at the Central School of Art and Design and at the Royal College of Art.

Member of the Board of Trade team working on textile designs for 'Utility' furniture.

1944 First woman engraver to be appointed a Royal Designer for Industry.

1946 Elected fellow of the Society of Industrial Artists and Designers.

1952 Designed a set of three stamps to mark the beginning of the reign of Queen Elizabeth II.

1955 Elected a member of the Society of Wood Engravers.

1960 – 1965 Served as Head of Department of textiles, dress and pottery design at the Croydon College of Art.

1965 – 1974 Engaged in lecturing on history of textiles at colleges in Winchester, Birmingham and NADFS.

MOORE, THOMAS STURGE

b 1870 in Sussex. d. 1944.

Poet, wood engraver and illustrator.

Brother of George Edward Moore (1873 to 1958), philosopher and leader of the philosophical revolution against idealism.

1885 Met Ricketts and Shannon who persuaded him to become a student with them at the Lambeth School of Art. Led to a lifelong friendship.

1897 – 1899 Joined the Dial Group.

1899 Wrote his first book of verse *The Vinedresser* (Art and Life) published by Methuen, London.

1905 Wrote a book on Dürer which was published in London by Duckworth.

1919 Published *Power of the Air* and *Tragic Mothers*.

1921 Herbert Furst published a small book *T. Sturge Moore* through the Morland Press series of Modern Woodcutters.

1924 Moved from Petersfield, Hampshire to Princes Risborough, Buckinghamshire.

1927 Opened the exhibition in Manchester of the Society of Wood Engravers.

MOORE, HENRY. OM, CH, FBA, Hon. ARIBA

b 1898

Artist and sculptor.

Holds a large number of honorary degrees from universities in Great Britain, USA and Germany.

Educated at the Castleford Grammar School.

1919 – 1921 Studied art at the Leeds College of Art.

1921 – 1925 Studied art at the Royal College of Art.
1928 Exhibition of work held in London. Has continued to have works exhibited in many countries.
1941 – 1956 Trustee of the Tate Gallery.
1947 Appointed a member of the Royal Fine Arts Commission continuing until 1971.
1948 Appointed an honorary associate of the Royal Institute of British Architects. Awarded the international sculpture prize of the twenty-fourth Venice Biennale.
1955 Appointed a trustee of the National Gallery serving until 1974.
1961 Elected honorary member of the American Academy of Arts and Letters and of the National Institute of Arts and Letters. Elected honorary member of the Akademie der Künste, Berlin.
1963 Awarded the Feltrinelli Prize in Italy.
1966 Elected a fellow of the British Academy.
1968 Awarded the Erasmus Prize in Holland.
Awarded the Grand Cross with Star Order of Merit of Federal Republic of Germany.

MORGAN, GWENDA. RE
b 1908 in Petworth, Sussex.
Wood engraver and painter.
1921 – 1926 Educated at Brighton and Hove High School.
1926 – 1929 Studied art at Goldsmiths' College School of Art.
1930 – 1936 Studied engraving at the Grosvenor School of Modern Art under Iain Macnab.
1935 Elected a member of the National Society of Painters, Sculptors and Engravers.
1939 – 1946 Enlisted in the Women's Land Army.
1950 Elected a member of the Society of Wood Engravers.
1952 Elected an associate of the Royal Society of Painter-Etchers and Engravers.
1961 Elected a fellow of the Royal Society of Painter-Etchers and Engravers.

MUNGAPEN, SHIRLEY. NDD, SRN
b 1933 in Boston, Lincolnshire.
Wood engraver, painter and State Registered Nurse.
1944 – 1949 Educated at Kesteven and Grantham Girls Grammar School.
1950 – 1954 Studied painting and engraving at the Nottingham College of Art and Craft. Engraving instructor Mr Thursby.
1956 – 1959 Nursed at Peterborough Memorial Hospital and qualified as a State Registered Nurse.
1959 – 1961 Studied for National Diploma of Design at Portsmouth College of Arts and Crafts under engraving instructor G. Tucker.
1961 – 1962 Art therapist at Birmingham All Saints Hospital. Short visit to Florence to study Fra Angelico.
1965 – 1966 Art therapist at St James Hospital, Portsmouth.
1968 Art therapist at St Mary's Hospital, Portsmouth.
1970 Art therapist at Queen Alexandra Hospital, Portsmouth.

NASH, JOHN. CBE, RA, Hon. FRCA
b 1893 in Kensington, London. d 1977.
Painter, wood engraver and book illustrator.
Educated at Wellington College.
1907 Encouraged by his brother Paul to take up painting.
1913 Exhibited (with Paul Nash) at the Dorien Leigh Gallery, South Kensington.
1914 Founder member of the London Group. First London exhibition held at the Goupil Gallery.
1915 Exhibited at the first exhibition of the Camden Town Group at the Goupil Gallery.
1916 Enlisted in the Artists Rifles and was on active service until 1918.

1918 Commissioned as an official war artist.
1920 Founder member of the newly-formed Society of Wood Engravers.
1921 First one-man show at the Goupil Gallery. Went to live at Meadle near Princes Risborough.
1930 One-man show at the Goupil Gallery.
1934 Taught in the Design School of the Royal College of Art.
1937 Designed a large decoration for the Paris Exhibition.
1939 Joined the Observer Corps.
1940 Appointed official war artist to the Admiralty. Elected associate of the Royal Academy.
1941 – 1945 Commissioned as Captain in 1941 and served in the Royal Marines.
1945 Went to live in Suffolk. Rejoined the staff at the Royal College of Art.
1951 Elected a Royal Academician.
1954 Retrospective exhibition at the Leicester Galleries.
1964 Awarded the CBE.
1967 Retrospective exhibition at the Royal Academy. Awarded an honorary degree by the University of Essex.

NASH, PAUL

b 1889 in Kensington, London. d 1946.

Painter, wood engraver and designer.

1901 – 1906 Educated at St Paul's School. Lived at Wood Lane House, Iver Heath, Bucks.
1906 Studied art as a part-time student at the Chelsea Polytechnic.
1908 Began to attend evening art classes at the Bolt Court School, Fleet Street.
1910 – 1911 Studied at the Slade School of Fine Art. Moved to Paultons Square, Chelsea.
1912 Held first one-man show at the Carfax Gallery. Left Chelsea. Invited to exhibit with the New English Art Club.
1914 Enlisted as a private in the Artists Rifles; detailed for service in UK. Married Margaret Theodosia Odeh.
1916 Gazetted 2nd Lieutenant in 3rd Hampshire Regiment.
1917 Posted to 15th Hampshire Regiment for service in the Ypres Salient. Invalided to London the same year. Later in the year he was invalided out of the Army and subsequently appointed war artist.
1918 Shared a studio with his brother John in Chalfont St Peter. Exhibition *Void of War*, Leicester Gallery.
1919 First wood engraving *Diseuse*. Returned to London to live in Fitzroy Street. Relinquished his appointment as war artist.
1921 Went to live at Dymchurch, Kent to recuperate from serious illness. Elected a member of the Society of Wood Engravers.
1924 Exhibition at the Leicester Gallery.
1925 Appointed lecturer in design at the Royal College of Art but resigned at the summer term. Went to live at The Cottage, Iden, near Rye, Sussex.
1928 Exhibition of wood engravings at the Redfern Gallery.
1930 Death of his father. Began abstract and constructive series of paintings and drawings. Last dated wood engraving print.
1931 Visited the United States as a British representative on the International Jury for the Pittsburg International Exhibition.
1932 First serious attack of bronchial asthma.
1933 Founder member of Unit One Group. Elected President of the Society of Industrial Artists and Designers.
1934 Short time spent in France, Spain and Morocco.
1935 Disintegration of Unit One.
1936 Moved to 3 Eldon Grove, Hampstead. Participated in the International Surrealist Exhibition in London.
1938 Resumed teaching at the Royal College of Art in January.
1939 Moved to 106 Banbury Road, Oxford at the outbreak of war.

1940 Resigned teaching post at the Royal College of Art. Commissioned as artist to the Royal Air Force. Later became attached to War Artists Advisory Committee.
1946 Taken seriously ill in January and died the same year.
1948 Memorial exhibition held at the Tate Gallery in March.

NICHOLSON, SIR WILLIAM NEWZAM PRIOR
b 1872 in Newark-on-Trent. d 1949.
Painter and engraver.
1888 Studied art at Herkomer's Art School, Bushey.
1893 Secretly married Mabel Pryde, (sister of James Pryde the painter) at Ruislip, Middlesex. Lived at the Eight Bells, a small public house at Denham, Bucks. James Pryde arrived for a weekend and remained for two years.
Nicholson and Pryde collaborated in poster design, and the two men worked under the pseudonym the Beggerstaff brothers.
1894 Ben Nicolson born.
1920 Bought North End House, Rottingdean, Sussex.
1929 Illustrated Sassoon's book *Memoirs of a Foxhunting Man.*

NIEKERK, SARAH VAN
b 1934 in London.
Wood engraver.
Educated at Bedales School.
1951 – 1954 Studied art at the Central School of Art and Design and engraving under Gertrude Hermes.
1954 – 1955 Studied at the Slade School of Fine Art. Studied with Anthony Gross and Lynton Lamb.
1974 Elected a member of the Society of Wood Engravers and Relief Printers.

O'CONNOR, JOHN. ARCA, RWS
b 1913 in Leicester.
Painter, wood engraver, writer and teacher.
1930 – 1933 Studied art at the Leicester College of Art.
1933 – 1937 Studied engraving at the Royal College of Art under Eric Ravilious and John Nash.
1937 – 1938 Taught at Birmingham.
1938 – 1941 Taught at Bristol.
1941 – 1945 Served in the Royal Air Force.
1946 – 1948 Taught at Hastings.
1948 – 1964 Head of the Colchester School of Art.
1964 Taught at St Martin's School of Art.

PALMER, GARRICK S. NDD, RE
b 1933 in Portsmouth.
Wood engraver, painter and teacher.
Educated at St John's College, Southsea.
1955 – 1958 Studied painting and engraving at Portsmouth College of Art, and obtained the National Diploma in Design.
1958 – 1959 Studied painting and engraving at the Royal Academy Schools, gaining the certificate. Awarded the David Murray Landscape Scholarships 1955/6 and 1957. Obtained the Royal Academy Gold Medal and awarded the Edward Stott Travelling Scholarship (Italy) in 1958.
1963 Elected associate of the Royal Society of Painter-Etchers and Engravers.
1969 – 1970 Two visits to Holland. Elected a fellow of the Royal Society of Painter-Etchers and Engravers.
1973 Visited Istanbul.
1974 Visited the Orkney Islands. Appointed as Head of the Foundation Department of the Winchester School of Art.

PARKER, AGNES MILLER. DA (Glasgow), RE
b 1895 in Irvine, Ayrshire.
Wood engraver, painter in oil and tempera.
Educated at Whitehill Higher Grade School, Glasgow.

1914 – 1918	Studied art at the Glasgow School of Art. Awarded Diploma of Art and the Haldane Scholarship.
1918 – 1920	Teaching post at the Glasgow School of Art.
1920 – 1928	Teaching post at Maltmans Green School, Gerrards Cross, Bucks.
1926	Studied wood engraving under Gertrude Hermes and Blair Hughes-Stanton. Visited Paris.
1927	Visited Paris and St Tropez.
1928 – 1930	Teaching post at Clapham High School, London. Went to Italy and visited Florence and Venice.
1930 – 1933	Did teaching and engraving at the Gregynog Press, Newton, Montgomeryshire. Elected a member of the Society of Wood Engravers. Visited Norway.
1939	Lived at Pheasants Hill, Hambleden, Henley-on-Thames. Elected an associate of the Royal Society of Painter-Etchers and Engravers.
1962	Lived at 31 Riddrie Knowes, Glasgow E.3. Married William MacCance DA (Glasgow), painter, sculptor and typographer, and subsequently moved to the Isle of Arran, Scotland.

PAYNTER, HILARY. NDD, ATC
b 1943 in Dunfermline.
Wood engraver and art therapist.

1949 – 1951	Resident in China.
1956 – 1958	Resident in Malta.
1959 – 1964	Studied art at the Portsmouth College of Art under Gerry Tucker.
1964 – 1965	Studied for the Diploma in Education of Maladjusted Children at Tavistock Institute, London University.
1965 – 1967	Taught art at the Elliott School, Putney.
1967 – 1969	Resident artist governess to children in Manchester, USA.
1967 – 1972	Teacher in charge at Hammersmith Remand Home.
1972	Elected member of the Society of Wood Engravers.
1974	Appointed as Head of Remedial Department at Girls Comprehensive School, Richmond.

PETTS, JOHN. ARE
b 1914, in Hornsey, North London.
Sculptor, painter, wood engraver and designer of stained glass.

1930 – 1933	Studied art at Hornsey College of Art and Crafts. Studied engraving under Norman Janes and took the National Diploma of Design.
1933 – 1935	Studied art at the Royal Academy Schools and became a British Institution Scholar.
1934	Studied engraving at the Central School of Art and Design under W. F. Robins.
1938– 1942	Ran his own private press, The Caseg Press at Llanlleslind, in Gwynedd, North Wales.
1945 – 1946	Enlisted, and served in the 6th Airborne Division in the Middle East, Israel, Greece and Egypt.
1948 – 1951	Restarted his private press at Llanystundury in Gwynedd, North Wales.
1951 – 1956	Appointed Assistant Director for Wales, Arts Council of Great Britain.
1953	Elected a member of the Society of Wood Engravers.
1957	Elected associate of the Royal Society of Painter-Etchers and Engravers.
1958 – 1961	Lecturer in Design and Crafts at Dyfed College of Art.
1964	Documentary film *Out of the Rock* made by Derek Trimby describing work of John Petts shown on BBC television.
1965	Designed the *Alabama Window* for the reconstructed Negro Church at Birmingham, USA.
1967	Awarded the Churchill Fellowship and travelled to USA and Mexico.
1973	*The Affirmative Way* with Joan Bakewell for BBC television.

PILKINGTON, MARGARET. OBE, MA (Honoris Causa), JP, EMA
b 1891 in Salford, Lancashire. d 1974.
Wood engraver and watercolour painter.
Educated at the High School and Crohamhurst School, Croydon.

1913 Studied art at the Slade School of Fine Art.

1914 Studied wood engraving at the Central School of Art and Design. First lesson in wood engraving from Lucien Pissarro. Afterwards studied under Noel Rooke at the Central School.

1920 Print from a wood engraving hung in the first exhibition of the newly formed Society of Wood Engravers.

1922 Invited to membership of the Society of Wood Engravers. Founder member of the Red Rose Guild of Craftsmen in Manchester.

1924 Elected as Honorary Secretary to the Society of Wood Engravers on the retirement of Robert Gibbings.

1925 Elected a governor of the Whitworth Art Gallery, Manchester.

1927 Member of the Manchester City Art Galleries Committee.

1935 Director of the Whitworth Art Gallery from 1935 to 1959. Formed a collection of the work of members of the Society of Wood Engravers.

1942 Awarded MA (Honoris Causa) by the University of Manchester.

1952 Elected Chairman of the Society of Wood Engravers.

1954 Awarded the OBE.

1965 Member of the Art Workers' Guild.

PISSARRO, LUCIEN
b 1863 in Osny, near Pontoise. d 1944.
Wood engraver, painter, book designer and typographer.

1870 First visit to England aged seven years.

1883 Came to London for one year to learn English and stayed with his Uncle Phineas Isaacson in Holloway.

1884 Family move to Eragny near Gisors. Lucien returned to France for several years and was employed in the publishing firm of the art dealer Manzi.

1890 Returned to England.

1892 Married a young English woman Esther Bensusan.

1893 Finally settled in England. Daughter born (Orovida).

1894 Founded the Eragny Press, and designed his own type. Press named after the Pissarro home in Normandy.

1895 Had his portrait painted by Charles Shannon.

1897 Contributed wood engravings for the spring issue of *L'Image*, an artistic and literary revue produced by Auguste Lepère and Tony Beltrand. Lucien contracted a serious illness in London.

1901 Spent several weeks with his father in France.

1907 La Societé des Cents Bibliophiles commissioned Lucien to produce and design colour wood engravings for the book *Histoire de la Reine du Matin et de Soliman, Prince des Génies,* by G. de Nerval.

1920 Founder member of the Society of Wood Engravers.

PLENDERLEITH, THOMAS DONALD. RE, ATD
b 1921 in Peebles, Scotland.
Wood engraver, etcher and painter.
Educated at St Clement Danes Grammar School.

1936 – 1939 Studied art at the Ealing Art College. Awarded NDD in painting. Wood engraving instructor James Bostock.

1939 – 1945 Bomber pilot in the Royal Air Force.

1945 – 1946 Studied art at the Hornsey College of Art and Crafts. Instructor in etching Norman Janes.

1947 Awarded the Art Teacher's Diploma of the Hornsey College.

1947 – 1954 Taught art at Pinner Grammar School.

1962 Elected a fellow of the Royal Society of Painter-Etchers and Engravers.

1954 – 1974 Appointed as Head of Art Department at St Nicholas Grammar School.

POOLE, MONICA. ARE

b 1921 in Canterbury.

Wood engraver and illustrator.

Educated at Abbotsford, Broadstairs.

1945 – 1949 Studied art at the Central School of Art and Design and was awarded the Diploma in Illustration. Studied under John Farleigh.

1967 Elected an associate of the Royal Society of Painter-Etchers and Engravers.

1970 Elected a member of the Art Workers' Guild.

RAVERAT, GWENDOLEN MARY. RE

b 1885 in Cambridge. d 1957.

Wood engraver, artist and art critic.

Childhood spent in Newnham Grange, Cambridge. Started drawing at the age of ten years.

1908 Studied art at the Slade School of Fine Art under Frederick Brown and Henry Tonks.

1911 Married Jacques Pierre Raverat, whom she met at the Sorbonne where both were students.

1915 Went to live in Le Havre and later returned to England and lived at Weston near Baldock during the rest of the war. Two daughters were born.

1920 Went to live in Venice where Jacques Raverat died in 1925. Founder member of the Society of Wood Engravers. Elected an associate of the Royal Society of Painter-Etchers and Engravers.

1925 Returned to England and lived at the Old Rectory, Harlton, Cambridge until 1941.

1928 – 1939 Art critic for *Time and Tide*.

1934 Elected a fellow of the Royal Society of Painter-Etchers and Engravers.

1942 Returned to her place of birth and lived at the Old Granary in Newnham Grange, Cambridge.

1951 Suffered a stroke and could no longer engrave.

RAVILIOUS, ERIC

b 1903 in Acton. d 1942.

Painter, engraver and designer.

Early childhood spent in Acton.

1920 – 1922 Studied art at the Eastbourne Art School. Won a scholarship to the Royal College of Art.

1922 – 1925 Studied art at the Royal College of Art under the newly appointed William Rothenstein. Won a travelling scholarship to Italy. Married the wood engraver Tirzah Garwood.

1926 First commissions included illustrations for novel called *Desert* and work for the Golden Cockerel Press.

1930 – 1937 Taught at the Royal College of Art. Designer of Wedgwood pottery.

1936 Stayed at Newhaven with Edward Bawden.

1937 Designed wall decoration for the British Pavilion at the Paris Exhibition.

1938 Moved from Castle Hedingham (a small village in Essex) to Rye Harbour, Kent.

1939 Served for a few months in the Observer Corps.

1940 Commissioned into the Royal Marines.

1942 Given the rank of Flying Officer as an official war artist but killed whilst on a flight to Iceland to record the naval air operations there.

RAWLINSON, WILLIAM THOMAS

b 1912 in Liverpool.

Wood engraver, painter and teacher.

1929 – 1935 Studied art at the Liverpool College of Art. Awarded the college art scholarship in design 1931 and Senior City Art Travelling Scholarship 1932 also Board of Education drawing certificate and painting certificate. Studied in France, Italy, Austria, Czechoslovakia and Germany. Gold medallist Paris Salon, (engraving).

1935 – 1941 Appointed as art master at the Liverpool Institute High School.
1941 – 1946 Joined the Royal Air Force. Served in Egypt, North Africa, Sicily and Italy. Drawings for the Ministry of Information.
1943 – 1946 Worked as an official war artist for the RAF. Fourteen paintings commissioned by the Director General of Signals for the War Artists Advisory Committee for the Imperial War Museum.
1947 – 1948 Appointed as Art Lecturer for the Wimpole Park Technical College, Cambridgeshire.
1948 – 1951 Served as County Organiser for Art and Craft, Cheshire County Council.
1951 – 1952 Appointed HM Inspector of Schools.
1953 – 1966 Art master at the Harry Chesture County Secondary School for Girls, Kidderminster.
1966 Appointed Head of Art Department, Stratford-upon-Avon High School for Girls.
1972 Invited to membership of the Society of Wood Engravers and Relief Printers.

RECKITT, RACHEL
b 1908 in St Albans.
Wood engraver, sculptor, and designer of wrought iron work.
1933 – 1937 Studied wood engraving at the Grosvenor School of Modern Art under Iain Macnab.
1945 – 1950 Studied stone sculpture at Hammersmith School of Building Crafts, and lithography at the Central School of Art and Design.
1950 Elected a member of Society of Wood Engravers.
1969 – 1974 Studied wrought iron and welding under Mrs Horrobin, Rockwater, Waterditch, Somerset.
1932 – 1970 Short periods spent in France, Italy, Greece, Portugal, Spain, Yugoslavia and Sweden.

REDDICK, PETER. RE, DFA (Slade)
b 1924 in Essex.
Wood engraver, illustrator and teacher.
Educated at the Royal Liberty School, Romford, Essex.
1947 – 1948 Studied art in Cardiff.
Studied art and engraving at the Slade School of Fine Art under Norman Janes and John Buckland-Wright.
1951 Awarded diploma in fine art.
1953 Elected a member of the Society of Wood Engravers.
1960 – 1962 Taught at the Kumasi University, Ghana.
1963 – 1967 Taught at the Glasgow School of Art.
1967 Taught in the Faculty of Art and Design, Bristol Polytechnic.
1970 Elected an associate of the Royal Society of Painter-Etchers and Engravers and a fellow in 1973.

RICE, BERNARD
b 1900 in Innsbruck, Austria.
Wood engraver, painter, sculptor and stained glass designer.
1914 – 1915 Learned the technique of stained glass in his father's studio.
1915 – 1918 Studied wood engraving, woodcut, painting, drawing and modelling at art school in Innsbruck.
1919 – 1920 Studied art at the Westminster School of Art.
1921 – 1922 Studied art at the Royal Academy Schools.
1922 – 1926 Designing furniture in a craft school in Bosnia, Yugoslavia.
1926 – 1927 Studied etching and related techniques at the Royal College of Art.
1927 Competed in the Prix de Rome Final.
1927 – 1928 Returned to Yugoslavia for one year.
1929 – 1939 Went to Cairo, to teach wood engraving, copper engraving, etching and fresco painting at the Ecole Supérieure des Beaux Arts, Egyptian Ministry of Education.

1932 – 1934 Reconstructed the gold canopy of Queen Hetepheres (5000 BC) for the Boston-Harvard Expedition.

1939 – 1948 Engaged on war work but during this period produced some paintings and a large woodcut *Rammuda* (70mm x 125mm).

1949 – 1952 Taught wood engraving at the Sir John Cass School.

1952 Elected a member of the Society of Wood Engravers.

1954 Awarded second prize in the Giles Bequest Competition.

RICKETTS, CHARLES. RA

b 1866 in Geneva. d 1951.

Painter, wood engraver and book designer.

1884 Met Charles Shannon at the Lambeth School of Art.

1888 Ricketts and Shannon moved to Whistler's house, The Vale, Chelsea.

1894 William Rothenstein persuaded Llewellyn Hacon to lend Ricketts a thousand pounds to start the Vale Press.

1897 – 1902 Dial Group formed comprising Shannon, Ricketts, Sturge Moore and Lucien Pissarro. Ricketts and Shannon published five numbers of *The Dial* periodical.

ROOKE, NOEL. ARE

b 1881 in London. d 1953.

Wood engraver, painter, book designer and teacher.

Educated at Lycée de Chartres and Godolphin Schools.

Studied art at the Slade School of Fine Art.

1898 Studied art at the Central School of Art and Design, under W. R. Lethaby and Edward Johnston.

1904 Turned his attention to wood engraving.

1905 Appointed teacher of book illustration at the Central School of Art and Design.

1912 Given permission to teach wood engraving at the Central School of Art and Design.

1914 Experimented with colour in wood engraving. Became Head of the School of Book Production at the Central School of Art and Design.

1915 Elected a member of the Design and Industries Association.

1920 Founder member of the Society of Wood Engravers. Elected an associate of the Royal Society of Painter-Etchers and Engravers.

1923 Work was exhibited at the Royal Academy Exhibition of Decorative Art.

1924 – 1925 His wood engravings were shown in the British Empire Exhibition at Wembley.

Honorary Secretary of the Arts and Crafts Exhibition Society.

1932 Married Miss Celia Mary Twisleton-Wykeham-Fiennes.

SANDFORD, LETTICE

b 1902 in St Albans.

Wood engraver.

1926 – 1929 Studied at the Chelsea Polytechnic under Robert Day and Graham Sutherland.

Married the book designer and typographer Christopher Sandford of the Chiswick Press, Boar's Head Press and the Golden Cockerel Press.

SEKALSKI, JOZEF. ARE, SSA

b 1904 in Turek, Poland. d 1973.

Wood engraver, mural painter and designer.

Educated at Turek Boys Grammar School.

1925 – 1928 Studied medicine.

1929 – 1934 Graduated in art at the Faculty of Fine Arts, Wilno University; painting instructor Ludomir Slendzinski, lettering instructor Bonawentura Lenart, engraving instructor Jerzy Hoppen (to whom he became assistant in his final year).

1934 – 1937 Painted murals under Professor Mehoffer in Turek. Doleszczyn and Poreba churches in Poland.
1937 – 1939 In charge of an Artists-Designers Studio in Lodz. Visited Vienna and Italy.
1940 Escaped from German-occupied Poland but was recaptured.
1942 Reached England after escaping for the third time.
1944 – 1945 Worked as illustrator and designer for the Polish Library and Publishing Company in Glasgow.
1947 – 1951 With some difficulty he obtained work at two preparatory schools and teaching handicrafts at evening classes. Visited Belgium and Holland.
1949 Elected an associate of the Royal Society of Painter-Etchers and Engravers.
1950 Elected a member of the Society of Scottish Artists.

SHANNON, CHARLES HAZELWOOD. RA
b 1863. d 1937.
Painter, wood engraver and book designer.
1884 Met Ricketts at the Lambeth Art School.
1885 Met Thomas Sturge Moore.
1888 Shannon and Ricketts moved to Whistler's house, The Vale, Chelsea.
1897 – 1899 Dial Group formed. Publication of five numbers of *The Dial* periodical.

SMITH, RICHARD SHIRLEY
b 1935.
Wood engraver, etcher and painter.
1949 – 1954 Educated at Harrow School. Made many visits to David Jones while at Harrow.
1954 Called up for National Service and sent to Bremen, Germany. Commissioned in the Royal Artillery.
1956 – 1960 On completion of National Service studied drawing, painting and etching under Anthony Gross at the Slade School of Fine Art.
1960 – 1962 Spent two years' individual study in Rome where he taught himself wood engraving.
1962 – 1966 Studied lithography at the Central School of Art and Design, taught part-time typography and lithography at the St Albans and Watford Schools of Art, and gave extra-mural art appreciation lectures for London and Bristol Universities.
1966 – 1970 Appointed as Head of Art Department at Marlborough College.
1969 – 1971 Produced a series of slide strips, *Villas of the Veneto* for Visual Publications, London.

STONE, REYNOLDS ALAN. CBE, RDI
b 1909 in Eton, Buckinghamshire.
Wood engraver, illustrator, designer, and lettering craftsman in stone.
Educated at Eton and Magdalene College, Cambridge.
Became a printer and worked with the Cambridge University Press.
Self-taught engraver influenced by Thomas Bewick and Edward Calvert.
1932 Received first engraving commission.
1940 Elected a member of the Art Workers' Guild.
1948 Elected a member of the Society of Wood Engravers.
1950 Taught lettering at the Royal College of Art.
1956 Appointed as a Royal Designer for Industry.

TUTE, GEORGE WILLIAM. ARE, ARWA
b 1933 in Hull, Yorkshire.
Painter, wood engraver and teacher.
Educated at Baines Grammar School, Lancs.
1949 – 1953 Studied art at the Blackpool School of Art. Obtained the National Diploma in Painting.
1953 – 1958 Studied art at the Royal Academy Schools under Sir Henry Rushbury; awarded the Silver Certificate, taught himself wood engraving.

1954 – 1955 Three months each year spent in France, St Paul de Vence.
1960 – 1962 Part-time lecturer in Graphics at York School of Art.
1962 – 1974 Appointed Senior Lecturer in Graphic Design at the Bristol Polytechnic. Elected a member of the Society of Wood Engravers and an associate of the Royal Society of Painter-Etchers and Engravers.
1970 – 1971 Year spent in Germany and Italy.

UNDERWOOD, LEON

b 1890 in Shepherds Bush, London. d 1975.

Sculptor, painter, wood engraver, teacher and writer.

1907 – 1910 Studied art at the Regent Street Polytechnic Art School.
1910 – 1913 Studied art at the Royal College of Art.
1913 – 1914 Travelled to Poland.
1919 – 1920 Studied art at the Slade School of Fine Art.
1920 – 1925 Conducted a private school of drawing from life at Girdler's Road, Hammersmith.
1925 – 1928 Spent three years in the United States.
1926 Visited the Altamira Cave. John Day and Co, New York publish *Music from behind the Moon* by James Branch Cabell describing Underwood's work.
1927 Wrote and illustrated a novel *The Siamese Cat.*
1927 – 1928 Journey through Mexico with the author Phillips Russell, using a variety of means of transport.
1928 – 1939 Reopened his private school in Girdler's Road, Hammersmith.
1929 Illustrated Phillips Russell's book *The Red Tiger*, published by Brentano, New York.
1931 Prints designed for his magazine *The Island.*
1934 Faber published *Art for heaven's sake* by R. H. Wilenski, being the collected thoughts and drawings from Leon Underwood's studio.
1939 Worked at the Ministry of Home Security, Civil Defence Camouflage Establishment, Leamington Spa. Invited to join the Society of Wood Engravers. Travelled to Iceland.
1945 Travelled to West Africa. Now recognised as an authority on African sculpture.
1961 Elected honorary fellow of the Royal Society of British Sculptors.
1966 Awarded the Jean Masson Davidson Medal by the Society of Portrait Sculptors.

UNWIN, NORA S. ARCA, RE, ANA

b 1907 in Surbiton, Surrey.

Wood engraver, painter in watercolour, writer and teacher.

1914 – 1917 Educated at Surbiton High School.
1923 – 1925 Studied art at Leon Underwood's School with Blair Hughes-Stanton.
1925 – 1927 Studied art at the Kingston School of Art and graduated to the Royal College of Art.
1927 – 1931 Studied art at the Royal College of Art.
1930 First exhibited with the Society of Wood Engravers.
1932 Awarded associateship of the Royal College of Art.
1933 Elected an associate of the Royal Society of Painter-Etchers and Engravers.
1946 Decided to emigrate to the United States of America and to settle in New Hampshire.
1952 Elected a member of the Society of American Graphic Artists.
1953 Elected an associate of the National Academy of Design, New York.
1956 Spent three months in Mexico and made short visits to Britain, Iceland, France, Germany, Greece, Italy and Bavaria.
1957 – 1959 Appointed Head of Art Department, Tenacre Country Day School, USA.
1962 Engaged by the Sharon Arts Centre, Peterborough, New Hampshire, to teach printmaking.
1962 – 1963 Part-time teacher of watercolour at Manchester Institute of Arts and Sciences, Wellesle, New Hampshire.

1963 Elected a member of the Society of Wood Engravers and the Boston Watercolour Society, USA.

WADSWORTH, EDWARD. ARA

b 1889 in Cleckheaton, Yorkshire. d 1949.

Painter and wood engraver.

Studied engineering at Munich.

1906 Attended evening classes in art at the Knirr School, Munich.

1907 Returned to England and studied at the Bradford School of Art.

1908 – 1912 Gained a scholarship to the Slade School of Fine Art, and won first prize in figure painting.

1910 – 1913 Influenced by the lectures given by Marinetti in London.

1912 Exhibited at Roger Fry's Second Post-Impressionist Exhibition in October at the Grafton Galleries.

1913 Exhibited at Frank Rutter's Post-Impressionist and Futurist exhibition in October at the Doré Galleries.

1914 – 1916 Met Wyndham Lewis at Roger Fry's Omega Workshops and joined Lewis's 'Rebel Art Centre'. Foundation member of the London Group. Repudiated the Futurist manifesto *Vital English Art* and signed the Vorticist manifesto in *Blast* No 1 June 1914 in which he published translations of extracts from Kandinsky's *Uber das Geistige in der Kunst*. Represented in the Vorticist and Group X exhibitions as a member.

1915 May: work shown in the first and only Vorticist Group exhibition at the Doré Galleries.

1917 Served in the RNVR but invalided out after a short period.

1918 Employed on camouflage work. Moved away from Vorticism, changed his style and became associated with Unit One.

1920 Work shown in the exhibition of Group X at the Mansard Gallery. Published *The Black Country* a book of drawings.

1943 Elected an associate of the Royal Academy. Travelled constantly in Italy and France.

WALES, GEOFFREY. RE, ARCA

b 1912 in Margate, Kent.

Wood engraver, illustrator and teacher.

1924 – 1929 Educated at Chatham House School, Ramsgate.

1929 – 1933 Studied art at the Thanet School of Art.

1933 – 1937 Studied at the Royal College of Art under Malcolm Osborne, Robert Austin, John Nash, Eric Ravilious and Edward Bawden.

1937 – 1953 Taught in the Canterbury Group of Art Schools.

1940 – 1946 Enlisted in the Royal Air Force.

1946 Elected a member of the Society of Wood Engravers.

1961 Elected a fellow of the Royal Society of Painter-Etchers and Engravers.

WEBB, CLIFFORD. RE, RBA

b 1895 in London. d 1972.

Wood engraver, lithographer and painter.

Educated at Chigwell Grammar School.

Apprenticed to a London firm of lithographers.

1914 – 1919 Served in the Grenadier Guards and later was commissioned in the Wiltshire Regiment. Fought at Mons, Gallipoli, and Mesopotamia. Wounded four times and mentioned in Dispatches. Served in India as a captain. Spent his spare time painting in oils and watercolours.

1919 – 1922 Studied art at the Westminster School of Art under Walter Bayes. Began wood engraving.

1923 – 1926 Taught drawing, specialising in animals, at the Birmingham School of Art.

1927 – 1933 Worked as a freelance artist in London.

1928 First exhibited with the Society of Wood Engravers.

1934 – 1939 Taught drawing and engraving at the Westminster School of Art.

1935 Elected a member of the Society of Wood Engravers.

1936	Elected a member of the Royal Society of British Artists.
1938	Elected an associate of the Royal Society of Painter-Etchers and Engravers.
1939 – 1945	Worked in Newcastle as Controller of Petrol for the North of England.
1945 – 1965	Taught drawing and engraving at the St Martin's School of Art until his retirement at the age of 70 years.
1948	Elected a fellow of the Royal Society of Painter-Etchers and Engravers.

WHITE, ETHELBERT. RWS, NEAC
b 1891. d 1972.
Painter, wood engraver and printmaker.

1920	Two wood engravings in first exhibition of the Society of Wood Engravers.
1921	Elected a member of the Society of Wood Engravers.
	Elected a member of the New English Art Club.
1925	Resigned from the Society of Wood Engravers and joined the newly formed English Wood Engraving Society. Visited Algeria.
1930	Last year of the production of wood engravings.
1932	Exhibited at the first Society of Wood Engravers linocut exhibition at the Redfern Gallery, exhibiting with the English Wood Engraving Society. Recommenced exhibiting with the original Society.
1934	Elected a member of the Royal Watercolour Society.
1935	Re-elected a member of the Society of Wood Engravers.

WORSDELL, GUY
b 1908 in York.
Wood engraver and painter.

1930 – 1933	Studied art at the Central School of Art and Design under Noel Rooke and John Farleigh.
1936 – 1938	Further training in wood engraving from John Beedham.
1971	Elected a member of the Society of Wood Engravers.

INDEX

INDEX OF SUBJECTS

THEATRE

INDEX OF PERSONS

PAPER AND PRINTS

PRIVATE PRESS

SCHOOLS